D1606389

SIMON BARUCH

History of American Science and Technology Series

General Editor, LESTER D. STEPHENS

SIMON BARUCH
Rebel in the Ranks of Medicine, 1840–1921

PATRICIA SPAIN WARD

The University of Alabama Press

Tuscaloosa and London

Library of Congress Cataloging-in-Publication Data

Ward, Patricia Spain.
    Simon Baruch : rebel in the ranks of medicine, 1840–1921 /
Patricia Spain Ward.
        p.   cm.—(History of American science and technology series)
    Includes bibliographical references and index.
    ISBN 0-8173-0589-0
    1. Baruch, Simon, 1840–1921.   2. Physicians—United States—
Biography.   3. Medicine—Southern States—History—19th century.
4. Balneology—United States—History.   I. Title.   II. Series.
R154.B3317W37   1994
610.'92—dc20
[B]   93-31300

British Library Cataloguing-in-Publication Data available

To the memory
of
Marceda Liguori Spain, M.D.,
who imparted to me
his love for the practice of medicine
and for its history

Contents

Preface

How to write a preface in 1991 for the long-deferred publication of a manuscript written between 1956 and 1961: it is a puzzlement. In the three intervening decades, the history of medicine—initially slow to develop despite the pervasive centrality of health to our daily lives—has at last gained recognition as a scholarly discipline. Alongside intellectual and social history and as a part of them both, health history now holds its own place within an academic field once dominated by the political, the military, and the economic.

Since 1961 Americans have celebrated the one hundredth anniversary of the Civil War and a national bicentennial, emerging from these commemorations with a heightened sense of the value of the past. Concomitantly, the historical literature has mushroomed on almost every subject that concerned Simon Baruch. It would be possible to rewrite the entire context of his life by substituting secondary works published after 1961 for those I initially used. I have not attempted to do this. Instead, wherever more recent scholarship has seemed particularly relevant, I have tried to integrate it either in the text or the notes, probably with more success in my own field of medical history than in areas more peripheral to Baruch's life. Because the civil rights movement and the women's movement have swept away such earlier usages as "Negro" and "lady," I have revised my language accordingly.

Physical medicine, rehabilitation, and the treatment of chronic disease were bare infants a decade after World War II, when I began this biography of one of their founders. Although historians have yet to do justice to these fields, we now take them for granted in a culture in which law mandates equal employment opportunities and physical access for disabled persons. In the years since Simon Baruch's death in 1921, medicine has benefited from technological advances he could scarcely have imagined. Nevertheless, the current holistic health movement and popular concern with "right living" embody his thinking to a degree that would astonish his contemporaries, who sometimes ridiculed his preoccupation with diet, exercise, fresh air, and water. Ironically, had this story been published earlier, amid the boundless optimism for curative medicine inspired by antibiotics and the seeming miracles of surgery in the 1950s and 1960s, Baruch's ideas would have seemed less "modern" than they do now, as we approach the twenty-first century with grudging awareness that even surgical and pharmaceutical "miracles" have their limitations—and that we cannot always afford them, in any case.

Spa therapy, on the other hand, has not yet found the wide acceptance Baruch sought for it among American physicians. Despite our rich natural endowment with a wide variety of mineral springs, the United States continues to trail Western Europe and the former Soviet Union in balneology. This long-standing discrepancy spurred Baruch to press for the development of Saratoga Springs during World War I and inspired Henry Sigerist to write repeatedly about American spas between 1941 and 1952. Yet no American president has made spa development for the benefit of the working classes a matter of government policy, as V. I. Lenin did in Russia in 1919; nor, in the years since Franklin Delano Roosevelt's resort to Warm Springs, Georgia, for buoyancy therapy for his paralyzed legs, have we had any record of spa patronage by political leaders to match Mikhail Gorbachev's use of Russian watering places for political advancement and personal health (*Vanity Fair,* February 1990, pp. 186–87).

The free public baths which Baruch did so much to secure for tenement dwellers were closing in the decade after World War II. They seemed anachronistic in those prosperous years, when almost all Americans had some form of housing, most of it with full plumbing: as historian Nelson Blake wrote in 1956 in his *Water for the Cities,* "it was not the public bath house but the private bath room that was destined to become a great American institution." In 1991, however, amid a large and growing population of homeless Americans (one-third of them women and children), we have renewed understanding of the importance of public baths to the immigrants who crowded our cities at the turn of the last century. And the movement Baruch pioneered has at last found a full accounting in Marilyn Thornton Williams, *Washing "The Great Unwashed": Public Baths in Urban America, 1840–1920* (1991).

More difficult to bridge than any of these gaps between 1961 and 1991 is the adult lifetime that separates me from the person who wrote this book in her twenties. Over many months of revision, I have repeatedly echoed the distress of Ebenezer Scrooge, who cried out at the close of his mandatory one-night autobiographical retrospective: "Spirit! hear me! I am not the man I was." A sympathetic colleague described the difficulty poetically (and in gender-neutral language): "You now speak with a different voice." Far less certain about right and wrong than I was thirty years ago, and no longer so .critical of those who, like Baruch, press openly for recognition of their contributions, I have attempted with mixed success to alter the tone of this very long manuscript to reflect my present, older, "voice."

In the course of this protracted work, I have amassed a commensurate number of intellectual creditors. These include two undergraduate professors at the University of Colorado: Hal Bridges, whose gentle passion for biography touched me in 1954 and has never left me; and Frank Pegues, who introduced me to the history of science and technology at that critical point in my life at which I turned from the pursuit of medicine itself to the study of its history.

At The Johns Hopkins University, Richard H. Shryock supported both my choice of Simon Baruch as the subject of my doctoral dissertation and my application for the research grant from the National Institute of Mental Health that enabled my researches in South Carolina and Virginia between 1958 and 1961. Upon Professor Shryock's departure from Hopkins soon after I started my research, C. Vann Woodward generously shouldered the burden of guiding a long dissertation only tangentially related to his own scholarly interests. His thoughtful comments led me to many useful materials and helped me pare away literary excesses born of my youthful determination to "write readable history" and "make science and medicine understandable."

Two of my best critics were fellow graduate students, Willie Lee Rose and Frank Albrecht. They read every chapter, always tempering their criticisms with helpful suggestions and enthusiasm for my subject. Willie Rose directed me to many invaluable sources which she encountered while working on *Rehearsal for Reconstruction:* my accounts of Baruch's medical student days and Reconstruction practice owe much to her keen eye for materials of likely use to me. Other Hopkins colleagues who gave the manuscript thoughtful readings were Doris Thibodeau and Gert Brieger.

To Ronald L. Numbers I owe a debt I can never repay, for reviving my academic aspirations and patiently urging me toward publication over the past sixteen years. In 1974, during a postdoctoral fellowship year at

The Johns Hopkins University Institute of the History of Medicine, he read the by-then dusty Baruch typescript. He subsequently supported my candidacy for a Maurice L. Richardson Fellowship that enabled me to resume doctoral studies, at the University of Wisconsin in 1976, and chaired the dissertation committee at Madison that included Judith Walzer Leavitt, John Parascandola, Vanessa N. Gamble, Victor Hilts and John Scarborough. To all of these readers I am indebted for encouragement and for many helpful suggestions.

For their forbearance through endless delays and their enthusiastic help in converting this aged and lengthy manuscript into a book, I thank Lester Stephens, editor of The University of Alabama Press series in the History of American Science and Technology, and the staff at The University of Alabama Press. The outside readers for that series and its copyeditor, Trudie Calvert, have saved me from many errors.

Like all historians I bear a heavy debt to archivists and librarians. These include staff at the Eisenhower Library and the William H. Welch Medical Library of The Johns Hopkins University; the Library of the Medical College of South Carolina in Charleston (now the Waring Historical Library of the Medical University of South Carolina); the South Caroliniana Library in Columbia; the Tompkins-McCaw Library of the Medical College of Virginia in Richmond; the Enoch Pratt Free Library in Baltimore; the Library of the New York Academy of Medicine; the Library of Congress; the National Archives; the National Library of Medicine; the Robert H. Woodruff Library, Emory University, Atlanta; the Middleton Health Sciences Library of the University of Wisconsin, Madison; the Wisconsin State Historical Society; the Library of the Health Sciences, University of Illinois at Chicago; the Museum of The City of New York; and the Camden Archives and Museum, Camden, South Carolina. Out of her expert knowledge of historical photographs available in the Washington, D.C., area, Diane Hamilton led me to a wealth of Civil War illustrations from which to choose.

For typing or entering on computer the earlier versions through which this book has passed over the decades, I have grateful memories of Catherine Grover of Baltimore, Linda Reigstad of Madison, and Valerie Smith and James C. Fisher, Jr., of Chicago. I can never adequately thank Ronald P. Legon who, as Associate Vice Chancellor for Academic Affairs at the University of Illinois at Chicago, provided personal encouragement and administrative support as I struggled with the massive revision required to shape this final version for submission as my doctoral dissertation at the University of Wisconsin-Madison and as a manuscript for publication by The University of Alabama Press.

My daughter, Lydia Ward-Chene, has enthusiastically supported my many research projects over more than a quarter-century. Although I had finished the original Baruch manuscript before she was born, many times throughout her growing-up years she cheerfully helped me move and store masses of Baruch materials, never questioning that they would eventually serve some purpose. Now well launched on her own career as a clinical psychologist, she remains one of my best readers and most valued critics. To Lydia and my mother, Nola Lensch Spain, and to Robert F. Ward, Willie Rose, Patti Levington Atwater, Rima Apple, Sharon Stern, Ruth Andrews, Joan Campbell, Florence Scala, Norman Gevitz, Suzanne Poirier, Guenter Risse, and James Harvey Young, I send thanks for their sustaining faith that I would someday complete my formal education and publish the "Baruch book."

Erwin Ackerknecht, himself the biographer of Rudolf Virchow, once said that "Every biography disfigures history." I trust that readers will find this life of Simon Baruch an exception to Ackerknecht's general rule, in the sense that I have attempted to avoid exaggerating Baruch's importance in medical history. I have, however, been unable to correct several distortions arising from deficiencies in surviving manuscript materials. Among the papers which Simon's second son, Bernard, gathered in 1956 for my use in this work, very few were personal apart from Simon's love letter of 1867 to his future wife, Belle Wolfe, and some "memos" he wrote to her late in life. Worse yet, except for his physician's casebooks, Simon apparently saved no manuscripts when moving to New York City in 1881. Thus I have literally had to create his first forty years out of the other materials described in endnotes and in the Note on Sources. The length and detail of the Civil War and Reconstruction chapters are products of the numerous Civil War recollections Baruch wrote late in life and the series of long, thoughtful letters he wrote to a South Carolina colleague, Alexander S. Salley, Sr., in the difficult years after the war, letters fortunately preserved in the South Caroliniana Library. For many of the years between 1865 and 1881, there are no materials other than Baruch's presentations at the South Carolina Medical Association; hence association matters may appear even more dominant than they probably were in Baruch's life. The emphasis on public baths, hydrotherapy, and spa therapy was dictated by the importance those subjects held for Baruch, as reflected in the professional correspondence, press clippings, and scrapbooks that made up a large part of his surviving papers. (On the present location of these papers, see Notes on Sources.)

In the larger sense intended by Ackerknecht, I hope that Simon Baruch's life will illustrate history rather than disfigure it, making concrete in one doctor's story many of the dilemmas of theory and practice that confronted all American practitioners in the last half of the nineteenth century—and some that were peculiar to those who served in the Civil War and later worked in the Reconstruction South.

It was my own curiosity in the 1950s about how earlier practitioners had actually treated the sick and conducted their professional lives that led me to select the articulate Baruch as my subject, hoping that his story might provide readers with some idea of what doctors did in those days. Thanks to the diligence of historians over the three intervening decades, we now have a much more comprehensive picture of nineteenth-century health care: indeed, upon reading John Harley Warner's recent book, *The Therapeutic Perspective: Medical Practice, Knowledge, and Identity in America, 1820–1885,* I toyed with the idea of retitling this book *Simon Baruch: The Therapeutic Perspective Exemplified.* In continually evaluating his own therapeutic practices and sharing his conclusions by publishing them (he called it "contributing to the general stock of knowledge"), Simon Baruch was hardly a typical American physician; but because of this habit, he left an unusually comprehensive record of what it was like to practice medicine in the United States during the budding of what it pleases us to call "modern medicine."

Although it was the potential value of Baruch's life as a mirror for medical history that first drew me to him, it was ultimately his human development that captivated me. As I worked my way through his writings, I decided to follow a chronological structure for this book so as to portray the actual course of his life as closely as possible. Against the advice of several critics, I have retained this arrangement; while it will force readers interested in a particular topic during Baruch's South Carolina years to check many different index entries (for bloodletting, for example, or for contract practice), it has seemed to me the best way to show the evolution of his thought. In the last six chapters, devoted to the New York years when he tended to concentrate on only one or two major interests at a time, the chronological happily coincides more frequently with the topical.

Patricia Spain Ward
University of Illinois at Chicago

SIMON BARUCH

"Amerika, du hast es besser"

As the Staten Island ferry pulled away from the Manhattan shoreline on Saturday mornings during the second decade of the present century, the regular passengers included a tall, distinguished gentleman in his seventies. From his appearance alone, his fellow passengers could tell that he was a man of marked personality. Everything about his erect figure bespoke mental and physical vigor, from the high polish of his shoes to the broad-brimmed black Stetson that left only the ends of his long, white hair to the mercies of the sea breeze. His trousers were sharply creased, his coat the proper if somewhat outmoded frock. Above a beard no less lustrous than his hair, his light eyes, piercing yet benign, looked out through small, wire-rimmed spectacles. As he traveled to his weekly duties at Sea View, the city's tuberculosis hospital on Staten Island, Dr. Simon Baruch looked the typical southern gentleman.[1]

Nothing could have been farther from his view of himself. He was no more concerned with being a southerner or a New Yorker by residence than with being a European Jew by birth. Labels dependent on such accidents of life held little interest for him. He was what he had made himself: a scholar and a physician, dedicated to the study of medicine, its philosophy, history, and practice. He was also a crusader, indefatigable and uncompromising wherever medical matters touched the welfare of the people.

Yet Baruch was by no means a selfless man. Altruism and ambition were so mingled in his nature that neither alone could account for his many achievements. Had he cared to examine his life critically—which he did not—he would have seen in it a paradox, a constant and often

I

simultaneous flickering of two inner lights. At one and the same time, he was capable of the noblest motivation and the most blatant obsession with self-aggrandizement. He devoted long years to medical practice among the poor of South Carolina—black and white—and among the tenement dwellers of New York City; yet he readily confessed to a craving for a more "respectable clientele." Within him, disinterested intellectual curiosity competed with a passionate yearning for a niche in the annals of medicine's great; the energy he poured into his unceasing search for improved knowledge and therapeutic methods sprang from the one as much as the other. Throughout his long, crowded lifetime, his devotion to causes was inseparable from his concern for the credit he might earn in their service.

Few traces remain of the roots of Baruch's paradoxical nature, for the roots were laid down in the eternally troubled soil of central Europe, midway between Warsaw and Berlin, during the fifteen years following his birth in 1840. Records of the Jewish community in his native village were destroyed during World War II, together with the archives of the Gymnasium where he received his education.[2] In 1933, when the last survivors of his immediate family fled the Nazi terror, they left behind family papers of three generations. Photographs, letters, diaries—all were lost.[3] In scattered historical remnants, in recollections of Baruchs still living in the 1950s, there were more questions than answers, though the questions themselves held some clue to the puzzle of Baruch's nature.

Simon Baruch was the first of nine children born to Bernhard and Theresa (Gruen) Baruch in the little town of Schwersenz, on a lovely lake not far from Posen, capital city of the province of Posen. In the various wars and treaties that devoured Poland in the late eighteenth century, the province was taken by Prussia; yet it remained one of the most patriotic parts of the territory once known as Great Poland, flourishing in the nineteenth century partly as the natural center of a great agricultural region, partly as a bulwark of the Poles in their struggle against German domination. Though Simon was born and raised at the center of this national "resistance," he does not seem to have thought of himself as a part of it. He spoke of his native village not as the Polish "Swarzedz" but as the Prussian "Schwersenz" and of the province and its capital not as "Poznan" but as "Posen."[4]

Simon's father, Bernhard, was a tall, ruddy brunet of scholarly tendencies and unknown occupation, who seemed far more interested in the Baruchs' heritage as Jews than as Poles or Germans. Among Bernhard's most cherished possessions was a human skull, inscribed in many tongues, including Hebrew, Portuguese, Spanish, and German, and purporting to trace the genealogy of the Baruch family through many nations and centuries.[5] Yet Simon became an agnostic and a reformed Jew, less concerned about his Sephardic ancestry than about his role as a citizen in the communities where he later made his home.[6]

Bernhard Baruch's most perceptibly enduring legacy to his children was neither land nor money but wealth in the realm of the intellect. His dark, nearsighted eyes corrected by thick glasses, he never tired of reading, and he held books and education to be matters of great importance. On his own initiative, without benefit of formal schooling, he indulged a flair for languages and a love for the law. In the days before his marriage, he was an ardent theatergoer, sometimes catching a lift atop a loaded wood-lorry traveling to Posen, the cultural heart of the province, sometimes making the long trek on foot through the woodland. Whatever the price of the journey, he paid it gladly, usually returning to make enthusiastic diary entries in German about the plays and the actors. His diary also carried comments in Polish and in Hebrew and—when he wanted to describe Theresa, his future bride—in French. For his children he sought the advantages of formal education which he had been denied. He enrolled Simon and the three other boys in the classical curriculum of the Royal Friedrich Wilhelm Gymnasium in Posen, regretful that there were no similar opportunities for his five daughters.[7]

Simon was probably no older than six or seven when he entered the Vorschule (preparatory school) of the Gymnasium. He was almost certainly too young to grasp the irony of the trip that carried him away from Schwersenz toward Posen. Yet he may have learned from his Jewish elders that Schwersenz had been only a tiny manorial village until 1621, when its magnanimous Protestant lord transformed it into a religious haven for Jewish refugees from the crowded Posen ghetto. Twenty years later the same lord extended his hospitality to include the Protestants of Posen. By guaranteeing the religious and civic freedom of both groups, he made Schwersenz a living experiment in toleration, an effective rebuke to the excesses of Roman Catholicism in the provincial capital.[8] Two centuries later, when Simon began his education in Posen, the religious elements of the city were in better balance. Although he saw all about him the Renaissance architecture in which the capital was rebuilt after the great fires of the sixteenth century, he would soon perceive that the hand of Martin Luther's Reformation had touched the population and come to rest on the Gymnasium.

From the time of its founding in 1834 as a part of the network of state-supported Prussian schools, the Friedrich Wilhelm Gymnasium viewed itself as an instrument of the evolution of German culture, created to awaken and strengthen in students a love for the "glorious ancestral ruling race" and to plant in their souls the seeds of a staunch religious feeling, a "true Christian sense." Except for a brief period during the 1840s, when a few Catholics were permitted on the faculty, the staff of regular teachers consisted almost solely of Lutherans. If this fact accounted for the persistently small number of Polish nationals in the student body, it did nothing to diminish the trust in which Jews—of the province as well as the city—seemed to hold the Gymnasium. Hebrew fathers of the region presented their sons to the evangelical faculty in numbers that sometimes surpassed those of the Christians.[9]

Except for a high concentration of Jewish students, the Posen Gymnasium differed little from other schools in the Prussian system. It was governed by the same rigid principles in the administration of the same curriculum of Latin, Greek, and the humanities. In physical facilities it typified the pre-1860s paradox of all Prussian education: excellent instruction carried on in hopelessly inadequate buildings. The house where it opened in 1834, at the busy intersection of the Schützenstrasse and the Schiessgasse, was but one ramshackle part of the ramshackle establishment. Originally a private home, the main building held six classrooms on the ground floor, the director's residence on the second floor, a pair of rooms under the roof, and a basement for the school servants. A newer building, with an entryway from the courtyard outside, contained the so-called great lecture hall. For the students' use during recess, the only space provided was a small, wretched, plastered courtyard, running from the main building to the rear of the property. Until 1857, when the school at last enlarged its facilities, the faculty was forced to teach divided classes, morning and afternoon, and summer as well as winter sessions.[10]

Simon attended the Friedrich Wilhelm Gymnasium during some of its most difficult years. Because of the peculiar circumstances of the province, the aftermath of the political upheaval of the 1840s persisted well into the next decade. Between 1850 and 1856, the Gymnasium was plagued by natural calamities as well. During a flood that robbed it of courtyard, garden, and cellar, it was obliged to give up several classrooms to shelter families driven from their nearby homes by the hungry waters. In the summer of 1852 an extraordinarily violent outbreak of cholera reduced attendance from 523 to fewer than 200, disrupting the normal course of the summer session for almost three months.[11]

In 1855, apparently having made the decision that would govern the course of his life to come, Simon withdrew from the Gymnasium. He left before taking the *Abiturientenexamen,* the final comprehensive examination required for admission to Prussian universities.[12] Perhaps he had read a lesson about the fate of Jews in his homeland from the example of his father, a learned man without professional or community status, even in the little town of Schwersenz. Simon had no wish to follow that fruitless path. Along with the intellectual bent that characterized his father, he shared certain traits of his mother's. Like her, he was hardworking, practical, down-to-earth. He wanted not merely to study medicine but also to practice it, a course closed to Jews in his native country. Before the Prussian government had a chance to interrupt his studies by compulsory military service, he made his decision.[13]

The horizon that beckoned him was more distant than that of Paris or Montpellier, where many of his young countrymen were flocking in pursuit of medical knowledge.[14] *"Amerika, du hast es besser,"* wrote Goethe early in the nineteenth century. Dejected over the upheaval, the age-old unabating strife that had long been the story of Europe, Goethe looked to the New World with an almost wistful hope.[15] In hardier expectations of improvement, three million immigrants entered the United States in the decade after 1845. One of them was Mannes Baum, a friend and townsman of the Baruchs. He was not disappointed in his new life. Happily established as a merchant, he wrote glowing reports to his friends back home about opportunities the New World held for the young and energetic and about the social and professional freedom Jews enjoyed there. He urged his ambitious young friend to join him.

Simon read the letters over and over again. The lure was irresistible. At the age of fifteen, he left his family, his friends, and his home, setting off for a new land where the only soul he knew lived in a town called Camden in the state of South Carolina.[16]

2 To Become a Doctor

Camden was a pretty little town on the tawny Wateree River, in the heart of the longleaf pine region. From its monuments to revolutionary heroes, it was apparent that Camden had a history, as history was measured in the New World. Even the name had a historic ring. The Irish Quakers who made the first permanent settlement in 1758 had called it Pine Tree Hill, but the name that stuck was the one given in honor of the colonists' friend Lord Camden in a charter granted by George III ten years later. Side by side with reminders of the past were cotton mills in the part of town called Factory Village, indicating that Camden also had a future. Within a year after the railroad came through from Columbia in 1850, the population climbed from 1,165 to between 2,000 and 3,000, including a few inhabitants of foreign birth. A piedmont town as well as a county seat, Camden was a stopping-off place for planters en route from their tidewater homes to the spas and resorts of the up-country. From those aristocrat-refugees who extended their stopovers into permanent summer homes, Camden derived some of its prosperity and much of its social tone.[1]

Simon Baruch stated in his naturalization petition in 1871 that he had arrived in America on December 23, 1855, but he later recalled not having reached Camden until July 1859. Perhaps he spent some time in New York after landing there, or perhaps he lingered in Georgetown, South Carolina, which he listed as one of his places of residence on becoming an American citizen. According to family legend, he worked for a time in the Baum general store in Camden before beginning his medical studies. As that story goes, he showed so much more interest in the books he kept under the counter than in the customers that it soon

6

became clear "he was no born business man."[2] As he remembered many years later, it was "on the morning after" his arrival that Mannes Baum took him to meet Dr. Thomas J. Workman. A medical graduate of the University of Pennsylvania in 1846, Workman had since become a successful Camden practitioner. He agreed to act as Simon's preceptor for the required period of apprenticeship.[3]

For some aspiring physicians, apprenticeship was the sole preparation for medical practice in this period. During the 1830s and 1840s, coincident with rapid westward expansion and what is called "the rise of the common man," most states revoked or failed to enforce medical licensure laws enacted early in the national period. For the most part, anyone who wished to practice medicine could do so, although many first pursued a formal medical education, including a required period of apprenticeship begun before entering medical school and often continued between terms. Through apprenticeship students could learn materia medica, that is, the names of drugs in common use, their dosages and effects, and the diseases for which they were used. If the preceptor's office or the local hospital had a skeleton, the apprentice might also learn the names of bones and of the muscles attached to them.[4]

Simon's apprenticeship combined the study of medicine with the problem of mastering the English language. In Dr. Workman's office, situated on the front portion of a large hall and lighted by tall, narrow windows on either side of the door, he pored over the books Dr. Workman advised him to read. Beginning at the rate of twenty pages a day, he relied less and less as time went by on his English-German dictionary, but he always kept his English dictionary and Robley Dunglison's *Medical Dictionary* at his side.[5]

It was probably during the fifteen months spent thus in study that he apprenticed himself to a second preceptor, Dr. Lynch Horry Deas, an older man than Workman and one of Camden's best beloved physicians.[6] Deas had rounded out his medical education at the Medical College of South Carolina and the University of Pennsylvania with a year of training in Paris during the ascendancy of French medicine. Simon found him a "most sympathetic physician," the "courtliest of gentlemen," and a "man of intelligence," although he would later come to feel that Deas's ideas were "antiquated and in many instances, very queer."[7]

The apprenticeship system proved to have its weaknesses. Both Deas and Workman were better doctors than teachers, but their example taught Simon ethical principles and professional obligations—"self-sacrifice, soulful devotion, genial spirit and lessons of tact"—which he would long remember.[8]

During his apprenticeship, Simon lived as a "foster son" in the modest

Baum home, along with the younger brothers, Herman and Marcus, who had followed Mannes from Schwersenz to Camden and joined him in business. Before long the deepening sectional controversy found its way into the everyday lives of the new Americans. In early October 1860, the brothers Baum advised readers of the (Camden) *Weekly Journal* that a purchase from their large assortment of "Fancy and Domestic Dry Goods, Clothing, Hats and Caps, Boots and Shoes, Tin, Hard Glass and Crockery Ware, Saddlery, Etc." would bring "as much satisfaction as the election of BRECKINRIDGE AND LANE, the only true Democratic Candidates, would afford to the South."[9] Such was the pitch of local political tensions that M. Baum & Bros. doubtless flourished. Their financial success was greatly to Simon's interest, for it was the Baums who sent him to medical school in the fall of 1860.[10]

Perhaps because it was nearest, or because Dr. Deas had studied there, Simon chose to attend the Medical College of South Carolina in Charleston, 150 miles to the southeast. When he left the sandy, rolling countryside of Camden and traveled through the pine barrens, cypress swamps, and stately rows of moss-draped oaks that marked the way to Charleston, the election of Abraham Lincoln and the first lectures of the winter session were already past. It was the middle of November, and secession fever ran high in the port that was then one of America's leading cities. There had been signs of the same disease back in Camden, where the diarist Mary Boykin Chesnut found her Camden townsmen "busy and frantic with excitement, drilling, marching, arming, and wearing high blue cockades"; where "red sashes, guns, and swords" soon became "ordinary fireside accompaniments."[11] In Charleston the fever was more virulent yet. On November 10, when the legislature called for a December convention to consider secession, Charleston celebrated with fireworks and parades. Business came to a near halt, and military preparations took on an air of frenzy at rumors that March 4, the day of Lincoln's inauguration, had been set as the date for a slave insurrection. With ordinary affairs already neglected, Charleston's shipping soon fell to one-third its usual volume, only one-fourth of the accustomed cotton standing on its wharves.[12]

Amid what Chesnut called the "phospherescent" atmosphere surrounding secession, the Medical College proceeded with its affairs as it had during every session since 1824, when it was established as the first medical school in the South. Around midcentury Charleston had ranked, along with Boston, New Haven, and Philadelphia, as one of America's great intellectual centers, site of the third annual meeting of the American Association for the Advancement of Science. The college, too, had reached a peak of prosperity and repute at this time, drawing Louis Agassiz from Harvard to spend his winter vacation of 1852–53 teaching comparative anatomy on the same faculty with such outstanding South Carolinians as Samuel Henry Dickson, a medical reformer of wide renown and an officer of the American Medical Association on its founding in 1847. When Simon enrolled in the Medical College in 1860, it remained one of the finest in the nation, boasting excellent clinical facilities and many European-trained professors of long experience and great ability.[13] Yet he found admission to the student body of 247 a simple matter. There were no requirements at all, although the faculty prided itself on the fact that some of its students were graduates of literary institutions and "nearly all of them have received *liberal* and *classical* educations." To begin work Simon had only to pay fifteen dollars a ticket for each of the seven lecture courses—anatomy, chemistry, physiology, materia medica, surgery, and theory and practice of medicine—and two five-dollar fees, one the formal matriculation fee, the other for the privilege of observing surgical cases in the Roper Hospital adjoining the college.[14]

Meeting the requirements for graduation was another matter. A candidate had to be twenty-one years old and of good moral character, having had three years of study with "some respectable practitioner" and a course of dissections at the college; and he must offer a thesis on some medical or surgical subject before taking his examinations. To distinguish itself from medical schools that awarded degrees after a short period of study, the college insisted on two full courses of lectures at a "respectable Medical School," the last course to be in residence in Charleston. "But in no case will a course from a college delivering two courses in one year, graduating students thereupon, be recognized as an equivalent to one in this College."[15]

The requirement of two full sessions did not mean that the curriculum was a graded one, wherein students progressed to different courses in the second year. That fruit of medical reform was not achieved until later in the century. When Simon was in medical school, students heard the same lecture courses two years in succession. Another flaw was the brevity of the term, in most schools only five months, even shorter in Charleston, where it opened on the first of November and closed on the first Saturday in March. From its inception in 1847 the American Medical Association had pressed for longer sessions, but all such efforts failed because medical schools, then often owned and operated by faculty members, feared destructive competition. Many physician-teachers, who fully realized the inadequacy of the short terms, could not afford to drive students to less demanding institutions by raising their own standards too high, particularly in an era of lax licensure laws.[16]

There was also a practical reason for limiting the session to a few months, a factor more urgent in the South than elsewhere. Anatomists then had no effective methods of preserving materials. Until formaldehyde began to be used for tissue fixation in 1893, even the most dedicated investigator suffered while dissecting a cadaver more than a few days old, even during the coldest months of the year. When schools frankly stated their requirements in terms of "so many winter sessions," they meant simply "so much anatomical teaching." Even in England the *annus medicus* traditionally extended only from autumn to spring. In semitropical Charleston the problem was more acute.[17] The Charleston faculty did its best to compensate. The 1859–60 circular announced that a legislative appropriation had made it possible to enlarge and renovate the Anatomical Theatre, where demonstrations were held—changes intended to "secure free ventilation." With the same appropriation the faculty made additions to the Anatomical Museum, where wax models, odorless and nondecomposable, supplemented work at the dissection table.

Five weekly lectures were given by John Edwards Holbrook, a founder of the college and its first professor of anatomy. Considered North America's most noted herpetologist, Holbrook had studied at Edinburgh and in England, France, and Germany after taking his M.D. at the University of Pennsylvania in 1818. He blended accurate description with a grace of expression that "made the dull details of anatomy glow with an unsuspected beauty."[18] "Practical anatomy" was required by the college as early as 1835, yet the catalog was silent on the question of dissection by students, probably because the legal supply of bodies was inadequate to this purpose.[19] In Charleston, as elsewhere, it was probably supplemented by "resurrection," a cooperative arrangement between the anatomist and the local grave digger—sometimes including the school janitor and students as well. Medical students at the University of Louisville, working in groups of six to a cadaver, paid the demonstrator of anatomy a dollar apiece to reimburse him for the price paid to the graveyard sexton. At the end of days given over to lectures and demonstrations, the real work began:

After supper, we returned to the college building, and dissected dead bodies in the suit [sic] of dissecting rooms, that occupied the basement room of the large college building. The dissecting rooms were large—; with brick floors—; 6 or 8 of them, opening into each other, and into a hall that ran between them—; there were from 4 to 6 dissecting classes in each room. Each class consisted of 6 young men—; who were dressed with black cambric aprons over their clothes, fitting with close buttons at the wrists & neck, & a band tied round the waist—, & a black cap generally—; the dead body lay on a long narrow table, about 2 ft. wide & 6 long—; they sat around the body on tall stools—; some dissecting & some reading aloud from the Anatomy, to guide the matter of dissecting—; the flesh & refuse matter left over after each night's work, was carried into the *dead* room, where there was an immensely deep dry well, into which it was dumped, & a close cover laid over the top—; before returning home, we went through a vigorous process of ablution—; there was a force pump of prodigious power, that knocked the filth and bad smell from the fingers; but it was very hard to get rid of—; could sometimes, in spite of hard washing, smell the stench on our fingers even at the table.[20]

Whether through infection entering broken skin on ungloved hands or some other illness, most medical classes of that era lost several members each year: "Buried Finney this morning . . . Dr. Humphreys delivered a very appropriate address from Job . . . 'Thy purposes are broken off &c'. . . . We marched from College to the graveyard in long & solemn procession . . . following to his last long home one who but a few days ago was mingling in our midst. Just two weeks ago too, we buried Dowdy. . . . Alas, 'all flesh is as grass.'"[21] Yet the students usually drew lots at the end of the session to see who of the six would take the remnants of their cadaver home for the summer. Although the winner was able to improve his knowledge by preparing a skeleton, the job was not a pleasant pastime in warm weather. A medical student from Tuskegee, Alabama, tried to make light of his discomfort in "scraping bones, though they aint half macerated, & a precious business it is, sitting on a plank in the stable, with an old case-knife in my hand diligently scraping the fragrant members as I take them dripping from the barrel."[22]

Another Charleston faculty member who had done postgraduate work abroad was Simon's professor of surgery, J. Julian Chisolm. Already one of Charleston's leading surgeons and co-owner of a hospital for plantation slaves, Chisolm gave his four weekly lectures with an enthusiasm born of full practical experience. Within a year he would write a manual of surgery for Confederate medical officers and devise a chloroform inhaler that ranks as one of the few medical innovations of the war. In connection with Chisolm's lectures, students saw surgical cases in the Marine Hospital and the newly opened College Ward of the Roper Hospital. Completed in 1858, the Roper was a large, handsome, well-arranged building set in a tasteful garden at the corner of Queen and Mazyck streets. The first floor housed physicians' offices; the second, the library of the Medical Society; and the third, a large amphitheater for clinical lectures. In the east and west wings were spacious, well-ventilated wards with broad, sunny piazzas looking southward. Here, the faculty promised, students would see "an unusual number of capital operations" during the winter. Privately practicing physicians as well as faculty members performed operations "on any day of the week" and taught postoperative care "from the bedside."[23]

Simon would remember these occasions all through his life: "'Little' [Francis] Peyre Porcher earnestly peering through his spectacles at the 'facies' [the drawn, pinched *facies Hippocratica* indicative of impending death] of a patient in the Marine Hospital and counseling the students to act early before danger menaced—Elegant T. L. Ogier, the typical Southern doctor; Dr. [St. Julien] Ravenel's fine example for young aspirants like myself, later the kindliest of men but nervous." It is unclear whether Simon fully realized how extraordinary this faculty was. Francis Peyre Porcher (1824–95) was a student of Pierre Louis, an early proponent of the germ theory, co-owner with Chisolm of the Charleston hospital for slaves, and a gifted botanist. In his history of drug supplies in the Confederacy, Norman Franke has estimated that Porcher's *Resources of the Southern Fields and Forests* (a guide to indigenous medicinal plants commissioned by Confederate surgeon-general Samuel Preston Moore and published in Richmond and Charleston in 1863) "saved the Confederacy for two years"; David Hufford quotes Edward Croom, who called Porcher's guide "the most complete list of useful plants written on any region of the country." Thomas Lewis Ogier (1810–1900), who appeared to be merely a "typical Southern doctor," had acted as prosector to François Magendie in France in the 1830s; during the war he would become medical director of the Confederate army for the states of South Carolina, Georgia, and Florida. St. Julien Ravenel (1819–82), a pupil of Agassiz, was a chemist as well as a physician; he entered the Confederate medical service at the outbreak of the war but later directed the Columbia laboratory that prepared medical supplies for the blockaded South.[24]

Proper surgical technique was often controversial, the choice of one method over another resting on individual preference. Whenever this was the case, the Charleston faculty promised that all operative procedures would be described, along with the reasons for employing one rather than another. "The physician . . . does not only explain his own peculiar treatment, in any case, but endeavors to inform them what other modes of treatment are recommended."[25]

Drugs were even more widely debated than the proper use of the lancet. In the course of his thirty-six years as professor of materia medica, Henry Rutledge Frost had witnessed far-reaching changes in concepts of dosing. He had watched the rising star of mild homeopathic remedies and the decline of heroic medicine—the administration of massive quantities of depletive drugs, which around 1800 had inspired the charge that medicine was an "art founded on conjecture and improved by murder."[26]

Some subjects in the curriculum were not so controversial. One of these was chemistry, taught during Simon's year at Charleston by Charles Upham Shepard, a physicist, chemist, botanist, and mineralogist and former assistant in the Yale laboratory of Benjamin Silliman. Another was obstetrics, taught by Thomas G. Prioleau, who was reportedly "inefficient" even though he had been on the faculty since 1824. In addition to hearing his three lectures a week, students were given obstetrical cases when possible "under the immediate direction of the Surgeon of the Institution."[27]

Eli Geddings, Simon's professor of the theory and practice of medicine, was one of the most outstanding members of this outstanding faculty. Geddings received a license to practice medicine before entering medical school and later attended a course of lectures at the University of Pennsylvania. In 1825 he took the first degree awarded by the new Medical College of South Carolina. After a year in the hospitals of Paris and London, he launched into a teaching career that included anatomy and physiology at the University of Maryland and, at various times, chairs of pathological anatomy, medical jurisprudence, surgery, and practice of medicine in Charleston. His knowledge of Latin, Greek, French, and German gave him access to the classics of medical literature, and he believed that students should be trained in foreign languages.[28]

Geddings was, in fact, a reformer. He criticized the short terms common in American medical schools, the content of the curriculum, the idea of equating a diploma from medical school with a license to practice medicine, and the illogic of apprenticeship, which presented advanced problems before fundamentals. He favored the more rigorous system of the Prussian and Austrian universities and urged many reforms modeled on them in American medical education—reforms not generally achieved until after The Johns Hopkins Medical School opened in 1893. Among the admission requirements he considered "indispensable" were a good working knowledge of English, literature, geography, history (ancient and modern), elementary chemistry and physics, and a reading knowledge of Latin. He thought a student entering with deficiencies in any of these subjects should make them up in the first term or be dismissed. And finally, as desirable if not "indispensable," he added botany, zoology, mineralogy, geology, more Latin, some Greek, and "above all, a familiarity with the French and German languages."[29]

In the manner of the times, Geddings wrote out his lectures on the "Institutes and Practice of Medicine," delivering them mainly from the manuscript. Nonetheless, he was known not only as a "ready and forcible writer" but as a "fluent speaker, full of enthusiasm, possessed of an imaginative and an accurate memory, which was never at fault for a word or a name, holding the attention of his auditors from the opening to the close." Simon found Geddings "skilled in diagnosis and learned" but "plain spoken" despite his erudition. From his lectures, characterized by "earnest delivery, painstaking illustrations, chaste eloquence and scholastic precision," Simon took full notes which he often consulted in later years and prized beyond any work in his medical library.[30]

Geddings's subject was one of the most important in the entire curriculum. It was also one of the most difficult. Both the theory and the practice of medicine were in a state of flux. Pathology, advanced especially in France in the early part of the century, offered a new approach to the study of disease by revealing organic changes in the body after death. By studying these local pathological lesions and correlating them with signs and symptoms observed in the patient before death, investigators opened the way for concepts of disease quite different from those that had prevailed before. Their researches tended to discredit theories such as that of Benjamin Rush, which lumped ills together as results either of too much or too little "tension." Just as the generalized concept of disease had called forth the excesses of heroic medicine, so the newer, more specialized concept called for specific therapy.[31]

Unfortunately for the practitioner and his patients, there were few known specifics. Quinine was recognized as effective in treating malaria, but doctors then lacked the knowledge necessary to understand how it works: that it enters the bloodstream, where it attacks tiny organisms that live and reproduce within the circulatory system, thus causing malaria. In later years of the century, as bacteriologists isolated one microorganism after another and other investigators began to find specific drugs to act against the newly isolated organisms, physicians would at last be able to attack the cause in many diseases in which their predecessors could only treat symptoms. In the meantime, for more than half a century, therapeutics wavered uncertainly between the discrediting of old methods and the establishment of new ones. In 1835 the French clinician Pierre Louis contributed to the decline of therapeutic confidence by using medical statistics to show that bloodletting was not effective in treating pneumonia. The old rationale of treatment suffered still another blow in the apparent success of homeopathic remedies, so dilute that their potency seemed negligible. In the face of this evidence, few physicians could cling to the antiphlogistic idea, based on the illusory "healing" force of emesis, catharsis, salivation, perspiration, blistering, or bleeding. Did patients not recover just as well—and far less painfully—on homeopathic soup (so thin, as Abraham Lincoln said, that it might have been "made by boiling the shadow of a pigeon that had starved to death")?[32]

This was the dilemma of the profession Simon was about to enter. In Europe, where disillusionment with their tools led many physicians to a complete loss of faith in their ability to treat illness, quackery flourished apace with the therapeutic nihilism of the regulars. Respect for the profession thus fell to a low ebb near the very centers where researchers were laying the foundation for future progress in therapeutics. In the United States a public dazzled by technological advances—the telegraph, steam engine, cable, harvester, sewing machine—could scarcely be expected to perceive the value of medical research that threw over old methods without furnishing better ones.

The extent to which therapeutic nihilism pervaded American medical thought is still a question among medical historians. Certainly it was somehow modified, like all things European, in the rough, open reaches of the New World. In 1860 Oliver Wendell Holmes told the Massachusetts Medical Society that the extreme opposite of nihilism—heroic medicine— was a natural concomitant of the American character. No one, Holmes contended, could expect a people "which has a revolution once in four years, . . . has contrived the Bowie knife and the revolver, . . . has chewed the juice out of all the superlatives in the language in Fourth of July orations," to be content with anything less than the heroic in medicine. "What wonder that the stars and stripes wave over doses of ninety grains of sulphate of quinine, and that the American eagle screams with delight to see three drachms of calomel given at a single mouthful?"[33]

Despite Holmes's colorful accounting for heroic medicine in America, these drastically depletive measures seem to have fallen into disfavor in the urban centers and academic bastions of the New World just as they had in comparable areas of Europe. Certainly Eli Geddings was one of their outspoken opponents. Yet he must have felt that they still had many adherents, for he larded his lectures with admonitions. His own approach was one of compromise: "In my early life," he told Simon's class, perhaps referring to his year in Paris and London in the 1820s, "I found that truth lies in the middle."[34] Whether discussing calomel or cold baths, bloodletting or surgical procedures, Geddings always noted the current variety of opinion, thus giving his students an excellent picture of American medical thought and practice in 1860. Most important, he told them his own moderate ideas, ideas that had a lasting influence on Simon's thought. Geddings the pathologist gave his classes a careful clinical-pathological description of each disease he discussed, but he did so in order that Geddings the clinician might teach them to make a correct diagnosis and select the best treatment. Although Simon would dabble in and publish about many aspects of medicine, the clinician would always be supreme in him as it was in Dr. Geddings.

Through these lectures Simon learned to use all the new methods of physical diagnosis, with special emphasis on percussion and auscultation—the thumping and listening process that discloses hidden morbid changes in the chest and abdomen. Dr. Geddings apparently did not use the stethoscope, invented by René Laënnec in 1819. The early form of this instrument, later greatly improved, was a rigid wooden tube that transmitted physical movement as well as sound, a failing that made it inferior to the unaided ear pressed directly on the chest. Dr. Geddings apparently preferred the latter method (as did the Harvard Medical School, which did not have a stethoscope until 1868). Geddings did instruct his students to use the microscope (not used at Harvard until 1869), but he did not advocate technique to the exclusion of individual considerations. Heredity played an important role, he said, in gout and rheumatism, in epilepsy and consumption. From him Simon learned to pay close attention to the habits, occupation, and "constitutional endowments" of the patient.[35]

If Dr. Geddings shared any of the racist views in vogue among some southern medical educators in the 1850s, he did not bring them into his lectures. Certainly Simon and his classmates did not need reminders of the growing sectional breach. The South Carolina secession convention had barely assembled in Columbia on December 17 when a smallpox epidemic forced it to vacate the capital in favor of Charleston. (Mary Boykin Chesnut wryly observed that "The men who are all, like Pickens, 'insensible to fear,' are very sensible in case of smallpox." But they were, she added, "all our wisest and best . . . the ablest men, the good men and true. Patriotism aside, it makes society delightful.") The medical students doubtless cared less about "society" than about the convention's actual presence in Charleston, which made it hard to concentrate on studies. On December 20, when the delegates unanimously voted to dissolve South Carolina's bond with the Union, Simon noted beside the title of the day's lecture on yellow fever that his transcription was neither "precise nor full." For a day at least, politics superseded the routine of work.[36]

It was a day for Charleston medical students to remember. Fifteen minutes after the secession ordinance was passed, Robert Barnwell Rhett's *Charleston Mercury* began rolling copies off the press as an extra. Crowds of citizens and militia surged through narrow, cobbled streets to the accompaniment of cannon and church bells. When some of his fellow

students decided to join the festivities, Simon marched along beside
them, his young mind registering a lifelong impression of the banner
they carried: "There Is a Point Beyond Which Endurance Ceases to Be a
Virtue."[37]

Outwardly at least, the faculty of the Medical College took no notice
of secession. Classes went on as before, with no longer than the customary interval between lectures at Christmas and school as usual on New
Year's Day.

As the year advanced, Simon's neatly written notes rapidly multiplied.
They bear witness to two striking characteristics of Dr. Geddings's lectures: uncertainty about the origin of disease and a strong conviction that
the *via media* was the right way in therapeutics. Throughout the notes,
intimations of the germ theory abound, in references to the "animalcules
in the air" (as a source of diseases of the nervous system) or to the
"parasytic vegetable growth" that formed in the throats of diphtheria
victims. But the origin of "periodical fevers," Geddings felt certain, lay
in the noxious miasms or effluvia produced by the sun's action on stagnant water or moist, low-lying soil. The peculiar principle of malaria was
"not yet determined, and still very obscure"; of all the theories proposed,
he said, vegetable decomposition received "most sanction from pathologists."[38] Dr. Geddings spent so much time rebutting the arguments
advanced by others for the possibility of contagion and the necessity of
quarantine in yellow fever that Simon was confused and, with all respect
to the professor, unconvinced. To himself he noted: "All the remarks on
this subject have not been taken down, as they are merely an argument in
favor of a pet opinion, still I have no doubt, but that Dr. G. has substantiated his belief before he asserted it."[39]

Simon felt no such hesitation about Geddings's philosophy of moderation in therapy. This he adopted for his own, along with the two concepts
that supported it: the *vis medicatrix naturae,* or healing power of nature,
and the self-limiting nature of disease.[40] He came to see the physician as
Geddings did, in terms of the Hippocratic ideal, as nature's handmaiden,
whose aim is not so much to wage war against disease as it is to aid the
patient's "natural powers" and "vital energy." It was not easy to implement this philosophy with the medical equipment of the time. Having no
alternative to the depletive measures of the day, Geddings always urged
his students to use these debilitating techniques with moderation, *never*
dosing or bleeding or cupping or blistering to the detriment of the
"powers of life."[41]

Of the few preventives known to medicine in 1860, vaccination for
smallpox was the most important. Practiced correctly, it could prevent

Eli Geddings, M.D. (1799–1878), Simon Baruch's Professor of the Theory and Practice of Medicine at the Medical College of South Carolina and a medical purveyor for General Robert E. Lee during the Civil War. (Courtesy of the Waring Historical Library, Medical University of South Carolina, Charleston.)

this virulent blight that, when it did not kill, disfigured beyond the capacity of later generations to imagine.[42] Because vaccination was often performed improperly, Geddings took great pains to teach his students the correct method, insisting that they make revaccination a policy whenever smallpox was epidemic. This lesson, too, made a lasting impression on Simon.

In contrast, Dr. Geddings's opinion of the therapeutic use of water was scarcely calculated to make of Simon the "apostle of hydrotherapy" he eventually became. In fact, Simon's later advocacy of rational scientific hydrotherapy constitutes a striking departure from the views of his teacher. Geddings, finding the idea of cold applications in pneumonia "altogether incompatible with our views of the treatment of the inflammatory affections of the chest," mentioned it only to caution students against a remedy "strongly advocated by others." He admitted that certain mild forms of hydrotherapy were sometimes useful in nervous diseases like epilepsy, catalepsy, and hysteria, and even in typhoid, typhus, and yellow fevers; yet his reason for applying it in fevers rested on the "antiphlogistic" theory of "abstracting inflammation." Simon would later supply an altogether different rationale.[43]

Because surgery did not properly fall within Dr. Geddings's realm during Simon's term in Charleston, he avoided discussing it except where medical methods were inadequate. This was the case, for example, when strangulation threatened a victim of croup, diphtheria, or epilepsy. Here Geddings advised resort to tracheotomy, a small incision for the insertion of a tube into the windpipe at a point between the lungs and the obstruction. He could not exactly be called an enthusiast: "Where the patient is threatened with suffocation, laryngotomy or tracheotomy must be performed, to save him; but this should only be a dernier resort. [Armand] Trousseau [the first to perform tracheotomy, in Paris in 1831] claims a high degree of success for the operation; others do not think it so efficient." Practicing physicians had good reason to reserve judgment. Because of its dramatic nature (it seemed drastic indeed to cut into the patient's throat even as he was struggling for breath), tracheotomy required courage on the physician's part and cooperation from the patient, often a child, and from his family as well. The operation was so slow to gain general acceptance that even Dr. Geddings's cautious commendation seems unusual for the time.[44]

Geddings's attitude toward tracheotomy, like his views of the *vis medicatrix naturae,* the self-limitation of disease, and the imperative need for moderation in therapy, became a part of Simon's medical thought. Yet in later years he credited his views to the men with whom they had originated—Hippocrates, Louis, Bigelow, Holmes, and others—rather than to the teacher through whom they came to him. Apart from a tribute written at the time of Geddings's death, Baruch's published writings are unencumbered by the professor's name.

To Simon, events in Charleston Harbor following secession probably meant no more than occasional dinner conversation. Like medical students everywhere, he lived in a world too full to admit political concerns. There were lectures, sometimes eight a day, and quizzes, and the reading necessary to keep up with them. For at least twelve hours a day, sometimes for thirteen or fourteen hours for four or five days at a stretch, there was medicine in one form or another. All through the week the hectic routine repeated itself: up early to make a fire and study by candlelight before the boardinghouse breakfast; dash to the first lecture of the day; rush from one lecture room to another; jostle for position on the stairway to the amphitheater; leap downward over the semicircles of seats to the front row, nearest the professor and his revolving table. After supper it was back to the college for dissection. Then long, solitary hours of study, hours broken only by the watchman's cry—"Past one o'clock and a starlight morning"—"Past two o'clock, and a bright moonlight morning"—until it was "time even for a student to go to bed."

There were occasional tasks, too: having scalpels ground, replenishing the supply of notebooks and Faber pencils, buying and trading texts. Through it all ran the universal themes of student life, the eternal borrowing and lending among friends until the funds were too thin to be juggled any longer. Then the inevitable letter home, like this one from another Charleston student, and the effort to account for the vanished:

Your letter with the money came in very good time, for I have borrowed twenty dollars from McKay & have not ten of that left. I have to pay a high price for board—have to buy my own firewood & light—have taken some private tickets and have had to buy, necessarily, more books, than I had any idea of. I shall be obliged to buy one more high priced one, & that, I reckon will be the last. I have tried to be economical—have not been to but one place of amusement since I have been in the City, where I had to pay a cent. . . . But some how my money goes very fast. . . . I will have to hand in with my "Thesis" thirty dollars ($30.00) by the 1st Feb. & will be much obliged to you sir, if you will send me more money by that time.[45]

Like other students, Simon and his contemporaries found time for social life. Younger than the medical students of a later day and not so well educated before entering medical school, they took their amusements in less sophisticated ways. To the more devoutly religious among them there was food for hours of thought and discussion in a sermon entitled "Is the Study of Medicine Favourable to Skepticism?" In the homes of local citizens—especially those with marriageable daughters—the young doctors-to-be found a ready welcome in their leisure hours. Although some of them welcomed the occasional temptations of an oyster supper with quantities of hot whiskey punch, most would submit to sessions with the girls at piano and flute and songbook—or even to a game of "mock-wedding"—with no inducement other than tea and cakes or blackberries and ice cream.

Among themselves the boys arranged serenades and rowing contests. Despite an occasional fistfight, they presented a solid front of professional skepticism at one-night stands of such humbugs as the traveling "animal magnetizers." In their banter, as in their letters and journals, they pretended to have forgotten terms once familiar. Abandoning the layman's short Anglo-Saxon words, they loved to ripple off the long, impressive Latin and Greek derivatives of the medical nomenclature. Within the first year of study, the eyelids of old became "palpebrae"—but either way, they were always heavy.

The life was rich enough to make everyone who liked it wish he could get along with six hours of sleep or less. Although the established facts of medicine were few compared to a later day, the medical student of the nineteenth century had only eight months to learn what was known. For the most part, politics was a world apart. If Simon found time to stroll up and down the neatly fenced promenades of Charleston's Battery, or the long stone quay, reputed to be the finest sea walk on the Atlantic Coast, he was probably too preoccupied with thoughts of work to notice the fortifications going up along the shore or the ironclad floating battery, finished just as the term ended.[46]

Simon was once again in Camden, at work as Dr. Deas's apprentice, when the bombardment of Fort Sumter on April 12 put an end to medical education in Charleston. With many of its faculty, including the sixty-two-year-old Geddings, entering the Confederate service, the Medical College of South Carolina ceased operation for the duration of hostilities. Simon had to decide what to do. His school was closed. Many of his friends and classmates were going off to war. On July 29 he would be twenty-one and a good part of the way toward the goal that had brought him to America. He could join in the fight and return to his work when it ended, as others planned to do. But what was the war to him? Was its purpose the right to secede or the right to hold slaves? Suppose it should go on and on, perhaps for years instead of months? Once he learned that the Medical College of Virginia, in the capital of the Confederacy, would remain open, he decided to continue his education there.

There was probably no city in all the South more exciting than Richmond in the first year of the war. To visiting Frenchmen, it seemed like Paris in miniature. Its prewar population of forty thousand was swelled by all classes of people, some come to provide the Confederacy with their inventions, some to staff the giant Chimborazo Hospital, constructed on the heights above the James River in October, the month of Simon's arrival in the city. With a capacity of over eight thousand beds, the Chimborazo was reputed to be the largest military hospital organized up to that time. It offered rich opportunities for clinical observation to medical students, some of whom served as "medical stewards."[47]

Until the addition of its own hospital (called the College Infirmary) in the spring of 1861, the Medical College of Virginia consisted of a single extraordinary building. Erected in 1845, according to the design of Thomas S. Stewart of Philadelphia, the Egyptian Building towered like a great gray mausoleum over the section of Richmond east of Shockoe Hill. In 1860 this unique structure at the northeast corner of Academy Square housed functions now spread over many city blocks. Laboratories and museum, lecture halls and administrative offices, a hospital ward closed only when the infirmary building opened in 1861; even the dissecting rooms were in the Egyptian Building.[48]

A few blocks to the northeast stood the White House of the Confederacy; a short distance south, the capitol of Virginia, a monument in marble to Thomas Jefferson's preference for the elegant simplicity of neoclassic architecture. In the immediate neighborhood of the Egyptian Building were the boardinghouses where Simon and his classmates studied, ate, and slept and the new College Infirmary, which was to serve more than a thousand Confederate sick and wounded in the first year of war. Nearby, too, was the cemetery, rumored to be the source of dissection material, and the almshouse, which had been transformed into a Confederate hospital at the outbreak of war.[49]

Unlike earlier classes, which had doubled or tripled in size with the influx of southern students "seceding" from northern medical schools, Simon's class was the smallest of all between 1859 and 1865—a commentary on the widespread belief that the war would pose but a brief interruption to studies. Of his sixty-seven classmates, only fourteen had already completed one year of study north of the Mason-Dixon line.[50]

He probably did not find much difference between the Richmond and Charleston schools. Because of the ungraded curriculum, he repeated the same courses and paid approximately the same fee for each professor's ticket. The Richmond college circular estimated the cost of food and lodging at between four and five dollars a week, a surprisingly low figure in view of wartime inflation. The Richmond faculty, like that of the Charleston school, included several outstanding members, many of them with long teaching experience. For the good of the Confederacy it was fortunate that the war faculty was a strong one, for one by one the medical schools of the South followed the example of the Medical College of South Carolina and closed, leaving the Richmond school alone to train doctors to care for unprecedented numbers of sick and wounded produced by the war.[51]

While David Hunter Tucker perhaps fell short of the standard Eli Geddings set in Charleston, the Richmond professor of theory and practice of medicine was well qualified, boasting two medical degrees and several years of postgraduate work in Paris. The professor of materia medica and therapeutics from 1854 to 1868 was Beverly Randolph Wellford, a medical graduate of the University of Maryland and an early president of the American Medical Association. Levin S. Joynes, who had studied for two and a half years in Dublin and Paris, was dean of the college, professor of the institutes of medicine and medical jurisprudence, and a medical historian by avocation. James Brown McCaw, professor of chemistry, had studied with Valentine Mott, a New York surgeon famed for ligating the great arteries. McCaw was commandant and medical chief of the Chimborazo Hospital, reputed to be a model of efficiency.[52]

The man Simon remembered best of all his teachers in Richmond was Charles Bell Gibson, professor of surgery and surgical anatomy, one of the first in Virginia to use anesthetics, and surgeon general of the state until its medical affairs were merged with those of the Confederacy. Gibson's two weekly lectures were supplemented by demonstrations and operations "of every grade" frequently performed before the class. Even before the war the proportion of surgical cases in Richmond's hospitals was usually large and varied, including amputations of every sort, removal of tumors and operations for cataract, fistulas, polyps, pterygium (a growth over the surface of the eye), ovariotomy, and many operations of "less magnitude." The College Infirmary, an eighty-bed, three-story brick building completed in April 1861, was open to student observers "free of charge." Admitting both races and all medical and surgical cases except insanity and infectious disease, it accommodated 1,254 patients during 1861, 1,015 of them soldiers of the Confederacy. Soon after it opened, the need for beds outran its capacity, and the college had to reopen its own hospital ward to accommodate sick and wounded soldiers.[53]

In addition to Gibson's lectures and demonstrations in surgical anatomy, the Richmond faculty offered general and special anatomy and "unsurpassed" facilities for practical anatomy. "The supply of subjects for dissection is abundant, and at a very trifling cost to the student. The dissecting-room is spacious, well lighted and complete in all its arrangements." It is surprising to find such statements boldly published in the faculty circular for 1859, for the Virginia legislature did not provide for anatomical material for students until 1885. Before that time this state-chartered medical school, like many others in America, required its graduates to learn anatomy by dissecting human cadavers procured illegally. The janitor of the Richmond school, who received equal billing with the faculty in the catalog of 1860–61, probably carried on the tradition of the faithful *Diener,* "armed with pick, spade, and lantern," who "fared forth alone or accompanied by a few adventurous medical students" to resurrect a recently interred body.[54]

The problem of preservation plagued the study of anatomy in Richmond as elsewhere. Although their geographical location cannot have made more than a few hours' difference in the lasting power of cadavers, the faculty assured prospective students that Richmond's "winter temperature is far more favorable for the study of Practical Anatomy than that of any city south of Virginia."[55]

In one respect Richmond appears to have fallen short of Charleston: while the Medical College of South Carolina had created a chair of pathological anatomy for Eli Geddings in 1837, the Medical College of Virginia did not incorporate this important study until 1867. There can be little doubt that both schools failed—in the manner of the times—to provide the clinical work and practical experience students needed. When Simon received his M.D. on March 6, 1862, he did so, he said later, "before ever treating a sick person or even having lanced a boil."[56]

At graduation, the customary fifty-dollar prizes were awarded to the two graduates who submitted the best essays, one in the theory and practice of medicine, the other in surgery. Simon did not win a prize, perhaps because he chose a topic insufficiently attuned to the times. The winning essays dealt with camp fever and the nature and treatment of gunshot wounds.[57] Military medicine was clearly the order of the day.

On March 8 the southern frigate *Merrimac,* converted to an ironclad, sank the Federal *Cumberland* in the stretch of water called Hampton Roads, a victory reversed the next day when the *Monitor* obliged the *Merrimac* to withdraw. At the same time, on the western front, Confederate forces lost the bloodiest battle yet seen in the war—the supposedly short war now almost one year old. In Columbia, Mary Boykin Chesnut heard the news from Pea Ridge and Hampton Roads and noted in her diary that "the handful left at home are rushing to arms at last."[58]

Baruch was one of the handful who could no longer stand apart. His flight from the disabilities of Jews in Prussia had led him to the center of a struggle involving his friends, his classmates, his teachers, and his adopted state. If he had failed to avoid military service—which was one of his reasons for coming to America—he had at least postponed it long enough to become a doctor. Whatever the true war aim of the Confederacy, he could have had little more than a vicarious interest in the outcome, for he was neither slaveowner nor southerner. It was by mere chance that he lived in South Carolina at all: the Baums had happened to settle there, and he had followed where they led. All the same, it was there that he had enjoyed friendships and a foster home. It was there that he had found a life his own land would have denied him because he was a Jew. "South Carolina gave me all I have," he said. "I'll go with my state."[59]

Whether he realized it or not, the war would be a sort of postgraduate course in the practical medicine he had failed to get as a student. In places he had never heard of in March 1862, he would have his share—and more—of clinical experience. Ahead of him lay Second Manassas and Chancellorsville and Gettysburg and the Wilderness.

3 Confederate Surgeon

Within a month of his March graduation from the Medical College of Virginia, Baruch presented himself at the Charleston office of Dr. Robert Alexander Kinloch to be examined for commission in the Confederate medical service. Kinloch, who was one of the most distinguished surgeons of his day, was joined in giving the examination by Dr. Thomas T. Robertson of Winnsboro and by Baruch's beloved professor Eli Geddings. Baruch thought the exam "rigid," and it no doubt was. In the early months of the war, anxiety to acquire medical officers had contributed to admission standards so low that reexamination and dismissals occurred frequently. Soon, however, Secretary of War Judah P. Benjamin was able to report to President Jefferson Davis that "the efficiency of the Corps has been greatly increased by the purgation it has undergone." Standards had risen sufficiently by April 1862 to preclude any necessity for frequent "purgation." By the end of 1861 examinations had become so difficult that one candidate who was "pitched" consoled himself with the admission of one of his examiners that "four out of five wer [sic] thrown."[1]

It would be hard to say just how difficult Baruch's examination was, for standards varied from place to place. Examinations usually consisted of both written and oral portions and were intended primarily to test practical knowledge. Yet a candidate might be asked to describe the microscopic appearance of the brain and the distribution of its nerves or the anatomical structure of the eye with the possible inflammations of its various coats and their differential diagnosis. Such knowledge was easier to measure than a doctor's probable efficiency in amputating limbs or probing for minié balls under chaotic battle conditions.[2]

26

Baruch passed his examination and on April 4, 1862, assumed the duties of assistant surgeon in the Confederate States Army.[3] He thus became part of a medical staff which, though essential to the survival of the military arm, was relegated to an inferior place by its leaders. Unlike officers in the quartermaster and commissary departments, medical men held no actual rank. They were assigned "assimilated rank" only to simplify matters of pay and post allowances. Jefferson Davis has been blamed for this effort to "deprive the medical officers of his army of their actual rank," but doctors in the Union army fared no better. The traditionally and enduringly unsympathetic attitude of military leaders toward army doctors was understandable in an era when physicians merited little esteem even in peacetime.[4]

Enlisted men too occasionally gave vent to their feelings about the medical service. One of them wrote that the surgeon's responsibilities were, first, to purchase a full supply of liquors "under the names of drugs and medicines"; second, "To cause all private cellars to be searched, and all good brandies found there to be confiscated, lest the owners should smuggle them to the soldiers, give them away and make the whole army drunk"; and third, "To see that he and his assistants drink up all of said liquors."[5]

The Confederate medical service did in truth include some bad doctors. But from the time when official boards began to examine surgeons for competence, as opposed to their popular election by the men themselves and the haphazard methods of selection of the early war months, qualified men came into preponderance over the hacks. Not even the most dedicated enemy of the profession could accuse medical officers of avarice, for civilian practice back home paid extravagant returns in comparison with army doctors' salaries.[6]

Baruch's commission as assistant surgeon gave him status comparable to that of a captain of cavalry, with pay allowance from $110 to $150 a month. His pay was calculated on the minimum figure, giving him considerably less than enough to purchase a uniform, which cost at least $200 in Richmond during the winter of 1861–62. Perhaps because of this financial discrepancy—or because of their long friendship—Mannes Baum, who had put Baruch through medical school, also provided him with a uniform and sword. Military discrimination against army medical men did not extend to their dress, which included the finest regalia. The gray fabric and cut of the double-breasted tunic worn by doctors were the same as those of the regular officers, except that the collar and cuffs and the trouser stripes were black, to distinguish them from the light blue of the infantry, the scarlet of the artillery, and the buff of the cavalry. Two rows of gold braid on his coat sleeves and three gold bars on the front ends of his collar made the assistant surgeon equal, at least in official insignia, to the captain of cavalry.[7]

Not yet twenty-two years of age, Baruch was tall with the sprightliness of a short-waisted, long-legged man and perhaps a bit vain with the knowledge of his own good looks. He parted his thick, dark, slightly wavy hair on the side and surrounded his sensitive mouth with a neatly trimmed Vandyke. His eyes, wide-set and so light as to appear almost colorless, gave his face an intensity of awareness accentuated by fine, black, slightly arched eyebrows. With the saber of the light cavalry officer suspended from the medical officer's green silk sash about his waist, he was the quintessence of the youthful, earnest military surgeon. Even in a brief meeting, he gave the impression of being "a promising young man."[8]

His first assignment was somewhat less exciting than he might have hoped. Under the interlocking organization of Confederate field and general hospital services existing during the first two years of the war, he was attached to the Third South Carolina Infantry Battalion. His first post—remote from the troops in camp—was at the Rikersville Hospital in Charleston. Here merely doing the paperwork was an exhausting task. The regulations of the Confederate Medical Department required monthly, quarterly, and consolidated monthly reports of sick and wounded, returns of medical officers and of medical and hospital property, abstracts of medical and hospital property, requisitions for medical and hospital supplies, certificates of disability, and hospital muster rolls. Each hospital was also required to keep a register of patients, a prescription and diet book, a case of copies of requisitions, annual returns, reports of sick and wounded, and an order and letter book.[9]

The paperwork was not all, of course. Patients had to be cared for, but even this was not particularly dramatic, for they were far more likely to be suffering from disease than from battle wounds. Pneumonia was especially prevalent, and the mortality ran high. Then classified as an inflammation, pneumonia was treated accordingly by antiphlogistics, believed to abstract inflammation by relieving congestion. In view of the high mortality under this treatment, which consisted mainly of bleeding and purging, some surgeons eventually decided that wartime pneumonia was different and gave up heroic methods in favor of sustaining aids such as liquor, opium, and quinine.[10]

Before the new therapy came into vogue, Baruch saw a pneumonia patient at the Rikersville Hospital who was more a victim of doctors than of disease. There may have been many similar cases, but the one that most impressed Baruch involved a hardy young mountaineer. On orders of the chief surgeon, Baruch applied a poultice or blister to the man's chest and gave him a mercurial purgative. He followed this by massive doses of nitrous powder—a potent mixture of potassium nitrate, calomel, and "tartarized antimony"—given every three hours until salivation ensued. As a final form of "the doctors' blows upon the enemy," Baruch was told to apply wet cups to the area over the affected lung. As he worked with the flush peculiar to the young medical graduate treating patients for the first time, one of the hospital's volunteer nurses appeared at the bedside and suggested "out of the goodness of her heart and fullness of her knowledge" that he apply "crabs eyes." What humiliation! He did not even know what that was. After a confused retreat to consult his dispensatory (which told him that it meant merely prepared chalk, or powdered calcium carbonate), he made an embarrassed reappearance and proceeded with the treatment. But he never afterward overcame his antagonism toward untrained nurses.[11]

Despite the variety and potency of the prescribed measures, they were either inadequate or excessive, and the outcome of the mountaineer's bout with pneumonia was unhappy. One lung recovered, but the other was attacked, as the doctors pursued the elusive enemy with the same violent tactics, omitting only the blister as a concession to the patient's weakened condition. Baruch ruefully recalled later, "the disease was practically cured, but the patient died from sheer depletion."[12]

In addition to well-meant but medically ineffective efforts of volunteer nurses and inadequate therapeutic methods, Baruch soon recognized that Confederate surgeons faced still another handicap. The South appeared to be headed for a serious drug shortage. On April 2, 1862, just two days before Baruch's examination for commission, Confederate surgeon general Samuel Preston Moore issued a circular urging the collection of "Indigenous Medical Substances of the Vegetable Kingdom." The circular did not specifically mention Lincoln's designation of medicines as contraband of war, but Moore evidently feared the effects of this ban, for he soon commissioned Francis Peyre Porcher, one of Baruch's Charleston professors, to write an entire volume on indigenous medicinal herbs. The surgeon general believed that the forests and savannas of the South could furnish an abundant supply of certain drugs, notably "Tonics, Astringents, Aromatics and Demulcents," and a moderate number of narcotics and sedatives. He urged that local areas also be examined for herbs to be used as "Anodynes, Emetics, and Cathartics."[13]

Moore's idea was not original. The belief that there are plants in every land to cure the diseases found there is one of the most enduring in human history. Centuries before Christ, the author of Ecclesiastes wrote,

"The Lord has created medicines out of the earth, and a sensible man will not refuse them," and in twentieth-century Ireland the belief written by the poets prevails: "Wherever you find the disease you will find the cure."[14] The concept found favor with many southerners, and Moore was apparently one of its enthusiasts. One hospital steward felt that the idea of native remedies sat "like a nightmare upon the brain of the Surgeon-General." Moore did indeed seem to put great emphasis on it. In a pamphlet enclosed with the circular and distributed to medical officers, he described the most important indigenous plants, requesting that his men gather and send them to medical purveyors for preparation and distribution. The purveyors in turn advertised high prices for Georgia bark, white willow, Indian physic, skunk cabbage, wild cherry bark, pipsissewa, and cranesbill, employing agents and even circuit riders to collect plants and encourage country people to do likewise.[15]

The interest spurred by the surgeon general's campaign served indirectly to embarrass Baruch, for the second time in his first two weeks of military service. When a Charleston woman prominent in war relief applied to him for directions in gathering and preparing herbs, he could not locate a copy of the pamphlet for her. Furthermore, he did not even have time to look for one, for he had been ordered to join Lieutenant Colonel George James's Battalion. Still, Mary Amarinthia Snowden was just the sort of person one ought to help, and he did his best. Pleading an unfamiliarity with South Carolina flora, he recommended the few he knew: blackberry root and root of cranesbill (used for diarrhea and dysentery, the most common and debilitating illnesses in the Confederate army); snakeroot (depending on the type, used for phthisis, coughs and colds, nephritis and gonorrhea); wild cherry bark (a sedative and expectorant in gastric weakness, general irritability, and coughs); bloodroot or "Puccoon Root" (for pneumonia, coughs, bronchitis, and jaundice); and slippery elm bark (used for the ubiquitous "camp itch," which could have been prevented by occasional baths).[16]

An army man for barely two weeks, Baruch had already grasped one of the fundamentals. He concluded his note to Mrs. Snowden with the hope that, in ministering to the sick, she would not forget the members of James's Battalion. "Any favors conferred upon the sick under my charge," he wrote, "will not only be gratefully received by them, but place me also under many obligations to you."[17]

Mrs. Snowden did not forget. Among her correspondence—and the remaining record of her work is by no means complete—is a long list of men in the Seventh South Carolina Battalion to whom she sent shirts and socks. The September 16, 1862, *Charleston Mercury* noted that she had gone to Virginia, carrying hospital stores for South Carolinians stationed there.[18]

Baruch had already received his first pay—$66, calculated on the basis of $110 a month from April 4 to 21—when he was transferred from hospital to camp duty. His new post was that of assistant surgeon attached to James's Battalion of Kershaw's Brigade of McLaws's Division of Longstreet's Corps of the Army of Northern Virginia. On his way north from Charleston to Virginia he stopped to say good-bye to the seventeen-year-old brother who had followed him to America. Simon asked him to promise not "to be carried away with the existing enthusiasm," and Herman gave his word not to join the army without Simon's consent.[19]

From Camden, Baruch proceeded northward to join in the last war to be fought in the "medical middle ages."[20] Despite rapidly expanding medical knowledge, physicians in the Civil War period had only a few better therapeutic tools than those at the disposal of physicians during the revolutionary period, among them anesthesia, quinine, and the hypodermic syringe. Despite the excellent work of pathologists early in the century, the headquarters of the U.S. Army Medical Bureau did not employ one until 1863. Historians of Civil War medicine have estimated that the number of clinical thermometers used by northern physicians was not more than twenty. Only the better-educated army surgeons used percussion and auscultation to examine the chest—not to mention the stethoscope. For all the advantages the hypodermic syringe offered, most surgeons persisted in older methods, giving opium in pill form and dusting morphine directly into wounds. Shortages of drugs and supplies within the Confederacy sometimes negated entirely the seeming preventive properties of quinine and the merciful work of the anesthetics.[21]

In addition to gaps in his own armamentarium, the Civil War surgeon also had to contend with the pernicious influences of army life on the human economy. Baruch's particular task was to care for the physical well-being of five hundred infantrymen who would, at various times and to varying degrees, be ill-fed, inadequately clothed, infrequently bathed, and constantly exposed to infections against which they had lowered resistance or none at all. When a medical man dared to suggest sanitary improvements that would lower the disease rate, he more often than not encountered official military resistance of the most hardheaded sort. As the medical director of the northern forces summarized: "The general idea seemed to be that it was the duty of the doctor to physic every man who chose to report sick and to sign such papers as the colonel directed him to sign. To superintend the sanitary condition of the regiment, to call upon the commanding officer to abate nuisances, to take measures for the prevention of disease was in many instances considered impertinent and obtrusive." Like other medical men just coming to the field, Baruch had to learn two elementary lessons: first, how to manage without supplies and equipment; second, that talk as he might, soldiers would still do as they pleased with regard to sanitary matters—and officials would, for the most part, defend this freedom for their men. [22]

Among his other duties was that of keeping records, for even in the field, medical officers had to do a great deal of paperwork. Early each morning the men with complaints presented themselves at sick call. Examination was usually cursory, the rapid diagnosis and prescription governed to a great degree by the supply of medicines on hand. In addition to writing up daily reports after morning sick call, the medical officer was expected to make weekly, monthly, and quarterly reports to the senior surgeon of the brigade, who consolidated and forwarded them to the chief surgeon of the division. [23]

It was not until the end of the summer of 1862 that the war really began for Baruch. On August 23, General Robert E. Lee called up several divisions, among them McLaws's, to join his army along the Rappahannock. Baruch accompanied his men on the march—as assistant surgeons were expected to do—on horseback. Early in the afternoon of the twenty-eighth, as they approached the field of Manassas, they reached the pass cut through Bull Run Mountain called Thoroughfare Gap. The brigade suddenly halted under orders to make preparations for battle. Leaving his command at the mouth of the gap, Baruch took his steward and two litter bearers toward the rear of the column to obtain battlefield supplies from the medical supply wagon. [24]

The general plan of both medical services in the Civil War called for the full surgeon to select some building or site for his field hospital at a "safe distance" to the rear of the fighting—"safe" being beyond the range of enemy artillery, or about one and a half to two miles. At the same time, assistant surgeons like Baruch were to establish a "primary station" just outside musketry range, where the wounded could get first aid and be loaded into regimental ambulances for transport back to the safer, better-equipped field hospital. During the battle Baruch was to provide temporary control of hemorrhage by ligature, tourniquet, or bandage and compress; adjust and temporarily fix fractured limbs; give water, anodynes, or stimulants; and see that the wounded were promptly carried to the rear, either by ambulance or by an infirmary detail. The detail consisted of about thirty men, usually those "least effective under arms." Each member carried a canteen of water, a tin cup, and a knapsack containing lint, bandages, sponges, tourniquets, four splints, and a pint of alcoholic stimulants. There was one litter to every two men. Besides all this equipment, the assistant surgeon himself was expected to carry onto the field a pocket case of instruments, ligatures, needles, pins, chloroform, morphine, alcohol, tourniquets, bandages, lint, and splints.[25]

When Baruch returned from the rear with his supplies, he learned that the troops had already marched into the gap. Those who remained outside warned him that he would "find it very hot in there." He went in to find himself in a narrow gorge formed by two high faces of rock rising from one hundred to three hundred feet on either side. In places along the face of the canyon wild ivy grew out of the deep fissures, breaking the stern grayness of the basalt walls. It was a place of almost breathtaking beauty, but it was wasted on Baruch, who had never been under fire before. He found no place for a "primary station." Accompanied by his infirmary corps of unarmed men (distinguished from the rest of the command only by badges), he moved about giving first aid and supervising the removal of the wounded amid the shellbursts, which "demanded frequent prostration on the ground to escape the rattling fragments."[26]

Because of the delay at Thoroughfare Gap, General John Pope's army was already in full retreat when Baruch and his brigade reached the battlefield of Second Manassas on August 29. Shells thrown by retreating artillery burst here and there, apparently harmless to the latecomers beginning to cross the field. Seeing neither dead nor wounded, Baruch felt lighthearted as he watched the enemy flee into the dust-enveloped distance. His horse withstood the occasional shells and wild rebel victory cries with less equanimity. Momentarily preoccupied with his uneasy mount and the loss of his blanket, insecurely tied to the saddle in the haste of the morning's march, he suddenly became aware of a whizzing sound, strange and awesome to the unpracticed ear. Veterans around him whispered, "Minié balls! The enemy is making a stand." He saw the enthusiasm of victory quickly give way to an oppressive solemnity wherever the minié ball sang its "diabolical mosquito song."[27]

Ducking and dodging to avoid the invisible foe, Baruch's command hurried to shelter, where they received orders to form in battle line. Once safe in a wooded spot, Baruch dismounted. Minié balls and grapeshot flew through the treetops, showering the ground with leaves and massive branches. Looking about, he saw his white blanket not far away on the field, but he had no chance to rescue it. A moment later, two litter bearers came into view carrying a wounded man. Baruch directed them to put him down in the shelter of a rail fence. Just as he began to dress the wound, a solid shot fell on the other side of the fence, throwing earth over patient and doctor. With a caution born of his experience at Thoroughfare Gap, he had the man moved to a more sheltered place before continuing his work.

That night he camped with the men on the battlefield. He awoke the next morning to the ghastly scenes of war. Long lines of ambulances, which Lee had permitted to come up from Washington under flag of truce, were carrying away the Union wounded. Because the supply of regular ambulances soon proved inadequate, Union forces called on makeshifts: hacks, omnibuses, beer trucks, and delivery trucks. Still there were not enough. Three days after the battle, some three thousand wounded remained on the field, mostly unfed and almost all without surgical attention. Baruch's mind registered every detail as he watched men from both sides burying the dead amid scenes of horror: "Mere remnants of men and animals; arms flung away in the mad retreat; blood pools that were less horrible than the shattered bodies with vermin at feast."[28]

In search of instructions, he visited an improvised field hospital. Passing by the wounded, who lay outside patiently waiting their turn for whatever help medicine and surgery could give, he entered the small house. There, on a table formed by laying a door over a box and a barrel, one of the wounded was receiving chloroform, the preferred anesthetic among southern surgeons. A doctor stood nearby, ready to operate. Surveying Baruch's slight form and pale face, he banteringly offered him the knife, saying, "Perhaps you would like to operate, Doctor." Baruch took off his coat, rolled up his sleeves, and proceeded with the amputation according to the technique he had learned from Charles Bell Gibson at the Medical College of Virginia. When he finished the amputation— his first surgical operation of any kind—the surgeon commended his work.[29]

In the massive repair work that followed the battle, Baruch learned that veterans had good reason to fear the whistle of the minié balls. Unlike the round musket ball, the faster-moving, conoidal, rifle-driven minié was apt to shatter, splinter, and split long bones, causing greater shock and more risk of infection than had ever been known before. None of the musket balls of the day had the comparative advantages of the modern bullet, which travels at such high velocity that it is sterilized by heat and, being encased in steel, does not spread on contact but merely drills a neat aseptic path through tissue and bone alike. During the Civil War, the vast area of laceration and the track, altogether out of proportion to the caliber of the projectile itself, soon convinced surgeons that early amputation to avoid infection was the only hopeful course. The probability of hospital gangrene and other prevalent sequelae to amputation increased markedly if an operation was delayed more than twenty-four hours after the wound occurred.[30]

A few days after Manassas, the Confederates were on the march again, this time toward Maryland. Tired and gloomy at the outset of a journey begun in rain and hunger, the troops became more cheerful as they approached the harvest-heavy fields across the border from Virginia. By the fifth and sixth of September, when they crossed the Potomac by the fords near Leesburg, the strains of "Maryland, My Maryland" echoed from one end of the long columns to the other.[31]

On the march to Boonsboro, Baruch's job was to act as surgeon to the rear guard, charged with picking up stragglers. Of the three aims which all military doctrines are said to have in common—to frighten, to wound, and to kill—he had seen a good bit of the last two in his five months of war. He did not realize the power of fright until this march revealed a disease new to his inexperienced eye. Never before had he been called on to examine so many men who complained of feeling too ill to march or to carry their gear. With his penchant for foreign phrases, he named this new symptom-complex *"mal de bataille."* The first cases appeared when the thunder of distant artillery drew near; they soon increased in number, becoming unmanageable when the march brought the men within earshot of rattling musketry.[32]

After a weary march in which the rear guard rounded up a large number of stragglers, they reached the battlefield of South Mountain only to find their men already in retreat. "On came the shrill and high-pitched Union cheer—rushing soldiers, flying artillery—sullen mien of the line that still held formation. On came the screech of the shells . . . nearer and nearer the terrific explosions." Baruch wheeled about and joined the retreat.[33]

Stopping in front of an abandoned house from which flew the yellow flag of the hospital, he rummaged in the closets until he found half a loaf of bread and some apple butter. He had just begun to eat when a shell struck the chimney and sent a shower of bricks thundering down the roof. Baruch forgot his hunger. He mounted his horse and galloped to the wagon train in the rear. Exhausted by the day's march and excitement, he crawled beneath a wagon and slept. During the night a young adjutant shook him into wakefulness long enough to present him with an order to remain with the wounded, but he was too tired to comprehend the significance of the message. He returned to his wheeled shelter and awakened only when it moved away.[34]

Faint streaks of day were lighting the gloomy sky as he made the first round of his "hospital," Boonsboro's brick Disciples Church. Seventy-five seriously wounded men lay outside on the lawn and on the floor within. Although their wounds had been hastily dressed on the battlefield, most of them required immediate attention. By unhinging the door from an adjacent house abandoned during the battle, Baruch built an operating table like the one he had seen at Second Manassas. Laying the door across two barrels, he ordered the most seriously wounded man to be placed on the table by two soldier nurses. While the patient was receiving chloroform, he prepared his instruments, barely aware of the retreat going on about him—the tramp of the orderly troops and the rumble of wagons and artillery trains.

Suddenly his concentration on the stern task before him was broken by the clatter of hoofs and the spray of bullets against the upper walls and roofs of nearby houses. Despite the advantages of operating outside in the daylight, where the moving open air would dilute the anesthetic, Baruch and his assistants carried the chloroformed patient inside. [35]

The clash of Union troops with Lee's retreating rear guard was over as quickly as it began, and the narrow streets of Boonsboro rapidly filled with Federal cavalry. Now Baruch understood the full meaning of his assignment to stay with the wounded. Even before his appointment as assistant surgeon had been confirmed and his commission made official, he was a prisoner of the enemy.

All day and all night General George B. McClellan's troops tramped through the streets. When Baruch requested that a Union guard be placed at the church gate, the reply was "Too busy," but no one interrupted his treatment of the wounded. The following day, while the guns of Antietam boomed in the distance, he learned that "courtesy and consideration" were the rule toward captured medical officers. Side by side with him in the rain, Union surgeon J. P. Daly helped him care for his patients. Daly, a jolly, kindhearted Irishman, seemed not only humane but even "sympathetic and cordial." [36]

For nearly two months Baruch remained a prisoner in Boonsboro. He and his Confederate colleagues took their meals, at "Uncle Sam's" expense, in the little country hotel where they met Union medical officers socially as well as professionally. Passing through the columns at rest in the street, the captive surgeons often overheard whispers of "See the Rebs," whispers intended less to give offense than to express satisfied curiosity. Baruch frankly enjoyed the "social amenities to which some lovely Maryland 'sympathizers' of the gentler sex materially contributed." Except for an illness, he considered his stay in Boonsboro one of the most delightful of his war experiences. [37]

From a purely professional viewpoint, it was not always so satisfying. In contrast to the efficacy with which men smashed each other's bodies, nature was not always equal to the task of mending. The so-called surgical fevers—tetanus, erysipelas, hospital gangrene, and pyemia—took a

Civilian volunteers often gathered to help remove the wounded from the battlefield. After the fighting at Sharpsburg, Maryland (called Antietam in the North), Alfred R. Waud made this pencil and Chinese white drawing (published as an engraving in *Harper's Weekly,* October 11, 1862) to depict volunteers unloading an ambulance while surgeons at the left amputated a soldier's leg. Shortly before this battle, which left some 7,000 dead and 17,000 wounded, Baruch and the 75 wounded Confederates in his care were captured in Boonsboro, about six miles to the northeast. (Courtesy of the Library of Congress.)

high toll among postoperative cases, despite surgeons' efforts to enforce cleanliness. Many of the procedures used to disinfect wounds or remove gangrenous tissue were agonizing to the patients.[38]

Baruch felt particular compassion for the amputees, who experienced prolonged torment in the postoperative care they received. For the first two or three days after amputation, the stump was left at rest in a water dressing. Then began the work of warding off infection, according to the best methods of the day:

Each stump was exposed by removing the bandages, now soiled and saturated with decomposing fluids; sponges were plied and water was poured in order to cleanse the stump, which lay quivering and trembling within the hands of an assistant. The openings from which dangled the silk ligatures, and which were intended for drainage, were, in many instances, so closed by swelling that it was necessary to cut some of the sutures. The stump being clean, it was again bandaged and replaced. Day after day the poor patient was subjected to the same ordeal, perhaps intensified by the injection of some "disinfectant" . . . solution through the stump. This undressing and redressing was continued from day to day, sometimes several times daily, for weeks, until the patient either succumbed or the stump healed, while he was reduced to the last extreme of debility.[39]

Baruch thought all this disturbance robbed nature of the working advantage it might have had with complete rest. Even with such constant attention, the few cases that healed without the formation of pus were displayed as remarkable. Many never recovered at all.[40]

By the middle of November, only a few wounded remained to occupy the little cluster of surgeons. Many had recovered sufficiently to go to Federal prisons and many others lay in Boonsboro graves when the last of the convalescents and their doctors bade their northern friends good-bye and left in a horse-drawn ambulance. At Frederick City a Union lieutenant took charge of escorting them by train to Baltimore.[41] Before the train pulled out, the surgeons somehow got word that Baltimore sympathizers would have carriages waiting near the station to take them to the homes of friends.

The lieutenant in charge had other ideas. He claimed them as prisoners of war and insisted that he was duty bound to deliver them along with the other prisoners to the provost marshal. Their plea of noncombatant status failed to sway him, although it was justified under the then-existing agreement between North and South. Only after much coaxing did he agree to accompany Baruch and another medical officer to the Eutaw House to see General Morris, the commanding general of the department. Morris ordered all the surgeons released, asking only that they report at the quartermaster's office the next morning for transportation to the appointed place of exchange. Free men at last, the southern doctors scattered over the friendly border city.[42]

Baruch and his companion, Dr. Bailey, went to the home of a prominent Baltimore druggist, where ladies and gentlemen in evening dress received them as honored guests. After a hot oyster supper, they danced until two in the morning. The next day their hostess announced that they were expected to drive out for a rapid view of the city. In an open victoria drawn by a splendid team of horses, they rode down Baltimore Street in full uniform, "the observed of all observers." At Bendann's Gallery they left the carriage to have their pictures taken as a memento of the visit. After the sitting, they found themselves surrounded by a group of Baltimore ladies who clamored for their photographs and assured them of their sympathy by "many a gentle pressure of the hand."[43]

The doctors were understandably reluctant to leave such "delightful 'captivity,'" but that afternoon, as they had promised, they boarded the bay boat *Louisiana* and sailed out into Chesapeake Bay. A trip of fifteen hours brought them to Fortress Monroe, where they could enjoy a view embracing the mouths of the James and Elizabeth rivers and the entire space of Hampton Roads. Here the exchange officer, James Mulford, supervised their transfer from the *Louisiana* to another boat which carried them up the James to Aiken's Landing below Dutch Gap.[44]

Baruch was again with his brigade on December 13, when they drove back the repeated assaults of General Ambrose E. Burnside's men on Marye's Heights above Fredericksburg. That night a south wind warmed the air to the temperature of spring, and the northern lights shone on the scene of Confederate victory. The next afternoon was a proud one for everyone from Kershaw County, when one of their own boys risked his life to carry water to ease the suffering of the Union wounded on the field. Confederate losses, though small compared with the massacre of northerners, totaled some forty-two hundred, enough to keep the doctors busy behind the lines.[45]

The winter at Fredericksburg was pleasant for Baruch despite cold and hunger and smallpox. The men amused themselves with dramas, minstrel shows, and snowball fights, for the snow was a phenomenon of unusual interest to those from the Deep South, if not to the Prussian immigrant. There were religious meetings and vigorous political discussions of President Lincoln's Emancipation Proclamation. In an effort to compensate for the lack of medical periodical literature, some of the doctors banded together in "societies" to discuss medical and surgical subjects, using the plentiful supply of cadavers for "scientific and educational purposes." What impressed Baruch most was the "amenities of civilized warfare," the unwarlike conduct of the Union and Confederate pickets ranged along opposite sides of the Rappahannock. "Our men would fashion little wooden boats, place tobacco upon them and push them over a narrow part of the river to receive in return coffee."[46]

During the winter lull, Baruch returned to Camden, where he found his young brother Herman in the uniform of the cavalry, a courier on the staff of General Pierre G. T. Beauregard. When Baruch rebuked him for his disobedience, Herman said, "Brother, I could no longer stand it, I could not look into the faces of the ladies." Anxiety to please the ladies was scarcely grounds for reprimand in the Baruch family. Simon himself enjoyed the admiration lavished on him by Mrs. Mannes Baum's young

Winnsboro niece, Belle Wolfe, who was painting a portrait of the handsome surgeon.[47]

When he visited in the winter of 1862–63, Baruch found Camden a
changed place. Like nearby Winnsboro, Camden was a terminal point
along the railroad that carried wounded and sick soldiers back from the
field in ever-growing numbers. To care for those unable to go farther by
themselves, the women of both towns set up wayside hospitals and
auxiliary relief associations; among the most active in collecting and
distributing food, clothing, and medical supplies to South Carolina
troops were the women of the Baum and Wolfe families.[48]

Because Baruch wore the uniform of the Confederacy, and because his
Jewish friends and "adopted" family were also active in support of the
cause, they may have been spared the lash of a rising current of anti-
Semitism in the South. This wave of feeling, seemingly unprecedented in
the history of the region, was directed particularly against Jews of German and Polish ancestry who were engaged in trade. Indignant over the
twin evils of extortion and speculation that mushroomed in the time of
the blockade, many native southerners could not admit that any of their
own people would stoop to profiteering in necessities of life while the
South was struggling for existence. Immigrant Jews among the southern
merchant class received the lion's share of the blame. Even in the army,
anti-Semitism erupted occasionally. The anonymous author of an essay
written for the *Army Argus* listed as one of the duties of the southern
people "to surrender the entire trade in shoes and clothing—on which
trade the army is dependent—to that patriotic class of men known as
Jews, who are too conscientious to charge the government or the army a
profit exceeding two thousand percent." If Baruch felt any of these gibes,
he left no record of it. With revolutions raging anew back in Europe and
his people there centuries behind American Jews in every sort of freedom, he could be well content with the path he had chosen.[49]

After spending some time at Camp Brooks, South Carolina, Baruch
returned to Fredericksburg. There, through the slowly deepening spring
of March and April, the opposing armies lay as quiet as the balloons that
drifted above the lines. On April 27, when General Joseph Hooker
moved his troops across the Rappahannock to attack, the long rest came
to an end.[50]

Shortly before sunrise on the first day of May, three brigades of
McLaws's Division, among them Kershaw's, marched up to join the three
of R. H. Anderson's Division on the Old Turnpike near the crossroads
called Chancellorsville. Outnumbered by more than two to one, Lee's
forces fought a hard three-day battle that gave the South its most costly

victory. In addition to an estimated thirteen thousand casualties among their own men, the southern surgeons assumed the burden of caring for about twenty-five hundred of the Union wounded.[51]

Baruch worked inside the little Salem Church, where Kershaw's Brigade had helped to drive back a strong attack. In his anxiety to repay the kindness shown him and his men by Union surgeons at Boonsboro, he assisted captured Union surgeons "with all the means in my power." Lafayette Guild, medical director of the Army of Northern Virginia, was well pleased with the conduct of his officers, who, he said, would "compare favorably with any other similar organization upon this continent." But the long, grueling hours of work were beginning to take their toll. On the second day of the battle at Chancellorsville, Baruch began to be troubled with a malady of his right eye—a malady that would grow progressively worse and eventually threaten him with blindness.[52]

On the morning of June 3, McLaws's Division quietly broke camp and moved toward Culpeper Court House. Along with the First Corps—Longstreet's freshly organized "great rock"—Baruch joined in the northward march up the firm, broad roads of the Shenandoah Valley. By June 19 they had reached Ashby's Gap in the Blue Ridge. The next day they forded the Shenandoah and camped on its left bank. At Hagerstown in Maryland the three corps of Lee's army converged and continued their march until the twenty-seventh, when they rested in Chambersburg, Pennsylvania. Here, while the southern surgeons scouted up molasses and whiskey for their sick, Baruch watched with amusement as the Chambersburg women displayed Union flags on their bosoms. Seemingly in preparation for march on the twenty-ninth, Longstreet had his men turn in early on the night before, but they were still in Chambersburg, twenty-four miles from the town of Gettysburg, on the night of June 30.[53]

It was already late in the first day of fighting at Gettysburg when Kershaw's Brigade reached the battlefield. They camped for the night in a dew-covered meadow. The next day, after considerable marching and countermarching that gave Baruch a good view of the battle preparations, they formed a line opposite the Peach Orchard. Baruch was at his first aid station, not far behind the line, when Kershaw's men attacked the battery in the orchard. Watching this charge of an entire division (the first he had ever witnessed), he saw the enemy artillery belch fire and the men begin to fall. When several shells burst near his own position, he was relieved to be ordered to the division hospital, far behind the lines in the Black Horse Tavern.[54]

A wayside hotel about three miles west and slightly south of the town of Gettysburg, on the Fairfield Road at the crossing of Marsh Creek, the tavern included a stone house, a barn, and several wooden outbuildings. To the north and west were orchards. Imperfect though it was, the sixty-year-old tavern made a better hospital than many of the houses, hotels, and churches being pressed into use elsewhere around the battlefield. Baruch and his companion surgeons hastily opened their supplies and set up operating tables. They had already finished when the first ambulance loads of wounded began to arrive.[55]

Some of the men were able to tell the surgeons why nearly all of them were wounded on the left side. Having captured the battery in the Peach Orchard and put to flight a Wisconsin brigade supporting it, they were ordered to close a gap on the right of the line. This deflected the charging column and enabled the retreating artillerymen to return and send an enfilade into the Confederate left flank. It was a hard day for what Joseph B. Kershaw sadly and affectionately called his "doomed regiments. Hundreds of the bravest and best men of South Carolina fell," he lamented, "victims to this fatal blunder." Those of his men who survived to fight on found heavy opposition on Cemetery Ridge. Kershaw lost about half of his brigade strength. More than six hundred of his men were killed and wounded. In one company of the Second South Carolina, only four men of the forty who marched out across Emmitsburg Road survived to bury their fallen comrades.[56]

All day on July 2—and all that night by the light of sperm candles—surgeons worked at the field hospital. On July 3 wounded continued to pour into the yard of the Black Horse Tavern. Everywhere around the little town of Gettysburg—normal population, 2,400—the story was the same. Exhausted surgeons worked with incredible endurance. Both armies would soon move out, and Union medical director Jonathan Letterman, expecting another big battle, could leave a mere 106 medical people, only about one-third of them operating surgeons, to care for the estimated 14,500 Union wounded. And there were 6,000 or more casualties among the Confederates.[57]

There was a pitiful discrepancy, as General Carl Schurz observed, between the handful of doctors and the masses of wounded who needed immediate attention:

Most of the operating tables were placed in the open where the light was best, some of them partially protected against the rain by tarpaulins or blankets stretched upon poles. There stood the surgeons, their sleeves rolled up to their elbows, their bare arms as well as their linen aprons smeared with blood, their knives not seldom held between their teeth, while they were helping a patient on or off the table or had their hands otherwise occupied. . . . As a wounded man

The Black Horse Tavern, where westbound horse-drawn conveyances had found food and lodging throughout the nineteenth century, became a field hospital for Baruch, two fellow surgeons, and some 576 Confederate soldiers wounded during the Battle of Gettysburg. Today it is a private residence designated as a historic landmark. (Photograph, taken in 1863, courtesy of Bill Leonard, present proprietor and resident of Black Horse Tavern Farm. My thanks also to James M. McPherson, who first called my attention to this picture when it appeared in an article entitled, "Bernard Baruch's Father Recounts His Experiences as a Confederate Surgeon," *Civil War Times Illustrated,* October 1965.)

was lifted on the table, often shrieking with pain as the attendants handled him, the surgeon quickly examined the wound and resolved upon cutting off the injured limb. Some ether was administered and the body put in position in a moment. The surgeon snatched his knife from between his teeth . . . wiped it rapidly once or twice across his blood-stained apron, and the cutting began. The operation accomplished, the surgeon would look around with a deep sigh, and then—"Next!"[58]

For thirty-six straight hours Baruch worked at the Black Horse Tavern, tending Union men along with his own. The pace was so frantic that the only case recorded under his name, out of the many he cared for, is that of a twenty-one-year-old private who survived the ordeal of the gallant Second South Carolina Regiment—minus the lower third of his left leg.[59]

At sundown on July 3 Baruch threw himself down on a pile of hay and slept. When he awoke, he found that he was one of three medical officers ordered to stay behind with the wounded at the tavern. Out of the 576 division casualties brought to the hospital during the three days, about 222 wounded remained, all of them too badly hurt to accompany the retreating Army of Northern Virginia or even to be moved to the safety of general hospitals behind the lines.[60]

Everything seemed quiet about the tavern. The July sun shone brightly, birds twittered in the orchard, and fragrant blossoms scented the air. Baruch and his colleagues, Surgeon J. F. Pearce and Assistant Surgeon H. J. Nott of the Eighth and Second South Carolina regiments respectively, commissioned the hospital cook to prepare their first meal in some time. For the main course they had caught a peacock that had strutted too near the tavern. In the deserted kitchen they had found some cold biscuits, coffee, and sugar. They seated themselves and prepared to begin this feast, but just as Baruch raised his knife to carve, a shell shrieked through the morning silence and exploded in a field nearby. Deserting the breakfast table, the doctors scrambled to the top of the barn and hoisted a yellow cloth—the hospital emblem of pre–Red Cross days—from its lightning rod. As they hurried on to reassure the wounded, they saw two Confederate scouts, field glasses in hand, dash away from the hill in front of the orchard.[61]

Except for their patients, these were the last Confederates the doctors were to see for a long time. Once again, for the second time within a year, Baruch was a Federal prisoner.[62]

Gettysburg to Appomattox

4

Even after the yellow flag flew plainly from the top of the barn, six more shells landed nearby. Then all grew quiet and Doctors Pearce, Nott, and Baruch returned to their cold breakfast in the orchard.

They had barely finished eating when the hill opposite them began to bristle with a line of cavalry, weapons shimmering in the brilliant July sun. Slowly the line rode down the hill. Dr. Pearce, the ranking officer, directed Baruch (who, he believed, could better "understand these Yankees") to meet the pickets and surrender. Straightening his gray coat and green sash as he went, Baruch approached the line and asked to speak to the commanding officer. A captain galloped to his side, saluted, and demanded to know if there were many rebels around. To Baruch's reply that there were only wounded and medical personnel, the captain declared, "We'll see to that ourselves," and ordered his men to fall in. The bugle sounded and the cavalcade dashed away, to return about an hour later, followed by what Baruch took for the "entire 6th Corps" of General John Sedgwick.

Among the brilliantly attired staff officers who filled the yard of the tavern, Baruch tried to find the medical director. Failing this, he addressed his complaint about the shelling of the hospital to the adjutant general, who politely stated that they had not noticed the yellow flag and were only trying to dislodge troops they suspected to be behind the hill, where they had seen scouts.[1]

The amenities and the surrender completed, everyone turned to the grave problem of feeding the wounded. The first few days after the fighting were anxious ones, but at least there was plenty of food to be had, however slow it might be in coming. By contrast, the South could not always provide adequate supplies even for the general hospitals far removed from front-line emergency areas, leaving at least one convalescent to feel that he "would just as soon lie on my back and let the moon shine in my mouth" as try to satisfy his hunger with hospital meals.[2] The tremendous concentration of wounded in the small area around Gettysburg made for an acute food shortage in the days immediately following the battle, a shortage softened only theoretically by the intention of the Federal government to furnish enough for all the wounded, northerners and southerners alike. As one nurse put it, "Uncle Sam is very rich, but very slow."[3]

Fortunately, private philanthropy moved in to fill the gap. On the morning of July 5, Baruch was called to the flap door of his tent by an officer in a chaplain's uniform, a kindly looking gentleman with beaming face who came from the Christian Commission depot, set up in town to distribute supplies to the impromptu field hospitals. Two hours later, Baruch and an orderly rode into Gettysburg on horses hired by paying a shoulder of bacon, a commodity left in "needlessly abundant supply" by the retreating Confederate commissary. A stop at Christian Commission headquarters netted them several bags of supplies and the suggestion that they also try the Sanitary Commission depot.[4]

The suggestion proved immensely helpful. As Baruch approached the warehouse of the Sanitary Commission, he saw that the sidewalk and even the street outside were crowded with barrels and boxes of provisions. Standing in the busy crowd where blue uniforms pressed against gray and army wagons were loaded to bursting with supplies, he scanned with amazement the mounds of "everything a sick or wounded man could ask for." A commission clerk took down the location of the hospital, the names of the surgeons, and the number of wounded.[5] From the quartermaster Baruch secured the use of a wagon, which commission agents loaded as courteously as if Baruch were "a merchant purchasing goods." Everything he asked for was given: a barrel of eggs packed in sawdust; a lemon box half filled with lemons, half with butter packed in thick paper and covered with ice. Ice itself, usually brought into the South by ship from New England, was a luxury to blockaded Confederates, especially to the thirsty feverish wounded.[6] Some items were offered above and beyond necessities: a keg of tamarinds imported from the West Indies to be used as refrigerants and diluents in fever; wines and jellies—delicacies from the kitchens of the North.[7]

On the advice of the officer in charge, Baruch went to enter a request for medical supplies. He was ushered in to see Jonathan Letterman, medical director of the Army of the Potomac, the man who created a model ambulance service, reorganized the medical supply system, and molded an efficient division field hospital structure. Letterman handed him a blank requisition, showed him how to make it out, approved it, and sent it to be filled by a medical purveyor. The only medicine not available was calomel, stricken from the Federal medical service supply table by Surgeon General William A. Hammond because of its frequent abuse. Baruch never forgot the magnanimous treatment accorded the southern wounded by Letterman, a "true soldier . . . and a true physician."[8]

Along with food from the Christian and Sanitary commissions and medical supplies from the Army of the Potomac, Baruch received still another gift, this time a personal one. After Gettysburg as after many Civil War battles, civilian surgeons from nearby towns flocked to the great gatherings of wounded. Among those who came up from Baltimore was a "Dr. F.," who watched Baruch perform an operation and complimented him on his skill.[9] The following day, Dr. F. returned and presented Baruch with "a splendid Tiemann field operating case" with his name engraved on the cover. This was probably the most useful gift anyone could have given a Confederate surgeon; the shortage of surgical instruments in the South had begun early in the war and was the most constant and universal shortage of all medical equipment. Baruch counted himself fortunate to acquire such a fine set—a product of the house of Tiemann & Co., celebrated New York instrument makers—at a time when so many of his colleagues had none at all.[10]

There was a shortage of nurses, too, a shortage which placed an extra burden on the already strained surgeons, inducing Federal authorities to permit paroled Confederate soldiers to act as nurses. After the Gettysburg holocaust the government even allowed southern women to enter the area to tend their wounded. Here again, the friendly city of Baltimore came to Baruch's rescue.[11] A few days after the battle, two women of the Howard family traveled up with an English nurse to volunteer their services at the Black Horse Tavern. They were totally unlike the "fussy female notoriety seekers" and the "quarrelsome, meddlesome, busybodies" surgeons so often complained of; nor were they "wretched females" who plagued others with their "simple" wants— "simply a room, a bed, a looking glass, someone to get their meals and do little things for them."[12] Undaunted by the fact that all the buildings were occupied by wounded, the Misses Howard asked to be assigned quarters in the garret, directly under a roof receiving the full force of the summer sun. They began at once, without ostentation, nourishing the feeble, encouraging the homesick, cheering the despondent, and giving religious consolation to the dying. Under their attention the crude straw pallets spread upon the floor of the barn and on the ground in the orchard soon assumed an air of orderliness and comfort.[13]

Even with the aid of volunteer nurses, civilian surgeons, and several philanthropic commissions, many of the wounded could not be saved. Tetanus, caused by a bacillus carried in the intestines of cattle and horses, occurred rarely during the war, probably because much of the fighting took place on virgin soil, unplowed and unmanured. When it did strike, the fatality ran to 89 percent. Baffled doctors blamed it on a variety of causes: exposure to excessive heat or cold; night air and drafts; neglect of thorough and early cleansing of wounds (which was closest to the truth); pressure on nerves by missiles, bone splinters, or bandages; or injuries to nerves while the surgeon probed or operated. When six of Baruch's most severely wounded charges developed tetanus, he had to treat them without the knowledge that their muscular convulsions and horrible fixed smiles came from toxins produced by an anaerobic bacillus planted deep in their wounds on the field where they fell or perhaps in the very yard of the tavern. Baruch applied the usual inadequate treatment: mild dressings over the wound, large doses of brandy and opium, and feeding through nose tubes to prevent starvation. Despite his efforts, every one of the six men died.[14]

Except for the tragic losses that continued long after the battle ended, Baruch enjoyed the six weeks he spent around Gettysburg. It was a unique medical community. The Confederate wounded alone were scattered in twenty-four different camps within an area of twelve miles, and close association with other surgeons filled his days with interesting ethical and surgical adventures. Sectional barriers mattered little here. When the last of the wounded were well enough to travel, he regretted leaving some of the United States Army surgeons he had come to know. As he and Pearce and Nott prepared to leave the tavern, the Baltimore nurses produced a roll of money, insisting that the men take whatever they expected to need. Confident of an early exchange, Baruch at first declined. Only after much urging did he consent to take five dollars. He might have been less chivalrous had he known what the future held.[15]

Late at night the band of Confederate surgeons—numbering about one hundred—and several chaplains boarded a train crowded with convalescents. Throughout the trip, which brought them to Baltimore early the next morning, Baruch rode in an open-top cattle car. At the Baltimore depot a file of soldiers met them and separated the surgeons from the others, confirming Baruch's belief that, as before, they would be treated as noncombatants and exchanged at once. Instead, the guards escorted them to Barnum's Hotel on Monument Square, temporarily used as a prison, and locked them up.

About noon a "dirty negro" appeared with a basket containing bacon and bread. Taking a piece of bread in one hand, he placed a piece of bacon on it by pushing it off the fork with his thumb, serving each man in his turn. The surgeons and chaplains were unaccustomed to such treatment, but because they had had no breakfast, they ate gladly. Afterward they held a meeting ("the usual thing with Americans," Baruch observed) and passed resolutions protesting this "cruel treatment" of noncombatants. That afternoon they were made to march from Barnum's through town to Fort McHenry. To the doctors, accustomed to doing their marching on horseback, the three-mile tramp over Baltimore streets steaming in the August sun seemed endless. To Baruch it was a dark contrast to the triumphal carriage ride of the preceding year, when he had gloried in being one of the "petted prisoners of the fashionable world."[16]

Still puzzled that they were not to be exchanged at once, they arrived at the fort, answered to roll call, and moved into a long barracks near the left of the gate, a building destined to be their quarters for some time. Baruch's bunk adjoined that of one of the Union officers who occupied part of the same building. The double-decker bunks consisted of a frame of strong posts with crossbeams supporting two-board floors. Having neither mattresses nor straw, the men made great to-do over "finding the soft side of the planks." The only doctor who seemed to sleep comfortably was A. B. Johns, whose ninety-nine-pound frame rested lightly over a horizontal distance of six feet two inches.[17]

McHenry inmates were drawn from all classes. They included privates, officers, chaplains, surgeons, and citizens suspected of disloyalty to the Union—altogether a sort of prisoner elite. Nonetheless, the menu left something to be desired. Breakfast consisted of an unlimited quantity of hardtack and the sweetened black coffee that each man dipped from a large can with his one-pint tin cup. Supper differed only in that it was served at a different time. Dinner consisted of corned beef and potatoes, or pork and potatoes, or rice soup with beef. Sometimes the soup was garnished with "very big green flies" or worms, but the men ate anyway in the hope that "what would not kill would fatten."[18]

Aside from the food, Baruch considered the early weeks of his confinement like a "summer spent at a seaside resort." The men were free to roam the entire grounds between the brick enclosure and the river. They could swim, play ball, walk around the docks, listen to the band music at guard-mounting and dress parade, and stare back at the crowds who came to stare at them. At night they sometimes entertained themselves with formal debates or language classes. German was especially useful to prisoners in Baltimore. On one occasion Baruch acted as translator for a prisoner who wanted to buy apples but who spoke German no better than the old woman peddler spoke English.[19]

The prisoners also had the privilege of buying whatever they could pay for in the sutler's store, and Baruch was grateful for the money he had accepted from the Misses Howard. Some of the surgeons received money from friends in the North who saw their names among prisoner lists, but money sent did not always arrive. Not until after the war did Baruch learn that a former Charleston friend, living in New York during the war, had sent him money. Fortunately, he received ample assistance from a certain "Miss M." of Baltimore, whose gifts reached him through her black laundress.[20]

Many McHenry inmates enjoyed daily visits from Baltimore sympathizers. These women drove up to the office of the provost and sent their cards through him to the men they wished to see. In honor of the occasion, the prisoners usually shaved and even put on fresh paper collars. Although guards were always present, they were courteous enough to stay out of earshot. Not content with such brief pleasantries, one of the women bribed a sergeant on duty at the gate to permit one or more of the prisoners to attend an evening party in the city and return to the fort before morning. The evenings out became a frequent practice, and before long three of the ten chaplains failed to return.

When an order came for the clergymen to prepare to leave the fort, three surgeons, one of them a fiery Texan with a most unclerical vocabulary, offered to replace the missing men. The substitution eluded detection, and all might have gone well except that, a few weeks later, one of the departed surgeons was called to appear as a witness in a case of opium theft from the dispensary. While Federal guards searched for the missing Dr. Guild around the prison grounds and in the water, the captive doctors elected one of their members, "the dean by age of the 'medical faculty of Fort McHenry,'" to inform the provost marshal that Dr. Guild was "absent without leave" and that the search for him was in vain. A file of guards soon marched into the barracks and called the roll of surgeons. One after another came the replies of "absent," interspersed with an occasional "gone where the woodbine twineth."[21]

Retribution was swift. Carrying their baggage on their backs, the doctors were marched to a brick artillery stable occupied by deserters and bounty jumpers, a lowly class of prisoners driven to work every day in a chain gang. The dreary, unheated loft of this stable was the doctors' new residence hall. They also found their outside activities drastically curtailed. After two weeks of severe confinement, they sent the commanding officer a petition asking for relaxed discipline in exchange for their parole of honor not to escape. The guards were then withdrawn and the men again permitted to roam out-of-doors, though in a more restricted space than before.

Despite the relative pleasantness of their captivity, Baruch and his fellow inmates found themselves growing irritated. The waste entailed in such a long internment of so many medical officers was a mystery. Neither side had surgeons to spare. After September 19 and 20, when the battle of Chickamauga placed more than one hundred Union surgeons in the hands of General Braxton Bragg's army, officials made an effort to effect an exchange, but still the surgeons were held.

It was late autumn, cold and gray, when at last they received an order to pack their things and prepare to leave.[22] Immediately after the chain gang left for its day's work, a colonel in charge of artillery at the fort entered the lower part of the stable with his staff and called the prisoners down two by two. Peering through a knothole from above, one of the doctors saw that a sergeant was examining all baggage and confiscating new purchases and money—but he was not examining the prisoner's persons. Amid great scurrying in the loft at this realization, Baruch placed an extra hat in his boot leg, replaced his old flannel shirt with two new ones, donned several undervests and a new civilian coat, and stuffed his bulging form into his "ample" military overcoat. Trembling for his beautiful instrument case, he concealed it in a roll of blankets. When his turn came for inspection, he diverted the sergeant's attention to his roll of Confederate bills, and, signaling the next prisoner to open his bag for inspection, he quickly moved the blanket roll over to the side of things passed.

He managed to save the instruments, but it would not have mattered had he failed. When the prisoners sailed out into Chesapeake Bay, they saw their confiscated articles heaped on deck. When they stopped at Fortress Monroe, as Baruch had done only a year before, the exchange officer obtained release of all their property. The men gleefully scrambled to sort out their belongings as the friendly vessel carried them up the James River toward Aiken's Landing.[23]

Upon their arrival in Richmond, they were summoned to the office of Surgeon General Samuel Preston Moore, a gentleman whose "spit and polish" attitude made him the terror of medical officers of every rank. From their number Moore appointed a committee, including Baruch, to tour Libby Prison, then the butt of much northern criticism for its alleged maltreatment of Union inmates. After comparing its conditions with those they had just experienced at Fort McHenry, the committee brought a favorable verdict for Libby.[24]

Safe at last in Confederate territory, Baruch was concerned for the surgical instruments "Dr. F." of Baltimore had given him. Whether or not he knew that some medical units of the Army of Northern Virginia were compelled to do without any surgical equipment in the field, he did recall in later years having been fully aware that his recent acquisitions were of "inestimable value since they could not be procured in the Confederacy, except through running the blockade." As he recounted the incident, it was in the face of this knowledge that he promptly sent the entire set to Camden, "for safekeeping until needed." He already had instruments for his own use, and it apparently did not occur to him that he might release them to another surgeon and use the new Tiemann kit himself. Or perhaps the great probability of loss—for both sides hastened to confiscate instruments at every opportunity—dissuaded him from making the sacrifice. At any rate, into storage the instruments went, at a time when the Confederacy had no greater medical need.[25]

On December 5, 1863, Baruch was ordered to report to the surgeon in charge of hospitals at Newnan, Georgia, a small town on the railroad running southwest from Atlanta to Montgomery.[26] By this stage of the war, the number of wounded who poured into Newnan and the surrounding area filled all of the churches and made of it a most fashionable haven for convalescent officers. Despite the bitter cold (the winter of 1863–64 was the most severe of the war), the many gatherings of patients and doctors were cheered by the warmth of camaraderie. One of the women nurses brought an abandoned piano into her room, where it "contributed largely to the pleasure of the soldiers, also serving for sacred music when needed."[27]

Occasionally personal feuds disrupted the general goodwill. At a New Year's Eve party, two army officers became so involved over the question of a lady's honor that they insisted on fighting a duel. One of them asked Baruch to act as his surgeon. Unable to change his friend's mind, Baruch finally agreed, but he never got to the field of honor. Instead, he spent the appointed hour in the household where he was a guest, home to one of the participants. In a sequence of scenes that might have inspired an early movie melodrama, the young doctor rushed about pouring pitchers of cold water on various female members of the family who suffered alternate fits of hysteria and fainting spells. Fortunately, his friend managed to pick another surgeon en route to the duel to care for him when he was wounded at the first fire.[28]

More disturbing than occasional duels were rumors that from eight to ten thousand Georgians capable of bearing arms were avoiding service, an army of "listless lookers on." In Atlanta, where Baruch indulged in holiday cheer at the Kimball House the day after the duel, many businessmen were reportedly willing to pay as much as four to five thousand dollars apiece for army substitutes.[29]

Sometime in the spring of 1864, Baruch left his Georgia hospital post. He was once again with the Army of Northern Virginia when it moved into the Wilderness, the forest between Orange Court House and Fredericksburg. Here, where the woods trembled with the roar of artillery, he saw his friend Marcus Baum for the last time. Dashing up to the field hospital, Marcus begged to know where he might find his chief, General Kershaw. Despite Baruch's warning that he must not try to reach the front, Marcus set off in that direction. He succeeded in joining Kershaw, only to be caught in the accidental firing by Confederates that wounded General James Longstreet. Several hours later, Baum's white horse returned to camp, his neck spotted with blood. Baum's body was never recovered.[30]

After the Wilderness came five days of trench warfare and bayonet charges at Spotsylvania. On May 8 Baruch saw a number of wounded who had been bayoneted, two of them through the chest. He treated their shock with stimulants and anodynes, immobilized them completely, and made continued applications of cold water, disdaining the current fashion of sealing chest wounds "hermetically." As the days went by, he frequently checked by auscultation and percussion for signs of pleural inflammation or pneumonia. He found neither, and both cases healed without the formation of pus. By May 19, the men had recovered sufficiently to be moved to a general hospital.[31]

Throughout May and June, Baruch pondered the successful outcome of these cases and others like them. Their easy recovery was not what men in the lines usually expected of bayonet wounds. Brave and seasoned though Kershaw's men were, Baruch had often observed that "the determined approach of a line of glistening steel makes the cheek blanch and causes the bravest hearts to waver." In view of the rapid healing he had seen, he pondered this phenomenon: "Why do we in every battle witness the rout of lines that have unflinchingly withstood a continued galling fire of musketry and artillery, as soon as the opposing line approaches closely with fixed bayonets?" Other observers, too, noted the fear of cold steel. Some even considered it a peculiarly American trait, resulting in a lower incidence of bayonet wounds in American than in European conflicts. There were indeed few bayonet wounds in the American Civil War—so few that saber and bayonet wounds together accounted for only

0.4 percent of the total of wounds inflicted on both sides throughout the entire conflict.[32]

Baruch believed, perhaps naively, that inordinate fear of cold steel sprang from the idea that bayonet wounds were more often fatal than gunshot wounds.[33] Leaving to others the task of showing that few bayoneted corpses, easily recognizable by their "peculiarly contorted" appearance, were found on any battlefield, he set out to show the relatively high recovery rate of those who came into his field hospital with bayonet wounds. In July he submitted a detailed account of recoveries to the *Confederate States Medical and Surgical Journal,* edited by James Brown McCaw, one of his former professors and commandant of the Chimborazo Hospital in Richmond.[34]

In relating his case histories in this, his first article, Baruch used his newfound mastery of English to dispel the prevalent "dread of tranfixion." Bayonet wounds, he assured his readers, were less harmful than the "ploughed tracks which the terrible minie bores through the tissues. The bayonet is easily diverted from a straight course by bony, cartilaginous and tendinous tissues, and forms a smooth track whilst the minie is relentless in its course, whirling with unimpeded force through all opposing structures, crushing, tearing and maiming all." Because bayonet wounds involved less tissue damage, he said, they were less frequently followed by dangerous sequelae. "A bayonet wound almost invariably heals by first intention under auspicious circumstances, and leaves no deformity behind, whilst the simplest ball wound requires weeks for complete recovery, and then perhaps, leaves the sufferer with a contracted and useless limb." In the bayonet wounds he had seen at Spotsylvania, he observed "no irregular gluing of muscular fibres, no permanent or even temporary contraction of muscles and tendons."[35]

By the time Baruch wrote his article, he was able to add that both men who had been wounded in the chest were back on duty with their commands. Of the less serious bayonet cases he had observed, "nearly all . . . recovered at the field infirmary and were returned to duty." Although chest wounds might seem far more threatening than those of the head, loins, and shoulder, he found that they usually healed more rapidly. Why? The young surgeon confessed with what must have been a good bit of chagrin that men with minor punctures "would not obey my injunctions to keep quiet."[36]

Baruch intended his little contribution to give physiological support to a plea for moral courage in the face of cold steel. Whether or not it ever made its way to the men in the lines for whom he apparently meant it, he must have had a sizable audience, for it was published by the only medical journal in the Confederacy.

On July 18, 1864, Baruch was promoted from assistant surgeon to full surgeon. His salary increase, from $110 to $162 monthly, was doubtless more than offset by the inflated economy of the ailing Confederacy and by the government's growing difficulty in paying its soldiers and doctors. Now assigned to the Thirteenth Mississippi Infantry Regiment of Colonel G. S. Barksdale, he exchanged the twin bars of the captain for the major's star. On August 11, 1864, he was ordered to report to Medical Director J. S. Dorsey Cullen of Longstreet's corps.[37]

At this time, although Baruch still looked strong and well, there were indications that his health could not continue to bear demands of the kind his more than two years of service had placed upon it. The trouble that had appeared in his right eye during the fighting at Chancellorsville had grown progressively worse. Now, in early October 1864, he was admitted to a Richmond hospital with a severe attack of diarrhea, the universal plague of Billy Yank and Johnny Reb alike. While other infectious diseases took their toll early in the war, leaving survivors with some degree of immunity, the twin scourges of diarrhea and dysentery became increasingly widespread among veterans, their health progressively weakened by poor diet, exposure, and exhaustion.[38]

Although Baruch's eye trouble lingered on, he recovered from the intestinal attack after only eight days in the hospital. He was well enough to ride to Cedar Run, where, on October 18, he "foolishly undertook with a colleague to check the flight of a group of soldiers" whom General Jubal Early was trying to urge back from retreat. Galloping toward their front, Baruch was shouting, "Rally men for God's sake, Rally," when a close shellburst frightened his horse into a retreat of its own. The men shouted after the vanishing doctor, "Why in the hell don't you rally!"[39]

In attempting to stop a rout, Baruch was acting outside the surgeon's normal duties, but he did have some assigned tasks that were not directly connected with the care of the wounded and sick. One of these was to reject requests for spurious sick leaves, another to recommend the release of those who, for reasons of health, would be more effective elsewhere. On November 24, 1864, from a camp near Richmond, he addressed an appeal to Secretary of War James A. Seddon in behalf of J. C. Calhoun, acting hospital steward of the Thirteenth Mississippi Regiment: "I would respectfully recommend that Hosp. steward J. C. Calhoun be allowed to attend lectures this winter. He is, in my opinion, unfit for active duties of an infantry soldier, being constitutionally weak and liable to attacks of spasmodic pain caused by stone in the bladder. In a medical capacity he has always proved efficient." The hospital steward, the only man permanently assigned to the surgeon, was a warrant officer with rank above first company sergeant. His duties included exclusive charge of the dispensary; applying bandages and dressings, cups and leeches; pulling teeth; and occasionally superintending the cooking. Although he was not exactly an "infantry soldier," his duties in the field would be rigorous for a victim of kidney stones. On November 28 Surgeon General Moore granted Calhoun permission to reenter the Medical College of Virginia to continue the studies he had started in Alabama before entering Confederate service.[40]

Before another month had passed, Baruch had occasion to write a similar letter in his own behalf. On December 8 his eye ailment led to his admission to private officers' quarters in Richmond. The next day an examining board of army doctors diagnosed the trouble as "amaurosis," a loss of vision without perceptible physical cause. The board recommended a leave of absence to give Baruch "change of air, scene & diet." On December 10 an assistant adjutant general approved the recommendation, but, for some reason, the permission necessary to apply to the board for a medical certificate was delayed. Without the certificate, Baruch could not file formal application for leave. For two weeks he waited. In the meantime, he was moved from private quarters to a Richmond wayside and receiving hospital, then back to private quarters again. As the waiting wore him down, his fear turned to panic. Nearsighted at best, he could not risk further damage to his eyes.[41]

At last he could no longer bear inaction. On December 22, the day Savannah fell to William Tecumseh Sherman's men, Baruch addressed a personal plea to the secretary of war:

Sir

I am suffering from a disease of the eye (amaurosis) which threatens me with blindness & which I contracted in the service. Two weeks ago Surgeon Crenshaw's Med. Examg. Board advised . . . a leave of absence, which has not yet reached me. My case being very urgent, the board have today again recommended a leave. I would respectfully ask of you, Sir, to give me permission to procure the Med. Certificate from the board (without which permission I cannot get it), and to bring my application before you for action. (The urgency of my symptoms alone prompt [sic] me to take this step for an early attention to them. I am entirely dependent on my profession and should I lose my sight, it would be a fatal loss to me. Hence my anxiety.

Hoping for an immediate & favorable consideration I am, Sir,

Very Respectfully
Your obdt Surgeon
S Baruch
Surgeon 13th Miss Regt

Baruch must have felt desperate indeed as he wrote this request. The grammatical errors, inaccurate punctuation, and hurried hand were altogether alien to his usual precision. Whatever the cause of his failing vision, he seemed certain that a leave would be beneficial. In this conviction, he had professional support: along with his letter to Secretary Seddon went a certificate signed by two surgeons attesting that he was unfit for duty and unable to resume his work in less than thirty days.[42]

This last appeal brought prompt action. It reached the secretary's office on December 23. The same day, orders were issued granting Baruch a month's furlough, and he started toward Camden once more.[43] It was a gloomy journey; discontent over the crumbling war effort was at a high pitch. The very day his leave began, South Carolina virtually nullified an act of the Confederate Congress. Hardships carried lightly at first were beginning to grow irksome. It was a cheerless Christmas in Camden, where the people, once appalled at being reduced to using tallow candles for light, now had to rely on smoky terrabine lamps burning a preparation of turpentine. As the days wore on into January, the ever-tightening blockade brought greater hunger, and there was news of riots and demonstrations in the cities.[44]

The hardships of civilian life did not deter Baruch from overstaying his furlough. Very likely he was still in Camden in mid-January 1865, when General Sherman turned northward into South Carolina, bringing the war in the direction of the nearby state capital at Columbia. On January 23, Baruch became a part of the vast number, North and South, of medical officers absent without leave. On January 29 he had still not reported back to his post in Humphrey's Brigade, perhaps because it was impossible to do so. In February he reappeared at last, only to join another large and growing army of medical officers applying for transfer from field service to hospital work behind the lines.[45]

Baruch had doubtless encountered the contemptuous attitude field surgeons often displayed toward men who chose hospital service. With the pride that was such a striking component of his character, he must have felt desperate to request such a transfer. Even in 1864, Surgeon General Moore had tried every possible means to bring more surgeons from the hospitals into the field; it does not seem likely that the situation had eased in the intervening year.[46] Nevertheless, Baruch got his transfer. On February 27 the surgeon general signed an order approved by General Lee, relieving Baruch from duty with the Army of Northern Virginia on a certificate of disability and directing him to report to Peter E. Hines, medical director of North Carolina hospitals, in Raleigh.[47]

Baruch's new post was a smallpox hospital in Goldsboro, a small town of strategic importance at the intersection of the North Carolina Railroad, the Wilmington and Weldon Railroad, and the Neuse River, which leads inland from the coast. Just sixty miles downriver from Goldsboro was New Bern, a coastal city that had been occupied by Federal troops within the first year of the war. After Baruch reached the hospital, he received one full order of supplies by means of the railroad, an order lacking only the six yards of gutta-percha cloth he needed to mask the faces of smallpox victims to prevent pitting. According to the original organization of the Confederate medical service, the personnel of a general hospital was to include a steward (usually a medical student or someone familiar with drugs), ward masters, one nurse to every ten patients, one matron to twenty, and one cook to thirty. Few hospitals in the Confederacy could boast anything like a full staff in March 1865; a month earlier a nurse in Georgia noted "so much irregularity as far as hospital organization was concerned that one scarcely knew how best to serve the sick."[48]

To aggravate the disorganization Baruch must have experienced at his new post, he was forced to leave even before acknowledging the medical supplies he had received. After the fall of Wilmington on February 22, Federal troops under General J. D. Cox moved inland from New Bern toward Goldsboro in an effort to open that arm of the railroad for northern use. For two days after March 8, with Robert F. Hoke's division and a part of John B. Hood's troops under D. H. Hill, General Braxton Bragg engaged Cox's men in fighting on the south side of the Neuse at Kinston, only thirty miles downriver from Goldsboro. It was an unequal fight. On the night of the tenth, Bragg retreated toward Goldsboro, bringing with him a number of wounded, many of them Union prisoners who spoke only Baruch's native German.[49]

General John M. Schofield occupied Kinston on the fourteenth and moved on toward Goldsboro. At the same time, Sherman's men were marching northward and eastward. There was no hope of maintaining the Goldsboro hospital. Under orders to evacuate and take along the high-ranking Union wounded, Baruch and his charges boarded a train on the North Carolina Railroad and fled inland. They were fortunate to have access to a train at all, but the journey was not an easy one. Long trips in crowded cars without heat and water were agonizing for the wounded and for the medical officers who could do little to ease their suffering. The capture and destruction of many southern rail lines meant greater congestion and confusion on those that remained: as early as 1863 the surviving lines were so overloaded that delays sometimes cost the lives of men who might have recovered under more favorable circumstances. When one of the wounded under Baruch's care, the colonel of a

Massachusetts regiment, became extremely ill on the train, Baruch left him behind in more comfortable lodging at High Point, North Carolina, about 150 miles inland from Goldsboro.[50]

Baruch had orders to proceed to Thomasville to prepare hospital accommodations for Joseph E. Johnston's men, who were attempting to block Sherman's drive into North Carolina. Men wounded in these running engagements were often sent to general hospitals without adequate arrangements for their reception, sometimes with tragic consequences. Earlier in the war such errors were common because the military arm failed to notify the medical service of anticipated troop movements. Now the reason was different. North Carolina medical director Hines did his best to have adequate facilities ready for the casualties incurred in Johnston's rapid maneuvers, but he often could not provide for them because of "the want of straw for beds and lumber for fitting up houses for hospital purposes." It was another symptom of the Confederacy's failing vital powers, a symptom which made improvisation the essence of military medicine.[51]

Arriving in Thomasville with six partly disabled soldiers assigned to assist him, Baruch found himself in a "straggling village containing several churches and factories and a college for women." Like hundreds of his fellow surgeons in other towns like Thomasville, he quickly set about using the tools at hand. Within a few days of his arrival, he had built a bake oven and cleaned out some factories and a hotel for use as hospitals. He had barely finished these preparations when Medical Director Hines sent word that more than two hundred wounded from the fighting at Averasboro on March 16 were on the train to Thomasville.

Baruch immediately ordered all the men and boys of the town brought to his headquarters. Explaining his need for their help in his hasty preparations, he commandeered two wagons, put two men on each, and sent one to gather pine knots, the other pine straw. Young women from the school stuffed the pine straw into sacks, which they arranged on the floors of factories and churches cleared of machinery and pews for the emergency. In front of the makeshift hospitals Baruch had pine knots placed in piles that could be set on fire to give light for unloading the wounded. He himself went from house to house, urging the townswomen to assist him by baking bread and preparing rye coffee and bacon.

When the train clattered into Thomasville, its tragic freight of wounded lay on loose cotton supplied at the battlefield hospital. Only two surgeons accompanied the men. Aided by the older women of the town, the three doctors worked until daylight. Before Baruch retired, he saw that every man who could eat had been fed and that all were as comfortable as possible.[52]

After two hours of sleep, Baruch organized the hospital and started the inevitable surgery, working all day and far into the night. The next day he awoke feeling ill. His head throbbing with pain, he dictated a telegram to Hines requesting a replacement. Then he lapsed into the unconsciousness of typhoid fever.[53] Like the other intestinal infections of the war, typhoid seemed to increase in virulence as time went on, and the treatment seemed calculated to weed out the weak: Dover's powders or other opiates for the accompanying diarrhea; hot fomentations, blisters, and cupping for the abdominal pain; cold applications to the head and frequent spraying of the body with water for the fever; doses of turpentine taken by mouth to sear the intestinal ulcers; and, on the first sign that collapse was imminent, warmth and friction to the body, capsicum, ammonia, or brandy internally.[54]

For two weeks Baruch raved in delirium, so ill at one point that the other doctors gave up hope for his life. When he again became aware of the world about him, he learned that George Stoneman's cavalry had passed through Thomasville and paroled all Confederates. Lee had surrendered. The long war was over at last. Too weak to walk without crutches, Baruch started back home to Camden.

The New York Interlude

5

Baruch's homeward journey took him straight through Sherman's wasteland. The countryside was ravaged and deserted, a far cry from the bountiful land he had so recently come to call home. Travelers along the road from Chester to Winnsboro saw "nothing but solitude, nothing but tall blackened chimneys." Between Winnsboro and Camden, where the landscape looked a bit more like its antebellum self, blacks were working in the fields, plowing and hoeing corn almost as if there had been no war. Nature, seemingly anxious to help their work along, had provided an early spring. Spared from the nip of frost since March 7, the lush Carolina vegetation pushed ahead of its usual April growth, covering the land with a moist, fresh green and giving promise of crops that would be badly needed.[1]

Within Camden the war had left lasting scars. Like other towns in the central part of the state, Camden had been a wartime storehouse for the valuables of the low country. Here, as in Columbia to the southwest and Cheraw to the northeast, vacant rooms and attics had been stuffed with cotton and goods—rich finds for Sherman's scavengers. Along with the other treasures, someone had put away the precious surgical instruments Baruch had sent home for safekeeping after his release from Fort McHenry. They were no longer there when he returned. He never learned whether one of Sherman's men got them, or whether they vanished with one of Robert Brown Potter's raiders, who had come through Camden after Johnston's surrender, taking away even books and letters. He only knew that after the marauders had done their work, the instruments were gone, along with whatever wealth remained in Camden by the last months of the war.[2]

61

Baruch once again made his home with the two surviving Baum brothers, Herman and Mannes, and their families. He set up his practice and tried to get started, although the circumstances were hardly promising. Neither his personal ambition and energy nor his professional knowledge and skill stood much chance in the prostrate Camden of 1865. When President Andrew Johnson issued his proclamation of amnesty on May 29, most Camden citizens took the loyalty oath before the provost marshals. Yet the military occupation dragged on through June and into July. On July 12 a group of townspeople, presided over by Baruch's former preceptor, Dr. Lynch Horry Deas, adopted resolutions to be sent to the president. Stating that all industry was paralyzed and social life in chaos, they requested that he appoint a provisional governor and re-establish civil government. The request was granted even before it was received, but still the restoration was far from complete. "We are shut in here," wrote a Camden resident, "turned with our faces to a dead wall. No mails. . . . All railroads have been destroyed . . . and the bridges are gone." A group of enterprising Carolinians established a line of wagons linking Aiken, Columbia, and Orangeburg, but Camden remained in isolation.[3]

These conditions made the launching of a medical practice—difficult in the best of circumstances—all but impossible for Baruch. Most of Camden's formerly wealthy inhabitants were too impoverished to pay for medical care. The few who still had means tended to rely on the older established physicians.[4] As a beginner, Baruch was left with whites and blacks of the "poorer and middling classes," who could provide plenty of work, if the freedmen could pay for the medical care they needed.[5] Few of them, however, had acquired habits of personal responsibility to match their independence. They had never had to take care of themselves, and they did not suddenly learn how to do so at the moment of emancipation. According to a representative of the American Freedmen's Aid Commission, the blacks of Kershaw District were "the finest in the State. Physicians who practice among them receive their pay as among whites." This was a dubious compliment to Camden blacks, for few whites could afford medical care during the first summer of peace.[6]

As Baruch soon learned, there was still another drawback to practice in Camden. Although the plentiful supply of physicians should have assured him a rewarding professional existence, he found his local colleagues disappointing. Camden had a reputation for producing "a pattern of gentlemen singularly sweet and gracious of manner," soft-spoken men who were "cultivated and courtly." Baruch found them slow and unenterprising, courteous gentlemen all, polite and genteel, but sadly lacking

in intellectual curiosity.[7] Nor was there a state or county medical society
to compensate for the lack of stimulation in Camden's day-to-day life.
All through the South such organizations had ceased operating during
the war. Until they revived, there would be no relief from the intellectual
stagnation Baruch loathed. Even medical literature was scarce. Southern
medical journals, unable to bring paper, ink, and machinery from the
North during the war, now found it difficult to resume publication.[8]

Gloomy as professional prospects appeared in those spring and summer months, Baruch found pleasant distraction in the company of Belle
Wolfe, a dark-eyed, spirited Winnsboro girl, who often came to Camden
to visit her aunt, Mrs. Mannes Baum. As a stimulus to young love, the
southern spring was ideal. The sweet scents of opopanax, violets, roses,
and jasmine filled the air along Camden's streets, still thronged as late as
June with refugees from the low country. Like many another youth home
from the war, Baruch dedicated himself to a cause not yet lost. He set
about wooing Belle away from her memories of the "good Yankee" who
had treated her with kindness in a moment of danger.[9]

As spring moved into summer and summer into fall, Baruch found his
work increasingly unsatisfactory. He had always hoped to practice in a
city. In contrast to the dream, he found the reality of Camden's intellectual and economic poverty unbearably harsh.[10] Perhaps the drives he felt
were intensified by his deepening affection for Belle. To win her he must
do well, for her father had been a man of position and wealth before the
war. The Wolfes prided themselves on their descent from the Sephar-
dim—the Jews of Spain and Portugal—and traced their American fore-
bears back to the late seventeenth century.[11] A recent immigrant from
Prussian Poland might well wish for some degree of professional attainment to strengthen his hand in courting the daughter of such a family.

Since Camden seemed an unlikely place to seek his fortune, Baruch
decided to leave. There were countless cities he might have chosen, but
he would not settle for a mere step up the ladder. In the autumn of 1865
he leaped to the top: "I made a bold attempt . . . to establish myself in
New York."[12]

Baruch found New York far more prosperous than Camden but not
much more receptive to young, unproven physicians. Although New
York had a large population able to pay for medical treatment, it also
had more than its quota of established doctors. The young man from
Camden had neither the political nor the social or family influence that
have been called "the *sine qua non* for real success in medicine, in New
York as elsewhere." Because good hospital appointments were rarely

open to men without these nonprofessional assets, the best entrée for Baruch was a post in one of the city dispensaries.[13]

Financed by revenue from a quarantine tax first imposed in 1754 on seamen and passengers entering the port of New York, municipal dispensaries provided free medical care for huge numbers of sick every day. Most dispensary patients could not afford a private physician, but that was not true of all; some were referred by their doctors because they could not pay for a specialist's attention. Although dispensary doctors were forbidden to solicit private practice, the temptations their positions offered were widely acknowledged as irresistible.[14] Partly because of this and partly because of the experience dispensaries offered, competition was fierce for every staff opening. The one Baruch set his cap for at the North-Western Dispensary was no exception. Although the surrounding neighborhood was dangerous (boys deprived of space for hockey and football sometimes stoned dispensary doctors and policemen) and the position carried no salary, Baruch found his rivals "as ravenous for it, as a wolf is for prey." Somehow, by what he called "a sheer piece of good fortune," he got the job.[15]

A physician who held a similar post in later years described the typical dispensary routine:

The number of patients daily was enormous, a line forming outside the door long before it opened. We were so rushed that it was impossible to give anything but snap diagnosis and treatment. I would stand with two other physicians, side by side in a narrow room, our elbows touching, with stethoscopes around our necks and pads and pencils in our hands, our pockets stuffed with tongue depressors. The sick children, guided by or in the arms of older people, would be admitted in three lines, one for each doctor, and after advice was given they would be let out the side door. Children were brought to us in all stages of disease, sick, moribund and even dead. There were few mornings, indeed, without a dead baby.[16]

Baruch's work at the North-Western Dispensary, established in 1852, had a special flavor, for the building stood at Ninth Avenue and Thirty-sixth Street, in the area known as Hell's Kitchen.[17] Not long before midcentury this part of Manhattan was still rural, a green and peaceful land boasting more cows than people. In 1851 the Hudson River Railroad opened a station at Thirtieth Street and Tenth Avenue. By 1859 the railroads and the encroaching waterfront, the influx of industry and immigrants, the rumbling trains and the clattering, horse-drawn trucks had brought soot, smoke, and the malty fumes of breweries to the formerly peaceful pastures of old Bloomingdale. When Commodore Cornelius Vanderbilt acquired control of the Hudson line in 1863, he scorned those who objected to putting a railroad through such "unpromising" country.

Put the road there, he maintained, and people would go there to live. The commodore was right. Within a few years lumberyards, stables, distilleries, brickyards, warehouses, and slaughterhouses pressed in around the Hudson River Railroad's tracks. Side by side with them grew the tenements that housed their laboring forces.[18]

In the wartime 1860s New York's population numbered some 813,000 souls. Many of the 203,000 Irish and 169,000 Germans who helped make up that total lived in Hell's Kitchen, established by the time of the Civil War as "one of the most wretched slums in America."[19] The postwar period may have been the "Spittoon Era" in higher circles, but Baruch found that Hell's Kitchen lacked even more fundamental sanitary equipment. As dispensary surgeon he spent every morning trudging up and down the dark stairways and halls of the tenements surrounding the dispensary. The buildings usually had four stories and a cellar; each floor was divided into four apartments. The bedrooms, dark and unventilated, were located in the center of the row of rooms. From the single faucet on each floor, located over a sink in the dimly lighted hall, four families drew water for cooking and whatever washing the squalor around them might inspire. The outdoor privies seemed "as primitive as in the smallest village, namely, unconnected with the sewer."[20] In this world of the tenements, where mere existence was a painful struggle, Baruch found his work little improvement over practice in Camden. It did not even offer pleasant surroundings as compensation for financial distress.

Fortunately, there were professional advantages. New York's libraries and hospitals were gloriously rich in all that he had missed in Camden, and he made good use of them. At this period of his life he was especially interested in what is today called internal medicine. In New York he found many opportunities to add to the knowledge and ideas he had acquired from Professor Geddings at the Medical College of South Carolina five years earlier. His frequent contacts with such men as Alfred Lebbeus Loomis, Erasmus Darwin Hudson, and Austin Flint illuminated the latest methods of diagnosis and treatment in fevers and respiratory and circulatory afflictions. The treatment in vogue was a far cry from the bloodletting, antimony, mercury, blisters, and starvation of the early nineteenth century. Dr. Geddings had taught that no therapy should be carried to the point of damaging the patient's "vital powers," but now Baruch learned that the pendulum had swung still farther from the old extremes of heroic medicine. Strict expectancy, meaning that the doctor largely left the disease to run its natural course, was the order of the hour among the leaders of the profession.[21]

It was a philosophy of therapy with great appeal for Baruch. During his early days in the Confederacy, he had literally doctored a hardy young man to death in a vain effort to abort his pneumonia. From that time on, he had felt particularly impotent in dealing with this disease. Because there was no adequate medical means for combating it, its fatality rate ran so high throughout the war that he "no longer entered the fray with a stout heart." He admitted that "a cowardly pessimism would have overwhelmed me amid the continuous fatalities" if life had not been counted so cheap in the days of Shiloh and Gettysburg and Antietam. Now the expectant treatment, which seemed to yield astonishing results when compared with older, spoliative practices, offered some hope for pneumonia victims.[22]

Along with expectant therapy in disease, doctors were coming to place more emphasis on healthy habits of living. But Baruch was not free to use this new approach in his dispensary work. Any doctor who suggested that a sickly resident of Hell's Kitchen eat better food and get more sunshine and fresh air would be laughed out of town. Irritable stomach resulting from the use of alcohol was endemic. The unceasing struggle for survival in New York slums, with the debilitation it entailed, was one obstacle to the practice of enlightened preventive or expectant medicine. In acute disease, the obstacle was the more universal psychological aspect of the patient–doctor relationship, which is often more powerful than physical factors. As Leo Tolstoy observed, doctors are useful not because they make the patient swallow drugs but because they satisfy "that eternal human need of hope for relief, that need for sympathetic action that is felt in the presence of suffering."[23] Inaction, however sympathetic and judicious, is an inadequate substitute. Like the young doctor of today who meets with difficulty when refusing, on excellent medical grounds, to give antibiotics for viral infections, Baruch soon learned that patients are not always ready to accept what the doctor thinks best. Only a physician of rare courage could practice truly expectant medicine, or as Baruch put it, "stand idly by and see nature do the work for him," for it was a rare patient who would be "content to pay a doctor for watching nature cure him."[24] Inaction would drive people into the open arms of quackery as effectively as the excesses of heroic medicine had done earlier in the century. Someone fully committed to the most extreme implications of Social Darwinism might commend quackeries for the way they "suck in the botched, and help them on to bliss eternal," but Baruch's concern was the survival of the unfit, and he felt harshly limited by conditions in the tenements.[25]

At the winter's end, he surveyed his situation and realized it would require "about ten years (with all qualifications) to get into a respectable practice"—which was what he wanted. Even at the age of twenty-five, he had no illusions about practicing medicine purely for the joy of helping suffering humanity. He wanted to stay on in New York, but ten years was a long time to manage in a position without a salary. He did not have enough money of his own to last even three or four years. Around the end of March, he yielded to the urging of his Camden friends and left New York "in disgust."[26]

The brief episode that closed with Baruch's return trip southward had depleted his stock of youthful optimism, but it had also enriched his knowledge. It had not quenched either his confidence or his ambition to succeed. He had failed not through any professional shortcoming but because he was a nobody with no money. If the dream of big-city practice had proved to be beyond him for the moment, its very elusiveness fired his determination to return.

First, he must squeeze his aspirations back into the smaller mold of Camden and concentrate on earning the price of his dream.

6 "No balm in Gilead"

Once back in Camden, Baruch had to adjust downward from New York's lively professional life, with its clinics and libraries and societies, to the leisurely pace of his South Carolina colleagues. Through a small, properly professional announcement in the *Camden Weekly Journal,* he gave public notice of his return. As of April 30, 1866, the newspaper item said,

> DR. S. BARUCH
> Has RESUMED HIS PRACTICE in this town.
> Office two doors below Baum, Bro. & Co.[1]

His return offered some consolations. He had friends in South Carolina, from the Old World and the New, from before, during, and after the war. And in contrast to the bitter cold winter in the dingy tenements of Hell's Kitchen, Camden's spring was gloriously bright and fresh. As he would admit in later life, "The country doctor has certain privileges which the city doctor misses." He probably did not appreciate it in his frustrated return from New York, but he later owned that the rural practitioner, "in constant communion with Nature, in the forest, the hills and valleys and streams he traverses," gains "the placidity and contentment which close contact with Nature alone may lend to the mind."[2] For all his railing against the intellectual poverty of country life, it provided a tranquility—psychological as well as physical—to counterbalance his own tendency toward instability. He freely admitted his dependence on the countrified calm of his friend Dr. Salley, an Orangeburg practitioner he had met during the war, to tone down his own "occasional wild & extravagant ideas."[3]

Wherever Miss Isabel Wolfe was concerned, Baruch's emotional equilibrium was subject to marked disturbance. During the summer of 1866, when she left her home in nearby Winnsboro to visit relatives in Long Branch, New Jersey, Baruch smarted with uncertainty while she was away, even though they were now engaged. Belle was only sixteen, ten years his junior, and he felt painful doubts of her devotion. In July, after two weeks without a letter from her, he could not contain his apprehension. "Is it thus you treat him who has laid his all, his highest love, his sublimest aspirations, his fondest hopes at your feet? The tortures of the past few weeks have wrought a change in my spirit; the hopeful joyous cast of my disposition has turned into despairing bitter feeling, that unmans me and makes me no longer fit to live." Perhaps Belle had written him so frequently up to that time that two weeks without word seemed reasonable cause for concern. Whatever the source of his anxiety, it remains a mystery. Of the many letters that must have passed between them, his alone remains: only one, long, hasty outpouring of words. But if it were a book of memoirs, it could not tell more—and would likely tell less—of his love and pride and possessiveness and torment of insecurity. Her silence must be the result of "foul play"; someone had intercepted his letters or whispered slander in her ear. "Believe them not, my treasured love, believe them not; for it will make you as miserable to cease loving me as it would make me." Whatever others said, he cared for no one but Belle. "If I have ever been harsh to you, love, you know it is caused by my superabundance of love, and I have never scolded you but for neglect of me. Is this alone not a proof of love?"[4]

Life in general was depressing enough to intensify his fear of losing Belle. Although parts of the South Carolina Railroad were again intact, Camden remained isolated, and it seemed the little town would never prosper again. A northern teacher reported that "times are hard in this District, both for *white* and *colored*. No one is making money except the merchants, who put *it on unmercifully*. Money is scarce among the people at large, and goods are very high."[5] Prosperity for the Baums only meant more trouble for physicians like Baruch. One of Camden's doctors had already begun to look beyond medicine for his livelihood.[6]

Everywhere in the South, economic difficulties were reflected in the condition of the medical profession. Journals struggling to resume publication all too often met the same response: "I am too poor to subscribe." In December 1866, at the end of its first postwar year, the *Richmond Medical Journal* informed readers that "the past year has been

particularly unfavourable for the origination of any literary enterprise."
Many of the men who would ordinarily support a professional periodical
were impoverished or bankrupt. Of those who had subscribed, not a few
did so "at the sacrifice of physical ease and domestic comfort. Thousands
in the Profession, who have hitherto, after a year's hard labour, received
an ample remuneration, from the opulent agriculturist, are now dependent upon the precarious collections, from those who have not yet
acquired that important requisite in social stability—pecuniary responsibility."[7] With her doctors preoccupied by the struggle for bread, South
Carolina still had no state medical association. Baruch turned hopefully
toward the move to organize the doctors of Kershaw County, for he was
starved for the opportunity to exchange ideas. He also began to seek
professional stimulation through correspondence with Dr. Alexander S.
Salley. In his forties when the two met during the war, Salley had returned in 1865 to practice in his native town of Orangeburg. Baruch felt
unbounded respect for his tall, stern-looking elder, who was the very
picture of professional and personal integrity. He addressed him in December 1866 almost as a student might an honored teacher: "There is no
gentleman of my acquaintance, whose opinions on social, political and
professional topics I value more highly, than yours. Hence I desire to
open a regular correspondence with you in order to exchange views and
(I must be candid enough to confess) partly to derive advantage from
your valuable opinions."[8] Dr. Salley reciprocated with expressions of
friendship and esteem, and Baruch poured out his professional worries.

How to make practice pay: that was the biggest problem. For Baruch it
boiled down to making practice pay among blacks, for they made up a
majority of his patients. In antebellum days, physicians had made contracts with plantation owners, agreeing to give whatever medical care
their family and slaves might need, either for a prearranged fee for a
year's work or for so much per person per call.[9] Now that blacks were
free, employees rather than slaves, Baruch's colleagues seemed to scorn
the idea of contracts, with unhappy results for blacks and doctors alike.
"The practice on slaves was formerly very remunerative & no doubt did
much to increase the number of physicians. It is now almost nil, and I
think it is a duty we owe to ourselves (at least to those of us who are
compelled to earn a support by our professional labors) to reclaim that
practice by some means, honorable alike and profitable." The honorable
part presented real difficulty, for the opposition of Baruch's colleagues to
contract practice also precluded him from working in that way, unless he
wanted to break with accepted local standards.[10]

If all employers took the same personal interest in the freedmen's wel-

Doctor Alexander S. Salley (1818–1895) of Orangeburg, South
Carolina, whom Baruch met during the Civil War and afterward frequently sought out through correspondence and visits
for the "talk of physic" he missed in Camden. (Courtesy of the
South Caroliniana Library, University of South Carolina, Columbia. Reproduced from Alexander S. Salley, Jr., *The History
of Orangeburg County, South Carolina, from Its First Settlement
to the Close of the Revolutionary War,* Orangeburg, 1898, facing
page 128.)

fare that masters had taken in their slaves, physicians would have no cause for worry. Most employers, however, did not. The botanist Henry William Ravenel was an exception. At the war's end he called his former slaves together and told them "to consider it over & let me know what they will be willing to take, either by week or by month, either deducting lost days or not, & either paying their own Doctors bills or not." Most employers knew, as Ravenel did, that blacks "have no experience in taking care of themselves & providing for the future," but few employers were willing to assume the responsibility he shouldered.[11]

It was far more common for former slaveowners to "prove"—by abandoning the personal bonds of early days—that blacks had been better off as slaves than they were as freedmen. For every employer who rose to the task Ravenel assumed, there must have been hundreds who felt or pretended to feel, with Mary Boykin Chesnut, that emancipation was "a good riddance. A hired man would be a good deal cheaper," she said, "than a man whose father and mother, wife and twelve children have to be fed, clothed, housed, and nursed, their taxes paid, and their doctor's bills, all for his half-done slovenly, lazy work. For years we have thought negroes a nuisance that did not pay." In March 1865 the physicians of the area around Aiken and Pineville agreed not to attend any calls not authorized by plantation proprietors "unless the fee is paid in advance. They adopt this course," botanist Ravenel noted, "to bring to the notice of the negroes, their dependent condition & to check the feeling of irresponsibility now prevalent."[12]

Baruch was realistic in his estimate of the situation: the doctors who practiced among blacks must take the initiative in arranging for payment of fees or, in most cases, there would be no payment. Because he did not find contract practice forbidden in the American Medical Association Code of Ethics, he was all the more infuriated by his colleagues' refusal to consider it. He was by no means blind to the reasons given against contracts: that they might serve "to impair the dignity of our profession and reduce it to the level of a common trade or barter." He was always in favor of elevating the profession and "rendering it worthy of the highest intellects," for he believed that professional dignity tended to foster "a certain relation between patient & physician that cannot but conduce to *mutual* benefit." Still, for all these legitimate objections, Baruch believed it was "almost impossible to practice medicine at the present time in the country without some system of that kind."[13]

This was not a conclusion reached hastily or without good reason. "I have practiced the whole summer much on negroes," he wrote Dr. Salley, "and I find that I would be willing to take 150 Doll for my practice (worth about $1000.) This is labor wasted & were I not a beginner here, I would not do it." Older physicians could afford "to wait for some improvement in the social condition of the country to improve the negro practice." It was not so easy for the beginners, who perforce relied on practice among blacks for the majority of their work. "Deprived of the former advantages among these, we are almost entirely without support."

The freedmen of Kershaw District were not wholly to blame for their financial problems. One of the teachers in Camden's freedmen's schools observed that some of the shoemakers and tailors "work not only through the day, but in the 'hurrying' season, through the night. Others, working on contracts after their day's labor for their employers, cultivate a piece of ground, working on until late at night." Many reportedly did this without pay, others for a half dollar a month. All of the freedmen on plantations and most of them in town worked crops on contracts and were not able to raise money until the crops were in, and, as one Camden teacher reported, "the crops in this District are very light." To make matters still worse, "some of the unprincipled 'Buckra' [whites] resort to all manner of means to defraud the hard working negro of the fruits of his toil—striving by wrongs and provocations to make him break his contract so that they may get all the crops themselves." Especially on the plantations in the fall of 1866, "the [Negro] people have no money now."[14]

The freedman's inability to pay for his own medical care was more than an immediate economic hardship for doctors. From personal experience Baruch knew that a black would frequently die before he would send for a physician "& even if he is not so obstinate, where is the common plantation negro with a family of six to twelve, that can afford to pay (out of his earnings) a doctors bill in case of an epidemic or even in case of serious illness or surgical injury?" Judging from his observations, there was none. Other physicians had observed the same neglect, either through carelessness or inability to pay. During the winter of 1865–66, the surgeon in charge of City Hospital in Charleston saw six blacks with frostbitten extremities which, he said, "in our climate and during so mild a Winter, is a suggestive commentary upon their capacity to take care of themselves."[15]

Baruch saw in this threat to the welfare of blacks a threat to the South itself. "I do not agree with those gentlemen who hold that the extermination of the negro is our salvation." In his opinion, South Carolina could ill afford to neglect the health of its blacks when many were already leaving the state, victims of "Florida fever."[16] He did not think the whites alone could provide for themselves. "No, Sir, until we have a system of immigration of whites in good working order, we are dependent on the negro for our sustenance; for there are not a sufficient number of whites in this State, even if they were willing to work (which, you know, three fourths will not do) to make more than enough provisions to support them, even leaving the production of cotton off altogether." So it was actually out of civic as well as professional self-interest that physicians should "do all we can to maintain them [blacks] in *working* integrity and to elevate them morally, if possible."[17]

With no personal sources other than Baruch's letters to his revered friend Salley, member of an old, established South Carolina family and a former slave owner, it is difficult to assess Baruch's attitude toward blacks. Although he freely wrote Dr. Salley his criticisms of his Camden colleagues—and of South Carolina whites in general—on grounds that they were all lacking in energy and enterprise, he seemed to vacillate when discussing blacks. He denied that he lacked the compassion and self-sacrifice appropriate to the character of a physician: "None of us would refuse to attend a poor wretch be he ever so lost and obnoxious to us." But neither did he want to appear guilty of an unseemly egalitarianism: "You know well I am no negro lover, and deprecate as much as anyone the miserable fate that places us on political equality with them." Baruch seemed to be telling Salley that it was expediency, not a wayward European liberalism, that prompted his worry.

The arrangement he proposed was a simple one, which, like any other form of remuneration, could be made proof against exploitation. It would consist of a fee schedule, "a deviation from which is to be treated & looked upon in the same light as a deviation from the established rate of the feebill." He suggested a standard charge for mileage, perhaps one dollar per mile, and a fixed rate for the care of sick plantation hands, "$2 or 3 or 4 per head &ct." "Fortified against inroads of selfishness" by this stated schedule of prices, his system, he felt sure, would withstand the dangers of "underbidding."[18]

That the economic situation should necessitate such measures made him unhappy enough. The political situation, "here as elsewhere in our miserable, downtrodden South . . . only thought of with a shudder" was still more discouraging. "Our enemies are not satisfied with our ruin, but they thirst for our humiliation. God knows, we have had enough of that too, when our Davis is languishing in prison, and our Lee is branded a traitor and our Hampton is muzzled by a Northern General. Where will it end? Is there no balm in Gilead to heal our many wounds?" The only hope was to "trust to God alone," work hard, avoid politics, and "go along in the 'even (crooked?) tenor of our ways' until something turns up." Baruch would try to content himself with gaining "a little reputation" and continue the "uphill work" to overcome what he perceived as popular prejudice against young, unmarried physicians. The number of paying patients seemed particularly scant because Camden, in January 1867, had four practicing physicians besides Baruch: there was his old preceptor, Dr. Lynch Horry Deas, as well as Drs. Salmond, D. L. DeSaussure, and A. A. Moore. If the black practice could be made available, every one of them could have enough to do. As it was, he said, "two active men" could do it all.[19]

Encouraged by Dr. Salley's approval, Baruch determined to present his contract idea to the January meeting of the newly organized Medical Association of Kershaw District. He needed the consent of these men before launching a departure from the ethics prevailing in local practice. But when the meeting of the association failed to produce a quorum, no business could be transacted, and he seemed relieved not to have to voice his unorthodox views. "I apprehend that they would have fallen through, from the fact that the physicians of this place are so wedded to 'old ideas' that they hold on to them with a tenacity that would lead one to suppose their very existence depended on them."[20]

Putting tradition before self-preservation was incomprehensible foolishness to this young immigrant. "We live in a new era, our country is completely revolutionized, socially and politically, and it is our duty to cast about us to find new ideas to conform with this great and radical change, with this unexampled metamorphosis of condition." Baruch was willing to learn from the past but not to sacrifice the future to its memory. "I think that they who will adhere to old notions must sink and those men who can . . . look our unfortunate fate calmly in the face, will reap the benefits of such a course."

Despite all obstacles to prosperity, Baruch soon had reason to be surprised at his own success. "My practice this year," he wrote Dr. Salley in January 1867, "will fork up (in cash practice) about $2000.00." This was "very good for a beginner," and Baruch had accomplished it even though, not being married, he got "very little family practice." The brief storm over Belle's neglect during her Long Branch vacation had passed, and he was looking forward to their marriage as soon as his finances would permit. His dissatisfaction with Camden practice persisted despite his 1867 income, and he continued to speak of money in his letters to Salley, but not as though it was the mere fact of dollars that mattered: it was his energy that was frustrated. "There is no field here for enterprise, and sometimes I almost make up my mind to leave." Yet when openings appeared in Memphis and Atlanta, he contented himself to stay on in

Camden. He wrote that it was a case of the proverbial "bird in the hand," but he may have been thinking that Camden was as good a place as Memphis or Atlanta until he was ready for another try at New York City. In February he permitted himself the luxury of another short trip there to "walk the hospitals" and pay particular attention to eye surgery. Yet he made no effort to stay. Before doing that he would have to have a number of $2,000 years.[21]

By June 1867 the crops prepared with great energy in the severe cold and snow of January had begun to show promise. With cotton and corn doing well, Baruch longed to see the promise of prosperity fulfilled by a political settlement "involving complete restoration." He marveled at Dr. Salley's description of Orangeburg as a "growing town" with plenty of work to be done. "I really did not think that there was a growing town in this God forsaken state of ours." The political agitation that seemed to hinder progress at every step also kept outsiders from coming to South Carolina and (still worse, in Baruch's opinion) from investing their capital.[22]

Professional matters at least offered profitable subjects for discussion. Unlike the low country around Orangeburg, Camden in June had not yet gone into the "intermittent" (malaria) season: "Our principal disease has been dysentery," he told Salley. Although not of epidemic proportions, "there were quite a number of sporadic cases, and a good many among children." Less concerned about this malady than he would be in later years, he found that the best treatment—not exactly strict expectancy—was castor oil or "salts," laudanum, or other opiates, "of course adding always Poultices & careful diet [limewater and milk in the early stages]." A case of very oblique fracture of the tibia had given him the chance to devise an apparatus for traction so successful that, after a month, he found the leg healed with "not the least shortening." And he asked Dr. Salley's "impartial opinion" of the usefulness of veratrum viride, a drug made from the roots of the plant by the same name, used for high blood pressure and in rheumatism, typhoid fever, and pneumonia.[23]

In June 1867 Baruch had the pleasure of seeing the *Richmond Medical Journal* print his article advocating hypodermic medication, his first publication since the war. Introduced in Europe in 1845 by Francis Rynd, an Irish physician, and into America by several physicians during the late 1850s and 1860s, the hypodermic syringe was still not widely used outside large cities.[24] Although medical conservatism stood against it, Baruch, who had probably seen it used in New York, thought the new method would "confer untold blessings" on the human race. His discovery that many doctors were not yet using it set him to writing "in order to enlist for it a more universal adoption by the Profession." It was, he noted, by no means new in cities ("the centres of science as well as of commerce"), yet it was "still unknown in the more rural districts, where innovations seldom find a ready welcome. Especially is this true in the South where we have been almost entirely deprived of reports on the subject during the past few years."[25]

In his presentation of the case for hypodermic medication Baruch displayed Germanic thoroughness and a wide familiarity with medical history. He described earlier methods used to introduce medicines into the body, listed their disadvantages, and described the structure of the syringe and the steps entailed in using it. He even listed the unpleasant effects of hypodermic injection—largely minor and transitory—and concluded with a brief discussion of the drugs most frequently given in this way and the diseases in which it was most helpful.

By an irony of the times, the very economic pinch that had kept so many southern medical journals out of publication probably assured Baruch's paper a wide audience. Under the able editorship of Edwin S. Gaillard and W. S. McChesney, the *Richmond Medical Journal* continued in existence after others had collapsed following short life spans. Whatever its reception among the profession, the article elicited a fine response in the scientific column of the *Charleston News.* "Well-conceived, well-arranged, and admirably executed," said the reviewer, "and if the little we can say in his commendation can induce him to try his pen again, we know we shall do the profession a service." To this the *Charleston News* added praise of Baruch's work in the Confederate medical corps, where "his early promotion, notwithstanding his youth, gives proof that his worth found acknowledgment." This was excellent publicity, indeed, for a "mere country practitioner."[26]

Of course, a good review was not as satisfying as a good-paying practice, but the one often contributes toward the other. In the summer of 1867, Baruch could use every assistance. In preparation for his marriage to Belle Wolfe in the fall, he bought a large two-story house on Lyttleton Street and began the expensive task of furnishing it for their occupancy.[27] The transition from his simple life with the Baums to the support of a household for Miss Belle was a costly one for Baruch. Nor was her family able to help, for she was one of twelve children, and her father had emerged from the war heavily in debt.[28]

Perhaps this was the reason the young couple decided to be married far away. In November, Baruch once again journeyed to New York City, where, on November 27, he took the seventeen-year-old Belle as his bride. The ceremony was performed by a "Minister Isaacs" of a New York synagogue, witnessed by Isaacs's wife and one member of Belle's

family.[29] It seems strange that the oldest daughter of a large family as
well-known as the Wolfes should be married far from home, especially
when Baruch lived in Camden and the Wolfes in Winnsboro, only thirty
miles away. Perhaps Mr. Wolfe's financial distress made any other arrangement impossible. Or it may be that Belle's family had not yet
accepted the prospect of her "marrying down" (as they doubtless viewed
it). At any rate, Simon at last had Belle all to himself.

If he had stopped to analyze their chances for happiness, he might have
harbored grave doubts. There was ferocious pride in them both: in Simon, the pride of the future, of the poor but well-educated immigrant
Jew, recently arrived from eastern Europe and burning to gain a share of
fame; in Belle, the pride of the past, of Sephardic blood, of colonial
ancestors, of long-established wealth and position. Added to these disparate backgrounds were Belle's vanity and Simon's almost inordinate
need for affection, for constant reassurances of her devotion. It was a
dangerous combination, but Simon did not seem concerned. In mid-
December he wrote Dr. Salley: "Well, doctor, I am married and I am
delighted with the happy change of my life. My wife is, as everybody's
wife, the most perfect woman on earth."[30]

In December the newlyweds found Camden frozen with sleet and
snow; nonetheless, Baruch wrote Salley, the honeymoon, "proverbially a
happy period of laziness & abandonment to pleasure," was not a disappointment, at least "so far as the happiness is concerned." Laziness was so
foreign to Baruch's nature that he could not indulge in it, even in the early
days of marriage. He kept busy with correspondence, complaining that
"there is nothing doing here in practice; no sickness. It is duller than ever
I saw it." Money was a real problem now. "Collections are very, very
dull. I cannot collect enough to meet current expenses and were it not for
an occasional fee of ten, fifteen or 20 Dolls. for a gonorrhea or syphilis
case, I would be a blank." He was apparently running strong competition
to Dr. Cornelius Kollock, a gynecological surgeon in Cheraw, approximately fifty miles to the northeast of Camden, who was reputed to be
especially skillful, drawing patients "from distant parts." In Baruch's
own estimation, he had himself built up "quite a reputation in this
line."[31]

His success is symptomatic of a changing attitude toward venereal
disease, an attitude bound up in every age with prevailing views of sexual
activity. In America up to about 1850, most doctors thought "these
diseases were divine punishment for licentious living and as such should
be left to run their course."[32] As late as the early 1900s, this corset-bound
morality deprived one of New York's large dispensaries of a genitouri-

nary department because the trustees refused to "foster vice by curing the diseases produced by ungodly conduct." But the confusion between sin and disease had begun to clear long before the twentieth century. Even in the antebellum South, some doctors accepted cases of syphilis, despite its supposedly divine origin. Their heroic mercury treatment, often more debilitating than the disease, sent droves of patients to try the milder approaches of quacks.[33] Although Baruch did not describe his methods to Dr. Salley (saying only that he had had "some unique incidents in this branch of practice"), he evidently did not attack "private diseases" with gigantic doses of mercury. Had he done so, his patients would not have continued to come from distances of "30 x 25 miles . . . in other districts."[34]

With business slack except for venereal diseases, Baruch devoted his excess energy and time to experimentation. He failed to find a substitute for quinine, the costly remedy for malaria, but he managed to convert a related discovery into an item published in the correspondence columns of the New York *Medical Record,* one of the country's leading medical journals. He was always interested in new drugs and apparatus; as long as they promised to be therapeutically useful, it mattered little whether they were major innovations. Not even Dr. Salley kept so thoroughly abreast of the times. In March 1868 Baruch described to him the "new" treatment by inhalation, especially useful in "purely local disease" such as "Asthma, Chronic Bronchitis, Laryngitis, Pharyngitis, and even Phthisis [pulmonary tuberculosis]. . . . You get an apparatus called an 'Atomizer,' which sends a minute spray of any solution into the mouth & thus the fluid is inhaled." He was also experimenting with a "special apparatus" for use in tuberculosis, a method he did not describe because it was still very much "on trial."[35]

Baruch's enthusiasm and energy in therapeutics were not altogether wasted on his patients. During one month in early 1868, his practice "among the more substantial whites & blacks" brought him $648, an astounding sum (and probably not a typical one). It was especially good, he thought, for the youngest practitioner in Camden. As far as he could tell, he had "collected as much as any physician (if not more) here." Having been "thrown back considerably in financial matters by the expense of furnishing a house & getting married," he could accept his paying—if not exclusive—clientele gratefully and temper his frustrated aim for a "respectable practice" with the knowledge that, in Camden, it was "the better (?) classes, who generally dont pay their bills."[36]

To Dr. Salley's inquiry about his "nigger practice," he replied that he had more success in collecting from them than from the whites, partly because, as he put it, he was "not afraid of dunning people." From town blacks he took payment in kind. "One fellow furnishes me beef, another one (a woman) washes, another sews for me &ct." Conditions were such that he could collect as effectively as he did only "by strict and watchful attention" to business. "That's the point, be after them early & late; I see what they have; I take hay, corn, fodder, eggs, chickens, anything, for I have to buy these anyhow."

Still it was not enough. Even as a bachelor Baruch had found it hard to bear his colleagues' resignation to the nonpayment of plantation blacks' fees. In March 1868, with Belle expecting their first child, his impatience took on a tone of desperation. How it galled him that these "gentlemen" would persist in practicing as though former masters cared what now became of their former slaves: "They are blind to the fact that the employer cares less for his negro laborer than he does for his horse, or dog." Not one of his medical associates would help him in "leading by degrees the minds of the employers to recognize the fact that *it is* to their interest to have their employees receive proper medical attention when sick." He did not blame the employers for refusing to contract in advance to pay the medical bill of a worker, for without some prior agreement with the doctor as to the total bill, the employer might find himself liable for fees worth twice the worker's dues at the end of the year. Nor could the worker, who lost twice by being ill, be reasonably expected to assume the full burden of a doctor's bill; in some instances, the cost of medical care might "swallow up his whole years earnings," even if the crop brought more than enough to cover the lien of his employer. The doctors must simply learn not to look for full payment of the "regular charges" of one dollar per mile and two per visit. Medical ethics permitted deductions for indigent people, and Baruch said he would gladly settle for half, in exchange for the certainty of being paid anything at all. As it was, he rarely got even half because the planters refused responsibility and the freedmen were often unable to pay "even moderate bills."

There were at least two different ways to solve the dilemma. One was to say to the employer and freedmen on a plantation where the annual practice averaged about $500, "I will practice in this place for $250.00 a year, which would be about $2.00 a head." The employer could then charge each black in accordance with this rate *at once* in his book, or the blacks might agree to let the employer pay entire bill. Either way, he would know ahead of time "precisely for how much he is responsible for each of his hands" and could take this into account in making advances to them throughout the year. If the doctors would propose such an arrangement, the employer would stand "on sure footing & cannot with reason refuse his sanction & responsibility."

"But, no, our fogies are frightened of the *name* 'Contract.' They see in it dangers that threaten to swallow them up bodily, and they prefer starving & 'looking on' (as they say) & 'waiting for the employer to get to his senses.' What folly!" They were "the nicest gentlemen" Baruch had ever known, but they had "no energy and less business tact." Some of them gave as a serious objection to contracts the fact that they would often be called out unnecessarily. Baruch found this hard to believe, "because negroes won't, for trifling ailments, leave their work & lose time, nor will the employer let them have mules to go for a doctor." And even if contracts did involve the doctors in a few needless trips, "What would be the consequence? They would be riding on the road instead of loafing at the drug & other stores the whole day; they would at least be attending to business instead of doing themselves injury by idleness."

Unlike doctors of later years, deluged with a medical literature vast beyond the reading time available even in limited practices, Baruch's colleagues had little to do, and they apparently neglected even that. Baruch seemed to feel that they wasted their leisure hours as foolishly as the North Carolina doctor who wrote that, in an especially healthy period, "neither myself nor my co-partner are doing anything save drinking liquor and swapping horses." For himself, Baruch would not object to a few extra calls: "My horse has to be fed anyhow & I would a great deal rather spend my idle time in going on professional business, though it be bootless and unprofitable for *it is* profitable in the end." The others were "peaceful, gentlemanly & harmonious," but it aggravated him to see them "acting so suicidally" and forcing him to do the same. Their lethargy made him indignant. "Thank God, *I* am not starving, and am willing for the sake of harmony in the profession to 'look on' too, and to 'let the grass grow, while the horse is starving.'"[37]

Out of his frustration Baruch devised still another plan, one with a mid-twentieth-century ring. He would make "each negro laborer sign his responsibility for the payment of an equal share of the doctor's bill of the place whether he or his family have been sick or not. For instance if there are 100 head, and the bill is $200.00, each head pays $2.00, then the head of a family of 6 pays $12.00, a family of 10 pays $20.00 &ct. Thus it is a sort of mutual benefit association and comes easier on them." But this, too, had its drawbacks, for no definite sum could be fixed in advance of the year's crop of ills, "and hence there is but one place on which I think I'll be able to practice in this way, during the present year. It is really a hard case for me to lose the practice of five or six places, because we dont practice by contract, but this is the last year I will stand it. I have a family now and must do the best I can. I am willing to do all in my power to uphold the dignity of my profession & do not wish to do aught against the ethical rules of it."[38]

It made Baruch frantic to be so bound down, to have his contract proposals condemned, while some physicians worked on salary in institutions such as insane asylums. He would try once more to persuade the Kershaw District Medical Society ("Society forsooth! It has been in existence two years, and has been able to get up but two meetings . . . since then we have never been able to get a quorum"). Failing an improbable success with them, he vowed to "strike out independently for myself & risk the consequences; I will secede & next year practice on my own merits & my own fee bill."[39]

Apart from Baruch's failure to earn what he thought he should, his practice flourished. He saw his town blacks, "mostly uterine cases," in his office clinic, allotting certain days of the week so that he would not be out of town when they came. As an obstetrician, he was quite successful. In two years only one of his patients had developed puerperal convulsions, the curse of childbearing, and that one he had treated successfully with chloroform. From the works of Friedrich Wilhelm Scanzoni and Carl Braun von Fernwald, he had learned of the role of kidney disease in these convulsions; through accounts of the work of Sir James Y. Simpson in 1847, he became aware of the help chloroform could give when convulsions occurred. Simpson was a special hero to Baruch, who found the anesthetic an invaluable aid, particularly in the toxemia and convulsions of pregnancy, then called eclampsia. "I am sure," he wrote Dr. Salley, "I shall never treat a case of this kind without chloroform, if it can be had, there being no point in practice on which I am clearer."[40]

Obstetrics and gynecology constituted much of general practice in the 1860s, but Baruch's rural practice called for every sort of medical and surgical skill. Very delicate surgical maneuvers, however, like the ones he performed in a case of traumatic aneurysm of the posterior occipital artery, were not to his liking. Even after the patient recovered, Baruch shivered to think of the "ticklish business" of ligating the left primitive carotid, a major blood vessel of the neck: "to see the swollen internal jugular lying on the artery & to know that a mere pricking of its coats would send my patient into eternity." The surgeon's thrill at being "environed by dangers at every step," at moving with painstaking care through the veins and arteries and nerves, was not for Baruch. "The only safety lies in laying the knife aside as soon as you open the sheath; then use the handle of the aneurism needle & separate the tissues as little as possible." Although he was proud enough of his success to write about it to Dr. Salley, it was clearly not the work of the surgeon that he sought for his life's occupation.[41]

In July 1868 Baruch's hope for the political millennium flared briefly when he heard rumors that New York was undergoing a "revulsion of feeling in favor of the South." He could readily imagine such a "revulsion," but not through any love for the South: "I think it is more an effort to achieve their own salvation, for they can see into the future and know full well, that Radical rule has sapped the foundation of this government and if it continues it will crumble to the dust, and bury their magnificent city & its grand prospects under its ruins." New Yorkers could already see "destruction looming up in the distance, whence the valiant Ulysses is coming with a lot of horses & a box of segars, which are to be his oracles of Delphi in questions of state policy." The fall election must return a Democrat to the office of president or the South would cease to be a place for white men: "We will have a perfect pandemonium down here, under nigger rule." Baruch had no love for Ulysses S. Grant, "the horse and segar man," predicting that he would be but a "pliant tool in the hands of the Jacobins." If Grant should win the election, "niggerism, miscegenation, free-lovism and all the modern schisms of destruction & death will reign rampant in this poor land"—the same land, the immigrant lamented, "where peace & prosperity were wont to smile and beckon strangers to their loss."[42]

Whenever he wrote Dr. Salley about a situation in which he felt trapped and impotent, whether it was his colleagues' opposition to contracts or the political plight of southern whites, Baruch's discretion flowed away in an undertow of anger and frustration. The very thought of a Radical Republican victory in the 1868 election sent his pen racing hotly ahead of his reason: "There is yet one resource, that has once failed us, but may now succeed; at any rate it is worth a trial when all is lost—I mean the sword. What boots it to live under such tyranny, such moral and physical oppression, when we can be much happier in the consciousness of dying for such a cause." Despite the "horrors & privations" of war, he said, "I am not willing to submit, when I have a remedy left. For God & the right then will we strike & with Gods help we will conquer." The Radicals won the November election, and the "horse and segar" man moved into the White House. But Baruch neither struck nor conquered, except in the safe white anonymity of the Ku Klux Klansman.[43]

Nor did he carry out his threat to flaunt local medical custom and enter practice on his own terms. Although practice by contract was by no means unknown elsewhere in South Carolina, in Camden it apparently would have meant professional ostracism. However unrewarding the company of his colleagues, Baruch could not bring himself to alienate them. Instead he settled into a smugly bitter satisfaction when three large plantations came into the hands of "a nigger-quack-doctor, because I refused to take them on contract." The local medical group, "mostly averse" to medical discussion, was "one of the 'Rip Van Winkle' kind," which would—deservedly, he thought—"wake up astonished some of these fine mornings, when some Yankee doctor will come here & take all niggerdom on contract."[44]

Despite the difficulty of collecting fees, Camden had ten physicians by the end of 1868. Five of them, like Baruch, lived wholly from their practice, which he estimated at about $4,500 for all five together. The others, who had incomes apart from medicine, still made not less than $1,000 among them. An aggregate income of $5,500 for the physicians of Camden and its environs seems a surprisingly high figure for the time, but it was poor compared to antebellum earnings. In 1860, during Baruch's preceptorship, he had seen that Dr. Deas's account list usually showed $3,500 or $4,000. Now, in 1868, he surmised that Dr. Deas seldom collected over $1,000 annually. The doctors were still *earning* the fees they had once received, and earning them under the difficult conditions of country practice, but the people had no money to pay.

It set Baruch thinking again about the direction his life was taking. Dr. Salley was the only practitioner in Orangeburg. By long years of service in the community, he had reached a place of respect and authority which his young Camden friend greatly envied: "Aside from the pecuniary (and most important) benefit accruing therefrom, it must be a great satisfaction to look back upon all the trials and struggles of embryonic, youthful and even matured professional life, and see them all in the distance, surrounded by that splendor (?) which only the *distant* contemplation of such hardships can produce." Such a position was Baruch's highest goal, the "pinnacle of ambitious desires." But in country practice the occupant of this Olympian post faced hardships, too: "In fact, it becomes rather the most laborious period of a country doctor's life, when he is called upon," as Dr. Salley was, "to do the whole practice of a community."[45]

Medical practice was physically exhausting then in a way unimaginable today. Trained nurses were a thing of the future. The alternative of hospitalization was available only to practitioners in large communities. The country doctor, who knew that imperfect nursing by family or servants often hampered recovery or contributed directly to a fatal outcome, still bore the full brunt of caring for the patient. He not only had to make an examination and diagnosis and prescribe accordingly; in many cases he had to stay with the patient to see that the proper dosages were administered to the proper part of the body at the proper time.[46]

While Baruch hoped to have his hands and mind constantly occupied in his declining years, he could not bring himself to associate "that time of life with laborious country practice." He wanted to have a good city practice in old age, though he did not have much hope of it. For someone like Dr. Salley, "in vigorous health," a large country practice lost some of its unpleasantness. Baruch did not consider himself so blessed. During the war he had suffered severe and recurring attacks of diarrhea and had barely survived a bout with typhoid fever—but these were common enough during those days and need not be taken as a sign of poor health. More telling for his constitution was his wartime affliction with an eye ailment of uncertain origin. After the war, he continued to suffer from imperfect vision and frequent headaches, sometimes severe enough to keep him from working.[47] He had tremendous energy, to be sure, but his physical machinery seemed extraordinarily susceptible to breakdown under long hours of hard work and prolonged situations of insecurity.

After the arrival of his firstborn, Hartwig, in 1868, when the pressure of earning bore in more heavily than ever, he took a contract post—one that was considered ethically acceptable—as examining physician for the Southern Stock and Mutual Life Insurance Company.[48] It at least provided a steady source of income, even if a small one. He would soon have occasion to be especially grateful for it. Before the year was out, the slim hope he still had of entering into contract practice in Camden vanished. With it went his prospects of quickly earning enough over the cost of supporting himself and his family to start the life he wanted in New York City.

As in a nightmare, the faster he raced toward his goal, the faster it seemed to recede beyond his reach.

7 "Let us be up and doing"

Early in the spring of 1869, Baruch took steps to provide a respite from Camden's intellectual sluggishness. As corresponding secretary of the Kershaw District Medical Association, he wrote to members of the Charleston Medical Society, urging efforts to revive the state medical association. Within two months the Charleston doctors arranged for a reorganization meeting. They could not determine who the officers were (the association had not met since February 1860, before Baruch entered medical school), but they gathered contributions for refreshments and arranged for reduced railroad fare to encourage attendance. Despite these inducements, the turnout was disappointing. When Baruch reached Charleston for the meeting on May 20, he found that only eleven men had taken advantage of the opportunity to travel at half-fare in the shabby, stale-smelling cars of South Carolina's rail lines. Even at half-fare, the trip was evidently too costly for many. Counting Charleston's delegation of twenty-seven, a total of thirty-eight physicians came together, representing only eight of the state's more than twenty-nine counties. As if the attendance were not sufficiently disheartening, those who had not seen Charleston since the war found much to grieve them in the appearance of that once beautiful city. Fire and war had worked special hardships on the proud seaport of earlier days, as the roofless houses and gaping window frames testified. After four full years of peace, the wide swath of buildings burned in the fire of 1861 had not yet been repaired.[1]

Over deeply rutted streets, filled with holes that made even a buggy ride hazardous, the men came together to the convention site in the Roper Hospital. Here, where Baruch had started his medical training in

1860, he saw several of his former professors, Thomas Lewis Ogier and Francis Peyre Porcher, as well as Robert Alexander Kinloch, who had examined him for commission in the Confederate medical service. Here too was Eli Geddings, who had lost the treasures of a long and laborious academic career in the conflict to which he gave four years of his old age. Even his library, "then one of the choicest in the South," and his instruments and teaching apparatus had been burned in Columbia, where he had sent them for safekeeping. His home in Charleston had been plundered and all his surgical instruments stolen. Yet Geddings was one of the few older men sufficiently spirited to enter into the reorganization effort. Although Baruch's Orangeburg friend, Dr. Salley, was unable to attend, he sent along a letter asking to be enrolled as a member.[2]

Of all the practitioners in Kershaw County, Baruch was the only one who attended the Charleston meeting, a fact that did nothing to improve his opinion of his colleagues. Their absence, however, gave him opportunities he might not have had otherwise. Two committees essential to reorganization—one on nominations, the other on a new constitution—were set up to include one man from each of the counties represented. As the sole spokesman from Kershaw County, "S. Baruch" became a member of both. Although absent, Dr. Salley was elected one of the two vice-presidents. Baruch did not receive an office, at least not at first. After the slate of officers, including two vice-presidents, was filled, the committee on the constitution—of which he was a member—wrote still a third vice-president into the document they created. The committee on nominations—of which he was also a member—then held a special meeting and returned his name, which the membership approved. It was a minor office but a start in the right direction.[3]

Despite scanty attendance, the members set up general requirements: all "regular diplomated physicians of good standing" could join by subscribing to the constitution and paying a year's assessment of five dollars. They adopted the code of ethics of the American Medical Association. By way of enforcement they provided that "any member knowingly violating the Code of Ethics, or found guilty of unprofessional or ungentlemanly conduct, or gross neglect of duty, shall be punished by reprimand, suspension, or expulsion, as the Association may determine." Any physician accused of offense would have a hearing, with punishment to be meted out by no less than a two-thirds vote of the members present, the yeas and nays to be called out and recorded.[4]

Since Baruch had often expressed his intent to conform entirely to the American Medical Association code, he was most certainly among the supporters of this provision, although there is no record of the discussion that must have preceded its passage. Ironically, it was through this action that he was to be irrevocably denied the opportunity for contract practice; even as the South Carolina Medical Association was agreeing to abide by the national code, the American Medical Association, in annual session in New Orleans, was adding the stipulation "that all contract physicians, as well as those guilty of bidding for practice at less rates than those established by a majority of regular graduates of the same locality, be classed as irregular practitioners."[5] Baruch might have decided to risk this stigma to gain the financial security contracts would give him, but the constitution he himself had just helped to write contained a further proviso: that county societies, to be entitled to representation in the state body, must adopt both the national code and "a constitution which shall in no particular, contravene that of this [the state] Association."[6] This clause killed any chance of contracts or mutual payment plans.

Of course Baruch could not know the implications of the new constitution until he later heard of the AMA ruling on contracts. Otherwise the Charleston meeting was a satisfying experience, filled with the "talk of physic" that he missed at home. There was a lively discussion of veratrum viride, the drug he had asked Dr. Salley about a few years before. Indigenous in swampy districts of almost every area in the United States, veratrum was known by a multitude of names: American hellebore, swamp hellebore, Indian poke, poke weed, bear weed, itch weed, tickle weed, earth gall, devilbit, wolfbane, and puppet root. Its properties, like those of the entire genus veratrum, were emetic and purgative, but in the late 1850s it came into use in the South as a sedative in inflammatory diseases.[7] Dr. W. C. Norwood of Abbeville County, one of its proponents, precipitated a debate by distributing pamphlets to the group and speaking ("at some length") in praise of its properties. Norwood's advocacy brought a protest from Eli Geddings. When Geddings had finished his rebuttal, little remained to recommend the "universality" of usage Norwood had urged. It was a good lesson to Baruch, who was himself in occasional danger of being swept away by excessive therapeutic enthusiasm.[8]

Although Baruch returned from the meeting refreshed by seeing old friends and participating in their earnest talk of medicine, the ruling on contracts, when he learned of it, must have been a bitter disappointment, especially in the worsening economic conditions that summer of 1869. Fortunately, now that he was a family man, he was consulted more frequently in obstetrical and gynecological cases. This increased business, together with his salary as an examining physician for the Southern Stock and Mutual Life Insurance Company, helped him weather the financial maelstrom that struck Camden that fall. Not all of the town's doctors were so fortunate: on September 2, 1869, Dr. Thomas J. Workman, Baruch's former preceptor, joined the growing number of those whose bankruptcy declarations dotted the Camden newspapers.[9]

Perhaps to alleviate the distress of those who would willingly take work if they could get it, the commissioners of Kershaw County expanded official activities. On November 1 they opened accounts with local persons to "diet" prisoners in the county jail; to repair roads and bridges; to manage elections; to furnish coffins for prisoners, paupers, and other charges of the county; and to collect firewood for the jail. The commissioners also contracted with doctors to care for the inmates of county institutions. Once again Baruch placed himself on payroll, as physician at the county poorhouse and at the jail. On January 15, 1870, he collected $125 for his services to the county of Kershaw.[10]

There were few bright spots at the beginning of the new year. Belle was pregnant again, surely a mixed blessing in such unpromising times. As the economic situation worsened, local reaction to Radical government, and especially to southerners who supported it in any way, reached a high pitch of heat and bitterness. Amid these depressing circumstances, Baruch welcomed a visit from Dr. Salley and his son in late January. In their correspondence Baruch often expressed a wish for such a visit, so that the two might talk about their many common interests.

One subject the doctors often discussed was the prospect of making the South Carolina Medical Association a going concern. It seemed "disgraceful" to Baruch "to think that ours is the only state that is so deficient in enterprise and scientific attainment of its Medical men, that it cannot boast of a Med. Society as a flourishing Institution." They must find a way to elevate professional standards and arouse that "spirit of emulation" so essential to "enlightened Medical Practice." Baruch asked Salley to help in recruiting members: "We owe it to ourselves and our prosperity to be vigilant, lest we lapse into ignorance and . . . be left far behind by the progressive spirits of other states. Surely we are not so fallen and degraded, but that we still have some pride to uphold the fair fame of the medical men of South Carolina. Let us be up and doing, even if our only reward lies in the consciousness of having done our duty."[11]

In February the *Richmond and Louisville Medical Journal* noted the collapse, "either from neglect or inanition," of seven southern medical periodicals since the close of the war. The times were difficult indeed. In March 1870, when the association again convened in Columbia, only seventeen out of forty-four members were present. Once more Baruch was the only physician representing Kershaw County.[12] To this small audience he exhibited a device designed to facilitate the placement of a uterine sponge-tent, one of the contributions of his revered James Y. Simpson. Such devices, unheard-of today, were frequently needed to remedy birth injuries in an era of imperfect obstetrical methods. In some circles a reaction was under way against the torrent of gynecological apparatus, the "burning and cauterizing, cutting and slashing, and splitting and skewering" that threatened to consign the "old-fashioned womb" to a place in history and make a "Chinese toy-shop" of a woman's body. One physician whose views received a wide hearing demanded a return to the days when "our grandmothers never knew they had a womb, only as they were reminded of it by a healthy foetus . . . which," he added, "they always held on to." Baruch's colleagues were apparently not yet caught up in the reaction. They received his demonstration without unfavorable discussion and asked him to write it up for publication in the *Transactions*.[13]

In August 1870 Baruch had the belated pleasure of seeing the *Richmond and Louisville Medical Journal* take up the cause of contract practice which he had vainly championed for so long. Editor Gaillard even argued from the same evidence: that blacks were not receiving adequate medical care and that southern physicians were suffering "untold, inexpressible poverty." The mutual payment plan Gaillard proposed was similar too, but he had begun his agitation too late, for the American Medical Association had officially excluded contract practice.[14]

Fortunately, Baruch seems to have been successful in collecting fees despite the difficult times. By autumn of 1870, he needed a larger house, for Belle had borne him a second son, Bernard, in August. On November 11, Baruch bought a three-story house which, together with its 100-by-573-foot lot, cost him $4,000. Built in Charleston style with the front door facing inward on the garden rather than onto the street, this rambling house of whitewashed brick was one of Camden's finest homes. By January 1871, the growing family was settled beneath the hipped roof and large chimneys in a comfortable setting of huge old shade trees and a brick-walled flower garden stretching southward from the broad veranda.[15]

A large part of Baruch's practice at this time consisted of uterine disease, the subject of an article he wrote for the *Richmond and Louisville Medical Journal*. The current status of therapy in this field was discouraging to a young physician who harbored ideals far removed from therapeutic skepticism. So many different theories were thrust forward that they threatened to leave him "vacillating upon a sea of conflicting elements"; yet he remained certain that experience would guide him to the truth. In the spirit of Eli Geddings, he expected that the truth would lie somewhere between the extremes; that "there is no absolute doctrine of uterine disease, but that these affections are to be rationally dealt with on the same sound pathological principles which guide us in the study of other affections."[16]

Practicing among what he called the "lower classes" of whites and blacks, Baruch could see that the proverbial ounce of prevention would be far more effective than all the remedies he could apply. Unfortunately, poverty contributed more heavily to uterine maladies than any other single factor: strenuous exertion too soon after childbirth, frequent pregnancy and criminal abortion, lack of cleanliness, insufficient food and clothing, excessive and premature exposure to "viccissitudes of weather"—all were more or less directly connected with the terrible poverty for which there was no remedy. The most intractable uterine diseases he saw were those caused by gonorrheal infections, treated before he saw them, if at all, by "old negroes and other quacks that abound in the country." Under prevailing economic conditions, Baruch was surprised that uterine disease was not even more widespread. The answer, he said, lay in education and prevention rather than in therapy for the unhappy victims.[17]

The 1871 meeting of the South Carolina Medical Association shed little light on the particular problems Baruch faced in his work. Once again, out of the state's 583 physicians, only a small number attended. As a result, Baruch again served on numerous committees. George E. Trescot, a Charleston physician who was professor of materia medica and therapeutics at the medical college, read a paper condemning extreme enthusiasts and therapeutic skeptics alike. He asserted that both seemed to be victims of the delusion that medicine would one day be able to account for all the phenomena of disease. "Now I do not believe that day is ever coming," said Dr. Trescot, "unless it be in the morning when Prof. [Thomas] Huxley has succeeded in artificially creating life." Trescot disdained certainty in any form. "The man who, at the bed-side of the sick, puts on a grave face, and says, 'You are very ill, but I will cure you,' and the man who says, 'In this disease so many will die, and so many recover, so I will do nothing,' are both unfit to practice medicine." Through the ages therapeutics had suffered at the hands of men who persisted in looking for or thinking they had found the medical panacea. Trescot warned his audience to avoid this error. They must content themselves with the knowledge that, although medicine would never know all the answers, it would always be true that "there is no disease so trifling that it may not end in death, and none so severe that we cannot do something to relieve."[18]

Exceptions to this last rule are rare. Yet Baruch had no more than returned home from the meeting when he confronted such an exception in the strange case of Edward Nash. A sixty-year-old black, tall and athletic, Nash had been severely brain damaged at birth. Upon the death of his kindly master, who had employed him as a wood carrier and cattle driver and allowed him "many privileges on account of his imbecility," Nash refused both food and drink for a full week. At the end of this time, he was brought to the poorhouse. Baruch made every effort to sustain him with food, "but he obstinately, persistently, though not violently refused anything to pass his mouth. His teeth could not be forced open." For eleven days he rejected the food and water, coffee and milk placed daily by the keeper on a bench near his cot. In the entire time he neither said a word nor made the feeblest attempt to move from his room. "Three days before his death," Baruch recorded in his casebook, "delirium supervened, he exclaimed I am so hot, so hot, so hot, I am dying, I am dying, I am dying." Not even in the last delirium of his self-inflicted death throes did he ask for succor. The only sounds he made were those he knew best—the lowing of cattle, the bellowing of bulls, the braying of asses, and the bleating of sheep. [19]

Such inconsolable grief at separation from the master was rare in South Carolina in 1871. Black militia units had organized throughout the state, and on July 4, during a parade demonstration to celebrate their independence, Camden's black militia became embroiled in a scuffle that quickly snowballed into a free-for-all with clearly drawn color lines. It was only one of many unhappy omens that year. In August the first issue of the *Camden Journal* published under the new ownership of John Kershaw carried a front-page article smugly entitled "The Darwinian Theory— The Monkeys Hear of it, and are Much Agitated in Consequence." Though ostensibly intended as a gibe at evolution, the article was really a less-than-subtle satire on the political and intellectual aspirations of blacks. It clearly illustrated Kershaw's avowed "conservative" point of view, at the same time belying his aim to make the *Journal* serve as "a reflex of the latest thought and sentiments which agitate the world." [20] The "latest thought" in the world outside Camden no longer looked on Darwinism as a joke with crude atavistic implications.

In October 1871 activities of the Ku Klux Klan reached such proportions in up-country South Carolina that President Grant proclaimed "a condition of lawlessness and terror" existent in nine counties of the state, three of them bordering Kershaw County. Federal authorities suspended habeas corpus in all nine and began to arrest suspected Klansmen. Continuing poverty went hand in hand with political chaos, until at last even the Medical College of South Carolina gave up the struggle to maintain standards and consented to lower its fees. [21]

The year 1871 was also discouraging for the doctors of Charleston, who found themselves questioning their concept of yellow fever. Despite the quarantine that many of them believed would protect them, the summer had brought a veritable plague of yellow fever upon the population of nearly forty-five thousand. Looking for contagion of a different sort, the physicians did not understand how this disease, also called the "black vomit," moved through the filth and sewage and garbage abounding the city's streets.[22]

Even as Charleston doctors were looking for the weak link in their quarantine system—or wondering whether yellow jack was "imported" at all—Baruch was questioning his attitude toward bloodletting. At one time he had thought it was almost universally bad, justifiable only in very special cases and then only in negligible quantities. Now he was not so sure. Five years earlier, imbued with the teaching of Austin Flint and Chambers and John Hughes Bennett, he would have agreed with a *Richmond Medical Journal* editorial rejoicing at the recent and growing proscription of the lancet.[23] From his entry into practice until 1871, Baruch had "so seldom drawn blood . . . that the operation of venesection" seemed "almost formidable!!" Yet he was haunted by the thought of two or three patients whom he might have saved, or at least relieved, had he not been so strictly opposed to bleeding. Especially troubling was the memory of a patient with pulmonary congestion as a consequence of heart disease, a patient whose "dusky countenance, distended nostrils, foaming mouth and serous exudation from the lungs" cried out to Baruch to bleed. But Baruch had been unable to cast off the lessons of his youth: "With timidity I opened a vein in the foot and allowed the blood to flow, after having cupped in three preceding paroxysms." It was such a severe case that he had not hoped for a "curative impression." Yet he could not forget "the agonies, the unspeakable horrors that gleamed from the patient's anxious countenance." Could these, he asked himself in 1871, have been eased by free bloodletting?[24]

In puerperal convulsions too, "this terrible disease" as he called it, he was coming to think that bleeding might have saved expectant or laboring mothers whose suffering had seemed to be eased but not ended by the chloral hydrate, potassium bromide, and morphine injections with which he customarily treated them. Chloroform, which he had once considered the answer, had disappointed him. Dr. Thomas Robertson of Winnsboro, "who has had a large experience in this disease," used bloodletting. Although Dr. Salley seemed to prefer injections of morphine, Baruch gradually began to use venesection to stop the shattering convulsions that seemed to kill by producing exhaustion.[25]

In pneumonia the "restorative treatment" Baruch had learned early in his career had borne up better under the test of experience. By 1871 he had cared for numerous cases, slight and severe, many of them among blacks, to whom bleeding was supposed to be especially hazardous: Bridget, "feeble mulatto woman, my cook"; Henry Mitchell, a "tall, thin man, carpenter"; Charles Chesnut, "strong mulatto—bricklayer—addicted to drinking"; Ananias; Sandy. Recoveries in all of these patients attested to Baruch's therapeutic judgment; he used mercurial purge ("I always deem it important to have bowels in good condition"), chicken, tea, milk, whiskey or brandy, quinine, morphine, poultices, and an occasional blister. Neither strictly expectant nor heroic, this mode of treatment seemed ideally suited to blacks with pneumonia. There was occasionally an unresponsive case like that of Celia, "stewardess on the train, addicted to drinking," who "would not take food or stimulants" and died the day after falling ill. And there were disheartening relapses like that of Ebenezer Cantey, "a strong robust fellow," who was recovering when he "arose one day & was exposed to a driving rain which entered the room & drenched him." This brought on "oedema of the glottis," which carried him off two days later. The same fate overtook John Lever, a "decrepid [sic] mulatto," who, after a steady recovery for eight days, "got up & sat by the fire in an open room, where the wind blew down the large chimney & through the many openings in the walls."[26] No degree of medical skill could succeed where shelter against the elements was wanting.

For all his success with the restorative treatment in pneumonia, Baruch sometimes wondered whether he did not observe too rigidly the proscription on bleeding which he was taught to apply to all blacks. There was, for example, the case of Josh Williams, a prisoner at the jail. Even with double pneumonia, Josh was "one of the most robust negroes" Baruch had ever seen. Baruch had used restorative treatment, but because this was a case that "would certainly have tempted any one to the anti-phlogistic treatment," he found himself asking whether he was truly doing justice to the patient by refraining from bleeding. It happened that Josh's recovery was rapid and uninterrupted, proving as well as any single case could that the restorative treatment was sufficient for blacks. Still, Baruch kept turning over in his mind the question of bleeding whites. In October 1871, he confessed that "even in pneumonia, though I deem the stimulant and supporting plan the best, I think that in a robust subject (white) one may with advantage draw blood, as long as there is only a slight crepitation [the sound heard in a lung affected with pneumonia]."[27]

Baruch's indulgence in these occasional reviews and reevaluations of his therapeutic methods is a tribute to the industry and conscientious attention he devoted to his work. Mere practice filled the hours most country practitioners gave to their profession in those days—practice and the eternal problem of collecting for their services. In early 1872 Baruch's colleagues at last faced up to the impossibility of their financial situation, as he had long predicted they would someday have to do. At a "regular meeting" on January 9, the Kershaw District Medical Association unanimously adopted the following preamble and resolutions: "Owing to necessities of the times it is necessary that the collection of medical fees should be regularly made, and believing that it would be better both for physicians and patients that they *should be made* at least once a month, it is therefore RESOLVED That the members of this Association are required to make out and present there [sic] bills for medical attention on the first of every month and collect the same."[28]

Although monthly bills, certainly not much easier to collect than annual ones, fell far short of the drastic steps Baruch had advocated in the 1860s, there was no better alternative. Before the AMA outlawed contracts, southern physicians (who would suffer most from such a ruling) might have bargained to prevent its adoption: the profession in the South knew that the North wanted them back in the AMA, and they might have stipulated AMA approval of contracts—or, at the least, official silence on the matter—as their price for reunion. Now it was too late. Indeed, the national body seemed bent on making medical practice purely charitable. At its 1872 meeting the AMA committee on ethics proposed classifying as irregular and disqualifying from membership in national, county, or city societies all "members of the profession hired by the month or year for definite, stipulated wages, by individuals, families, railroad or manufacturing corporations, or any other money-making institutions whatever, for ordinary medical or surgical practice (always excepting benevolent and eleemosynary institutions, and medical officers of the Army and Navy)." The AMA did not immediately act on this drastic measure, which would seem to include even such posts as examining physician for an insurance company, referring it instead to the various state societies.[29]

On the last day of the national meeting, opposition to the ethics committee's stance arose even among northerners. It was a Pennsylvanian who moved that, since the report on ethics seemed to cover the whole subject of contract practice, "every thing relative to this subject be rescinded or stricken from the ordinances of this Association." If passed, this motion would have given another chance to those who favored contract practice, perhaps even allowing them to have the idea reinstated. But they were not to have that opportunity. The Pennsylvania doctor's motion was tabled, and the anticontract amendment of 1869 stood firmly attached to the AMA code of ethics.[30]

The annual state association convention was held in Columbia in April

1872. Out of its official roster of seventy-five members, fewer than a third attended. On behalf of the Kershaw District Medical Association, Baruch invited the members to hold their next meeting in Camden; but Charleston and Columbia, which took turns as hosts and certainly had the best facilities and the largest representation, retained their monopoly.[31]

There was scarcely a small town in South Carolina that would not have profited from a gathering of professional men on an annual outing, even if the outing was not lavish. As it happened, Camden needed the boost more than anyone suspected. During the summer of 1872 the *Camden Journal* published an item to the effect that Camden and its environs, formerly considered a good resort area by prosperous northerners, were "very unhealthy." Other papers quickly picked up the notice and reprinted it, with "such unfortunate results" that the Kershaw District Medical Association felt compelled to issue a refutation. "Inasmuch as statements have inadvertently been made relative to the health of Camden and its vicinity, calculated to injure its reputation and affect its business, we, the undersigned practising physicians in the town and neighborhood do certify that the season so far has been an *unusually healthy* one, and the two cases of sudden death which, we presume, gave rise to the report, were exceptional in their character and not to be attributed to local causes." Signed by Drs. A. A. Moore, L. H. Deas, S. Baruch, E. C. Hughes, E. M. Boykin, and D. L. DeSaussure, the denial appeared in the *Journal* on September 5, along with a note from the editor, who had been away when the "error" occurred. He was, he said, "surprised to learn that Camden was so unhealthy." Immediately upon his return, he asked that all papers that had copied the error also copy the correction, a request repeated in a later issue.[32] The doctors and the editor had good reason to worry. Rumors of unhealthy climate, however unfounded, were more devastating than fire or flood to small towns with few commercial or industrial assets. The little town of Pineville had never recovered its former prosperity after the fatal summer of 1834 destroyed confidence in the health of the village. Camden was more fortunate. There the old year closed in a flurry of sleet and snow, which brought out skates and sleighs and laid to rest rumors of the sickly climate.[33]

Baruch's concern over Camden's prosperity is easy to understand. At the end of 1872 he was in his thirty-third year and still a long way from realizing his goals. Keeping to their regular pattern of a child every two years, he and Belle had had a third son, Herman. Even with three children, they were hardly needy—as need went in South Carolina in those days. Baruch collected fees in cash whenever he could, accepting other remuneration in the form of goods and services. The family lived in a fine house. They had enough servants to give Belle time for activities such as the Camden Histrionic Club, dramatics being one of her favorite indulgences. By Camden's standards, Dr. Baruch was a success. By his own, he still had a long way to go. Never again in his lifetime would a period of eight years elapse with the publication of so few as the mere four articles he had produced between 1864 and 1872.

8   The Therapeutic Optimist

When the South Carolina Medical Association met in Charleston on April 8, 1873, Baruch was more active and conspicuous than ever. This time, however, his contributions were not well received. His part of the assigned report on a gynecological apparatus of considerable current interest prompted unfavorable discussion. When he read the report of a committee set up the preceding year to study hypodermic medication, he was drawn into debate with Francis Peyre Porcher, his former professor, and with George Trescot, professor of materia medica and therapeutics and dean of the faculty at Charleston. The debate raged on so long that the day's meeting was adjourned in the middle of it. The next day, when Baruch called for the question on submitting the controversial report to the committee on publication, the report was deferred—tantamount to a refusal to publish it, something that had never happened to a paper he had prepared for the association.[1]

Practically the only good thing that happened to Baruch at the 1873 meeting happened through a quirk. As chairman of the committee on nominations, he reported the committee's choice of Robert A. Kinloch for president. When Kinloch declined the honor, the committee returned with Baruch's name. The assembly approved the nomination, and Dr. Simon Baruch became president of the South Carolina Medical Association at the age of thirty-three. His election merited notice in the *Camden Journal:* "Such a tribute to the worth of one so young in the profession, and of foreign birth, is a compliment alike creditable to him and to those bestowing it, and gratifying to the Doctor's many friends."[2]

Camden newspapers seemed to have excellent rapport with Baruch's medical world. Along with noting his election (in a manner all the more flattering because it referred to his "youth" and "foreign birth"), the *Journal* announced that Baruch had a paper in the April issue of the *Charleston Medical Journal and Review,* a periodical just coming back to life under the editorship of Francis Peyre Porcher eight years after the war.[3] This article, "Subinvolution of the Uterus," was a continuation and development of Baruch's earlier work on uterine disease among the lower classes, with a still broader sociological bent. He reported that, although both rich and poor women were victims of uterine ailments, these conditions occurred far more often among blacks and lower-class whites, partly because of their poor living conditions and the inadequate care they received as expectant and recently delivered mothers and partly because low moral standards and unwanted pregnancies caused frequent resort to indigenous plants believed to produce abortion.[4]

Baruch deplored feticide, and he claimed a certain provincial pride in the fact that, in the South, it was at least restricted to those at the bottom of the social ladder. "Judging from the startling reports we receive from other points, it has become so general among the upper classes as to threaten terrible inroads upon the population." He said that, in this respect, South Carolina was fortunate to be "remote from the centres of 'civilization,'" for isolation kept the area "shielded against the wiles of this hydraheaded monster, that throttles a human being at the very dawn of existence."[5] Raising moral standards and preventing abortions, he said, would prevent much of the uterine disease that was so difficult to treat, but those tasks fell outside the doctor's realm.

A more immediate problem troubling Baruch in the summer of 1873 was the severe intestinal disease of newborn infants and very young children, descriptively and inexactly called "infant diarrhoea and dysentery." This dread malady, which struck especially in the summer months, had concerned him from his entry into practice. It was terrible enough to be unable to help the children of his friends and neighbors, but now he himself had three sons between the ages of one and five. What could he do even for his own, when he so often found the usual treatment by astringents and opiates unavailing? In August he confided in his physician's register: "Four cases have proved fatal in spite of all my efforts, besides several others in the hands of other colleagues and one seen in consultation." Reflecting on the futility of his therapeutic methods, he concluded that "there must be something erroneous in my conception of the pathology of this disease." There must be a better approach. "Should we not endeavor to check these terrible evacuations which not only drain the life blood of these feeble children, but exhaust them by the accompanying pain?" He knew what needed to be done, but he did not know how to do it. "We steer between Scylla and Charybdis. In vain have I looked for a true unfailing guide. I feel discouraged but shall continue to reflect, study and analyze cases."[6]

Baruch had other reasons to feel depressed in 1873. South Carolina's return to prosperity seemed as dimly distant as an effective treatment for infant dysentery. Some years before, Baruch had written his friend Dr. Salley that southerners must look to immigration to revive their failing fortunes. Nothing had happened in the intervening years to change his mind, but the failure of the state immigration commission headed by General John A. Wagener had dampened his hopes. A German-born Confederate veteran, Wagener had tried to attract newcomers into the state from the war's end until 1868, when his office was abolished by the Radicals. Even with the support of planters, land speculators, railroad interests, and industrialists, Wagener was able to bring in only about four hundred people. Apparently determined to succeed where Wagener had failed, a group of Camden citizens, including Baruch, met in January 1874 to consider the need for directing immigration into their state. Along with Mannes Baum and one of the Kershaws, Baruch agreed to investigate the best methods for attracting new people.[7]

Less than a year before, a northerner by the name of James Shepherd Pike had visited the state and published a book describing his experience there. Despite the title of his work *(The Prostrate State)*, Pike praised South Carolina's attributes: the moderate climate and fine soil; the low price of both land and labor; the high return for agricultural products. Pike wrote of the other side, too: the factors that prevented all but a few of the three hundred thousand people who annually entered the United States from choosing to live in the South. He told his wide audience that blacks opposed any measures calculated to encourage white immigration for fear that it would contribute to their political downfall. Nor did the majority of whites welcome outsiders, an attitude Pike attributed partially to hostility aroused by carpetbaggers.[8]

Judging from the Wagener commission's abortive efforts immediately after the war, opposition to outsiders was rooted far below the topsoil of Reconstruction miseries. Wagener considered local prejudice against foreigners the chief obstacle to his program. Pike, too, noted that newcomers were repelled by "the habit of the old South Carolinian to feel that the State, in all its franchises, potentialities, and future possibilities, belongs to him alone."[9] Although planters were as eager as other southern economic leaders for fresh supplies of manpower, in 1873 the British consul in New Orleans reported that to southern planters "a labourer is a labourer; . . . whether he be French or German, Italian or Norwegian, British or Chinese, he is to be housed, fed, and treated just as the black race used to be." Promises of opportunity for enterprising newcomers rang hollow in the face of such evidence. Even before bursting into the open later in the century, southern hostility toward foreigners made efforts to encourage immigration a "minor and futile phase in the New South."[10]

Even as Baruch confronted the immigration problem, he was trying, as association president, to rally membership. With the organization languishing for want of participants, he did not hesitate to exploit the appeal to former Confederate ties. Yet even that usually responsive chord sometimes failed. One of his wartime acquaintances, Dr. J. A. James of Indiantown, joshed him about his purported anguish over their long separation. "I think, 'Simon,'" wrote James, "you piled on the *'agony'* a little too heavy, but as I am considerably fatter than when you saw me last I reckon I can carry it." Dr. James had fond memories of their association in the "splendid failure" of the Confederacy, and he would like to see his friend again, but he could not afford to "'splurge' yet at Columbia & Camden." At the end of the war he had been sadly *"impecuniosed."* Now, with five boys and two girls to support, he found life a "struggle to keep my head above the waters of absolute want." Although his practice kept him busy ("My reputation here is national—ie covers the whole district"), it did not keep him from "thinking of going to Dallas Texas." "Dont you want to go with me?" he asked.[11]

Texas was not the object of Baruch's ambition, nor was he anxious to leave South Carolina while he held the presidential chair of the state medical association. For two days in April he presided over the annual convention, this time in Columbia. The treasurer's report opened the meeting on a cheerless note: a bare 50 percent of ninety-two active members had paid dues the preceding year. Because of haphazard election methods, many men around the state did not even know that the association had voted them into membership. Some who could afford to pay dues ignored the matter entirely; others simply did not have the money.[12]

The next report indirectly explained the treasurer's problem. It was a response to an extraordinary petition presented to the association the year before, in which the doctors of Anderson County had asked that the association pressure the state legislature to pass "some act whereby our profession may have payment secured for services rendered to that class of our population who are protected by the homestead law of our State." Protesting that they should no more be expected to work for nothing than "the common farm labourer, to whom we are expected to pay full value for labor whenever and to whomever rendered," Anderson County doctors wanted the legislature to "make the services of a physician in common with that of a farm laborer a lien, not only upon the crop of the person to whom the service is rendered, but upon any property that he may be found seized or possessed of, and that, as with farm labor, it may be regarded a prior lien to any other that may exist." After what must have been a stunned silence, the 1873 assembly had gingerly passed this ethical hot potato to a committee, "to report as soon as practicable."[13]

Now, in April 1874, with Dr. Baruch presiding, the report came out of committee, together with a memorial the committee intended for the state legislature. Whatever the memorial said, a motion to adopt it set off such heated discussion that it was not included in the minutes. An attempt was made to refer the memorial back to the Anderson County society with the sanction of the association, but this action was voted down. Those who felt that the association should act in behalf of impoverished practitioners once again brought up the original motion to petition the legislature. Once again it met defeat.[14] The economic pinch was sharper in 1874 than ever before, but any action to bring relief smacked too much of the unprofessional to win association approval.

The same was true of a preamble and resolutions in which the Medical Society of Columbia proposed to charge interest on all accounts not settled in ninety days. From a mild initial motion that the document be "received as information," the association progressed to a formal statement that it "sympathized in the action taken by the Medical Society of Columbia." Farther than this it would not go.[15]

The young man who presided over these strained responses to the plight of South Carolina physicians had threatened, not long before, to bolt legitimate medical circles, "to secede & practice on my own merits & my own fee bill," rather than be ground between old-fashioned ethics and altered economic conditions. Now that he held the highest post in organized medicine in the state, he could only join his colleagues in extending sympathy to hard-pressed practitioners.

In his presidential address, although Baruch denounced the forces that made the physician "the worst paid individual in every community," the solution he proposed was a moderate one, suggesting a man mellowed either by age or position. To resist "the dangers which threaten them financially" and "the encroachments daily made upon them by an exacting and ungrateful public," he could only recommend that his colleagues form a "self-protecting guild," a "solid phalanx" that could "establish a fair and remunerative schedule of fees, and adhere to them with uniformity; preserve inviolate the strict rule of the code of ethics, and spurn, with all your influence, the tricks of trade, resorted to by some men to obtain a cliency." As a beginner in his twenties, Baruch had been full of schemes for contracts and mutual payment plans to make practice remunerative. As president of the association at the age of thirty-three, his major concern was the status of the profession.[16]

Baruch called his address "Methods of Fostering the Interests of Medical Science and Its Votaries." Every line was charged with his awareness of the high calling of medicine; of the challenge of the times ("an age of vast intellectual force"); of an urgent obligation to contribute to and draw from growing stores of knowledge. Bursting with impatience, he tugged and pulled at his audience, reminding them that their state had once stood high on the horizon of American medicine. Now, everywhere around them, he said, fallacious doctrines were "succumbing to the onslaughts of modern chemistry, physiology and microscopy, and their resultant, a sound pathology." Despite the hardships of Reconstruction, they must find a way to add to the work. "Light! light! is the watchword emblazoned upon the banners of the present generation! In all departments of research, more light is anxiously sought. The gentle flame of inquiry is stirred into a seething blaze by an all-pervading skepticism, which subjects all ideas and propositions, however sacred and time-honored, to its relentless attacks."[17]

Judged by later standards of literary economy, Baruch's extravagant words sound insincere, but he could not have been more earnest, even in his rhetorical questions. "Shall we stand idle, while the tide of progress and enlightenment is rushing past us?" This was not his wish, either for South Carolina or for himself. More than anything, he feared drifting out of the mainstream of life to stagnate in the quiet, mossy pools at its edge. The "tide of progress" set the pace to which all must step. Of the three means of professional improvement he discussed—medical organizations, medical journals, and medical education—Baruch gave greatest attention to the first. "Human maladies are so exceedingly complex, and the human mind so variously constituted," that close and frequent professional association could do far more to advance medical knowledge than any man acting alone. Once again the personal sense of onrushing time lent urgency to Baruch's argument: "Life is indeed short; it is a dream upon earth. As shadows that float upon the waves, we pass away; we measure our lazy steps by space and time, and find ourselves, ere we realize it, in the midst of eternity."

Acting under his conviction that the physician was obliged to present the results of his experience for discussion by his peers, Baruch brought his evolving philosophy of eclecticism before the association. He cautioned the members to avoid wholesale rejection of the work of charlatans, "lest the quick eye of the public discover a latent jealousy in our apparent zeal for truth." Although he knew that the organized medical profession was likely to frown on efforts to cross the boundary it had drawn between "regular" and "irregular," he invited his colleagues to join him in straddling the line, taking the useful from both sides: "It behooves us to cull in *all* fields; not alone from the beautiful and well arranged parterre of systematic and orthodox medicine, but even from amidst the tangled wilderness and noxious weeds of those empirical systems, in which some truth is hidden under mysticism and charlatanism." Baruch went even further, turning the criticism regulars often leveled at quacks against the regulars themselves. The history of medicine, he observed, was cluttered with discredited theories that had once been accepted by the most orthodox of the regulars.[18]

To illustrate the good to be found in sects, Baruch briefly traced the contribution of homeopathy to the evolution of expectant medicine. Then he turned to the empirical "water-cure," scorned by regulars in the South as elsewhere, perhaps because its most noted exponent, Vincenz Priessnitz, was an unlettered Silesian peasant who had made a sizable fortune from his ability to heal, sometimes when the regulars had failed. The rancor of licensed physicians against the followers of Priessnitz was understandable, but, at least in Baruch's eyes, it was also unreasonable. He urged his audience to "descend from the self-constituted height of pure orthodoxy," itself entangled in error, and give the hydropaths a hearing. "You will be astounded that so much truth can be unearthed from so much empirical rubbish." Granting that it was never wise to base therapeutics on a single measure, Baruch asserted that the hydropaths had a system in which "remarkable results" had been achieved "by the influence of pure air, cleanliness, attention to hygienic and dietetic management, and the effect of those intricate and powerful elements—cold, heat, and moisture." Far from finding these simple means worthy of the contempt they received from many in the profession, he predicted that to their *"proper appreciation, the therapeusis of the future will yet owe many signal triumphs."*[19]

Baruch appealed to medical history to support these ideas. Starting with Hippocrates, he cited a long list of noted writers, "regular" physicians all, "to establish the fact that the hydropathic system, absurd as it may seem under the leadership of a Priessnitz, possesses undoubted merit." With a trace of the determination that would grow with the passing years, Baruch almost threatened those who ignored the virtues of hydropathy: "To regard the system with indifference and scorn, would be criminal; it is the part of wisdom to penetrate beneath the cloak of charlatanism, and search for the golden truth."[20]

When Baruch finished speaking, the association voted to submit his address to the committee on publication. He had asked his audience for "friendly criticism" to "deal gently with our errors of judgement, and wrap the mantle of charity around our shortcomings, if, perchance, we should have blundered"; but no discussion of hydropathy was recorded.[21] Although some of his words must have fallen hard on the assembled doctors (the bastion of orthodox medicine in South Carolina), his patent reverence for the profession may have blunted his criticism of their tendency toward dogmatism. Or perhaps his radical suggestions seemed less offensive because he was so young. In any case, a certain amount of eclecticism was not incompatible with orthodoxy. As he several times noted, Hippocrates himself had said that judgment is difficult.

After his address, Baruch seemed exhilarated and outspoken when discussing the effect of chloroform anesthesia during childbirth. Although disappointed in the action of chloroform in puerperal convulsions, he remained its "firm and unwavering" advocate in normal deliveries. In a bantering tone he attacked the testimony of C. D. Meigs, a leading obstetrician, who was cited in the discussion as having adduced "a few cases of the fatal effects of chloroform upon the foetus." Reliable though Meigs might be on other points in this field, Baruch put little stock in these observations, remembering that Dr. Meigs opposed anesthesia during labor because Genesis said, "'In sorrow thou shalt bring forth children.'" Baruch wryly observed that Dr. Meigs, "not unlike the other descendants of Adam," did not feel compelled to honor the biblical sentence on the male: "'In the sweat of thy face shalt thou eat bread.'"[22]

Dismissing the opinion of a man who would subvert medical progress to biblical fiat, Baruch said that he did not know of a single recorded case in which a newborn death could be traced directly to chloroform. Although statistics could be misleading, he considered those gathered by French and English obstetricians as "incontrovertible proof of the innocuousness of chloroform upon the foetus during and prior to labor." Baruch made no concession to those who opposed Sir James Y. Simpson's innovation, except to note that chloroform sometimes indirectly harmed the child through the mother's milk.

Several of his colleagues did not find the evidence so decisive, among them his former obstetrics professor, Jacob Ford Prioleau, and two of the men who had examined him for a Confederate commission, Thomas Robertson and Robert Kinloch. Robertson had seen a patient who needed so much chloroform during childbirth that he feared it was responsible for the baby's death shortly afterward. Kinloch raised the crucial question: how could they know, in the case of a stillborn fetus or a baby who died soon after delivery, whether chloroform was to blame? The problem of cause and effect, difficult even in the most carefully controlled experiments in the physical sciences, seemed almost insuperable in the varied and unpredictable realm of human life.[23]

If either his interest in hydropathy or his uncompromising stand on anesthesia in childbirth had won Baruch enemies, he came off with honors in spite of them. He was appointed to a committee of three to report on puerperal convulsions at the next meeting and was chosen to represent the association at the American Medical Association meeting and at the New York Medical Society.[24]

As the Columbia meeting drew to a close, and with it Baruch's term as president, he departed from precedent by indulging in a lengthy "farewell address." He said he had been called to the chair "without the slightest preparation for its high duties; without the faintest anticipation that you would bestow the honor upon one so unworthy as myself." Pleading "inexperience in deliberative assemblies" and only "humble attainments in the science," he said that he would have preferred to remain an "obscure but faithful laborer in the ranks, especially as I saw around me, men whose active zeal for our science, and whose warm interest in our Association, rendered them more worthy of this position." But he admitted "that the occupancy of this high and noble office at some future time, was among my bright anticipations," and, for all his humble words, Baruch surrendered the president's chair with the air of a man who felt eminently fitted for the job he had done.[25]

Within the year, Baruch had occasion to show how strongly he felt the therapeutic hope expressed in his address. As he read the *Charleston Medical Journal and Review* of October 1874, he bristled at an article questioning whether medicine had made any progress in the nineteenth century.[26] The author, Dr. M. Reynolds, thought that many changes were losses rather than gains. "The physician of to-day," Reynolds said, "may have a more classical education than his great grandfather of the last century, but his real knowledge of how to cure disease is probably less, and the remedies at his command for accomplishing that end as nearly as possible the same."[27]

According to Reynolds, the idea that medicine had kept pace with science was a grand delusion. He had once believed (in what he called the "sanguine temperament of youth") that medicine merited its tribute as "the Godlike science," the "divine art." He had entered the profession "'hoping all things, trusting all things, believing all things,'—with the most perfect and extravagant confidence in medication, and the exhibition of remedies." Now he spoke with the voice of disenchantment. The new pathology had merely revealed "conditions of structural deterioration over which medicine could exercise not the slightest control!" Advances in surgery and especially in obstetrics were of little avail in many conditions unaided also by medicine. With these points Baruch could not disagree entirely. But when Reynolds charged that, within the area of actual medical treatment, neither new additions to the materia medica nor the late radical revolution in treatment had "given us a more advantageous position in our relation to disease," Baruch could not ignore the challenge.[28] His youthful idealism afire, he sat down to write a retort.

Charging that the recently introduced hypnotic, chloral hydrate, was worthless because it caused bad dreams, Reynolds had used the lines of Clarence in *Richard III* to describe the patient's reaction:

> I would not spend another such a night,
> Though 'twere to buy a world of happy days;
> So full of dismal horrors was the time.

In reply, Baruch gave his own professional opinion and copious citation from others to show that chloral surpassed "any known agent in hypnotic properties." Had it been known in Elizabethan times, said Baruch, Shakespeare might have provided even the guilt-ridden Macbeth with the slumber he vainly sought:

> Sleep that knits up the ravell'd sleave of care,
> The death of each day's life, sore labour's bath.[29]

To Reynolds's dismissal of hypodermic medication as a "professional triviality," Baruch snapped " 'Trivialities,' forsooth!" He directed Reynolds "and his followers (if he has any)" to the vast literature on the subject "for conversion and repentance . . . ere he favors the profession with the future discussion of it which he promises." Reynolds had deplored the fact that "the whole land is flooded" with pills and powders. Baruch responded with an antiphon of praise for ergot, mercury, quinine, and digitalis. Reynolds had even denied that veratrum viride was useful for controlling the heart—but an editor's note saved Baruch the trouble of rebuttal: ("Dr. R. must reconsider this. Its special power over the heart is undoubted.").[30]

Reynolds had questioned not only contemporary but even future therapeutics. Medicine, he contended, could never hope for results like those of the physical scientists. "They deal with material structure and law in their more pronounced manifestations and phenomena, and the crucible, microscope and scalpel may carry them far; we, with the subtle essence of vitality itself." Like the essential principle of life, the working of disease was hidden from man by what Reynolds considered an "impenetrable screen." Although therapeutics would always be a mysterious business, Reynolds hoped that medicine would clarify etiology and find more practical applications for pathological research. Above all, he looked to the day when physicians, by attention to sanitary reform, would become "more the conservators of health than the dispensers of physic."[31]

Baruch was not yet the mystic, the vitalist, which long years of practice often make of young materialistic physicians. He expected to see vast progress in therapeutics—and soon: "We stand breathless upon the eve of great and glorious events! We peer into the future, and behold the bright promise of a more perfect system of healing." Even in appraising the scene about him, he was more optimistic than Dr. Reynolds. Comparing medical practices in 1874 with those of the 1820s, Baruch concluded that no one could fail to see marks of progress. "Facts are accumulating, great stores of knowledge derived from exact experimentation are being hoarded, the various developments of the cognate sciences are brought to bear upon the elucidation of hitherto obscure points." Although practicing physicians could not immediately apply the latest scientific findings to their sick patients, it was largely because of the recent flood of knowledge, Baruch said, that the average doctor had "adopted a conservative course, unwilling to be longer enslaved by the trammels of orthodoxy or heterodoxy." If all the scientific contributions of the nineteenth century had not yet led to better ways of treatment, they had at least revealed the folly of former practices, making the contemporary physician's therapeutic procedures "essentially eclectic." From the hydropaths, Baruch observed, doctors had borrowed the cold bath in typhoid fever; from the bleeders, the lancet to relieve congestion. And there were new tools: the thermometer, the sphygmograph (to record the movements of the arterial pulse), the microscope, and—from the bacteriologists—the concept of the parasitic origin of disease.[32]

Baruch supported his argument with citations from German, French, and English journals, both clinical and experimental. Although he did not deny that problems remained, he viewed the overall progress of medicine in the nineteenth century as a matter for pride, not censure. In Reynolds's own terms of medical advancement, "in relation to the great object of curing the sick," Baruch saw progress enough "to be clearly traced in the recent history of various remedial agents, in 'new points of departure in practice,' and in the contributions of valuable drugs and methods of medication."

Baruch's reply to Reynolds was spirited, hopeful, almost naively optimistic, a reflection of his buoyant resistance to therapeutic nihilism. He was genuinely confident that doctors *could* help the sick, and he wanted others to share his assurance. At the next association meeting, in the spring of 1875, he presented accounts of two cases of serious disease that had responded well to current therapeutic means. One was a husky thirty-five-year-old man who had suffered from acute articular rheumatism since the Civil War. Even after developing cardiac complications and high fever, he seemed to benefit from Baruch's use of cold baths, ice bags, and large doses of potassium iodide. Baruch offered this example as an antidote to the prevailing therapeutic doldrums, "when routinism as the one extreme and nihilism as the other, bewilder the candid searcher after truth and render him skeptical as to the efficacy of therapeutic procedures." In such times even a small success was important. Baruch hoped that his colleagues might draw from it, as he had, "encouragement and strength for the daily battle with disease and death."[33]

The second case concerned a mulatto boy, referred to Baruch for removal of a tumor on his upper left jaw. Using chloroform anesthesia (an advance even Dr. Reynolds could not deny), Baruch operated. For about two weeks the patient seemed to be recovering. Then tetanus set in, yielding only after a week of treatment with potassium bromide and chloral hydrate. Baruch's point was that it did yield. This case aroused so much interest at the meeting that the association asked Baruch to prepare a report devoted wholly to tetanus.[34]

He did prepare the paper, but he did not appear at the 1876 meeting to present it. This, the first convention he had missed since the association's postwar reorganization in 1869, marked the group's most strenuous venture up to that time into the realm of preventive medicine. During his absence, Baruch was appointed to the standing committee on state medicine and public hygiene. The committee had already started to work and was ready to provide each doctor at the meeting with a questionnaire about various aspects of public health. Some of the questions would have been unnecessary if the state had provided for the registration of vital statistics; others, such as those concerned with the comparative incidence of alcohol consumption, syphilis, and fecundity among whites and blacks, seemed to have as many political as medical implications.[35]

The committee also hoped to determine the total numbers of whites, blacks, and "mixed" in the 1876 population, as compared with their numbers in 1865. The ostensible plan was to include in the public health work a study of the miscegenation rate over the years since the Radicals first gave legal status to racial intermarriage.[36] Whether or not the association thought of this as a purely medical matter, it was almost certain to provide fuel for growing political activity among the state's conservatives.

Resentment against the Radicals, exacerbated throughout 1875 by outbreaks of incendiarism and race rioting, reached a pitch in December, when the Republican-dominated legislature appointed two circuit judges over public opposition. Though neither man was seated, this action served to unite irate conservatives. After a bitter, violent campaign in 1876 and an election honored by visiting voters from Georgia and North Carolina, the Democrats succeeded in electing Wade Hampton as governor of South Carolina.[37]

This appeared to be the political break Baruch had looked for ten years earlier, at the impatient age of twenty-seven. When the election news came into Camden by telegraph, the town burst into jubilation that proved somewhat premature. For the next five months, while Republicans contested the returns from several counties, the state had two governments—and thus no government. Like the disputed presidential election, which the Democrats claimed for Samuel J. Tilden and the Republicans for Rutherford B. Hayes, the South Carolina governor's contest dragged on into 1877. It was settled at last by a compromise putting Hayes into the White House and Hampton into the governor's mansion in Columbia.[38]

As a part of this "compromise of 1877," Hayes on April 10 ordered Federal troops to withdraw from South Carolina. Military Reconstruction came to an end, and South Carolina was once again her own mistress.

Reunion and Reform

9

On the day when Federal troops withdrew, Baruch was in Charleston, attending the annual South Carolina Medical Association meeting. April 1877—the end of Reconstruction: it was one of those watersheds that seem to evoke a mood of summing up, a pervasive sense of retrospect and prospect. The doctors were clearly under the spell. Banqueting at the Hibernian Hall, they talked of days past and of the work before them: "Hosts and guests, with hearts opened by the Exercises of the Evening, protracted the 'flow of soul' till the 'wee sma hours,' when—with characteristic moderation—they quietly adjourned."[1]

In his presidential address, John Frederick Meckel Geddings surveyed the state of science and medicine in South Carolina. It was a cheerless picture, "with the scientific and literary institutions of the State languishing or closed—with neither hospitals, laboratories or extensive libraries, public or private—with poverty and distress arising from the most monstrous and outrageous government that ever afflicted a civilized people." No one need look here, Geddings said, for "that mature intellectual development and culture, so strikingly manifested in happier lands." Few physicians had formally committed themselves to a code of ethics by joining the association. In Charleston, the number of registered stillbirths was sufficiently disproportionate to the total number of births to evoke suspicion of widespread criminal neglect. All the more reason to strengthen the coroner system. Yet the government had discontinued the practice of holding inquests: an economy measure, officials said. Geddings wanted a return to the active role coroners had once played in such cases. Unhappily he saw "little prospect of a memorial from this body

meeting with favor in the General Assembly. It has ever been the misfor-
tune of South Carolina to be represented by parties who take but little
interest in matters outside of their immediate pursuits."[2]

Despite such discouragements, the doctors were filled with hope for
reform. Most of them had gained a hearty respect for sanitation during
their war years, and, now that the state was once again governed by
South Carolinians, they wanted to improve its public health. The most
difficult part was deciding where and how to begin. In addition to the
needs marked out by President Geddings (an improved coroner system
was only one), they heard about numerous trouble spots from the Committee on State Medicine and Public Hygiene. This group of five association members, including Baruch, had found the state lacking in almost
every phase of public health they had investigated: "South Carolina, one
of the old original thirteen States, is among the last to range herself in the
march of progress, and to follow in the rear of one of the grandest
features of civilization." The committee viewed her failure to match the
advances of other states "not with the blush of shame, but rather with the
flush of indignation, that mounts up, again to fade away in the despon-
dency that results from the crush of spirit . . . the long period of oppression . . . the stop that has been put to the advance of civilization in a once
proud commonwealth."[3]

Baruch and his fellow committeemen had made a vain attempt to
assemble population statistics. Only four association members had returned the previous year's questionnaire asking about births and deaths of
whites, blacks, and "mixed"; only two had had sufficient information to
answer all the queries. Lacking any other source of demographic data,
the committee had turned to mortuary records, which indicated that
since 1860 mortality rates had risen faster for whites than for blacks,
while stillbirth and infant death rates were higher among blacks than
whites. Clearly, South Carolina needed to reestablish the registration of
vital statistics disrupted by the war.[4]

The committee's report on harbor quarantine shows evidence of the
hand of Baruch, the former New York City dweller. On paper, South
Carolina's harbor quarantine system looked fine; it looked, in fact, very
much like New York's, with a fifteen-day waiting period to New York's
ten. Yet the means provided for implementing the South Carolina laws
were so "absurd in their feebleness and poverty" that the actual protection did not compare in any way to New York's "wonderful and almost
perfect system." The efficacy of quarantine depends on active disinfection, not on the mere time a ship lies in harbor, and active disinfection
often means that ships must be unloaded, which requires labor, money,
and equipment. "The law of South Carolina stops short of this point."

Instead of the $8,ooo needed for effective operation of the state's four quarantine stations, the legislature usually allowed only $2,ooo and had recently cut even that in half. Thus the entire quarantine force in Charleston consisted of one physician and two boat hands.[5]

Within the city itself sewage accumulated in troughs along the streets, to be gathered into supposedly airtight carts. Referring to the trails of black, concentrated filth which these vehicles left in their wake, the committee sarcastically commended the Charleston Board of Health for having "solved the problem with great simplicity. . . . They dispose of it by emptying it within a few feet of the doors of the people." Laws for the inspection of slaughterhouses were equally poorly enforced, with the result that tapeworm infection was on the rise. As a final indictment of the status quo, meals prepared for the sick in "the filth-hole designated as the hospital" were far below even minimum standards. Without actually naming the Radical Republicans, the report blamed all these sins of commission and omission on "iconoclastic hands, guided by a policy, the theory and practical application of which may be expressed in the words, 'to the victor belong the spoils.'"

To seek solutions to these problems, the committee proposed that the legislature be asked to constitute the entire association as the "South Carolina State Board of Health." For greater effectiveness, the board's powers would be delegated to an Executive Committee, consisting of seven association members chosen at large. These men would divide the state into health districts and appoint a sub-board of health for each, to supervise such local activities as registration of vital statistics and meat inspection. With legislative support, within a few years the state could have a statistical foundation for devising a still more effective system. The association assigned Baruch's committee the task of approaching the legislature at its next session.

In addition to his work on public health, Baruch presented the 1877 meeting with a plea for reform in the teaching of forensic medicine. Modern science was making criminals more and more skillful (closely followed by the legal profession, with its "progressive spirit"), but medical schools neglected this important field. Called upon to give expert testimony, doctors often found themselves unable to combat the lawyer's efforts "by sophistical reasoning and adroit management of the evidence, to so obscure the true merits of the case, as frequently to snatch his client from the doom that awaits him." Considerations of justice aside, Baruch knew from recent personal experience how humiliating this could be. Ostensibly to save his colleagues from the same fate, he said, "I desire to bring before the Society the details of an interesting case of homicide."[6]

It began on February 29, 1876, when the coroner summoned Baruch to examine a man who lay dead twelve miles from Camden. J. B. Hendricks had been a habitual drinker, occasionally an excessive one. On a visit to Camden the day before his death, he had indulged freely. On the morning of the twenty-ninth he sought consolation in a flask of whiskey hidden in the barn. He discovered, "after having swallowed a good draught," that the whiskey was bitter. Concluding that he had been poisoned, he walked rapidly to the home of a friend nearby, told him what had happened, and persuaded him to stay with him until he died. Shortly afterward, Hendricks suffered convulsions and seemed to be in great pain. The friend gave him coffee but did not call for medical assistance. Within an hour Hendricks was dead.

Baruch suspected strychnine poisoning, but the autopsy he performed was inconclusive, except that rigor mortis was complete while the body was still warm. Knowing that the law demanded actual demonstration of the presence of poison, Baruch paid special attention to the stomach, tying both ends, removing the entire organ, and emptying its contents into a bottle. He also took a sample from the flask. "Not being able to obtain an analysis, by an expert chemist, on account of the dilapidated condition of our county treasury," he did the work himself, "reluctantly, and urged only by the strongest sense of duty." Nonetheless, Baruch described the details of the analysis with the verve of a Sherlock Holmes. After all the mixing and filtering and evaporating came a final color test that proved what he suspected: Hendricks's stomach and the flask from which he took his last drink both contained strychnine.

Implicated by circumstantial evidence, Mrs. Hendricks eventually came to trial on the charge of murdering her husband. Baruch was called to testify. Expecting simply to report the findings of the autopsy and analysis, he found the defense led by the "most able criminal lawyer of our bar," who indulged in "some ingenious mystifications of the uses of chemical analysis in general," which Baruch was unprepared to refute.

He was still less prepared to hear the foreman of the jury ask whether strychnine was not ordinarily used in the manufacture of common whiskey. Baruch knew of this popular belief but had found no basis for it in texts on medical jurisprudence. The foreman, "a gentleman of considerable intellectual force and learning," displayed "an interest and acumen rarely witnessed on such occasions." As though he had received a positive answer to his first question, he asked if the quantity of strychnine in a drachm of common whiskey "would not probably yield all the characteristic color tests of the strychnine." Baruch had no choice but to spring the trap: his analytical methods, he confessed, could detect as little as 1/30,000 grain.

Because the defense had failed to prove that strychnine was ever found in the whiskey purchased from a dealer, the court ruled out this last testimony. Subsequent events, however, showed that "the learned foreman" continued to insist, despite the ruling, that manufacturers commonly used strychnine to increase "the spirit" of their whiskey and that if a habitual drinker of "bad whiskey" died under suspicious circumstances, the mere presence of strychnine in his stomach could not serve as proof of poisoning.

A man "of much learning and great scientific attainments," the foreman was also the editor of a journal in which he later attacked Baruch's testimony and reasserted his own theory that such adulteration was common. "Finding that the popular error was so firmly rooted in the mind of many intelligent persons," Baruch felt compelled to vindicate himself. He bought and "analyzed carefully five different specimens of the meanest whiskey to be found in our town." Not a trace of strychnine did he find in any of them. He then wrote an article in his own defense, using this evidence to support his contentions that no one had ever demonstrated the presence of strychnine in manufactured whiskey; no work on medical jurisprudence mentioned such adulteration; and if strychnine were added to the malt-wort, it would probably not survive the distilling process.

Baruch was "astonished to find that not a single one of the numerous persons with whom I conversed upon the subject, was free from the belief of this adulteration." Fearful of "the important bearing of such a popular fallacy in future trials" and "stimulated by other considerations," he sought the expert opinion of "a number of practical distillers" and of the well-known Boston chemist James Robinson Nichols. Their answers bore out his conviction. Final proof came with the publication of a book on the chemical examination of alcoholic liquors by Albert Benjamin Prescott, dean of the University of Michigan School of Pharmacy: "There is no evidence that strychnine has ever been used in the making up of whiskey, or other distilled liquors, and no probability that it will ever be so used. Its intentional addition to the malt-wort could only arise from gross ignorance, and would not at all affect the distillate."

Baruch gathered this information only after the trial and publication of the foreman's subsequent journal article, too late to prevent Mrs. Hendricks's acquittal and his own humiliation. The trial and the foreman's article reinforced the fallacious idea, propagated by "well-meaning temperance lecturers," that whiskey usually contains strychnine, while Baruch's exposure of the truth came too late for anyone's benefit outside of his association audience.

Baruch also presented the 1877 assembly with the tetanus report he had prepared for the preceding meeting. Although fairly uncommon, tetanus was highly fatal. Because it sometimes followed even minor surgical procedures, it was the subject of special interest at a time when anesthesia and antisepsis enabled surgeons to try more daring explorations of the human body. Unaware that their own contaminated catgut sutures often introduced the tetanus bacillus into the airless places where it thrives, surgeons sought to cure what they did not know how to prevent. Baruch's report was not encouraging. After surveying the literature, he found nothing to recommend except the two antispasmodics, chloral hydrate and potassium bromide, which he had already reported using in 1874 in his successful treatment of tetanus following his removal of a tumor of the jaw.[7]

Even a short paper like this one took time to prepare, for Baruch usually prefaced his contributions with summaries of the foreign-language literature. Still, he was always anxious to take on association work. At the 1877 meeting he agreed to present the legislature with a bill recommending establishment of a board of health. In addition, he accepted several other association projects. These, together with his large practice and his family duties as the father of four sons, would seem to make work enough for anyone. Yet Baruch retained the post of examiner for the New York Universal Life Insurance Company and, in July 1877, became a director of the newly formed Camden Building and Loan Association.[8]

He even permitted himself the luxury of a hobby, though by no means a frivolous one. In 1876 he began to invest in land where he could engage in small-scale farming, an interest he may have learned from his father. His father had been so skillful in growing "everything" and in supplying his family with fresh fruits and vegetables that the family said he had "green fingers."[9] Dr. Baruch's approach was somewhat different: he farmed more as an experimentalist than a provider, keeping his farm journals beside his medical books, as though he considered the two pursuits equally scientific. In agricultural journals and even in local newspapers, he found denunciations of the one-crop system and suggestions for crossbreeding and different combinations of fertilizer, seed, soil, and water. On the little land he had, Baruch put in various crops and is said to have been among the first in South Carolina to use tile drainage. This method of laying ceramic pottery under the soil was a costly process when a Scotsman named John Johnston first tried it on his New York State farm in 1835. When machine-made tiles became available ten years later, tiling provided a cheap way to promote intensive cultivation in clay soil, making way for corn and clover where only hay or pasture had grown before.[10]

Baruch seemed to do well at farming. In later years one of his sons remembered that his cotton, corn, oats, and cane sometimes won prizes at the county fair—and that Belle felt that the Doctor might better spend his time on medicine. But he enjoyed his hobby, even enlarging it to include a little herd of Alderney cows. With four growing boys to feed, he could honestly claim that dairying was a profitable pastime. In 1878 he devised plans for a truck farm and dairy farm and stock-breeding business, to be run by a Camden couple, Charles and Marie Barbot, with Baruch acting as a silent partner. Besides $800 in capital, Baruch was to furnish stock mortgaged to him by a relative of the Barbots: "one Bull, one Cow named Pansey, one named Daisy, one named Rose one named Tulip one named Flirt one Cow named Buttercup all of which are termed and known as Jersey Cattle."[11]

Another of Baruch's nonprofessional pursuits was the Hebrew Benevolent Association, formed by the "Israelites of Camden" in October 1877. The association's constitution, which Baruch helped to write, outlined needs of Jews in the community. Camden had no synagogue. In 1871 Yom Kippur and New Year's services (said to be the first in the town's history) were held in the Baruch home, the next year at the Baums' and from that time on in the Masonic Hall. One of the first needs of the association was a lot for a Hebrew cemetery, which Baruch promptly procured. His financial affairs were apparently improving, for he donated lumber to fence it.[12]

As the new organization became an active concern, Baruch rarely missed a meeting, but neither this nor any of his other activities kept him from work for the South Carolina Medical Association. When the 1878 meeting convened, the committee appointed to urge the legislature to create a state board of health reported that it had failed. The chairman took the bill's defeat as proof that association members had "overestimated their influence, weight, and importance," bitterly observing that they had been presumptuous to expect that, "as the representatives of the medical profession of the State of South Carolina, their recommendations and suggestions on matters pertaining to medicine were worthy of consideration."[13]

Actually, although Governor W. D. Simpson had neglected to mention the bill in his message to the legislature, it had passed the House and received a good bit of consideration. The mayor of Charleston had even sent a representative to Columbia to oppose its passage. While Baruch and the other association lobbyists argued for the bill before the entire senate and separately before the Charleston delegation, the mayor's spokesman (a Charleston alderman) was busy protesting "that it would take the management of Health affairs of this and other places out of the hands of their own people, leaving them entirely under the control of people from the middle country, up country, or anywhere the Legislature choose." Charleston interests won the day. "Partisan influence and narrow-minded policy" blocked passage of the bill in the senate.[14]

The bill's failure unified the association in its determination to have a board of health. Acting as a committee of the whole, it resolved that the South Carolina medical profession, "both individually and collectively," should exert all possible pressure on the legislature to pass the bill. To facilitate quick action, the association gave the drafting committee discretionary power "to act in the interim of the meetings of the Association." For distribution among legislators the association authorized the publication of three hundred copies of the 1878 report on state medicine and public hygiene. On Baruch's motion they agreed to include those portions of the 1877 report which disclosed the disgraceful absence of vital statistics, inadequacy of quarantine measures, and deplorable sanitary conditions in Charleston and in public institutions throughout the state. They voted to ask the governor to call special attention to the bill in his annual address before the legislature and to have the bill published in newspapers of Charleston and the counties. Several members went so far as to pledge that the legislative delegates from their counties would support the bill on its second run.[15] There was no channel open to their influence that they did not attempt to use.

The pity was that only 15 percent of the state's doctors belonged to the association. When clout depended on numbers, as it did in lobbying, professional apathy was a serious handicap. President Geddings had called attention to this problem in his address the year before. In 1878 Baruch suggested that it was not so much lack of interest as the "terribly depressed conditions of the people under robber rule" that prevented many from joining the association. With returning prosperity, more doctors would have time and money for membership. In the meantime, he proposed an unrelenting recruitment campaign. "By thus constantly agitating this important subject and keeping it before the minds of our professional brethren, our membership will be rapidly and surely increased."[16]

Baruch proposed specific ways to implement Geddings's recommendation that the coroner system be revived. Since it was the coroner who started homicide proceedings, he should be a man of integrity and clear judgment, with medical training and experience, criteria very different from those prevailing, which provided South Carolina with coroners "distinguished . . . only for their ignorance."[17] As Baruch explained this singular distinction, "the office is frequently bestowed upon some hanger-on of a political party—some political aspirant who must be rewarded for services, after the principal spoils have been divided." He suggested that the association memorialize the legislature to empower the board of health—once the legislature agreed to create such a board—to appoint coroners and make rules governing their work. Each candidate should be a physician "in good standing," with authority to conduct all postmortems and consult other physicians in difficult cases.[18]

On another recommendation from Geddings's address of the previous year, Baruch reported adversely. Unlike Geddings, Baruch did not think the state needed " 'a plan by which the sick poor in the several counties, outside of towns and cities, may be provided with medical attendance.' " Existing state laws authorized county commissioners to use county funds to pay physicians for this work, and Baruch apparently thought this system adequate. (Although he did not mention it, he worked under such an arrangement with the commissioners of Kershaw County, and it provided him with a small but reliable income.)[19]

As for the proposed state board of health, Baruch suggested that any member who might be a legislator at the next session be added to the association committee supporting the bill. Probably neither Baruch nor anyone else at the meeting in 1878 was aware that even as they prepared to launch their second attempt in the legislature, a force stronger than their own was working for its passage. Epidemics have a way of persuading people to heed medical advice they otherwise ignore. In the spring of 1878 yellow fever was beginning a march up the Mississippi Valley. Only the year before, it had struck Port Royal, one of the sea islands off the Carolina coast, but its small toll of 25 deaths there did not convince lawmakers of the need for public health legislation. The epidemic of 1878 was a different matter. Out of a population of about 50,000 in Memphis, where the epidemic was most intense, approximately 30,000 fled. In a space of three months, 17,500 of those remaining succumbed to the disease, and more than 5,000 died. Before the frosts of autumn put an end to its ravages, the black vomit felled more than 100,000 men, women, and children from New Orleans on up the river. The figures were awesome enough to end turf battles between up-country, middle country, and low country. Before the year was out, the association got the state board of health legislation it had wanted for so long.[20]

Another alarm that may have prodded South Carolina legislators to this rapid change of mind was federal legislation, namely "An Act to prevent the introduction of contagious or infectious diseases into the United States," passed by the House of Representatives on March 27, 1878. Read into the minutes and discussed at the association meeting in April, it might have been entitled "An act for the suppression of state sovereignty" for the reaction it provoked. Association members raised objections remarkably like those put forward by Charleston interests against the idea of a state health authority. One of them said that the act appeared to constitute "the entering wedge for turning over the quarantine regulations to national authority." Protest took the form of a committee, including Dr. Baruch, instructed to examine and report on the provisions of the act at the next meeting.[21]

The committee never had a chance. Before the month of April was out, the National Quarantine Act passed the Senate and went into effect as the law of the land. Under its provisions, United States consular officials abroad were to report the sailing date and American destination of any vessel leaving a foreign port in which contagious or infectious disease existed. With this information, the surgeon general of the Marine Hospital Service could prevent the entry of infected ships into American harbors. No funds were appropriated for enforcement, however, and the bill was further crippled by a proviso stating that its rules should not interfere with those of any state or local system. Without funds and without authority, the law became practically a dead letter.

The real "entering wedge" did not come until March 1879, when Congress, energized by the same Mississippi Valley yellow fever epidemic that moved the South Carolina legislature to create a state board of health, passed a bill creating the National Board of Health. The new bill made detailed provision for regulating harbor quarantine and local sanitary conditions. While urging cooperation between the national board and local and state health boards, it placed full power in the hands of the national group.[22]

In 1878 it had been primarily southerners who were troubled by the prospect of federal intervention in local health matters. In 1879, when the threat of intervention became a law with teeth in it, cries of protest arose from Yankeedom. "Every port or State ought to take care of itself," ran the argument in the northern press, "and furnish the means for doing it." John Shaw Billings, planner of the new Johns Hopkins Hospital and of the embryonic Surgeon General's Library, came to the rescue of the principle implicit in the new law. He showed that the mere interest on money raised in the North since 1865 to aid southern communities stricken with yellow fever would more than pay the expenses of the proposed quarantine system. Random charity, Billings asserted, was neither the cheapest nor the most effective way of securing the nation's health. "In sanitary matters, no single man, city, state or nation can protect itself, except by non-intercourse and not always even by that. To get the best results with the least cost and interference with freedom, we must help one another."[23]

When the South Carolina Medical Association convened in April 1879, it did so for the first time as the legally constituted State Board of Health. Before proceeding to the work before it in its new capacity, the association paused for a backward glance. In the death of Eli Geddings the previous October, the state had lost one of its brightest medical lights and the association one of its most dedicated supporters. Geddings was one of the few older physicians in South Carolina who had helped the younger men bring the association back to life after the war. From that time until his death, he had maintained an active interest in its welfare. "Even in his declining years, when bowed down by the infirmities of age," he continued to enrich its proceedings with his wisdom and inspiration. To Baruch, Geddings had been a figure of awesome stature. First Geddings's student at the Medical College of South Carolina only a year after arriving in America, then his colleague in the association after the war, Baruch had greater respect for Geddings than for any other physician in the state—save perhaps Dr. Salley.

His admiration was more than professional. As he revealed in the memorial address he presented on behalf of the association, there was a deeply personal appeal for Baruch in Geddings's life story. "His career presents a brave, a grand, yes, a magnificent struggle with opposing elements; a struggle, whose triumphant issue will, in the . . . future, nerve the heart of the aspiring youth, inspire the weary seeker after fame, and sustain his faint endeavors, despite most adverse environments." Even more than to Baruch the physician it was to Baruch the immigrant that the life of Geddings spoke. It told him "that a man may, if he be true to his nature, steadfast in his purpose, single-hearted in his devotion to his profession, lift himself from an humble position in life to the highest pinnacle of fame, and when his life is spent, leave to his loved ones an heritage as proud as the proudest."[24]

Baruch sought to leave the heritage of a writer. In the manner of a man "steadfast in his purpose," he presented the 1879 meeting with another paper on obstetrics. The year before, he had reported his observation that quinine sometimes induces uterine contractions and might therefore be used to hasten or facilitate labor.[25] In 1879 his subject was the management of retained secundines (placenta or afterbirth) in miscarriages occurring during very early pregnancy. Because of its place in folklore, particularly among blacks, the expulsion of the placenta was an especially important part of childbirth in the South. Very often Baruch would see a man dash up to his door, mounted on a mule "whose heaving flanks, distended nostrils and foam-covered body" portended emergency. An anxious friend or husband would announce that "'the after-birth has grown fast'" and that the midwife (frequently the only attendant among blacks and what Baruch characterized as the "poorer class" of whites) needed Baruch's help. Off he would dash, sometimes for a journey of six, eight, or ten miles, to find the patient with excited pulse, anxious countenance, and apprehensive eyes, indicating an alarm reflected in the "lugubrious faces" of her friends and neighbors gathered round. On examining her he invariably found the umbilical cord firmly tied to her thigh by strong tape or twine. Superstition dictated that this must be done, lest the imperfectly expelled placenta slip back into the innermost recesses of her body, to be recovered only at great risk to the new mother.[26]

The management of "retained secundines" was a matter of current medical controversy. The method Baruch advocated was that of Fordyce Barker, a noted obstetrician whose work he had come to know in New York City. Like Barker, Baruch believed that the rigid rule of emptying the uterus immediately after childbirth too often meant forcing nature with excessive doses of ergot or mechanical interference. These means, in turn, accounted for many of the wretched postpartum diseases of the day. Baruch advised his colleagues to wait: the connections between uterus and placenta would soften, he said, and the exhausted uterus would regain strength to expel the placenta by itself.[27]

Several vigorous discussions marked the association's 1879 meeting. Baruch was a firm proponent of adopting the metric system of weights and measures in the United States, but he was apparently silent during a heated debate over the question of euthanasia. The committee report that introduced the subject was neutral: mercy killing was forbidden by law, and though there was something to be said for doing for humans what is customarily done for animals, the practice might open the way for grave abuses. In short, the committee felt much more discussion was in order before a decision in favor of euthanasia could be justified. Dr. Baruch's old friend from Winnsboro, Dr. T. T. Robertson, disagreed. He thought the committee's caution was just so much pussyfooting. Euthanasia, he said, was as sure to be accepted as the doctrine of evolution, and evolution as certain as the Copernican system of astronomy. He believed in Darwinism himself, Robertson admitted.[28]

By his unfortunate choice of analogy, Robertson offended association members who were antievolutionists as well as those who opposed euthanasia. His remarks set off the dispute in earnest. Was it the duty of medical men to form public opinion—in this case to practice euthanasia and lead the public to accept it? Or should physicians conform to prevailing mores, as expressed in the law? Should they refrain from mercy killing, even when it seemed inhumane to do so? Some association members confessed that they did not fear to chloroform patients who were suffering terribly with cancer or some other incurable disease. Others, believing that he who shortens life takes life, doubted that doctors could ever be sure that a patient would not recover if not helped to die. It was difficult indeed to discern the line between prolonging life and prolonging the act of dying. When one timid soul expressed concern lest their discussion be made public, J. F. M. Geddings, Eli's son, replied that he had never known of a medical body doing anything it feared to have known. "[Applause]," the secretary noted. It was a tortured question, as it remains more than a century later. The discussion ended without result, other than a general rise in blood pressure and an atmosphere of irritation that carried over into the next year's meeting.[29]

In their new capacity as the State Board of Health, the twenty-eight association members present set about their duties as sanitarians. By legislative act they were now sole advisers to the state in questions of public health, their powers vested in an Executive Committee to which they elected Baruch and six others. These seven, together with the attorney general and comptroller general, were to investigate the problems discussed in 1877 and 1878 by the association president and its Committee on State Health and Public Hygiene: the endemic and epidemic diseases plaguing South Carolina; the influence on health of climate and location, occupation, and personal habits; drainage, scavenging, water supply, heating, and ventilation; and the general hygienic condition of state charitable institutions as well as those operated at public expense. The law even charged the board with general supervision of quarantine, which, by this time, had at least partially fallen into the hands of federal authority.[30]

In early May Baruch received official notification from Governor W. D. Simpson of his appointment to the Executive Committee. On June 10, in the comptroller's office in the capitol building, the committee convened for its first meeting.[31] Following the election of J. F. M. Geddings as chair, each member was instructed to appoint sub-boards of health in certain counties, Baruch in his own county of Kershaw as well as Fairfield, Lancaster, York, and Union. Of the small standing committees, Baruch was assigned to the one on epidemic and endemic diseases and the one on adulteration of food and drink.[32]

At the second Executive Committee meeting, on October 21, only three of the nine members appeared in Charleston. A plea went out for an extra session before the state legislature convened, and on November 10 seven members were present to approve appointments. Because the counties under Baruch's jurisdiction were so sparsely populated, each having only one town with over five hundred people, he needed only one sub-board in each county. Yet, between June and November, he had not been able to get any appointments accepted in his own county.[33]

The committee heard a report on sanitary and working conditions among penitentiary prisoners hired out on the Greenwood and Augusta Railroad. Once the investigator had seen how these victims of the convict-lease system lived, he found it easy to explain why their death rate ran as high as 60 percent in some months of the year. His findings had already persuaded officials of the South Carolina Penitentiary to demand that the railroad directors return forty-one of the forty-nine prisoners. Apparently impressed with the committee's usefulness, the Comptroller General moved that they petition the legislature for an appropriation of $2,800 to assist them in their work.[34]

By the time the committee met again in February 1880, its chair, J. F. M. Geddings, and Manning Simons (both Charlestonians) had submitted their resignations to the governor.[35] With Dr. B. W. Taylor as acting chair, the remaining five men moved to the business before them, this time mostly the result of Baruch's work as head of the Committee on Epidemic and Endemic Diseases. He reported that the greatest public health menace in South Carolina was widespread susceptibility to smallpox. Of all known contagious and infectious diseases, smallpox was the easiest to prevent. Yet, "outside of our larger towns and cities I believe that *not one-eighth part of our population is vaccinated.* Vaccination is never thought of unless an epidemic of small-pox is threatening. *I doubt if there is another portion of the civilized world, claiming to possess enlightenment, whose people are so completely at the mercy of this terrible scourge as the rural population of our State.*" Baruch pictured a fertile countryside innocently awaiting the introduction of a disease which "among the ignorant whites and among the negro population would spread like wild-fire if once beyond the control of quarantine." The "negligence of all hygienic rules" and the "well-known migratory propensities" of these people would make ordinary quarantine impossible. "The pestilence will fly upon the wings of the wind and outstrip the vaccinator so far that pursuit for the purpose of limiting the spread of the epidemic would be futile."[36]

Baruch considered the situation so dangerous that he asked the Executive Committee to give a vaccination campaign priority over every other public health need. "A supply of lymph should be obtained from reliable sources, or a vaccine farm should be established as a central depot, from which the lymph should be distributed gratuitously." Through local newspapers the sub-boards of health should call attention to the importance of vaccination, and their medical members should visit public schools on appointed days, vaccinating each child ("unless the parents object; which, in our State, will rarely be the case") and keeping records of their work. The sub-boards should make it clear in their newspaper announcements and circulars that "all others desiring to be protected may be invited to attend at the school-house or some other convenient place of meeting." By this plan Baruch felt certain that a large proportion of the population could be immunized quickly and at a trifling cost compared with the enormous losses an epidemic would entail. For the necessary funds, he looked to the legislature: "I can readily establish the economy of legislation, and of an appropriation of money for carrying it into effect."

In the discussion that followed Baruch's report, the committee showed special concern over the unique economic threat a smallpox epidemic would pose to the South, a threat that hinged on the capacity of the smallpox virus to travel over long distances on inanimate objects called "fomites." Like clothing and furniture, cotton was a fomite; it would take only a few cases of smallpox in South Carolina to destroy the market value of thousands of bales. Appalled at this prospect, the committee asked Baruch to prepare a second report, elaborating his skeleton plan for a general vaccination.[37]

Baruch also reported on adulteration of food and drink. He wanted the Executive Committee to procure the services of the State Board of Agriculture chemist to investigate the purity of various substances distributed for human consumption. Because there were no funds for this project, he moved that the committee address circulars to circuit judges, telling them to instruct grand juries that the state law relative to the sale of drugs and medicine was frequently violated, threatening the health and sometimes even the lives of the people.[38]

In view of the dispatch with which Baruch had handled the investigations assigned him, it is not surprising that the Executive Committee elected him interim chairman. When the next quarterly meeting failed for want of a quorum, Baruch called an extra session within five days and began to drive the committee as he drove himself. For two days, from ten in the morning until seven at night, he kept his members busy. From the attorney general he asked for a clear, full explanation of the powers of the Board of Health according to the law that created it. He promoted discussion of a sanitary code to be proposed for legislative action. He brought in the Charleston health officer to explain quarantine matters and discuss the new federal Quarantine Act. With the powers granted by the Health Act, he wrote to health officers of the various South Carolina ports, asking for special reports on their work. Because the Harris and Acklen Amendment then before the Congress would give the National Board of Health vast power in matters of quarantine (powers he knew South Carolina would wish to keep for itself), he asked South Carolina congressman John H. Evins to use delaying tactics until the State Board of Health could form an official opinion on the bill. Finally, as part of his own work on epidemic and endemic diseases, he sent out circulars to all sub-board chairmen in the state, asking information about the need for smallpox vaccination in their areas and suggestions as to how it might best be done.[39]

Baruch worked the committee hard, but he also arranged compensation for its members beyond their three dollars a day. "A most excellent dinner was provided by friends of the Columbia Medical Society. The Committee met with a warm welcome from their hosts, and sat down to an entertainment which was characterized by elegance and taste, and were soon engaged in testing the qualities of the tempting cheer presented in great profusion. Several hours were spent in convivial enjoyment and when the hour for departure arrived, it seemed all too soon to leave."[40]

One week later, when Executive Committee members returned to Columbia for the annual association meeting, Baruch was ready with a report on the year's work. With the establishment of thirty-six sub-boards in twenty-five counties, almost every section of the state was in direct communication with the State Board of Health. Referring to the provision for lay as well as medical sub-board members, Baruch noted that it was "very wise . . . to engage the public in the work, and to interest it in the sanitary supervision of the State."[41]

This last provision, however, was practically all he could find to praise in the history of relations between the medical profession and the state legislature. Measures proposed by doctors had had a high mortality rate in the South Carolina assembly:

Legislators, who would wax warm in the advocacy of measures for the repression of glanders and pleuro-pneumonia, and who would vote vast sums for the protection of cattle, will hesitate when they are asked to advocate a Board of Health, and to vote a paltry sum for protecting the people's health. Legislators, who will expend thousands in the pursuit of the potato bug and the cotton worm, will ponder and grow suddenly economical when they are entreated by disinterested parties, to expend much smaller sums to insure safety against yellow fever or small-pox.

If South Carolina's lawmakers were as interested in safeguarding the purity of food and drink for human consumption as they were in protecting the farmer against "sophistication of fertilizers," sanitary medicine would not still be in its infancy. Baruch almost gloated over the fact that recent epidemics had begun to awaken the lay public, making the sanitarian a "welcome and honored adviser of legislative bodies." So long as fear gave them an attentive audience, Baruch advised his colleagues to seize the chance and press three special projects in the legislature.

First was a law to provide for smallpox immunization. He had not yet finished collecting statistics, but all the data he had gathered so far showed "the crying need of a system of general vaccination."

Second was a "Sanitary Code or Ordinance" enumerating "in plain and unmistakable terms" various nuisances endangering public health. Without a law defining "degrees of gravity" and specifying punishment for offenders, the Board of Health would be impotent. To get such legislation, Baruch knew the association must first penetrate the "ignorance existing in the minds of the people, on the subject of sanitary medicine. It is certainly not fair to grow angry, and abuse the average legislator, because he cannot see our position in its true light, when we have taken no pains to educate him, or the people whom he has been chosen to represent."

The third measure Baruch wanted to see before the legislature was a plan for "the thorough organization of a system of Vital Statistics, throughout the State." When the former committee chairman had recommended this to the legislature, the Medical Committee of the House had reported unfavorably, "on the ground, as I am informed, that such registration of births, deaths and marriages would give the country doctor too much trouble, and that the United States Government had undertaken a similar work." Baruch did not believe that South Carolina doctors would, on such trivial grounds, frustrate "the great object of registration of Vital Statistics." Practitioners in sparsely settled "country districts" would willingly make such records, he said, for they would benefit from them materially as well as scientifically; it was for lack of vital statistics that "South Carolina is regarded abroad as the home of yellow fever and malaria, as a State in which no foreigner could survive a summer." Outsiders interpreted the absence of statistics as a confirmation of these beliefs. Baruch believed that the facts would actually show

that yellow fever is only an occasional visitor in our seaport towns, and has never spread as an epidemic in the interior; that malarial diseases are confined chiefly to the narrow limits of the paludal lands bordering on some of the water-courses; that the larger portion of this State presents a climate that cannot be surpassed for its salubrity, and that in the mountainous regions of the upper part of this State can be found an atmosphere which, for purity and bracing effect, might vie with the lovely Alpine mountains and valley retreats of Switzerland.

Baruch had arguments to persuade city practitioners too. "If a human being is much more valuable to the State than is a bale of cotton, then statistics of the human crop would prove much more valuable than statistics of the cotton crop; and yet every newspaper can and does furnish statistics as to the cotton crop, such as no man can now anywhere procure as to our human crop." Vital statistics were essential to ascertain "the fecundity of whole peoples and of the races thereof"; "the influence of meteorology, occupation, locality, in generating disease and improving health"; "and the approach of morbific storms, by ignorance of which negligent cities and even nations have been destroyed." Vital statistics were important to "the resident and the immigrant, the capitalist and the laborer, the politician and the statesman, the moralist and the scientist. Ignored and disparaged by the average American legislator, they have been advocated and supported by Napoleon and Thiers, by Bismarck and Cavour, by Gladstone and Disraeli; and their establishment has become a test of the degree of civilization reached by a people and their rulers."

In contrast to the progressive measures he recommended—smallpox vaccination, a sanitary code, and the registration of vital statistics—Baruch closed his report with a statement opposing the Acklen and Harris Amendment. Intended to strengthen the National Quarantine Act, this amendment embodied recommendations made by the National Academy of Science and the National Board of Health after the National Quarantine Act of June 1879 had been in effect for some time. It would empower the president, acting in concert with the National Board of Health, to restrict passage of goods and persons into and out of areas declared dangerously infected with contagious or infectious disease. Commerce in an area so designated would be forbidden under penalties imposed by federal courts, "unless such transportation is carried on in accordance with rules and regulations approved by the National Board of Health." Proponents claimed that this measure was intended merely to prevent local authorities from hurting their own areas by declaring quarantine unnecessarily: "It was never intended to give the [National Health] board more power," one of them said.[42]

Opposition to the Acklen and Harris Amendment, springing from fear of interference with states' rights, was immediate and strong. The Georgia Medical Society printed a statement of protest. It was unlike Baruch to join in the obstructionist tactics of these medical men—

doctors, John Shaw Billings bitterly observed, "whose solicitude lest local self-government should be interfered with seems to have been much greater than that of business men or politicians." But Baruch did join the opposition. Perhaps he truly objected to federal authority in state health affairs (although he certainly did not do so in later years); or perhaps he realized that the colleagues who elected him expected him to oppose federal power over South Carolina commerce. At any rate, he offered a resolution for the association to send to South Carolina's representatives in both houses of Congress: "That, whilst the State Board of Health approves of the establishment of a National Board of Health, and desires it to be endowed with full power to protect the people by sanitary regulations and investigations, we do protest against the establishment of any quarantine in this State without the previous consent of the Governor and of the Executive Committee of the State Board of Health of this State."

Baruch confessed that the work of the Executive Committee, though "onerous and exacting," had as yet achieved "no result evident to the public." He expressed confidence that its proposals, "when matured," would demonstrate that the committee members had "labored with an eye single to the well-being of their beloved State, whose most vital interests are in their keeping."

In less than a year, in a state that had never before had a public health organization, the Executive Committee had accomplished a great deal. Association president F. M. Robertson, in his address before the annual meeting in Columbia in 1880, might have praised the committee's work. He might have urged members to support the projects proposed. He might at least have spoken on a topic related to their aims. But he did none of these. He was apparently too preoccupied with the previous year's discussion of euthanasia to notice the progress of the public health movement in South Carolina. It was not even euthanasia itself, admittedly an appropriate medical concern, that troubled him. The elderly Robertson (who had been the first secretary of the association at its formation in 1848) felt compelled by religious conviction to challenge the implicit acceptance of Darwinian ideas which Dr. T. T. Robertson had indirectly introduced in supporting euthanasia at the preceding annual meeting.[43]

With these remarks, said President Robertson, "the glove was boldly, if not defiantly, thrown down." He felt obligated to take it up, "as a firm believer in the existence of an omnipotent, omniscient and omni-present God—or in other words, the Jehovah of the Bible." For this reason, he made his presidential address an "endeavor to show that there are several

links missing in the chain of the evolution scheme, which destroys its
unity as well as its continuity, and, consequently, the claims of the doctrine to be ranked as a scientific truth." Evolution was "nothing more
than a hypothesis, and by no means a demonstrated fact in science."
Given a real test, he believed, it would "vanish like the morning mist
before the brightness of Jehovah's sun." Ignoring biological arguments
appropriate to a medical audience, he concluded, on the basis of protracted astronomical and geological reasoning, that evolutionists would
not merit serious attention until they could explain the creation of life out
of dead matter. His brief condemnation of euthanasia came almost as an
afterthought: "In the absence of all moral support to this arbitrary and
premature extinction of human life for reasons that are untenable, we
appeal with confidence to the utter fallacy of basing it upon the unproven
and unscientific doctrine of evolution."

A majority of association members may have held views on evolution
similar to the president's; recent scholarship has described the persistence
of anti-Darwinism to the turn of the century and beyond. Nonetheless,
the president apologized for his choice of subject. It almost certainly
offended the friends of T. T. Robertson, who had been association president in 1870 (and one of Baruch's three examiners for the Confederate
medical service in 1862). Nonetheless, as though pulling the final stop in
a religious revival, the president of the South Carolina Medical Association ended his version of the Almighty versus Charles Darwin with a
quotation from the German poet Johann Paul Friedrich Richter:

> End is there none to the universe of God.
> Lo! Also, there is no beginning.[44]

Smallpox and the New South 10

Throughout the early summer of 1880 Baruch buried himself in his study of the need for smallpox vaccination in South Carolina. He corresponded with every sub-board of health in the state and from their replies began to weave a full report for the Executive Committee meeting in July. The absence of vital statistics made it impossible for sub-board members to document estimates of immunity in their locales, but most of them were practicing physicians of high standing and long residence in the communities they served—"the ablest medical men in the various Counties in this State," Baruch said, "better versed in matters of this kind than [are] any others." They gave him all the confirmation he needed for his idea that the state was poorly protected against smallpox. Even allowing for exaggeration, their estimates of nonimmunity were astounding: from a mere one-third in the Greenville area the proportion soared to three-fourths in York and nine-tenths or more in Bennetsville, Abbeyville, Blackville, Manning, and Greenwood. In the area of the Walhalla sub-board, where there had not been a general vaccination since 1865, almost everyone under the age of fifteen was unprotected. In Lancaster County, in the northern part of the state, the last vaccination had taken place under threat of a smallpox siege in Charlotte, North Carolina, thirty years earlier.[1]

Some of the sub-board reports came from areas that until a short time before had known only the most primitive medical care. The Grahamville group stated that no blacks had been vaccinated since emancipation, and the poorer whites "have never realized the value of this protection." During the winter of 1865–66, when the only practitioner in the area was

131

a United States Army surgeon, a smallpox outbreak had taken so many lives that apparently only one effort was made to check the spread of the disease: "In some instances, houses containing corpses were destroyed by fire to avoid the necessity for burial and the attendant risk of infection." Immunity among the survivors was the only protection in the population in 1880. According to the Walterboro sub-board, a similar outbreak had occurred immediately after the war among blacks along the Combahee and Ashepoo rivers. Those who lived on in immunity, plus the few who were vaccinated, constituted an estimated half of the population.

On the sea islands off the Carolina coast, constantly exposed to the danger of infection through trade in long-staple cotton and through northern missionaries and teachers, the large proportion of unvaccinated blacks lowered the immune population to a dangerous level. The Port Royal board reported that there had been "no vaccination done here since the late war." Although the town had a population of only about six hundred, few of the preponderant number of blacks had been immunized—and then, it was said, not since the days of slavery, when masters had arranged it for infants and small children. Protection was more common among the whites, who came from "various States and nationalities." Vaccination of sea-island blacks posed particular problems: "No negro would ride a mile to have his child vaccinated unless he were paid for it, so perfectly indifferent is he to the subject of hygiene and prophylactics. He is more of a fatalist than the Turk!" To have even a chance of success, vaccination at Port Royal would have to be offered at public expense. Because of Beaufort's larger population, the situation was still more critical in that sea-island city where, out of an estimated twenty thousand blacks, only one-twentieth had been vaccinated.

The Orangeburg and Marlboro sub-boards opposed Baruch's plan, arguing that isolation from the "great thoroughfares of traffic and travel" made their areas safe. Baruch answered this objection with examples of smallpox devastation in the most remote areas imaginable. He also raised the possibility that South Carolina might not always be a poor land of isolated rural communities. Even if the gentlemen from Orangeburg and Marlboro saw no present need for immunization, they must think of the South of the future: "Our aim is to vaccinate them now and continue our work, and transfer it to those who may succeed us as conservators of the public health." Baruch looked to better days, when "the new era, which is now but dawning upon us, will fill our towns with thriving, bustling communities, when Orangeburg, it is to be hoped, and other now sparsely populated towns, will resound with the busy hum of machinery, which will require thousands to serve and supply it with material and to distribute its manufactured goods." For the sake of the New South, the Old must begin to make ready. Smallpox might pose a great threat to this bright vision of commerce and industry. Even in 1880, it could frighten South Carolinians of one section into boycotting another: "Trade stagnates when the news of even one case of smallpox reaches the interior of the county. Great discomfort and anxiety are felt by all; the happiness and prosperity of the community are damaged; for even if the authorities succeed in limiting the disease by isolation, two months elapse ere the danger is believed to have passed."

Baruch's words were not idle fear-mongering. Shortly before beginning his work on smallpox, he had attended a woman from Charleston who fell ill while visiting in Camden. His examination left no doubt that she had smallpox. When he tried to forestall its spread by vaccination, he found that there was "not a particle of vaccine lymph or crust" in Camden. He sent to Charleston. There was none there either, so he telegraphed New York. Three days later the lymph arrived. In the meantime, everyone attending the case had been exposed. Each in turn became the center of an ever-widening circle of exposure. In no time, a single isolated case became a real threat, "for revaccination had never been practiced in this section." Although local authorities did their best to establish strict quarantine, cases soon sprang up in other parts of town. By great exertion and expense every case was finally isolated and the spread checked by vaccination, but Camden might as well have had a full-scale epidemic: "For two months the people of the interior of the county were unwilling to visit the town, depriving the latter not only of much trade, but also preventing their purchasing country produce, which is very necessary for the actual support of families." In addition to the expense of isolation and vaccination, Camden had to bear a loss of trade and the threat of dwindling food supplies, until the alarm at last subsided.[2]

The New South Baruch envisaged would stand to lose even more by a smallpox visitation. Already, in 1880, the region was growing less and less isolated. "The passenger traffic through our State has of late been greatly increased," he noted. "Especially during the winter months, thousands emigrate from the North to the sunny climes of Florida and other Southern resorts." These travelers, from cities and towns in every section of the Union, could easily carry infection, and they would come in increasing numbers "when rates of travel and board at the South will be cheapened, as eventually they must be by competition."

Apart from the resort traffic, there was still another potent source of contagion. "Take, for instance, clothing which is sewed by poor seamstresses in the Northern cities." From his experience in a New York City dispensary during the winter of 1865–66, Baruch knew that smallpox was a frequent visitor in the tenements. Clothing from one contaminated sweatshop could bring disease and death to hundreds of merchants and consumers in the South.

Baruch also felt compelled to answer arguments that vaccination did not give true immunity to the disease. To a world ravaged by epidemics, Edward Jenner's method had come as a deliverance, but with the subsequent decline of smallpox, people forgot that vaccination was an exact procedure, effective only when properly performed. They forgot, too, that Jenner never claimed it would produce permanent immunity. When those who had been improperly vaccinated or had gradually lost their immunity fell victim to smallpox, opponents claimed that Jenner was wrong. From this misapplication of his idea and consequent disillusionment with it, vaccination had fallen into disuse. As increasing population placed the vaccinated in the minority, the second and third quarters of the nineteenth century saw a return to the cycle of epidemics that had marked the era before vaccination.[3]

Baruch's report was filled with the evidence of neglect, continuing into the 1870s, measured in numbers of cases and deaths in Switzerland, Italy, Bohemia, Germany, England, Holland, Peru, Chile, and every major city of the United States. Other medical members of the Executive Committee were already aware of these facts. Baruch wrote for a broader audience: "The people must be educated to the necessity and importance of this protective measure." It was for "popular use" that he filled his report with refutations of the antivaccination forces.[4]

Why bother with "the people"? Unlike many of his colleagues, Baruch did not desire compulsory vaccination. He wanted his plan to succeed because the public accepted it. From the history of vaccination, he knew that mandatory legislation only strengthened resistance inspired by fear or ignorance. "The opposition to vaccination," he warned, "was rendered violent and aggressive just so soon as its benefits were being *forced* upon the people." Coercion ran counter to the current of nineteenth-century liberalism, eliciting belligerent responses even from such a man as Alfred Russel Wallace, an early formulator of the theory of evolution by means of natural selection. In his *Vaccination a Delusion, Its Penal Enforcement a Crime,* Wallace snorted: "Liberty is in my mind a far greater and more important thing than science." Baruch considered such a sentiment "imbued by a fanaticism as unreasoning as it is dangerous . . . mostly under the leadership of believers in spiritualism and other isms which attract the modern dreamer"—but he did not underestimate its popular influence.[5]

Baruch knew that legislators, even more than the people they represent, are susceptible to economic considerations. Unfortunately, it was difficult to determine the cost of an epidemic, depending as it did on the value of labor, property, and human life. Someone had made such a study of the Philadelphia epidemic of 1871–72, however, and Baruch reproduced the resulting figures to show that a thorough program of prevention would have required only $618,000. Lacking such protection, the city lost more than $21 million. Bringing the issue still closer to home, he reported that the 1874–75 epidemic cost Mobile approximately fifty times as much as the vaccination program that could have prevented it.

On the basis of his study, Baruch recommended legislation to provide for a program of popular education to be followed by statewide voluntary immunization. The first step was to "impress upon our law-makers the lessons taught by the history of vaccination."[6] In detail of execution his plan followed that of the veteran American sanitarian Elisha Harris. One of the organizers of the United States Sanitary Commission—the "fifth wheel" of Lincoln's war chariot—Harris later arranged what has been considered the first free public vaccination service. Largely through his work, between fifty and sixty thousand New Yorkers were vaccinated in the single year of 1869.[7] Like Harris, Baruch wanted to see all adults and medical practitioners provided with "such necessary means of information and instruction as shall suitably prepare them to understand and perform their duties." By this he meant every South Carolinian: "No barriers of poverty, ignorance, or the inaccessibility of means, shall prevent the vaccination which each child needs."[8]

To assure that the quality of lymph was carefully controlled through a central authority, Baruch urged that the Executive Committee appoint "a well-informed and energetic physician as Chief of the Vaccinating Department of the State Board of Health." The appointee, a man with "all necessary professional qualifications for the office, with executive capacity," should reside at Columbia and receive "sufficient compensation" so that he could give most of his time to the work of vaccination. From the central lymph supply, he should distribute carefully inspected allotments to sub-boards of health and private physicians all over the state, together with instructions and forms for recording and preserving the facts of each vaccination. The chief would also act as inspector of vaccination, visiting each sub-board at least once a year.[9]

On the local level, the medical members of the sub-boards, or two substitutes appointed by them, should be constituted public vaccinators in their respective counties. "They should visit all the schools in the County, giving previously written notice to the teachers through the County School Commissioner, of the appointed days." Baruch wanted copies of this written notice distributed among editors, teachers, and ministers ("who may thus be induced to cooperate in the laudable work") and notifications sent, in advance of the appointed vaccination day, to the various school precincts. In this way everyone in the state could learn that not only the schoolchildren but any other persons ("especially infants") might receive free immunization at the schoolhouse. Eight days after vaccination day, those who received lymph should reassemble at the schoolhouse to be examined by a vaccinator, who would note whether the vaccination had taken. At the same time, he would gather lymph from the arms of the "healthiest subjects for maintaining the general supply" and report names, ages, and verification of all who came. For each day's work, these local vaccinators would receive a fee of five dollars.

At the end of his report, Baruch referred to it as a "rough outline" for the Executive Committee to use in "constructing a more detailed organization." Actually, as he must have realized, it was anything but "rough." When he was first assigned to the Committee on Epidemic and Endemic Diseases in June 1879, he had thought his job was to organize medical care in South Carolina cities stricken with plagues. For that reason he had suggested that some other member take his place—preferably someone from Charleston, a location more likely than Camden to be invaded by epidemics.[10] But once he had begun to conceive of his work as preventive, a little study had showed him that South Carolina stood wide open to smallpox, the one infectious disease medicine could prevent. Asked for more proof of his preliminary assertion, he had launched into the project with his accustomed energy and thoroughness, overlooking nothing from the extent of susceptibility to the best means—psychological as well as medical—for providing immunity. His mild deprecation of the final report notwithstanding, he had every reason to consider it adequate.

Given happier economic conditions, Baruch's work on vaccination might have brought immediate results. Although it has been credited with producing South Carolina's "first legislative action" on the subject, the earliest vaccination law on record was not passed until 1905.[11] If it came through Baruch's efforts, it came too late for him to enjoy the victory—and too late to prevent the smallpox outbreaks that plagued South Carolina from 1888 into the twentieth century.[12]

"No field for enterprise"

Less than five months after completing his work on smallpox, Baruch at last moved to the North. It seems strange that he should decide to leave South Carolina at just this time. As chairman of the Executive Committee of the State Board of Health under an interim appointment that had apparently become permanent, he possessed more power and prestige than any other physician in the state. And he enjoyed the prestige. He had envelopes addressed to himself in extrabold Roman type, with his name in capitals over the rest of the address: "Chairman Ex. Committee, State Board of Health, Camden, S.C."[1]

His success as a private practitioner was no less remarkable. From his work he had managed to wring a return that more than supported his needs and those of his family. With the surplus he bought land: a tract on the edge of town in 1877; twenty-nine acres on Pine Tree Creek in 1878; twenty-eight acres on Camden's eastern boundary and twenty-five acres on Cheraw Road in 1880; and he owned several lots within the city.[2]

One did not need a fortune to buy land in South Carolina in the years just after Reconstruction. The large holdings of earlier times were being broken up and sold, and, as Wilbur Cash said in his chronicle of the southern mind and mores, the land went, "in this world of poverty, for a song." But even in small portions, even at the going rate of "a song," it went only to "hard, pushing, horse-trading men"—the ones who had been able, even in the roughest financial waters, to "gather and hold a little mobile capital." The main chance came only to those "remarkable for thrift, acumen, energy, undeviating desire for acquisition and power." Some had made their money "by painful toil and a single eye to gain," some by chicanery.[3] Baruch had made his honestly but not accidentally. He had worked hard. He had had his days of "dunning people." While his gentlemanly, unbusinesslike colleagues stood by, waiting for better days, he had kept busy. He had collected fees in kind by taking "hay, corn, fodder, eggs, chickens, anything." In the long run his energy and careful attention to detail had made his practice pay—handsomely.[4]

If it was not financial dissatisfaction that prompted him to leave, perhaps it was, as some have suggested, his desire for broader fields in which to study and practice hydrotherapy.[5] Certainly he had devoted an extraordinarily large portion of his 1874 presidential address to the medical usefulness of water; but it had not yet become a passion with him, to judge from the fact that, for some time after leaving the South, he continued to devote himself to a wide range of medical topics just as he had done in Camden.

His son Bernard has said that it was the duel between Colonel E. B. C. Cash and Dr. Baruch's friend Colonel William Shannon that led him to abandon Camden for New York.[6] This incident was the most infamous of an epidemic of duels marking a breakdown, between 1878 and 1880, in the cordial relations which common misfortunes had seemed to enjoin on Camdenites during Reconstruction. The duel, deliberately provoked by Cash, resulted in Shannon's death. According to two Camden historians writing in 1926, it "caused a profound sensation throughout the State, such perhaps as was never produced by the death of any other of her citizens, before or since."[7] Dr. Baruch detested violence. Shannon's death must have seemed especially bitter to him if it is true that he tried to prevent the duel by secretly notifying the sheriff of the time and place. Although the sheriff arrived too late to save Shannon, Baruch at least succeeded in dissuading a party of vengeful lynchers from going after Cash. If it was the shock of the duel that prompted Baruch to leave, it was slow to mold his judgment, for it happened in July, and in October he accepted reelection as president of the Camden Hebrew Benevolent Association.[8]

In his autobiography Bernard Baruch recalled that for some time before 1880 his mother had been urging his father "to go North where opportunities would be greater."[9] Perhaps Belle did urge him, but not because he lacked ambition of his own. His dissatisfaction with the South, as he poured it out to Dr. Salley in the years just after the war, indicates that he needed no urging from anyone. His reasons for leaving in 1880 probably did not differ from those he gave for his flight to the city less than six months after Appomattox. Then he had seized the first opportunity to leave the South and try to establish himself in New York

City. He had failed, but only because he lacked capital to support himself while he made a start. Now, after fifteen years in which his every published work bespoke ambition, he had the money for a second try.

He also had a wife and four sons, a beautiful home, and a thriving practice. It would have been easier to slow to the leisurely pace of Camden life and stay on where he had established himself so successfully. But the "tide of progress" still beckoned to him, and it rushed on at such a distance from South Carolina that he knew he could never join it there. The atmosphere of intellectual stagnation that had vexed him in his twenties was enough to madden a man of forty who had come only a little of the way he wanted to go. In 1880 one could hardly continue to blame the war or the Radicals for this inertia of the mind. What one of Ellen Glasgow's Virginians called "mental malaria" did indeed seem endemic in the South.[10] Like the malaria of the body, it weakened without killing, but it was neither intermittent nor remittent nor treatable by quinine.

Another ambitious immigrant had chafed under the slow, steady erosion of "mental malaria," not in Camden in the hard days after the war but in the college town of Columbia twenty-five years before secession. Even as a teacher in academic surroundings, Francis Lieber had felt oppressed by the intellectual "leadenness" of the people. Lieber was a scholar, a political scientist, but he had in common with Baruch a desire to write and a dependence on his immediate environment for stimulation. It simply did not exist, either for Lieber in Columbia before the war or for Baruch in Camden afterward. "We live in an absolute desert here," Lieber wrote to a friend in the North. "My book . . . I have been obliged to spin solitarily out of my brain, as a spider spins its cobweb, without one cheering conversation, one word of friendly advice,—in utter mental isolation." There was no one near him, he complained, "from whom I could derive stirring knowledge in my sphere."[11]

Baruch, too, had a painful sense of intellectual exile. In 1868 he wrote Salley that "there is not a single physician here, whose knowledge of medicine (I mean aside from practice & empiricism) enables him to hold a decent conversation in Medicine." They were "fogies" and "mere empirics." Still worse, they had "no energy." He yearned for companionship, "for as I am situated here I never get an opportunity to 'talk physic,' our doctors being mostly averse to such recreation." For a time, he had hoped that the Kershaw County Medical Association would rouse his colleagues from their lethargy, but he was soon disillusioned. "I am disgusted with our society, for I cant learn anything there & that was my object in joining it & working for its maintenance." It had proved to be "one of the 'Rip Van Winkle' kind . . . entirely oblivious to progress," devoted "principally to the ante-bellum notion of things." No one in Camden shared Baruch's ravenous appetite for medical literature. To obtain a copy of the *Surgical History of the War of the Rebellion,* he was obliged to barter away two early works from his medical library to the Surgeon General's Library in Washington.[12]

After 1869 Baruch had turned for intellectual stimulation to the state medical association. Although association meetings provided the most exciting days of the year, they were still poorly attended fifteen years after Appomattox. To measures the association recommended in its capacity as the State Board of Health, the legislature turned a persistently unresponsive ear. Baruch's urgent appeal for smallpox vaccination failed to bring action. The state made no legal provision for preventing the spread of syphilis and ignored repeated proposals for the collection and compilation of vital statistics and the protection of public health.[13]

To a man with Baruch's distaste for mixing religion with science, the 1880 association meeting had presented a sorry spectacle, and it did not much matter that the refutation of Darwinism which constituted F. M. Robertson's presidential address was only one of many such expressions in the South at that time. In 1878 the trustees of Vanderbilt University had summarily abolished the chair of Alexander Winchell, an active and eminent geologist, an action widely attributed to objections by the influential trustee Bishop McTyeire to Winchell's advocacy of evolution. Andrew Dickson White, seeing in Winchell's plight a parallel to that of Galileo, sardonically marveled at the progression from a Roman Catholic cardinal to a Methodist bishop.[14] But at least it was a churchman who had sent Winchell and his ideas packing out of Tennessee into the less confining atmosphere of Michigan. Vanderbilt was a denominational school and so was the South Carolina College and Theological Seminary in Columbia, where, in 1884, James Woodrow was to be tried and found guilty of heresy, that is, of teaching "with undue sympathy for the Darwinian school, in contravention of the scriptural account of creation."[15] Incompatible though both cases were with the spirit of free inquiry, they could be written off as intradenominational conflicts.

President Robertson's address was another matter. In disputing evolution on religious grounds before a professional gathering, he disavowed the spirit of enlightenment and progress which Baruch had urged in his own address six years earlier. Baruch himself was neither a Christian nor an Orthodox Jew. Like Robertson, Baruch professed belief in "One, Great, Omniscient, Omnipresent, Unchangeable God, the one Jehovah," but he did not let this belief interfere with his work, and he resented those who did.[16] He went out of his way to mock the man who would withhold anesthesia from a woman in labor so that she might bring forth children "in sorrow," as the Old Testament decreed. He probably did not even approve of churchmen meddling in the faculty affairs of denominational schools, and he must certainly have been appalled to hear Dr. Robertson address the state medical association as though he were speaking to an evangelical gathering.

What a contrast there was between this display and the intellectual richness of the American Medical Association convention which Baruch attended in June. And how different was New York, the AMA convention site, from Camden—or Columbia—or even Charleston! In fact, New York in 1880 was different from the city Baruch had known in the first winter after the war; or in 1867, when he and Belle were married there; or even in 1868, when he went there to "'walk the hospitals.'" It was a growing city in a land of promise, a magnet for many of the South's most eminent physicians. It was, Baruch thought, one of the "great intellectual workshops of the world."[17]

"There is no field here for enterprise," he had written from Camden in 1867. Less than six years out of medical school, he had confessed to a persistent "ambition to practice my profession in a city." Even in his youth, the rigors of rural practice had held no charms for him. He looked forward to the time when he would be regarded as the highest medical authority in the community, but "in a country practice, this pleasure is far from being unalloyed; in fact it becomes rather the most laborious period of a country doctor's life." This was not what he wanted, "though I would, no doubt, be well enough contented to have my hands constantly full in the decline of my life, yet, somehow I cannot associate in my mind, that time of life with a laborious country practice." At twenty-eight he had feared that he might "never reach such good luck" as to have the city practice he had always wanted.[18]

By 1880, twelve years after confiding this fear to Dr. Salley, Baruch knew that hard work had much more to do with it than luck, and, for all his forty years, his capacity for hard work was undiminished. He was extremely careful about his health, adhering rigidly to the simple diet of his youth, scorning fried foods and pastries in favor of fruits, vegetables, and berries—fresh when in season, otherwise simply preserved. From the milk which his herd of Alderneys provided, he prepared a cheese he often ate in preference to meat at breakfast or supper. To retain the minerals that lie just beneath the husk of each wheat kernel, he used only partially bolted flour. During hot southern summers, he often made an entire meal of wheat bread, butter, cheese, and milk or coffee. Unlike Belle, who was growing round and soft, he remained a lean, long-legged, vigorous high-stepper, a striking figure of a man, with far more energy than he needed for all the work South Carolina could give him.[19]

Even though he was far along in life to make a new start, there was nothing to keep him from trying. He had lots of ideas in his head—perhaps even a book—and he did not want to sit, like Francis Lieber, and spin them out alone, "as a spider spins its cobweb."

On December 4 Baruch sold his house, his "farm," and his practice. Together with his savings, the sale gave him $18,000 to last through the difficult transition he faced. Leaving Belle and the four boys to follow when he found a place for them to live, he set off once again for New York City.[20]

Baruch Makes His Mark   12

Despite his success in fifteen years of practice in South Carolina, Baruch knew it would be almost as difficult to establish himself in New York City in 1881 as it had been in 1865. This time he had money, but he also had a wife and four sons, the youngest of them barely seven, the oldest only thirteen. Beginning his new life cautiously, he settled his family in two modest rooms on the fourth floor of a brownstone boardinghouse at 144 West Forty-third Street. Then he enrolled in a number of New York's many clinics, the postgraduate courses of that time. Baruch missed scarcely a specialty. He studied ophthalmology with Cornelius Rea Agnew and Edward Greeley Loring; gynecology with two of New York's prominent transplanted southerners, T. Gaillard Thomas and Thomas Addis Emmet; pathology with Carl Heitzman; neurology with Edward Constant Seguin; surgery with Henry Burton Sands and Charles McBurney; and dermatology with Lucius Duncan Bulkley.[1] Apart from the medicine he could learn from these men (which included much of the best knowledge of the day), he could have found no better way into New York's inner professional circle.

Unexpectedly, his work in the ophthalmology clinic resulted in a "cure" for the persistent "migraine" headaches that had long kept him from work several times a week. "Two eminent oculists" had once assured him that the trouble was a simple matter of nearsightedness in his right eye, which he would do well to leave as it was. Now he was surprised to discover that he suffered from double astigmatism. With the aid of glasses prescribed by an ophthalmologist whom he met at the clinic, he suddenly had perfect vision and no more headaches.[2]

143

Then something far more serious than faulty vision threatened him. He had not been in New York long when he began to suffer chest pains, which he interpreted as symptomatic of heart disease. The first physician he consulted confirmed his fears. Convinced that he did not have long to live, Baruch began to think of returning to South Carolina, where his death would not leave his wife and sons alone among strangers. Before making a final decision, he had the diagnosis checked by Alfred Lebbeus Loomis, an eminent clinician and diagnostician, particularly skilled in diseases of the heart and chest. Loomis saw at once that the seat of the pain was the stomach, not the heart. Baruch had dyspepsia: severe, chronic indigestion, probably arising from professional worries. According to his son Bernard, the illness disappeared as soon as Dr. Baruch's practice began to flourish.[3]

To build a practice quickly, Baruch began to look for a dispensary position like the one he had held fifteen years earlier. This time he had help in the competition. He had, in fact, a blanket recommendation from the son of Willard Parker, noted surgical innovator and medical educator.

My dear Sir
I take great pleasure in introducing to you my friend Dr. Simon Baruch formerly of Camden S.C.
I became acquainted with him during a recent winter spent in the South and can most cordially endorse his application for any position he may seek
Truly yours
Willard Parker, Jr.[4]

Whether through Parker's intercession or his own medical and linguistic skills, Baruch soon moved into the post of "surgeon for eye, ear and throat diseases" at the North-Eastern Dispensary, reportedly "one of the largest and in prospect, wealthiest in the city." He was so proud of the affiliation that he took care to list it in a paper he wrote for the South Carolina State Board of Health in April 1881, even though the paper had nothing to do with the eye, the ear, or the throat.[5]

In the course of its 1881 meeting, the South Carolina Medical Association officially received Baruch's resignation and chose replacements for him on the many committees on which he had served. They also elected him an honorary member, putting him in the notable company of Edwin S. Gaillard, founder and editor of the *Richmond Medical Journal* (later the *Richmond and Louisville Medical Journal,* and, finally, in New York City, *Gaillard's Medical Journal*); of the scientists John and Joseph LeConte and Charles Upham Shepard; of J. Marion Sims, whose surgical triumphs had brought him out of Alabama to a place among the leading surgeons of Europe; and of T. Gaillard Thomas, Baruch's postgraduate professor of gynecology in New York.[6]

Much as Baruch welcomed this honor from his southern colleagues, he now had to move ahead in a different world, and he did not find it easy. American physicians in the 1880s lacked the status that the later combination of "scientific medicine" and popular science worship would give their successors. In the last decades of the nineteenth century, low prestige and low compensation so plagued doctors that many turned to other work soon after leaving medical school. Baruch's dispensary post paid no salary, but this time he did not mind, for he was primarily interested in using it to attract a "respectable practice." Many in the profession believed that there was widespread abuse of free dispensary care by those who could afford to pay a physician. Baruch doubtless expected to win private patients from those he would first see at the dispensary.[7]

In the spring of 1881 another door to a "better" clientele opened when Dr. William Frothingham gave Baruch charge of his summer practice, "up north" in Washington Heights (between the Hudson and Harlem rivers from 145th Street north to the upper part of Manhattan island). On June 18 the Baruchs moved out of the steaming city into summer quarters at 157th Street and Nicholas Avenue, overlooking the woodland where the Polo Grounds would later stand. There, just south of the scattered farms and quiet countryside of the Bronx, the four boys could romp in the open while Baruch attended to Dr. Frothingham's patients. At about the same time, Baruch became medical attendant to several public institutions, among them the New York Juvenile Asylum. Little by little, he began to attract wealthy patients whose trips to Bermuda, South America, the Adirondacks, and the Continent he noted in his casebooks. As he later described it, his practice ranged "from the denizen of the crowded tenement to the palatial home of the millionaire."[8]

The next year brought still better fortune. On January 7, 1882, the *Medical Record* published Baruch's "Plea for Improved Vaccination" as its lead article. Deploring the current antivaccination campaign, Baruch nonetheless admitted some statistical justification for the opposition: from 1818 to 1870 the average smallpox mortality had been only about 4 percent; from 1870 to 1880 it had risen to more than 12. Perhaps physicians had grown careless in choosing lymph and verifying results. Or was the profit motive at fault, as Baruch suspected? "In these days of mercenary traffic in all things, human life is but too often regarded as naught when placed in the scale against profit. The tottering tenements, the rotten ships, the rusty boilers and frail bridges which have sent their victims into eternity, bear witness to this fact. Is it not possible—yes, probable—that this mercenary spirit has touched the dealers in 'vaccine virus' and rendered them careless regarding the maintenance of its purity and efficiency?" Out of thirty-five vaccinations Baruch had performed during the preceding winter, no fewer than ten had proved faulty, though he had used "bovine 'virus' purchased from one of the most reliable drug-houses in this city." For lack of anything like a Food and Drug Administration to enforce standards of purity, Baruch urged physicians to choose vaccine with care and assure patients of effective protection by checking the vesicles: "No medical student should be allowed to graduate who does not exhibit a full appreciation of the importance of vaccination and a thorough knowledge of all its details."[9]

Drawing from his experience in eye, ear, and throat diseases at the North-Eastern Dispensary, Baruch wrote a treatise on the treatment of catarrh for the South Carolina Medical Association in April.[10] But an even greater advantage arose from his affiliation with this dispensary, self-advertised as "one of the largest in the city, treating over 20,000 cases annually, and having an attending staff of twenty-five physicians." From these facilities there emerged the Medical Polyclinic of the North-Eastern Dispensary, a single set of buildings with its own staff, where doctors and medical students could study many of the specialties Baruch had had to pursue in various locations the preceding year. Baruch, who considered himself one of the polyclinic organizers, called it "the First Post Graduate School." The opening announcement stated his official position as head of the eye, ear, and throat clinic. Classes, limited or divided "so as not to exceed four," took place in a room adjoining the dispensary building at 222 East Fifty-ninth Street. For all the clinics of a single term, including five clinics weekly for eight weeks, the cost was $25. Though not the first, the Medical Polyclinic of the North-Eastern Dispensary was one of the earliest organized systems of postgraduate clinical instruction in the United States. It opened on October 27, 1882, only four days later than its widely recognized predecessor, the New York Polyclinic, which was founded by the transplanted Alabama surgeon John Allen Wyeth and staffed in major part by Wyeth's fellow southern émigrés: Thomas Addis Emmet, Edward L. Keyes, H. Marion Sims, T. Gaillard Thomas, and Walker Gill Wylie.[11]

As if Baruch did not have enough to do with his work at the polyclinic, at the New York Juvenile Asylum, and in Dr. Frothingham's summer practice, he took on a job as assistant to Dr. Walker Gill Wylie in his clinic for the diseases of women at the DeMilt Dispensary. Wylie was a South Carolinian, eight years Baruch's junior. A boy of twelve when the Civil War began, he was still an undergraduate at the University of South

Carolina when Baruch was establishing his postwar practice. Unlike Baruch, Wylie had left South Carolina early in his career, graduating from Bellevue Hospital Medical College in 1871. By 1882, when the graying Baruch was just getting started in New York City, Wylie was well established. The discrepancy between the age and achievements of the two might have made their relationship difficult, especially since Wylie was a keen critic, reportedly given to swearing at assistants when he became exasperated during an operation; but they got on well together. When Wylie was away during the summer of 1882, Baruch took over the DeMilt women's clinic, keeping up a full attendance there. In November, when Wylie resigned to become visiting gynecologist to Bellevue, he recommended Baruch as his successor.[12]

A position at the DeMilt was considered "one of the best appointments in the city," and there was the usual heavy competition for the opening. Judging from the support Baruch marshaled among his formidable network of former southerners, he wanted the job badly. On November 19, T. Gaillard Thomas wrote in his behalf, calling him "thoroughly competent to fulfill the requirements of the place." Eight days later, Thomas Addis Emmet informed the committee on applications that he had "personal knowledge" of Baruch as "an accomplished & highly educated physician with an accurate knowledge of the treatment of the diseases & injuries peculiar to women. Notwithstanding I have already signed the application of another candidate for the position," Emmet added, "I do not hesitate to vouch for Dr. Baruch's being well fitted to fill the position." Still, there seemed to be doubt of Baruch's appointment. On November 30, Wylie again wrote the committee, fearing that his first letter had been lost or overlooked: "I have known Dr. Baruch for a number of years. Besides being an accomplished and experienced physician he has given special attention to diseases of women. In my opinion he is decidedly the best man that I know of for the position."[13] With three of New York's best-known gynecologists writing in his behalf, Baruch got the job.

In other places, too, his tremendous energy began to bring results. By the end of two years in New York he was prosperous enough to move his family north from 144 West Forty-third Street to 158 West Fifty-fourth. Together with an increasing work load came a reputation. On December 19, George Shrady, one of America's most prominent and successful medical editors, invited Baruch to write several articles for the *Medical Record*. Founded by Shrady in 1866, the *Record* was one of the first well-organized weekly medical journals in the country. Even while living in South Carolina, Baruch had read it and contributed correspondence to its

columns. Now he was to be honored as one of the "many distinguished
gentlemen," the "men of larger experience," whom Shrady had chosen
to write a series on the pathology and treatment of "many of the com-
moner diseases which are met with in general practice."[14]

Baruch elected to write about malaria, but not without first doing a
great deal of research. Of the two papers he wrote on this subject for
Shrady, the first was not ready until November 1883. In an editorial of
August 18, 1883, Shrady had stated that malaria had recently become a
"bugbear" in the "Middle and Eastern States." "It is always with us on
Manhattan Island and its surrounding regions."[15] Baruch's articles contended that, despite city death certificates attributing some five hundred
annual fatalities to malaria, the disease was not common in New York;
many doctors, he said, simply could not distinguish malaria from other
fevers. They confused it with typhoid, acute tuberculosis, tubercular
meningitis, peri-nephritic or hepatic abscess, and other febrile conditions.

Unlike many of his New York colleagues, Baruch explained, he had
had ample experience with the real thing: since his graduation from
medical school, he had spent three years "in active service as a military
surgeon in the camps of Virginia" and fifteen "in an extensive practice at
Camden, S.C., and upon the plantations on the banks of the Wateree
River, where I had medical charge of many hundreds of laborers and
planters." After coming to New York, he had practiced "in those so-
called malarious suburbs, Washington Heights and Fort Washington,
where I had under my medical charge three institutions, which contain
about fifteen hundred children, teachers, and other employees." Out of
all this experience, he was absolutely convinced that there was no justification for calling New York City "malarious."[16]

Baruch was right, but for the wrong reason. Like many of his contemporaries, he believed that malaria was borne in the noxious air or miasms
arising from decaying organic matter or stagnant pools of water. We now
know that malaria does occur in such settings, but only when transmitted
by mosquitoes bearing the *Plasmodium* parasite. All the same, Baruch
correctly reasoned that the relatively small proportion of actual malaria
sufferers in the city—and the absence of swamps, the proximity of buildings, and the low winter temperatures—made it unlikely that five hundred New Yorkers were dying yearly from malaria.

Baruch portrayed the unfortunate psychological effects of widespread
misdiagnosis: "Malaria is supposed to be the omnipotent, ubiquitous
enemy lurking in every household. In the luxurious dwellings of the
rich as well as in the humble tenements of the poor, in the crowded

schoolhouses, in the prisons and courtrooms, in the railway stations, in the beautiful parks of this great city, and even in its snow-clad streets . . . malaria is believed to contaminate the air with its noxious elements." In their anxiety to "exorcise this potent yet hidden terror," the people were consumed with a "quinomania" as avid as the bloodletting craze of an earlier era. "In the show-windows of the retail druggist quinine is heralded, as a panacea, in various seductive forms. Pills, capsules, compressed powders, tablets, elixirs, syrups of quinine are regularly sold to the anxious seeker after health without a physician's prescription. A schedule of prices may be seen prominently displayed in the windows of many druggists, offering quinine pills as the grocer offers eggs."

People in all walks of life were taking quinine as a later generation would take aspirin. Believing that "the reckless diagnosis of malarial fever by many physicians" was to blame for widespread public apprehension, Baruch devoted his second article to differential diagnosis. How could physicians distinguish the real thing? Without knowing anything about the *Plasmodium,* or the fact that its different varieties cause different chill-fever cycles, Baruch settled the question empirically by observing the effect of quinine. Here, too, he was right without knowing precisely why. Quinine is truly specific for malaria: it enters the bloodstream and kills the causative organism. It could have no therapeutic effect on other fevers seen in New York City. Baruch gave a careful clinical description of malaria, particularly of the characteristic early morning remission that affords the best time for giving quinine. "Woe unto the patient if these brief hours of respite glide by unused for treatment. Sad experience has taught me that the morning remission of remittent (true malaria) fever affords at once a pathognomonic symptom and a therapeutic opportunity." [17]

In calling attention to current errors of diagnosis in one of the most widely read medical journals of the day, Baruch's malaria articles made hundreds of physicians aware of his background and experience and of the impressive depth of his reading in the medical literature of the United States, England, and the Continent. In late 1883 and early 1884, he began aiming criticism at the current practice of applying antiseptics during and after normal childbirth. By the time Joseph Lister's antiseptic method at last achieved wide acceptance in America in the mid-1880s, leaders among the profession had already begun seeking a place for it in their own special fields. On Baruch's arrival in New York, such outstanding obstetricians as T. Gaillard Thomas and Fordyce Barker were teaching that normal labor and childbirth should be regarded in the same light as major surgery: that is, they advocated antiseptic applications to the torn membranes of the birth canal.

Baruch had delivered approximately nine hundred babies in South Carolina without using this method. He had encountered only one maternal death from the puerperal fever (septicemia) which advocates of puerperal antisepsis believed would result from the failure to apply antiseptics. Actually, by his extreme caution in keeping his instruments and hands clean, Baruch was approximating the surgical ideal of asepsis. He had no need of harsh chemicals to disinfect what he had never infected. Yet he decided to give the highly recommended methods of puerperal antisepsis a try in his New York practice. Then the difficulties began: "While I formerly had rarely encountered severe febrile processes after labor, I at once found myself favored in this direction. Six cases of severe fever, of undoubted septic origin, occurring from the fifth to the ninth day, rewarded my innovation."[18]

Here, as in the case of malaria, Baruch was unafraid to challenge authority when he found its dictates in conflict with experience. First at a meeting of the New York County Medical Society on December 21, 1883, then as a guest—an outsider—at the New York Academy of Medicine in early January 1884, he spoke out against puerperal antisepsis. On January 5 he wrote a protest for publication in the *New York Medical Journal*.

With a view to prevent the mischief which is likely to be done by the indiscriminate washing of the vagina after labor, among the younger members of the profession, I raise my voice of warning at this juncture. Guided by the justly eminent gentlemen who advocate antiseptic vaginal prophylaxis, every new-fledged obstetrician, in country and town, will rush to the rescue of 'septically *threatened* parturient' women (all), and scorn everyone else who does not pursue this practice as an old fogy. The various therapeutic fashions which have flourished since the beginning of medicine bear witness to the probability of this unhappy result. I plead for a pause of reflection, and would urge upon our leading obstetricians to stem the tide ere it be too late.[19]

On the day that this piece was published, George Shrady's *Medical Record* ran a lead editorial, summarizing Baruch's part in the two medical society discussions and supporting his views.[20] As though fearful of missing his main target, Baruch sent copies to Fordyce Barker, one of the founders and the first president of the American Gynecological Society and president of the New York Academy of Medicine, whom Baruch considered the "Coryphaeus" of puerperal antisepsis in America. Barker's reply left little to be desired. Far from being displeased that Baruch had challenged his view, Barker confessed to having "read with great interest and warm approval your very able papers." There was to be another academy meeting on the subject, and Barker wanted Baruch to be there: "You have anticipated several points which I had intended to make, and as there are many of our Fellows who wish to take part in the discussion and as [T. Gaillard] Thomas must have time to reply at the close, I shall be compelled to condense my ideas as closely as possible."[21]

Barker wanted to meet Baruch. He asked (how welcome it must have been to the forty-three-year-old Baruch), "Why have you not joined the Academy?" Baruch did not join at once, but he did attend the meeting to debate his views with an impressive group: William Thompson Lusk, author of an early English textbook explaining the phenomena of gestation and labor in accord with physiological laws; Paul Fortunatus Mundé, formerly Barker's assistant surgeon at the Woman's Hospital and an outstanding gynecologist in his own right; and James Bradbridge Hunter, assistant surgeon to T. Gaillard Thomas and editor of the *New York Medical Journal,* which had published Baruch's first protest against puerperal antisepsis.[22]

Whether or not Baruch won the battle at the academy, he apparently did not yet believe he had won the war. On February 16 he summarized his campaign in the *Medical Record:* "Thus far I find myself feebly supported in the societies and entirely unsupported in the public prints"—with the exception of the *Medical Record* editorial of January 5. On February 11 Barker wrote Baruch of his hope that the controversy, in addition to its scientific and practical value, might prove that "the rancor and animosity which unfortunately characterizes most scientific discussions" was unnecessary and that such differences could be settled "sharply, keenly and even with good humoured sarcasm, but with kindness and courtesy."[23]

T. Gaillard Thomas eventually withdrew his approval of puerperal antisepsis, but still Baruch campaigned. In March he published the results of a survey of maternity hospitals in Paris, Prague, Berlin, Parma, Glasgow, Copenhagen, and New York. The relative incidence of puerperal fever was markedly higher where antiseptic measures were applied routinely after birth than where precautions were limited to asepsis. It was a nice statistical case for his theory that obstetricians would do better to brush their fingernails with an antiseptic solution than to disturb the new mother for days after birth with applications of strong chemicals.[24]

Eventually Baruch's view became dominant (and asepsis became much easier with William S. Halsted's introduction of rubber gloves at the turn of the century). Baruch took great pride in "this sudden change of front of the foremost teacher in obstetrics" and the resultant "saving of distress and of life." He received due credit, too. From Texas a doctor wrote to assure him "that the great body of the most eminent physicians in this state adhere to your views and are strict followers of the principles which you have so plainly laid down."[25]

After several years in New York, Baruch found his work bringing practical rewards. When the Montefiore Home for Chronic Invalids opened on October 26, 1884, in honor of the one hundredth birthday of the indestructible philanthropist Sir Moses Montefiore, Baruch was on the staff as attending physician. In April 1885 he was elected chief of the Montefiore staff.[26] Twice in the first four months of 1885 he received special invitations to attend meetings of the Practitioners' Society of New York, an exclusive group founded by several doctors including George Shrady of the *Medical Record*. In 1885 the society consisted of nineteen members, including many of the finest medical minds of the day. Charles Loomis Dana, the neurologist who was Baruch's colleague in the Medical Polyclinic of the North-Eastern Dispensary, invited him to the February meeting, where, instead of the regular paper, there was to be a discussion of fevers characterized by skin eruption. In April he was asked to participate in the society's discussion of the complications and sequelae of scarlet fever. Baruch treasured these invitations among his papers, but apparently he did not join the Practitioners' Society.

As though stimulated rather than satisfied by success, Baruch began to drive himself harder than ever. In the fall of 1884, he published an article about the use of tracheotomy in croup and diphtheria, a practice well-known for several decades, yet still feared or abhorred by many. He drew much of the material for his article from his large practical experience among children at the North-Eastern Dispensary, but he also showed familiarity with the *Index-Catalogue of the Surgeon-General's Library*, just then coming out in serial fashion.[27] In April 1885, he leaped off again to obstetrics, publishing "The Management of the Third Stage of Labor" in the *American Journal of Obstetrics*, a periodical edited by a member of the Practitioners' Society. In June and July his two-part article on the cervical follicles appeared in the *New York Medical Journal*, and in July he published a final word on puerperal antisepsis, still occasionally advocated in normal childbirth despite the attention he had called to its dangers.[28]

After Baruch became a Fellow of the New York Academy of Medicine on November 5, 1885, his publication rate slowed somewhat.[29] In early 1886, in an article for the *Medical Record*, he challenged the theory that Lister's carbolic acid applications prevented infection by acting as "a moderate stimulus to the cut surfaces." On the contrary, Baruch believed Lister's method worked by making it possible to leave wounded tissues at rest, without interference from man or microbe. Recalling the anguish of

Civil War amputees during continual cleansing and dressing of their wounds, he said, "I rejoice that I have lived to see this happy era in surgery."[30]

A year later, writing about methods to lower temperature in typhoid fever, Baruch took special pains to condemn the widely discussed cold-bath technique proposed by Ernest Brand, a German clinician.[31] He would one day be persuaded to reverse this judgment, just as he had persuaded T. Gaillard Thomas and Fordyce Barker to recant in the matter of puerperal antisepsis.

In the autumn of 1887, identifying himself as visiting physician to the New York Juvenile Asylum and to the Manhattan (now Knickerbocker) Hospital, Baruch wrote a paper about hysteria, a psychoneurosis sometimes marked by the conversion of unconscious conflicts into physical symptoms. This article differs from most of his writings in two respects: it is concerned solely with mental illness, and he prepared it with a collaborator. Dr. Edward S. Peck was a Vermonter whose interest in ophthalmology had taken him to England and the Continent in the 1870s, when the study of hysteria occupied some of Europe's best medical minds. Even as the *Medical Record* published the Baruch-Peck article, Sigmund Freud was embarking on an English translation of Hippolyte Bernheim's *Hypnotismus, Suggestion und Psychotherapie,* a work primarily concerned with the treatment of hysteria.[32]

Baruch and Peck were prompted to write their article by the case of a man with hysterical blindness. In the 1860s, they said, physicians had believed that hysteria was linked with the uterus and therefore peculiar to females, but the two intervening decades had marked a change: "We know today that hysteria has no more connection with the uterus than with any other organ, not even with the now fashionable ovary." The two authors applauded this development, or perhaps it would be more accurate to say that Baruch applauded it, for at this point in the article, the editorial "we" gives way to first-person singular, and the tone becomes that of the older man: "Far be it from me to deny that we may frequently discover in utero-ovarian diseases sources of ill-health from which originate severe hysterical manifestations. But I desire to emphasize the point, that too much attention has been, and is still, directed by medical men to the sexual organs of women as well as of men, and that the introspection incident to this attention has aggravated the sufferings of our patients and diminished the effect of our therapeutic measures." Baruch deplored the approach illustrated by J. Marion Sims, who in 1882 called Baruch to see a young woman whose hysteria Sims had treated by a surgical section of the cervix. Although Baruch conceded that physical disturbances should be treated *"when they are clearly productive of health depreciation,"* he believed that hysteria was "a functional disease of the general nervous system, which has its origin in psychical influences connected or unconnected with physical disturbances." Baruch and Peck succeeded in treating their male victim of hysterical blindness by the simple practice of suggestion. During consultation, in voices just loud enough to permit him to "overhear" them, they repeatedly spoke of his certain recovery. After six days of these "doses of cheer," as Baruch called them, the patient recovered his vision.[33]

In December 1887, again in the *Medical Record,* Baruch turned to the problem of diphtheria. In less than a decade Emil von Behring and Shibasaburo Kitasato would produce an antitoxin to be made available on a grand scale. In the meantime, physicians differed as to the best method of treating diphtheria: "The skeptic stands arrayed versus the expectant, the conservative against the sanguine, therapeutist." Baruch himself was "uncompromisingly opposed to the plan of idly watching this fell destroyer, or meeting him with half-hearted resistance." Once the disciple of expectancy in almost every disease, he had been convinced of diphtheria's destructive power by several virulent cases. "The modern physician does not stand resigned in the presence of these diseases. It is true that he no longer seeks for specifics to cure them; but he adopts such therapeutic measures as are rationally indicated to diminish the dangers of the disease and to ameliorate the sufferings of the patient." Although long an advocate of tracheotomy, he was concerned to prevent the disease from progressing to the point at which such drastic surgical intervention became necessary. Claiming support from Robert Koch and others, he asserted that internal doses of turpentine would retard the multiplication of the disease-causing organisms without harming the patient. The idea smacks of horse-doctoring; yet Baruch had been persuaded to try it by "favorable reports in the German medical journals," *Virchow's Archiv* in particular. In recommending it to his non-German-reading confreres, he gave several case histories of his own to illustrate its efficacy.[34]

For all of Baruch's hard work, one of his greatest advancements came through sheer chance. It started in Christmas week of 1887, when friends came up from Charlotte, North Carolina, for a visit. Samuel Wittkowsky, formerly of Camden, was now a partner in a Charlotte business with Dr. Baruch's brother Herman. On the evening of December 28, the Wittkowskys' nine-year-old son Gerard ate dinner with his parents and the Baruchs, saying nothing to them of his stomachache. He spent a miserable night, vomiting and suffering severe abdominal pain, which his mother interpreted as another of his frequent attacks of acute indigestion.

The next morning Dr. Baruch found Gerard's pulse racing at 120 and his temperature at 102.4. Baruch made a diagnosis of "perityphlitis," the term then used for an inflammation of the peritoneum around that portion of the large intestine known as the cecum. For half a century, the word *perityphlitis* had obscured the true nature of such cases by drawing attention to the entire cecum rather than to the appendix. Only the year before, Reginald Fitz of Harvard had clarified the pathology of so-called perityphlitis, correctly placing the blame on the appendix.[35] Baruch apparently did not yet know of Fitz's work. Giving Mrs. Wittkowsky an unfavorable prognosis, he withheld food for the next twenty-four hours, administered poultices to Gerard's abdomen, and gave him a turpentine enema. The next morning, free of pain and vomiting, Gerard still had a fast pulse, a high temperature, and decided tenderness in the lower right abdomen. Baruch thought he saw signs of impending collapse.[36]

He was frightened, and for good reason. This illness was beginning to resemble that of five other patients he had seen in the preceding six years. In each case he had called in as medical consultant a leading physician and diagnostician. He had treated all six patients according to the best medical knowledge of the day: with leeches, ice bags, poultices, and opiates. One man of fifty-two died of diffuse peritonitis within two days. A boy of eleven died the same terrible death after five days. In March 1884 came the worst case of all: a young boy, a patient for only six hours, died while Baruch and Abraham Jacobi, the pioneer of American pediatrics, were consulting in the next room.

Medicine was clearly unable to save the victims of perityphlitis so Baruch decided to give surgery a try. With the Wittkowskys' consent, he called in his former mentor, Henry Burton Sands. Now in the last year of his life and suffering the effects of a stroke, Sands was still considered by many as the leading surgeon in New York City.[37] He met Baruch at noon, examined Gerard, and made a diagnosis of "acute septic peritonitis, caused by perforation of the vermiform appendix." The prognosis was grave: Sands advised immediate resort to an extensive exploratory abdominal incision called laparotomy.

Baruch replied that the family would require further counsel before consenting to so serious an operation. While Sands waited and the necessary preparations were made for surgery, Baruch began a nightmarish race to find consultants. From the fashionable boardinghouse at 14 East Forty-second Street where the Wittowskys were staying, he drove to 191 Lexington Avenue, only to find that the surgeon he sought was not in.

He then hurried on to the Thirty-third Street office of Dr. William Tillinghast Bull, a private pupil of Sands and a surgeon especially well-known for his work with intestinal lesions.[38] Bull came along at once.

Although there was some discussion among the three doctors as to the best type of incision to use, they all agreed on the need for surgery and at last reached a compromise. At 4:00 P.M., about forty-eight hours after the onset of illness, Sands operated under ether anesthesia. The incision revealed peritonitis, not yet widespread but with no sign of adhesions forming to seal it off. Within the appendix, Sands found the source of the inflammation: two fecal concretions, which he picked out with forceps. Because the appendix was not gangrenous, he merely trimmed the edges of the perforation and closed it with silk sutures. He then washed the inflamed intestines with warm water, rinsed them with a dilute antiseptic solution, and closed the upper incision with silver sutures. The rest of the opening he dusted with idoform and packed with idoform gauze.

Within an hour, Gerard's temperature fell to 98.5. In a few hours more, his pulse and temperature were almost normal. From that time on his convalescence progressed without serious interruption. On February 8, 1888, Sands presented his account of the case to the New York Surgical Society. He also presented the patient, fully recovered and about to return to his North Carolina home. Sands attributed a part of the success to Dr. Baruch, "a gentleman who appreciated the necessity of obtaining surgical advice without delay." It was, Sands thought, the first case on record in which "a perforative peritonitis, due to disease of the appendix, has been diagnosticated, and treated by laparotomy with a favorable result."[39]

Four years later, John Allen Wyeth would describe Gerard's operation in the *International Journal of Surgery* because of its "historic value" and because "it was the first case in which the operation had been done after a diagnosis of perforation of the appendix."[40] This case was eventually to be the source of a priority controversy, but the dispute over Baruch's contribution to the history of appendectomy lay in the future. For the present, it was enough that Gerard lived. So much the better if his remarkable recovery was earning attention from the profession at large.

Almost before Baruch had time to grasp the significance of Gerard's operation, he found himself swept into the heart of a second widely publicized incident. Because this one involved the musical prodigy, pianist Josef Casimir Hofmann, it immediately drew public attention. In the fall of 1887 the eleven-year-old Josef came with his parents to tour American concert stages under a contract with a managerial firm headed by Henry Abbey, a brilliant but erratic impresario whose gambles often

cost him fortunes. Josef promised to be one of Abbey's better investments. Born to two professional musicians in 1876 in Podgorze, Poland,
Josef was only seven when he attracted the attention of Anton Rubinstein. By the age of ten he was playing concerts all over Europe, ac-
claimed as the greatest child pianist since Mozart.[41]

American audiences were equally enthusiastic. "Little Josef" seemed to
thrive on his rigorous existence, practicing three hours a day, playing
long concerts, improvising on themes given him by the audience, conducting the orchestra, and performing some of the most difficult pieces
in the repertory in addition to his own compositions. Abbey could have
attracted unlimited audiences, with receipts between $2,000 and $3,000
per performance, if he had not been restrained by a license limiting Josef
to no more than four concerts weekly in New York City. Since Abbey
had contracted to pay the Hofmanns only $250 per concert plus expenses,
it is not surprising that Josef soon found himself supplementing his restricted New York schedule with concerts on alternate days in Boston,
Philadelphia, and Washington. Nor is it surprising that Abbey soon col-
lided with the Society for the Prevention of Cruelty to Children, recently
risen to prominence under the leadership of Commodore Elbridge T.
Gerry.[42]

In late January, after two months in which Josef played about half of
the eighty concerts called for in his contract, Gerry called Mayor Abram
Hewitt's attention to the boy's out-of-town performances. Gerry had
heard rumors that Josef looked tired and that he had been seen to cry
often and easily. Hewitt consented to order Abbey to present Josef for an
examination by several medical experts. The appointed date was Thurs-
day, February 2, during a week when Josef played in Boston on Monday,
New Haven on Tuesday, and New York on Wednesday. Scenting a story,
the New York newspapers moved in. On January 29 the *Herald* scoffed at
Gerry, insisting that Josef had as much fun playing concerts as other boys
did marbles. The same day a *Tribune* reporter found Josef looking well,
an impression Josef's father seemed anxious to confirm. A man from the
Times heard Josef's cheery denials of illness but noted ominously that his
eyes were darkly circled, his face pale.

The physicians chosen to perform in what the *Times* called the
"Mayor's medical matinee" were four of New York's best: Lewis A.
Sayre, resident physician of New York City under four successive mayors
and so-called "father of American orthopedic surgery"; Allan McLane
Hamilton, a specialist in nervous diseases; Edward Gamaliel Janeway, one
of the foremost clinical teachers and consultants of his generation; and
Joseph Decatur Bryant, health commissioner and one of the country's

leading surgeons.[43] These four concluded that, although Josef's health was sound, he should give only four concerts weekly, with free days in between. Abbey consented.

Casimir Hofmann may have been relieved to learn that his son was well, but he was distracted by the news Gerry is said to have given him during the examination; news that an anonymous music lover had offered to provide $50,000 for Josef's future education, on condition that he be withdrawn from the stage at once. Hofmann reportedly responded that it would take at least $100,000. Fine and happy at the beginning of the examination, Josef was reduced to tears after being stripped and examined before Mayor Hewitt, Manager Abbey and his three assistants, Commodore Gerry, and Mr. Hofmann.[44] Nonetheless, he went on to play before ever larger and more sympathetic audiences.

Then, suddenly and unexpectedly, the tour halted. On Sunday morning, February 19, following an especially brilliant performance by Josef at the Metropolitan the previous night, Mr. Hofmann sent Abbey a note terminating their contract. He was withdrawing Josef from the stage on advice of "one of the first doctors." Abbey was stunned. When he learned the identity of the physician recommended to the Hofmanns by a mutual friend, he was doubly stunned. Who, pray tell, was Dr. Simon Baruch? Abbey promptly had the Hofmanns' baggage attached and attempted to freeze their bank assets. Considering the money at stake, roundly estimated at $57,000 in the breach-of-contract suit he threatened, Abbey felt reluctant to accept the word of Hofmann's "own physician," a man whose reputation was unknown to him.[45]

Baruch later wrote this about the affair:

The manager, recognizing the great financial loss resulting from the withdrawal, "moved heaven and earth" to prevent it. His agents importuned me to modify my orders and the musical people beset me with prayers and threats to save his "genius." The newspapers were enlisted in this agitation and every night a large number of reporters awaited my return from the patient to obtain information on his condition. A prominent medical journal had espoused the cause of the manager, and a commission, consisting of an eminent neurologist, prominent physiologist, and a surgeon convened with my consent at Dr. Sayre's office to discuss the feasibility of my modifying the interdiction.[46]

Two of these men, Lewis Sayre and Allan McLane Hamilton, had participated in the original "Mayor's medical matinee" on February 2. The "physiologist" was Austin Flint, Sr., author of several medical textbooks and one of New York's most noted teachers and practitioners—with a strong "physiological" bent based on his studies in Germany, where natural remedies had attracted his interest.[47] As Baruch recalled the incident (and as medical ethics would dictate), the others saw Josef with Baruch's consent; but according to the *Tribune* of February 23, it was the others who, for "professional and business reasons," invited Dr. Baruch to join them.

The four met at eight in the evening on Monday, February 20. They examined Josef and agreed on his symptoms: his temperature was a bit high and his pulse irregular. All four agreed, too, that, despite certain other unspecified "irregularities," he was not suffering from any organic disease. There the great minds ceased to meet. The conclusion Baruch drew from these facts was irreconcilable with that of his colleagues: they thought that a slight reduction in work would take care of the trouble; Baruch believed Josef must give up playing altogether, at least for a time, or risk a complete breakdown. After hours of debate, Sayre, Hamilton, and Flint stood by their prognosis. Baruch left the meeting alone at 2:30 in the morning.

All four physicians refused to talk to reporters before meeting the next night to write a carefully worded report. When they finished at last, long after midnight on Tuesday, the report remained a secret among the doctors, the manager, and the Hofmanns. To an anxious press, awaited in turn by an anxious public, Abbey's attorney at last released what purported to be a summary of the physicians' findings. At best an inadequate statement of a complex medical problem, it became still less adequate in the frenetic rush of some papers to press. No organic disease became no disease at all, and Baruch was said to have agreed that Josef might continue playing concerts.[48]

To clarify his position, Baruch released a minority report which appeared in the *Times* and almost every other New York newspaper on February 23. "Only the reflection that I should be culpable in the highest degree should I permit this child's health to be jeopardized overcomes my repugnance to this public dissent from my worthy and eminent colleagues." Sayre, Hamilton, and Flint were indeed worthy and eminent, and Baruch's position was difficult. He explained his belief that Josef was overworked; that he was suffering from "nervous exhaustion"; that he should play no concerts for three weeks and then only when he wanted to; that he must have complete rest from the piano and an opportunity to recover from "the legitimate effects of the enormous mental strain imposed on him by an almost continuous appearance in concerts since May 17, 1887."[49]

"L'affaire Hofmann" was a boon to newspaper sales. "Hofmann's Finale," screamed *New York Journal* headlines on February 22: "Little Josef Plays No More and Doting Ladies Weep." "Never to hear him till he's a horrid man with a mustache. Oh, how cruel," said a disappointed fan. The disagreement among the doctors made the controversy all the more readable. "Josef's Big, Weak Arm" made headlines in the *Morning Journal:* "It knocks out three of Mr. Abbey's physicians; they meet and make a favorable report, but Dr. Baruch declines to compromise." The *Daily Tribune* of February 24 took a serious view: "The difference of opinion between these distinguished physicians and Dr. Baruch, who leans to the Hofmann view of the case, is a legitimate subject for difference of opinion." The *Star* added its conviction that "the side to err on, if there be any error, is that of being overcareful, if anything, of the boy's health. The musical world can do without concerts from Josef Hofmann for a time, but it would be sorry to know that it must do without him altogether, and that might easily be the result of too much forcing."[50]

To describe his own feelings amid the uproar, Josef could have found no better text than the opening lines of Pope's "Epistle to Dr. Arbuthnot":

> Shut, shut the door, good, John! fatigued, I said,
> Tie up the knocker, say I'm sick, I'm dead.

He came close to a paraphrase in asking a reporter from the *World* to "tell Mr. Abbey he must please excuse me from playing as I died this morning."[51] In the *World* of February 24 Baruch said, "I believe the boy is sick; that work makes him sick, and it is a truth of medicine that you cannot treat a disease without removing the cause. Hence, I say, stop his work."

Popular sympathy did not need bolstering. It had grown day by day, stimulated by headlines and interviews and editorials. On the other hand, Baruch's dissent from his colleagues was a continuing source of embarrassment to him. It only increased with Mayor Hewitt's statement (the inspiration for an editorial in the *Sun*) that someone had done a "tremendous amount of lying" somewhere along the way.[52] Equally awkward was Abbey's statement in the *Star* of February 24 that "no sensible person expects me, after the time and money I have spent on young Hofmann, to accept the statement made by a physician whom I do not know to the effect that the boy's health has broken down, when the most eminent physicians in the city declare that he is in perfect health." When Abbey called the whole thing "a put up job," the senior Hofmann was not as helpful as Baruch might have wished: "I do not care what other physicians say," he replied weakly. "The opinion of my own physician is good enough for me."

Although no paper, either in article or editorial, directly accused Baruch of implication in the "Hofmann conspiracy," he needed support for his position. According to records he kept while seeing Josef (every day but two between February 17 and March 11), Josef complained of "frightful dreams especially 'when lying on his heart'": dreams that the moon took on odd shapes, that the sun fell upon the earth. Baruch never mentioned these in the press, but the *Evening Sun* of February 24 published a lengthy illustrated analysis, apparently written by a reporter, of the sketches to which Josef turned his attention when he first stopped playing. In one of them a great snake with forked, quivering tongue pursues a frightened man. Said the reporter-analyst, "If Josef Hofmann had never been terror stricken himself, his hand could not have guided the pencil in making that face." In another sketch, Josef depicted himself trying to sleep in a Pullman car under the threatening gaze of "an able-bodied ghoul who came in the shape of a nightmare to the tired boy." Small black devils and drunken Indians were favorite subjects. Stranger still, the reporter noted, Josef drew the hands of them all with one or more fingers missing.

Whatever such behavior might mean to post-Freudian observers, it puzzled alienists of Hofmann's day. Allan McLane Hamilton discounted it altogether.[53] For fear of causing Josef more embarrassment than he had already suffered during the incessant peering of press and public, Baruch could not mention what was probably the most significant symptom of all. The physician's casebook alone carried the full story. Between the "Mayor's medical matinee" and the day, two weeks later, when the Hofmanns brought Josef to Dr. Baruch, the boy began to suffer from urinary incontinence. When he played the piano, either during concerts or for himself or his friends, he suffered an involuntary loss of bladder control. This was the clearest danger signal of all. Yet, as Baruch wrote in his history of the case, "This 'irregularity' was omitted from the published report for obvious reasons."[54] Though Drs. Sayre, Hamilton, and Flint knew of it, they apparently considered it unimportant.

In search of support for his position, Baruch turned to his friend, George Shrady, editor of the *Medical Record*. On Saturday, February 25, Shrady examined Josef. That same day he published an editorial titled "The Overworked Boy Pianist." With an admirable blend of frankness and discretion, Shrady stated the full facts of the case in the only proper place: a professional journal available to the New York physicians who previously had to judge Baruch's action in the dim light of newspaper accounts. Shrady concluded that "the advice of the gentleman having charge of the case—to give the little hard-worked boy complete rest—is eminently sound. With ordinary boys of his age who are overtasked at school, there would be no question as to the policy to be pursued, but with the boy pianist, whose performances are worth so much money, it appears to be an altogether different matter."[55] Baruch was grateful to Shrady for "setting forth the true status of this matter so clearly that all agitation ceased." As he later put it, "the *Record* aided materially in saving to art a child, who was at that time regarded as a second Mozart."[56]

There were a few last sour comments on the case. On February 26, the *World* ran a cartoon showing "the overworked prodigy" seated at the piano, looking rested, well-fed, and well-dressed. Grouped around his picture were photographs of haggard, malnourished child laborers clad in filthy rags: baby nurses, tenement tobacco strippers, "The Newsboy All Day and Night," and coal sorters at work in the mines. The caption read: "A Few Studies from Nature for Philanthropists to Contemplate." But public opinion was in overwhelming sympathy with Josef's temporary retirement, however suspect his father's motives. Manager Abbey knew that he could gain nothing but a reputation for villainy by refusing to give up the contract without a court fight.

While Abbey and Hofmann worked out their financial difficulties, Josef stayed in the Baruch home at 47 East Sixtieth Street. He soon made friends with the four boys (the youngest of them only a little older than himself), sliding down the banisters just as noisily as the others. The long practice sessions of former times were forbidden, and he received only rare permission to touch the piano. To fill the suddenly empty hours, he often went along on calls in Dr. Baruch's buggy. Once, while they were driving up Fifth Avenue, the doctor gave in to Josef's teasing to hold the reins. The eleven-year-old proved a dangerous chauffeur. "He wanted to go fast, and he urged the horse to fly. Before I knew what he was about he was almost in a smash with another carriage." When Dr. Baruch reprimanded him, Josef said he had only wanted "to see how close I could come."[57]

In late March, Josef returned to Europe with his parents, to study under Anton Rubinstein and Moritz Moszkowski in preparation for concert work that would mark him as one of the rare artists who fulfill the promise of precocity. Reviewing events of 1887 and early 1888, Baruch had much to ponder. For twenty-five years he had devoted himself to medicine. Yet it seemed that mere chance—an inflamed appendix in the child of a friend from Camden and the near breakdown of a prodigy from his native land—had suddenly brought him closer to his goals than he had ever been before.

The Apostle of Cleanliness   13

Midway through the elegant 1880s, Baruch's rising fortunes enabled him to summer with his family in the resort town of Long Branch, New Jersey, a sea-blown shorefront settlement blessed with an excellent beach and a thirty-five-foot bluff celebrated by Winslow Homer. Later surpassed in size and popularity by Asbury Park to the south, Long Branch in the time of President Ulysses S. Grant was the rollicking summer capital of the nation, gambling and racing mecca of the country's newest rich. When the Baruchs became summer residents of Long Branch, the lots along the broad promenade called Ocean Avenue were rapidly filling with "cottages," huge thirty-room buildings laden with turrets, cupolas, balconies, and latticework. Although its rambling hotels and muddy streets lacked the solidity and refinement of Saratoga or Newport, Long Branch in the 1870s became more popular than either; popular, but not exclusive: "Brass bands on the lawns of hotels, tents where pop and gingerbread were sold, shooting galleries, and hundreds of red, white and blue flags and pennons waving from the hotel, carriages swirling in the dust along Ocean Avenue—such a scene along the ocean front surely bespoke Broadway rather than Fifth Avenue. It was a brave and showy effort in the direction of Newport that never quite managed to lose sight of Coney Island."[1]

Long Branch was not the equal of Saratoga or Newport, but it was closer to New York City than either of them, and that is probably why Baruch chose it. Though *Harper's* exaggerated the proximity of the two cities in describing Long Branch as "the great marine suburb of the great metropolis," it was possible after 1882 to travel between them without much trouble. Once the Pennsylvania Railroad completed its final unit of shoreline, Long Branch became the resort best situated to keep Baruch in touch with the "great intellectual workshop" of New York City.[2]

Not content to be idle even in the laziest months of the year, Baruch carried on a summer practice at the West End Hotel. A fittingly progressive residence for a progressive physician, the West End in 1880 set up direct telegraph service with the New York Stock Exchange. Two years later, when the New York and New Jersey Telephone Company inaugurated service in the West End section of Long Branch, the hotel was one of the original subscribers. By 1884 long distance service made it possible for anyone with "lusty lungs and good vocal chords" to talk directly to New York City and Philadelphia.[3]

Baruch made good use of the new medium, especially in appendicitis cases, which often seemed to flare up at night, too late for a New York surgeon to catch the last regular train out from the city. After watching several victims of appendicitis die under medical treatment and seeing Gerard Wittkowsky's remarkable recovery after surgery in 1887, Baruch became such a staunch advocate of surgery in appendicitis that William Tillinghast Bull twitted him with having "a penchant for seeing appendices removed." Although he occasionally sounded a false alarm via long distance, the surgeons he brought roaring out on special engines from the city often arrived just in time to prevent the fatal effects of perforation.[4]

Apart from the difficulty of finding surgeons to perform emergency operations, Baruch's practice at the shore differed little from his city work—with the notable exception of the all-pervading cult of the sea. Long Branch had its devotees of parties and flirtations, gambling casinos and promenades, but it was the air and the water, not the social whirl, that drew growing numbers of city dwellers who poured off trains and boats for a Sunday at the shore. As a Long Branch citizen with social aspirations, Baruch might deplore the area's growing reputation as a weekend watering place and recreation area for the rising middle class; as a physician, he could only rejoice that so many people could escape from the steaming city into a world of bathing and beaches.[5]

For the rich and near-rich, the escape was hardly a necessity, even though their city apartments were, in Baruch's words, no better than "gilded tenements."[6] Those who lived in the real tenements had no exit. The average tenement family was crowded with all its belongings and six or eight boarders into three rooms of a row house. Beds, bedding, and clothing, often dirty and alive with vermin, filled two inner rooms relieved by neither light nor air. If the third room was on the front or back of the building and had a window to the outside, it served as kitchen, dining room, sitting room, workroom, and laundry room for the entire family—and as a bedroom for boarders, who helped out with the rent in exchange for the privilege of sleeping on the floor. Always heavy with sewer gas, cooking odors, and thick kerosene fumes, the atmosphere in these cramped surroundings became stifling in the summer heat.

During the sweltering days of July and August, the absence of bathrooms seemed even worse than the lack of light, air, and privacy. For the people living on a single floor, whether twelve or fifty in number, the usual source of water was a faucet in the dark hallway. Even for a sponge bath, the tenement dweller had to carry water from the garbage-laden hall sink to the stove, heat it, bathe in a washtub or dishpan in crowded quarters, and return the dirty water to the hall. At such a price, not even the dustiest, sweatiest workers—the coal heavers, ragpickers, scow trimmers, or longshoremen—could be expected to treat themselves to an "all-over" more often than once a week.[7]

Over one million New Yorkers lived under such conditions. They had a mortality rate nearly twice as high as the nontenement population of the city, and they died principally of diseases fostered by poverty, ignorance, slums, and filth. The great killers were pulmonary tuberculosis, bacillary dysentery, and typhoid fever. Largely because of diarrheal diseases of infancy and infectious diseases of childhood (especially scarlet fever, diphtheria, and lobar pneumonia), 65 percent of all tenement house children died before their fifth year. When it became clear, especially in the decade after 1880, that living conditions fostered this mass mortality, New York's growing civic conscience responded with "model" tenement projects and with legislation setting minimal requirements for tenement construction. Both measures failed to effect rapid change. The ordinary tenement paid a higher profit than other dwellings, even those in the most desirable part of the city, and it threatened to perpetuate itself as long as there were people to inhabit it.[8]

From his first service as a dispensary physician on the squalid East Side during the winter of 1865–66, Baruch had been concerned about the people of the tenements. In the summer of 1889, he set out to determine exactly what bathing facilities were available to those who had none at home. He learned that in 1870, faced with a huge and growing bathless population, the city had made a "feeble step" to provide the poor with means to bathe and cool themselves during the summer by setting up fifteen floating baths in various rivers and harbors, especially in the North and East rivers, as near as possible to the most crowded districts. Open throughout the warm weather, these baths accommodated women on Monday, Wednesday, and Friday and men at all other times. Bathers were limited to twenty minutes in the water. When the baths were crowded with working people during the early and late hours, children were excluded. During one summer alone, more than two and a half million water-starved New Yorkers availed themselves of the floating baths, disregarding the filthy water in which they were anchored. In 1872 the Association for Improving the Condition of the Poor (AICP) had built a pay bath in Mott Street, offering a less repulsive alternative to bathing off the shores of Manhattan (which Baruch described as "a body of land surrounded by sewage"). Observing that only the strong and vigorous could enjoy floating baths; that they were open only three months in the year; and that bathing suits and the condition of the water prevented thorough washing, Baruch decided that they were hopelessly inadequate for maintaining personal cleanliness.[9]

Many European cities had met the problem of large tenement populations by building indoor public baths that operated year-round. Similar proposals had been offered for New York, notably in a series of articles in the *New York World*. But it would take more than newspaper articles to bring the baths into being. It would take someone with sufficient single-mindedness and drive to withstand prolonged disappointment and discouragement. Baruch launched his crusade to help the great unwashed without realizing that he had these qualities or that he would need them.

On August 24, 1889, as New York editor of the *Philadelphia* [medical] *Times and Register,* Baruch made his first statement for public baths: "As in modern statesmanship, the great problem is the attainment of 'the greatest good to the greatest number,' so it is the aim of modern medicine to achieve the same end by the prevention rather than the cure of disease." Using historical data to show that the modern world had fallen far behind former ages in standards of personal cleanliness, he urged New York City to construct showers (he called them rain or spray baths) like those used in the German army and in many German cities. He intimated that public baths were necessary to avert class war. All about him, he said, were "unrest and discontent, which are but the muttering of a storm that will sooner or later sweep with devastating fury over our prosperous land." Public baths would prove "that they whom fortune has favored bear a kindly interest in those who are tottering under the heavy burden of poverty and its inevitable train, misery and death."[10]

In this opening plea for baths, Baruch was careful to pay tribute to "the press, that most potent agitator of the rights of the people." He particularly praised the *World* for the "energetic and brilliant initiative" that paper had shown in publishing its recent series of "well-written articles upon this subject." On August 30, six days after his editorial appeared, the *World* published a summary of it, emphasizing the superiority of showers over tubs and the need for such baths in the schools of tenement districts. The *World* also reproduced Baruch's tribute to the press. In the bond thus forged between two agents of reform, the bath cause was to find a potent champion.

In June 1890 Baruch learned that other New Yorkers were working for baths. One of them was John Brisben Walker, a dynamic, adventurous crusader for social justice who owned, edited, and published *Cosmopolitan Magazine*. To Baruch's inquiry Walker replied that he was only one of a group, "somewhat yet in embryo, and largely in the hands of Bishop Potter."[11] Soon afterward, in a paper Baruch gave before the Health Department of the Social Science Association at its annual meeting in Saratoga Springs, he mentioned the need for public baths in New York and the recent efforts of Walker, Bishop Potter, Cornelius Vanderbilt, and others.[12]

With his customary thoroughness, Baruch had commissioned a New York architectural firm to draft rain bath designs for him to show his Social Science Association audience. Referring to the "germ of discontent which is now breeding untold misery for all classes," he suggested that if the anarchist was a "dirty, long-haired individual" (as cartoonists then implied), proponents of baths might "succeed in transforming his destructive bent by encouraging personal cleanliness as the first step." Because the constitution of the Social Science Association, drawn in 1865, contained a specific provision for the study of public baths, Baruch expressed the hope that his presentation might "be the means of arousing your interest in furthering this important movement for civilizing the people by soap and water" so that "one of the objects of your Society will attain realization."[13]

The hint fell short of its mark. When the society did not choose to publish his paper in its transactions, Baruch sought other outlets for his ideas. At the New York Juvenile Asylum at 176th Street and Tenth Avenue, where he was medical attendant to more than a thousand children, he arranged for showers to be substituted for tubs. Sixty-eight overhead sprinklers, spaced twenty inches apart, made it possible to bathe 180 children in an hour with only one-eighth the water formerly required to give tub baths to eighty an hour.[14]

In the late summer and early autumn of 1890, accompanied by his eighteen-year-old son, Bernard, Baruch toured Europe, visiting his parents, studying the use of hydrotherapy, and observing "numerous baths in which persons in moderate circumstances may obtain cleansing for a small sum." He pronounced the Vienna Central-Bad "the most substantial, elegant and complete bath in the world." Hamburg, Magdeburg, Leipzig, Hanover, Cologne, Bremen, Nuremberg, and Dortmund also had public pay baths, but the one he chose as a model for New York was Vienna's "humble *Volksbad* in the *Mondscheingasse*." Situated in a building in the center of the working population, with separate entrances for men and women, the Volksbad had seventy bath cells. For five kreuzer (then about two cents) bathers received a towel, a key to a clothes locker, and an apron or mantle to wear between locker and shower cell. Showers, which were replacing tubs in many German cities and even in some large factories, saved time, water, and space, as well as expense for construction and maintenance.[15]

On his return to America, Baruch immediately tried to promote his bath plans through his position as chairman of the Committee on Hygiene of the powerful Medical Society of the County of New York. In a committee report in October, he recommended that New York build public baths like the Vienna Volksbad in all of its populous tenement districts: convenient, inexpensive, year-round bathing facilities for "the people especially who have literally 'earned their bread by the sweat of their brow.'" It was at this time, just after his travels in Germany, that Baruch moved beyond hygienic considerations and talk of appeasing the restive masses to a constitutional justification for baths. He urged that existing safeguards to life, liberty, and property be extended to include a fourth: "that their health, more precious than all these, be protected." It was a new idea, he said, "whose dawn gives promise of better and brighter days for the poor and lowly, who, owing to their helplessness, should be our special care."[16]

To support his proposal of school baths, Baruch had visited nine public schools in various sections of New York City. The conditions he had discovered were appalling. Overcrowding alone, most severe in the very areas where children had no way to bathe at home, made it hard "to comprehend how teachers and scholars can remain for hours in the polluted air of these rooms and not become ill." (Despite a Board of Education rule that restricted classes to no more than 75 students, Public School 69, on Fifty-fourth Street between Sixth and Seventh avenues, held 188 small children in its two main classrooms.) Most of the classrooms Baruch inspected had neither fresh air nor adequate natural light. Even on bright days it was necessary to use gas lamps, "which, with the poor ventilation, made the atmosphere almost unbearable." Until the city could provide large, light, airy, well-equipped schools, baths would make life more pleasant for teachers and students alike. Crowded together with their wraps in dark, unventilated rooms, on benches too high for their legs, the students would return from the showers refreshed for studies—and perhaps they would bear new habits of cleanliness to homes badly in need of them.[17]

Although Baruch's report again praised J. Brisben Walker and the other "benevolent gentlemen [who] have formed a society for the promotion of public baths," this group soon dropped out of the work.[18] Baruch found a new ally in Cyrus Edson, a member of his committee in the county medical society and chief inspector of the city health department.[19] Baruch's report aroused interest elsewhere, too. In late October 1890, the Executive Committee of the Association for Improving the Condition of the Poor, which had established a pay bath in Mott Street, invited him to present his ideas. Baruch so impressed the AICP that the committee asked him to draw up plans, and several of the members asked the city to provide free water for an association-built bathhouse. When the Board of Managers of the AICP met on December 2, the president, John Paton, announced that a number of charitable organizations had endorsed the project, and the AICP would construct a building to house showers, to be known as the People's Baths.[20]

The next day the *Sun* gave a full account of the proposed "Cheap Baths for the Poor." The *World* thought it "a greatly good and civilized project," warranted by the public's eager use of the floating baths, by the threat of filth-borne disease, and by "those worse effects which befall the character when one reconciles himself to uncleanliness as a natural condition." The *World* urged everyone to contribute toward the estimated cost of $20,000, not only out of unselfishness but because "it is every one's interest that every one should 'wash and be clean.'"[21]

With the press supporting it, the AICP bathwagon seemed to be off to a rolling start. On December 5 Baruch addressed the New York Academy of Medicine's Section on Public Health and Hygiene with a paper called "A Plea for Public Baths, Together with an Inexpensive Method for their Hygienic Utilization." Far longer and more exhaustive than any of his previous statements on baths, this one began with general praise for the "equalization of political rights among all classes" and for those "movements for ameliorating the condition of that portion of the community which is waging an unequal struggle for existence. . . . What are the bathing facilities of our people, taking the city of New York—the imperial city, as we proudly term it—as an example?" The wealthy had one or more bathtubs in their homes. The middle classes, "living in so-called apartments, which are but a higher grade of tenements, have a dark room called a bathroom, to which a water-closet is the invariable accessory, and to resort to which is surely not a pleasing procedure." The poor, "that overwhelming majority of our population, have no bathing facilities whatever."[22]

Other great cities of the world had acted long before: London, Glasgow, Brussels, and a number of German cities had made some provision for public bathing (though not always by methods Baruch considered ideal). If New York was to have bathhouses, Baruch told the academy, they must contain showers, not tubs. He praised the bath designed by Dr. Oscar Lassar, president of the Berlin Society for People's Baths, and exhibited at the Hygienic Exhibition in Berlin in 1883. Writing in 1960, a historian of "the bathroom and the water closet" described the corrugated tin Lassar bath as "about as inviting as a public urinal, but better than nothing at a time when Germany had one public bath per 30,000 inhabitants."[23] Baruch judged it less harshly, observing that ten thousand persons used it during the exhibition, as many as several hundred on some days. Between 1883 and 1890, German garrisons and factories had adopted Lassar's model, which was also used in the public baths of Vienna, Berlin, Weimar, and Frankfurt and the public schools of Göttingen. It was inexpensive to build (6,300 marks or $1,499) and easy to maintain. Baruch did not demand that New York's bathhouses be corrugated tin, but he was specific about other requirements: they must be unpretentious, neat, clean, inviting, easily accessible to the laboring classes, and open "every day and night, so long as people are abroad in the streets."[24]

On December 6, the day after Baruch addressed the academy, the *Herald* hailed his plan and published an exclusive account of the discussion that followed his paper. On the same day, the *Medical Record* described the baths planned by the Association for Improving the Condition of the Poor. In addition to bathing facilities, the proposed building would have "a large reading room, with an open fireplace, and twenty-four large apartments for the bathers." Five cents admission would pay for a towel, a cake of soap, and a shower—plus hot coffee, "which will be given to those who desire it on leaving the bath in winter months." According to the *Record*, the AICP expected to accommodate a thousand bathers daily. For this, "much credit is due to Dr. S. Baruch, of this city, for his earnest agitation of this subject."[25]

Baruch never stopped agitating. On December 20, presumably through the intercession of Cyrus Edson, he presented the case for municipal baths to the New York City Board of Health, whose vice-president, Joseph Decatur Bryant, was surgeon general of New York State. Meanwhile, the AICP Bath Committee located a prospective site at Number 9 Centre Market Place, between Broome and Grand streets, near the famous Tombs Prison. By March the AICP was attacking such fundamentals as water pressure and the angle of shower heads.[26]

Throughout these months of planning, baths continued to receive publicity in the New York newspapers, most of it excellent. The *Sun* of March 31, however, went too far. Alleging that fortunes were "wasted wantonly" every year on new hospitals and dispensaries, the *Sun* called it a "crying shame" that five hundred thousand people were treated annually, free of charge, "and treated for diseases that would never have been contracted but for the want of public baths. If sixty of the sixty-two dispensaries of this city were wiped out of existence, and bathing houses erected in their stead, it would mark an era in our mortality statistics and in the advance of philanthropy." This proposal was not likely to enlist the support of Baruch's medical colleagues, but there was nothing objectionable in the *Sun*'s suggestion that New York's rich provide bathhouses in every dispensary and station house, "with the requirements that every night-lodger should partake of its benefits. We want opportunities and means for transforming some of these grimy Anarchists, and some of these Poles, Russians, and Italians into good Americans; but how can we expect to make patriotic citizens out of individuals to whom so much of their native land still clings, unless methods are provided for ridding them of these foreign reminiscences?" Less than a week after publishing this editorial, the *Sun* carried a "leaked" verbatim copy of Baruch's report to the New York County Medical Society the preceding November. A week later, Baruch gave the *Herald* an interview that ran five full columns.[27]

Like most crusaders, Baruch did not champion causes solely out of altruism, but these plays for the press were extraordinarily blatant manifestations of his ambition. In actuality, he was reacting to his eclipse in the AICP bath project by Colonel William Gaston Hamilton, a grandson of Alexander Hamilton and a retired businessman who was chairman of the Committee on Baths. Baruch had made a great deal of informed and influential propaganda for baths before the AICP entered the picture in late 1890. He had also played an important part in the inner deliberations that led the AICP to build the People's Baths. Yet, after the initial stages of planning, he seemed to be shunted out of the organization's activities, his advice more submitted to than sought.[28]

As soon as Baruch realized that he was being pushed aside by the AICP, even before an open clash with Hamilton, he began to turn his energy to the cause of government-supported baths. In March he inquired of the *Herald* about chances for getting bath legislation. De Francias Folsom, the reporter who answered Baruch, foresaw difficulties:

Gov. Hill will not sign mandatory bills in reference to the city because of his alleged concern for "Home Rule." The bill should authorize the Commissioners of the Sinking Fund to erect a building and equip it for the use of a public bath and then the Commissioners are left to exercise their own will.

Of course this board is very conservative and may resist expenditures of any sort which has [sic] not the requisite backing.

Baruch did not yet have necessary backing, and he doubtless welcomed Folsom's offer of help: "When you get ready for me with your announcement of the public bath scheme, let me know."[29]

The *Sun's* appeal of March 31 to "wealthy philanthropists" brought a letter and a check for $250 from Henry Flegenheimer, a member of the New York Board of Aldermen. When Baruch saw Flegenheimer's letter in the *Sun* on April 1, he wrote to him at once. Flegenheimer replied the next day, promising his full cooperation.

This cheering offer of aldermanic assistance arrived just as Baruch and Hamilton were exchanging the letters that ended Baruch's already faded connection with the AICP and the People's Baths. He now gave Folsom his "announcement of the bath scheme." It appeared in the form of an interview in the *Herald* on Sunday, April 12, under headlines:

Safe Free Baths For All The People

Within a Twelvemonth New York Will Have Accommodations
For All Who Desire To Be Clean and Healthy

No Tubs, But Only Showers Used

Dr. Simon Baruch, Who Is At the Head of This Hygienic
Movement, Tells of His Plans And What He Hopes To Accomplish

The text, when it mentioned the People's Baths at all, emphasized Baruch's role in planning them, neglecting the architects who designed the building actually under construction in favor of those who had drawn Baruch's preliminary design.[30] The article also stated that Mayor Hugh Grant and the Board of Estimate and Apportionment would be requested "within a week" to erect free baths in all crowded parts of the city.

Despite the literature Baruch sent to Mayor Grant before they finally met on April 20, the Tammany-controlled mayor was not interested in the idea of baths.[31] Baruch's collaboration with the press, however, was stirring public interest. A reader of the *Evening Post* wondered if the city should not only build baths but also empower the Board of Health "to compel the people to use these when sanitary conditions require it." (The writer wanted the criminal code amended so that persons convicted of drunkenness, formerly sentenced to ten days of confinement, would instead spend "ten days in the bath-house, with a cold shower everyday, which would effectually sober them up, and at the same time turn them out upon the public again in a cleaner and wiser condition, with a degree of self-respect not obtainable" otherwise.)[32]

Baruch continued to work closely with Alderman Flegenheimer, who agreed to propose that the Board of Aldermen appropriate $2,500 for the construction of a municipal bath under the supervision of a group of prominent citizens. When the aldermen granted the appropriation on May 12, Flegenheimer asked Baruch for a list of interested citizens to place before Mayor Grant.[33] One week later, while Baruch was still trying to round up volunteers, Flegenheimer met with the mayor in what proved to be an unsatisfactory interview: "I conclude from his language that he is not inclined to favor our project." Mayor Grant did not commit himself one way or another. He said he wanted to "await the result of the experiment about to be made [the People's Baths], and intimated that some of the friends of the free bath movement have urged him to take no action for the present."[34]

Immediately after meeting with the mayor, Flegenheimer was anxious to "bring the strongest possible pressure to bear upon him to appoint the Citizens Committee." By the next day, when he received Baruch's list of five names, he had changed his mind, fearing that the mayor would not act on the matter unless pushed by public sentiment. "The press of the city must be aroused to urge the movement and medical and charitable societies ought to be induced to pass resolutions in approval of it."[35]

Baruch had already arranged to publish the paper he had given at the New York Academy of Medicine the preceding December. Ten large journal pages long, forty-five pages in reprint, the article as it appeared in the *Dietetic Gazette* included all that Baruch had said earlier, plus a great deal more. Although he lauded the People's Baths, he emphasized that New York City, "so over-crowded with the poor and needy, is too vast to be left to one benevolent body." Hammering at the government's responsibility for health, Baruch insisted that the city could easily convert ordinary tenement buildings into bathhouses.[36]

While Baruch used his medical editorship of several journals to sustain interest, De Francias Folsom kept the subject alive in the *Herald* and also at City Hall. On May 25 he wrote Baruch that he had seen Mayor Grant and found him anxious to confer with Baruch again before naming a citizens' committee. Baruch was having trouble adding to his list of five volunteers, which Flegenheimer feared would not give the mayor enough choice. Still worse, the alderman said, "Hasty action is necessary as I understand the Mayor is soon to leave on a long vacation."[37]

Baruch fared better at public relations than at recruiting. Although he failed to corral the desired number of citizens, he engineered a strong publicity campaign in late May and early June, using the *Medical Record* and the *Herald* to reach both physicians and the public. Picking up the theme in a lyrical piece headed "Give the People Baths," the *Sun* declared: "It is idle to talk about other reforms until you can get people clean. Soap can wash away more false theories, more blind ways of looking at life, more harsh feelings, than all the reform clubs and missions." The *Sun's* suggestion that "it would almost pay a big soap manufactory to build a bath house as an advertisement"—though it would do credit to Madison Avenue in a later era—went unheeded by the cleanser magnates of the day.[38]

During the summer of 1891, while the mayor was on the predicted long vacation, Baruch ground out more bath propaganda. Under his editorship the June issue of *Gaillard's Medical Journal* published a purported eulogy of the AICP, which was, in reality, a subtle appreciation of Baruch's insufficiently known contribution. The AICP was doing "pioneer work" and deserved "lasting credit," *Gaillard's* said, while asking readers to note that the People's Baths were modeled on those "advocated by [Baruch's] report of the Committee on Hygiene of the County Medical Society last fall." *Gaillard's* also announced that the city authorities had been asked to establish free public winter baths based on the same pattern. "Let the good work go on!"[39]

Following his own editorial urging, Baruch sent literature about the bath campaign and his part in it to people all over the country. The responses showed a gratifying level of interest and an appreciation of his contribution. From Berlin, Professor Oscar Lassar, who had designed the Volksbad showers, wrote of his pleasure "that my ideas have crossed the ocean and found such eloquent interpolation." D. Sulzberger of the Philadelphia Hebrew Education Society asked Baruch how to convert into showers the pool which his society was building when Baruch's letter arrived. The president of the Medical Society of the County of New York said he would be pleased to speak of the work "as one of the advances made during the present year." Edward Fenner, president of the New Orleans Auxiliary Sanitary Association and heir to a name famous in Louisiana medical history, described the bath his group had just completed as "very large, adapted to our peculiar situation. The bath has two swimming pools respectively 70 x 40 and 60 x 40 feet." Beside bathing blacks and whites separately and somewhat unequally, New Orleans used waste water from its public baths to flush drains and sewers that carried away "the liquid filth of premises." Formerly using water pumped from the Mississippi at an annual cost of $10,000 to $12,000, New Orleans now cleansed the city's gutters with used bath water, cheaply obtained from artesian wells.[40]

Despite the interest and admiration expressed in such replies, Baruch was unable to overcome his resentment of the AICP. Invited to attend the grand opening of the People's Baths on August 17, he sent regrets and warm endorsement of the work.[41]

Several of Baruch's colleagues tried to compensate him for his isolation from the AICP at the moment of its triumph. In the September issue of the *Medical News* of Philadelphia, editor George M. Gould portrayed Baruch as the moving spirit behind the AICP's bath work. According to Gould, it was Baruch who "made it possible for a New York working-man or boy to have the best kind of a bath, cold or warm, with pure water, in a private room, with a new cake of soap and a clean towel—'all for five cents, and if the five cents is hard to find, the bath may be had scot-free.'"[42] On September 19 A. N. Bell wrote Baruch that he in-tended to call the AICP bath "the Baruch bath" in editorials in the *Sanitarian* and the *Journal of Balneology and Dietary.* In order to describe Baruch's idea thoroughly and precisely at a forthcoming meeting of the American Public Health Association, Bell asked for an interview. Baruch was more than obliging. Defying raw autumn weather, he personally escorted Bell to the lower precincts of the city for a tour of the People's Baths that embodied Baruch's ideas.[43]

In late October, with Mayor Grant back in town, Baruch once again took up his duties as representative of the people versus City Hall. Henry Flegenheimer had succeeded in wringing another appropriation from the Board of Aldermen, and Baruch wondered how they might best "circumvent" the mayor in putting the $25,000 to immediate use. Flegenheimer urged getting "the strongest and largest possible delegation of citizens together to call on the Mayor as quickly as possible before the election."[44]

Such a delegation should not have been necessary. Both of the new charity-run baths were popular successes. After a slow start, the two-story People's Baths in Centre Market Place had proved itself many times over. At first, the people had been timid. They came around only after a pioneer had passed through the arched doorway into the rooms of light enamel brick, braved a drenching in the all-iron bathroom, and emerged to show that the process was not fatal. A short time later, even the most skeptical were using the baths, to the number of 140 a day, with as many as 1,074 in one memorable twenty-four-hour period. The patrons were Germans, native ("unspecified"), Irish, Italians, and Jews, in that order of frequency. Frowsy men who went in with dejected step came out saying that they felt good—"vera gooda," "wery gut," "domned good." The Bowery boy fresh from the shower declared that he felt "fit fer a scrap." Among the bathers from as far away as Jersey City and Brooklyn was a blind man, who made a regular weekly trip from Jersey City Heights just to take a shower. Similar scenes, with ethnic variations, occurred at the Baron de Hirsch Baths at Henry and Market streets, where German, Polish, and Russian Jews were soon taking seventy thousand baths a year. City Hall could no longer doubt the people's desire for cleanliness.[45]

If further proof were needed, Baruch's idea had support from people all over the country. The American Public Health Association responded with interest and enthusiasm to Dr. Bell's presentation on October 23. Soon afterward rain baths were introduced into several large institutions in the United States and Canada.[46] The press—the *Sun,* the *World,* the *Telegram,* and the *Mail and Express*—espoused the cause fully and warmly.

In the face of so much evidence, even in the preelection crisis of November 1891, City Hall rejected the idea of municipal baths. Perhaps defeat at this time was inevitable. Tammany was at the height of its power, and, as one writer put it, Tammany "had other fish to fry—fish that did not need washing."[47] Perhaps Baruch was foolish to think that he could persuade Tammany Hall, which was not noted for being health-conscious. (Jacob Riis remembered the Tammany-appointed head of the Health Department primarily for his response to a discussion of the work of the great German bacteriologist: "Koch," the health officer said irritably, "who is that man Koch you are talking about?"[48]) The city administration was hopeless. Public baths would have to come through Albany.

The first chance for state action came in the spring of 1892, when an energetic, ministerial-looking Buffalo lawyer named Goodwin Brown, a graduate of Cornell University, took up the cause in the state assembly. Brown's interest in showers had begun when Governor Grover Cleveland appointed him to work on the State Commission on Lunacy. While investigating state institutions for the insane, he was struck with the hazards of tub baths, in which water flowing in from the bottom could be hot though the surface was deceptively cool. Mental patients had been scalded and one or two paretics, bereft of sensation, had been cruelly burned. Noticing an "unwholesome looking bathroom and dirty bath tub" at a county poorhouse for the insane, Brown asked how the attendant managed to bathe all his charges in a limited time with a limited quantity of water. The attendant replied "that he frequently bathed five or six in the same water, but that he always exercised care to bathe those with skin diseases last." On the basis of Brown's findings, the State Commission on Lunacy substituted showers for tubs in all state hospitals for the insane.

From his position on the lunacy commission, Brown had exerted pressure in the assembly for a bill mandating the construction of free public baths in all cities of fifty thousand or over and permitting it in smaller cities and towns. As Baruch could have predicted had he known of Brown's efforts, the governor found the mandatory clause unacceptable. Governor Flower did sign a redrafted bill that merely permitted the expenditure of public funds for baths and hence did not infringe on New York City's right of "home rule." For the same reason, the bill was useless.[49]

Just at this time, as the prospect of free public baths in New York City seemed most remote, the ugly visage of plague gave hope to the cause once more. As yellow fever had aided the public health movement in South Carolina in the late 1870s, so in 1892 the threat of cholera surpassed Baruch's best efforts. Today, when cholera is unknown in the Industrial world, it is difficult to imagine the terror inspired by an impending epidemic. It was quite different in the nineteenth century, not by coincidence both the century of industrialization and urbanization and the century of great epidemics. Time and again between 1800 and 1890 cholera struck the United States, most notably in 1832, 1847, 1866, and 1873. Survivors of these epidemics carried a lasting fear of cholera, whose course, though short, was unforgettable, with vomiting and diarrhea so violent that some of its victims died of prostration and dehydration within a few hours. Through the virulent contagious material expelled by the dying, the disease spread quickly from one victim to the next. Ordinary people acted accordingly: where a contaminated community water supply left only a few fortunate survivors, the few often refused—wisely, if not humanely—to assist the dying or even to bury the dead.[50]

Cholera began to spread again in 1891. In 1892, when it devastated European Russia, Americans began to grow apprehensive. Having suffered so many disappointments in three years of work for public baths, Baruch might have exploited their fears. He knew that it is easy "to enforce lessons of cleanliness" among panic-stricken people, and there was certainly truth in his claim that showers for the masses would reduce the tremendous plague potential of the New York tenements. Yet he did not press the advantage, at least not in the first frenzy that swept America. On the contrary, in an editorial in the *Dietetic and Hygienic Gazette* in September 1892, he attempted to allay apprehension, assuring the public that it was adequately protected by such men as Cyrus Edson, chief of the Sanitary Bureau and Baruch's coeditor on the *Gazette*. Baruch said he had Edson's personal assurance that "our city authorities are wide-awake, and will meet the enemy with all the forces which modern sanitation furnishes."[51]

Only in October, after the scare had abated, did Baruch refer to it as a "blessing in disguise, inasmuch as it has offered an opportunity for attracting the attention of the public to the crying need of affording the poor more abundant opportunities for keeping clean, and of teaching the people that the most virulent disease may be fought off by attention to the minutiae of cleanliness in food, drink and clothing."[52] The same point was made in an article in the *Evening Telegram* on October 31. Under headlines noting the success of the People's Baths, the *Telegram* "wondered" why nothing had been done with the $25,000 appropriation voted for baths the preceding winter and "hoped" that the incoming administration would prove more energetic in complying with the wishes of the Board of Aldermen and the needs of the people. In language very like Baruch's, the *Telegram* warned that "the recent cholera scare which has left as an indelible lesson the imperative need of affording the poor better opportunities for cultivating cleanliness is 'the writing on the wall.'"

The language sounded like Baruch's because it was Baruch's, transmitted by his reporter friend De Francias Folsom, who had left the *Herald* for the *Evening Telegram*. Folsom also arranged for an editorial attacking the subject from a new angle: the city must build baths in order to break down class distinctions, to blur the social extremes connoted by the terms "'daily bath man'" and "'the great unwashed.'" Thanks to the People's Baths, the *Telegram* said, "this line of social demarcation is happily becoming obliterated. The humblest citizen may now be as clean as the millionnaire, and cleaner than, it is to be feared, some millionnaires choose to be."[53]

Bath promoters, with their condescending talk of washing alien soil and alien ideas from anarchists and foreigners, had formerly appealed primarily to the sense of superiority of the more prosperous classes; an appeal to noblesse oblige was the perfect approach for any charitable enterprise. For Baruch's evolving concept of government responsibility for health, however, the argument that baths could help to blur class lines was far more effective. It also promised to enlist the masses in creating the public sentiment Baruch needed to sway elective officials.

This new approach coincided with an upsurge in the spirit of reform. In the first week of November 1892, during the heat of the mayoral campaign in New York, Baruch launched again into what he called "prodding the authorities." He called the *Telegram* article and editorial to the attention of the faithful Alderman Flegenheimer, who passed Baruch's letter on to his former secretary, Otto Kempner, an Austro-Hungarian immigrant and a lawyer, who was an anti-Tammany candidate for the legislature. On November 9, safely elected to a seat in Albany, Kempner wrote Baruch that he was "ready at any time to cooperate with you in furtherance of your scheme of public baths."[54]

Baruch obliged with an editorial for the *Dietetic and Hygienic Gazette* describing the success of the People's Baths. In one year it had given 40,455 baths to men, 7,575 to women, 6,203 to boys, 2,043 to girls, and 4,950 to small children, all in an area measuring only sixty-seven by twenty-one feet. The AICP had charged only five cents and had collected $2,813.80, thus fulfilling Baruch's prophecy that the people *would* bathe, even at a price. Baruch urged the incoming administration to take note.[55]

In late November a New York attorney who was interested in baths advised Baruch that it was "vitally necessary" for him to confer with Mayor-elect Thomas F. Gilroy. The governor would need the approval of Gilroy, a Tammany politician but also a former commissioner of public works closely identified with the floating baths, before signing legislation for New York City. Though Gilroy was not to take office until March, the attorney urged Baruch to meet with him as soon as he could round up an "influential" committee, "formed of doctors and prominent citizens who make matters of charity subjects of study and of practice."[56]

By December 8 Otto Kempner was preparing to introduce bath legislation in the state assembly. His bill provided for the establishment of thirty public baths, one in each district of New York City, and for an office of public bath superintendent. By mid-February the bill had passed a first reading and was referred to the Committee on Affairs of Cities. As it then stood, it provided for a bureau of public baths under the control and supervision of the city Board of Health, but the superintendent was to be a three-year mayoral appointee, at an annual salary of $3,000. He would make regulations for the management and maintenance of the baths and appoint a deputy superintendent at an annual salary of $1,500 and four attendants for each bath at $900. The bill failed to spell out any other administrative aspect of the bath bureau.[57]

Because neither Baruch nor Kempner had previous legislative experience, Baruch should not have been surprised to learn that the bill was inadequate. Health commissioner Joseph Decatur Bryant wrote Baruch that it was "so full of defects, that in case it be not possible to correct them, it should be consigned to the waste paper basket of the Assembly Chamber." Bryant objected that the bill failed to give the Health Department power to appoint the superintendent and make regulations and that it provided for "unnecessary places" at "exorbitant" salaries: "You will please understand Doctor, that this is a personal opinion of myself alone, and is not expressed in my official capacity in any sense whatever." But, Bryant added, he would give the same opinion "if speaking upon the full import of the bill, either in the Health Department of New York City or at Albany, in the presence of the Committee." Although Kempner protested that the appointment of the superintendent by the mayor was a necessary "concession to Tammany Hall" and denied providing for "unnecessary places at unusual salaries," he admitted to Baruch that "the bill is susceptible of amendment" and expressed his willingness to accept "any final suggestions."[58]

Apparently Baruch was not anxious to suggest changes, even though Bryant's objections were both justified and well-intended. If the bill were passed as it stood in February, the superintendent's office would become a political plaything. Perhaps Baruch's growing reputation as the "Apostle of Bathing" led him to hope that he would be the mayor's choice as bath superintendent. Whatever his reason, he apparently hoped to convince the Board of Health to accept the bill as it stood, instead of trying to make it acceptable to the board.[59]

Still another threat confronted the Kempner bill on March 11, when the *Medical Record* urged that the building of baths be left to charities: "It is hardly within the functions of the government to wash the masses, if the cleansing process can be effected in any other way." Editor Shrady said he would support the bill because it was important to educate the people in habits of cleanliness, but he found the involvement of the state in personal health an affront to his "ideas of the duties and limitations of popular government."[60]

Although Baruch lost no time in answering Shrady, he did not press the idea of government responsibility in matters of health. Instead, he reminded Shrady that the existing charity baths charged admission and that the AICP proposed to set still higher fees in future baths in the hope of reaping profits for other benevolent purposes. While five or ten cents might not be much to a "hard-worked doctor," Baruch said, "it is not a nominal sum to the laborer who has a family to bathe, or to the poor shop-girl who earns $3.50 a week." He quoted Goodwin Brown, father of the emasculated bath bill of 1892, who had said "'that even the small sum of five cents is too great an amount for the majority of the people who should avail themselves of the privileges of public baths.'" The average laborer earned between $1.00 and $1.50 a day. "'Five cents will buy a loaf of bread, and though cleanliness is to be desired, yet the cravings of hunger must be satisfied.'"[61]

There was a still more telling comparison. As a settlement worker observed, "It takes many a man some time to make up his mind to spend five cents for a bath instead of a glass of beer, and several trials to find that he feels better for the bath than for the beer."[62] This argument, in an age of careful distinction between the "poor" and the "worthy poor," would scarcely have strengthened Baruch's case, and he did not use it. Instead, while carefully praising the AICP for its benevolence, Baruch condemned its use of baths as investments and all but begged a retraction from the *Record,* "a journal whose influence on the medical [and] lay public is so powerful." He was painfully aware that "the lukewarmness of the average legislator in sanitary matters will induce him to grasp at any objection."

Baruch had additional reason to be upset by Shrady's editorial, for it appeared just two days before Baruch was to meet with Mayor Gilroy. He need not have concerned himself. Although Gilroy had seemed interested in baths when he was commissioner of public works, as mayor he proved as intransigent as his predecessor. Baruch argued long and earnestly, but he could not persuade Gilroy that the masses needed bathhouses. "People like that won't wash," the mayor said.[63]

Thus dismissed, Baruch once again turned to the press for help, this time with the appeal to public fears that he had formerly disdained. On March 17, under a headline reading, "Free Baths Needed for the Poor: Prepare for an Epidemic—City Officials Should Act Promptly," the *Mail and Express* ran an "interview" with a "leading doctor" who described the plan presented by Dr. Baruch and rejected by the mayor despite the support of "the medical profession." The unnamed interviewee referred ominously to cholera ("'the medical fraternity appears to be unanimous in the expectation of the approach of the dire disease next summer'") and to the speed with which it would spread by the "'intimate intercourse of all classes, by means of workmen, servants, laundresses, dressmakers and other tradespeople.'" He was astounded to hear that "'Mayor Gilroy was not impressed by Dr. Baruch's arguments. . . . In a matter of such vital import to the entire community no personal or political considerations should be permitted to interfere with the bounden duty of the city officials to protect us by any important hygienic measure that promises immunity from disease.'" If the mayor and his advisers did not at once establish free baths, the "leading doctor" said, they would have to answer for any epidemic spread by "'the great unwashed in this city.'"

Only Baruch could have known so much about Gilroy's reaction. Indeed, on the following day the *Evening Telegram* indirectly identified Baruch as the anonymous doctor:

An old saying tells us that even His Majesty of the lower regions is not so black as he is painted.

Many of our hard-working fellow citizens who are rather more grimy than we could wish are not so from choice. Dr. Simon Baruch, whose eminence in his profession gives weight to any utterance of his on the subject of public health, gave the reason yesterday.

The TELEGRAM seconds his appeal for free public baths all the year round. They are urgently needed. The Centre Market Place baths are doing excellent work, but they are not free and they serve only a fraction of the population.

More baths are demanded and we cannot have them too soon.

Even if Baruch had desired anonymity—and he was conspicuously not anonymous most of the time—he was now too busy to care. Before the Kempner bill came up for a committee hearing in April, he privately sought support from such men as Felix Adler, founder of the Society for Ethical Culture, and Roman Catholic archbishop M. A. Corrigan. He again put the medical journals he edited to work for the cause. In the March issue of *Gaillard's Medical Journal,* he reprinted the entire Kempner bill, calling on legislators to note its "grand possibilities for doing lasting good to their constituencies, be they rich or poor." He ventured to hope that the men in Albany would see that the principle of the greatest good to the largest number "finds its fullest illustration in the provisions of an act which secures to the humblest individual the right and privilege to be clean of body." He also asked that his physician readers "use their influence for the furtherance of any legislative action which would promote free baths for the poor."[64]

In the March *Journal of Balneology* Baruch concentrated on epidemiological reasons for supporting the bill: the "threatened approach of cholera and the presence of typhus in the city—both diseases due to and promoted by filth." If lawmakers truly believed that the function of the government was to protect the lives and property of the people, their "reason and true statesmanship" would lead them "to embrace with eagerness" the opportunity Kempner's bill offered.[65]

Through personal and professional channels and through the press, Baruch whipped up a storm of interest in the bill. Yet he did nothing to amend it to meet Commissioner Bryant's criticisms. The result was disastrous. On April 10 Kempner wrote Baruch: "Our bill may be considered dead. There is no possibility of having any action taken in regard to it. I may have the opportunity of saying a few words in its favor in open session, but even that is doubtful. I expect a different kind of a legislature here next year."

The legislature was not really to blame. Bitter opposition from city authorities had killed the bill in committee hearing.[66] Though Baruch blamed Mayor Gilroy, he himself was partly responsible. Without an office of superintendent appointed by the mayor and independent of the Health Department, the bill might have had enough support from the Board of Health to counterbalance the inevitable opposition of City Hall. Perhaps Baruch thought that press agitation and public sentiment would carry the bill over the opposition of politicians and physicians alike. If his personal hopes had prevented him from giving up the offensive provision, his ambition to head a municipal bath domain had cost that domain its existence, at least for a time.

14   "Ikey, Ikey, save the soap"

For a time, the failure of the Kempner bill sent Baruch's energy pulsating into other channels. During the spring and summer of 1893, he wrote articles and editorials about hydrotherapy and contaminated food and milk, but he did not stop thinking about public baths. If New York would not listen to him, perhaps other cities would. After all, New York did not have the only slums in America. When he inquired about baths in Philadelphia, he learned that the city of brotherly love had not a single one, despite a provision for them in the estate Benjamin Franklin had left more than a century before.[1]

Baruch did not have to write to Chicago, for it had already come to him, with promise of better results than he had reason to hope for in New York. Chicago had come, in December 1892, in the person of Gertrude Gail Wellington, a gynecologist whose plump, dimpled vivacity belied the stereotype of the mannish woman doctor. She came to Baruch to learn from the master, and, on her return to Chicago, recruited several able disciples from the "influential and public-spirited" women's Municipal Order League. Together with Dr. Sarah Hackett Stevenson, Dr. Julia Howe, Jane Addams, and Mrs. W. H. Duncanson, Dr. Wellington besieged the committee rooms of the city council and "wrestled with the gigantic aldermanic brain" to persuade it of the need for baths. These women soon won the support of four aldermen, all members of the Finance Committee of the City Council. Four other aldermen also endorsed the scheme, as did the chief and assistant chief of police and the president of the Park Board of the West Side, Chicago's vast immigrant dumping ground, where Dr. Wellington especially wanted to build baths.

By the spring of 1893 she had finagled an appropriation of $12,000 and conferred with the mayor and other municipal officers about spending $5,000 of it for a bath on the West Side, $5,000 for another on the South Side, and the remainder to improve a summer bathhouse on the North Side at the foot of Chicago Avenue. With the addition of municipal baths to those already located in the basement of Hull-House, Jane Addams's settlement house in the heart of the teeming Jewish and Italian Near West Side, and the ones to be installed in the Hull-House annex going up on Polk Street, Chicago would offer more public baths than New York. The efficacy of the women's campaign filled even Dr. Baruch with admiration.[2]

Perhaps it was their success that inspired Baruch to work for similar facilities through the Riverside Association, a new organization of New Yorkers anxious "to help the working man and his family to help themselves." In the settlement house tradition, the Riverside Association building on West Sixty-ninth Street between Amsterdam and West End avenues housed a free public library, a kindergarten, sewing and cooking classes, and a social club for working girls. In 1893 the Working Girls' Guild consisted of 120 "poor little women" who worked in mills, factories, shops, and stores. Primarily for these "handicapped daughters of toil," but also for men and boys, Baruch arranged to have showers installed in the association building. They opened in September 1893, free to members every day of the year from 6:00 A.M. to 10:30 P.M. and "supplied with hot and cold water and an inexhaustible stock of soap and towels." In less than a year men and boys alone were averaging fifty showers a day in these limited facilities.[3]

When Baruch visited Chicago in January 1894, he told a reporter that the special advantages of the rain bath (showers) would soon induce health officials to insist on their installation in every large tenement house. He predicted that rain baths would someday be as common as beer halls. Describing the People's Baths, he suggested that the New York Association for Improving the Condition of the Poor could treble attendance if it would remove the word "Poor" from the arched entrance. "People who bathe themselves are too proud to be patronized. They would rather go in a sub-cellar and pay 15 cents for a dip in second-hand water." In actuality, the AICP baths were flourishing, with 122,323 patrons during 1893, nearly 13,000 alone in a single summer month of 1894.[4]

Even more than the success of the People's Baths, events of the late summer and early autumn of 1894 gave Baruch reason to rejoice. On August 30, Richard Gilder, chairman of New York's newly created Tene-

More than thirty years after Jane Addams installed free public baths
(showers for adults, tubs for children) in Hull-House in 1892, the
women of Chicago's Near West Side continued to bathe their children
in these Hull-House tubs. Prodded by Hull-House residents and by
three women physicians including Gertrude Gail Wellington, Chicago
opened the nation's first free municipal showerbaths in 1894. Mayor
Carter Harrison had intended to name them in honor of Simon Baruch,
but after Harrison's assassination in 1893, the first bathhouse was named
for Harrison and a later one for Baruch. By 1920 Chicago had provided
the poor and working-class districts of the city with twenty-one of the
small, economical showerbaths Baruch advocated. (Courtesy of the
University Library, University of Illinois at Chicago, Jane Addams
Memorial Collection, Wallace Kirkland Papers.)

ment House Committee, wrote to ask if Baruch would like to appear
before the committee. At this, his first encouragement from city authorities, Baruch willingly agreed to receive a subpoena.[5] At almost the
same time, John M. Faure, secretary of the reform-minded Committee of
Seventy, called on Baruch to ask that he become a member of a subcommittee about to be formed to deal with "Baths and Lavatories." Baruch

was ill when Faure called, but he sent a conditional acceptance, "if his individual work then before the legislature would not be interfered with." Apparently unwilling either to hamper the yet-to-be-formed subcommittee with prior commitments or to "take any step that might interfere with the fruition or development of your ideas," Faure replied that the Committee of Seventy felt unable to name Baruch as a member—a decision that was destined to hamper the public bath movement in New York City.[6]

Except for his cooperation with the Gilder committee, Baruch had no prospect of work "before the legislature" when he answered Faure in November. Soon, however, he became involved again, in an effort more significant than the ill-fated Kempner bill. In January 1895 he began working with lunacy commissioner Goodwin Brown toward passage of Brown's bill mandating the erection of public baths in cities of fifty thousand inhabitants.[7] Because Baruch did not know about this bill before its introduction in January 1895, he did not have much time to promote it, but he kept the general subject of baths alive in the press through his plan to enlarge the Riverside Association baths to accommodate the public.

On January 29 the *Brooklyn Eagle* ran the gamut of reasons for baths: social, epidemiological, and the inevitable identification of bodily cleanliness with 100 percent Americanism:

New York has added to itself, within eight or ten years, many thousands of people who do not wash. When there was danger of cholera the hose was turned upon some of them before they came ashore, and it was the first approach to a bath that they had had in their lives. Some of them claim that they are forbidden by their religion to profane their bodies with soap, and others are of such a saving disposition that they long ago cut off such luxuries as wash basins and towels. If the people of this large and influential class can be weaned from their practice and made to comport themselves like self respecting Americans, it will be for their own good and for the good of the Americans, too.

The *Sun* of February 3 reminded residents of the area around the Riverside Association—fashionable West End Avenue from Seventieth Street up the side streets where "good living is the rule"—that only a few blocks away "life is only one degree less squalid and miserable than in the heart of the east side."[8]

On February 5 Brown invited Baruch to Albany for a hearing: "I think if we all take hold of this matter that such a bill may become a law this session." Because the bill made baths mandatory in every city over fifty thousand (in numbers to be decided by local health boards), Brown also planned to have notices sent out to these local officials. Baruch did not attend the hearing, but he sent material that helped Brown to secure passage of the bill, which included, at Baruch's insistence, the provision that river or ocean baths "shall not be deemed a compliance with the requirements."[9]

Despite fears that the bill might be considered unacceptable because it made public baths mandatory, the governor, perhaps influenced by a giant pro-bath rally that overflowed Cooper Union on March 27, signed it on April 18. The legislation Baruch had wanted for so long was on the books at last: Chapter 351 of the Laws of 1895. Brown made much of the "unanswerable arguments" Baruch had given him to lay before the committee: "To you I largely ascribe the credit of the most important measure of the session. . . . There is nothing to do now, except to point out to the aldermen of New York the necessity of at once establishing a free public bath."[10]

Unaware that yet another struggle lay ahead, Baruch was exultant, a mood reflected by the newspapermen who had supported his views through a long period of disappointments. "Free public baths and free all year round," crowed the *Herald* of April 21: "Places where poor persons may enter and in the utmost privacy bathe thoroughly with either hot or cold water; houses that shall be open at least fourteen hours every day in the week, so that any human being can partake of the advantages of cleanliness." The *Herald* reproduced the entire bill, with full credit to Dr. Baruch, together with an interview in which Baruch expressed his delighted certainty that New York City would have free public baths by autumn. The *Brooklyn Eagle* of April 22 attributed the bill solely to Brown's efforts and predicted that it would indirectly foster civic pride "because if a man be not clean personally, he does not see the importance of having everything else clean." On April 27 the *Albany Evening Journal* showed its hometown colors, boasting that it was Brown, "a resident of Albany," who started the movement resulting in the new law.[11]

Less than a week after Governor Morton signed the bill into law, Baruch sent a copy to the New York City Health Department. Replying that the Board of Estimate and Apportionment was already studying the number of baths needed and the best locations for them, Cyrus Edson said they wanted Baruch's opinion on both points, as well as a description of the design he considered best suited for the purpose. Edson added that "no time should be wasted in determining what is required for it will take time to issue bonds and erect the establishments." Two days later, he sent Baruch the sanitary superintendent's report so that Baruch might study it before meeting with the board on May 2.[12]

Baruch was undoubtedly grateful for the advance information, for his old rival Colonel William Gaston Hamilton turned up at the meeting in his capacity as vice-president of the AICP, whose bathhouse was considered a model by the Board of Health. Hamilton appeared just as eager as Baruch to advise the city. Also at the meeting were John M. Faure and William H. Tolman of the Committee of Seventy, who proposed six likely sites. The board postponed action until plans and specifications could be presented and sites chosen in executive session. After these preliminaries were settled and the approximate cost set for each bathhouse, the Board of Estimate and Apportionment would be asked to appropriate the necessary money. [13]

At this early point in the official proceedings, Baruch began negotiations with the architectural firm of Brunner and Tryon, apparently requesting that they make drawings for baths. Though reluctant to invest his effort prematurely, Arnold W. Brunner finally agreed. Baruch's anxiety to have Brunner as bath architect to the city probably arose from Brunner's championing of Baruch in a priority dispute with Goodwin Brown. Also, Baruch's press release had so slighted the major competitors, Messrs. Cady and Co., that they could certainly be counted in the camp of Colonel Hamilton. Apart from reasons of pure ego, Baruch hoped his advice would be taken over Hamilton's because he believed he knew more about baths. [14]

By the end of May, Brunner presented sketches for Baruch to show to the Board of Health. The *Sanitarian* for June reported that the health departments of New York and Brooklyn were "actively engaged in measures to render the law effective as speedily as possible." On June 22 the *Medical Record* reversed its earlier opposition to government-supported baths, hailing the new law as a landmark in public hygiene, a worthy successor to legislation concerning pure food and drink and tenement construction.

Unhappily, the bath law, like these other measures, was difficult to enforce. Although the *Record* urged New York officials to hurry bath construction, the summer passed without perceptible progress. At the same time, Baruch lost an important route of influence when Cyrus Edson left the Board of Health. On September 5 board president Charles Wilson returned the Brunner plans to Baruch with news that the board was having trouble acquiring property "in suitable locations and at fair prices." At the end of September, Baruch was still offering his advice, and the board was still promising to take it—if it ever got past the preliminaries. [15]

In the course of the board's fumblings, the bathball fell into the nimbler hands of the Committee of Seventy, anti-Tammany reformers who ran for office in 1894 on pledges to make the city more homelike by providing public baths and water closets. Although the Committee of Seventy members chosen by Mayor William L. Strong to constitute his Committee on Public Baths had done nothing toward bath construction, the reform party made baths a major issue in the campaign of 1895. If Baruch found any comfort in the fact that baths had become politically popular, it vanished when he learned that the mayor had appointed his arch-rival, Colonel William Gaston Hamilton, to chair the bath committee.[16]

On October 25 the Committee of Fifty (a streamlined Committee of Seventy) released a pamphlet telling voters "What Municipal Reform has done and will do for You: Blackmail Stopped. Grand Jury List Purified. Truck Nuisance Abated, with its accompanying wrong and immorality. Honest Police Justices. Better Tenement Houses. Clean Streets. New Parks Down Town. Pure Milk. Free Public Baths for a Million People. Plans Already approved for the First Public Bath of a Series of Seven. Also for Public Water Closets and Urinals. The Committee of Seventy began True Municipal Reform; the Fifty will continue it."[17]

Most of the pamphlet dealt with baths to be built in the six locations suggested to the Board of Health in May: "You will note how the welfare of the people is consulted by these." But the Committee of Fifty also used this publication to make political points: "In 1892, a law was passed by which you might have had Free Public Baths. TAMMANY REFUSED to give them to you, preferring to use the money for its bosses and henchmen." Implying that the legislation of 1895 was its own work, the Fifty promised facilities for twenty-five thousand baths a day. Reading the pamphlet, Baruch learned that the architects and engineers were to be Cady, Berg & See, who had built the AICP bath. Hamilton and his cohorts were to have things their way. In November 1895, when the electorate returned the reform forces to office, Baruch sent Brunner's drawings back with apologies. Brunner was sorry their plans had failed: "Of course it cannot be helped, but I hope to build some, sometime, somewhere."[18]

For all its campaign promises, the mayor's committee did not act quickly. Through the first five months of 1896, Baruch looked in vain for signs of construction in New York, while other cities—Buffalo, Yonkers, Pittsburgh, Trenton, Boston—moved ahead. The movement was progressing in Philadelphia, too, where the *Citizen* of January 1896 noted with alarm the emergence of the Japanese as rivals to the English in habits of cleanliness: "One advantage, however, John Bull must continue to have over the Jap; he will always look the cleaner of the two." (To ensure Anglo-Saxon supremacy, the *Citizen* endorsed the work of the Public Baths Association of Philadelphia.)[19]

On April 6, when Baruch asked the New York City Health Department about the delay, he learned that action awaited an appropriation. He also learned that another bath bill had been passed by the legislature on March 25. Baruch was furious at the thought of precious time wasted on the new bill, clumsy compared to the law of 1895 and altogether unnecessary. He was still more furious to hear from Chairman Hamilton that the mayor's committee would insist on the installation of tubs in every public bath built under its supervision because Hamilton considered them necessary for the infirm and for mothers with children (a consideration Baruch discounted even though Chicago's Near West Side mothers made frequent use of the tubs at Hull-House).[20]

Baruch was disconsolate that Hamilton was heading what Baruch considered *his* movement, in its hour of greatest promise. The two men differed on points that Baruch considered essential, and Hamilton had none of Baruch's fiery impatience to be on with it: to Baruch he seemed incomprehensibly lethargic. For nine months, Hamilton and his committee had wasted time on a second bath bill that was more likely to cancel than to clarify the legislation they were supposed to implement. Now, on June 12, 1896, Hamilton told Baruch that it would take still longer for the authorities to act, for the new bill would have to be amended to provide for the purchase of land. It was almost too much for poor Baruch. A bath disciple in Trenton complained that "apathy and hard times are *agin* us. . . . The city is dilatory," but Baruch could not believe that Trenton rivaled New York City in such matters.[21]

In Chicago, Dr. Wellington was having troubles of her own. The culprit was the commissioner of health, "a two by four man" anxious to exclude her from the work she had started. He refused to give her information Baruch wanted, "but that does not trouble as little a woman as I am." Knowing that Baruch was about to publish something about baths, she confessed, "I secretly glory in what you are about to do and—do me the honor to show an *Irishman* that a Jew and *an American* have a right to both feet on America's soil. Only insist on your recognition for what you have been ie the 'father of Rain baths in America'—and me as your right hand champion."[22]

The *Sanitarian* for June held recognition aplenty. Editor A. N. Bell published an article called "The Introduction of Public Baths in America" by Harvey E. Fisk, one of the founders of the Riverside Association. Working from Baruch's mass of bath correspondence and clippings, Fisk told the story of the bath movement as a friend of Dr. Baruch would tell it. References to William Gaston Hamilton and Goodwin Brown were few and muted.[23]

Although Fisk's article contained no untruths, Dr. Moreau Morris of the mayor's bath committee felt compelled to respond in the July issue of the *Sanitarian*. He charged Fisk with ignoring "the instrumentality of the Mayor's Committee in providing for the construction of the Rain Baths."[24] In the *Sanitarian* for September, Dr. Baruch's son Herman supported Fisk with more newspaper material praising Dr. Baruch, at the same time admonishing that "any rivalry or jealousy among the movers, introducers and promoters of this greatest hygienic movement of the day appears unseemly."[25]

When Dr. Wellington received a copy of the final article in the June-July-September exchange, she was "excessively pleased over the report—and more than gratified to see you protect yourself in this matter—and advise you to do so on every possible occasion." She was also pleased with the material about her work: "I am contemplating issuing a similar expression of our work and shall remember to quote you as frequently as possible—as the *supreme mover* in *pub baths of this country.*"[26]

By February 1897 Wellington and her co-workers had seen another free bathhouse through completion, this time on Chicago's South Side. The *Chicago Tribune* rejoiced that "in the months of hot weather coming the miserable little urchins abounding in the neighborhood of Thirty-ninth Street and Wentworth Avenue will not have to wade about in the small mud holes and shallow ponds of the vicinity to find out how water feels."[27] As Baruch read the clippings from Dr. Wellington, he chafed at New York's comparative inertia.

When the mayor's bath committee issued a report in May 1897, Baruch at last learned what it had been doing since 1895. In what he called a "pretentious volume of one hundred and ninety-six pages," the committee reported that it had investigated European baths, recommended a bath act of its own, and, after getting it passed on March 25, 1896, obtained an appropriation of $200,000 toward its execution. But the committee had done nothing with the appropriation, for it appeared that, through some error, its own legislation now required that baths be built only in public parks—and there were no parks in the areas where baths were needed.[28]

Baruch's mind reeled to think that the mayor's committeemen had spent two years legislating themselves into an impasse. Their errors threatened to undo everything he had worked for since 1889. They antagonized him further by claiming credit for the bath act of 1895. Chafing under these irritations and his long-smoldering resentment against

Chairman William Gaston Hamilton, Baruch turned three large editorial pages of the *Medical Record* of May 8 into as lively a tirade as readers of a medical journal were likely to see.[29]

He first referred to the work begun "about seven years ago" by "a physician of this city," but the name "Dr. Baruch" soon slipped in, as he recounted how Mayor Grant had "pigeonholed the measure, and turned a deaf ear to the personal appeals of the projector." When Baruch discussed the elections of 1895, which had put the Committee of Seventy into power, his account turned to vitriol: "Now came upon us the great reform movement which promised to purify city politics and bring untold blessings upon its inhabitants. The committee of seventy had promised the people public baths and lavatories. Unfortunately the law providing these had been passed without their assistance."

In two years the mayor's committee had accomplished nothing "except the obstruction of this great movement." Its investigation of European baths was worthless, "since this city already possessed the best examples of true public baths" (based, though he did not mention it, on his own European observations). Although the law of 1895 seemed adequate to others, it "evidently did not suit the 'reform' politicians to give the board of health control of so important a measure. Nine months the mayor's committees 'labored and brought forth a mouse,' in the shape of the clumsy act, passed March 25, 1896," empowering the commissioner of public works to decide the number and location of bathhouses and to take the initiative toward construction. "Thus a sanitary measure belonging to the board of health was wrested from its proper guardians and relegated to the politicians."

When the mayor's committee got a generous $200,000 appropriation to build baths under its own legislation, it spent a year producing nothing but a report in which it concluded that its own legislation prevented further action. "Wise Solons, these! We do not claim to be experts on public baths, as are these authors of the 'Report', but we do claim to understand English, and we fail to find one single reference in the act of March 25, 1896, either to a mandatory or other permissive use of the public parks for public baths." The only reference to parks in the bill concerned the location not of baths but of "structures for the promotion of public comfort"—and this was merely permissive, not mandatory.

As for the claims of "this sapient committee" to credit for the bath act of April 1895, Baruch noted that the committee was not created until July 1895: "A great sanitary movement, begun by a medical man, urged through medical channels, and auspiciously brought to a happy conclusion, [has] been wrecked by Mayor Strong's committee on baths."

Baruch called it "'The Mayor's Committee on Bath Literature'" and urged city authorities to seek a better guide.

The editorial was unsigned, but it was not really anonymous. No one involved with Baruch could fail to recognize his lethal style. Two days after his attack appeared in the *Record,* the *Herald* reproduced large portions of it, asking in a headline, "Are Reformers to Blame?" Mayor Strong told a reporter from the *Herald* that he was "surprised at the attack upon him by the *Medical Record.*" Through third persons, the mayor expressed regret that the committee had not succeeded in building baths, but he refused to comment on "the criticism made by the profession represented by the *Record* concerning the delay caused by his committee."[30]

Baruch's editorial did not represent the views of the entire profession. When Baruch sent it to George B. Fowler of the Health Department, expressing his intention to bring the matter before the Academy of Medicine, Fowler was dismayed. After conferring with the department's attorney, Fowler wrote Baruch that "we are all inclined to believe that you are in error in your contention." He asked Baruch to meet with him and the attorney in a few days and to refrain from public statements in the meantime. Fowler warned, "If I were in your place I should be very careful what I said to-morrow night at the Academy." A conversation with the attorney, Fowler thought, would persuade Baruch "that there is good reason why the provisions of the Laws of 1895 cannot practically be carried out by the city authorities." Baruch was too impatient to wait for the suggested meeting. He saw Fowler and the attorney the next day and, as he put it, "convinced them that they are in error."[31]

The same night, May 20, 1897, Baruch went before the academy and asked it to appoint a three-man committee "to urge upon the city authorities the necessity of immediately erecting the public baths authorized by the recent act of legislature of this State." Under academy rules, the resolution was tabled until the next meeting two weeks later, when it was discussed and passed, despite dissent from such leaders as Edward Gamaliel Janeway. The president appointed R. Van Santvoord and George B. Fowler to the committee, with Baruch as chairman.[32]

When Baruch marched his academy force to City Hall the next day, he found that Mayor Strong was in a conciliatory mood. Strong said he was already considering a lot in Rivington Street on the lower East Side. The committee left feeling that the mayor had given a "satisfactory interview."[33]

If Mayor Strong also went home in a glow of goodwill, the glow faded when he saw himself in a cartoon in the *Evening World,* gross and sprawling in an ornate bathtub piled high with ice, gleefully squirting himself with one of a series of selzer bottles. A bucket of "ice tea" and an overhead shower completed the picture of His Honor, cool and comfortable, "In His Cracked Ice Bath at 12 West Fifty-seventh Street." In an inset, *World* readers saw a head-to-toe view of the mayor's chubby form, clad in a wide-striped bathing suit, "Dancing in Seabright's Surf." The cartoon was titled "The Question of the Day Answered." The caption read: "Says Mayor Strong: 'It is true the free baths have not been built, though $200,000 appropriated. But what are free baths to me? I don't need free baths.'" Baruch later noted that the mayor's "position was misunderstood." Evidently so, for despite the abuse, Strong went ahead with his plans for the Rivington Street bath.[34]

On June 5, the day after the *World* cartoon appeared, the *New York Times* at last entered the eight-year-old bath controversy. Baruch professed a pleasure at the paper's interest which he could scarcely have felt, especially since the *Times* editorially advised the academy against action to spur bath construction. From its own reading of the law of March 1896, the *Times* believed that baths must be built in parks. This it opposed, cautioning the academy to study the law further before urging its fulfillment: "That it has been permitted to slumber for a year is, from that point of view, a subject for congratulation rather than regret."

Baruch responded with a mild letter to the editor written the day the *Times* editorial appeared. With patience and restraint, Baruch explained again that the reference to parks was permissive, not mandatory. The fiery anonymous author of the *Medical Record* editorial of May 8 was now a judicious signed letter writer, full of praise for Mayor Strong's "well-known and highly appreciated efforts" and the "able and energetic bath committee." He applauded the interest of "an influential journal like The Times" and hoped that it would "continue to aid the good cause and encourage the Mayor in his laudable effort for the betterment of the condition of the tenement population."[35]

On seeing Baruch's letter in the *Times*, Charles H. T. Collis, commissioner of public works, wrote him that the corporation counsel agreed with Baruch's interpretation: Collis need not place baths in parks if other city property was available. On this advice, Mayor Strong had already directed Collis to prepare plans for a bathhouse on the Rivington Street lot, owned in fee by the city.[36]

The delays that followed this development in June 1897 made Baruch terribly impatient. Bid letting is inevitably slow, and a transfer of the bath project from the Commission of Public Works to that of Public Building, Lighting and Supplies meant added delay. Fearful that the move would bog his plan in a department known for some of the richest graft in a graft-ridden city, Baruch began "prodding the authorities" again.[37] He learned that the expected cost of construction had climbed to $95,700 and the expected date of completion was receding into 1899, a full decade after he had launched his crusade in behalf of the unwashed.[38]

While official bumbling deprived New York of bathhouses, the public bath movement succeeded elsewhere to a degree that only made Baruch more miserable. When Philadelphia's first bathhouse opened in April 1898 on one of the worst streets in the city, blacks and whites, clerks and street urchins, Jews and gentiles, the shabby and the well-dressed stood in line together. Coal heavers who went in black with grime, their clean clothes wrapped in newspaper, were almost unrecognizable when they emerged some twenty minutes later. Jews, who always predominated on Friday, set a record on September 14, when they came out more than four hundred strong in raw cold weather to wash and be clean for their New Year the following day.[39] In November 1898, the Baltimore Free Public Bath Commission drafted a newspaper advertisement noting that in some sections of the city 90 percent of the homes lacked bathrooms. The commission urged Baltimoreans to match Boston's annual $35,000 expenditure for public baths or New York City's $48,000 (such was the image of New York that it had to do little to stand as an example).[40]

In March 1899 Baruch requested an appointment for his academy committee to see Mayor Robert Van Wyck, who had successfully run on the slogan "To Hell with Reform" in 1898. Although a Tammany man, Van Wyck received the committee with "courteous attention, and with every manifestation of a deep interest in public baths." He promised to promote construction of two small, inexpensive bathhouses on the East and West sides in locations recommended by the committee.[41]

When nothing had come of the mayor's genial words by May, Baruch's impatience flowed over in a letter to the *Tribune*. The soft-spoken author of the letter to the *Times* nearly two years before now reverted to his role of gadfly. Sparing Mayor Strong and his successor, as well as the current commissioner of public works ("who received the plans and contracts as a legacy from the last administration"), Baruch laid all the blame for delay on the mayor's bath committee—William Gaston Hamilton and his cohorts. Thanks to their errors, Baruch said, the city was about to spend nearly $100,000 for a bath in Rivington Street which might have been built long before for only $27,000.[42]

The summer of 1899 bloomed and faded into fall without the bathhouse Baruch had been promised by Commissioner Henry S. Kearney the preceding October. Reform was discredited, and the police were once again directed by Tammany. As the author of a book about Hell's Kitchen put it, "Mob action and street fighting made New York's thoroughfares unsafe, on the East Side as well as the West, just at the time the nation was proclaiming its determination to bring law and order to Cuba, Puerto Rico and the Philippines."[43] Reformers like Jacob Riis, who had looked to baths to promote self-respect and hence respect for law, could chalk up the failure of the citizens to the failure of the city itself.

Early in 1900 Baruch went to Europe, where he arranged to have an exhibit on American public baths included in the Paris Exposition. In early April he accepted an invitation to inspect Buffalo's bathhouse, the first to be built under New York State's mandatory act of 1895. After the tour, in a newspaper interview aimed at his own unappreciative Manhattan, Baruch promised to make Buffalo famous for its bathhouses on the Terrace.[44]

When Dr. Wellington learned that Chicago, too, was a candidate for international fame via Baruch's exhibit at the Paris Exposition, she wrote, "It was a bright thing for you to think of, and do, and I secretly enthuse over it." She was still having troubles of her own, like Baruch's with the mayor's bath committee. "I felt so deeply *your* humiliation, and have so indignantly resented mine—the 'cheek' evinced has been so glairing [sic] and pronounced that it is patent to all observers that it savors of the 'All Hog' of Chicago. Now Dr. Stand for your rights in this respect— and if you will permit me, I will write to the Manager of the 'World' of N.Y. and have him do you what honor he can through the Press—He's a right royal fellow (Mr. Van Bruthuysen)—and a good friend of mine— but keep hammering away and the Mayors Committee will soon be non est."[45]

Baruch's rival in the spring of 1900 was not William Gaston Hamilton of the mayor's committee, but the Albany lawyer and commissioner of lunacy, Goodwin Brown. When Brown, in the *New York Times* of April 29, claimed to be the originator of the entire public bath system in America, Baruch rallied his supporters in medical journalism. Labeling Brown's claims as "absurd," the *Medical Record* of May 12 said it was voicing the sentiment of the medical profession "in defending one of its members against encroachment, and insisting that credit be not withheld from the man who has so valiantly and successfully made the fight for this great sanitary boon."[46]

The *Sanitarian* for July outdid its rival journal in unique fashion. Editor A. N. Bell chided the *Record* for neglecting to contrast Brown's grasping spirit with Baruch's magnanimity, as illustrated by a letter Baruch had written in 1895 protesting that he did not deserve sole credit for the

In 1901, long after other cities had acted, New York City at last opened
its first municipal public bath at 326 Rivington Street on the Lower East
Side. Note the separate entrances for women and men. In 1917 the city
re-dedicated this building, painting out the original sign and mounting
Baruch's name above it. Although architecturally modest compared
with New York's later monumental bathhouses, the Rivington Street
Bath was too lavish to suit Baruch. He wanted many small,
inexpensive, unpretentious shower facilities to be scattered throughout
the most crowded districts of the city. (Courtesy of the Museum of the
City of New York.)

passage of the bath act introduced by Brown. "In short," Bell wrote in 1900, "Dr. Baruch was so gratified with the success of the enterprise, that, like Schley, on the result of the conflict with the Spanish fleet, he thought there was honor enough in it for all the participants." Whether this approach was Bell's idea or Baruch's, it was masterful, giving Baruch the credit and, at the same time, credit for not wanting the credit.[47]

On November 17, 1900, the *Sun* announced that Baruch had won a silver medal for his public bath exhibit at the Paris Exposition.[48] Four months later, the long years of political infighting and priority disputes faded into insignificance, when, on March 23, 1901, New York City opened its first free municipal bathhouse, on Rivington Street near Goerck Street, within a block of the East River. At last Baruch saw the realization of a dream he had promoted over more than a decade of prodding, haggling, and pleading with five successive administrations. Where children swarmed in front of the tenements and peddlers chattered in Yiddish along the curb, the Rivington Street bathhouse at last stood open to the people, and the people flocked inside. On the first day there were 150, on the second 250, on the third, more than 700. Men came mostly at night, women in the early morning. Children—especially boys—came all day long, some of them trying to get in three or four times in a single day. Through all the open hours, attendants were on hand, ready to show young and old how to take what was for many the first shower of their lives.

A newspaper reporter, in a piece titled "A Story in Municipal Sociology," found the three-day-old bathhouse "thronged, and already established as an institution." Outside, where pushcart men scrambled up on the sidewalk to escape a fire engine and tender clattering through the street, the air was a din of polyglot. Six ragged urchins romped down the bathhouse steps, their wet hair slicked down over their foreheads, their bright faces the envy of a group who could not get in because they had no towels. Inside the door a big policeman stood next to the shirt-sleeved attendant, who gave out small pieces of soap as the eager boys filed in. As each boy got his soap, he marched down the stone steps leading to a long corridor, lined with individual showers. The floors were mosaic, the walls slabs of clean, hard slate.

In the women's and girl's corridor there was little sound except the steady drip, drip, drip of the showers. The men were quiet, too, but the boys made a happy, deafening clamor: "Izzy, come in, the water's great!" "Here comes Chumpsie, Turn the hot water on Chumpsie." "Ikey, Ikey, save the soap, take it home!" There were boys of every description, most of them Russian or Polish Jews, with threadbare coats and trousers, scuffed shoes, and ragged stockings. They all went in

Top: Baltimore's public bath pioneers were unique in combining private funding with municipal management and in experimenting with portability. After extemporizing baths by connecting gospel tents to city fireplugs, they built inexpensive, light-frame structures that the city could transport from one vacant lot to another and maintain for only $30 weekly. Bottom: Workmen filled the waiting rooms of public baths that opened in Buffalo in 1897, two years after the New York State legislature mandated free public showerbaths in all first- and second-class cities (New York City, Brooklyn, Buffalo, Rochester, Syracuse, Troy, and Utica). Many of the bath patrons wore the derby hat that was becoming a sign of middle-class status. The spittoon at the center of the room was a ubiquitous sanitary convenience that, for many English observers, epitomized Americans of that era: loud-voiced, money-centered braggarts, spitting tobacco juice and lacking both manners and education. (Both photographs courtesy of the late Frances A. Hellebrandt, M.D., in author's possession.)

grime-dirty and came out clean. And some of them saved the soap and took it home.[49]

The popularity of the new bathhouse did not flag with familiarity. In the first five months of 1902 (winter months at that), 224,876 of the people Jacob Riis called the "Sweaters of Jewtown" used the showers, 66,256 of them women and girls. "The 'great unwashed' were not so from choice," Riis observed. Writing *The Battle with the Slum* in 1902, he was thankful for the long-awaited building and hopeful that "godliness will have a chance to move in with cleanliness. The two are neighbors everywhere, but in the slum the last must come first."[50]

Over the next five years Baruch maintained his vigilance, the city extended its efforts, and more bathhouses went up: on the outskirts of Hell's Kitchen, at West Forty-first Street near Ninth Avenue, in November 1904; on East 109th Street in the swarming, squalid Italian quarter in March 1905; on East Eleventh Street near Avenue A in December 1905; on East Seventy-sixth Street, among Hungarians, Bohemians, garbage cart drivers, longshoremen, and hands from the river tugs and steamers, in January 1906; on West Sixtieth Street in June 1906. By 1908 the East Eleventh Street bath had five thousand patrons daily during the summer, with waiting lines running a block down the street. At the East Side baths, where regulations were posted in both Yiddish and English, attendants could scarcely keep up with the crowds on the eve of Yom Kippur. Every happy cry of "Ikey, Ikey, save the soap, take it home" supported the *Outlook*'s prediction that "the days of the Great Unwashed are numbered" and Jacob Riis's idea that each bathhouse was "a nail in the coffin of the slum."[51]

Baruch had started his public bath crusade at the age of forty-nine. When the first free municipal bathhouse opened in New York City, he was almost sixty-one, his hair and beard snowy white, his once black eyebrows steel gray. Known as the "Apostle of Bathing" in places as far away as San Francisco, New Orleans, and Puerto Rico, he was cheered by crowds in Chicago's Eleventh Ward, where he had never set foot before the opening of a bathhouse named for him there in 1910.[52]

Baruch loved it all. He never tired of collecting clippings and letters and pictures, carefully preserving them in "public bath" scrapbooks along with typewritten accounts of the many failures that preceded the final success. At one time he wrote: "I consider that I have done more to save life and prevent the spread of disease in my work for public baths than in all my work as a physician."[53] He had worked long and hard to realize his splendid dream, and he was rightly called the "pioneer of free public rain baths in America." Yet it was a triumph of fleeting historical significance. The sturdy brick buildings he had helped to give the people would serve only as long as the people needed them. Public baths were self-destructive: they bred discontent with the very living conditions that had called them into being. Even as Baruch gloried in his achievements, he knew that prosperity and growing government responsibility for individual welfare would relegate them to obsolescence. Within four decades the bathhouses he was so proud of would serve mainly as reminders of a crowded and colorful era in American history.[54]

The Gospel of Hydrotherapy   15

Throughout his years of crusading for free public baths, Baruch also poured enormous energy into a purely medical cause. He was deeply concerned about the lag between advancing medical knowledge and outmoded forms of therapy. With few new methods of treatment to replace older, discredited, depletive measures, many physicians had lost confidence in their usefulness as healers. Because the American physician's identity was closely tied to therapeutic intervention, Baruch could not view this loss of therapeutic confidence solely as a healthy reaction to the former excesses of heroic medicine. New sects were springing up—chiropractors, osteopaths, Christian Scientists, and a host of patent medicine vendors—to woo the sick with exuberant promises of help. While the regulars groped for a firm therapeutic footing, sectarians multiplied and quacks prospered.[1]

To Baruch, the existence of the regular profession seemed in jeopardy. The lesson he drew from the extremes illustrated in the history of medicine was the one the *Richmond and Louisville Medical Journal* expressed in 1866: "It is better to be taught by the voice of Nature than to seek wisdom from man's ingenuity."[2] In his presidential address before the South Carolina Medical Association in 1874, Baruch strongly endorsed this conclusion. As late as 1892, he still agreed that medicine had taken a giant step forward when it abandoned heroic methods in favor of expectant treatment based on the assumption that "the physician cannot throttle disease, but must watch and wait for a point of vantage, when he may come to the rescue of the system which is battling against it." But while he applauded the aims of expectant practice ("To weaken the influence of the disease, to strengthen the resistance of the [human] organism"), he had learned from personal experience that the physician could not merely watch and wait. He had tried it and found it "expectant" indeed, "in the sense that I personally expected some complication or failure of the vital powers to turn up at any time and I expected, too, to be powerless to meet it."[3]

Like other practicing physicians, Baruch compromised: for pneumonia, he used smaller doses of drugs but calmed the sleepless patient with morphia and chloral, wrapped her in a hot poultice or warm cotton jacket, fed her milk and broth, and gave stimulants when death seemed imminent. This, the remnant of expectant methods under the duress of actual practice in acute disease, was so unsatisfactory that in the 1880s the introduction of the coal-tar drugs for lowering fever revived some of the old abuses of dosage.[4]

Baruch sought a better "via media" in therapeutics. By 1889 he thought he had found the answer in hydrotherapy. Two years earlier, appalled at a mortality of over 34 percent in typhoid patients treated by expectant methods, he had suggested that it might be lowered by moderating the temperature of cold baths and the dosage of antipyretic drugs. In the *Medical Record* in January 1887, he had urged doctors to content themselves with reducing the patient's temperature to 102 degrees, leaving the rest "to that good old handmaiden of the doctor, the vis medicatrix naturae." The cold baths used with success by Ernst Brand of Stettin had not met with Baruch's approval in 1887: "The sudden submergence of a typhoid patient with a temperature of 104 degrees into a bath of 60 degrees several times a day, may not weaken a German soldier, but it is not so well adapted to an American constitution, if we may judge from our own hospital reports."[5]

By 1889 Baruch was ready to retract these views. One of the things that changed his mind was a lecture on the general pathology of fever, delivered by William Welch at Columbia College of Physicians and Surgeons on April 12, 1888. With his co-workers at the Johns Hopkins Hospital, Welch had discovered that animals could be kept at high temperatures for at least three weeks without manifesting serious symptoms or any functional disturbance attributable to elevated temperature other than frequent respiration and quickened pulse. Welch cautioned physicians not to abandon antipyretic treatment on the basis of these experimental results, however, for the so-called antipyretics had many functions other than temperature reduction: "I need only to refer to the powerful influence of cold baths upon the circulation, and the nervous system, and to the action of antipyrine and other anti-thermic drugs upon the nervous system."[6]

The second cause of Baruch's about-face was his more careful study of the work of Ernst Brand. Brand's procedure of immersing the typhoid patient for five minutes in 65-degree water whenever the temperature exceeded 103 degrees (or every three hours as long as the temperature continued to exceed 103) had originally led Baruch to believe that Brand's sole purpose was antipyretic; that is, to reduce the patient's temperature. This, he now discovered, was not true, though many outstanding clinicians, including Theodor Juergensen of Kiel, Hugo von Ziemssen of Munich, and even Carl von Liebermeister of Basel, "the high priest of the altar of antipyresis," were guilty of the same misinterpretation. Brand's low mortality—7.8 percent in 19,017 cases, 3.9 in another group of 5,573—depended on something else.[7]

Brand himself did not understand exactly how cold baths aided patients in the struggle against typhoid, but no one could know this without knowing more about the nature of the disease—and about human physiology. When Baruch recanted his opposition to Brand before the Medical Society of the State of New York in February 1889, he suggested that the cold bath treatment combated "these very effects of the infective and toxic agencies, with whose true entity we have not yet been brought face to face. . . . It has been clearly demonstrated by numerous trustworthy observers, that the reflex stimulus aroused by the shock to the extensive peripheral nerve-endings so energizes the nerve centers which furnish innervation for circulation, respiration, digestion, tissue formation and excretion, that the system is enabled to tide over the dangers which would ensue from failure of these functions."[8]

Baruch was sufficiently committed to this hypothesis to enter a plea with his colleagues. Despite the difficulties they would encounter—time required for giving baths; resistance by the patient, his family, and friends; difficulties in diagnosing cases before the fifth day, when baths must begin to assure good results—Baruch urged them to treat all typhoid patients with the unmodified Brand bath: "The history of medicine does not present a parallel to the application of statistics for the elucidation of a question of therapeutics which Brand had presented and which I have amplified. The evidence is before us, clear and uncontrovertible."[9] With unmistakable conviction, Baruch thus entered upon what was to prove the most significant medical crusade in a lifetime of crusades.

As he hoped, his advocacy of Brand baths aroused wide discussion, reaching even to Stettin, where it elicited a response from Brand himself.[10] Brand, who had heard of Baruch's earlier opposition, chided him good-naturedly for doubting whether Americans could bear the rigors of cold water. Having treated babies and old people as well as soldiers,

Brand "wondered" whether adult Americans had more delicate constitutions than German babies. The objections Baruch anticipated did not seem likely to Brand: "Do we fear chloroform because the patient is nearer death than life, and looks like a corpse? . . . Do we fear the knife because it causes blood to flow?" As for the idea that Brand baths could not be carried out by poor people, Brand told of being called to the fourth story of a miserable house in Stettin, where a family of six lived in one room and a dark closet, the three children cared for by an old, deaf, crippled grandmother, while the parents worked as day laborers. The six-year-old girl lay ill with typhoid. Her eleven-year-old brother declined to have her sent to the hospital. Instead, he cared for her himself, bathing her, feeding her, and keeping the temperature charts. When his older sister also fell ill, he cared for them both and for his own mild fever as well. "The little hero's name is Franz Witte," Brand wrote. "He is today a printer in the Rede establishment, and I have kept the histories written by him as a memorial." [11]

In relaying this letter through the *Medical Record* of April 20, 1889, Baruch added Brand's warning that hospitals must not expect as low a mortality as private physicians because the Brand method should be started early in the course of the disease, whereas patients usually entered the hospital late. Still, a mortality of only 4 or 5 percent in patients treated by Brand's method was a mere third of the death rate under expectant treatment. "If a hospital physician thoroughly understands the method," Brand added, "he only loses the peritonitis and hemorrhage cases, of the others only exceptionally one." Despite difficulties in securing hospital cases early, Austin Flint and Charles Loomis Dana at Bellevue Hospital and George Livingston Peabody at the New York Hospital soon introduced the Brand method. [12]

It was probably the success of Brand baths which led Baruch to a broader advocacy of water in therapeutics and a renewed effort to distinguish what he called "hydrotherapy" from the "hydropathy" practiced by irregular physicians and laymen. At the New York Academy of Medicine on November 7, 1889, he invoked history to teach his colleagues a lesson. In the first half of the nineteenth century, he said, a Silesian peasant named Vincenz Priessnitz had enjoyed so much success with hydropathy in treating gout and rheumatism, especially among high-ranking Englishmen, Frenchmen, and Germans, that his reputation had spread far and wide: "In 1840 he had treated over 1,500 patients from all parts of the world by the methods he had invented, and when he died, twelve years later, he had amassed several millions. . . . The government built roads to facilitate access to his establishment; monuments and fountains were erected to his memory." Physicians, too, had come to see Priessnitz's work, and they were sometimes converted. But when several regulars petitioned the French government for permission to open institutions similar to the one at Grafenburg, their colleagues had opposed the idea until a hospital trial of the new methods resulted in a favorable report and the withdrawal of the interdiction. "Thus has it ever been," Baruch said, "when the biased views of inexperienced opponents were met by clinical demonstrations in hydrotherapy."[13]

Whether the popular cult of hydropathy had been merely a part of the sweeping "return to nature" or a reaction against heroic treatment (and its opposite, therapeutic skepticism), it had posed a threat to the regular profession: in the wake of Priessnitz, European watering places were popular even among such people as Thomas Carlyle and Charles Darwin, and a veritable "water-cure craze" swept the United States.[14] In 1889, when other medical sects were threatening the position of the regulars, Baruch saw hydrotherapy as a possible means of professional salvation. He called his paper before the academy "A Plea for the Practical Utilization of Hydrotherapy." Earnestly endorsing "this most gifted child of medicine" on historical, physiological, and clinical grounds, he hoped to retrieve it from "its empirical union with hydropathy" and establish it on a rational, scientific basis.[15]

With practiced hand Baruch guided his audience through centuries of medical opinion about water in disease, ranging from Hippocrates to contemporary teachers of medicine "in the best schools of Germany, Italy and France—men, too, who are known everywhere as representatives of good clinical teaching. If the history of medicine were the subject of a few lectures in the medical course, much unnecessary labor and groping in darkness would be spared the student and future investigators, and much good would accrue to his future patients." By concentrating on new discoveries to the exclusion of their own professional history, he said, physicians were shortchanging themselves: "No subject can be logically and scientifically discussed without a knowledge of previous achievements in its line."[16]

Throughout history the persistence of hydrotherapy rested on purely empirical grounds; over and over again, physicians used it simply because it seemed to work. At last, in Baruch's time, physiological experiments were preparing the way for rational scientific explanation. Researchers were studying the effects of water on such measurable functions as respiration and circulation, in animals and in humans. Supporting these ideas were subsidiary physiological investigations by Carl von Liebermeister, Ernst Felix Immanuel Hoppe-Seyler, Franz König, Juergensen, and others. In their work Baruch found proof that water was a most versatile substance, useful in various forms and at various temperatures to affect cardiac action, vascular tension, the quality and distribution of the blood supply, heat production, elimination, and the condition of the nervous system. Some of these effects were clearly understood in 1889. Others such as certain reactions of the nervous system and resistance to toxic effects, as in typhoid fever, have not yet been fully explained, although they still play an important part in successful treatment.[17]

To support effects still awaiting physiological explanation and to give practitioners information more important to them than either history or physiology, Baruch offered pages of clinical evidence. Almost reluctant to use this form of argument (which often formed a basis for the claims of quacks and empirics), he disavowed any intent to claim that hydrotherapy was a "*universal remedy.* I stand second to no one in high appreciation of the medicinal agents, which the practice and custom of many years have established as reliable, and especially of those more modern products of the pharmacist whose effects have been demonstrated with so much precision." Cautiously, he claimed for hydrotherapy "only the position of a valuable but an indispensable auxiliary to other treatment."[18]

In presenting the clinical evidence for hydrotherapy, Baruch borrowed two categories of therapeutic action from the German author F. A. Hoffman: direct methods, which act by removing the cause of disease; and indirect ones, which influence the circulation and nutrition of an organ, causing general tissue change and thus removing disease or causing it to recede. To these categories Baruch added a third, "by which we may so impress the various functions of the body, chiefly through the innervation which governs them all, as to enhance the resisting power of the patient and thus enable him to escape the dangers which are known to be lethal."[19]

The only conditions directly benefited by hydrotherapy were gastric and intestinal diseases. In those involving toxic products produced when microorganisms were ingested with food or milk, especially during the summer, intestinal irrigations were effective even in advanced and threatening cases. In adults with dyspepsia, sipping hot water before meals removed products of fermentation and restored tone and vigor to the lining of the stomach, enabling "the natural forces to come into play."[20]

In the category of indirect action, Baruch saw a role for hydrotherapy in such diseases as "neurasthenia and other nervous diseases," rheumatism, gout, anemia, obesity, and scrofula. Through his own experience in treating neurasthenia, he had devised two diagnostic categories, calling for two different forms of hydrotherapy. In the "erithic" type, characterized by "an instability of the nerve forces," Baruch used soothing measures such as cool ablutions, prolonged wet packs, and half-baths at 65 or 70 degrees, once or twice a day. (Half a century later, William Bierman's textbook of physical medicine for the general practitioner would explain the soothing effects of water in mental illness "on the basis that in the patient's mind the bath is a return to his mother's womb, thus abating anxiety and producing muscular relaxation and mental appeasement." Baruch was content to achieve the effect without trying to explain it.)[21]

In the "asthenic" type of neurasthenia, characterized by an "enfeeblement" of the nerve forces, Baruch submerged the patient in "a mass of cold water for a brief period," sometimes also employing "general faradization" or electrotherapy. For "intermediate" cases, he applied various treatments which he failed to describe clearly, perhaps because of disagreements among those who used hydrotherapy in treating nervous disease.[22] "Hysteria in its protean forms," Baruch said, "presents a wide field for hydrotherapy." Wet packs calmed excited patients; brisk showers, alternating cold and warm, stimulated those who were depressed. In neuralgia and sciatica, there was strong clinical evidence of hydrotherapy's benefits. In cases of anemia not dependent on organic disease, Baruch proposed specific measures which, in his experience, rarely failed to produce weight gain and general improvement. He could not tell whether this was because hydrotherapy affected the blood supply, as demonstrated by physiological experiments, or because it produced palpable but ill-understood effects on the appetite and digestion.

For tuberculosis, the "white plague" of the cities, Baruch presented ample clinical evidence, in addition to his own selected successful cases. Hugo von Ziemssen, Wilhelm W. Winternitz, and Dettweiler had recorded cases in which the disease process seemed to recede under hydrotherapy. In others the fever and night sweats abated, and the patient gained in weight and strength. In maladies as disparate as rheumatism, gout, constipation, and morphine addiction, Baruch gave one or two case histories of each to show his success. In these diseases, as in neurasthenia, however, he failed to give his listeners anything that could be called a strict hydrotherapeutic technique for dealing with them.[23]

Although he then considered fevers the most fruitful field for hydrotherapy, Baruch devoted only a little of his academy address to them because he had written so much about them elsewhere. He emphasized the fact that the object of the Brand bath for typhoid was not so much to reduce temperature as to "*refresh the nervous system* and enable the organism to withstand the lethal influence at work in the regular process of disease."[24]

In conclusion, Baruch said he had showed that hydrotherapy was no longer empirical, that it had become a rational science "in its true sense"—an impossible claim for many therapeutic measures then and even today, after a century of additional investigation. From the evidence Baruch presented in 1889—indeed, from the best knowledge of health and disease available to him and his contemporaries—it was not true that hydrotherapy boasted anything like a complete rationale. It was true that certain physiological effects of water in health were established beyond a doubt, as Baruch showed, but the connection between these effects and the clinical results he and others achieved in treating disease by water was altogether unproved and was then unprovable, partly because "doses" of hydrotherapy were difficult to regulate, partly because of imperfect knowledge of the life processes in health and in disease. Hydrotherapy was certainly worth a trial, if only because of its empirical superiority to the expectant method: in typhoid, for example, Baruch was right to urge his colleagues to test it "fairly and fearlessly," for its proven physiological action gave doctors a way to influence the vital processes without risking the dangers inherent in some of the drugs then in use. But he exaggerated in claiming a complete rationale for the "maltreated and neglected" hydrotherapy.

If Baruch had relied on his intelligence alone, he would have made no such claims, but he was above all a healer in an era when healing threatened to become a lost art, and his heart was as much involved as his head. One case appears over and over in his pleas for hydrotherapy, particularly for Brand baths. He was tormented by the memory of a beautiful young woman who fell ill with typhoid one summer at Long Branch. After making a diagnosis on the second day, he decided to treat her by cold baths, but in the several days required to locate a tub, he kept her temperature down with antipyrin (a coal-tar drug introduced in 1884). When the tub at last arrived, she seemed to be recovering, so he decided not to disturb her by baths: "I was still under the dominion of the antipyretic idea and had not realized the value of the cold bath as a refreshing and invigorating measure." For two weeks antipyrin kept her temperature down. Then her pulse began to fail, and she had chills followed by a temperature of 106. This, too, yielded to the coal-tar drug, but when her young heart failed again, Baruch could do nothing. When she died, he blamed himself: "The tub which would have saved life stood empty and unused in one corner of the room."[25]

This experience, so painfully marked in his memory, apparently led him to confuse the true purposes of scientific investigation with the poet's "sublime and irrefutable passion of belief." Once engulfed in this confusion, which historian Fielding H. Garrison has called "one of the saddest things in the history of medicine," Baruch never recovered.[26] He continued with his crusade, apparently unaware that he was wishfully supplying a link between physiological evidence and empirical therapeutic results which did not yet exist. Encouraged in his "passion of belief" by the continued success of the Brand bath and the increasing number of physicians who accepted it, he again publicly regretted his earlier opposition to Brand: "I propose to devote all the energy of my nature, because I am a proselyte myself." He was undeterred even when Alfred Loomis twitted him for being an enthusiast on the subject, "willing to go as far as the law allows, and even a little farther."[27]

At the end of the summer of 1890, Baruch went abroad "to ascertain the true status of hydrotherapy in Europe, and to observe the practical working of the methods adopted by prominent specialists in this line." After talking with physicians and patients, he wrote the *Medical Record* that hydrotherapy was "almost exclusively relied upon" in the treatment of chronic disease, even among such eminent neurologists as Jean Charcot and Wilhelm Heinrich Erb. Yet in acute diseases, hydrotherapy seemed to have lost favor in Germany between 1880 and 1890—a paradox Baruch understood only when he discovered that even in Germany physicians still erroneously assumed that the purpose of the Brand bath was to lower temperature. Professor Albert Fränkel, at the new Staedtische Krankenhaus zu Urban in Berlin, told Baruch that, although as a pupil of Ludwig Traube he had learned to value hydrotherapy, he now rejected baths in fever, "'because in Germany, we have come to be opposed to all antipyretics in typhoid fever.'" In effect, Baruch said, hydrotherapy was being penalized for the failure of antipyrine and the other antifebrile chemicals to live up "to the trust so unscientifically imposed upon them." Instead of saving life by combating fever, these drugs often merely permitted the patient to die with a normal temperature. In Germany as in America, Baruch had to explain again and again that the Brand bath was a refreshing agent, acting through reflex action from the periphery upon the nerve centers, "from which the whole machinery of the body receives its tone, its force, its very life."[28]

In Paris in September, Baruch saw encouraging signs that the French were coming to accept hydrotherapy, despite its German origin. A discussion at the Société Médical des Hôpitaux brought out facts supporting the views of men he considered the best clinical teachers in Germany: "that until we can find an anti-infectious specific, the cold bath is our best

remedy in typhoid fever." Under the influence of Paris, Baruch's enthusiasm got a bit out of hand, and he ventured the prediction that hydrotherapy in acute disease was in a transition stage from which "it will
emerge as a remedial measure that will endure for ages."

In Vienna, Baruch visited Wilhelm W. Winternitz, a man only six years
his senior, who had written a study destined to rank for several decades as
the best scientific treatise on hydrotherapy.[29] In his youth as a navy
physician, Winternitz had confronted an epidemic of influenza on board
ship. He applied affusions and baths with a success that led him to read
the classical English works on hydrotherapy by Wright and James Currie
of Liverpool (1798). He then went to Grafenburg, the center of operations of Vincenz Priessnitz, to set the extraordinarily successful results of
the Silesian peasant on a scientific footing. Winternitz was a careful investigator. His work with the sphygmograph (a device for recording the
pulse) and exact mathematical and chemical tests so impressed Baruch
that Baruch predicted Winternitz's modifications of the Brand bath
would make it more acceptable to the profession and the public.[30]

While Baruch was in Germany, Brand invited him to Stettin and offered to help him in his study of hydrotherapy, but Baruch did not
accept. He did visit the garrison hospital in Munich, where Dr. A. Vogl
administered the Brand bath on a mass scale, in wooden pavilions so
filled with windows that they looked almost like greenhouses. Vogl's
patients, many of them German soldiers, furnished large bodies of data
on the low mortality in typhoid treated by the Brand bath. Baruch was
convinced by his inquiry into Vogl's statistical method that the results
were reliable.

Baruch found European physicians divided on methods of applying
hydrotherapy in chronic disease: Germans used wet packs, footbaths, sitz
baths, and other local baths, as well as showers; the French, following
Fleury, used showers almost exclusively. Baruch saw virtues in both
schools of thought. The German way allowed many subtle modifications
of hydrotherapy. The French system, as he observed on his visit at the
Institute Hydrotherapeutique de l'Arc de Triomphe, took less time for
both physician and patient.

Besides visiting hydrotherapeutic establishments directed by regular
physicians, Baruch took several looks at the competition. Lay "water-
cure" establishments had suddenly multiplied in Germany after 1869,
when legislation aimed at something else incidentally smoothed the way
for anyone who might claim to treat disease. Tremendous numbers of
nature healers blossomed under this Kurierfreiheit: faith healers, exorcists,
masseurs, devotees of nudism and blue and green electricity, and oc-

cultists of every sort.[31] Baruch was alarmed at the pronounced and increasing influence of the *Naturärzte,* usually teachers, clergymen, or ordinary laborers, some of them highly effective healers but without medical education. An institution Baruch visited at Gera was presided over by a weaver whose success as a therapist had enabled him to buy the building. Impressed by this uneducated man, Baruch went to Chemnitz in Saxony to see "the fountain-head of the 'Nature-doctors.'"

The Von Zimmerman Institute was an imposing building surrounded by beautiful gardens, high on a mountain overlooking a lovely valley on one side and smoking factory funnels and distant mountains on the other. It was endowed by a wealthy merchant who had found relief in water treatments for a disease the "regular faculty" had unfortunately pronounced incurable. Accommodations for patients were no less impressive than the exterior of the building, but Baruch found the equipment disappointingly crude and badly maintained. One of the attendants told Baruch that he used no thermometer, relying simply on his sense of touch; the temperature was not important anyway, he said. Despite their ignorance, these men achieved good results in treating functional nervous disease, anemia, gout, dyspepsia, and rheumatism—results Baruch attributed to "cleanliness, regulation of diet, improved habits, and abstention from medication."

In a letter to the *Medical Record,* Baruch described the work of Father Sebastian Kneipp, a simple Bavarian parish priest who was reviving at Wörishofen what Priessnitz had done at Grafenburg. Unlike Priessnitz, who had made several millions in the water-cure business, Father Kneipp refused payment for his services. Although he did not advertise, patients came to him by the score. In October 1886, when he published the first edition of *My Water-Cure,* Kneipp expressed the hope that a physician would relieve him of the work of physical healing: "I should be so happy," he said, "if at last these professional men would begin to study the system of hydropathy thoroughly and put it in practice under their inspection." A fifth edition (six thousand copies) of *My Water-Cure* sold out in five weeks. By April 1889, no longer able to answer the flood of requests for medical advice, Kneipp put out a seventh edition. By that time, the number of physicians becoming interested in his system led him to hope that it would gradually pass over to the "professionals." This, he said, "will be my greatest consolation."[32]

When Baruch was in Europe, between the printing of the twelfth edition in December 1889 and the twenty-seventh in February 1891, Father Kneipp's success was "the theme of all circles." Baruch attributed Kneipp's results to the novelty of the treatment, the compulsory outdoor exercise, and "not a little of the faith cure." From the patient's viewpoint, there was great virtue in the fact that Kneipp neither made nor attempted to make a diagnosis but merely prescribed according to the complaint the patient considered significant. There was a lesson for physicians in this, but Baruch did not note it until later.[33]

Shortly after Baruch returned to America late in the autumn of 1890, the medical world went agog over a discovery that would indirectly serve to strengthen his "passion of belief" in hydrotherapy. On December 13, 1890, at the Tenth International Medical Congress in Berlin, Robert Koch announced that he had discovered a substance that offered protection against tuberculosis and might even provide a cure in early cases. The reaction in medical and lay circles was immediate. Koch already ranked as "the pope of medical science" for his work on the anthrax bacillus in 1876 and the development of culture and staining methods that enabled him to discover the tubercle bacillus in 1882. Although public health measures were sending tuberculosis incidence into a slight and still imperceptible decline, it remained the world's leading cause of death, and the world paid Koch proportional homage for his discovery. At first, he refused to reveal the nature of his miraculous substance. He was so well regarded, however, that the considerable experimental evidence he presented sufficed to vouch for tuberculin (also called Koch's lymph), bringing hopeful consumptive patients to Berlin from all corners of Europe.[34]

Shortly after his announcement, Koch let out samples for clinical testing in America. New York City physicians scrambled to try the sherry-colored lymph on their tubercular patients. Popular interest ran at such a pitch that city newspapers tried to give full coverage to the trials. The *Herald* published articles daily, telling lay readers how tuberculin was delivered exclusively by a Berlin chemist after six weeks of preparation; how it was injected; and how sputum samples were prepared and examined microscopically by Theophil Mitchell Prudden, a co-worker of Koch in 1882 and more recently a founder of the pathology department at Columbia College of Physicians and Surgeons. When doctors using the lymph would permit it, the *Herald* interviewed them as well. Dr. Abraham Jacobi was not cooperative, taking "great precautions during all his experiments to make them as mysterious as possible." Dr. Kinnicutt of St. Luke's Hospital "got a little ahead of Dr. Jacobi by as much as an hour and a half, whereat Dr. Kinnicutt and all his friends were very much pleased." Dr. George F. Shrady, Baruch's friend and editor of the *Medical Record,* used the lymph at St. Francis Hospital. Alfred Loomis's son Harry was both enthusiastic and optimistic about his results with tuberculin at Bellevue.[35]

As chief of the medical staff at Montefiore Home for Chronic Invalids
(then attracting some of New York's best physicians for patient care,
teaching, and research), Baruch had a large and likely field for a tuberculin trial. Montefiore admitted only those who had diseases considered
incurable, many of them with advanced pulmonary tuberculosis. On
December 27, after a week of testing, Baruch told the *Herald* that he had
enough patients to enable him to determine the worth of the lymph
"without endangering the chances of improvement by other means." ·
Apparently, he was using tuberculin only in otherwise untreatable patients, for he added that, though he would not hesitate to devote most of
Montefiore to tuberculosis treatment once the worth of tuberculin was
proved, he would in the meantime assume "no uncalled for responsibility."[36]

While he was giving injections to nine patients who had been under
treatment and to one new patient who had personally requested it, Baruch clearly harbored mixed feelings about tuberculin. He was attempting to make Montefiore the first fully equipped hydrotherapeutic clinical
laboratory in the country, and tuberculosis was one of the diseases in
which he had had excellent results. In 1890, six patients admitted with
what was considered hopeless consumption became well enough after
hydrotherapy and nourishing diet to return to their homes.[37] Baruch
reported in *Gaillard's Medical Journal* in December 1890 that even if the
lymph should prove capable of breaking down pockets of tubercles in the
lungs, "the vital forces must still be brought to bear upon the expulsion
of the debris." Presumably, physicians would still need hydrotherapy to
stimulate these vital forces.[38]

Starting in January 1891, Baruch gave his impressions of the tuberculin
experiment mainly through editorials and articles in the *Dietetic Gazette:
A Monthly Journal of Physiological Medicine.* He had taken up the editorship
of the *Gazette* with the sole aim of making it useful to practicing physicians, and he interpreted the journal's title in the broadest possible sense,
using "diet" to mean "the employment of everything necessary for the
preservation of health and life," including such man-made contributions
as tuberculin.[39] The *Gazette* of January 1891 carried both his first editorial and an article summarizing his tuberculin experience. From the
two hundred injections he had given and from reports of other physicians
in Europe and America, he was almost convinced that the lymph was
drawn to living tubercular tissue, where it set up local inflammatory
processes. It was too early to say whether this inflammation would result
in the removal of the diseased tissue, but, all in all, it appeared to Baruch
that Koch's hopes would be fulfilled: "I believe with Ewald, 'that Koch's
remedy stirs up the tuberculous deposits, just as the dog does the badger

in his burrows.' Every day brings new proof thereof." Baruch noted the negative evidence, too: that several deaths had been reported; that tuberculin was "a two edged sword, and requires a skilful and judicious hand"; that Koch's method, born of reason and logical deduction, must be nurtured and developed and applied in the same way; that the lymph did not seek out the bacilli, but only diseased tissue, and was therefore not a true specific.[40]

Charges against Koch for his secrecy—ugly allegations of German profit-seeking at the expense of human life—hit Baruch at a sensitive spot. In an article in the *Dietetic Gazette,* he quoted portions of the apologia made by the German minister of culture, who had dissuaded Koch from freely and openly describing tuberculin production. "It was not a matter of money," the minister said, "for millions are taken by swindlers, but far greater was the danger of suffering humanity." Baruch believed that Minister Von Gossler had tried to "prevent imitation of the remedy" only for the good of mankind. He praised Von Gossler's widespread distribution of tuberculin samples for testing and Koch's arrangement to prevent its becoming a remedy for the rich. "Surely," Baruch urged, "even the French cavillers must hide their little heads in shame and hiss their accusations of German selfishness and unseemly haste in silence, while the contempt of the whole world lights upon them for the misdirected patriotism which would doubt the sincerity of a man like Koch."

Elsewhere in the *Gazette,* Baruch used one of his first editorials to dramatize ongoing tuberculin trials. He wrote of a "great struggle" in progress: "not the hand of man raised against his fellow man, but the mighty hand of science arrayed against the most insatiable and relentless foe of mankind. . . . In the hospitals of the civilized world, in the silent wards, beside the couch of suffering thousands, the battle is being fought with the hypodermic syringe as the weapon, charged with the minutest portions of a potent fluid." Physicians who were led into the editorial by this startling example of medical journalism found themselves reading Baruch's plan to perfect Koch's weapon. Koch would provide the mortal attack on tuberculosis tissues, leaving them necrosed but still dangerous to uninfected surrounding areas; Baruch would come in with hydrotherapy and other "well-proven non-medicinal remedies" to spur the body's mopping-up operation. Baruch had even found a quotation from Koch saying that "mountain climate, fresh air treatment, special diet etc." might "be highly advantageous when combined with the new treatment."[41]

On January 12 the *Herald* reprinted Baruch's article from the *Dietetic Gazette,* describing it as "the first review of the Koch treatment in New

York as compared with the attainable data of the experiments abroad." Above two full columns of newsprint stood five headlines, among them "Koch's Fluid Doing Its Work Well" and "Results as Dr. Simon Baruch Sees Them."

As weeks passed and tuberculin fell short of performing the miracle expected of it, popular optimism, inflated by an overzealous press, turned into popular dejection. Baruch was as slow to give up on the lymph as he had been to accept it. His own therapeutic ideas made him hesitant to follow Koch; yet he seemed unwilling to see Koch fail. In the *Dietetic Gazette* for February he defended Koch again, warning against confusion between deaths caused by lymph and deaths that merely happened to occur under lymph treatment. Although Baruch reiterated his belief that tuberculin, as Koch said, sought out diseased tissues and set up a local reaction, he saw "no evidence of a curative tendency" in the more than thirty cases under his care. Still, he thought it was too soon to judge. Admitting that the "possibility of fallibility" was increasingly apparent, he reminded readers that such a possibility was "a necessary attribute of all therapeutic agents devised by the finite human mind." Rather wistfully, he predicted that, if tuberculin should fail, "this same human mind, prompted by the unrest which had given the world its greatest discoveries, will cast about in other directions for means of conquering this greatest enemy of the human race."[42]

For some time Baruch continued to waver between the ingenuity of man and the voice of nature. In February 1891 he made much of the importance of fresh air in tuberculosis, calling it "the kernel of rational therapy."[43] In early April, showing a reporter from the *Herald* a bottle of lymph which he intended to use in his private practice, he said, "That does not look as if I didn't believe in it." But he reserved judgment: "We will not be satisfied that the lymph cures phthisis until years have elapsed. Nor shall we be willing to condemn it until ample time has been afforded for these experiments."[44]

In June 1891, when Koch revealed that tuberculin was a glycerine extract of tubercle bacilli, many New York physicians were disappointed that he did not provide the exact formula so as to prevent the manufacture and sale of fraudulent imitations. Baruch again sprang to Koch's defense: he did not think that lymph could be made solely on the basis of written instructions, and he was certain that Koch would soon throw his laboratory open so that others could learn the preparation and administration of lymph from the master. "This will tend to make his theories and treatment known all over the world, and then the lymph will become one of the standard remedies for tuberculous troubles."

As the tuberculin experiment wore on, data pouring in from all parts of the world proved more and more disappointing. "Koch's lymph" did not produce cures; worse, it sometimes proved highly toxic to persons already harboring the tubercle bacillus. Debilitated patients died in the nausea, vomiting, and fever of reaction; dormant cases became active; tubercular ulcers, healed over and forgotten for years, flared up and opened again. Parts of the medical press berated Koch for bad judgment and premature announcement, but his reputation was too great to be badly damaged by a single failure, and it rebounded with the later discovery that tuberculin was a valuable diagnostic agent.[45]

Although Baruch saw some of his Montefiore patients set back by tuberculin, he never expressed bitterness toward Koch.[46] Following the lymph fiasco, however, he turned more and more from the "ingenuity of man" to the "voice of nature." The hopeful young physician who had challenged therapeutic skepticism in 1873 had come full circle by January 1892: "To-day we stand in breathless expectancy, awaiting the dawn of precision in therapeutics. This hope is vain! Recent experience has demonstrated the fallacy of specific therapeutics after it had been promulgated by a master-mind and adopted as an experiment by the best clinicians in every part of the globe."[47]

Far from leading Baruch to doubt his own usefulness as a physician, his disenchantment with specific therapy strengthened his "passion of belief" in physiological agents—primarily hydrotherapy. From January through May 1892, the *Dietetic and Hygienic Gazette* serialized a long article he wrote about such therapies.[48] Significantly, the first two articles and part of the third were concerned with tuberculosis. The rest of the third and all of the fourth dealt with gout, rheumatism, diabetes, and gastric ulcers. In all of these conditions, which he had rich opportunities to study at Montefiore, Baruch contrasted his own success with the frequently halfhearted, hopeless approach of his colleagues. The healing power of nature was as potent a force for recovery in these conditions as in typhoid fever, he said; physicians had only to believe in it and cooperate with it.

In the last section of this five-part article, Baruch discussed what he called "functional disease." His inclusion of anemia excepted, the term *functional* seems to have meant to him what it does today: illness having no discernible physical or organic origin, hence sometimes inexactly called "psychosomatic." Unlike physicians who believed that diversion of the mind was the major goal in treating such conditions, Baruch emphasized the need for systematic therapy, exemplified in the methodical rest cure of the neurologist S. Weir Mitchell. Though functional disease was without apparent physical origin, it often responded well to physical treatment. In the dyspepsia frequently seen among students and professional people, for example, Baruch claimed effectiveness for external applications of cold water used in combination with warm water stomach lavage. He noticed that these patients benefited by seeing physical proof, through lavage, that, despite their symptoms, their food was being digested.[49]

Baruch treated a growing number of neurasthenics in the years after 1890. Their stories abound in his casebooks and publications, and his correspondence contains letters of referral from doctors such as S. Weir Mitchell and Charles McBurney. From these colleagues and many others Baruch took these difficult cases and usually—but not always—had some success with them. It was not reasonable to expect hydrotherapy to help all the time; like every other treatment for mental illness, it rested on a purely trial-and-error basis. In 1868 the American Medical Association had published a report stating that "moral causes" brought about "physical changes" that in turn caused disease of the mind. The predominant moral causes listed were ill health of various kinds; intemperance; grief; sorrow and anxiety; "female derangements"; causes "connected with religion"; "anxieties, struggles, trials, poverty"; and "vicious indulgence [masturbation]."[50] In its 1869 code of ethics, the AMA inserted a clause urging patients to communicate to their physician the supposed cause of their disease: "This is the more important, as many diseases of a mental origin simulate those depending on external causes, and yet are only to be cured by ministering to the mind diseased."[51] Through the work of a few pioneers, understanding of mental illness had advanced in the intervening years, but it was far from complete; even though Sigmund Freud was aware of the possibilities of hypnosis in the early 1890s, he was still using electrotherapy, hydrotherapy, and massage to treat his patients.[52]

For the desperate souls who came to Baruch with morphine addiction incurred in a long and fearsome flight from pain or insomnia, he prescribed codeine and tonic hydrotherapy. From dysmenorrhea to indigestion, these were the neglected conditions, sometimes considered imaginary because they involved no physical evidence of disease. Baruch's surprising number of successes is attested by his letters from the "cured": warm, happy, grateful letters emphasizing the weight gain he particularly valued because, though only symptomatic, it was often a legitimate index of well-being in patients formerly unable to enjoy food or even to eat. That his patients so often mentioned it is indicative, too, of their desire to please him. Their letters often said how proud he would be to see them in health. The personal element was undoubtedly important in Baruch's ability to heal, as it is in the therapy of every successful physician.

By 1903 Baruch's methods had replaced restraint and chemical sedation at the Manhattan State Hospital for the Insane on Ward's Island.[53] Was there a reason for this success apart from Baruch's personal dynamism? Although the return-to-the-womb theory of a later day may explain some of hydrotherapy's successes, it is also true that Baruch did things which many of his colleagues did not do. He was interested in patients and listened to their symptoms; he did not go as far as Father Kneipp, ignoring diagnosis altogether, but he did gear treatment to symptoms, even classifying neurasthenia into types according to response to treatment. Because of his hope for hydrotherapy, Baruch was enthusiastic in his practice. He plainly expected patients to improve, and many of them did.

Physiological remedies were particularly well suited to combat the sort of complaint voiced at the turn of the century by the sagacious Mr. Dooley: "Father Kelley says th' styles iv medicine changes like th' styles iv hats. . . He says they ought to enforce th' law iv assault with a deadly weapin' again th' doctors. He says that if they knew less about pizen and more about gruel an' opened fewer patients and more windows, they'd not be so many Christyan Scientists. He says th' diff'rence between Christyan Scientists an' doctors is that Christyan Scientists thinks they'se no such thing as disease an' doctors thinks there ain't anything else."[54]

Baruch was so certain that hydrotherapy was an answer to many current therapeutic dilemmas that he pressed his views at every possible opportunity throughout the 1890s and into the twentieth century. Always emphasizing that water's therapeutic usefulness derived from its action on the nervous system, not from mere antipyretic properties, he embodied ideas based on his clinical experience and on his travels in three books laced with citations to other writers, European and American. Because he was sometimes charged with riding a hobby in medicine, he carefully disavowed any intent to establish a system of healing. As he stated in 1892 in the preface to *The Uses of Water in Modern Medicine,* his first book on hydrotherapy: "Of all men the physician should be broad and liberal, and should shrink from all exclusive or universal remedies."[55] Nonetheless, a review in the *New York Medical Journal* charged that Baruch's claims for the Brand bath might induce investigators to give up the search for a specific against the typhoid bacillus.[56]

In January 1893, when Baruch read a paper before the Medical Society of the County of New York, he seemed to sense a "recent revival of hydrotherapy": "Three years ago, the first paper, giving a general review of the uses of water, external and internal, by lavage, irrigation, baths, etc., was read before this society. Articles on this same subject have now become numerous. A new journal has appeared on balneology, and a department in that magnificent specimen of American journalism, the *Annual of the Universal Medical Sciences,* chronicles the advances in this therapeutic specialty."[57] Nonetheless, in a presentation called "Therapeutic Reflections" before the New York Academy of Medicine in the fall of 1893, he complained that too many physicians still relied on symptomatic medicinal treatment. No nihilist himself, he said he fully appreciated the value of some drugs: "I would only inveigh against the thousand and one impotent drugs with which the sick are deluged; drugs without ascertainable effects upon the economy, though many frogs and dogs may have died and lived under their experimental use, have no charms for me."[58]

For too many practitioners, the proper use of hydrotherapy was still a *"terra incognita."* As Brand had recently written Baruch, "Who reads what we write? Who acts upon it? No one." Brand was an old man, bitter that he had spent thirty years of "labor, debate, discussion and polemics" on his treatment of typhoid, time wasted in an age of symptomatic thinking which still wrongly considered his treatment primarily antipyretic. Baruch called the attention of his academy audience to evidence supporting Brand's typhoid therapy in recent work of William Sidney Thayer at the Johns Hopkins Hospital. Building on Elie Metchnikoff's demonstration of the role of leucocytes in the body's reaction to irritation or infection (1884), Thayer had showed that the number of circulating leucocytes more than doubled after a Brand bath, while chemical antipyretics destroyed leucocytes and hampered natural defenses by affecting the heart and kidneys. It angered Baruch that physicians ignored results like these in favor of new drugs that poured out "in alluring forms and rapid succession."[59]

In the discussion following Baruch's paper at the academy in 1893, Alfred Loomis concurred in Baruch's indictment of coal-tar antipyretics. As the physician who in 1881 had diagnosed Baruch's chest pain as nervous indigestion rather than heart disease, Loomis was responsible for Baruch's staying on in New York. He now said charitably that if Baruch had gone "a little 'crazy' on the use of water in his treatment of disease," Loomis himself was "a little off on fresh air, climate, change of surrounding, etc." Baruch replied: "If I am crazy on water, then there are a good many lunatics in Europe. . . . I reiterate that enthusiasm in therapeutics is unwarranted, but that the evidence in favor of the bath treatment in acute and chronic diseases is unimpeachable."[60]

The *New York World* of October 6, 1893, praised Baruch's academy paper in article and headline, but in November the *Medical Record* printed a letter of criticism. A physician named Gustavus Eliot asserted that only a callous physician would subject protesting patients to cold baths. Sounding rather callous himself, Eliot wrote that "this may answer very well in hospitals, where it makes no particular difference whether any individual patient dies or gets well," but private practitioners could not indulge in such heartless coercion. In a long reply, fiery and defensive, Baruch stated that "sentiment and pathos must yield to logic and common sense in medicine."[61]

A friend from Boston soon came to Baruch's rescue with an article supporting the Brand bath. In the *Medical Record* in April 1894, Charles E. Page phrased his argument in terms calculated to make opponents feel like outsiders: the Brand bath, he said, was too simple for the "super-scientific youngsters" and not mysterious enough "to impress the mind of the average medical man, whose head had been so crammed at school with drug theories . . . that there is little room left for common-sense innovations after leaving alma mater." Quoting Baruch on the dangers of antipyretic medication, Page commented: "This is not the off-hand fling at medicine of a tyro, or quack, but the careful statement of a veteran among New York's leading physicians." Page proclaimed that the real quack was the physician who ignored the lessons of Priessnitz and Kneipp, lessons confirmed by several of "the most eminent men in the regular profession."[62]

In 1895 the Riverside Association extended its settlement facilities to include a "hydriatric department" under Baruch's supervision. Most of his patients were poor people with chronic disease—"neurasthenia, chronic rheumatism and gout, neuritis, chlorosis, bronchitis, lumbago, sciatica, hysteria, locomotor ataxia"—referred from dispensaries and from outpatient departments of the large city hospitals. When a "prominent physician," apparently as a joke, sent Baruch a patient with a *"prescription for the Kneipp treatment,"* Baruch vented his anger in an article about Kneipp. He said the Bavarian priest (whose book was then in its fortieth edition) was not a swindler in the material sense, "but there are other motives that may bring a good man to charlatanism—namely, ambition and vanity." Kneipp was guilty of both, Baruch was sure. Bad as Kneipp's failures were, his successes were still worse, for they made it more difficult to secure a place for hydrotherapy in the realm of regular therapeutics.[63]

Despite the apathy and antipathy of many of his colleagues, Baruch's second and larger book, *The Principles and Practice of Hydrotherapy: A Guide to the Application of Water in Disease for Students and Practitioners of*

Medicine, met with considerable success. Published in 1898 by William Wood and Company, the New York edition of this first systematic English-language work on hydrotherapy went through a second printing a year later. A London edition came out in 1900, a second New York edition in 1903. A third, in 1908, was translated into French and published in Paris in 1910.[64] Baruch continued to write articles about hydrotherapy and speak about it wherever he was asked: in Albany, San Francisco, Buffalo, Los Angeles, Boston, Pasadena, Baltimore, St. Louis, Atlantic City, Brooklyn, Charleston and Columbia, South Carolina, and Salisbury and Charlotte, North Carolina—even in Carlsbad, Bohemia. His work in the hydriatric clinic of the Riverside Association increased rapidly, from 2,146 treatments in 1895 to 16,012 in 1902. In the Park Avenue Hydriatric Institute, established in 1892 for the use of hydrotherapy in chronic disease, Baruch had by 1908 supervised more than 100,000 treatments for patients referred by more than a hundred physicians.[65]

Despite all these trappings of success, Baruch still earned only a modest living by the practice of medicine. His fee for hydriatric treatments ranged from a mere $1 to a rare $35; judging from his frequent worries about money, he could not have made much from this work. In 1892, even before he began the clinic work, he wrote about the appalling financial prospects of the physician in what he called a "practical, utilitarian, money hunting age."[66] During the 1890s, perhaps as much for prestige as for money, he served in an editorial capacity with at least five different medical journals, several of them concurrently.[67] From his articles and books he made little or nothing, despite degrading squabbles with publishers who failed to pay him what he considered proper.[68] Although he often complained about the amount of gratis work expected of physicians by people who could afford to pay for medical services, he apparently did not adhere to the "soak-the-rich" theory of compensation. His fees often arrived with notes saying that the bill was reasonable or even too low. Around 1900 he turned over an entire ledger of unpaid bills to a lawyer who had little success collecting, not because the patients had no money but because it would have required court action to prove that they did.[69]

Some of the bitterness Baruch began showing toward surgeons at this period hinged on the growing discrepancy between their earnings and those of physicians, especially general practitioners and family doctors. The *New York Herald* of September 1, 1904, quoted him as saying that "intellectual work" should bring better wages than "mechanical work," in medicine as in other areas of life: "It is to the great credit of the medical profession that the doctor has long been content with the 'grateful appreciation' of his patients and has gone on with his self consuming labors until advancing years reminded him painfully that his race is run and he had not received material reward sufficient to afford him in his declining years that ease and comfort which he has fairly earned."

The man who wrote this had but recently been relieved of the arduous work of earning his livelihood by medical practice. Around the turn of the century, Dr. Baruch's second son, Bernard, announced to his tired father that Bernard's skills as a speculator had made him "worth a million dollars" at the age of thirty. As Bernard remembers the incident, his father's uninterested response made Bernard dissatisfied with mere money and led him to ask himself what good he might do with it. Bernard considered his father's mind the best "with which I had ever come into contact, and his life the most useful that could be imagined." Dr. Baruch had worked very hard for a long time, and so Bernard offered to buy his freedom from work, effectively paying him to retire from practice. At what must have been great cost to his pride, Dr. Baruch accepted the offer.[70] He gave up all but a few of his patients, supposedly to devote his newfound leisure to rest and research. But he was too energetic to rest. He could not do research either, not in the laboratory sense, for he was a clinician. He had been a clinician for forty years and had never wanted to be anything else. Although he continued his work at the hydriatric clinic in the Riverside Association, his literary output dropped sharply. He acted more like a man suddenly burdened than one freed from care.

In September 1902 he attended the Congress of German Naturalists and Physicians in Carlsbad. Even in the Section on Internal Medicine, therapeutics was overshadowed by the bacteriological, chemical, physiological, and philosophical aspects of medicine. Writing from Berlin in mid-October, Baruch described an "alarming absence of bedside workers, while every eye is strained, every ambition is spurred, every thought concentrated on laboratory research." One of the few encouraging signs he saw was progress in disease prevention through public sanitation. Another was the special place given to hydrotherapy in German universities, where it was sometimes required in the regular medical curriculum. Some universities had even created chairs of hydrotherapy.[71] This discovery stirred an old fire of ambition. Many times in the past, as early as 1893, Baruch had urged the teaching of hydrotherapy in American medical schools and postgraduate clinics. He was professor of hydrotherapeutics at the New York Post-Graduate Medical School and Hospital, but he longed to teach medical undergraduates, the impressionable young doctors of the future who would approach his ideas with fresh, unbiased minds. Above all, he wanted to inspire some young disciple to carry on the cause of rational scientific hydrotherapy after he was gone.[72]

In 1907 his chance came. Columbia College of Physicians and Surgeons, the one-hundred-year-old medical school of Columbia University, created a chair of hydrotherapy in the Department of Materia Medica and Therapeutics, appointing Baruch professor for a three-year term starting July 1 at an annual salary of $1,000 "chargeable to gifts." His course was required for fourth-year medical students, who would attend in groups of ten or more on Monday, Wednesday, and Friday afternoons throughout the spring term, either to hear Baruch lecture or to watch him demonstrate new hydrotherapeutic equipment installed in the basement of the Vanderbilt Clinic at Sixtieth Street and Amsterdam Avenue. On the final examination, graduating seniors would be required to answer at least two questions on hydrotherapy.[73]

Though only a few years short of his "allotted three score years and ten," Baruch launched into the new work with vigor. In his introductory lecture, "The Claims of Water as a Therapeutic Agent," he spoke of the versatility of water as a therapeutic agent—stimulant, depressant, sedative, tonic, diaphoretic, emetic, purgative, antipyretic, and antiseptic— and recounted historical reasons for believing that whenever the profession ignores hydrotherapy, patients turn to quackery. He did not claim that water was comparable to the great specifics (mercury for syphilis; quinine for malaria; opium and the anesthetics as painkillers). But even if water could not replace these "Sampsons of the Materia Medica," Baruch told his students that, by using it wisely, they might hope to cure their patients, *"tuto, cito, et jucunde,* and to add to the sum of practical achievement of our calling in the saving of life and alleviation of suffering."[74]

For the most part, Baruch followed the organizational scheme of his 1898 textbook, by then in its third edition. He devoted each lecture to the use of hydrotherapy in a single disease and always pointed out errors concerning hydrotherapy in current textbooks on therapeutics. In his lecture on heatstroke he recalled the steaming summer of 1896, when the temperature in New York stayed in the nineties for ten consecutive days. While the mortality from sunstroke averaged 33 to 41 percent in cases treated antithermically in hospitals, it was only 6 percent in 197 patients whom Baruch treated with procedures aimed at overcoming circulatory failure, not merely at lowering temperature. Yet the higher death rate, which he called "absolutely indefensible," was inevitable if one followed procedures prescribed in any of the leading texts from which he quoted.

Every one of seven prominent authors, William Osler among them, advocated plunging the heatstroke victim into a bath with ice floating in it; that is, into water forty degrees Fahrenheit or colder. Baruch gave physiological reasons for the fatality of such ice baths, carefully explaining his alternative method. "The medical mind," he told the students, "appears to be slow in accepting the best established clinical facts."[75]

At the end of almost every lecture Baruch made a plea for converts: "If you are convinced of a truth by positive clinical observation sustained as are certain propositions in hydrotherapy by physiological rationale, do not hesitate to speak out again and again until you are heard. It is your mission to guard and preserve the most valued possessions—life and health. Do your duty fearlessly as men and physicians."[76]

Baruch seemed well adapted to his role as professor. Indeed, his major bibliographer has suggested that, but for the accidents of Civil War and Reconstruction, Baruch, equipped with the "independence of taste, catholic spirit, and disciplined mind of the university professor," might have entered academic medicine as a youth.[77] He was a striking figure in the lecture room, vital and enthusiastic for all his years. With a sense of drama and an earnestness that was quickly apparent to his impressionable students, he spoke slowly but fluently and convincingly. Although he occasionally said "outdoor" department for "outpatient," "borderland" for "borderline," and "outhouse" for "outbuilding," his extraordinary command of English usually lent force rather than humor to his speech. When he mentioned his experience as a medical officer in the Civil War, the students—mostly northerners—burst into applause, to the great amusement of one young Southron, who knew that Baruch had been a Confederate surgeon.[78]

In joining the Columbia faculty, Baruch had hoped that his work there would soon make the time "ripe for establishing the chair of Hydrotherapy permanently." In this he was disappointed. When his first three-year term ended in 1910, he felt a certain "discomfiture" for reasons he disclosed in confidence to Dr. Samuel W. Lambert, head of the Department of Materia Medica and Therapeutics. On Lambert's urging, Baruch accepted appointment for another term, but in April 1913, when he learned that hydrotherapy had been changed from a required to an elective subject, he decided that any future efforts would be "absolutely barren of results." He wrote Lambert that he interpreted the change as evidence "that Hydrotherapy is not regarded of sufficient importance to warrant the time taken from other subjects, and it confirms my misgivings which have recently crystalised into conviction that the permanency of the Chair on Hydrotherapy is impossible. This episode is but another painful chapter in the sad if not disgraceful history of Therapeutics which was inaugurated by venesection. I fondly hope that it may soon be redeemed by the present laboratory activities."[79]

What were Baruch's misgivings? He wrote Lambert that they were "in no wise related to the curriculum." Reluctant to commit them to paper, Baruch discussed them in person with Lambert. Two of Baruch's assistants later remembered an incident in which students hurled a bag of water at Baruch during a lecture, crying, "Water is good, inside and out." This water-bag treatment allegedly became standard hazing technique for all students who continued to attend Baruch's lectures.[80] Not one out of twenty graduates of the Class of 1913 recalls such incidents, though many of them remember Dr. Baruch: his kindly face and pleasant attitude toward students; his intense interest in and enthusiasm for his specialty; his fondness for the new equipment; the broken English in which he described the essentials of the Brand bath ("cold mit friction"); his tall figure, impressively well-groomed and erect, "like a typical Southern Colonel." Baruch was unlucky in that his course fell in the spring term of the senior year, just before the last crucial medical school examinations. One former student candidly admits that "like most students at this time . . . I probably was more concerned about final examinations in the heavier subjects." The graduating Class of 1908 numbered only ninety-three, reflecting the enrollment decline that afflicted Columbia (along with other American medical schools then beginning to raise admission requirements); hence Baruch's first students were better trained in the basic sciences than former classes had been, a fact that may have contributed to a scornful attitude toward therapies not yet firmly grounded in physiology and biochemistry. Still, it is many steps from indifference or even resentment to open attack.[81]

It seems more likely, as several former students suggest, that Baruch sensed that the rest of the faculty paid little heed to his ideas. The author of the water-bag story says that the incident was "inspired" by medical conservatives and reactionaries displeased by Baruch's activities. Outspoken and peppery by nature, increasingly so as he aged, Baruch certainly did little to ingratiate himself with his more conventional colleagues. Addressing the Chicago Medical Society in 1910, he said: "Hippocrates taught 23 centuries ago 'Nature Heals.' The neglect of this grand therapeutic truth has filled more graves than all the battles of history, and its tardy recognition during the last half century has saved more lives than all the drugs in the materia medica."[82] Such statements were not likely to endear him to his orthodox brethren, nor was his allegation in November 1912 that prejudice against hydrotherapy "simply demonstrates that medical men are *sui generis* in their moss-grown, falsely-termed, Conservatism."[83] These things were written for publication, and they are only examples snatched from an endless stream. They indicate that the professional custom of overlooking colleagues' errors had no appeal for Baruch (he called it "false courtesy that must inure to the discredit of the doctor, and damage to the patient").[84] What Baruch said off the record—and the reaction of the Columbia faculty—can only be imagined.

Shortly after April 28 Dr. Lambert visited Baruch to discuss his reasons for resigning. Baruch spent the next few days "canvassing the situation." On May 4 he wrote Lambert his "painful" decision that "the interests of Hydrotherapy and the University" demanded his resignation. On May 8 he opened his lecture on tuberculosis with one of his last thrusts at the medical profession from the shelter of academe: "Gentlemen: It has been repeatedly my painful duty during this course to inveigh against the criminal indifference of medical men to the uses of water in the treatment of disease and to point out by precept and by example that the result of this neglect is too often loss of life."[85] At the end of the term, Baruch packed up his work at Columbia and prepared for a trip to England. His resignation from the faculty became effective on June 30, 1913. The chair of hydrotherapy, "dependent on gift," went out of existence.

On his return from Europe, Baruch found an expression of sympathy from Columbia president Nicholas Murray Butler: "Without being my-self a medical man, I have had a feeling that the branch of therapeutics with which you were dealing was one of much promise, and I wish it might have had a longer period of testing and development." Summer travels had not softened Baruch's disappointment. Replying to Butler, he once again reviewed the reasons for his resignation: the faculty's action in making his course an elective; "the detailed reason for my despair," confided only to Dr. Lambert; the students' lack of interest. "Not a line has been (spontaneously) published by my teaching staff, only one graduate expressed interest and for financial reasons only." And Baruch was begin-ning to feel the effects of age: "If I were even ten years younger, I would not have resigned."[86]

Baruch might have been twenty years younger at this point in his career if he had not spent his twenties and thirties in Camden, South Carolina, far from the mainstream of American medicine. But if he had had an opportunity to teach at Columbia at fifty, rather than seventy, would it have changed the likelihood of winning a place for hydrotherapy within regular medicine? In chronic diseases, perhaps so; it is in this area, in sports medicine, and in mental illness that hydrotherapy finds its widest use today. It is doubtful that a younger Baruch could have gained hydrotherapy wider or more lasting acceptance in treating acute disease at the turn of the century, for bacteriologists and pharmacologists were looking for specific answers: vaccines for prevention, antitoxins, and chemotherapeutic remedies like arsphenamine (Salvarsan), introduced in 1910 for the treatment of syphilis. Until the introduction of chloramphenicol in 1948, however, the treatment of typhoid fever remained symptomatic and supportive. In the absence of any effective specific treatment for almost three decades after Baruch's death, hydrotherapy remained an essential, life-saving measure.[87]

Judged in the light of subsequent medical advances, the major value of hydrotherapy in acute disease was its offer of therapeutic hope instead of therapeutic skepticism, of common sense and moderation instead of new polypharmaceutical abuses reminiscent of heroic medicine. Baruch's work found a transient reward in the physicians he taught to use hydrotherapy and in the lives saved that might otherwise have been lost to typhoid fever or heatstroke. Useful though it was in his lifetime and for several subsequent decades, hydrotherapy in acute disease was a stopgap in medicine, just as municipal baths were in public health. Baruch's sense of failure, of "despair," stemmed from expecting too much of it.

16 The Wizard of Spas

Even before resigning from the faculty of Columbia College of Physicians and Surgeons in 1913, Baruch began to explore another outlet for his fascination with the therapeutic uses of water. Through the Reservation Commission created by Governor Charles Evans Hughes in 1909, New York State was planning to restore Saratoga Springs as a health resort. Baruch called Hughes's action "the first step in the recognition by the State of the immense value and importance of mineral springs to the welfare of the people." Having long favored state ownership, Baruch now began to dream of a Saratoga transformed: an "American Nauheim," with facilities and personnel to provide the same wide variety of treatments available in many of the great European spas. Especially in Germany, where scientific hydrotherapy had gained wide popularity, "taking the waters" had come to mean more than the old luxurious vacation with perhaps an occasional mineral-water catharsis. Baruch wanted it to mean more at Saratoga, too. In March 1912 he expressed the hope that "ere long Saratoga may become as famous among physicians for the health-giving properties of its waters as it was in its golden prime for its cuisines, its fine hotels, and good sports to the seekers after pleasure." He wanted to see Saratoga's reclamation marked by "the true American spirit of utility to the largest numbers."[1]

Saratoga was not Baruch's first effort at creating spas. In January 1906 he had traveled to California, where he instructed physicians in the use of the waters at Paso Robles and inspected various potential health resorts whose virtues he reported to local medical societies and newspapers. The *San Francisco Chronicle* quoted his view that California springs rivaled those of Baden-Baden, Bad-Nauheim, Carlsbad, and Cannes, statements that sent the *San Francisco Call* into raptures over the "wine and honey, sugar and fruit furnished by our plains and medicine gushing from our mountains, crying out with the voice of many waters to the sick to come and be healed." The *Independent* of Santa Barbara headlined Baruch's opinion that "California leads the world in mineral springs." Lay and medical groups alike showed California's gratitude. He was invited to speak at the Medical College of the University of Southern California. He enjoyed privileges at the prestigious Bohemian Club in San Francisco and met the mayor over luncheon at the Union-Pacific Club. State officials asked his advice on such topics as the best use of $10,000 for hydrotherapeutic equipment.[2]

All these incidents, Baruch said, made his journey "a labor of love," undertaken "solely in the interest of scientific experiment and for the alleviation of the sick and suffering." Although California newspapers repeatedly mentioned that Baruch had come at the suggestion of the Southern Pacific Railroad, he denied any such involvement. He insisted that he had paid his own expenses and would not accept compensation for his work—which may have been true but was somewhat misleading.[3] As he went about his meetings and speeches and interviews, he carried a letter from the general eastern passenger agent of the Southern Pacific Railroad Company, asking that every courtesy be shown Dr. Simon Baruch, who was "en route to Paso Robles, California, at the instance of our Company." Baruch, the letter added, would "have charge of the installation of the cold-water treatment at Paso Robles."[4]

Baruch's endeavor for Saratoga was free of commercial taint. In fact, his ideas for reviving the "village" as a health resort required a curtailment of its former commercial attractions, once as overdeveloped as the springs of California were neglected. For two generations after the completion of the Erie Canal, Saratoga had been a favorite gaming place for big spenders and high livers, an unexcelled social escalator and matrimonial mart.[5] The Saratoga Baruch hoped to transform into an American Nauheim had been famed for its racetrack, its faro and roulette, its traditions of grand dining and drinking, and its processions of four-in-hand drags and barouches. In 1865, *Godey's Lady's Book* considered Saratoga and Newport "the Sodom and Gomorrah of our Union," but *Godey's* was excessively prim. Saratoga had flourished for years through a delicate "adjustment of the moralities and the realities." Its standards were such that those who wanted a good time could have it without risk to reputation.[6]

Although Saratoga had outlived many other American resorts by being neither prudish nor daring, it had fallen on hard times when Baruch first joined in the reclamation effort. After the Racing Commission closed in 1911 and gambling declined in the wake of nationwide reform, the business index sagged. The village had lost the patronage of the sick even earlier, when it was discovered that the waters were being adulterated, the springs first depleted by bottling companies, then "reinforced" by the addition of Epsom salts.[7] Formerly hostile to cleanup campaigns, the citizens of Saratoga emerged from the lean years ready for any suggestion—perhaps even for Baruch's plan to make the town a quiet but prosperous haven for the unhealthy. Although reform efforts by the Reservation Commission, created in 1909, had ceased in 1911 after the death of its chairman, Spencer Trask, Trask's successor, George Foster Peabody, was preparing the commission for action again when Baruch made his first attempt to join in the work.

En route to New York City from Lake Placid in August 1912, Baruch stopped at Saratoga to place his ideas before the commissioners. Finding neither Chairman Peabody nor Commissioner Benjamin F. Tracy, he told a reporter from the *Saratogian* of his ideas for "the erection of a modern bathhouse with a large well-equipped system of sanitary baths under the direction of a corps of doctors and nurses, trained in that line." This, he asserted, "would attract people from far and near as nothing else would. It would be something concrete to work on and would give immediate results."

"Great Bathhouse Needed Here Now, says Water Expert," read the *Saratogian* headline on August 29. The second headline identified Baruch as a "worldwide authority on baths," and the text called him "professor of hydrotherapy in Columbia University and writer on medical topics for the New York Sun." Baruch was in fact newly hired as medical editor of the *Sun*, one of the first physicians to hold such a position and someone who might be of great service to the commission. On the day when the *Saratogian* interview appeared, Chairman Peabody wrote to express his regrets at having missed Baruch's visit. The commissioners, Peabody said, had reached the stage of needing "expert advice" on the therapeutic uses of water. He invited Baruch to call at General Tracy's New York City office.[8]

When Baruch's Columbia tenure ended in the spring of 1913, he set out in earnest pursuit of his Saratoga dream. On May 14, in a *Sun* editorial called "The Rehabilitation of Saratoga Springs," he reviewed the achievement of the commissioners in restoring the springs vitiated by pumping and bottling. He praised Saratoga's assets, verging at some points on the advertisement disguised as news which, as medical editor, he was supposed to keep out of the *Sun:* "The prospect of probable restoration of the greatest American spa to its former prestige as a health resort makes the old timer's heart leap with joy; he has visions of daily pilgrimages to the Congress, Hathorn or other springs; he sees a ruddier face mirroring returning vigor to his jaded vitality, and his mind revels in reminiscences of former joys." Baruch made Saratoga waters sound almost as promising as goat gland transplants. Anyone who had visited the outstanding European spas, he said, "will realize that none surpass and few equal Saratoga in the variety of mineral waters and easily utilized possibilities." However much the commission might ask the state to spend in making Saratoga a modern spa, "the investment will assuredly prove profitable financially."

Before the month of May was out, the Saratoga Springs Medical Society invited Baruch to deliver the principal address at a banquet to honor the reservation commissioners. The society spared neither expense nor effort. Besides the commissioners and Baruch, the guest list of over one hundred included lawyers, clergymen, senators, assemblymen, state officials, leading Saratoga citizens, and many physicians from neighboring towns. In the ornate, high-ceilinged dining room of the Casino (a lively gambling and dining establishment built for half a million dollars in Saratoga's heyday), the society members stood as a reception committee, not a single member absent. After caviar and cocktails, the assembly sat down to a lavish dinner, accompanied by a sparkling mineral water from a newly developed spring. The food, one of the doctors said, was the sort contraindicated for patients.[9]

Afterward, Baruch again praised Saratoga's natural assets, but he noted that they were wasted without physicians trained in hydrotherapeutic techniques: "It is more important for the family physician who sends a patient to a health resort to be informed on the mental composition of the doctor than to know the chemical composition of the waters." He admitted that because American physicians were not as skilled as Europeans in this work, he sent patients abroad to Carlsbad for waters they might have gotten in America. True or not, this hardly seemed the thing to say after a feast at the expense of the local doctors, and Baruch made it worse by lecturing them. He warned against laudatory advertisements that might raise doubts of Saratoga's true worth and called attention to treatments of his own devising for which he claimed a great deal. Although the *Saratoga Sun* of June 18 reproduced portions of the address under the front-page headline, "Dr. Simon Baruch Eulogizes Saratoga's Great Springs at Medical Society Dinner," comments quoted from members of his audience suggest that his remarks left them either baffled or resentful.

In late June 1913, less than a month after leaving the Columbia faculty, Baruch boarded the S.S. *Mauretania* for London, where he planned to attend the Seventeenth International Medical Congress in August. (He had decided not to go when the title of his paper was omitted from the tentative program, but he changed his mind on receiving a cable from Sir Thomas Lauder Brunton, president of the Section on Therapeutics of the congress, knight, baronet, and master of the application of pharmacology in the practice of internal medicine. Sir Thomas cabled simply, "Please come to Congress—Lauder Brunton," and Baruch went.)[10] He cut an odd figure there, with his frock coat, his long legs clad in narrow, old-fashioned trousers, his soft, broad-brimmed hat, and his long white hair curling over the back of his high collar. He criticized English physicians as "drug-ridden," talked about the "benighted condition of British therapeutics," found fault with the Library of the Royal College of Physicians and even with *Encyclopaedia Britannica*—all in the name of neglected hydrotherapy. Whatever British physicians thought, the British press enjoyed him. The *London Express* said he was " 'Uncle Sam' like in appearance, and vigorous and pointed, as American doctors usually are."[11] He was indeed vigorous for seventy-three and even more pointed than an Englishman might expect an American to be.

Before leaving New York, Baruch had suggested to the Saratoga commission that he remain abroad to study the spas of Europe. He left before the commissioners had time to consider the offer, but they cabled their approval to London. On the basis of his report, the commissioners hoped to present the next legislature with a comprehensive plan for the development of Saratoga.[12] On August 16, Chairman Peabody wrote Baruch, asking that he get "authentic analyses" and all possible information about the physiological effects and therapeutic value of the waters at Vichy, Aix-les-bains, Carlsbad, Marienbad, Ems, Nauheim, Hamburg, Kreuznach, and Baden-Baden, as well as any other spas Baruch might consider important. In addition, Peabody asked for information about everything from the physical arrangements, engineering details, and price of treatments to hotel and pension rates and methods of bottling waters.[13]

Even with young Dr. Albert J. Wittson acting as his secretary, Baruch could scarcely have done everything the commission asked in less than a year—yet he did a great deal in a short time. He had already started on his work before the commission's authorization arrived. On August 2, in advance of the congress, he visited Bath. On August 11, the day before it ended, he went to Paris. On the thirteenth he visited Vichy. On the sixteenth, as Peabody was writing his instructions from Saratoga to

London, Baruch was on his way to Baden-Baden; on the nineteenth, Wiesbaden; the twenty-first, Hamburg; the twenty-fourth, Nauheim; the twenty-seventh, Kissingen; the thirtieth, Carlsbad. During the first ten days of September he visited Marienbad, Franzensbad, Berlin, and London. He lectured to a group of physicians at Harrogate on September 11 and sailed from Liverpool on the S.S. *Lusitania* on the thirteenth.[14]

Five days later, he arrived in New York City with a trunk full of notes and a head full of plans for Saratoga. That same day (September 18) Chairman Peabody wrote that the commission had employed Dr. Albert Warren Ferris as "Medical Expert" while Baruch was abroad. Though formerly "hydrotherapy expert" at a resort, Ferris was not a specialist in hydrotherapy. Furthermore, his ideas on the subject differed from Baruch's. The irony of his appointment was sharpened because Ferris, like Baruch's rival in his public bath campaign two decades earlier, had previously served on the New York State Lunacy Commission.[15] Though Baruch wrote Peabody on September 24 that he considered Ferris a good choice, in the *New York Times* of September 28 he said that no good European spa employed a medical man for advisory or administrative work. Some layperson of executive ability was usually *Kurdirektor,* with the task of supervising parks, gardens, amusements, and all external affairs, while a trained technician had charge of employees of the baths and all internal matters. "Thus the individual physician was unhampered in his management of patients, while all medical matters were decided by a vote of the local medical society."[16]

Neither the commission nor the Saratoga Springs Medical Society acted on Baruch's broad hints, but it is not likely that his remarks escaped the attention of Dr. Ferris, who—although he lacked Baruch's way with the press as well as Baruch's striking appearance—had the eight-month appointment Baruch had perhaps hoped for. At first, Baruch did not deign to correspond with Ferris, but he could not refuse to meet with him to discuss bringing Dr. Paul Haertl, director of the State Chemical and Balneological Laboratories of Bavaria, to visit Saratoga. It was Baruch's idea that Haertl, whom he had met in Bad-Kissingen, should advise the commission on hydrodynamics as he himself had hoped to advise it on therapeutics. When Peabody empowered Ferris to make financial arrangements for Haertl's trip, Baruch had no alternative to their suggested meeting. Then, however, and throughout his service to the commission, he used the press to compensate for his want of official status.[17]

On September 20, two days after Baruch returned from his lightning tour of European spas, the *New York Times* printed an interview in which

Baruch told Saratoga how to become a great health resort. Presumably because he had not yet had time to look over his notes, the advice was brief: forgo the races. By September 28 he had something more for the *Times:* he described the spas he had visited; their administration, usually by cities or states; the physicians who sent patients; and finally the patients themselves. Because everyone had been so helpful, he had been able in a short time to gather a great deal of data that he thought might prove "of the utmost value" to the commission. He reported that many of the Americans he had met were delighted to hear the plans for Saratoga, which they had regretfully given up "by reason of mismanagement due to contentions between the respective owners of the springs and the deficient and antiquated hotels." Most of these Americans abroad considered Saratoga so blessed with natural assets, Baruch said, that the commission need only supply "modern business methods" to make the New York spa prominent among the world's health and recreation centers. Baruch drew a moral from the fact that Baden-Baden had "barely escaped becoming a Monte Carlo" and that Nauheim, too, had once been a huge "temple of fortune." Cooperation between the government and the local medical society had saved them both, he said, as it could save Saratoga.

Baruch continued for some time to act as an important if unofficial adviser to the Saratoga commission, mainly through Chairman George Foster Peabody. Peabody was a dedicated philanthropist; a corporation director who advocated government ownership of railroads; an active promoter of higher education for southerners, black and white; and a supporter of free trade, woman suffrage, and the peace movement. He had originally accepted the commission chair out of loyalty to the memory of his friend and former partner, Spencer Trask, who had died in an accident while on commission business in 1909. Peabody soon developed an interest in the work for its own sake and retained this interest for many years. (He was later to bring his friend Franklin Delano Roosevelt to Warm Springs, Georgia, working with him to make it a health resort.) Only twelve years Baruch's junior, Peabody was a tall, handsome man with a mustache, a pointed beard, and an air of quiet dignity.[18] He responded to Baruch's energetic flow of questions and advice with seemingly boundless patience, never missing an opportunity to say something kind about Baruch's gratuitous services to the commission. He made Baruch welcome at commission meetings and expressed concern over the illness Baruch suffered after his energetic European tour: "I fear that you threw yourself into the work too vigorously."[19]

For many months Peabody said nothing about Baruch's reluctance to correspond with anyone else on commission business, even on matters of primary concern to someone other than Peabody. He was grateful to Baruch for bringing Dr. Haertl to them. He knew that only a man of Baruch's knowledge and experience could have learned so much about European spas so quickly and that most men with such qualifications would not have given their services without remuneration. Baruch was also generous in using the press for Saratoga's benefit. He arranged to have his report on springs of the United States published in the New York *Medical Times* of October 1913 and frequently used his medical editorship of the *Sun* to publicize the Saratoga restoration.[20] On January 28, 1914, a *Sun* editorial entitled "The Future of Saratoga Springs" urged the legislature to appropriate funds needed to lay new pipes and make other improvements suggested by Dr. Haertl. The editorial said that the legislature, for perhaps the first time in its history, could look for a return on an investment—a return to the entire state, not just to Saratoga. (The last point especially gratified Peabody, who, among other harassments, had to avoid charges of seeking pork-barrel legislation.)[21]

Always alert for opportunities to help, Baruch sprang to the defense of the commissioners when the *Albany Argus* used letters and an editorial to criticize their request for $235,000. The *Argus* urged the legislature to concentrate less on developing Saratoga Springs and more on bottling waters for profit. To counter this pressure on the governor—who was already showing a disinclination to sign the appropriations bill—Baruch wrote to the *Argus* explaining that Saratoga's superb resources would be wasted without the costly hydrotherapeutic equipment needed to compete with European spas. In a long letter published on the editorial page where the governor could not miss it, Baruch said: "The preparation has been completed at great but judicious outlay; the harvest is sure if experience is worth anything at all. To stop or be niggardly now in the last preparations would but result in weeds overgrowing the land." Baruch promised that baths would bring greater profit than bottled waters and that suffering humanity would benefit far more: "The baths should be the first consideration according to my humble judgment, derived from studying this subject and writing upon and teaching it for a quarter of a century." Bearing in mind the pork-barrel problem, he made a special point of saying that he would not trouble to write at all "were the prospective benefits confined to the hotels or the people of Saratoga." Since private enterprise would care little for the work that needed to be done, the state must take it up and finish it. This last statement, he later wrote a Saratoga physician, was to placate "the governor's known desire to avoid local appropriations for local benefits. This of course is *entre nous.*" Before the middle of April, the governor signed the appropriations bill.[22]

Again, on May 13, Baruch included some good words for Saratoga in a *Sun* editorial on the general subject of American mineral spring resorts and the need to submit their claims to analysis by impartial government experts. Endorsing a proposal that the United States Public Health Service undertake this activity, Baruch pointed to Saratoga as a good example—the only one, he said—of an American spring being supervised by a state hygienic laboratory. He predicted that the legislature's appropriation of funds asked by the Saratoga commission would "stimulate the development of other spas throughout the United States."[23]

Despite Peabody's unmistakably genuine gratitude for Baruch's services, a shadow of impatience appeared in his letters during the summer of 1914, when Baruch apparently expressed an unwillingness to deal with Ferris.[24] On July 3 Peabody sent a gentle ultimatum. Worn down by commission duties that had proved three times as demanding as he had expected them to be, he said that his new duties as a member of the Board of Directors of the Federal Reserve Bank would force him to reduce his Saratoga work. In the future he hoped "to have the work of the Commission attended to by those whom the State pays for their services, under our direction." Tactfully but firmly, he told Baruch to make up his mind to work with Ferris. Since Peabody could no longer act as intermediary, the two physicians would have to work out their professional disagreements: "You will realize that having selected him as having a broad knowledge of medical thought and practice, and particularly because he was not confined to any one aspect of practice, we shall have to confirm his position by being completely frank with him. Therefore all 'cooperation' with him will have to be directly and not through any orders from above, which of course would not be suitable from the lay Commissioners respecting professional statements."[25]

Baruch was stung—perhaps most by the indirect aspersion on his preoccupation with hydrotherapy. Resolving to let the chairman write the next letter between them, he set himself the unpromising task of persuading Ferris to accept his views. He began by chiding Ferris for hiring a bath attendant uninstructed in the hydrotherapeutic techniques Baruch and others had devised in the preceding decades. He also reminded Ferris that he had urged him over and over to install the apparatus used for neurovascular training—the so-called needle-spray or "douche" apparatus so popular in Europe and among Baruch's patients in New York City. Without this innovation, Baruch warned, Ferris could not meet the competition likely to come from a Saratoga hotel owner (brother of the manager of the Plaza in New York, where this form of hydrotherapy had met with great success): "These shrewd men will not be slow to see the financial and other advantages of adding one to their basement." Baruch wrote thus frankly, he said, "because you are at a turning point that for the sake of a few hundred dollars may set back this great and costly enterprise for years."[26]

Baruch made some progress with Ferris concerning the controversial equipment. Ferris in turn tried to indulge Baruch, asking for and praising his opinions, sometimes addressing him as *"Geehrter Kollege"* and referring to their relationship as that of master and pupil. But their rivalry often surfaced on subjects other than their mutual interest in hydrotherapy. On August 21, 1914, in response to something Ferris had written about events in Europe, Baruch snapped: "I am not at all sanguine about the Czar's promises and I hope he'll get another good licking to bring him to his senses. The whole world appears to be against Germany but the Kaiser's ancestor Frederick the Great conquered Austria, Russia and France combined. Wilhelm would have done it also if he had brought his siege guns to Liege in the beginning." Ferris replied: "I see that although you are a Pole, you are also a good German."[27] By the end of the summer, the two men were openly disagreeing on hydrotherapeutic matters, too, and writing letters of unprecedented brevity.

It must have been a great relief to Baruch when, in mid-September, Peabody wrote to ask that Baruch "stir up the physicians" of Saratoga, who seemed afraid to prescribe the new hydrotherapeutic equipment. Baruch reminded Peabody that he had hoped "to forestall this obstacle" by offering to instruct the Saratoga doctors if the commission would arrange it.[28] He preferred to discuss the subject in person and asked that Peabody consider confidential even his veiled references to "the medical mind of the average doctor." Baruch suspected that Peabody, because of his "catholic and perhaps too ingenuous mind," failed "to grasp the situation."

Both Peabody and Baruch feared that Saratoga, having come so far in a few years, might fail now because of the hostility or indifference of the local doctors. Suggesting that "Dr. Jacobi's advice would be of great value at this point," Baruch offered as "proof" of his own lack of bias a copy of a "letter I wrote on a sickbed and which resulted in the publication of the article on the following day." The article in question was a *Sun* editorial which Baruch had sent in on September 5. When it had not appeared by September 13, he asked the *Sun's* owner, William Charles Reick, to publish it, for the "good will of the medical profession is the most important element in the future success of the Saratoga Springs."

He also wrote Reick: "This is the psychological moment to impress upon the public and the profession the value and importance of furthering the development of these springs. I hoped that the Sun may utilize it. Other papers have done so (See inclosed clipping from yesterday's Telegram) and I had hoped to see the Sun in advance of others." Baruch later wrote Peabody that this note had prompted Reick to telephone orders to publish the editorial.[29]

Baruch took his inspiration for the editorial from a recent issue of the *Journal of the American Medical Association* praising the Saratoga commission for its "policy of candor and publicity." Expanding on this happy agreement between organized medicine and reservation officials, Baruch told *Sun* readers of the AMA's work in ferreting out frauds, "undaunted by the wealth or position of brazen advertisers of deceptive preparations, pursuing some even into the pages of respectable medical journals." When such an organization gave its approval to Saratoga, physicians could be assured that they "may well confide their patients to the care of these men with confidence that their and their patients' interests will be safeguarded."[30]

Peabody, who was the first of the commissioners to see Baruch's "splendid" editorial, had already had the pleasure of passing it around. It appeared in the evening *Saratogian* as well as the morning *Sun* and, Peabody wrote Baruch, "I am sure did much good for the cause which you have at heart."[31]

Though Baruch's support might be helpful among the doctors of the nation, it was more like a millstone in Saratoga, where the local practitioners' attitude toward Baruch was, as Peabody finally admitted, "discouraging, particularly in view of the most public spirited manner in which you gave of your wisdom and experience to counsel them."[32] For some time Baruch did not seem to realize how the local physicians felt, perhaps because he was preoccupied with Ferris; the "Medical Expert's" original eight-month appointment had stretched out over a year and seemed likely to go on indefinitely.[33] On October 9, 1914, Peabody felt compelled to explain again to Baruch that the commissioners had to hire Ferris because they had "no way of commanding the confidence of the medical profession excepting through the direct association with us day by day of some man of eminence in the profession." Baruch objected that Ferris was not truly an expert in hydrotherapy, but Peabody, again reflecting the low standing of Baruch's "special concentration," reminded him that there was "a stupid lack of interest in this country in hydrotherapy and it was necessary to have an M.D. of public standing outside of that particular branch of practice to arouse them to a situation which we are creating." Only when Ferris left the commission in 1915 did it become clear that the "local situation" was as great an obstacle to Baruch's plans for Saratoga as Ferris had been—and the situation persisted despite Baruch's best efforts.

When growing turmoil abroad gave America a rare chance to win the displaced patrons of European spas, Baruch worked harder than ever to gain wide recognition for Saratoga in lay and professional circles. In the Sunday *Sun,* November 22, 1914, he labeled as nonsense current anxiety about not getting to spas because of the war; Europe had no mineral spas the United States could not match, he said, with "Paso Robles, on the Southern Pacific," the three Virginia spas—White Sulphur Springs, Greenbrier Springs, and Hot Springs—and Saratoga Springs in New York State. "It may savor of Yankee spreadeagleism, but it is nevertheless true to say that in regard to variety of mineral and gaseous content and of temperature . . . some of the springs in the United States excel the best on the Continent." In a *Sun* editorial on March 16, 1915, he said that Europe had no cold springs with more valuable curative properties than Saratoga, "where persons who have been in the habit of spending the summer at Kissingen, Vichy, Hamburg, Marienbad or Nauheim, may find the carbonic acid waters of these resorts which aggregated 160,000 patients in 1911." Saratoga physicians who read this in the *Sun* or the *Saratogian* might have been pleased if only Baruch had not repeated what he had said at the banquet in 1913 about the importance of the "mental composition of the doctor to whom the patient goes." This time he made himself even more offensive by adding, "So long as this important branch of therapeutics is not taught in the medical colleges so long will the prescription of our mineral and thermal springs languish."[34]

One of Saratoga's greatest assets was its carbon dioxide waters, which resembled the springs that had made Nauheim famous since the mid-nineteenth century for the treatment of heart disease. At a symposium, "The Treatment of the Failing Heart," at the New York Academy of Medicine on May 20, 1915, Baruch said, "The only Nauheim bath in this country is at Saratoga Springs." He predicted that proper development of its resources would enable Americans to "live independent of Germany in the care of our hearts."[35]

Despite these efforts that would benefit Saratoga's doctors, Baruch appealed in vain for their support in May 1916. On the basis of tests done by the commission chemist, Herbert Ant, Baruch believed certain salts must be added to make Saratoga's carbonic acid baths as effective in treating heart disease as the famous Nauheim waters. On May 21, when he presented his findings to George D. Pratt, chairman of the State

Conservation Department that took charge of Saratoga that spring, Pratt, fearing a scandal like the one that had resulted from the secret Epsom salt "reinforcement," opposed any addition to the waters. If patients came with prescriptions for the familiar "Nauheim baths," Pratt said he would ask the referring physician to provide both a prescription for the desired additions and the salts themselves.[36]

Baruch believed that such a course would almost certainly cost Saratoga the chance to become the American Nauheim. Refusing to let his hopes for Saratoga be shattered by a politician of questionable integrity and no medical knowledge, he wrote directly to several Saratoga doctors, asking that they urge Pratt to provide all the bathhouses with salts and with bath managers instructed in their use.[37]

Saratoga's physicians could not have been less cooperative. Their responses fell on Baruch like an avalanche. Dr. Douglas C. Moriarta opposed adding salts because he preferred "to have Saratoga's future as a health resort stand upon her own marvelous natural resources." Influential both as a former health officer of the village and as a favored crony— along with J. Pierpont Morgan and John W. Gates—of gambler and entrepreneur Richard Canfield, Moriarta sent a copy of his letter to Pratt. From Maine, where he was enjoying his annual fishing trip, Dr. Calvin S. May wrote that "as a matter of good faith" and consistent with claims of the preeminent advantages of the waters and air of Saratoga, "I would not add to or take from its waters any element, or percentage of an element." Dr. May, too, sent a copy to Pratt. Herbert H. Baright, medical director of the Saratoga Springs Medical Sanitarium, thought it would be "wiser from all standpoints for the profession, both within and without Saratoga Springs, to advise their patients to take the mineral water baths here in natural, unmodified water." Baright added that Saratoga should refuse to "trade on 'Nauheim' or on any other reputation."[38]

Even before all the replies were in, Baruch knew that he was beaten. Four days after Baruch sent his letter, Commissioner Pratt issued a statement to the press declaring the commission's decision to maintain the waters in their natural state, which Pratt said was adequate to every purpose. Pratt warned that even adding salines on a physician's prescription would be "entirely upon his own responsibility, and will affect no other than his own individual patient." On June 10 a Saratoga physician wrote Baruch that the Saratoga Medical Society had unanimously endorsed Pratt's statement. "We hope you will join with us," the doctor said, "in dropping the name 'Nauheim' and in cultivating by every means possible, the efficiency of the Saratoga mineral water bath."[39]

Although Baruch dismissed the opposition as that of "a few sentimen-

tal Saratoga doctors" who were provincially proud of their native resources, he must have known that more was involved.[40] Two years later,
he received a warning to stay out of the Saratoga imbroglio because the
physicians did not like him, the people did not like him, and the commissioner did not like him.[41] The feelings of Commissioner Pratt are not
surprising; but some explanation is required for the fact that Baruch had
somehow incurred the hostility of physicians and townspeople alike in
the course of work that promised to bring patients to the doctors and
prosperity to the villagers.

Some of the medical bad will must be attributed to Baruch's enthusiasm for his own particular specialty, an eternally potent source of intraprofessional enmity which doubtless contributed also to his difficulties
on the Columbia faculty. Although there is no surviving evidence of anti-
Semitism, that too may have contributed to the antipathy Baruch so
frequently encountered. His insistence on the superiority of Nauheim
waters and German physicians at a time when Germany and the United
States were about to go to war is yet another likely source of difficulty. In
addition to these considerations, the Saratoga situation seems to have
been another example of Baruch's tendency to alienate others, a tendency
that grew as he aged. Many ambitious men with equally palpable egos
escape such recurrent personality conflicts by choosing their actions and
their words with deliberate caution; Baruch was apparently so unaware
of his ego's intrusion into his work that he failed to anticipate his effect on
those he hoped to persuade or instruct.

If any Saratoga physicians had come out of his address at the Casino
banquet in 1913 without resenting his preaching at and patronizing them,
Baruch gave them other occasions to take offense. One of the most
striking came in May 1916, just before Baruch appealed to them to
oppose Commissioner Pratt. Speaking to the Saratoga Medical Society
about Nauheim baths, he claimed that it had been his "happy privilege to
open the 'boom' for Saratoga baths which had eventuated in the present
high state of development of your Spa." Not content with this boast,
Baruch warned in the *Saratogian* against efforts to attract "holiday crowds
of gay pleasure seekers, enjoying the gambling, the races and fine wine
dinners." Such patronage, he said, would be a torment to invalids who
were ordered to retire at 9:00 and rise at 6:00. Even with its praise for the
town and the waters, this interview was not likely to please either businessmen or physicians. Baruch repeated his worn aphorism about the
physician's skill being more important than the water he prescribed, now
adding an analogy: "Millet, when asked how he mixed his paints to
obtain the brilliant coloring that made him famous, said, 'I mix them

with brains.'" With no apparent sense of condescension, he further assured the reporter, "You have good physicians here who doubtless will accept the advice I have given them."[42]

It is a sufficient comment on Baruch's judgment of human nature (his own and others') that he said such things in the lay press three days before appealing to the town's physicians in the expectation that they would support his views.

Outwardly, Baruch explained the opposition of Saratoga's doctors as a manifestation of provincialism. Outwardly, he interpreted Commissioner Pratt's decision as a wise one, which would placate local sentiment without prohibiting physicians from prescribing individual additions.[43] But the protests he marshaled through the medical press indicate that he thought otherwise. An editorial in the *Medical Record* reviewed Pratt's ultimatum in the light of Baruch's article on the Nauheim method, expressing fear that the commissioner might object to salts being added even on prescription: "This open and avowed practice would be eminently ethical, and could in no sense be regarded as an adulteration. . . . If the effort to establish the Nauheim method at Saratoga fails through a mistake of this sort, the Spa will never attain the popularity which its friends are working to secure for it."[44]

In the lead article in the *New York Medical Journal* of June 10, Baruch listed the exact chemical composition of each spring at Saratoga, noting that the carbon dioxide waters must be strengthened by added salines for the best results in heart disease. The resumption of horse racing, against all his warnings, prompted a vengeful comment: "The month of August, being devoted to sport in Saratoga, is not favorable for invalids, who at other times may find there the most favorable environment."[45]

In the same issue an editorial drew attention to the resources Saratoga offered for heart patients cut off from Nauheim by war and for those who had formerly used "artificial" baths because they could not afford to travel to Nauheim. Making a distinction that must have delighted Baruch (if he did not actually write it), the editorial noted that Saratoga "Nauheim" baths achieved by the prescribed addition of salts were highly superior to artificial carbon dioxide baths. The day his article and the editorial appeared in the *New York Medical Journal,* the *Medical Record* published a letter by Baruch on the subject of Nauheim baths at Saratoga.[46]

While Commissioner Pratt and the Saratoga doctors had their day on May 26, Baruch had his all through the first half of June in New York's two leading medical weeklies. In addition to the other publications written or inspired by him, the *Medical Record* of June 17 published Baruch's rationale for Nauheim baths in treating cardiovascular disease. By absorption through the skin and by inhalation, he said, the baths exerted an influence on the respiration, which in turn "must influence favorably the entire intrathoracic circulation, more especially the venus [sic] flow. The right heart is unloaded and the diastole prolonged, all of which must bring great relief from stases, which, by their production of edema and retention of toxines from faulty tissue change, give the bedside clinician most anxiety, and but too often close the scene." Several German investigators had recently published work showing that carbon dioxide baths first raised blood pressure, then lowered it. On the basis of his own experiments, Baruch believed that carbonated waters constricted the unstriated muscular structure of the skin, which then offered "mild but positive resistance to the flow of blood in the large peripheral surface, with the result of enhancing cardiac energy." Physicians who accepted this rationale would accept the addition of salines, for there was also evidence that the retention of carbon dioxide and efficacy of the water rose with its saline content. According to experiments done by Baruch and Herbert Ant, the Saratoga Reservation chemist, the addition of salts could raise the CO_2 content from 5–7 percent to 20–25 percent, while also facilitating its absorption by the body.[47]

This deluge of publications supporting Baruch's views proved too much for the anti-additive forces to bear in silence. In a letter to the *Medical Record* of July 1, the officers of the Saratoga Springs Medical Society reasserted "their deliberate and emphatic conviction that for series of successive CO_2 baths given systematically our natural Saratoga Springs mineral water, etc., is fully efficient, and further that it should be used for such series of baths without addition of any salts, *unless* such additions are plainly ordered in the prescription of the physician."[48] The baths they referred to could only be the graduated series used in cardiac therapy, called Nauheim baths by everyone but Saratogians. Baruch did not answer the letter himself. Dr. Albert J. Wittson, his friend and secretary on the tour of European spas, did it for him: "Whether the American profession will be guided by this resolution of a small number of colleagues whose unpublished observations extend over a brief period of a few months in a resort that is still in its infancy so far as CO_2 baths for cardiac disease are concerned, or by the published observations of physicians and eminent specialists all over the world extending over a period of twenty-five years on a material of over a million recorded baths for heart cases alone, is not for me to point out." With sarcasm that would have done credit to Baruch himself, Wittson noted the "zeal of the Saratoga physicians for purism" in a therapy they knew little about: "In fact, the publication of two cases is all the literature I could find upon these baths contributed by Saratoga physicians outside of propaganda by an official of the reservation." Baruch's paper in the *Medical Record* of June 17, Wittson said, was the first rational explanation of the action of salines in the Nauheim bath, "since he has fortified the opinions established on reliable clinical evidence by physiological data and chemical experiment."[49]

Despite Wittson's gallant representation, Saratoga's doctors refused to add salines, and the 1916 season was disappointing. In late August Baruch heard that Saratoga, as in olden days, was concerned with one month of business alone—"August and the races." The bearer of the bad news was Louis W. Noland, former secretary of the Reservation Commission. He was now secretary-treasurer of the Saratoga State Waters Corporation, "Lessee of the Mineral Waters Bottling Privileges" with the right to advertise its product ("natural cathartic waters" as well as table waters) with the arms of the state of New York on every bottle. Still worse, a patient whom Baruch referred to Saratoga encountered an incompetent attendant who botched even the simple hot packs Baruch had prescribed.[50]

All of these incidents made Baruch's goals for Saratoga—the restraint of gambling, cessation of bottling, and employment of trained hydrotherapeutic personnel—seem more inaccessible than ever. In addition, no one seemed willing to do away with the enclosed, heated "Drink Hall"; the "beer garden like hall," Baruch wrote to Superintendent Jones, "which you inherited from the Anthony-Ferris regime." Baruch considered this arrangement absurd, "more like a crowded indoor soda-fountain than like the open pavilion," the *Trinkhalle* of German resorts, where the mineral waters were dispensed in paper cups and the absence of seats encouraged patrons to wander about the grounds as they drank.[51]

Early in 1917 Baruch "decided to give up my interest in Saratoga for which I have so long labored, as one of the disappointments of my life." Yet he needed only a little encouragement to turn to the dream once more, expanding on his plans for a magnificent and luxurious bathhouse, for a pavilion, for gardens and fountains and shaded walks. At the slightest prompting, he took up pencil and paper and sketched his ideas for the Saratoga of the future, but the time had passed for him to see the ideas translated into reality.[52]

In March 1918 reservation officials who wanted Baruch to interest his friend Army Surgeon General William C. Gorgas and his son Bernard (chairman of the War Industries Board) in establishing an army convalescent center at Saratoga showed a flurry of interest in his ideas, but it did not last long enough even to get a pavilion built. In December Baruch appealed to Sir William Osler to use his influence for Saratoga's development, probably assuming that Osler, who had lost his only son in the war, would want to see America rival "the Springs of the Central Powers." Osler was interested, but he was also busy. He referred the letter to someone else.[53]

Baruch then turned to a potential competitor of the Reservation Commission, sending one of his articles on hydrotherapeutic technique to the owner of Saratoga's Grand Union Hotel. He hinted that the owner might find in it ways to "prolong the SEASON in Saratoga which is now all too short for a hotel enterprise as you are aware. The reading of this pamphlet and in fact its reproduction as an ad to physicians would probably promote the hotel interests of Saratoga. . . . If you are interested I shall be glad to give you an interview."[54]

Though no longer officially connected with Saratoga, George Foster Peabody shared Baruch's lingering hope that it could somehow be made into a first-class health resort. Peabody's hopes centered on his expectation that New York's new governor, Alfred E. Smith, would soon "make an examination of the condition of the Conservation Dept." Writing with unaccustomed irritation about Commissioner Pratt and "his underling, Deputy Jones—a quite hopeless State Official," Peabody expected that Smith would investigate the Reservation Commission. In the meantime, he counseled Baruch to postpone suggestions: "If Gov. Smith takes hold of it, we all want to get together and pull for the one plan and have no division among the friends of the Saratoga waters. Gov. Smith is a strong man and will develop state support more rapidly than anyone else."[55]

While other duties occupied Governor Smith, Commissioner Pratt and Superintendent Jones let Saratoga lie fallow. Baruch's activities in its behalf, like his tenure at Columbia, ended on a note of embitterment. On August 17, 1919, the *New York Times Magazine* carried a long article on Saratoga, "Our American Spa," attributing progress at the springs solely to Pratt, despite illustrations showing areas acquired and developed before 1915 by the commission headed by Peabody and advised by Baruch. The author of the article quoted Pratt at length: what he said was what Baruch had been saying for years, but Baruch was not mentioned. Neither was Peabody or Spencer Trask, who had started it all. When Peabody saw the article, he wrote Baruch of his outrage "that all reference to your splendid public service and notable counsels of wisdom was omitted." Peabody also wrote a stinging rebuke—not for publication—to the *Times* and a letter to Governor Smith.[56] For the first time in his seventy-nine years of life, Baruch did not defend himself against a slight in the press. The last notice in his papers of his Saratoga saga is the *Times* article, flowing with praise for "the foresight and generosity of George D. Pratt."[57]

17 Dr. Baruch of the *Sun*

During six of his last ten years, Baruch found an outlet for his still teeming energy as medical editor of the *New York Sun,* a position previously held by his friend and fellow southerner Dr. John Allen Wyeth. In having a physician on its staff so early in the century, the *Sun* was several decades ahead of the trend that eventually brought competent science writers into the wire services and trained science editors into the large metropolitan dailies. Although the *New York Herald* had employed George Shrady as medical editor somewhat earlier, most medical and scientific reporting in the lay press during Baruch's years with the *Sun* between 1912 and 1918 continued to show the haste and inaccuracy characteristic of journalism in that period. Newspapers often printed garbled interviews with physicians and medical reports more fantastic than the popular science fiction stories of Jules Verne.[1]

It was Baruch's job to check all medical news coming into the *Sun* office: "The medical editor should not be a figurehead," he wrote in 1912; "to him should be submitted all items of medical news for final decision, as is done in the office with which I am connected. In the absence of such a provision I should have declined the position."[2]

In addition to guarding the accuracy of medical news, Baruch was to write unsigned leaders on sanitation, education, and ethics. Putting the broadest possible interpretation on all three, he frequently addressed the *Sun*'s more than two hundred thousand readers about matters of public health, precautions against disease, medical innovations, and even such issues as medical education and licensure. In those years of life when many men seek a chair beside the fire, Baruch used his newfound public

248

voice with joy and vigor. During 1912 alone, 121 medical editorials appeared on that page of the *Sun* once colored by the brilliance and wit of Charles A. Dana.[3]

Baruch's subjects did not always lend themselves to lively treatment, and his German linguistic heritage sometimes made for gigantic sentences. Yet his editorials were rarely dull. Especially in areas where medicine crossed paths with politics, where there was corruption to be fought or an appropriation to be fought for, Baruch's peppery pen ably advanced the *Sun*'s tradition of epithet. Dana had mocked Tammany with a rhyme ("No King, no Clown, to rule this Town") and persistently referred to the president of the United States who had been elected without benefit of a popular majority as "His Fraudulency Mr. Hayes." Baruch carried on the Dana tradition with withering editorials about "the aldermanic mind" and antivivisectionist "zoophiles" and "maudlin lovers of animals" foolishly devoted to their "precious monkey ancestors." When he ran out of names, he quoted Mark Twain on "the irresistible propensity of the human race to make an ass of itself every time it gets a chance."[4]

Of approximately six hundred medical editorials appearing in the *Sun* during Baruch's six-year editorship, half or more were devoted solely to informing the public in matters of health and disease. A death from hydrophobia in 1912 inspired the first of many editorials about the disease for which Louis Pasteur had devised a treatment more than twenty-five years before. Prevention, Baruch explained, was best accomplished by the destruction of unclaimed strays and by muzzling all dogs found roaming the streets, not by heeding the superstition that dogs were safe except in the "dog days" or when manifestly fearful of water. Treatment consisted in applying a tourniquet or cupping the bite until the victim could receive the Pasteur treatment, not in killing the dog or using the "madstone," a conglomeration of hair and vegetable fiber obtained from the stomach of various animals and cherished in some families for many generations.[5]

Even before organized medicine inaugurated a nationwide publicity campaign for cancer detection, Baruch warned readers "to submit every growth or tumor to the judgment of a competent physician." He hammered at this idea again and again, warning women especially to beware of abnormal bleeding and to disregard equally the restraints of womanly modesty and "the attitude of 'christian science' friends. Delay is dangerous." When costly patent preparations for cancer appeared on the market, playing on fear of surgery and boasting the curative contents of radium, the *Sun* carried a cartoon to complement Baruch's editorial condemnation. Standing in front of bulging money bags, his hand extended, the patent medicine vendor shared the picture with the specter of death approaching the light beam called "radium." The caption: "Trust to suffering humanity; 'Money or your life.'"[6]

On the subject of heart disease, Baruch tried to reassure the public that heart murmurs were not the same thing as coronary artery disease. He objected to the listing of "acute indigestion" as a cause of death; indigestion never caused death, he said, and many deaths so noted were the result of previously unnoticed conditions of the heart or blood vessels. These deceased should be subjected to autopsy so that the family could know whether to beware of heart disease. In 1915 he reported on the alarming incidence of enlarged heart among entering freshmen at the University of Wisconsin. Later, when the examination of candidates for military service in the world war confirmed this evidence and put it on a nationwide basis, Baruch warned of the harm being done by sporadic and strenuous competitive athletics, urging more systematic exercise in the school systems from the earliest grades on through college. When Dr. Walter B. Cannon told the New York Academy of Medicine about his work on the physiological action of the emotions, Baruch advocated more international athletic events to get the "war spirit" worked out of men.[7]

In an age when people still lived in fear of the "white plague" of tuberculosis and of the long hospitalization required for recovery, Baruch wrote hopeful words about prevention. Ordinances against spitting, he said, were less important than universal appreciation of the need for adequate diet, sunshine, and fresh air by day and by night. He also described the warning symptoms of tuberculosis so that parents could procure early medical care for children, the most susceptible age group. To give hope to those who contracted the disease, he described a treatment plan devised by the Association for Improving the Condition of the Poor, especially for disabled consumptives who were unable to get into a sanitorium. In apartments built by Vanderbilt, the association provided facilities where tubercular patients could receive medical care without being separated from their families. After the plan had been tried for one year, Baruch reported that the percentage of cures and improvement was higher than in sanitoria and that the children, brought from tenements into homes bathed in light and air and sun, were so much healthier that they were less susceptible to infection.[8]

The United States still had around five hundred thousand cases of typhoid fever yearly during Baruch's editorship, approximately thirty-five thousand of them fatal; yet numerous precautionary measures were available besides vaccination, which had been recently introduced and was not yet widely practiced. Time and again Baruch explained to *Sun* readers that the autumnal prevalence of typhoid resulted from hygienic carelessness during summer vacations. Noting the role of the housefly in typhoid transmission, he urged vacationers to insist on screened windows and covered food in their summer retreats. Like typhoid, dysentery and a host of other diseases were not so much a "'visitation of Providence'" as a "visitation of flies." Suggesting various ways to fight flies—kerosene over stable refuse, covers on food, screens at windows and doors, poison in the form of bread soaked in formaldehyde—he urged that *Sun* readers carry these hints to farmers in the rural areas, along with pressure for pasteurization. Besides flies and infected milk and contaminated oysters, Baruch warned against human carriers of typhoid; they were comparable to homicidal maniacs, he said, and should be dealt with by legislation providing for their detention and care by the state.[9]

In addition to specific diseases, Baruch's editorials covered a number of other matters relating to health. For the obesity of middle-aged women he had no advice but hard work and rigid diet. Reducing nostrums were worthless. Massage did more for the masseuse than for "fat society women"; unlike exercise, massage did not aid the circulation and assimilation and, for that reason, its benefits were only transitory. Between 1913 and 1915, when the high cost of living was a subject of great concern, Baruch related it to the wisdom of minimum food consumption, throwing in an actuarial correlation between obesity and cancer for added incentive to dieters. In reporting that forty thousand New York schoolchildren were malnourished, he relayed the Russell Sage Foundation finding that five cents worth of bread furnished the same nutritional value as fifteen cents worth of apple pie, eighteen cents worth of pork and beans, or sixty-one cents worth of club sandwiches.[10]

Although he condemned Turkish baths for encouraging the "especially pernicious and degrading practice of drinking," he approved of other forms of bathing. Without devoting an excessive number of editorials to the subject so dear to his heart, he took pains to dispute the Japanese scientist who claimed that there are more microbes on the skin after bathing than before. He rejoiced in Dr. Mazyck Ravenel's discovery that chlorine could be added to public swimming pools to keep them free from bacteria: the Ravenel method, Baruch said, removed his own earlier objections to pools as uneconomical and unsanitary. It also afforded cleansing opportunities to people not attracted by showers and, at the same time, permitted bathers to learn to swim.[11]

Baruch often attempted to dispel commonly held misapprehensions about diet or health. Unless coffee was drunk in huge quantities—by which he meant more than two large cups a day—or just before retiring, it would not cause wakefulness or other effects associated with over-stimulation. Although he himself did not smoke, he approved of it in moderation, "for in these strenuous days of wear and tear and nerve tension the weed has become indispensable and a veritable nerve re-storer." Drinkers found less consolation in the *Sun,* for Baruch thought occasional immoderation less harmful than habitual, restrained tippling. Dismissing the bugaboo of "aerial contagion" (the idea that diseases are transmitted by the air) and the still common practice of disinfecting sickrooms with burning sulfur, he emphasized the need for fresh air and urged that laws regarding light and air be strictly enforced for the benefit of the tenement resident, whom he called "the modern cave-dweller."[12]

Baruch also used his *Sun* editorials to fend off public panic. When bubonic plague appeared in Cuba and Puerto Rico in the summer of 1912, he assured readers that health authorities were taking precautions to exclude it from New York. On the basis of a current theory that polio was not contagious, he severely chided health officers of New York and surrounding states for permitting popular alarm to develop in the summer and fall of 1916.[13]

Whatever he learned of scientific advances that might be of use to laymen—such as methods for reviving victims of electric shock or gas poisoning—Baruch passed along to readers. Although it was his policy to avoid discussing medical treatment, he occasionally mentioned such encouraging developments as diphtheria antitoxin and a newly dis-covered chemical reported to kill the causative organism of pneumonia.[14]

Baruch often drew ideas from publications of the American Medical Association, which still carried out much of the nation's food and drug inspection, despite the federal law passed in 1906. From research published in the association's *Journal* in 1914, he formed an indictment of the use of wood alcohol in varnish and perfume.[15] Although he was happy to transmit the contents of New York Health Department bulletins through his columns, he believed that they should be distributed to the public as well as to physicians: "Like cholera and smallpox, typhoid fever, yellow fever and tuberculosis will surely be abolished when the people become sufficiently enlightened to aid the sanitary authorities." In 1914 he praised the Tenement House Department and Tenement House Commit-tee for undertaking a campaign to educate residents of two city districts in methods of sanitation. Their pamphlet was to be put "in the hands of every cave man [tenement dweller] in town. It ought to do good." When the city health department at last got enough money to distribute its own bulletins, Baruch was delighted with the idea of putting them in places of public transportation so that "He Who Runs May Read."[16]

Many of Baruch's editorials stressed the rising incidence of chronic disease. When life insurance companies initiated the practice of periodic physical examinations for their policyholders, Baruch publicized their endeavor, urging that the government and private corporations follow suit. He put so much trust in annual checkups for those beyond middle age that he gave the title "The Prolongation of Life" to an editorial about an organization called the Life Extension Institute, composed of businessmen as well as physicians. When the Committee on Public Health of the New York Academy of Medicine issued a report on industrial disease, Baruch reprinted the safety measures it recommended. After studying a chart published by German insurance companies, correlating the incidence of industrial accidents with hours of the workday, he tried to persuade businessmen among his readers that they could save time and money by providing their workers with leisurely, nourishing lunches, either outside or in pleasant, cheerful dining rooms; with ample supplies of fresh, cold drinking water; and with showers maintained at strong pressure.[17]

Despite the criticism implicit in his suggestions for improving working conditions, Baruch often defended business. At a time when the great corporations were smarting from the reprimands of Theodore Roosevelt (whom the *Sun* called Theodore Rex), Baruch's editorials on industrial disease often contained sharp attacks on labor leadership. In an editorial proposing an inspection system for reducing industrial accidents and disease, he commended the Electrical Association for its study of electric shock and methods of resuscitation. People who knew of the "numerous similar activities on the part of employers for protection of the working people will estimate at their true worth the calumnies and fulminations of the misguided if not anarchistic GOMPERS." Workmen who had "long been under the domination of loudmouthed agitators" should soon come to question "whether these men whose living depends upon fomenting discontent are really safe guides in matters which affect him vitally." From a journal devoted to practical hygiene, Baruch culled examples of industrial beneficence: "pleasant reading and fine pictures, the various sanitary appliances, the social clubs, libraries, model dwellings, churches, schools, lunch retreats, places for change of clothing before and after work, baths, lavatories, pools." He credited the pools with exerting "a civilizing influence upon the rough immigrants coming from squalid homes." Workers, he said, were transformed by such aids: "Their eyes are opened to the realization that life is not a round of dull drudgery to be relieved by drunken orgies. Their manhood is aroused by these manifestations of striving for their welfare and that of their wives and children on the part of their employers, and all these are enhanced by the elevating force of cleanliness which is next to godliness." In his admiration for such examples of beneficence as the pension and benefit funds Western Union established for its employees, Baruch did not seem to question the small percentage of American workers touched by them: "Those agitators who would have the working people regard the corporations as 'juggernauts' crushing out hope, health and life itself that dividends may be piled up, may all pause in the contemplation of the welfare work of great corporations, one of which alone has expended three millions for this purpose. If personal interest continues to dominate these disturbers of industrial peace the toilers will soon themselves recognize the truth and eliminate them from their councils."[18]

Not all of Baruch's editorials were intended solely for the edification of the people. His expressed aim was not only to "serve the interests of suffering humanity" but also "my colleagues incidentally." Fifty years of medical practice had convinced him "that physicians are the worst used members of every community." Although he believed that the fault was largely their own, he intended to change the situation, and he found much to be done.[19] At that time, before organized medicine achieved the power for which it later became notorious, its efforts for reform—intraprofessional as well as external—were often hampered by the strength and influence of other healing sects. The hostility of the regulars was a gauge of the extent to which they felt their interest threatened by these sects. One of the strongest was Christian Science, which a *Journal of the American Medical Association* editorial credited with having the "most alert press bureau of any organization in the world."[20] Impressive enough in numbers alone, Mary Baker Eddy's followers had a maddening immunity to tactics which the regulars, in the evolution of their professional self-consciousness, had devised against sects. Christian Scientists met any attempt at regulation with cries of religious persecution. In some states where regulars had to earn degrees and also pass state examinations, healers who used neither drugs nor knives were exempt from licensure requirements. Although the stipulation that they must not accept money for their work did not always prevent them from doing so, it meant that they broke the law by accepting payment—a fact of some consolation to the regulars.

In late 1911 or early 1912, even this consolation was denied by a federal ruling on medical practice in the Panama Canal Zone. The crucial clause of the ruling stated that as long as the sanitary regulations of the zone were obeyed, "nothing in this order shall be construed to prohibit the practice of religious tenets of any church in the ministration to the sick or suffering by mental or spiritual means without the use of any drug or material remedy, whether gratuitously or for compensation." The ruling excited bitter professional reaction because it militated against regulars in the very area they had made habitable. In 1905 the tropical diseases that made the Canal Zone popularly known as the "white man's grave" had brought construction on the canal to a halt, to be resumed only when malaria and yellow fever were eradicated through the efforts of physicians (regular medical doctors), some of whom gave their lives in the process. On January 12, 1912, the venerable and aged Abraham Jacobi, grizzled refugee from the Revolution of 1848, friend of Carl Schurz, and father of pediatrics, stated his colleagues' objections to the federal ruling at a dinner of the faculty of the New York Post-Graduate Medical School.[21] The next day Baruch carried the issue to the pages of the *Sun,* in a letter signed "B." rather than in an editorial. Although he noted the injustice done to regular physicians by the ruling, his main criticism rested on considerations of public health. Because the Canal Zone was a key point for the dissemination of epidemics, it was essential that every case of contagious disease be reported to the authorities, as existing regulations required. If Christian Scientists did not acknowledge the existence of disease, they could scarcely identify and report sick persons who should be in quarantine, and once the canal was opened to traffic, a single unreported case of contagious disease could endanger life in some distant part of the world.[22]

Baruch's letter reached high places. On January 19 the *Sun* printed a response from Secretary of War Henry L. Stimson, who assured "B." that obedience to the sanitary rules governing the Canal Zone would be "exacted at the pain of criminal prosecution of every practitioner, whether medical or Christian Science." Stimson did not explain how someone who denied the existence of disease and germs could be expected, even "at the pain of criminal prosecution," to diagnose and report cases of disease. Instead, he excused the new ruling on the ground that it "merely followed the legislation of a large and important number of States, as well as the tropical Territory of Hawaii."

"B." shot back a letter which the *Sun* printed on January 21. He had learned that " 'the large and important number of States' " included only Connecticut, New Hampshire, Maine, South Dakota, and Tennessee. "If comparisons were not odious, it might be averred that these are among the smallest and least important States of the Union"—and five states out of more than forty could not be called a large number. Baruch's main objection remained unanswered: a Christian Scientist "could not conscientiously recognize 'a mortal error of the mind' and report it as a disease."

There was no further reply from the secretary of war. A few healers who differed in their interpretation of *Science and Health with Key to the Scriptures* took the opportunity to discuss whether or not Mrs. Eddy would rise from the dead, and one disciple wrote the *Sun* advocating diagnosis by the laity on grounds of "divine right of popular majorities."[23] On April 2, Baruch closed that particular phase of hostilities with an editorial that was surprisingly neutral despite its plea that Christian Scientists follow Christ's teaching and "'Render unto Caesar.'"

In the summer of 1912, when the Bull Moose party produced a platform favoring the union of all public health agencies into a national health service "without discrimination against or for any one set of therapeutic methods, school of medicine or school of healing," Baruch detected a political ploy: "Thus would votes for THEODORE REX be multiplied." William Howard Taft had won approval of the "quacks and healers" by his medical regulation for the Canal Zone; now political exigency forced Roosevelt to make this provision for various sectarians, those "hitherto despised men of predatory wealth." By "expressing a most tender regard for their sensibilities, [Roosevelt] promises to shield them against discrimination by educated physicians." "Politics makes strange bed fellows indeed," Baruch said, asking readers to "Behold TAFT and ROOSEVELT under the same blanket." The *Sun* cartoonist did not even try.[24]

The "quack plank" earned Roosevelt the energetic loathing of the *Sun's* medical editor. When THEODORE REX said something proprietary about the Pure Food and Drug Law, Baruch told readers that Roosevelt, then governor of New York, had been the only state executive asked to participate in the national food and drug congress who had declined to send delegates. Roosevelt's only connection with the bill, the editorial inaccurately stated, had been to sign it in 1906, after it was worked out by the congress and carefully considered by nine United States Congresses: "A closer connection with and a warmer concern for reform than the illustrious Oyster Bay adapter can always show."[25]

The year 1912 seemed to be open season on politicians. A bill to create a national department of health was before the United States Senate, and the impassioned spokesman for the opposition was Senator Works of California, who believed that Christian Science had cured him and his wife of unspecified maladies and kept their son from drinking whiskey for seven years. For two days Works occupied his captive colleagues with his idea that the government, by creating a department to study and make known the causes of disease, would be "planting the seeds of disease and killing more innocent and unsuspecting people than drugs ever saved." Lectures by physicians had already made innocent schoolchildren their "victims," he said: "Instead of being encouraged they should be made a crime." Disease, according to Works, was bred by hatred, malice, fear, revenge, and other wrong thoughts, among them suggestions of "disease and its alleged causes." In what Baruch imagined was an anguished shriek, Works protested: "Mr. President, I cannot keep silent and allow this nation to become a party to this monstrous propaganda of fear and devastation of the people." The cover of Works's speech, printed and circulated at government expense, bore the news that "Jesus of Nazareth was persecuted and finally crucified for preaching and practicing his religious belief by healing the sick." To *Sun* readers, Baruch described the senator's "maunderings" as "absolute inanity," reminiscent of Salem witchcraft days.[26]

The senator and his home state soon became favorite targets. The condition of the little California resort town of Los Angeles, Baruch wrote on November 28, was "especially attributable to a certain newspaper which under the direction of a Christian Scientist editor preaches the non-existence of disease as an entity and exploits the doctrines of Senator Works." Summarizing an article in the *Southern California Practitioner,* Baruch explained that Los Angeles made a practice of driving tuberculars from the city and that it neglected vaccination despite warnings from the local board of health. Truck garden center though it was, it had only one inspector of fruit, and " 'Since there is nothing for him to do he probably plays pinochle with the cream inspector.' "[27]

Baruch treated sects such as Christian Science more gently in the *Sun* than he did in medical journals, where he did not hesitate to sign his name to a letter calling them "sanctimonious seekers after the shekels."[28] But he wrote acid editorials about discriminatory licensure practices. He once suggested that exemptions of healers who did not use drugs rested on the "old and absurd idea that the practice of medicine consists of prescribing drugs, and that the public needs to be protected against poisoning." The real public dangers, Baruch believed, were self-appointed healers, who, "by omitting the application of certain remedial agents, like anti-toxin in diphtheria, permit the patient to die." Yet these people, licensed without education or examination, were not held responsible for omissions that would bring charges of negligence against a regular physician. Baruch wanted the same requirements applied to everyone who wished to practice the art of healing. Over and over he urged that licensure laws be made uniform and all-inclusive. Those who shunned them were "freebooters in the practice of medicine," unworthy of the public trust. At the time of the flood and tornado at Dayton, Ohio, in April 1913, Baruch noted the scarcity of quacks at disaster scenes: "There has appeared no despatch announcing that 'a special train containing a hundred osteopaths is on the way to Dayton. All the sufferers will receive spinal adjustments.'" Nor did the Omaha blizzard bring an offer from Senator Works to send a special detachment of Christian Scientists from sunny California to pray away Nebraska frostbite. "The faddists are like the 'summer soldier and sunshine patriot' of THOMAS PAINE. Their conquests are wrought in gorgeous office or marble temple over maladies that result from peace and plenty; 'nervous prosperity' is the prolific source of their emoluments."[29]

Baruch also used his editorship to urge reform within his profession. He deplored the neglect or carelessness which abandoned children with curable deafness to needless lives of silence in institutions for incurables. He urged the city to withhold support from hospitals that kept their death rate down by sending hopeless cases to die in municipal institutions.[30] For every editorial opposing unfair licensure requirements, he wrote one arguing for elevated professional standards. Above all, he tried to show that the two were interdependent: physicians would improve themselves only if all aspiring healers stood equal before the law. In 1913, praising a symposium of the heads of various state licensure boards, he urged that standardized examinations place more emphasis on clinical knowledge and less on "book learning." Many of his editorials dealt with medical education. When the Flexner report exposed the poor condition of many American medical schools, Baruch brought its findings to *Sun* readers, endorsing the recommendation of a required fifth year of medical education—a year of clinical work, which became the internship requirement a few years later. When Sir William Osler spoke out for more clinics and fewer lectures, Baruch endorsed the proposal out of his own experience: "Every earnest practitioner who has spent years in freeing himself of the barnacles that have clogged his progress since he emerged from college must appreciate these words of wisdom and bid this militant reformer Godspeed." In his summary of the year's medical developments at the end of 1914, he observed with pleasure that the idea of the full-time professor, teaching and treating patients in a hospital affiliated with a medical school, had been tested thoroughly; he believed it would "contribute vastly" to the complete preparation of medical students.[31]

Baruch's unrelenting attack on the proprietary ("alias patent") drug industry was aimed at both medical and lay readers. When he condemned "radium preparations" for cancer or commercial sour milk products al-

leged to prolong life by preventing intestinal putrefaction; when he tried
to counteract public vulnerability to personal testimonials, he was writing for a general audience. But most of his writing about proprietary
drugs concentrated on two trends within the profession: the growing
practice of prescribing ready-made compounds and the increasing frequency with which such compounds were advertised in even the best
medical journals of the day. A resolution passed by the State Medical
Association of Missouri, calling it derogatory to the best interests of the
profession for its members to publish articles in journals carrying such
matter, struck Baruch as an example the AMA should follow. He also
found "an example of ethics for doctors" in the decision of an unnamed
drug house to manufacture only those drugs listed in the official phar-
macopoeia, because "the evils chargeable to patent medicines are likely to
continue so long as these products have free access to the channels of
publicity." Baruch added that the only proper way to prescribe for patients was in terms of single drugs, written out in Latin and dispensed by
trained pharmacists. He even advised his readers to dismiss any physician
who prescribed patent preparations on the grounds that he was probably
"too ignorant to construct his own formulas." In 1918, the publishers of
the *New York Medical Journal* asked Dr. Baruch to intercede with his son
Bernard, then chairman of the War Industries Board, for the exemption
of proprietary medicines from priority classification; Baruch did the opposite, writing Bernard that all of them, including laxatives, were "non-
essential," a "fruitful source of waste of money and health and life."[32]

Before the growing complexity of medicine had culminated in the
network of national boards that now examine and certify specialists, Baruch urged that specialists be required to take diplomas in their chosen
field. Since 1875, he told *Sun* readers, the University of Cambridge had
conferred degrees in tropical medicine and hygiene upon those who did
special work preparatory to practice in the British possessions. More
recently, Cambridge had added a degree in psychological medicine for
doctors of two years' standing who passed twelve months in asylum
service. Baruch hoped that American universities and medical schools
would inaugurate similar plans, particularly for specialists in public
health and for surgeons and mental practitioners. The last two groups
were, in his opinion, the least satisfactorily trained and the most likely to
be infiltrated by both "educated and uneducated pretenders." When certification of surgeons began with the establishment of the American
College of Surgeons in 1913, Baruch predicted that "many lives will be
saved" if people would learn to look for a certificate of specialization
when choosing their surgeon.[33]

Much of the inspiration for Baruch's editorials on professional matters came directly from his experience, some of it highly prejudicial. Although such surgical abuses as he decried doubtless existed, he could have warned the public to beware of them without generalizations about men entering surgery for money, prestige, or the adoration of women. He berated the small-town surgical hospital of the day, "where important organs and useful limbs may be removed and many wonderful surgical achievements attained that are conveyed with bated breath and fond pride from one woman admirer to another." Apart from his markedly sex-linked antipathy to surgeons, Baruch also seemed to blame them for the decline of general practice. Pioneer work in surgery, he told *Sun* readers, had been done by "general practitioners who in this evolution toward the fittest became submerged for the general good." Among the physicians who had helped to advance surgery—along with Sims, Fitz, Pasteur (who was not a physician), and Lister—he mentioned an unnamed New York family physician (he could only have meant himself) whose recommendation resulted in one of the early operations for appendicitis. The family physician's deterioration into a mere "distributor of cases to the specialist" filled him with resentment: borrowing the words of his friend Abraham Jacobi, he prophesied that " 'In 25 years he [the family doctor] will recover the place of honor which was his 50 years ago.' "[34] Again, in denouncing the abuse of medical charity by people who could afford to pay for a doctor's services, Baruch publicized an evil that needed correction, but he was excessively vehement about it, perhaps because of his arduous days as an unsalaried dispensary physician.[35]

Baruch's editorial essays in the history of medicine reflected his disillusionment at human failure to appreciate the achievements of medicine and science. Whenever he eulogized great physicians of the past and explained the work for which they deserved to be famous, he marveled at the custom of lavishing honor on military heroes while neglecting medical benefactors. Schoolboys unfamiliar even with the name of Hippocrates knew all about Alexander the Great, who "carried death and destruction wherever his conquering legions swept." In history books totally ignoring William Harvey's work on the circulation of blood, the deeds of Harvey's contemporary, the imperial general Albrecht Wenzel Eusebius von Wallenstein, "stand out in gory grandeur." For his role in the development of anesthesia, "which has delivered millions from pain and fear," William T. G. Morton was honored only by a modest shaft erected over his grave by his colleagues, while the public lionized Morton's contemporary, General Winfield Scott. "Which is the grander achievement," Baruch asked, the conquest of Mexico or the victory over pain? "Where are the monuments proclaiming to posterity the liberation of the world from that terrible scourge small pox?" He puzzled over this "psychical phenomenon." "Is it the primal element of savagery surviving in man that prompts him to exalt the destroyer?" In his zeal to rescue medical figures from oblivion, Baruch was sometimes inaccurate, but for the most part, his editorials were excellent antidotes to an astigmatic historicism.[36]

Baruch often sought as much to combat antiscientific movements as to inform readers. Medicine needed defenses of vivisection and vaccination in a period when *Life* ran frequent attacks on animal experimentation, picturing dogs struggling in agony to escape vicious mouth and head clamps while Vandyked surgeons smirked cruelly at their torture.[37] During the winter of 1911–12, the Board of Aldermen of New York City twice refused to appropriate the money Health Commissioner Ernst K. Lederle needed to conduct a campaign of smallpox vaccination. The Tammany alderman said he "'didn't want to see the kids scratched and he did not believe in vaccination anyway.'" From this starting point, Baruch wrote a series of editorials, giving medical and historical proofs of the efficacy of vaccination. When antivaccinationists wrote letters to the editor protesting against "scratching the kids," he answered them with figures from the surgeons general of the army and navy, George H. Torney and C. F. Stokes. Through Baruch, Torney assured *Sun* readers that "if the 40,000 men in the Philippines in 1899 had not been vaccinated, all military operations would have ceased within six weeks, and only a small and disfigured remnant would have again seen their native land." Baruch added that the appropriation "would not have exceeded the cost of the funerals of victims that could thus have been saved." In 1915, when antivaccinationist forces were lobbying in Albany for a bill providing that vaccination of schoolchildren be compulsory only when an epidemic threatened, Baruch called the idea as logical as a plan to purify water only when a typhoid epidemic was under way.[38]

He was more moderate in his support of typhoid vaccination, perhaps because it was newer and not so thoroughly tested, perhaps because there were other typhoid preventives to emphasize.[39] In addition to his campaign against houseflies and human typhoid carriers, he repeatedly attacked the problem of transmission through shellfish by urging the purification of the waters rimming New York's shoreline. Until they became something better than "diluted sewage," he warned, oyster lovers would do well to restrain their longings for "the delicious bivalve." With regret, for he, too, was fond of oysters, he concluded in 1912 that "shellfish culture in the harbor must be abandoned." To emphasize the severity of the problem, he noted that New York's waters received sewage from more than six million persons and many animals, an amount expected to double with the population before 1940. He gave readers some idea of its volume by "the calculation that it would fill Broadway to Grace Church to a depth of one hundred feet." The pollution problem had forced the city health commissioner to ban bathing on the Manhattan waterfront. This deprivation too would persist until New Yorkers developed—and paid taxes to support—a sewage disposal system "fit for a civilized people."[40]

Along with shellfish, milk was one of the most common carriers of typhoid contamination, and Baruch poured even more energy into his campaign for pasteurization than he did into the larger and more difficult sewerage problem. He was especially devoted to the idea of pure milk because it had provided an answer to the highly fatal condition called infant diarrhea, one of the most heartbreaking problems he had encountered in his early practice. His inability to help its tiny victims had haunted him throughout his practice in Camden and among New York's tenement dwellers. When pasteurization brought a solution, Baruch welcomed it wholeheartedly. In 1893 he returned from a trip abroad with what he believed was the first sterilizing bottle to be used in America and, as he joyfully phrased it, "began at once to feed babies with germ-free food." When a return to raw milk became fashionable among physicians, especially among pediatricians who wanted to force the production of pure milk rather than allow carelessly handled supplies to be sterilized, Baruch's memories of infant deaths in the time before pasteurization made him an earnest opponent of the new trend.[41]

Baruch had told the New York Academy of Medicine in 1907 that it was the duty of the city to provide pure milk for its citizens.[42] By the time of his medical editorship, the city had begun to assume this duty, at least for its less fortunate inhabitants. Through the efforts of physicians led by Abraham Jacobi, depots to provide free pure milk for poor New York children, first established by Nathan Straus in 1893, came under municipal control in 1910. By 1911 there were fifteen municipal milk depots; by 1912, fifty.[43] It was for the people not provided with free pasteurized milk that Baruch wrote editorials stressing the importance of pasteurization as a precaution, not only against infant diarrhea and typhoid fever but against a host of other diseases, including tuberculosis, scarlet fever, and diphtheria.

While aiming for the ideal of compulsory and universal pasteurization, he also kept readers informed about the less complete sanitary measures then used to safeguard milk. When Governor Dix vetoed the Wheeler milk bill, which would have nullified legislation requiring high standards of cleanliness in the processing of milk, Baruch praised Dix for resisting pressure from commercial interests. He urged the Board of Health to publish the names of hotels serving low grades of milk at high prices, especially the hotels that offered a high grade at half price in the bar. Baruch generally disapproved of grading milk: "Half measures are as indefensible in this warfare as they are in military campaigns. If 'war is hell' the shorter and more energetic the campaign the better for those who are involved. The same principle holds in the war with disease and death."[44]

The pasteurization controversy *was* war to Baruch. In the spirit of "all's fair," he used every weapon to manipulate that fear of disease which he recognized as the medical reformer's most potent ally. Although the great epidemics were over, newly recognized milk-borne diseases gave him a lever against public apathy. In the spring of 1912 he reported on a study by Professor Mazyck Ravenel linking bovine to human tuberculosis through milk; this made it imperative, in Baruch's opinion, to pasteurize all milk consumed by children under age sixteen. For those who could not obtain pasteurized milk, Baruch gave do-it-yourself instructions. When epidemics of "fatal sore throat" occurred in areas where milk was improperly pasteurized, he noted that "many dangerous diseases whose origin appears mysterious" might be transmitted by milk. In 1913 he interpreted recent deaths from typhoid, traced to the milk supply, as proof of "THE SUN'S" contention that the outlay required to begin pasteurizing all milk would be cheaper than the prevailing system. Five similar outbreaks in Boston in a five-month period moved him to repeat his warning, this time in biblical language: " 'Thou shalt write them upon the door posts of thine houses and upon thy gates.' Drink no raw milk."[45]

Another object of Baruch's crusading editorials was the New York quarantine authority. Because the quarantine station, like the rest of New York's harbor management, was the property of the party in office, it was often distinguished for corruption and inefficiency. More than fifty men had held the office of health inspector since colonial times, most of them appointed as a reward for political service. In January 1912, the first month of his editorship, Baruch announced that the time had come "to agitate the placing of the important office of Quarantine guardian in the hands of the Federal Government." One by one, the various seaboard states had yielded their stations to federal agents until only a few remained under state control. Except for New York, Boston, Baltimore, and Providence, all other Atlantic, Pacific, and Gulf ports were protected by the Public Health Service and the Marine Hospital Service (later merged as the United States Public Health Service). These cities were doubly protected because the Public Health Service and Marine Hospital Service, then under the Department of Treasury, were about to maintain representatives in foreign consulates, where ships could be checked for disease before departure for American ports.[46]

In January 1913, when rumors emanated from Albany that Governor Sulzer was about to transfer the New York station to federal authority, Baruch renewed his editorial support. This time he concentrated on what he liked to call the most sensitive nerve in the body—the "pocket nerve." "The [New York State] quarantine budget for 1912 was $2,314,180, and Dr. O'Connell has just asked for an appropriation of $2,000,000 for the quarantine station." These were "quite fat perquisites!" The health inspector had a lucrative post, no doubt about it. Further confirmation came from Carlisle, head of the board appointed by the governor to investigate the proposed transfer: "I expect something of an uproar when this proposition is broached," Carlisle said. The *Sun* thought this a tribute to Carlisle's "experience in politics." In a subsequent editorial called "'The Nigger in the Woodpile,'" Baruch dismissed the objection of home rule raised by some members of Carlisle's divided committee: "That the question of home rule is secondary in this vital matter is evidenced by the transfer of all but one of the quarantine stations of the South by a people who gave of their blood and treasure in defence of State rights." The opposition's real reason, he said, was "the rich plum of contracts and salaries which politicians naturally never yield without a struggle." Despite the *Sun*'s hopeful praise for Sulzer's "economy mindedness" and its insistence that the transfer would save New York State nearly $2.5 million annually, quarantine authority remained with the state.[47]

After Sulzer's impeachment, when the New York Academy of Medicine brought the need for the transfer before his successor, Governor Whitman, the *Sun* again reviewed the arguments, including several new ones Baruch had learned through correspondence with Rupert Blue, surgeon general of the United States Public Health Service. In addition to the superiority of medical "regulars" over "militia," the transfer would bring New York's future quarantine problems directly to "the central office in Washington, where Surgeon-General BLUE controls the situation completely." Even in the status quo, Baruch said, federal agents always had to come in to help with the "big" cases. After advocating the transfer again at the annual meeting of the American Association for the Promotion of Hygiene and Public Baths, Baruch wrote Blue that he was "still hammering at the transfer" but that "political plums bar the way."[48]

From 1914 to 1917, Baruch often slanted his propaganda for the transfer at the number of mental and physical defectives who slipped through quarantine during periods when immigration was so heavy that physicians at the station had to examine as many as three thousand persons in a single day.[49]

Baruch also advocated higher salaries for those serving in the Public Health Service. They were the elite corps, only two thousand in number at the time of America's entry into World War I, trained to do the public health work Baruch and other physicians had done as "amateurs" all their lives. On September 4, 1912, he reported with pleasure on the "one excellent bill passed by the Congress which has just ceased for a time its more or less pernicious activities." He was referring to the bill that incorporated the Marine Hospital Service into the Public Health Service, defined the duties and scope of the new organization, and authorized a pay increase for its members: "Unlike the soldier or officer who rushes into the fray fired with battle ardor and in ambitious anticipation of glory, these assailants of the plague, yellow fever, cholera and other life-destroying forces, march deliberately into the very jaws of death, and lay down their lives that others may live and be prosperous and happy." The people, he said, could not possibly pay such workers as much as they were truly worth.[50]

Whether it was a matter of bubonic plague in China and Cuba, typhoid fever in North Carolina and Chicago, tropical disease in Panama, or hookworm in Puerto Rico and the southern United States, Baruch kept *Sun* readers informed of the battles public health workers were fighting and winning. Sanitary improvements alone accounted for many of the victories, and, as a veteran sanitarian who had lived on into the age of its triumphs, Baruch fully appreciated the work of those who fought the lowly problems of rats and garbage and sewage and swamps. He also valued innovations like the conquest of beriberi in the Philippines by exempting unpolished rice from a tax imposed on the whitened, vitamin-stripped variety.[51]

The work that underlay such achievements as these rarely attracted attention: "It may not have the same appeal to the imagination; the quest after microbes, the chase of the mosquito and the fly, the draining of marshes and the disinfection of stagnant pools are not so romantic in their seeming as the ranging of the seas, the penetration of the jungle, wrestling with the elements or taming the wild races of mankind." Yet Baruch ventured a prediction: "Among the coming generations the quiet man of science may prove to tower above the navigator and the pioneer, and his name may be written larger in the books of the future." The work of Colonel William C. Gorgas in Panama had attracted more than the usual public notice because it enabled workmen to continue construction on the canal. But Baruch thought its final significance might be even greater than then suspected: "A new figure must be set on the earth's capacity to support mankind, and this means an expansion of the [white] race in the course of a century or two exceeding any that has taken place within historic times. . . . There may come a day when the greatest good of the Panama Canal will be thought to lie in the fact that because of it we learned to clean up the earth."[52]

Because most of his readers were New Yorkers, Baruch paid close attention to public health work within the city. For refusing to permit a tuberculosis hospital to be built near the city's Croton water supply; for instituting food inspections, particularly of chicken and sausage coming from outside the city; for enforcing the rule against spitting on streetcars; for expanding the Bureau of Child Hygiene to include physical examinations of schoolchildren and home visits: for these and many other efforts Baruch gave New York health officials notice and approbation on the *Sun*'s editorial page.[53]

Baruch could dispense blame as well, whenever errors or inefficiency warranted. He called it "a national disgrace" that Americans died in 1912 from a disease so easily prevented as malaria. In 1914, the spread of hoof and mouth disease into the herds of fourteen widely separated states inspired him to indict the "whole system of Federal, State and local cattle inspection" as "useless and ineffective." As in South Carolina in the 1870s, he repeatedly attacked the neglect of vital statistics. The handling of the polio epidemic by the New York City Health Department in 1916 brought a stream of abusive editorials, one of them entitled "Is Stupidity a Germ Disease?"[54]

In the course of his criticisms, Baruch usually mentioned that health officials did surprisingly well considering how little money they were given. In 1912 New York State spent 1.7 cents on the health of each citizen, while Massachusetts (always in the vanguard of public health in America) spent 4.2. When New York City's Health Department asked for two hundred food inspectors to supervise twenty-seven thousand points of supply, it received only thirty. Legislators, Baruch said, were promoting a "struggle between death and the dollar." When they perceived this distortion of values, they would "cease to prefer a high death rate to a slight and temporary increase in the tax rate." In 1914, when the city health budget soared to 64 cents a person, Baruch still considered it too low. For lack of $86,000, it was impossible to examine all New York City schoolchildren and treat those who needed it; the city then had to spend $3,675,000 to reeducate the 189,840 children who failed their grade, most of them because of poor health. Baruch noted similar false economies elsewhere in the nation: "The Kansas Legislature appropriated a large sum for the study and prevention of hog cholera after refusing to grant any appropriation for the manufacture of diphtheria antitoxin. The Illinois Legislature has recently voted $151,000 for the protection of fish and game and allowed the State Board of Health $120,000 for the protection of the State's 5,000,000 inhabitants."[55] It was the same sorry story Baruch had heard for almost half a century: legislators would lavish money on livestock while stinting on human health.

In addition to larger public health budgets, Baruch's editorials supported more highly centralized organization. One of his earliest editorials supported the creation of a federal cabinet post for the coordination of public health efforts. Such a bill before the Senate in February 1912 faced opposition by patent drug interests and by "healers." The drug interests did not want the bill at all, and the healers wanted an amendment to protect them from regulation and ensure that all appointments would be made without "discrimination against any school of medicine or of healing." Despite Baruch's request that readers "exert their personal influence upon their representatives in Congress by urging them to thwart the commercial and quack interests," the bill failed to pass.[56]

When the number of deaths from typhoid moved Governor Sulzer to appoint a commission to investigate the action of various health boards in New York State, Baruch urged the commission to recommend unification: "There is too much regard paid to dignity at the expense of the public good in the present relation or lack of relation of the town, city, county, and State boards of health." The commission eventually recommended the appointment of a state health commissioner, whose authority would extend even to the activities of local officers. Baruch supported the idea, except for the proposal that New York City be exempt. Much as Baruch respected Ernst K. Lederle, then head of New York City's Health Department, he thought the law should include all cities, for "times change and Health Commissioners change with them."[57]

Many of the reforms Baruch urged in his *Sun* editorials concerned medicine only indirectly. In his interrelated crusades against drug addiction and handguns, he tried to sharpen public awareness of the inadequacy of current legislation: "When a craving and a prohibition conflict, it is the common law that the craving is always the stronger force and will run to any extravagance for its gratification. Just as the Sullivan Law sent the 'gunmen' to New Jersey for their armaments, the Boylan Law sends the drug fiends thither for their 'dope.'" According to Baruch, the Boylan antidrug law of 1914 was doubly harmful: it failed to trap the guilty, yet it so complicated the prescription of legitimate drugs that much suffering and some deaths would inevitably result. He expected both difficulties to be removed by the Harrison Law, which took effect on March 1, 1915. When it failed to accomplish all that he expected of it, he continued to write about the problem and to work for a solution in his personal capacity as well.[58]

In August 1912, fearing that the Sullivan Law against carrying small arms would fail to halt the rising homicide rate in New York State, Baruch wrote an editorial proposing legislation against the manufacture of all small arms except those needed for military purposes. When a gunman's attack on Theodore Roosevelt gave dramatic emphasis to Baruch's view, support came from twelve readers who signed a letter asking the *Sun* to resume its anti-pistol campaign. Baruch willingly complied. In addition to editorials, for which the *Sun*'s editor, Edward P. Mitchell, supplied figures on the firearms industry, Baruch particularly tried to rally women's support. As president of the Knickerbocker Chapter of the Daughters of the American Revolution, Belle made an appeal, written with her husband's help, asking the women of the nation to take up the work their men had failed to accomplish. Despite her charge that it was their "imperative duty to remove this stain upon the civilization of our beloved country," the ready availability of firearms remains a subject of debate at the close of the twentieth century.[59]

Baruch's stand on alcohol was equally remote from medicine proper—and equally unavailing. He considered alcohol outdated in the practice of medicine, but he did not often discuss this point in the *Sun*. His editorials were moderate, more concerned with habitual drinking than immoderation, and sometimes less concerned with either than with the posture in which people consumed alcohol. He could not appreciate the fondness of the English-speaking nations for what he called "perpendicular drinking." In other countries, men sat down to drink in comfort and companionship. In English pubs and American bars, they pushed to the crowded counters and gulped their drinks, escaping as quickly as possible to more pleasant surroundings. Such habits, he said in George Sylvester Viereck's *American Monthly* in 1918, bred "useless talk, headaches and vain regret." "A man standing up cannot drink properly. He acknowledges this by avoiding the light wines, by gulping malt liquor that should be sipped; by accepting from the presiding genius between bar and mirror beer that is chilled to the point at which it loses its fragrance, its life and its characteristic taste."[60]

More a temperance man than a total prohibitionist, Baruch favored the exemption of wine and beer from a national ban on alcohol. In 1913 the *Sun* said, "We do not believe that any people is to be made sober by legislation." Under his own name in Viereck's, Baruch said that the history of human reliance on alcohol, coffee, tea, cocoa, tobacco, and other mild stimulants or sedatives indicated "that the craving for stimulants is omnipotent, and that it is especially [apparent] in its most active, energetic and spirited members." He believed that the evils of prohibition would be greater than those it purported to cure. In one editorial he blamed a race riot in Harristown, Mississippi, on the abuse of cocaine, "and it is asserted on seemingly respectable authority that indulgence in this vice is particularly prevalent where prohibition obtains."[61]

Baruch's answer was to ban the manufacture, importation, and sale of distilled alcohol (except for industrial purposes) and to transform bars and saloons into pleasant, comfortable gathering places for families and friends, where Americans could learn to drink properly in an environment similar to that of the Danish *afholdjen* (temperance houses serving light wine and beer). By 1917, when prohibition forces reached the Senate, Baruch had organized his arguments against the inclusion of beer in the ban. He maintained that because barley was not a popular food, farmers would cease to plant it except for export to other countries, where it would bring a high price for use in malting; that beer had, by custom and habit, become essential to working people, who used it as both food and drink; and that barley and other cereals lost little of their food value through the brewing process. He even claimed that the milling of all grain for bread would deprive the milk producers of their accustomed supply of bran and middlings and thus reduce milk output. Because milk was more essential than bread, this last seemed a strong argument, but after it met with opposition from Graham Lusk, professor of physiology at Cornell University Medical College, Baruch dropped it. He sent his other reasons in a long, carefully written letter to every member of the United States Senate.[62] Despite President Woodrow Wilson's known preference for partial prohibition, the prohibition act— the Eighteenth Amendment to the Constitution, passed December 18, 1917, and ratified January 29, 1919—included beer and wine. Baruch's letters, articles, editorials, and numerous other published statements were unavailing. All forms of beverage alcohol were legally prohibited from January 16, 1920, to the "Hundred Days" of Franklin Delano Roosevelt, when beer and wine up to 3.2 percent alcohol by weight were again legalized. The ban brought all the evils Baruch had foreseen and some his nineteenth-century mind could not have imagined.

Baruch's occasional strokes against the coroner's office were made more in the interest of justice than of public health. From his unhappy experience as medical expert in a murder case in South Carolina, he had personal knowledge of the coroner's importance in homicide proceedings. Thus he was quick to cry for reform in November 1914, when the man who had been coroner's physician in New York City for twenty-five years was accused of taking a bribe in a case in which he was officially concerned. Following the flurry over this case, further hearings into activities of the coroner's office gave proof—hardly needed, Baruch said—that it was inefficient "or worse." Baruch recommended that the office be remodeled on the system used in New Jersey or Massachusetts, with full responsibility centered in an expert in pathology and medical jurisprudence. New York needed a system "which will be unapproachable when the interests of justice demand rigid search. It will be a disaster if after the present blazing exposure of the Coroner's office it be not swept out of existence."[63]

Along with the coroner's office, another New York institution marked for demolition by the *Sun* was Sing Sing Prison. It was filthy and vermin-ridden, according to an editorial entitled "The People's Murder House and Insanity Shop." A cartoon opposite this editorial portrayed a victim of prison conditions: a cadaverous figure, now encumbered with society's gift of disease, emerged from the stone walls within which he had paid his debt to society. The caption asked, "Did the Punishment Fit the Crime?"[64]

The prevention of mental illness, Baruch told *Sun* readers, was "far more pressing and important than the elimination of any physical malady." He urged readers to see a mental hygiene exhibit at City College; he praised Henry Phipps for contributing money to establish a psychiatric clinic at the Johns Hopkins Hospital; he appealed for support for the National Committee for Mental Hygiene; he urged that experienced alienists—clinically experienced psychiatrists, not book-taught neurologists—be given a voice in criminal court cases and that insane criminals be committed to institutions for treatment, not punishment. Again and again he warned that immigrants should be examined carefully for mental disorders as well as contagious disease before admission to the United States.[65]

In the matter of mental deficiency, Baruch's reform instincts moved into high gear with an energetic promotion of the eugenics movement, which aimed at racial improvement by selective breeding. His rationale for this paralleled the one he gave for euthanasia. If people had the same right as animals to be spared the misery of slow, certain death, they also had a right to prevent the proliferation of defectives, which are eliminated in the animal world by the ineluctable rule of survival of the fittest.[66] Stemming from the work of Francis Galton (1822–1911), an English scientist and cousin of Charles Darwin, eugenics took impetus after 1900 from the rediscovery and widespread recognition of Gregor Mendel's work illustrating the mechanisms of heredity. When Baruch's editorship began in 1912, eugenics forces were strong and growing. A. H. Estabrook was preparing a sequel to Richard L. Dugdale's *The Jukes, A Study in Crime, Pauperism, Disease, and Heredity,* published in 1877. Even before H. H. Goddard's similar study of the Kallikak family was published in 1915, Baruch related some of its findings in an editorial opposing a tax cut that would reduce funds for the custodial care of the insane.[67]

Amid much emphasis on the control of character formation through control of the environment, Baruch reminded people that heredity, too, could be "modified." Although this ordinarily happened through the slow processes of evolution, change could be hastened by the enforcement of selective breeding. To that end, he said, "we should not be weak or irresolute in our course of action toward degenerates and criminals. The increase of the latter should be stopped by segregation and certain modern radical methods [sterilization], regardless of maudlin sentimentality." Every crack in the opposition received editorial notice: a law passed by the Pennsylvania legislature in 1913, which Baruch called the first in America to deny marriage licenses to persons afflicted with mental illness, mental deficiency, or transmissible disease; a statement by the attorney general in 1913 that "'it is the duty of the State to protect the community against acts of these persons who are not under the guidance of their reason.'" Baruch suggested that newly devised psychological tests should be used to determine whether a person's mental deficiency ought to preclude procreation; if so, he should be put in an institution or a colony—not a prison—unless his family could prevent him from mingling with society.[68]

Viewing sterilization as a logical corollary to Darwinism and a right and duty of society, Baruch initially considered the Brush Law for the sterilization of habitual criminals and mental and moral degenerates, passed in New York in 1912, an "excellent hygienic measure."[69] In 1913, however, when a similar statute was declared unconstitutional by the New Jersey Supreme Court, Baruch looked more closely at both laws and found their provisions for enforcement hopelessly inadequate. The New Jersey statute "for the sterilization of feeble minded (including idiots, imbeciles and morons), epileptics, rapists, certain criminals and other defectives" left the task of enforcement to a surgeon, a neurologist, the state commissioner of charities and correction, and the chief physician of the institution. The New York statute was no better: the board of examiners consisted of a surgeon, a neurologist, and a practitioner of medicine. These three were to receive $10 a day plus traveling expenses while engaged in the task phrased as follows:

To examine into the mental and physical condition and the record and the family history of the feeble minded, epileptic, criminal and other defective inmates confined in the several State hospitals for the insane, State prisons, reformatories and charitable and penal institutions in the State, and if in the opinion of said board procreation by any such person would produce children with an inherited tendency to crime, insanity, feeble mindedness, idiocy or imbecility, and there is no probability that the condition of any such person so examined will improve to such an extent as to render procreation by any such person advisable, or if the physical or mental condition of any such person, will be substantially improved thereby, then said board shall appoint one of its members to perform such operation for the prevention of procreation as shall be decided by said board to be most effective.

The most ardent anti-eugenicist could hardly have drafted a less satisfactory bill. Apart from the impossible number of decisions to be made, Baruch objected to the stipulated qualifications of the enforcers, not one of them specially trained in mental illness. He frankly sneered at the idea of their making "the 'judgement,' the infallible 'judgement'! We commend this statute to the consideration of citizens who are not aware of the robust march of 'progress.'"[70]

In 1914 Baruch concluded that "the time appears not yet ripe" for an effective system of sterilization. Thereafter he restricted his editorials to less drastic safeguards such as colonization and segregation. Nonetheless, Baruch's editorials helped to accomplish what one eugenicist called the most essential task during that period: "to educate public sentiment and to foster a public eugenic conscience in the absence of which the safeguards of the law must forever be largely without avail."[71]

In all of his editorials, Baruch furnished a badly needed link between the profession and the public. "The highest function of the medical journalist today," Fielding H. Garrison wrote in 1913, "is to introduce new currents of scientific ideas and to keep them in circulation."[72] Baruch did this and more. He began his editorial defense of such old scientific ideas as vivisection and vaccination in 1912, the year in which the old *Life* magazine (1883–1936) pictured medical progress as the onward march of physicians over the graves of victims slain by these and other means.[73] By the time he left the *Sun* six years later, he had ranged over most developments in medicine and public health in the first two decades of the twentieth century. Through him hundreds of thousands of laymen had learned—many of them for the first time—of simple preventive measures against contagious disease, of the importance of public health work, and of the warning signs of cancer and tuberculosis. They also learned of medical developments in all parts of the world and of the need for reform in public health and health care at city, state, and national levels. This, Baruch's last fling as a propagandist, was also the broadest in scope. Although he came to the *Sun* late, very late, in life, he gave it the best of his considerable energy and ability.

18 "Before I go hence"

After May 12, 1916, Baruch had a better reason to slow down than most seventy-six-year-olds would need. On that day, while he was in Baltimore to preside over the annual meeting of the American Association for Promoting Hygiene and Public Baths, he suffered a heart attack. This time it was not dyspepsia in disguise, like the "heart trouble" induced by the uncertainty of his future in New York in 1881; it was a legitimate protest from the physical machinery that had served him well and long. In many ways, he had been careful of the splendid constitution he had inherited. He drank moderately, smoked not at all, and ate the plain, nourishing foods he associated with simple, sturdy German peasants. But he had also put tremendous demands on his body. Hospital and clinic work, office practice and house calls, speaking tours and professional meetings had so filled his "workdays" that the many reading and writing tasks he set himself had to be done in his "leisure" hours. Even on vacation, he had often stayed at his typewriter through the night hours into the early morning.[1]

When the immitigable toll of these years of work showed itself in 1916, Baruch barely flinched. He retired to his room at the Emerson Hotel and canceled his trip to visit Surgeon General Rupert Blue in nearby Washington. A few days later, he was safely back in New York City, as busy as ever. He wrote his daughter-in-law that he "had a little spell in Baltimore but came up smiling in the afternoon, and am alright to-day, preparing for an address I am booked for next Wednesday in Saratoga before the State Medical Society."[2] A few days after giving this address he wrote

274

more than twenty Saratoga doctors, asking them to support the addition of salines to Saratoga's carbon dioxide baths for heart disease—an effort defeated by their unanimous rejection of additives.

Despite his Saratoga failure, Baruch's life by 1916 had brought more than enough successes to justify an easier existence. He had received widespread recognition among his fellow physicians. As early as the late 1880s colleagues had begun looking to him for advice on hydrotherapy. In 1890 he was asked to contribute to a leading textbook on therapeutics. In 1893 Dr. Mary Putnam Jacobi said that she had read everything Baruch had written on hydrotherapy, while other physicians, less prominent than she, often said the same, and a New York physician included Baruch in his canvass of the "leading authors of England, Germany and America." In 1906 John Harvey Kellogg's textbook on hydrotherapy listed all of Baruch's writings on the subject. Harry P. Loomis, professor of materia medica at Cornell University Medical College, asked Baruch to read his lecture notes on hydrotherapy and make comments and corrections. In 1908 Baruch received a coveted professional honor in the form of an invitation to address the Interurban Club, a select group of East Coast physicians and medical educators. In 1909, while he was in Boston to address the Massachusetts Medical Society, the leading men in medicine there attended a dinner in his honor at the Harvard University Club. By 1910 new books on hydrotherapy usually included either a full article by him or many references to and quotations from his work.[3] From the early 1890s on, laymen all around the country asked his advice on hydrotherapy. In 1907 his work received unique recognition when Governor Charles S. Deneen of Illinois, in his second biennial message to the General Assembly, urged the inclusion of hydrotherapy in the medical curriculum.[4]

Baruch's life was rich in personal as well as professional gratification. Judging from the clippings he saved, he took pride in his four sons: in Hartwig's dramatic performances, in Herman's medical career, in Bernard's financial success, in the prize-winning dancing of Sailing and his wife in Madison Square Garden. He was immensely pleased with the third generation of American Baruchs—six grandsons and four granddaughters—and even wrote poems inspired by good times the entire family enjoyed at Kamp Kill Kare in the Adirondacks and at Bernard's seventeen-thousand-acre Hobcaw Barony near Georgetown, South Carolina.[5] Although Baruch flourished amid the intellectual excitement of city life, he also exulted in the beauties of nature. He often tried to describe vacation scenes in poetry, perhaps in emulation of Oliver

The Baruch family around the turn of the century. From left to right:
Belle and Simon; Sailing; Hartwig; Annie Griffen Baruch (Mrs.
Bernard Baruch); Herman; Bernard. (Courtesy of the late Frances A.
Hellebrandt, M.D., in author's possession.)

Wendell Holmes, the physician-poet he so admired. At least one of his
poems, "The Doom of Care: An Adirondack Lay," was published and
paid for by the *New York Times:*

> When clouds of care are gathering fast,
> And hope's fair sky seems o'ercast,
> In mountain glen and forest deep
> Where brooks o'er stony courses leap,
> Carking care must quickly cease
> And troubled soul find sure release.[6]

Baruch's social life had attained a richness epitomized in the golden
wedding celebration given for him and Belle at Sherry's on November
27, 1917. On a dais in the large ballroom, in front of a basket of immense
golden chrysanthemums from President Wilson, the couple received a
thousand guests, including the Belgian minister, the Jacob H. Schiffs, the
Marcus M. Markses, the Daniel Guggenheims, the Nathan Strauses, and

the Felix M. Warburgs. With a flowing white beard and a heavy shock of satin-white hair, Baruch looked every inch the patriarch—minus his eternal broad-brimmed black Stetson. Beneath an ermine wrap, Belle wore a trailing gown of white and gold brocade, with diamond ornaments. Most of the masses of flowers came from Belle's various clubs. Baruch received less perishable gifts: a gold replica of the bronze plaque marking the Rivington Street Bath House named in his honor a few months before; an illuminated testimonial to his service from the directors of Montefiore Home and Hospital; and a gold loving cup from the hospital built in his honor in Camden, South Carolina, in 1913.[7]

It was undoubtedly Bernard's influence that attracted some of the guests and the flowers from the president. Indeed, Bernard was responsible for many of Dr. Baruch's personal gratifications in this period, such as the small dinner party at which Dr. Baruch met the English actor, manager, and playwright Harley Granville Granville-Barker. It was also probably through Bernard that Dr. Baruch became acquainted with two of the leading men around President Wilson. In the fall of 1912, when illness struck William F. McCombs, Wilson's campaign manager, Dr. Baruch prescribed what McCombs gratefully called "effective treatments." Later, Secretary of Treasury William J. McAdoo sent Baruch a brief but cordial letter on political matters. In August 1916 Baruch received a tribute at least partially his own from Rupert Blue, surgeon general of the United States Public Health Service. Blue wrote to ask Baruch's advice about the sciatica that had made work impossible for him at a time of crisis in national affairs:

> My condition of helplessness is extremely exasperating in view of the epidemic of infantile paralysis now prevailing in New York. I would like very much to be able to assist in eradicating the infection and in preventing the interstate spread of the disease.
> I shall be very grateful for any advice you may choose to give me.[8]

Baruch was happy to treat the surgeon general, but he was not content with that. Despite his heart attack, he could not resist entering the campaign against polio, both as medical editor and as clinician. Although the best and most recent study had failed to prove the human transmission of polio, New York and surrounding states had adopted drastic quarantines, threatening to close all schools and universities. In a stream of editorials in the late summer and fall, Baruch berated public health officials for fostering the "'psychology of the crowd'" and sought to allay what he called "unreasoning fear" among the people.[9]

He also attempted to investigate the therapeutic properties of yeast in treating polio, an idea apparently inspired by a United States Public Health bulletin dealing with the use of yeast to restore function in pigeons afflicted with paralytic polyneuritis. The idea brought a negative response from Samuel J. Meltzer, a physiologist and pharmacologist at the Rockefeller Institute for Medical Research. Meltzer did not think yeast would help in poliomyelitis "because the disease is apparently caused, not by a dietary deficiency, but by a definite filterable organism." Meltzer did concede that "'therapeutics is, after all, but empirical'"—and that was encouragement enough for Baruch, who empathized with Meltzer's embitterment at "the inimical attitude of our Department of Health to my therapeutic suggestions." From a lifetime of crusading, Baruch understood Meltzer's assertion that the "visible government" was not responsible for the opposition he encountered: "There is," the Rockefeller scientist dryly added, "an invisible government which I do not care to discuss."[10]

As a private investigator, subject neither to "visible" nor "invisible" government, Baruch worked on through August as the polio count rose in an epidemic that was to total at least twenty-nine thousand cases and six thousand deaths. He was buoyed by recognition from Lafayette B. Mendel of the Sheffield Laboratory of Physiological Chemistry at Yale University. Mendel, who was then working on the hormone and vitamin content of brewer's yeast, protested Baruch's efforts to identify himself ("Professor Baruch needed no introduction"). As though he were an experimentalist, like Koch whom he so admired, Baruch obtained samples of waste yeast from breweries, patiently washing, filtering, and drying it to make it resemble the preparation used in the paralysis of malnourished pigeons. In mid-September he sent samples to physicians with a letter suggesting the dosage to be used "immediately after discovery of paralytic manifestations."

If the paralysis is not diminished in four days, it is unsuitable for your case.

It is harmless. I say this on the authority of the Hygienic Laboratory [later the National Institute of Health of the United States Public Health Service], in Washington.

After obtaining sufficient data, the formula will be published.

If you or other colleagues want a further supply, you may obtain it from me free of cost.

It does not conflict with other treatment.[11]

The procedure Baruch followed closely resembled Koch's handling of the "tuberculin experiment" a quarter of a century earlier, as well as Paul Ehrlich's distribution of Salvarsan for testing in 1910.[12] The results of

Baruch's trial were no more successful than Koch's, but this time there were no deaths; as Baruch said, the substance was harmless.

For a man of many achievements, more than seventy-five years old and troubled with a failing heart, Baruch continued to pursue an astounding number of demanding projects. He was consulting physician to Knickerbocker Hospital (Manhattan General) and to Bellevue and Allied hospitals. He remained on the staff of Sea View Hospital, a city hospital for tuberculous patients on Staten Island, where, for several months after February 1918, he struggled with difficulties in machinery and in personnel in order to establish an efficient hydrotherapy department.[13]

He also continued to devote much time and energy to the activities of the American Association for Promoting Hygiene and Public Baths. From the time of his appearance at the inauguration of a hydrotherapeutic department at the Sheppard Pratt Hospital in Baltimore in 1906, supporters of baths in Baltimore had worked together with their New York counterparts toward their formal organization in 1912. Baruch always said that the idea of forming the association had begun in Baltimore and migrated from there to New York, but the members seemed to feel that he deserved most of the credit. When they elected him president year after year, he always accepted, although he sometimes contented himself with having arranged the meeting and did not trouble to preside over it. At the 1913 meeting in Baltimore, Baruch was entertaining a reporter with tales of his imprisonment in Fort McHenry when someone came out of the meeting to tell him that the session had opened. According to the reporter, Baruch "waved him aside, explaining that he was going over to the Hotel Emerson in a few minutes to 'pack up' to return to New York."[14] He had other things to do: he retained medical editorship of the *Sun* through 1918 and remained active in the reclamation of Saratoga Springs well into 1919.

As early as 1913, Baruch had begun using his medical editorials as vehicles for preparedness propaganda. In 1913 and again in 1917, his advocacy of "vacation soldiering for college students" had won praise from General Leonard Wood, who set up the first six-week summer camp to give students military experience.[15] When America entered the war in 1917 and the patriotism of "German-Americans" became suspect, Baruch's stand on preparedness should have been proof enough of his loyalty. In addition, in 1914 he had studied the subject of ventilation in submarines and submitted his findings to Secretary of the Navy Josephus Daniels, and in March 1917 he had offered suggestions about recruiting to Dr. Franklin Martin of the Advisory Commission of the Council on National Defense.[16]

It seems incredible that anyone would question the devotion of an old man so energetic in his country's behalf—a man whose son was a member of President Wilson's Advisory Council. Yet Baruch suddenly found that his birth in Germany seventy-seven years before had become a stigma. In 1917 the *Chronicle Magazine* selected from *Who's Who* and the Social Register the names of prominent persons of German birth or descent and sent each one a letter demanding an affirmation of loyalty. The *Chronicle* warned that it would transmit the names of those who failed to comply, together with any "disloyal" replies, to the Department of Justice. Baruch seemed to take the threat seriously, perhaps because he had addressed the Association of American Women of German Descent in 1914 and, as recently as February 5, 1917, had been invited to attend a regular meeting of the Deutsche Medizinische Gesellschaft der Stadt New York.[17] He drafted a reply and then redrafted and polished and embellished it. He confessed that he had had early feelings of sympathy for "my relatives and friends in my native land" but insisted that his sympathy had vanished with the abandonment of American neutrality: "I had become a citizen of the United States, with the treaty acquiescence of the King of Prussia. If he had had any claim upon me, he had several opportunities to assert it during my visits under passport."[18] Together with the story of the *Chronicle*'s vigilantism in the supposed interest of national security, the *New York Times* of October 1 published Baruch's declaration of loyalty: "If I did not stand ready to consecrate heart and soul and all that I possess to the defense of my adopted country, I would despise myself as a scoundrel and perjurer and regard myself as an ingrate to the Government that has for sixty years enhanced and protected my life, honor and happiness."

While the *Chronicle* was compiling its list of suspects, Baruch remained busy with war work. He offered to advise on the proposed installation of hydrotherapeutic apparatus in army hospitals and to train army medical personnel in its use. When he received twenty-four-hour notice from Army Surgeon General William Crawford Gorgas that such equipment was about to be installed at the newly established Camp Devens, near Boston, Baruch arrived at the camp by such an early train that the commanding officer had not yet reached his office.[19] Between November 1917 and February 1918, out of concern for security, Baruch succeeded in having the total strength of American forces deleted from published reports from the surgeon-general's office. He also worked out a device for improved trench sanitation.[20] On January 22, 1918, he wrote Franklin Martin that he wanted to do even more: "I would like to enter the Service for the purpose of devoting myself to the instruction of

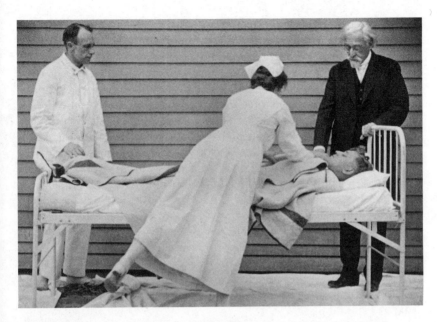

Baruch contributed to the war effort by teaching hydrotherapeutic techniques at federal installations. At Walter Reed General Hospital in May 1918, he demonstrated the wet-pack that he found effective in pneumonia, even in the toxic form characteristic of the influenza pandemic that began soon after this picture was taken. In the third edition of his *Principles and Practice of Hydrotherapy* (1908), he observed: "The patient cares little how he is healed; he certainly prefers to be cured by the empiric to being kept in continuous pilgrimage to the scientific doctor's office. A correct diagnosis does not interest a sick man so intensely as correct treatment." (Photograph courtesy of the late Frances A. Hellebrandt, M.D., in author's possession.)

physicians and assistants at the hospitals in which hydrotherapy is practiced, for it is usually practiced wrong and for this reason it is unsuccessful and is often abandoned. I would be willing to do this work without a commission, provided I could have one of my clinical assistants in hydrotherapy given the commission as my Adjutant." The assistant would travel to different cantonments where he would organize and maintain scientific hydrotherapy, "not only for ambulant cases but also to demonstrate its value in acute cases, e.g., Pneumonia, which," he observed prophetically, "appears to be very fatal in the Camps."

Addressing the staff of the base hospital at Camp Upton, New York, in

1918, Baruch appeared erect, handsome, and ready to work for his country. Nonetheless, with or without a commission, there was no place in the army for a man of seventy-eight, however vigorous. The army medical corps offered to use Baruch as an instructor when the Walter Reed General Hospital was completed, but Baruch was impatient. When he heard of plans for a reconstruction service that would use hydrotherapy to train and rehabilitate the wounded, he asked Franklin Martin outright: "Is there any way that I can become officially connected with this brand of Reconstruction work? With one or two young officers to assist me I could, in my humble opinion, be of great service in the organization and conduct of this important branch." He was beginning to feel desperate as plans for his work as instructor seemed to move unbearably slowly: "Our fine colleagues in the Department do not realize as I do that I may become physically disabled to start this work at any time and that when I reach that stage there will be no one to succeed me. To a man of my age," he added, "time is precious." Martin was grateful for Baruch's *Sun* editorials and his other attempts to promote the idea of increased rank and pay for medical officers, but he replied that he was "not always able to go as far as I should like."[21]

Apparently Baruch's sense of fleeting time was as much a torment to him in 1918 as it had been in his youth. He could not content himself with the fact that it had already carried him through an incredibly full lifetime. Even in his late seventies, he could not rest and enjoy the fruits of years spent in work and writing. Once in his life he had tried to stay home, and it had been such a miserable experience for him that, even after his heart attack in 1916, he apparently preferred the prospect of death from exertion. It was sometime between 1900 and 1914, after Bernard had freed him from the need to practice medicine, that he had first looked to Belle for daytime companionship. That unhappy period had taught him that, during his active years, she had learned to make other use of her time. By nature a joiner, active in Camden society even during the years when she was bearing and raising four sons, Belle had immersed herself in New York City's breathtaking array of women's activities. She was inspired, she told a *New York Times* reporter in 1914, by the "thoughtful and magnetic women speakers whom she heard in old-time Sorosis." At this club and others, she saw "a new and broader sphere of women" opening before her. The vision, she said, had "an almost hypnotic effect." After her sons were grown, she joined one organization after another until she belonged to more than thirty, requiring her to spend most of her mornings and afternoons away from home.[22] Thus in the years when Baruch began to slow down and look for company, he found himself alone except for the meetings he attended with Belle ("for the sake of appearances") or the evenings they spent at home together.[23]

Vain and quick to sense a slight, even in professional relationships, Baruch was a thousand times more sensitive about what he viewed as Belle's inattention. In his seventies he apparently needed reassurance of her love as much as he had in 1867, when two weeks without a letter during their engagement had put him into a frenzy of insecurity. In his later years, finding himself alone in his own home most of the time and in competition with servants and friends for Belle's attention during her hours at home, he grew bitter, especially as his tenure at Columbia drew to a close.

He often put his protests in the form of typewritten "memos," perhaps, as he claimed, because it was difficult to get near his busy spouse. Certainly his memos had more permanence than a vocal scene, and he made numerous carbons to remind Belle—after his death, he said—that she had abandoned her husband, leaving the servants to feed him like a "petted animal." Some of the memos traced in painful detail the instances in which he believed she had dragged him about in public and humiliated him by keeping him waiting in hallways, dressed for the street, while she chatted about club politics. Some of the memos reprimanded her for shaming him before others with stories—untrue, he said—about her father helping them financially early in their marriage and about giving music lessons herself to pay off the debts allegedly incurred in his medical education.[24] He resented her professions of pride in being Jewish ("tommyrot," he called it), while most of her friends were gentiles whom she sought to please by attending their churches or even joining them in communion. But for the most part, Baruch said that it was Belle's vanity, her egotism, and "high mightiness" that he objected to: he charged her with loving the friends and sons who flattered her, while resenting and avoiding the husband who told her the truth about herself.[25]

Of course, Baruch was hardly lacking in egotism himself. Although there are no surviving memos from Belle protesting his neglect of her, he could not have spent much time with her during the years when he was busy making his mark. No one, least of all Belle, could credit his protests in his last years that he had done it all for her. In a letter she wrote to him, probably in 1912, she professed regret at the deterioration of their relationship. Saddened by the recent deaths of several loved ones, she surveyed the course of their hectic, ambitious existence: "All these sad incidents crowd so fast as one grows old and if there is *no love* to soften and comfort what has life availed after all— *You and I* must realize this my dear, and both turn over a *brand* clean new leaf—I am ready—so there now." Belle wrote Bernard in 1919 that she was "a happy Mother and Wife"; that she had "prayed for my sons to be renowned among the Elders of the land—and God has answered me."[26] Although Dr. Baruch was proud of Bernard, he could not enjoy his triumph in the same way: to Belle, Bernard's financial success was the fulfillment of a mother's prophecy; to Simon it meant Belle's financial independence and the end of his own domination in the home.[27]

For lack of documentation, particularly of Belle's side of the story, it is impossible to say when things began to go wrong in their marriage. Whatever the source of the difficulty, Baruch thought of himself as a warm, loving man, made bitter and cynical by Belle's neglect. It made him wish, he said, for death to come quickly. In the last decade of his life, when the *Sun* editorship must have been a balm to his wounded ego, he wrote mocking, sarcastic editorials about suffrage and feminism. Although it may have been his German rearing or his life in South Carolina that initially formed his ideas of woman's proper place, his antifeminist editorials often sound very like his letters and memos describing Belle's activities in this period.[28]

On May 11, 1913, the *Sunday Sun* printed a long, prepared interview with Baruch, who "was at work upon a study of women as inventors." Before finishing the study—and very likely before starting it—Baruch concluded that women were not and never would be inventive.[29] Their strength was as "civilizers," as creators of the home and the family. It was his opinion that the female of the species lacked "the constructive germ plasm which leads to great creative discoveries."

Woman has been nursing babies from the beginning of time. Yet it was not a woman who perfected the ways of taking care of the babies.

For seventy-five years women have been studying medicine, while there is not one really great woman in the field of medical science.

With Havelock Ellis, Baruch believed that "'women take truth as they find it, while men want to create truth.'" It was "inconceivable, for instance, that a woman should have devised the Copernican system. It is still more difficult to recall a woman who for any abstract and intellectual end has fought for her way to success through obloquy and contempt, or without reaching success, like a Roger Bacon or a Galileo, a Wagner or an Ibsen." Baruch believed that women could be competent physicians or authors and that, in their own areas, they sometimes surpassed the male. "What John Brown could not accomplish with his savage, masculine methods, Harriet Beecher Stowe had accomplished by her feminine, noble and inspiring methods." Florence Nightingale had done in the Crimea "what all the skill and constructive capacity of the physicians" could not do. But invention or creativity? No. "The Biblical fiat will stand till the end of time: 'God created him in His image—in the image of God created He him; male and female created He them.'"[30]

During these years Belle publicly parroted her husband's ideas, linking suffrage and feminism pejoratively to socialism and contrasting both with the ideals of home, heaven, and mother.[31] When the New York City Federation of Women's Clubs hissed her statements at the Astor Hotel, the *New York Times* played down the news but inadvertently compounded the insult by attributing to her a statement she had actually set out to refute: that "the free power of selection in love is the true female franchise." In a letter to the editor, signed "Fairness," Baruch attempted to correct the error.[32]

On July 12, 1914, the *Sunday Times* carried a full-page interview with Belle, under the heading "Modern Womanhood Sadly Shirks Its Holy Duty." Belle explained that she had just resigned from seven clubs because she "found them to be taking more time and energy than should be expended upon selfish gratification. I believe the modern woman's aim in life should be to bring the modern man back home. To do that she must stay at home herself." Twelve days later, Dr. Baruch wrote bitterly to his son Hartwig: "If I did not love her and want to avoid scandal I should have quit long ago for what satisfaction is there in this kind of companionship?" He documented this charge with a chronicle of the "clubwoman's average day." Even with seven fewer clubs to compete with, he was losing the fight: "I spend my afternoons, somehow at a picture show, or other 'lovely' amusement—thats my fault." He complained that in the evenings, Belle dozed when he wanted to talk about ideas for editorials or articles. "Isn't it worth while living for after a man has labored for a woman for half a century?"[33]

For a time Baruch encountered little public opposition to his antifeminism, even when he said that Queen Elizabeth had "dragged womanhood in the mud" or that all the women monarchs of Europe could not compare with Frederick the Great of Prussia. He went unchallenged with arguments about "female incapacity to govern" and the absence of a female Raphael, Rubens, Velasquez, da Vinci, or Holbein as proof that women are incapable of creativity.[34]

Not until Baruch entered a controversy with Dr. Adolphus Knopf in the *New York Times* did he draw serious opposition. In one of his sallies against Knopf, Baruch tried to "discredit that ill-starred offspring of anarchism and socialism called feminism, which menaces the social fabric by its revolutionary teachings on the marital relation." He charged feminists with trying to change the marriage vow, disrupt family relations, and provide "various hair-brained schemes for the care of the offspring." When Baruch further insisted that "biological limitations (anatomy, physiology, and psychology)" predestined women for a limited sphere, he drew fire from Charles A. Beard, professor of history at Columbia University and husband of Mary Ritter Beard, herself a noted historian. Challenging Baruch's assertion that "women have made no inventions in the field of domestic labor," Beard referred Baruch to "the plain records of the Patent Office."[35]

Although Baruch never altered his basic premise, he did backtrack a bit. After the Beard exchange, he explained that by inventive or creative—or "illustrious," as the argument had run—he had meant to include only those who had done "epoch-making work": thus, even as *male* candidates for medical greatness, he considered only Hippocrates, Vesalius, Paré, Harvey, Jenner, Morton, Lister, Koch, and Carrel. He excluded Marie Curie from consideration because "she confesses participation with her husband."[36] Before making his last statement in the debate, however, he started a rear-guard action with a *Sun* editorial urging an end to discrimination against women doctors in "hospitals in which women are patients," a cause he asked the *Times* to support "with your powerful pen."[37]

Besides their common fight against feminism (which Belle abandoned when she accepted suffrage in 1916), both Baruchs were devoted to the current "cult of the South."[38] In 1913, as vice-president of the Southland Club, Belle gave a New Year's reception for club members. At home at 51 West Seventieth Street, she received her guests in "a Watteau frock of blue and white brocade, the exact copy of a costume worn by her mother in 1855 at a State ball in South Carolina." (According to newspaper accounts, the original dress had been destroyed during the ubiquitous Sherman's march.) Amid decorations of smilax, gray moss, bramble berries, and holly brought in from Bernard's South Carolina estate, the program began with a poem by Paul Hamilton Hayne, the southerner's poet of poets, and ended with a composition called "The Sunny South," all to the accompaniment of real southern eggnog.[39]

The New Year's party became a tradition. In 1915 Belle wore a pompadour of pink silk, a colonial model with two long curls draped gracefully over her shoulder. In anticipation of the 1916 celebration, the *Sun* printed an interview with Belle, "entirely the grande dame," that Baruch preserved in an undated clipping among his papers. "Her snow-white hair is dressed high and carefully. Her eyebrows are black swept arches above dark-brown eyes. Her mouth is that of an aristocrat and a gentlewoman." Belle explained to the reporter that the aim of the Southland Club had always been "philanthropy" as distinguished from "charity." With the international crisis, however, national interest had become paramount. As southerners, she said, members of the Southland Club had much to learn from the North. "'We also feel that we of the South have something to give the North'—she dropped her voice a full tone, adding gently, 'something to warm the blood of its patriotism, to thrill the spirit of its valor.'"

Dr. Baruch's southern cultism was different. Like Belle, he had read Thomas Dixon's *Leopard's Spots,* and, like her, he was pleased to be reminded, by a speech Senator John Sharpe Williams made in 1917, of Dixon's prophecy that the South would be the mainstay of the country in future emergencies.[40] But most of Baruch's thoughts about the South were less self-conscious and self-righteous. He had barely known the antebellum South and was, in fact, repelled by many aspects of southern culture which he saw in his fellow physicians in Camden. Although he repeatedly impressed people in the North as a "typical Southern gentleman," he certainly did not think of himself as one. Considering his revulsion at the ways of the South while he lived there, it seems peculiar that he should have grown devoted to any part of its memory, even out of the fondness age usually feels for remembered youth. Perhaps it was his misery with Belle—and it was misery to him—that made him look back with particular longing to the days when he was a young, strong Confederate surgeon, with all of life stretching before him and his sweetheart.

Whatever the reason, Baruch seemed to indulge his memories—not so much of Belle's South as of his war—most fully during the time of his greatest unhappiness at home. In 1912 he gave the *New York Times* a full-page interview relating his adventures as a captured Confederate surgeon. In 1913 he attended an encampment to commemorate the battle of Gettysburg. He became so excited at one of the scenes in *The Birth of a Nation,* D. W. Griffith's film epic of the Civil War (1915), that he leaped from his seat and gave the rebel yell. In 1914 he submitted an article called "A Surgeon's Story of Battle and Capture" to the *Confederate Veteran* magazine, and in 1915 the same magazine printed a letter from him asking to hear from men interned with him at Fort McHenry in 1863. Through the replies he received, he confirmed his memories of how the surgeons were sent there from Gettysburg; of their living conditions as prisoners, from the "two-story bunks" to the worms in the soup; of the stable loft where they were held as punishment for the escape of their comrades; of the "bull pen" where the Yankees "initiated their deserters and the uncivilized."[41]

In September 1915 Baruch spoke about his memories to a crowd of two hundred friends and members of the Long Branch Historical Society. While Belle entertained a group of Boy Scouts in one part of the Anchorage (the thirty-five room twelve-bathroom home where Belle and Simon spent their summers), Baruch regaled his audience in another, near a panel covered with his war mementos.[42] His public indulgence in the cult of the South reached a high point on January 19, 1919, when he gave the principal address before the Confederate Veteran Camp of New York, convened in the Hotel Astor to celebrate the 111th anniversary of the birth of Robert E. Lee. Though he spoke in prose long out of fashion, his intent was modern: to extract lessons for the present from the life of Lee and the circumstances that had brought him to greatness. The address was essentially a plea for support of President Wilson, its dominant theme the need for preparedness in 1919 and after; and for a strong regular army, even in peacetime, even if the proposed League of Nations should be established. "I beg of you friends not to lay one obstacle in the way of universal military service now that 'State Rights' as I shall show, are dead." According to Baruch, states' rights had died and risen from the dead several times, usually rising only during Democratic administrations. The final blow had come with President's Wilson's recent realization that, "in the evolution of this Nation, their sacrifice has become necessary and unavoidable." Baruch had accepted this fact, and he urged his fellow veterans to join him in putting aside states' rights in favor of national needs. "Now my comrades and friends the final lesson I would impress upon you is this: Neither the glories of war, nor the sanctity of the Lost Cause, nor the principles of the Lost Cause will endure."[43] Of the many speeches made around the country to honor Robert E. Lee that night, it seems safe to surmise that Baruch's was unique. Apart from a newspaper account of his search for the stable at Fort McHenry where he had lived as a prisoner, he made no other published remarks about the Civil War.[44]

In the last years of his life, Baruch's mind turned to other events of the past, especially to those of his accomplishments which savored of heroism or courage or originality. Although he already had living memorials in the Camden hospital and the Rivington Street public bath, he seemed to crave a larger niche in history.[45] He had the sense of mission that often accompanies a sense of history and, with it, an almost inordinate yearning to be remembered. As often as he referred openly to his mission, he still more often revealed it unwittingly. When the Rivington Street bathhouse was about to be dedicated to him in 1917, he recalled efforts by so-called "friends of public baths" to block the necessary $25,000 appropriation for public baths: these were the "blandishments of dillet-

To commemorate his father's early work and provide a place where Kershaw County doctors could make use of Captain John Burwell's bequest for health care for the sick poor "regardless of color," Bernard Baruch endowed Camden's first hospital. At Doctor Baruch's urging, it included a dispensary (an ambulatory outpatient department) where the poor could receive free attention for the "so-called minor ailments"—rheumatism and respiratory and digestive ills—that he knew often reduced earning capacity and made lives miserable. At the hospital's dedication in 1913 Doctor Baruch reminded "toilers of this community" that the new hospital was not a charity ("I hate that word," he said) but the offspring of philanthropy, a word he equated with "Love of Man." (Photograph, courtesy of the Camden Archives and Museum, shows the hospital as Bernard Baruch restored it after fire destroyed the original building in 1921.)

tante [sic] philanthropists, who desired the glory but failed of achievement." At the same time, he sent Manhattan Borough president Marcus Marks his view of the four great epochs in the history of bathing: the first, the Roman baths inaugurated by the Emperor Agrippa; the second, Oscar Lassar's demonstration of showers for public baths in nineteenth-century Berlin; "the third epoch began with the idea, which it was my happy privilege to promulgate, that it is the duty of a Municipality to furnish the people with free baths throughout the year, just as they do with free parks"; the fourth epoch was that begun by Marks himself.[46]

Baruch also thought that he deserved more credit than he had received for promoting the treatment of appendicitis by surgical rather than medical means. He felt inadequately appreciated despite numerous references to his contribution that were published between 1894 and 1907 by his friend Dr. John Allen Wyeth, one of them in an editorial in the *Sun*. Wyeth, who was president of the New York State Medical Association in 1900, of the American Medical Association in 1901, and of the New York Academy of Medicine from 1907 to 1911, had said in 1894 that to Baruch, "more than to any other one man, belongs the credit of having impressed on the general profession the fact that surgery is of the utmost importance in the successful treatment of appendicitis."[47] Still Baruch resented the acclamation surgeons received for the development of appendicitis treatment. When Wyeth wrote him in 1903 of his desire to give Baruch full credit for his work, Baruch replied acidly, "Such generosity is alas rare in our 'noble' profession." After supplying Wyeth with the details of the 1887 case on which his priority claim rested, Baruch said, "I think it may be claimed that I was the first to regard appendicitis as a surgical disease."[48]

In 1907, again preoccupied with priority, he wrote Dr. Albert J. Wittson, whose brother Gerard Wittkowsky had been the appendicitis patient in 1887. He had now modified his claim almost beyond recognition:

I was the first physician (not a surgeon) who made the earliest diagnosis of a successful case and whose early diagnosis bore fruit in that it prevented septic peritonitis which had always hitherto occurred, and I was the first physician who ever dared to insist on an operation for the disease and whose practice has since that time been followed. . . . Sometime before you reach my age you may hear the subject discussed, and when I have "passed to the great majority," you will be in possession of the facts of this classical case and then be able to speak from original and exact data.[49]

As appendectomy became a more common procedure, its history took on enlivened interest. Other doctors began turning up cases Baruch had never heard of, and medical historians tackled the difficult question of priority. When they failed to include the Wittkowsky case or to tell it as Baruch remembered it, he wrote them, asking that they carry corrections or additions in later editions.[50]

Even after a severe heart attack in March 1919, Baruch continued to press for wider acceptance of hydrotherapy. He had had singular success in treating pneumonia by hydrotherapeutic techniques carefully adjusted to suit each patient's condition. In twenty years of private practice, he had lost only two of these patients, one debilitated by age and alcohol, the other by three days of 105-degree temperature and a self-inflicted overdose of Epsom salts. When the 1918 influenza pandemic brought enormous fatality from pneumonia, his colleagues had frequently appealed to him to help them treat desperate cases. Despite his own failing health he had responded, traveling to patients' homes in New York and New Jersey, where he applied hourly chest compresses that proved effective even in cases marked by stupor before his arrival. Writing his last book, *An Epitome of Hydrotherapy for Physicians, Architects and Nurses* (1920), he explained his understanding of these remarkable results: "The pulmonary circulation is probably affected directly, in view of the fact that its vasomotor supply is derived from the second to the seventh dorsal ganglia, which are connected with the epigastric and scapular reflex area in the skin."[51]

In the introduction to the *Epitome,* Baruch said that it was his last message to his colleagues, his last effort to remove misunderstanding and ignorance of hydrotherapeutic technique and rationale. Like his other messages, the *Epitome* failed to achieve as much as he hoped for it. Efforts to establish hydrotherapy in the realm of regular American therapeutics were doomed because most physicians believed that hydrotherapy's rationale still rested largely on then ill-defined natural powers of resistance, powers that came to play an important part in medical thought only decades later. In 1926, Morris Fishbein, editor of the *Journal of the American Medical Association,* spoke for the medical orthodoxy of the day when he said: "On this tendency—the *vis medicatrix naturae* [healing power of nature]—all of the cults of history have floated their frail vessels."[52] Although the converse was not necessarily true (that everyone who relied on the healing power of nature was a cultist), most clinicians and researchers in the early twentieth century favored drug therapies. They never grasped Baruch's message that the use of water could be as precisely regulated as the use of drugs and with far less risk of damage to vital organs.

In 1914 Baruch admitted that his friends considered his work in hydrotherapy "a personal sacrifice" in the sense that his "large hospital experience would have brought me more fame and certainly more shekels if I had become a consultant in internal medicine."[53] The friends were almost certainly right, but the realization that he could do better by abandoning hydrotherapy seems to have made little difference. Although Baruch, like most ambitious people, scorned neither fame nor shekels, he was willing to give up both for the cause of furthering the rational use of physiological remedies, which he spoke of as his "mission."[54] He seemed to hope that he would be vindicated by history. Forty years after his death, the medical profession used hydrotherapy primarily in mental illness, in controlling temperature, and in physical therapy; hence Baruch would not have been surprised to see the popularity of saunas and hot tubs, or advertisements for home hydrotherapy units for the relief of arthritic pain and muscular strains, for those with a bent for do-it-yourself healing.[55]

Baruch's sense of mission bewitched him to the end of his life. When it was frustrated in his work, it cropped up elsewhere, often in the form of a drive for personal power. Sometime during the last two years of his life, he offered to use his influence with President Wilson in behalf of a friend seeking an appointment in the government: "My son advises [me] to write one letter to him and one to Dr. Grayson [Wilson's physician] instead of the president. He is convinced that the doctor will submit the matter to the president, who *will be certain* to accept my suggestion. If I were in good health," he added confidently, "I could make your cause like the famous line 'horse high, bull proud and pig tight.'"[56]

As late as 1919 or 1920, Baruch appeared hale and hearty as he sat absorbed in his reading at the Library of the New York Academy of Medicine.[57] In fact, he was often ill and harried by thoughts of all that he wanted to do before death came. In the spring of 1920 he wrote a letter to the *New York Times* on the subject of legislation banning the manufacture of small arms. To a response from George Le Brun, author of the Sullivan Law, Baruch replied: "I am now nearing my eightieth year and I would deem it a great achievement if I could before I go hence see an organization started with the determination to have the law I advocate enacted." He wanted Le Brun to call on him at once "because my 'hour may come' at any moment."[58] Nearly a year later, shortly after the inauguration of Warren G. Harding, a newspaper reporter found Baruch hard at work in his study, dictating letters to every member of Congress to arouse interest in anti-gun legislation.[59]

Early in May 1921 ill health put Baruch to bed. He was attended by his physician-son Herman, by Albert J. Wittson, who had accompanied him on his tour of European spas in 1913, and by Nathan Brill, who described the endemic form of typhus later known as Brill's disease. By the middle of May, Baruch knew that his hour was upon him. "As my 'sands are running low,'" he wrote Dr. Wyeth, "I want to establish the claim that you so kindly espoused in your great book on Surgery, in your able articles on Appendicitis, and in your editorial in the New York Sun in 1904, if I remember correctly." (Actually, the editorial had appeared in 1903.) The rest of the letter to Wyeth, in which Baruch reviewed the

Wittkowsky case still another time, was similarly marked by confusion, and the last sentence sprang from ambition apparently heightened by the illness that should have blunted it: "I should like to have the subject of my priority brought before the American College of Surgeons, at its next meeting, and would like you to espouse my cause, in any way you may deem proper."[60]

On May 16 Baruch wrote a long letter to one of his sons, setting forth his accomplishments one by one. There were the public baths: "Even in Rome the only baths that were free, were those donated by the Aristocrat-Adiles [sic], and by the Emperor, to the people. I have forced municipal authorities to give these baths free." There was the appendicitis case: "I made the first diagnosis of Appendicitis, which led to the first successful operation." There was the dinner at the University Club "to be tendered me by the faculty of Harvard University." And there was the "WAR WORK!"[61] These were the things he wanted people to remember.

On the day when Baruch wrote this professional summing up, the treasurer of the American Association for Promoting Hygiene and Public Baths sent the members a letter in Baruch's behalf: "Dr. Baruch has been dangerously ill for some time past, which doubtless accounts for your not having heard from him."[62] But even on his sickbed, Baruch did not neglect association matters entirely: he dictated the presidential address he would not be able to deliver in person on May 10 in Brookline, Massachusetts.[63]

On June 3 the *New York Times* reported that Baruch was in critical condition: "Three weeks ago he was seriously ill with an affection of the lungs that followed a heart attack." Bernard Baruch has recalled that Belle asked her sons to send for the rabbi to pray with Simon as his death approached. All four sons refused, honoring instead their earlier promise to their father; anticipating Belle's action, Simon had told them several days before, "The last thing I can do for you boys is to show you how to die"—adding, "There is no use trying to fool God at this late date."[64]

The *Times* of the next day carried his obituary. He had died shortly after one o'clock in the afternoon of June 3, at his home at 51 West Seventieth Street. The *Times* obituary ran a full column, describing contributions Baruch himself had probably forgotten. There were other tributes, too, even in South Carolina papers, but Baruch would probably have been most pleased by the *Medical Record* of June 11, which said he had been "for forty years one of New York's best known physicians."

Baruch's body was cremated after a simple funeral service at the West End Synagogue on June 5, conducted by Dr. Frederick de Sola Mendes, rabbi emeritus of the congregation and a longtime friend of Baruch. In the crowd that filled the synagogue were six Confederate veterans and Baruch's four sons. Belle, who was ill on another floor of their home when he died, was unable to attend. At the family's request, based on Dr. Baruch's wishes, Rabbi Mendes omitted a eulogy: "It would not be possible," he said, "justly to appreciate the achievements in science and the aid to suffering humanity of this man. Better leave them to a later generation to embalm in history."[65]

With a twinkle in his light eyes, Baruch would have objected to the good rabbi's choice of metaphor. "Embalmed" he could never be, least of all in history, where he had friends and mentors by the score. The history he knew and loved was as real to him as daily life, as vital as his sense perceptions of the world around him. His "achievements in science," his "aid to suffering humanity," could no more be embalmed than the body he arranged to have burned or the spirit he gave in every living moment, through babies he delivered, patients he treated, writings he published.

Baruch lived all of his eighty years in the service of one cause or another. What the more introspective Sigmund Freud said of himself was equally true of Baruch: "A man like me cannot live without a hobby-horse, a consuming passion—in Schiller's words a tyrant."[66] Unlike Freud, Baruch never found the perfect tyrant. He tried a whole succession of them and served each one well, but he did not lose himself in any, not even in hydrotherapy. Perhaps he was unable to lose himself. Perhaps that is why he was still in search of fulfillment at the end of so useful a life.

Notes

Abbreviations

AMB	*American Medical Biographies* (Kelly and Burrage)
BM&SJ	*Boston Medical and Surgical Journal*
CMJ&R	*Charleston Medical Journal and Review*
DAB	*Dictionary of American Biography*
DAMB	*Dictionary of American Medical Biography* (Kelly and Burrage)
DSB	*Dictionary of Scientific Biography*
DG	*Dietetic Gazette*
D&HG	*Dietetic and Hygienic Gazette*
GMJ	*Gaillard's Medical Journal*
JAAPH&PB	*Journal of the American Association for Promoting Hygiene and Public Baths*
JAMA	*Journal of the American Medical Association*
JB	*Journal of Balneology*
JSH	*Journal of Southern History*
MR	*Medical Record*
NYMJ	*New York Medical Journal*
ODJM&S	*Old Dominion Journal of Medicine and Surgery*
RBHSC	*Report of the Board of Health of South Carolina*
RMJ	*Richmond Medical Journal*
R&LMJ	*Richmond and Louisville Medical Journal*
TG	*Therapeutic Gazette*
Trans. AMA	*Transactions of the American Medical Association*
Trans. NYAM	*Transactions of the New York Academy of Medicine*
Trans. SCMA	*Transactions of the South Carolina Medical Association*

1. *"Amerika, du hast es besser"*

1. Louis Shalet, M.D., to author, October 26, 1959, recalled making these ferry trips with Dr. Baruch in 1914. Sea View Hospital opened with one thousand

beds in 1913; for details of plans to double its capacity only a few years later, see the *BM&SJ* 175 (September 14, 1916): 392.

2. I am indebted to Professors Zbigniew Czerwinski and J. Topolski (of the University of Pozan in 1958) for their assistance in the search for materials of this nature.

3. Martha Machol, daughter of Dr. Baruch's youngest sister, to author, May 1958.

4. Two early sketches of Baruch, for which he presumably supplied biographical data, carry these intimations of his identification with Prussia rather than Poland: see William B. Atkinson, ed., *The Physicians and Surgeons of the United States* (Philadelphia: Charles Robson, 1878), 164, and Irving A. Watson, *Physicians and Surgeons of America* (Concord, N.H.: Republican Press Association, 1896), 534–35.

5. Margaret L. Coit, *Mr. Baruch* (Boston: Houghton Mifflin, 1957), 54.

6. Baruch stated this in his letter of resignation as president of the Hebrew Benevolent Association of Camden, November 20, 1880, in association records kept by the secretary.

7. Martha Machol to author, May 1958.

8. Adolf Warschauer, "Die Entstehung einer judischen Gemeinde," in Ludwig Geiger, ed., *Zeitschrift für die Geschichte der Juden in Deutschland* (Braunschweig, 1890), 3:170–81. According to P. Hoffman, *Geschichte der Stadt Schwersenz und ihrer Schützengilden* (Posen, 1912), 5, weaving and brewing were the dominant industries of Schwersenz in the eighteenth century; to prevent conflict with the German craftsmen, Jews were forbidden to engage in weaving.

9. This description, including the quoted passages, comes from Hermann Starke, *Zur Geschichte des Königlichen Friedrich-Wilhelms-Gymnasiums zu Posen* (Posen: Herzbach, 1884), 6, 9, bound in [?] Schonborn, *Beiträge zur Geschichte der Schule* (in the Maria Hosmer Penniman Library at the Library of the University of Pennsylvania).

10. Ibid., 10. According to Kathryn M. Olesko, "Physics Instruction in Prussian Secondary Schools before 1859," *Osiris* 2d ser., 5 (1989): 105, the Posen Gymnasium in the early 1800s lacked equipment for physics demonstrations but nonetheless gave students information about available instruments.

11. Starke, *Zur Geschichte des Königlichen Friedrich-Wilhelms-Gymnasium,* 30–35.

12. Simon's name does not appear in Starke's list, ibid., 60–68, of all the Gymnasium's *Abiturienten* from 1835 to 1884. According to his naturalization papers, dated January 19, 1871, now in the South Caroliniana Library of the University of South Carolina, he arrived in America on December 23, 1855.

13. In a random search through the *Akta miejskie Swarzedza* (records of the community of Schwersenz, consisting of several hundred volumes handwritten in Gothic script), Professor Topolski found no indication that the Baruchs played an important role in the community. In "Reminiscences of a Confederate Surgeon," *Long Branch Record,* September 24, 1915, privately published reprint in Simon Baruch papers, Baruch said that he came to America to escape military service; in the *New York Times,* October 1, 1917, he said it would have been impossible to pursue a medical career in Prussia. Nathan Glazer, *American Judaism* (Chicago: University of Chicago Press, 1957), 23–24, discusses the circumstances underlying large-scale migrations of Jews to America from such areas as Simon's homeland beginning around 1840. On

the disappearance of Baruch's papers between 1961 and 1991 and their present location see Notes on Sources.

14. Stanislas Konopka, *Les relations culturelles entre la France et la Pologne dans le domaine de la médicine* (Warsaw: Société Polonaise d'Histoire de la Médicine, 1958), 13–16.
15. The quotation is the first line of Goethe's poem "Den Vereinigten Staaten."
16. Simon Baruch naturalization papers, dated January 19, 1871, in Simon Baruch Papers, South Caroliniana Library, University of South Carolina, Columbia; Bernard M. Baruch, *Baruch: My Own Story* (New York: Henry Holt, 1957), 4.

2. To Become a Doctor

1. Thomas J. Kirkland and Robert M. Kennedy, *Historic Camden*, 2 vols. (Columbia: State Co., 1905–26), 2:31–32, 41; William Watts Ball, *The State That Forgot: South Carolina's Surrender to Democracy* (Indianapolis: Bobbs Merrill, 1932), 103; Lawrence F. Brewster, "Planters from the Low-County and Their Summer Travels," *Proceedings of the South Carolina Historical Association* (1943): 35–41, esp. 36–37.
2. Simon Baruch naturalization papers; speech at the dedication of the Camden Hospital, reported in *Camden Chronicle*, December 5, 1913; Martha Machol, Dr. Baruch's niece, to author, May 1958; Bernard Baruch, *My Own Story*, 4.
3. *Camden Chronicle*, December 5, 1913. According to Henry Burnell Shafer, *The American Medical Profession, 1783–1850* (New York: Columbia University Press, 1936), 33–34, the payment usually made to preceptors for a three-year period was $150 in advance or $200 at the end of the term.
4. Richard Harrison Shryock, *The Development of Modern Medicine: An Interpretation of the Social and Scientific Factors Involved* (New York: Knopf, 1947), 258–59, 261–62; Charles Newman, *The Evolution of Medical Education in the Nineteenth Century* (London: Oxford University Press, 1957), 18, 24. On the frequently unsatisfactory nature of apprenticeship in this period, see Martin Kaufman, *American Medical Education: The Formative Years, 1765–1910* (Westport, Conn.: Greenwood Press, 1976), 45–46.
5. Baruch's remarks at the dedication of the Camden Hospital, *Camden Chronicle*, December 5, 1913; Shafer, *American Medical Profession*, 34. Robley Dunglison was an English physician who came at the invitation of Thomas Jefferson to teach at the University of Virginia; his *Medical Dictionary* (Boston, 1833), as edited by his son in 1847, was still considered in 1876 the "most convenient work of the kind in existence"; see Edward H. Clarke et al., *A Century of American Medicine, 1776–1876* (Philadelphia: H. C. Lea, 1876), 318–19.
6. At Dr. Baruch's request, the wards of the Camden Hospital built in his honor in 1913 were dedicated to four men, among them Workman and Deas. According to a plaque in the hospital, Workman was Baruch's preceptor from 1859 to 1860, Deas from 1860 to 1862. In the *Camden Chronicle* of December 5, 1913, Dr. Baruch stated that Deas became his preceptor after Workman's death; but Workman declared bankruptcy in 1869 (*Camden Journal*, September 2, 1869) and died the same year (Kirkland and Kennedy, *Historic Camden*, 2:445).

7. Kirkland and Kennedy, *Historic Camden*, 2:376. For a picture of Paris in 1830, when it was a mecca for an estimated five thousand medical students, see Shryock, *Development of Modern Medicine*, 153–54; letter from Dr. Baruch to Dr. Alexander Salley, March 5, 1868, in Simon Baruch Papers, South Caroliniana Library, Columbia; *Camden Chronicle*, December 5, 1913.

8. Simon Baruch, address to graduating class of Medical College of Virginia, published as "Lessons of Half a Century in Medicine," *Old Dominion Journal of Medicine and Surgery* 11 (July 1910): 1–23; *Camden Chronicle*, December 5, 1913. Although medical preceptors eventually went out of fashion as a requirement and then even as an occasional practice, some of their virtues were never duplicated in the formal curriculum, and the mid-twentieth century brought a partial return to the system. See W. Clarke Wescoe, "Preceptors as General Educators in Medicine," *Journal of Medical Education* 31 (September 1956): 598–603.

9. *Camden Chronicle*, December 5, 1913; *Camden Weekly Journal*, October 5, 1860.

10. For the question of which Baum brother financed Simon's medical education, see Coit, *Mr. Baruch*, 4–5.

11. Isabella D. Martin and Myrta Lockett Avary, eds., *A Diary from Dixie, as Written by Mary Boykin Chesnut, Wife of James Chesnut Jr., United States Senator from South Carolina, 1859–1861, and Afterward Aide to Jefferson Davis and a Brigadier General in the Confederate Army* (New York: D. Appleton, 1905), 3. Readers interested in a critical edition of this unique "diary" and in recent scholarship about its author should consult C. Vann Woodward, ed., *Mary Chesnut's Civil War* (New Haven: Yale University Press, 1981), and C. Vann Woodward and Elisabeth Muhlenfeld, *The Private Mary Chesnut: The Unpublished Civil War Diaries* (New York: Oxford University Press, 1984).

12. Earl Schenck Miers, *The Great Rebellion: The Emergence of the American Conscience* (Cleveland: World, 1958), 44–48.

13. Descriptions and appraisals of the Medical College of South Carolina are given by William F. Norwood, *Medical Education in the United States before the Civil War* (Philadelphia: University of Pennsylvania Press, 1944), 258, and Gabriel Edward Manigault, autobiography, 76, 92, in Manigault Family Papers, Southern Historical Collection, University of North Carolina Library, Chapel Hill; my thanks to Willie Lee Rose for locating this material. See also Joseph Ioor Waring, *A History of Medicine in South Carolina, 1825–1900* (Columbia: South Carolina Medical Association, 1967), 81–82; G. Edmund Gifford, Jr., "The Charleston Physician-Naturalists," *Bulletin of the History of Medicine* 49 (1975): 573 and n. 62; Michael O'Brien and David Moltke-Hansen, eds., *Intellectual Life in Antebellum Charleston* (Knoxville: University of Tennessee Press, 1986); and Robert Wilson, "Some Historical Aspects of the Medical College of the State of S.C.," in *A Brief History of the South Carolina Medical Association* (Charleston: South Carolina Medical Association, 1948), 142, 146.

14. Although none of the college records for the year 1860–61 survived the war, there is ample evidence of Simon's attendance: the following year he enrolled at the Medical College of Virginia with full credit for the "first course" at Charleston; he also kept a book of notes inscribed "On Lectures Delivered at the Medical College of South Carolina During the Term 1860–1861." The first

date in the notebook, now located in the Robert Woodruff Library, Emory University, Atlanta, is November 19, 1860, but several earlier lectures appear without dates. Annual faculty circulars (comparable to our catalogs but issued at the end of each term) still exist for the sessions from 1825 to 1883, exclusive of the years from 1860 to 1865. They are kept in a bound volume in the library of the Medical College in Charleston. Except for faculty changes, the circulars for the 1859–60 and 1865–66 sessions are so similar that I have drawn on them to describe general conditions in the college during 1860–61.

15. All material on fees and requirements is taken from the circular for 1859–60.
16. Shryock, *Development of Modern Medicine*, 258; Norwood, *Medical Education*, 257. The dean's report in the 1859–60 circular, 12–13, indicates that an additional session was held the preceding summer.
17. Newman, *Evolution of Medical Education*, 37; Wyndham B. Blanton, *Medicine in Virginia in the Nineteenth Century* (Richmond: Richard, Garrett and Massie, 1933), 69–70. Concerning the first use of formaldehyde, see Fielding H. Garrison and Leslie T. Morton, comps., *Medical Bibliography: An Annotated Check-List of Texts Illustrating the History of Medicine*, 2d ed. (London: Grafton, 1954).
18. The faculty for 1860–61 is listed in the *Centennial Memorial of the Medical College of the State of South Carolina, 1824–1924* (Charleston, 1924), 17. The sketch of Dr. Holbrook is taken from *DAMB*, 578; Waring, *Medicine in South Carolina, 1825–1900*, 243–45. See also *DSB*, s.v. "John Edwards Holbrook."
19. Norwood, *Medical Education*, 258. Shafer, *American Medical Profession*, 62, says that before 1850 blacks furnished "an easy and, to the whites, unembarrassing source of experimentation." He cites a Missouri statute of 1835 as indicative of the "general attitude of the South" that slaves' bodies might be dissected with the consent of the owner. This generalization is borne out in Todd L. Savitt, *Medicine and Slavery: The Diseases and Health Care of Blacks in Antebellum Virginia* (Urbana: University of Illinois Press, 1978), 290–93. See also John B. Blake, "Anatomy," in Ronald L. Numbers, ed., *The Education of American Physicians: Historical Essays* (Berkeley: University of California Press, 1980), 29–47.
20. Autobiography of Charles A. Hentz, typed copy, 1:104, 119–26, Hentz Family Papers and Books, Southern Historical Collection, University of North Carolina Library, Chapel Hill. My thanks to Willie Lee Rose for directing me to this material.
21. Diary of Charles A. Hentz, vol. 5 (1845–49), 150, ibid.
22. Ibid., 120.
23. *DAMB*, 222; Isobel Stevenson, "Medical Literature of the Civil War Era," *Ciba Symposia* 3 (April 1941): 909; H. H. Cunningham, *Doctors in Gray: The Confederate Medical Service* (Baton Rouge: Louisiana State University Press, 1958), 248. Joseph K. Barnes, et al., eds., *The Medical and Surgical History of the War of the Rebellion*, 6 vols. (Washington, D.C.: U.S. Government Printing Office, 1870–88), Part Third, Surgical Volume, 889; Medical College of South Carolina, 1859–60 circular, 16–17; Arthur Mazyck, comp., *Guide to Charleston Illustrated: Being a Sketch of the History of Charleston, S.C., with Some Account of Its Present Condition, with Numerous Engravings* (Charleston: Walker, Evans and Cogswell, 1875), 50–51. See also Waring, *Medicine in South Carolina, 1825–1900*, 212–14.

24. Simon Baruch to Yates Snowden, June 9, 1919, Yates Snowden Papers, South Caroliniana Library, University of South Carolina, Columbia; James H. Cassedy, *Medicine and American Growth, 1800–1860* (Madison: University of Wisconsin Press, 1986), 105; Waring, *Medicine in South Carolina, 1825–1900,* 230–32, 280, 282–86, 288–89; Norman H. Franke, *Pharmaceutical Conditions and Drug Supply in the Confederacy* (Madison: American Institute of the History of Pharmacy, 1955), 6–12; Edward Croom, quoted in David J. Hufford, *American Healing Systems: An Introduction and Exploration,* Conference Booklet (Philadelphia: University of Pennsylvania, 1984), 91. Originally published in 1863 in both Richmond and Charleston, Porcher's *Resources of the Southern Fields and Forests* was reprinted by Arno Press in 1970. For Ravenel's role in the controversy over priority in discovering and developing the phosphate deposits near Charleston, see Lester D. Stephens, *Ancient Animals and Other Wondrous Things: The Story of Francis Simmons Holmes, Paleontologist and Curator of the Charleston Museum* (Charleston: Charleston Museum, 1988), 44–48.
25. Medical College of South Carolina, 1859–60 circular, 17. Also Gert H. Brieger, "Surgery," in Numbers, ed., *Education of American Physicians,* 175–204.
26. *DAMB,* 439–40, 586; Newman, *Evolution of Medical Education,* 226. See also David L. Cowen, "Materia Medica and Pharmacology," in Numbers, ed., *Education of American Physicians,* 95–121. On Frost see Waring, *Medicine in South Carolina, 1825–1900,* 230–32.
27. *DAMB,* 1102; Medical College of South Carolina, 1859–60 circular; Manigault autobiography, 76. On Shepard, see Waring, *Medicine in South Carolina, 1825–1900,* 291–92. See also James Whorton, "Chemistry," and Lawrence D. Longo, "Obstetrics and Gynecology," in Numbers, ed., *Education of American Physicians,* 72–94 and 205–25 respectively.
28. *DAMB,* 458–59; this sketch of Geddings, written by a South Carolinian, notes that he rejected many offers of "foreign service," including the chairs of practice of medicine at Jefferson College, of anatomy at New York University and at Daniel Drake's newly organized Cincinnati College, and the choice of any chair he wanted at the University of Louisville. See also Waring, *Medicine in South Carolina, 1825–1900,* 235–38; the frontispiece of this book is a portrait of Geddings.
29. Eli Geddings, "Report of the Committee on Medical Education," *Trans. AMA* 22 (1871): 113–51.
30. J. M. Toner, "Obituary of Eli Geddings," *Trans. AMA* 30 (1879): 819–23; Simon Baruch, "Tribute to the Memory of Dr. Eli Geddings," *Trans. SCMA* (April 1879): xxv–xxvii.
31. A summary of the work that effected this transition appears in Fielding H. Garrison, *An Introduction to the History of Medicine,* 1st ed. (Philadelphia: W. B. Saunders, 1913), 338–50.
32. Many medical historians have noted regular medicine's indebtedness to the homeopaths, among them Newman, *Evolution of Medical Education,* 54–55; Shryock, *Development of Modern Medicine,* 164–270; William G. Rothstein, *American Physicians in the 19th Century: From Sects to Science* (Baltimore: Johns Hopkins University Press, 1972), 160–62, 235–36; and Martin Kaufman, *Homeopathy in America: The Rise and Fall of a Medical Heresy* (Baltimore: Johns Hopkins University Press, 1971). The Lincoln quote appears in Benjamin P. Thomas, *Abraham Lincoln* (New York: Knopf, 1952), 173.

33. Quoted in Cunningham, *Doctors in Gray,* 16. See also Alex Berman, "The Heroic Approach in 19th Century Therapeutics," in Judith Walzer Leavitt and Ronald L. Numbers, eds., *Sickness and Health in America: Readings in the History of Medicine and Public Health* (Madison: University of Wisconsin Press, 1978), 77–86.

34. Baruch's book of lecture notes, 153, Woodruff Library, Emory University, hereafter cited as "notebook." See also John Harley Warner, *The Therapeutic Perspective: Medical Practice, Knowledge, and Identity in America, 1820–1885* (Cambridge, Mass.: Harvard University Press, 1986), 171–72.

35. Notebook, 3, 44–45, 117, 145; Clarke et al., *Century of American Medicine,* 33. According to George Worthington Adams, "Confederate Medicine," *JSH* 6 (May 1940): 156, most Confederate surgeons also used direct auscultation; in *Doctors in Blue: The Medical History of the Union Army in the Civil War* (New York: Schuman, 1952), 49, Adams gives the dates mentioned in connection with the Harvard Medical School. See also Edward C. Atwater, "Internal Medicine," in Numbers, ed., *Education of American Physicians,* 143–74.

36. Martin and Avary, eds., *Diary from Dixie,* 3; notebook, 48.

37. *Camden Chronicle,* December 5, 1913; Richard Barksdale Harwell, ed., *The Confederate Reader* (New York: Longmans, 1957), 3–4; Arney Robinson Childs, ed., *The Private Journal of Henry William Ravenel, 1859–1887* (Columbia: University of South Carolina Press, 1947), 43–44.

38. Notebook, 7, 119, and passim; according to Major Greenwood, "Miasma and Contagion," in E. Ashworth Underwood, ed., *Science Medicine and History: Essays on the Evolution of Scientific Thought and Medical Practice,* 2 vols. (London: Oxford University Press, 1953), 2:501–8, both explanations of disease had numerous adherents up to the mid-1880s. See also Phyllis Allen Richmond, "American Attitudes toward the Germ Theory of Disease (1860–1880)," in Gert H. Brieger, ed., *Theory and Practice in American Medicine: Historical Studies from the Journal of the History of Medicine and Allied Sciences* (New York: Science History Publications, 1976), 58–84.

39. Notebook, 48–50. On prevailing concepts of the nature of yellow fever at this period, see John Duffy, *Sword of Pestilence: The New Orleans Yellow Fever Epidemic of 1853* (Baton Rouge: Louisiana State University Press, 1966).

40. Both concepts, though as old as the Hippocratic Corpus, had just begun to come back into favor. The idea that disease is largely self-limited was stated anew for the nineteenth century by Jacob Bigelow in 1835; it gave impetus to the trend away from heroic medicine by showing that certain diseases, once set in, would run their accustomed course regardless of the physician's efforts. See John Harley Warner, " 'The Nature-Trusting Heresy': American Physicians and the Concept of Healing Power of Nature in the 1850s and 1860s," *Perspectives in American History* 11 (1978): 291–324.

41. In his later zeal to reform medical practice Baruch often gave the impression that, as a student, he had heard not a word about the healing power of nature or about the self-limitation of disease; this may have been an effective exaggeration for his purposes, or he may actually have remembered it that way, but the notebook does not bear it out.

42. Page 60 of the notebook describes methods then used to prevent the terrible pitting that resulted when pocks became irritated or infected: one was to cauterize each pock with silver nitrate; another, used in the confluent form (where contiguous pocks cover large areas), was to mask the skin with mer-

cury ointment or collodion or a solution of gutta-percha (a latex resembling rubber).

43. Notebook, 156, 159. Dr. Geddings approved the use of hydrotherapy together with massage and "local electrization" to restore the function of paralyzed muscles. Electrotherapy was then practiced by applying one pole over the origin of the affected muscle, the other over its insertion, thus isolating the effect ("a gentle current only") to a single muscle (notebook, 81, 84).

44. Notebook, 95, 108, 121. The neglect of tracheotomy is suggested by the fact that in New York City in 1881, according to Franklin H. Top, ed., *The History of American Epidemiology* (St. Louis: Mosby, 1952), 86, more than 1 percent of children under age ten died of diphtheria.

45. Baruch left no record of his daily life as a student, nor do his papers contain any letters from that period. The material in the two paragraphs above is drawn from the diary (pp. 146, 155) and the autobiography (pp. 122–25) of Charles A. Hentz. The letter is from William Horn Battle, a medical student in Charleston, to his father in North Carolina, January 4, 1858, Battle Family Papers, Southern Historical Collection, University of North Carolina Library.

46. Hentz diary, 134, 147, 151, and, concerning social life, passim; William Battle to father, January 4, 1858; Martin and Avary, eds., *Diary from Dixie*, 21; Miers, *Great Rebellion*, 187–88, 211.

47. Harwell, ed., *Confederate Reader*, 60–62; H. H. Cunningham, "Confederate General Hospitals: Establishment and Organization," *JSH* 20 (August 1954): 382; Adams, "Confederate Medicine," 153–54.

48. Wyndham B. Blanton, "The Egyptian Building and Its Place in Medicine," *Bulletin of the Medical College of Virginia* 37 (February 15, 1940): 8–9. For a history of the college, see Thelma Vaine Hoke, comp. and ed., "The First 125 Years, 1838–1963," *Bulletin of the Medical College of Virginia* 61 (Fall 1963): 1–96.

49. Norwood, *Medical Education*, 271; Blanton, *Medicine in Virginia*, 211.

50. Handwritten book of matriculants (1855–71) in Dean's Office of the Medical College of Virginia, Richmond.

51. Bound volume of catalogs, 1854–82, ibid. The catalog for 1861–62 omits the list of requirements; the material in the text is based on those listed in the catalogs for 1858–59 and 1863–64, the nearest years for which they are given. The two are identical and doubtless applied also in 1861–62. The favorable assessment is from Blanton, *Medicine in Virginia*, 55; on p. 57, however, Blanton discusses the need for reform in the college, as does Norwood, *Medical Education*, 275, 427.

52. Hoke, comp. and ed., "First 125 Years," 30–31; Howard A. Kelly and Walter L. Burrage, eds., *American Medical Biographies* (Baltimore: Norman Remington Co., 1920), 1164; Medical College of Virginia, 1858–59 catalog, 10, 11, 12; *DAMB*, 1280, 681, 771; Medical College of Virginia, 1861–62 catalog, back cover.

53. *DAMB*, 464–65. Hoke, comp. and ed., "First 125 Years," 26–32. Patients with smallpox were excluded from the infirmary as "infectious," but those with tuberculosis, typhoid, erysipelas, dysentery, and others were admitted. Douglas Southall Freeman, *Lee's Lieutenants: A Study in Command*, 3 vols. (New York: C. Scribner's Sons, 1942–44), 2:439, calls Gibson one of the most renowned of southern surgeons.

54. The 1863–64 catalog, 12, assured students that "no fears need be entertained of a deficiency of material for dissection." See also Blanton, *Medicine in Virginia,* 69–70; Alan F. Guttmacher, *Bootlegging Bodies: A History of Bodysnatching* (Fort Wayne, Ind.: Public Library of Fort Wayne and Allen County, 1955), 11, 55–57; William T. Sanger, Chancellor Emeritus of the Medical College of Virginia, to author, November 12, 1959.
55. Medical College of Virginia, 1858–59 catalog, 13.
56. Ibid., 9–10; *DAMB,* 458; Blanton, *Medicine in Virginia,* 57. According to Toner, "Obituary of Eli Geddings," Geddings was among the earliest to teach pathology in America. See also handwritten register of graduates in the Dean's Office of the Medical College of Virginia; Simon Baruch, "Reminiscences of a Confederate Surgeon," *Long Branch* (N.J.) *Record,* September 24, 1915. Russell C. Maulitz, "Pathology," in Numbers, ed., *Education of American Physicians,* 122–42.
57. The Medical College of Virginia preserved only the winning essays; I found no record even of titles of the others in the handwritten register of graduates, Dean's Office.
58. Martin and Avary, eds., *Diary from Dixie,* 139.
59. Quoted in Coit, *Mr. Baruch,* 5.

3. Confederate Surgeon

1. S. P. Moore to Captain Withers, April 4, 1862, and to General S. Cooper, April 12, 1862, War Department Collection of Confederate Records, National Archives; Simon Baruch to Yates Snowden, June 9, 1919, Yates Snowden Papers, South Caroliniana Library, Columbia; Simon Baruch, "Reminiscences of a Confederate Surgeon," in Simon Baruch papers, reprinted from *Long Branch* (N.J.) *Record,* September 24, 1915; extracts of this text appeared under the title "The Experiences of a Confederate Surgeon," *Civil War Times Illustrated* 4 (October 1965): 41–47 (I am indebted to James M. McPherson for calling this article to my attention); Francis R. Packard, *History of Medicine in the United States,* 2 vols. (New York: Paul B. Hoeber, 1931), 2:1050; Cunningham, *Doctors in Gray,* 32.
2. Cunningham, *Doctors in Gray,* 34; Adams, *Doctors in Blue,* 48–49; Francis Trevelyan Miller, ed., *The Photographic History of the Civil War in Ten Volumes* (New York: Review of Reviews, 1911), 7:352.
3. Special Order 77/4 from Adjutant and Inspector General's Office, April 4, 1862, War Department Collection of Confederate Records, National Archives. Baruch's appointment became official only after it passed through the necessary channels; see letter from Executive Chamber, C.S.A., to Office of Secretary of War, September 30, 1862, ibid., which says the Senate confirmed his appointment on September 26, 1862.
4. Adams, *Doctors in Blue,* 34–35, 53–55; *Richmond and Louisville Medical Journal* 10 (August 1870): 211–12; Shryock, *Development of Modern Medicine,* 264.
5. Quoted in Harwell, ed., *Confederate Reader,* 127.
6. Miller, ed., *Photographic History,* vol. 7, Appendix D, 350–52; Adams, *Doctors in Blue,* 175.
7. Blanton, *Medicine in Virginia,* 273–74, 276–77; Harwell, ed., *Confederate Reader,* 62; Coit, *Mr. Baruch,* 5; Miller, ed., *Photographic History; Atlas to*

Accompany Official Records of the War of the Rebellion (Washington, D.C.: U.S. Government Printing Office, 1881), Plate CLXXII.

8. J. A. James to Dr. Baruch, February 14, 1874, in Simon Baruch's papers. Pictures of Baruch in Confederate uniform appear in Baruch, "Reminiscences of a Confederate Surgeon" and in his "A Surgeon's Story of Battle and Capture," *Confederate Veteran* 22 (December 1914): 545.

9. Miller, ed., *Photographic History*, vol. 7, Appendix D; Cunningham, *Doctors in Gray*, 106; Blanton, *Medicine in Virginia*, 276; Adams, "Confederate Medicine," 154. The only evidence of Baruch's Rikersville assignment is his letter . from there to Mary Snowden, April 20, 1862, in the Mary Amarinthia Snowden Papers, and a much later letter to Yates Snowden (June 9, 1919) in the Yates Snowden Papers, both at the South Caroliniana Library, University of South Carolina, Columbia.

10. Adams, "Confederate Medicine," 159–60.

11. Dr. Baruch to Yates Snowden, June 9, 1919, Yates Snowden Papers; Baruch, "The Management of Pneumonia Patients," *Medical News* (Philadelphia) 70 (January 2, 1897): 2–3; Baruch, "The Management of Pneumonia with Special Reference to Hydrotherapy," *Southern California Practitioner* 19 (March 1904): 79. According to the 1943 edition of the *U.S. Dispensatory*, 1237, "crabs eyes" also refers to the shiny, red, black-eyed seeds of abrus, which were used to cause inflammation and hence increase both circulation and absorption. It seems likely that it was this "counterirritant" that the nurse intended to suggest to Baruch.

12. Baruch, "Management of Pneumonia Patients," 2–3.

13. Cunningham, *Doctors in Gray*, 149, and illustration facing 212; Blanton, *Medicine in Virginia*, 279, n. 46. On the importance of Porcher's *Resources of the Southern Fields and Forests*, see chapter 2 at note 24.

14. The passage from Ecclesiastes is taken from Jacob Rader Marcus, *The Rise and Destiny of the German Jew* (Cincinnati: Jewish Publication Society of America, 1934), 166; Michael O'Donovan (pseud.), *The Stories of Frank O'Connor* (New York: Knopf, 1952), 183.

15. Cunningham, *Doctors in Gray*, 148–49 and passim. Writing in 1940, Adams, "Confederate Medicine," 155, says Confederate doctors felt the war experiment served only to prove the falsity of the herbalists' faith. By 1950 the development of tranquilizers and antihypertensives, growing out of the centuries-old use of rauwolfia by natives of the Himalayas, launched a new worldwide search for healing plants. For a popular contemporary account, see the full-page article "New Miracles in Jungle Medicine" on the front page of the Features Section, *Baltimore Sunday Sun*, October 25, 1959. See also *Remington's Pharmaceutical Sciences*, 15th ed. (Easton, Pa.: Mack, 1975), 439, 837–38.

16. *South Carolina Women in the Confederacy, Records Collected by Mrs. A. T. Smythe, Miss M. B. Poppenheim, and Mrs. Thomas Taylor* (Columbia, S.C.: State Co., 1903), 12, 61, 70–75, 139, 152, 160; Dr. Baruch to Mrs. H. A. Snowden, April 20, 1862, in Mary Amarinthia Snowden Papers. He also advised Mrs. Snowden to collect silkweed root, but I have been unable to learn its medicinal use. Every other herb he listed was still to be found in W. A. Newman Dorland, *The American Illustrated Medical Dictionary*, 22d ed. (Philadelphia: W. B. Saunders, 1951).

17. Baruch to Mrs. Snowden, April 20, 1862.
18. Much of her correspondence was destroyed in the Charleston earthquake of 1886. The remainder is discussed in *South Carolina Women in the Confederacy,* 70–75.
19. Voucher in Simon Baruch dust jacket, April 24, 1862, in War Department Collection of Confederate Records; Baruch, "Reminiscences of a Confederate Surgeon."
20. Adams, "Confederate Medicine," 151.
21. Concerning the neglect of vaccination see Cunningham, *Doctors in Gray,* 17; Adams, *Doctors in Blue,* 51, 195; Austin Flint, ed., *Sanitary Memoirs of the War of the Rebellion Collected and Published by the United States Sanitary Commission: Contributions Relating to the Causation and Prevention of Disease, and to Camp Diseases Together with a Report of the Diseases, etc., among the Prisoners at Andersonville, Georgia* (New York: United States Sanitary Commission, 1867), 142–44.
22. Medical Director Charles Stuart Tripler is quoted in Adams, *Doctors in Blue,* 53; Baruch's estimate of the number in the battalion ("Reminiscences," first page) seems somewhat high; Adams, "Confederate Medicine," 154; Cunningham, *Doctors in Gray,* 187, 207; William Quentin Maxwell, *Lincoln's Fifth Wheel: The Political History of the U.S. Sanitary Commission* (New York: Longmans, Green, 1956), 33–35.
23. Blanton, *Medicine in Virginia,* 278; Miller, ed., *Photographic History,* 7:349.
24. Blanton, *Medicine in Virginia,* 277; James Longstreet, *Manassas to Appomattox* (Philadelphia: J. B. Lippincott, 1896), 164–73; Baruch, "Reminiscences," first page; *New York Times* "interview" of Dr. Baruch (a full page of carefully prepared narrative), December 8, 1912, sec. 10, p. 14. For a list of medications to be carried in the field dispensing kit, see Franke, *Pharmaceutical Conditions,* 10–11.
25. Cunningham, *Doctors in Gray,* 114; Miller, ed., *Photographic History,* 7:350.
26. Baruch, "Reminiscences"; Longstreet, *Manassas to Appomattox,* 174.
27. Dr. Baruch gave the following account of Manassas in his "Reminiscences" and in the *Times* "interview." Basil Gildersleeve recalled the sound of the minié balls in *The Creed of the Old South, 1865–1915* (Baltimore: Johns Hopkins Press, 1915), 58. On the contribution of Charles E. Minié to the transition from smoothbore to rifled arms, and on the way the resulting increase in firing range escalated casualties, see James M. McPherson, *Battle Cry of Freedom: The Civil War Era* (New York: Oxford University Press, 1988), 471–77.
28. Freeman, *Lee's Lieutenants,* 2:340; Maxwell, *Lincoln's Fifth Wheel,* 177; Cunningham, *Doctors in Gray,* 221; Adams, *Doctors in Blue,* 75.
29. Simon Baruch, "Lessons of Half a Century in Medicine," *ODJM&S* 11 (July 1910): 4. On the Confederate preference for chloroform, see Barnes et al., eds., *Medical and Surgical History of the War of the Rebellion,* Part Third, Surgical Volume, 887–88, and Cunningham, *Doctors in Gray,* 225. Performing major surgery at field hospitals was not an ordinary part of the novice assistant surgeon's duty, though it undoubtedly happened with greater frequency as the war progressed.
30. Cunningham, *Doctors in Gray,* 220, 222; Adams, *Doctors in Blue,* 114–15.
31. Longstreet, *Manassas to Appomattox,* 199, 201–2.

32. Gildersleeve, *Creed of the Old South*, 63. In his *Times* "interview," December 8, 1912, Baruch equated this "fear syndrome" with the then-prevalent condition of neurasthenia; he attributed both to emotional disturbance. See also Barbara Sicherman, "The Uses of a Diagnosis: Doctors, Patients, and Neurasthenia," in Leavitt and Numbers, eds., *Sickness and Health in America*, 25–38.

33. Baruch, *Times* "interview."

34. Ibid.; Baruch, "Reminiscences."

35. Baruch, *Times* "interview"; Baruch, "Reminiscences."

36. Baruch, *Times* "interview"; Baruch, "Reminiscences." For other mention of cooperation between Union and Confederate surgeons see Miller, ed., *Photographic History*, 7:13; Thomas Marshall Hunter, "Medical Service for the Yankee Soldier" (Ph.D. dissertation, University of Maryland, 1952), 34, 89; E. E. Hume, *Victories of Army Medicine* (Philadelphia: J. B. Lippincott, 1943), 22.

37. Baruch, *Times* "interview."

38. Cunningham, *Doctors in Gray*, 236, 240–41.

39. Simon Baruch, "The Relation of Rest to Success of Antiseptic Surgery with Remarks on 'Listerism,'" *MR* 29 (January 30, 1886): 124–26, quotation on 125.

40. Flint, ed., *Sanitary Memoirs of the War of the Rebellion*, 61–62.

41. Baruch discusses this episode in the *Times* "interview" and in "Reminiscences."

42. Cunningham, *Doctors in Gray*, 129–31, outlines the series of events in May and June of 1862 which resulted in the mutual recognition of noncombatant status of medical officers.

43. Baruch, *Times* "interview"; Baruch, "Reminiscences." The Bendann Art Gallery, established in 1859, was still located at 105 East Baltimore Street in the 1950s; the pictures of Dr. Baruch and his companions were destroyed in the Baltimore fire of 1904.

44. The route the doctors followed is described in Lawrence Sangston, *The Battles of the North by a Member of the Maryland Legislature* (Baltimore: Ball, Kelly, Hedian and Pier, 1863), 9–10; U. S. Grant, "The Vicksburg Campaign," in Robert Underwood Johnson and Clarence Clough Buel, eds., *Battles and Leaders of the Civil War*, 4 vols. (New York: Century, 1887–88), 3:533, identifies Aiken's Landing.

45. Baruch, "Reminiscences"; Longstreet, *Manassas to Appomattox*, 297; Freeman, *Lee's Lieutenants*, 2:374, 378, 385.

46. Freeman, *Lee's Lieutenants*, 2:430–32; Cunningham, *Doctors in Gray*, 112, 265; Baruch, "Reminiscences."

47. The only evidence of this visit is in Baruch's "Reminiscences," in which he states that nine months after he bade Herman good-bye, he returned to find him in uniform. Baruch used this story to illustrate "the potent influence of woman over man." See also Kirkland and Kennedy, *Historic Camden*, 2:449; Bernard Baruch, *My Own Story*, 4; Coit, *Mr. Baruch*, 3. Belle's portrait of Dr. Baruch was destroyed during the war, but in later life he sat for several portrayals by J. Campbell Phillips (1873–1948).

48. Kirkland and Kennedy, *Historic Camden*, 2:161; *South Carolina Women in the Confederacy*, 151, 36–56.

49. E. Merton Coulter, *The Confederate States of America, 1861–1865* (Baton

Rouge: Louisiana State University Press, 1950), 223–29; Thomas Conn Bryan, *Confederate Georgia* (Athens: University of Georgia Press, 1953), 148; Harwell, ed., *Confederate Reader*, 287–89, 129; Bertram W. Korn, *American Jewry and the Civil War* (Cleveland: World, Meridian Paperback, 1961), chap. 7. According to Coit, *Mr. Baruch*, 23, South Carolinians viewed Simon Baruch as "one of us," not as alien.

50. Muster rolls, January 1 in Fredericksburg, February 28 in Camp Brooks, in Simon Baruch dust jacket, War Department Collection of Confederate Records; Freeman, *Lee's Lieutenants*, 2:519.

51. Freeman, *Lee's Lieutenants*, 2:625–27, 644.

52. Ibid., 2:531; Baruch, *Times* "interview"; Baruch, "Reminiscences"; Guild is quoted in Cunningham, *Doctors in Gray*, 261; Baruch to Secretary of War, December 23, 1864, War Department Collection of Confederate Records.

53. Freeman, *Lee's Lieutenants*, 2:714; Longstreet, *Manassas to Appomattox*, 334–35, 340–41; Clifford Dowdey, *Death of a Nation: The Story of Lee and His Men at Gettysburg* (New York: Knopf, 1958), 7, 344.

54. Baruch, *Times* "interview"; Baruch, "Reminiscences."

55. *Atlas to Accompany Official Records*, Plate XCV. The tavern still stands, now a private residence.

56. Kershaw is quoted in Dowdey, *Death of a Nation*, 222; Simon Baruch, "A Surgeon's Story of Battle and Capture," *Confederate Veteran* 22 (December 1914): 545; Baruch, *Times* "interview"; Baruch, "Reminiscences."

57. Baruch, "A Surgeon's Story of Battle and Capture"; Baruch, *Times* "interview"; Baruch, "Reminiscences"; Adams, *Doctors in Blue*, 91, 118; Cunningham, *Doctors in Gray*, 222; Dowdey, *Death of a Nation*, 78.

58. Quoted in Adams, *Doctors in Blue*, 118.

59. Barnes et al., eds., *Medical and Surgical History of the War of the Rebellion*, Part Third, Surgical Volume, 53. This case is included in a list of 335 similar operations. Baruch's patient was one of the 215 recorded survivors of this procedure.

60. U.S. War Department, *The War of the Rebellion: A Compilation of the Official Records of the Union and Confederate Armies*, 70 vols. in 128 bks. (Washington, D.C.: U.S. Government Printing Office, 1880–1901), ser. I, vol. 27, bk. 2, p. 364, Item 431, Report by Surgeon F. W. Patterson; Baruch, "A Surgeon's Story of Battle and Capture," 545; Baruch, *Times* "interview"; Baruch, "Reminiscences."

61. Baruch, "A Surgeon's Story of Battle and Capture," 545–46; Baruch, *Times* "interview"; Baruch, "Reminiscences."

62. Baruch's several experiences of capture and internment are exceptions to the generally accepted "Winchester Agreement," which held military surgeons of both sides noncombatants, not subject to capture as prisoners of war. According to William D. Sharpe, "Confederate Medical Services during the War between the States," *Academy of Medicine of New Jersey Bulletin* 11 (March 1965): 36, this agreement, worked out between Hunter Holmes McGuire and Federal medical officers in Winchester, Virginia, on May 31, 1862, was ratified by General Lee on June 17, 1862; it was incorporated by General Order 60 of the adjutant general in Washington on June 6, 1862, and by General Order 45 in Richmond on June 26, 1862. See also George H. Weaver, "Surgeons as Prisoners of War: Agreement Providing for Their Uncondi-

tional Release during the American Civil War," *Bulletin of the Society of Medical History of Chicago* 4 (January 1933): 249–55.

4. Gettysburg to Appomattox

1. Baruch recounts the breakfast and shelling incident in "Reminiscences," *Times* "interview," and "A Surgeon's Story of Battle and Capture," 545–46.
2. Quoted in Cunningham, *Doctors in Gray,* 86.
3. Henrietta Stratton Jacquette, ed., *South after Gettysburg: Letters of Cornelia Hancock, 1863–1868* (New York: T. Y. Crowell, 1956), 13; the quote is from a letter dated July 8. Adams, *Doctors in Blue,* 92, says it was six days before army supplies arrived to relieve the diet of beef and hardtack.
4. Baruch, "Reminiscences"; Baruch, *Times* "interview"; Baruch, "A Surgeon's Story of Battle and Capture," 546.
5. Baruch, "Reminiscences"; Baruch, *Times* "interview"; Baruch, "A Surgeon's Story of Battle and Capture"; Charles J. Stillé, *History of the U.S. Sanitary Commission: Being the General Report of Its Work during the War of the Rebellion* (Philadelphia: J. B. Lippincott, 1866), 385–86, describes Dr. Gordon Winslow and his work as well as the scenes in Gettysburg.
6. D. W. Brogan, *The American Character* (New York: Knopf, 1944), 40–41.
7. Baruch, "Reminiscences"; Baruch, *Times* "interview"; Baruch, "A Surgeon's Story of Battle and Capture," 546; Robley Dunglison, *Medical Lexicon: A Dictionary of Medical Science,* rev. ed. (Philadelphia: Blanchard and Lea, 1857), 899; Shafer, *American Medical Profession,* 99.
8. Baruch, "Reminiscences"; Baruch, *Times* "interview"; Baruch, "A Surgeon's Story of Battle and Capture," 546; and Baruch, "Lessons of Half a Century in Medicine," *ODJM&S* 11 (July 1910): 4; Maxwell, *Lincoln's Fifth Wheel,* 235. Jacquette, ed., *South after Gettysburg,* 26, tells of an inspection by Letterman (a "real alive man") in late August; he told hospital workers to feed the wounded, "*feed them,* I say, feed them. Feed them until they can't complain." On Hammond see Bonnie Ellen Blustein, *A New York Medical Man: William Alexander Hammond, M.D. (1828–1900), Neurologist* (Ann Arbor, Mich.: University Microfilms, 1979); and Gert H. Brieger, "Therapeutic Conflicts and the American Medical Profession in the 1860's," *Bulletin of the History of Medicine* 41 (May–June 1967): 215–22.
9. Maxwell, *Lincoln's Fifth Wheel,* 64–65; Jacob Rader Marcus, ed., *Memoirs of American Jews, 1775–1865,* 3 vols. (Philadelphia: Jewish Publication Society of America, 1955–56), 3:270–80, suggests that "Dr. F" was Dr. Aaron Friedenwald. In a letter to the author, July 23, 1958, Marcus said that this was merely "a conjecture," and I have not substantiated it.
10. Baruch, "A Surgeon's Story of Battle and Capture," 546, and Baruch, "Reminiscences." According to Cunningham, *Doctors in Gray,* 138, Confederates began to gain notoriety as instrument thieves as early as the first battle of Bull Run. Notice of George Tiemann's death appeared in the *R&LMJ* 7 (January 1869): 120. In 1989 Norman Publishing of San Francisco reissued the Tiemann instrument catalog that was first published in 1889 and subsequently became a classic; see George Tiemann & Co., *American Armamentarium Chirurgicum.*
11. Adams, *Doctors in Blue,* 69–70, 182–83. Jacquette, ed., *South after Gettysburg,*

11, says in a letter of July 7, "but nothing short of an order from Secy Stanton or General Halleck will let you through the lines."

12. Adams, *Doctors in Blue,* 182–83.

13. Ibid., 183. In his "Reminiscences," Baruch says the nurses were "two noble women of the most renowned Maryland ancestry in charge of an English nurse." In "A Surgeon's Story of Battle and Capture," 546–47, he names them as Howards but does not supply first names.

14. Adams, *Doctors in Blue,* 141–42; Cunningham, *Doctors in Gray,* 237; Baruch, "Reminiscences."

15. Stillé, *History of the U.S. Sanitary Commission,* 386; Baruch, *Times* "interview"; Baruch, "Reminiscences"; Baruch, "A Surgeon's Story of Battle and Capture," 546.

16. The phrase "dirty negro" appears in only one of Baruch's accounts, "A Surgeon's Story of Battle and Capture," 546. Baruch's comment on Americans' penchant for organizing (ibid.) was written in the 1900s. See also his "Reminiscences" and *Times* "interview."

17. Baruch, "Reminiscences"; Baruch, "A Surgeon's Story of Battle and Capture," 547; Baruch, *Times* "interview"; L. H. Hill to Baruch, August 14, 1915, in Baruch papers.

18. Miller, ed., *Photographic History,* 7:56; Hill to Baruch, August 14, 1915.

19. L. H. Hill to Baruch [1915?].

20. Baruch, "A Surgeon's Story of Battle and Capture," 547. While in Fort McHenry, Baruch was also permitted to correspond with relatives in Europe. These letters were confiscated when his descendants fled Germany for London in 1933.

21. Quotations in this paragraph and the next are from Baruch, "A Surgeon's Story of Battle and Capture," 548.

22. In his "Reminiscences" Baruch erroneously states that they were exchanged right after Chickamauga; in "A Surgeon's Story of Battle and Capture," 548, he says that it was October when they left. Cunningham, *Doctors in Gray,* 131–32, gives the entire story of the exchange question and says that no exchange took place until November 11. The Confederate archives do not contain any information about the date of Baruch's exchange.

23. Baruch, "Reminiscences"; Baruch, *Times* "interview"; Baruch, "A Surgeon's Story of Battle and Capture," 548.

24. Cunningham, *Doctors in Gray,* 30; Baruch to Yates Snowden, June 9, 1919, in Yates Snowden Papers, South Caroliniana Library, University of South Carolina, Columbia.

25. Blanton, *Medicine in Virginia,* 288; Baruch, "Reminiscences"; Baruch, *Times* "interview"; Baurch, "A Surgeon's Story of Battle and Capture," 548.

26. Bryan, *Confederate Georgia,* 110, says this railroad (the Atlanta and West Point) was a principal line in Georgia; War Department Collection of Confederate Records, National Archives, chap. 6, file no. 664, p. 78.

27. Bryan, *Confederate Georgia,* 196–241; Baruch, "Reminiscences"; Longstreet, *Manassas to Appomattox,* 524.

28. Baruch, "Reminiscences." This duel may be the one described in Bryan, *Confederate Georgia,* 199.

29. Baruch, "Reminiscences"; Bryan, *Confederate Georgia,* chap. 9, esp. 144; Longstreet, *Manassas to Appomattox,* 555.

30. Marcus, ed., *Memoirs of American Jews,* 3:280–81, reproduces this account from *Confederate Veteran* 22 (1914): 170. Baruch wrote it to correct Longstreet's error *(Manassas to Appomattox,* 564) in referring to Marcus Baum as "Bowen."

31. Simon Baruch, "Two Penetrating Bayonet Wounds of the Chest," *Confederate States Medical and Surgical Journal* 1 (September 1864): 133–34. According to Adams, *Doctors in Blue,* 51, only the better-educated doctors in the Civil War used auscultation and percussion.

32. Baruch, "Two Penetrating Bayonet Wounds"; Adams, *Doctors in Blue,* 113–14. David Donald, *Lincoln Reconsidered: Essays on the Civil War Era* (New York: Knopf, 1956), 96, states that bayonets were rarely used.

33. The idea was erroneous. Adams, *Doctors in Blue,* 136, says chest wounds made by cutting weapons were few in number, and only 9 percent were fatal; penetrating gunshot wounds numbered 8,700, and 62 percent of them were fatal.

34. Baruch, "Two Penetrating Bayonet Wounds." According to Franke, *Pharmaceutical Conditions,* 27, only four issues of this eight-page paper appeared before the paper shortage and other internal difficulties caused its demise.

35. Baruch, "Two Penetrating Bayonet Wounds."

36. Ibid.

37. According to the War Department Collection of Confederate Records (1-93-188, Report A.O.), Baruch was appointed surgeon on November 4, 1864, and confirmed December 17, 1864, to take rank retroactively to July 18, 1864. A pay voucher in the Simon Baruch dust jacket says that he was paid on November 18 for the first time since May 30 (at $110 a month up to July 17, $162 from then on). The assignment to Longstreet's corps was special order 189/42, August 11, 1864, from the Adjutant and Inspector General's Office.

38. War Department Collection of Confederate Records, chap. 6, file 178, p. 210, places Baruch in Richmond General Hospital No. 4 from October 6 to 14, 1864.

39. Baruch, "Reminiscences."

40. Baruch to Jas. A. Seddon, November 24, 1864, in War Department Collection of Confederate Records. The surgeon general's approval is noted on the back of the letter. See also Adams, *Doctors in Blue,* 67.

41. Abstract of Morning Report, December 8, 1864, Private Quarters, Richmond; Confederate Archives, chap. 6, file 145, p. 178; Confederate Archives, Morning Report of officers in private quarters, Richmond, December 14; Inspection Report P, no. 42, enclosure 13, all in War Department Collection of Confederate Records; Dunglison, *Medical Lexicon,* 185. For a similar instance of a surgeon whose health declined as the stresses of war extended into 1864, see James O. Breeden, *Joseph Jones, M.D.: Scientist of the Old South* (Lexington: University Press of Kentucky, 1975), 157.

42. Baruch to Secretary of War Seddon, Richmond, December 22, 1864, Secretary's Office, in War Department Collection of Confederate Records; appended to this letter is a recommendation for his leave signed by James Bolton and William S. Scott. See also Adams, *Doctors in Blue,* 156–57.

43. Leave was granted by Special Order 304/17, December 23, 1864, Adjutant and Inspector General's Office, War Department Collection of Confederate Records.

44. Martin and Avary, eds., *Diary from Dixie,* 333, 340; Childs, ed., *Private Journal of Ravenel,* 132.
45. Inspection Report P, no. 51 and no. 57, War Department Collection of Confederate Records, have him absent on January 21 and January 31 ("absent since Jan 17"); there is a record (1-7-183, Report A.O., February 3, 1865) of Baruch's application for transfer, but the application itself no longer exists.
46. H. H. Cunningham, "The Confederate Medical Officer in the Field," *U.S. Armed Forces Medical Journal* 9 (November 1958): 1587; Adams, *Doctors in Blue,* 45–46, 157.
47. Surgeon General S. P. Moore to General S. Cooper, February 27, 1865; and Special Order 48 (37), February 27, 1865, Adjutant and Inspector General's Office, War Department Collection of Confederate Records.
48. Baruch to Surgeon General S. P. Moore, March 25, 1865, in War Department Collection of Confederate Records; Blanton, *Medicine in Virginia,* 274; nurse Fannie Beers is quoted in H. H. Cunningham, "Confederate General Hospitals: Establishment and Organization," *JSH* 20 (August 1954): 393.
49. Baruch receipted the supplies from Thomasville on March 25; H. W. Slocum, "Final Operations of Sherman's Army," in Johnson and Buel, eds., *Battles and Leaders,* 4: editor's note, 754, and map, 694.
50. Cunningham, "Confederate Medical Officer," 1590–92; Baruch, "Reminiscences."
51. Cunningham, "Confederate Medical Officer," 1593–94; Cunningham, "Confederate General Hospitals," 393–94.
52. H. W. Slocum, "Sherman's March from Savannah to Bentonville," in Johnson and Buel, eds., *Battles and Leaders,* 4:691. In his "Reminiscences," written decades after the event, Baruch telescopes the chronology of events between the action at Averasboro on March 16 and his collapse sometime shortly before April 9.
53. In the War Department Collection of Confederate Records, Baruch is listed on a morning report of sick and wounded in Thomasville General Hospital, April 9, 1865 (Remarks: "Sick and unable to attend to duty").
54. Adams, *Doctors in Blue,* 15, 227. See also Breeden, *Joseph Jones,* 133–34, on the incidence and treatment of typhoid fever during the war.

5. The New York Interlude

1. Martin and Avary, eds., *Diary from Dixie,* 384–85.
2. Kirkland and Kennedy, *Historic Camden,* 2:167–68; Baruch, "Reminiscences."
3. Kirkland and Kennedy, *Historic Camden,* 2:197–98; Martin and Avary, eds., *Diary from Dixie,* 400; Childs, ed., *Private Journal of Ravenel,* 244.
4. Childs, ed., *Private Journal of Ravenel,* 112, 135, 160, describes the increased practice of self-medication in South Carolina during the war. See also Guenter B. Risse, Ronald L. Numbers, and Judith Walzer Leavitt, eds., *Medicine without Doctors: Home Health Care in American History* (New York: Science History Publications/USA, 1977); and Todd L. Savitt and James Harvey Young, eds., *Disease and Distinctiveness in the American South* (Knoxville: University of Tennessee Press, 1988).
5. Simon Baruch to Dr. A. S. Salley, December 18, 1866, in Simon Baruch

Collection, South Caroliniana Library, University of South Carolina, Columbia.

6. "Address of the American Freedmen's Aid Commission," in *Freedmen's Record* 1 (December 1865): 191.

7. Baruch to Salley, December 18, 1866; Ball, *The State That Forgot*, 21–22. The tendency of European physician émigrés to look down on the standards of American practitioners is noted in Charles E. Rosenberg, "The Practice of Medicine in New York a Century Ago," in Leavitt and Numbers, eds., *Sickness and Health in America*, 67.

8. *R&LMJ* (July 1866): 79. More than a year after the war's end, according to this editorial, only North Carolina and Georgia of all the southern states had moved to reestablish state medical associations. See also Frank Luther Mott, *A History of American Magazines, 1850–1865* (Cambridge, Mass.: Harvard University Press, 1930), 8, and 84, n. 174; Adams, "Confederate Medicine," 152–53.

9. Martin and Avary, eds., *Diary from Dixie*, 400. The story of Belle's feeling for the Yankee Captain Cantine (a tradition in the Baruch family) is told in Coit, *Mr. Baruch*, 4, and Bernard Baruch, *My Own Story*, 20–21. According to the latter, 21, Dr. Baruch was a guest of Belle's father, Saling Wolfe, before the war and at that time "had become interested" in Belle. If the birth date of March 4, 1850, which Bernard Baruch gives (p. 19) for Belle is correct, it would seem more likely that the romance did not begin until after the war.

10. Baruch to Dr. Salley, January 20, 1867.

11. Bernard Baruch, *My Own Story*, 13–20, describes the genealogy of his mother's people; see also Coit, *Mr. Baruch*, 10, 33–34.

12. Baruch to Dr. Salley, January 20, 1867. Rosenberg, "Practice of Medicine," 67, notes the particular attraction of New York City for transplanted European physicians, who, like Baruch, were often more interested in scholarship and investigation than their American colleagues.

13. Lewis G. Arrowsmith, "The Young Doctor in New York," *American Mercury* 22 (January 1931): 1; Rosenberg, "Practice of Medicine," 56–57.

14. Arrowsmith, "Young Doctor," 3–4; "The Abuses of Medical Charity," *Trans. AMA*, editorial 31 (1880): 987–1000, esp. 988–93; Ralph Chester Williams, *The United States Public Health Service, 1798–1950* (Washington, D.C.: Commissioned Officers Association of the U.S. Public Health Service, 1951), 56–67; Charles E. Rosenberg, "Social Class and Medical Care in 19th-Century America: The Rise and Fall of the Dispensary," in Leavitt and Numbers, eds., *Sickness and Health in America*, 165.

15. Baruch to Salley, January 20, 1867; Robert T. Paine, *Pauperism in Great Cities: Its Four Chief Causes* (N.p.: N.p. [1893?]), 6. See Rosenberg, "Social Class and Medical Care," 160–61, 170, on the desirability of dispensary posts and their monopolization by "a minority of well-connected physicians." Baruch's language skills (German and Yiddish) may have strengthened his application. On the need for translators in dispensaries, see Michael M. Davis, *Immigrant Health and the Community* (New York: Harper & Brothers, 1921), 332–33, 336.

16. Arrowsmith, "Young Doctor," 4.

17. Richard O'Connor, *Hell's Kitchen: The Roaring Days of New York's Wild West Side* (Philadelphia: Lippincott, 1958); in an author's "Note," O'Connor says

the north and south boundaries of this area are disputed, but the outermost limits are Twenty-third to Fifty-ninth streets between Eighth Avenue and the Hudson River. See also Jacob Riis, *The Battle with the Slum* (New York: Macmillan, 1902), 14..

18. O'Connor, *Hell's Kitchen*, 13–14.
19. New York Board of Health report quoted in Riis, *Battle with the Slum*, 14.
20. Benjamin De Casseres, "Ben Butler," *American Mercury* 20 (July 1930): 353–61; manuscript of speech in Baruch's papers, undated but after 1910; Simon Baruch, presidential address, *JAAPH&PB* (1921): 2:19–34. Rosenberg, "Social Class and Medical Care," 159, has noted that dispensary physicians were de facto social workers whose work often made them aware of public health needs unknown to the profession outside of the tenements.
21. Simon Baruch, "The Modern Management of Pneumonia," *ODJM&S* 13 (July 1911): 17. For a discussion of limitations on putting "strict expectancy" into practice, see Charles E. Rosenberg, "The Therapeutic Revolution: Medicine, Meaning, and Social Change in Nineteenth-Century America," in Morris J. Vogel and Charles E. Rosenberg, eds., *The Therapeutic Revolution: Essays in the Social History of American Medicine* (Philadelphia: University of Pennsylvania Press, 1979), 17–21; and Warner, *Therapeutic Perspective*.
22. Baruch, "Modern Management of Pneumonia."
23. Quoted in Newman, *Evolution of Medical Education*, 53, n. 101.
24. Baruch, "Modern Management of Pneumonia." See also Rosenberg, "Therapeutic Revolution," and Warner, *Therapeutic Perspective*, on the role of patients' expectations.
25. H. L. Mencken, *Prejudices: Sixth Series* (New York: Knopf, 1927), 220. Throughout his "Dives into Quackery" (217–39) Mencken showers mock praise on the various "healing sects" for their work in eliminating the unfit; he apparently felt even greater disdain for quackery than for the regular profession.
26. Baruch to Salley, January 20, 1867.

6. "No balm in Gilead"

1. This notice appeared in every issue of the *Camden Weekly Journal* from Friday, April 27, to Friday, July 27, 1866.
2. "Lessons of Half a Century of Medicine," address to Medical College of Virginia graduating class in the spring of 1910, typescript in Baruch papers, pp. 5–6.
3. Baruch to Dr. A. S. Salley, March 5, 1868.
4. Baruch's letter is dated July 25, 1866, Simon Baruch papers, copy in the author's possession.
5. Letter from Justus K. Jillson in report of B. F. Whittemore, Assistant Superintendent of Education of Eastern District of South Carolina, *Freedman's Record* 11 (November 1866): 192.
6. Childs, ed., *Private Journal of Ravenel*, 261, entry for December 29, 1865, tells of Dr. J. E. Matthews of Camden, who wrote Ravenel inquiring about his farm and "about the profits of fruit culture."
7. *RMJ* (November 1866): 449; ibid. (December 1866): editorial, 569–73. The

reference to annual remuneration probably indicates contract practice, which was widespread in the South before the war.

8. Alexander S. Salley, Jr., *The History of Orangeburg County, South Carolina, from Its First Settlement to the Close of the Revolutionary War* (Orangeburg, S.C.: R. L. Berry, Printer, 1898). This volume is dedicated to the author's grandfather, who was Baruch's friend and whose photograph appears facing page 28. Baruch to Salley, December 18, 1866.

9. Savitt, *Medicine and Slavery*, 198–201.

10. Baruch to Salley, December 18, 1866. According to Savitt, *Medicine and Slavery*, 200, n. 31, contract practice survived longer in the Lower South than in Virginia, where the kind of disapproval Baruch apparently felt in 1866 had set in before the war.

11. Childs, ed. *Private Journal of Ravenel*, 222, 247–48. See also Tamara Miner Haygood, *Henry William Ravenel, 1814–1887: South Carolina Scientist in the Civil War Era* (Tuscaloosa: University of Alabama Press, 1987), 113–15. Ravenel agreed to continue providing medical care (as well as housing, food, and clothing) for the freedmen he needed as full-time workers.

12. Martin and Avary, eds., *Diary from Dixie*, 387. Childs, ed., *Private Journal of Ravenel*, 222.

13. This paragraph and the seven following are taken from Baruch to Salley, December 18, 1866.

14. Letter from Ellen Gates, *Freedman's Record* 3 (June 1867): 103; letter from Sarah Babcock, ibid. (January 1867): 9; letter from Justus K. Jillson in Whittemore report, ibid. 2 (November 1866): 192.

15. *RMJ* (July 1866): 43. On the decline in black health during the first decade after the war, see Joel Williamson, *After Slavery: The Negro in South Carolina during Reconstruction, 1861–1877* (Chapel Hill: University of North Carolina Press, 1965), 318–21.

16. The exodus of blacks from the Camden area is discussed in letters from Justus K. Jillson, *Freedman's Record* 3 (March 1867): 39, and Reuben Tomlinson, ibid. (April 1867): 55.

17. For other comments on apparent inertia and distaste for work among South Carolinians see Jacquette, ed., *South after Gettysburg*, 263–64, and Martin and Avary, eds., *Diary from Dixie*, 165. On the role of white self-interest in maintaining the health of blacks, see J. Thomas May, "A 19th-Century Medical Care Program for Blacks: The Case of the Freedmen's Bureau," *Anthropological Quarterly* 46 (July 1973): 166.

18. According to Savitt, *Medicine and Slavery*, 196 and n. 23, recent historians of slavery agree that the average cost of medical care for slaves throughout the South was three or four dollars per year. Williamson, *After Slavery*, 320, describes a medical insurance system adopted by the workers on a plantation in Darlington County, immediately adjoining Kershaw County on the east; apparently there was sharp local divergence in the way medical societies viewed such arrangements.

19. Baruch to Salley, December 18, 1866.

20. Baruch to Salley, January 20, 1867. This letter is also the source for the next paragraph.

21. Baruch to Salley, January 20, June 21, December 18, 1867, March 5, 1868.

22. Baruch to Salley, June 21, 1867.

23. Ibid. On the debate over veratrum viride, see Warner, *Therapeutic Perspective,* 227–31.
24. Fielding H. Garrison, *An Introduction to the History of Medicine,* 2d ed. (Philadelphia: W. B. Saunders, 1917), 691. On American physicians' "ultra conservatism" toward hypodermic medication and their fear that it might lead to abuse of narcotic drugs, see James J. Walsh, *History of Medicine in New York: Three Centuries of Medical Progress,* 5 vols. (New York: National American Society, 1919), 1:260–61. As late as 1878, in the third edition of *A Practical Treatise on Materia Medica and Therapeutics,* 4, 10–11, Roberts Bartholow dwelled on the difficulties of hypodermic injection although apparently favoring it over blistering away the skin to facilitate absorption of local applications.
25. This paragraph and the one that follows are based on Simon Baruch, "Hypodermic Medication," *RMJ* 3 (June 1867): 515–19.
26. Ibid., 83–84. The journal cited in note 25 lists southern journals that had suspended or limited publication, a list reprinted from the *Medical and Surgical Reporter.* Baruch saved a clipping of the review, dated only 1867, in one of his scrapbooks.
27. Letter to author from Anna Young, a longtime Camden resident whose mother was a friend of Simon Baruch's wife, Belle Wolfe Baruch; Baruch to Salley, December 18, 1867.
28. Coit, *Mr. Baruch,* 7–8, 10–11. In *My Own Story,* 23, Bernard Baruch stated that up until the time of Sherman's raid, his mother's family was so well off that Belle had never even dressed herself but that after marriage she gave up most of her accustomed luxuries except for breakfast in bed.
29. Photocopy of marriage license and certificate in the Bureau of Records and Statistics of the Department of Health of the City of New York, Borough of Manhattan. The "S. Wolfe" who witnessed the ceremony may have been either Belle's father (Saling) or mother (Sarah), or a brother. I did not find the customary wedding notice in either Camden or Winnsboro newspapers.
30. Baruch to Salley, December 18, 1867.
31. Ibid.; *Camden Journal; Fairfield Herald* (Winnsboro), December 17, 1867. For brief biographical sketches of Kollock, see Packard, *History of Medicine,* 2:1048; and Waring, *Medicine in South Carolina, 1825–1900,* 254–55. Baruch's charges for treating venereal diseases reflect those specified around 1890 by the Kershaw County Medical Association. See George Rosen, *Fees and Fee Bills: Some Economic Aspects of Medical Practice in Nineteenth Century America,* Supp. 6 to the *Bulletin of the History of Medicine* (Baltimore: Johns Hopkins Press, 1946), 79; Waring, *Medicine in South Carolina, 1825–1900,* 195; and J. J. Taylor, *The Physician as a Business Man; Or, How to Obtain the Best Financial Results in the Practice of Medicine* (Philadelphia: Medical World, 1891), 52–55.
32. Shafer, *American Medical Profession,* 114. See also Owsei Temkin, "On the History of 'Morality of Syphilis,'" in Owsei Temkin, *The Double Face of Janus and Other Essays in the History of Medicine* (Baltimore: Johns Hopkins University Press, 1977), 472–84.
33. John Duffy, "Medical Practice in the Ante Bellum South," *JSH* 25 (February 1959): 53–72, esp. 70–71; and Duffy, "One Hundred Years of the *New Orleans Medical and Surgical Journal,*" *Louisiana Historical Quarterly* 40 (January 1957): 19–20 of reprint.

34. Baruch to Salley, December 18, 1867.
35. *MR* 2 (February 15, 1868): 575; Baruch to Salley, March 5, 1868. In an editorial summarizing medical advances, *RMJ* (December 1866): 570–72 described the new hope which "nebulization of medicated fluids" gave in the treatment of pulmonary disorders.
36. The quotations in this and the following paragraphs are from Baruch to Salley, March 5, 1868.
37. James W. Patton, "Facets of the South," *JSH* 23 (February 1957): 6; Baruch to Salley, March 5, 1868.
38. Baruch to Salley, March 5, 1868.
39. Ibid.
40. Ibid. Children also came to Baruch's clinic when they were able. He charged fifty to seventy-five cents for a prescription, "according to the means of the patients." The Kershaw County Medical Association fee bill specified a charge of one dollar for prescribing at the doctor's office, two dollars for prescribing on a home visit, and two dollars for prescribing from the doctor's home after 10:00 P.M.; see Rosen, *Fees and Fee Bills,* 78.
41. Baruch to Salley, March 5, 1868. Baruch's disavowal of surgery notwithstanding, Hillyer Rudisill, Jr., "Simon Baruch, M.D., July 29, 1840–June 4, 1921," *Library Bulletin of the Medical College of the State of South Carolina,* Baruch Number (September 1944): 7, notes that during his South Carolina years Baruch successfully resected elbow and hip joints; excised the upper jaw for cancer; ligated the common carotid; invented a "new" circumcision scissors; "improved the technique of tracheotomy"; and was an early practitioner of Listerian antisepsis.
42. Baruch to Salley, July 5, 1868; Baruch said he derived his impression of New York's changed attitude from remarks of the "Rev. Mr. Dickson." C. Vann Woodward, "The Political Legacy of Reconstruction," in Kenneth M. Stampp and Leon F. Litwack, eds., *Reconstruction: An Anthology of Revisionist Writings* (Baton Rouge: Louisiana State University Press, 1969), 525–26, has noted that none of these predicted consequences followed black enfranchisement, even in South Carolina, where blacks were a majority of the population and held a majority of seats in the lower house of the legislature.
43. Baruch to Salley, July 5, 1868. The only evidence of Dr. Baruch's alleged Klan activities (a matter of pride to his young son Bernard in the 1870s, when the Klan attacked carpetbaggers and scalawags, not blacks, Jews, and Catholics) appears in Coit, *Mr. Baruch,* 13, and Bernard Baruch, *My Own Story,* 32, 35. According to Kirkland and Kennedy, *Historic Camden,* 2:269, the Klan never operated in Kershaw County but was active in Union County, to the west of Kershaw. Francis B. Simkins and Robert H. Woody, *South Carolina during Reconstruction* (Chapel Hill: University of North Carolina Press, 1932), 444–45, describe Klan activities in South Carolina before the 1868 election.
44. Baruch to Salley, December 12, 1868.
45. Ibid.
46. Late in his life, in a speech to the graduating class of nurses at Monmouth Hospital School of Nursing in Long Branch, New Jersey (typescript in Baruch papers, date not given but around 1907), he spoke of the terrible mental and physical strain he had experienced in his early years of practice, when he had to be both nurse and doctor.

47. Baruch to Salley, December 12, 1868. In "The Relation of Peripheral Irritation to Disease; Considered from a Therapeutic Standpoint," *Medical News* (Philadelphia) 57 (July 12, 1890): 35, Baruch described his headaches as "migraine" but attributed them to imperfect vision and astigmatism.
48. *Camden Journal,* May 20, 1869.

7. "Let us be up and doing"

1. Baruch's letter to the Charleston Medical Society is described, together with activities preparatory to the organizational meeting, in South Carolina Medical Association, *A Brief History of the South Carolina Medical Association to which Are Added Short Historical Sketches of Various Medical Institutions and Societies of South Carolina* (Charleston: South Carolina Medical Association, 1948), 47. See also *Trans. SCMA* (1869): 3–4; Simkins and Woody, *South Carolina during Reconstruction,* 312–16, and map of the state's counties in 1867 facing p. 22; several new counties were created in 1868 (p. 101), but the number is not given.
2. *Trans. SCMA* (1869): 6; obituary of Geddings, *Trans. AMA* 30 (1879): 822–23.
3. *Trans. SCMA* (1869): 4, 6, 8.
4. Ibid., 1, 15, 16.
5. Because of its special interest for southern physicians, the *R&LMJ* 8 (1869): 164, published the verbatim addendum to the AMA code.
6. *Trans. SCMA* (1869): 16.
7. Robley Dunglison, *Medical Lexicon* (1857 ed.). See also the several indexed entries for veratrum viride in Warner, *Therapeutic Perspective.*
8. *Trans. SCMA* (1869): 7–8.
9. The *Camden Journal,* September 2, 1869, contains Dr. Workman's bankruptcy declaration; from September to the end of 1869 this paper is filled with bankruptcy notices. Kirkland and Kennedy, *Historic Camden,* 2:445, state that Dr. Workman died in 1869.
10. The *Camden Journal,* November 24, 1870, devotes half a page to the "Report of County Commissioners," mostly a list of names, services rendered, and amounts paid, from November 1, 1869, on. Baruch received payments of $125 on January 15, March 28, and August 15, 1870. Other payments listed for medical services ranged from $5 to $20. Baruch's Physician's Register no. 2, pp. 10 and 26, describes cases he undertook for the county.
11. Simkins and Woody, *South Carolina during Reconstruction,* 144, 448; *Camden Journal,* March 4, 1869; Baruch to Salley, January 25, 1870.
12. *R&LMJ* 9 (February 1870): 250; *Trans. SCMA* (1870): 3–4.
13. Address of Dr. W. D. Buck before the New Hampshire Medical Society, excerpted and reprinted in part in *R&LMJ* (December 1867): 559–60, with the heading, "Present Raid on the Uterus"; Simon Baruch, "An Improved Uterine Sponge-Tent Carrier," *Trans. SCMA* (1870): Paper E, 40–41. On the difficulties and hazards of obstetric methods in that period, see Judith Walzer Leavitt, *Brought to Bed: Child-Bearing in America, 1750–1950* (New York: Oxford University Press, 1986), esp. 142–54.
14. *R&LMJ* 10 (August 1870): 221–23.
15. Elizabeth Baum to author, May 12, 1958; Anna Young to author, June 27, 1958. Camden Court House records describe the lot as no. 726 with 100-foot

frontage on the west side of Broad Street, extending 573 feet back to Camp-bell Street. See also *Camden Journal,* January 19, 1871.

16. Simon Baruch, "Uterine Disease among the Lower Classes," *R&LMJ* (December 1870): 561–70.

17. Ibid.

18. George E. Trescot, "The Study and Value of Therapeutics; a Paper Read before the Medical Association of South Carolina," *Trans. SCMA* (1871): 88–103.

19. Baruch's Physician's Register no. 2, p. 26.

20. Simkins and Woody, *South Carolina during Reconstruction,* 451–52; *Camden Journal,* July 6, 1871.

21. Childs, ed., *Private Journal of Ravenel,* 354. An apologetic announcement of the fee reduction is bound in the back of *Trans. SCMA* (1872).

22. Manning Simons, "Report on the Climatology and Epidemics of South Carolina," *Trans. AMA* 23 (1872): 328–31.

23. *RMJ* 2 (July 1866): 79–84. Editor Gaillard's joy at the decline of bleeding was premature. The November 1869 issue of his journal (8:480–91 and 504–8) carried two articles on bleeding, one for and one against. On southern physicians' belief that blood loss was not well tolerated in southern climes, see John Harley Warner, "The Idea of Southern Medical Distinctiveness: Medical Knowledge and Practice in the Old South," in Ronald L. Numbers and Todd L. Savitt, eds., *Science and Medicine in the Old South* (Baton Rouge: Louisiana State University Press, 1989), 182–83.

24. Baruch's Physician's Register no. 2, p. 20 (entry for October 30, 1871). Pulmonary congestion resulting from cardiac insufficiency is one of the few conditions in which bleeding is still practiced.

25. Ibid., 4, 6, 8, 16. The toxemia of pregnancy is still not fully understood, but it is now usually prevented from progressing to convulsions by controlling salt intake and by antihypertensive drugs. For a woman who has not received prenatal care and in the absence of the drugs now used to treat convulsions, bloodletting remains a rational therapy.

26. Ibid., 10, 12, 14.

27. Ibid., 10, 20.

28. *Camden Journal,* January 11, 1872.

29. *Trans. AMA* 23 (1872): 55 (Item 6 of Report of Committee on Ethics). All this while, Baruch had continued to collect for his services to Kershaw County. According to the *Camden Journal* of December 19, 1872, he was paid $125 in fees on November 24, 1871, and on January 8 and April 10, 1872.

30. *Trans. AMA* 23 (1872): 62.

31. *Trans. SCMA* (1872): 11, 15.

32. *Camden Journal,* September 5, 1872.

33. Childs, ed., *Private Journal of Ravenel,* 92; Brewster, "Planters from the Low-Country and Their Summer Travels," 39; *Camden Journal,* January 2, 1873; James S. Pike, *The Prostrate State: South Carolina under Negro Government* (New York: D. Appleton, 1874), 9.

8. The Therapeutic Optimist

1. *Trans. SCMA* (1873): 11, 18–19. There is no summary of this report in the minutes, and it does not appear with the published papers at the end of the

transactions. On Trescot see Waring, *History of Medicine in South Carolina, 1825–1900*, 311–12.

2. *Trans. SCMA* (1873): 22; *Camden Journal*, April 17, 1873.

3. *Camden Journal*, April 17, 1873; the July 3 *Journal* noted publication of part two of the same article.

4. Simon Baruch, "Subinvolution of the Uterus," *CMJ&R* n.s., 1 (April 1873): 38–44, and (July 1873): 113–19; Robley Dunglison, *Medical Lexicon*, rev. ed. (1874) 467. One of these was *Gossypium arboreum*, the cotton tree, a decoction of whose root was used to promote menstruation and childbirth. Gossypol, derived from cottonseed oil, has become a subject of study in recent decades as a male contraceptive.

5. Baruch, "Subinvolution of the Uterus," 44. Abortion was illegal in New York (which Baruch probably had in mind here), but enforcement was inadequate; see Edward H. Parker, "The Relations of the Medical and Legal Professions to Criminal Abortion," *Trans. AMA* 31 (1880): 465–71. For the background of Baruch's remarks, see James C. Mohr, *Abortion in America: The Origins and Evolution of National Policy* (New York: Oxford University Press, 1978), esp. 159.

6. I was not able to locate this entry in his casebooks; the quotation, with the date he gave it, comes from the typescript of "Lessons of Half a Century in Medicine," 17, in his papers.

7. Rowland T. Berthoff, "Southern Attitudes toward Immigration, 1865–1914," *JSH* 17 (August 1951): 336–37; *Camden Journal*, January 8, 1874.

8. Pike, *Prostrate State*, chap. 24; Robert Franklin Durden, *James Shepherd Pike: Republicanism and the American Negro, 1850–1882* (Durham: Duke University Press, 1957), chap. 8, esp. 203–5.

9. Pike, *Prostrate State*, 55, 95–97; Durden, *James Shepherd Pike*, 211–12.

10. Berthoff, "Southern Attitudes toward Immigration," quote from 331.

11. J. A. James to Simon Baruch, February 14, 1874, in Baruch Papers.

12. *Trans. SCMA* (1874): 13–14. On physician poverty and low association membership, see South Carolina Medical Association, *Brief History*, 48–50; and Waring, *History of Medicine in South Carolina, 1825–1900*, 153–58.

13. *Trans. SCMA* (1873): 13–14.

14. Ibid. (1874): 15.

15. Ibid., 12–13.

16. Simon Baruch, "Methods of Fostering the Interests of Medical Science and Its Votaries," ibid., 47–48.

17. This paragraph and the following one are drawn from ibid., 35–36.

18. Ibid., 39–40.

19. Ibid., 42–43; Duffy, "Medical Practice in the Ante Bellum South," 67–70.

20. Baruch, "Methods of Fostering the Interests of Medical Science," 42–46.

21. *Trans. SCMA* (1874): 10–11.

22. This paragraph and the two that follow are taken from ibid., 20–22.

23. The discussion was summarized and paraphrased by the secretary in the minutes from which this account is taken. On Jacob Ford Prioleau, see Waring, *History of Medicine in South Carolina, 1825–1900*, 286–87. In the mid-twentieth century the consensus of obstetricians is that anesthesia is to be avoided as much as possible on the grounds that it may harm the baby. On the history of anesthesia in American obstetric practice, see Leavitt, *Brought to Bed*, 116–41.

24. *Trans. SCMA* (1874): 31, 33. Since the South Carolina Medical Association did not customarily send a delegate to the New York Medical Society, Baruch's election suggests that he was planning a trip to New York.
25. Ibid., 31.
26. M. Reynolds, "The Progress of Medical Science," *CMJ&R* n.s., 2 (October 1874): 199–212.
27. Reynolds's words are quoted from p. 317 of Dr. Baruch's article, "'The Progress of Medicine.' A Reply to Dr. M. Reynolds's Address," *CMJ&R* n.s., 2 (January 1875): 300–318.
28. Reynolds, "Progress of Medical Science," 202–3, 205.
29. Ibid., 206–7; Baruch, "'The Progress of Medicine,'" 316–17.
30. Reynolds, "Progress of Medical Science," 206, 208 (editor's note); Baruch, "'The Progress of Medicine,'" 315.
31. Reynolds, "Progress of Medical Science," 211–12.
32. This paragraph and the one following are based on Baruch, "'The Progress of Medicine,'" 303–6, 318.
33. Simon Baruch, "Acute Articular Rheumatism—with Cardiac Complication and Hyperpyrexia. Treatment by Cold Bath, Ice-Bags and Iod. Potassium in Large Doses," *Trans. SCMA* (1875): 241–46, quote on 244.
34. Simon Baruch, "Fibroma of the Left Upper Maxilla," *Trans. SCMA* (1875): 235–40; Baruch's Physician's Register no. 2, pp. 24, 27, 29, 31, 32.
35. *Trans. SCMA* (1876): 1. The questionnaire is on 29; page 33 of the president's address is devoted to hygiene and public health.
36. Walter Lynwood Fleming, *The Sequel of Appomattox: A Chronicle of the Reunion of the States* (New Haven: Yale University Press, 1919), 276. The Radical constitution of 1868 made no specific mention of intermarriage although, according to many authorities, miscegenation was thereby "legalized." Presumably Article I, Section 12, covered the subject adequately; see Francis N. Thorpe, comp. and ed., *The Federal and State Constitutions, Colonial Charters, and Other Organic Laws of the States, Territories, and Colonies Now or Heretofore Forming the United States of America, Compiled and Edited under the Act of Congress of June 30, 1905*, 7 vols. (Washington, D.C.: U.S. Government Printing Office, 1909), 7:3282.
37. Kirkland and Kennedy, *Historic Camden*, 2:217–23; Simkins and Woody, *South Carolina during Reconstruction*, 477–80, 485, and chap. 18, "The Campaign of 1876."
38. Kirkland and Kennedy, *Historic Camden*, 2:223; Simkins and Woody, *South Carolina during Reconstruction*, chap. 19, "The Dual Government." See also C. Vann Woodward, *Reunion and Reaction: The Compromise of 1877 and the End of Reconstruction* (Boston: Little, Brown, 1951). According to Coit, *Mr. Baruch*, 12, Wade Hampton was sometimes a guest in the Baruch home.

9. Reunion and Reform

1. Quoted in South Carolina Medical Association, *Brief History*, 51.
2. Address of the President, *Trans. SCMA* (1877): x–xi, xvii–xviii. For a brief biography of J. F. M. Geddings, see Waring, *Medicine in South Carolina, 1825–1900*, 238.
3. "Report of the Committee on State Medicine and Public Hygiene," *Trans.*

SCMA (1877): 2. For recent scholarship about the state of science in the prewar South, see Numbers and Savitt, eds., *Science and Medicine in the Old South*.

4. According to James H. Cassedy, *American Medicine and Statistical Thinking, 1800–1860* (Cambridge, Mass.: Harvard University Press, 1984), 203–5, South Carolina had a "reasonably well-established" system of vital statistics registration before the Civil War.

5. The material in this and the two succeeding paragraphs is from "Report of the Committee on State Medicine and Public Hygiene," 3–4, 23–25, 36–38, 53–54, 63, 65–66, 73–74.

6. The material in this and the following eight paragraphs is from Simon Baruch, "A Neglected Point in the Medico-Legal Aspect of Strychnine Poisoning, with Details of an Analysis," *Trans. SCMA* (1877): 85–94. The book Baruch was quoting from was Albert Benjamin Prescott, *Chemical Examination of Alcoholic Liquors: A Manual of the Constituents of the Distilled Spirits and Fermented Liquors of Commerce, and Their Qualitative and Quantitative Determination* (New York: D. Van Nostrand, 1875).

7. "Report of the Committee on Tetanus," *Trans. SCMA* (1877): 79–83.

8. *Trans. SCMA* (1877): xxiv–xxv; *Camden Journal and Gazette*, July 12, 1877. According to Atkinson, ed., *Physicians and Surgeons of the United States*, 164, Baruch had been examining physician for the Universal Life Insurance Company of New York since 1875.

9. The "experimental farm" which Dr. Baruch's son Bernard described in *My Own Story*, 1–2, is probably the area Dr. Baruch bought from S. M. Mathis at the corner of Haile and York streets. Gabriel Baum of Camden told the author in March 1958 that Dr. Baruch had also farmed "about six acres" on the southern edge of town. Dr. Baruch's niece Martha Machol to author, May 1958.

10. Bernard Baruch, *My Own Story*, 2; *Camden Journal*, August 12, 1869; *DAB*, 10:142–43; *Encyclopaedia Britannica* (Chicago: Encyclopaedia Britannica, Inc., 1957), 1:367–68, 6:854.

11. Bernard Baruch, *My Own Story*, 1–2; Simon Baruch, "A Clinical Study of the Etiology and Treatment of Summer Diarrhoea of Infants," *Medical News* (Philadelphia) 53 (July 7, 1888): 12; Simon Baruch, "Causes and Prevention of 'Liver Complaint' Among the Rural and Laboring Population of South Carolina," *Report of the State Board of Health of South Carolina* 2 (1880–81): 268–69, 276–77; draft of an agreement between Simon Baruch and Marie L. Barbot, December 1878, Manning Family Papers, South Caroliniana Library, University of South Carolina, Columbia.

12. Records of the Hebrew Benevolent Association, examined in March 1958 when they were in the possession of Trixie Schlosberg of Camden. According to Coit, *Mr. Baruch*, 24, Simon and Belle and the small boys attended the synagogue of Beth Elohim in Charleston before 1871.

13. Manning Simons (chairman), "Report of the Committee on State Medicine and Public Hygiene," *Trans. SCMA* (1878): 81–82.

14. Ibid., 82–84. Dr. Simons credited his knowledge of the Charleston opposition to the *Charleston News and Courier*, February 13, 1878; *Trans. SCMA* (1878): xx.

15. *Trans. SCMA* (1878): xx–xxi.

16. Simon Baruch (chairman), "Report of the Committee on Suggestions Contained in the President's Address of Last Year," *Trans. SCMA* (1878): xxi–xxiii.
17. South Carolina report in "Report on State Medicine and State Medical Societies," *Trans. AMA* 30 (1875): 350–51.
18. Baruch, "Report of the Committee on Suggestions," xxiv–xxv.
19. Ibid., xxv.
20. Williams, *United States Public Health Service,* 114–17. Dr. R. A. Kinloch of the South Carolina Medical Association reported in the *Trans. AMA* 33 (1882): 392 that the act of the General Assembly creating the South Carolina State Board of Health was approved on December 22, 1878. See also Waring, *History of Medicine in South Carolina, 1825–1900,* 174–76. For background on the impact of this epidemic, see John Duffy, "Yellow Fever in the Continental United States during the Nineteenth Century," *Bulletin of the New York Academy of Medicine* 44 (June 1968): 695–96, 700–701; John H. Ellis, "The New Orleans Yellow Fever Epidemic in 1878: A Note on the Affective History of Societies and Communities," *Clio Medica* 12 (June–September 1977): 189–216; and Jo Ann Carrigan, "Yellow Fever: Scourge of the South," in Savitt and Young, eds., *Disease and Distinctiveness in the American South,* 55–78.
21. This paragraph and the next one are based on Williams, *United States Public Health Service,* 74; *Trans. SCMA* (1878): xxi–xxiii; John Shaw Billings, "The National Board of Health and National Quarantine," *Trans. AMA* 31 (1880): 440.
22. Williams, *United States Public Health Service,* 76–77; Billings, "National Board of Health," 443. See also Manfred Waserman, "The Quest for a National Health Board in the Progressive Era," *Bulletin of the History of Medicine* 49 (Fall 1975): 353.
23. Billings, "National Board of Health," 452–55.
24. Simon Baruch, "Tribute to the Memory of Dr. Eli Geddings," *Trans. SCMA* (1879): xxv–xxvii.
25. Simon Baruch, "The Oxytocic Action of Quinia," *Trans. SCMA* (1878): 1–7.
26. Simon Baruch, "The Management of the Third Stage of Labor," *American Journal of Obstetrics* 18 (1885): 365–66.
27. Simon Baruch, "The Management of Retained Secundines in Abortion," *Trans. SCMA* (1879): 7–12. See also Leavitt, *Brought to Bed,* 144–49, on damage sometimes inflicted by improper use of ergot or forceps during delivery.
28. "Minutes of the Proceedings," *Trans. SCMA* (1879): xxiii. According to Bruce Fye, "Active Euthanasia: An Historical Survey of Its Conceptual Origins and Introduction to Medical Thought," *Bulletin of the History of Medicine* 52 (Winter 1978): 500, this was the earliest open discussion of euthanasia by a medical organization in the United States.
29. If Baruch participated in this discussion, his name does not appear in the minutes, xiv, xvi.
30. R. A. Kinloch, "Report on South Carolina Medicine," *Trans. AMA* 33 (1882): 392–93. The other six members were J. F. M. Geddings, R. L. Brodie, and H. D. Fraser, all of Charleston; J. F. Pearce of Marion; P. A. Wilhite of Anderson; and B. W. Taylor of Columbia.

31. Wade H.[?] Manning (private secretary to the governor of South Carolina), to Simon Baruch, May 2, 1879, in Simon Baruch papers.
32. Minutes of the Executive Committee meetings, *Trans. SCMA* (1880): xxxi–xxxiii.
33. Ibid., xxv–xli.
34. B. W. Taylor, "Report of the Committee on the Sanitary Condition of the State Penal and Charitable Institutions," *Trans. SCMA* (1880): Letter E.
35. Minutes of the Executive Committee meetings, *Trans. SCMA* (1880): xli.
36. This paragraph and the following one are based on Simon Baruch (chairman), "Preliminary Report of Committee on Epidemic and Endemic Diseases," *Trans. SCMA* (1880): 59–61.
37. Minutes of the Executive Committee meetings, *Trans. SCMA* (1880): xli.
38. Ibid., xlii.
39. Ibid., xliii. For a full discussion of the context of this debate, see Margaret Warner, "Local Control versus National Interest: The Debate over Southern Public Health, 1878–1884," *JSH* 50 (August 1984): 407–28.
40. Minutes of the Executive Committee meetings, *Trans. SCMA* (1880): xliii. It is possible that Baruch himself wrote this report.
41. This and the following four paragraphs are based on "Report of the Executive Committee of the State Board of Health," *Trans. SCMA* (1880): 31–35. The South Carolina Medical Association had been instrumental in securing vital statistics legislation in the antebellum period; see Waring, *History of Medicine in South Carolina, 1825–1900,* 67. For a recent study of the role yellow fever (the "southern pestilence") played in images of an unhealthy South, see Carrigan, "Yellow Fever."
42. This paragraph and the next are based on Billings, "National Board of Health," 450–51; Baruch, "Report of the Executive Committee," 36; Minutes of the Proceedings, *Trans. SCMA* (1880): xxvi.
43. This paragraph and the following one are based on "Address of President F. M. Robertson," *Trans. SCMA* (1880): 1, 2, 6, 8, 14–15.
44. For a recent analysis of the complex nature of opposition to evolutionary theory based on religious beliefs like Robertson's see James R. Moore, *The Post-Darwinian Controversies: A Study of the Protestant Struggle to Come to Terms with Darwin in Great Britain and America, 1870–1900* (Cambridge: Cambridge University Press, 1979), 193–216. See also Frederick Gregory, "The Impact of Darwinian Evolution on Protestant Theology in the Nineteenth Century," in David C. Lindberg and Ronald L. Numbers, eds., *God and Nature: Historical Essays on the Encounter between Christianity and Science* (Berkeley: University of California Press, 1986), 374–78.

10. Smallpox and the New South

1. This paragraph and the following three are based on Simon Baruch (Chairman), "Report of the Committee on Epidemic and Endemic Diseases," *Trans. SCMA* (1880): 449–56.
2. This paragraph and the following two are based on ibid., 447–49.
3. Duffy, "One Hundred Years of the *New Orleans Medical and Surgical Journal,*" 9, cites the case of "a prominent Louisiana physician" who denounced vac-

cination in 1879, claiming that it had "forfeited its claims to the confidence of every clear-sighted man." For another physician concerned with proper technique, see J. M. Toner, "A Paper on the Propriety and Necessity of Compulsory Vaccination," *Trans. AMA* 16 (1865): 325–30; my thanks to Judith Walzer Leavitt for this citation.

4. Baruch, "Report of the Committee on Epidemic and Endemic Diseases," 452, 454, 462–63.

5. B. J. Stern, *Should We Be Vaccinated?: A Study of the Controversy in Its Historical and Scientific Aspects* (New York: Harper & Brothers, 1927), quotes Wallace on 74; according to Stern, 145, the Anti-vaccination Society of America was founded in 1879.

6. Baruch, "Report of the Committee on Epidemic and Endemic Diseases," 466–69.

7. *DAB*, 8:307–8; Maxwell, *Lincoln's Fifth Wheel*, 333–34.

8. Baruch, "Report of the Committee on Epidemic and Endemic Diseases," 469.

9. This paragraph and the one following are based on ibid., 469–70.

10. Minutes of Executive Committee Meetings of June 10 and November 13, 1879, *Trans. SCMA* (1880): xxv–xxvi.

11. A sketch of Baruch in *The Jewish Encyclopedia* (New York: 1903), 561–62, credits him with causing the "first legislative action." M. Elizabeth Davis, health education consultant to the South Carolina State Board of Health, wrote the author on August 30, 1960, that the state's first smallpox law, approved by the governor on February 22, 1905, is No. 434, *Statutes of South Carolina* 24 (1903–5): 869–71; it provides for the compulsory vaccination which Baruch opposed.

12. Waring, *Medicine in South Carolina, 1825–1900*, 170.

11. "No field for enterprise"

1. One such envelope remained with Baruch's papers in 1956–61.

2. Records in the office of the Clerk of Court, Kershaw County. For a study of physicians' wealth in 1860 (including holdings in land, buildings, durable consumer goods, and intangibles), see E. Brooks Holifield, "The Wealth of Nineteenth-Century American Physicians," *Bulletin of the History of Medicine* 64 (Spring 1990): 79–85. The average wealth of antebellum southern physicians far surpassed that of their northern counterparts. I know of no comparable study for the postwar period.

3. W. J. Cash, *The Mind of the South* (1941; rpt. Garden City, N.Y.: Doubleday Anchor Books, 1954), 118–19.

4. Baruch-Salley correspondence, South Caroliniana Library, University of South Carolina, Columbia. Bernard Baruch, *My Own Story*, 24, 30, recalls that many of his father's black patients paid for their health care by working on the doctor's farms.

5. Hillyer Rudisill, Jr., M.D., "Simon Baruch, M.D.," *Library Bulletin of the Medical College of the State of South Carolina*, Baruch Number, Special Issue (September 1944): 2–8; Coit, *Mr. Baruch*, 30–31.

6. Bernard Baruch to author, 1956; Samuel Lubell, *Revolt of the Moderates* (New York, Harper, 1956), Appendix, 285. According to Marion Heyman, type-

script history of the Hebrew Benevolent Association in the association's minutes, 5, it was Shannon who sold the association the seventy-square-foot lot which Baruch then fenced for use as the Hebrew cemetery. Shannon charged the association only forty dollars.

7. Kirkland and Kennedy, *Historic Camden*, 2:234, 247–48.

8. Bernard Baruch, *My Own Story*, 37–39; minutes of Hebrew Benevolent Association, in possession of the secretary in Camden.

9. Bernard Baruch, *My Own Story*, 1.

10. Ellen Glasgow, *Barren Ground* (New York: Doubleday, Page, 1925), 286. Miers, *Great Rebellion*, 69–71, discusses similar ideas in the writings of Henry Adams and Wilbur Cash. On the role of various factors (slavery, climate, impoverishment) affecting the pursuit of science in the South, see Ronald L. Numbers and Janet S. Numbers, "Science in the Old South: A Reappraisal," *JSH* 48 (May 1982): 163–84. It appears that the absence of cities which troubled Baruch played a major part in discouraging scientific work.

11. William M. Geer, "Francis Lieber at the South Carolina College," *Proceedings of the South Carolina Historical Association* (1943): 11.

12. Baruch to Salley, March 5, December 12, 1868, Simon Baruch Papers, South Caroliniana Library, University of South Carolina, Columbia. According to Dorothy M. Schullian, "Unfolded Out of the Folds," *Bulletin of the Medical Library Association* 40 (April 1952): 138, the books Baruch sacrificed were Thomas Bartholin, *Opuscula nova anatomica de lacteis thoracicis et lymphaticis vasis* (Hafniae, 1670), and Jacob Reinhold Spielmann, *Institutiones materiae medicae . . .* (Argentorati, 1774). On the widely deleterious effect of the absence of libraries, see Numbers and Numbers, "Science in the Old South," 177. For yet another expression of distress at the kind of intellectual isolation Baruch felt, see Lester D. Stephens, *Joseph LeConte: Gentle Prophet of Evolution* (Baton Rouge: Louisiana State University Press, 1982), 101–2; an outstanding scientist, LeConte left the South for California in 1869.

13. "Report on South Carolina Medicine," *Trans. AMA* 33 (1882): 392. According to James O. Breeden, "Disease and Southern Distinctiveness," in Savitt and Young, eds., *Disease and Distinctiveness in the American South*, 11, significant steps to improve regional health conditions came only in the twentieth century and only with outside impetus.

14. Andrew Dickson White to Daniel Coit Gilman, July 24, 1878, in Gilman Manuscripts, Johns Hopkins University, Baltimore; Paul B. Sears, *Charles Darwin: The Naturalist as a Cultural Force* (New York: Scribner, 1950), 97, 100. On McTyeire and the role of White's *Warfare of Science and Theology in Christendom* (1896) in publicizing the Winchell case as a "prime exhibit of the suppression of free inquiry," see Paul K. Conkin, *Gone with the Ivy: A Biography of Vanderbilt University* (Knoxville: University of Tennessee Press, 1985), 60–63.

15. According to David N. Livingstone, *Darwin's Forgotten Defenders: The Encounter between Evangelical Theology and Evolutionary Thought* (Grand Rapids, Mich.: William B. Eerdmans, 1987), 86, a more likely cause of the Vanderbilt upheaval was the publication in 1878 of Winchell's *Adamites and Pre-adamites.* Recent scholarship indicates that a more complex relationship existed between theology and science than was earlier recognized: see Ronald L. Numbers, *Creation by Natural Law: Laplace's Nebular Hypothesis in American*

Thought (Seattle: University of Washington Press, 1977); Moore, *Post-Darwinian Controversies;* E. Brooks Holifield, "Science and Theology in the Old South," in Numbers and Savitt, eds., *Science and Medicine in the Old South,* 127–43; and Stephens, *Joseph LeConte,* 180–82. For a discussion of the Woodrow case and southern opposition to evolution in the context of regional cultural differences, see Livingstone, *Darwin's Forgotten Defenders,* 124. For a detailed account of the Woodrow case, see Jon H. Roberts, *Darwinism and the Divine in America: Protestant Intellectuals and Organic Evolution, 1859–1900* (Madison: University of Wisconsin Press, 1988), 224–29.

16. Simon Baruch, letter of resignation from the Hebrew Benevolent Association, November 20, 1880, in the records of that organization, Camden.

17. *Trans. AMA* 31 (1880): 40 of the minutes and passim; Simon Baruch, "Causes and Prevention of 'Liver Complaint' Among the Rural and Laboring Population of South Carolina," 2:268. Other eminent southern-born physicians who relocated to New York City (many of them at the urging of J. Marion Sims, who had gone north before the war) were Thomas Addis Emmet, Edward L. Keyes, H. Marion Sims, T. Gaillard Thomas, Walker Gill Wylie, John Thomson Darby, and John Allen Wyeth.

18. Baruch to Salley, January 20, 1867, December 12, 1868.

19. Baruch, "Causes and Prevention of 'Liver Complaint,'" 275–81; Gabriel Baum, son of Herman Baum, to author.

20. Records in the office of the Clerk of Court of Kershaw County; Bernard Baruch, *My Own Story,* 39. According to Holifield, "Wealth of Nineteenth-Century Physicians," 83, the average holdings of native-born physicians in four southern cities (including Spartanburg, South Carolina) in 1860 was $11,920; foreign-born physicians in the same cities just before the war averaged only $2,505 in wealth. Extrapolating on the basis of wealth lost in slaveholding and the generally depressed state of the southern economy during Reconstruction, Baruch's wealth of $18,000 in 1880 appears extraordinarily high for a first-generation immigrant.

12. Baruch Makes His Mark

1. Bernard Baruch, *My Own Story,* 42. Biographical sketch of Dr. Baruch in Columbia College of Physicians and Surgeons faculty announcement, no date, in Simon Baruch Papers.

2. Simon Baruch, "The Relation of Peripheral Irritation to Disease; Considered from a Therapeutic Standpoint," *Medical News* 57 (July 1890): 35.

3. Bernard Baruch, *My Own Story,* 42–43.

4. This letter is dated February 9, 1881; copy in Simon Baruch papers. On Willard Parker see Atkinson, ed., *Physicians and Surgeons of the United States,* 482–83. On the role of dispensary posts in physicians' career patterns see Rosenberg, "Social Class and Medical Care," 161.

5. Simon Baruch, "Causes and Prevention of 'Liver Complaint,'" 268–82. The description of the North-Eastern Dispensary appeared in the "Domestic Correspondence" of the *Chicago Medical Journal and Examiner* 45 (November 1882): 522–23. J. H. Gunning headed gynecology; Wooster Beach, skin diseases; Charles L. Dana, nervous diseases; and D. M. Camman, heart and lung diseases. Baruch's ability to speak German and Yiddish may have been a

special asset in his quest of a dispensary appointment: according to Davis, *Immigrant Health and the Community*, 332, 336, 340, Jews used New York's dispensaries more frequently than any other immigrant group; physicians with language skills like Baruch's saved dispensaries the expense of hiring interpreters.

6. *Trans. SCMA* (April 1881): 4. All of these native southerners had moved to New York City except the LeConte brothers, who left South Carolina for California in 1869.

7. Shryock, *Development of Modern Medicine*, 266; Committee on the Abuse of Medical Charity, "The Abuse of Medical Charities," *Trans. AMA* 31 (1880): 987–1000. On the status of the profession, see Rothstein, *American Physicians in the 19th Century*, and Rosenberg, "Practice of Medicine in New York."

8. Simon Baruch, "Malaria as an Etiological Factor in New York City," *Medical Record* 24 (November 10, 1883): 506; Bernard Baruch, *My Own Story*, 45, 47; Baruch's physician's casebook. In "The Differential Diagnosis of Malarial Fevers," *Medical Record* 25 (January 5, 1884): 2–3, Baruch mentions the institutional positions he held in 1881, 1882, and 1883.

9. Simon Baruch, "A Plea for Improved Vaccination," *Medical Record* 31 (January 7, 1882): 1–3. The *Medical Record* endorsed Baruch's views in an editorial, "The Necessities of Revaccination" 21 (January 21, 1882): 70–71. On the method of manufacturing "bovine 'virus' " in the 1880s and on controversies over contaminated vaccine and the 1902 legislation that regulated the production and sales of biologicals, see Jonathan Liebenau, *Medical Science and Medical Industry: The Formation of the American Pharmaceutical Industry* (Baltimore: Johns Hopkins University Press, 1987), 79–90.

10. Simon Baruch, "Practical Hints on the Treatment of Catarrh," *Trans. SCMA* (April 1882): 61–67.

11. On one printed announcement of the formation of the Medical Polyclinic of the North-Eastern Dispensary, Baruch wrote "The First Post Graduate School"; on another, "Dr. Baruch organised the first post-Graduate Medical School. Opened October 27, 1882." *DAMB*, 1340, and Garrison, *Introduction*, 2d ed., 761, credit John A. Wyeth with founding the first postgraduate medical school (the New York Polyclinic), which opened on October 23, 1882. The presence in New York of so many outstanding southern physicians says much about dissatisfaction with the post–Civil War South as an intellectual arena.

12. W. Gill Wylie to Chairman of the Committee on Applications of the DeMilt Dispensary, November 30, 1882, in Simon Baruch papers; *DAMB*, 1340–41.

13. Letters from Thomas, Emmet, and Wylie, dated November 19, 27, 30, in Simon Baruch papers. The evaluation of a DeMilt appointment appears in W. Morgan Hartshorn, comp. and ed., *History of the New York Polyclinic Medical School and Hospital* (New York and Camden, N.J.: Haddon Craftsmen, 1942), 112.

14. *DAMB*, 1108–9; editorial, "The New Volume of the Record," *MR* 23 (January 6, 1883): 12.

15. *MR* 24 (August 18, 1883): 187.

16. This paragraph and the next are from Simon Baruch, "Malaria as an Etiological Factor in New York City," *MR* 24 (November 10, 1883): 505–9.

17. Simon Baruch, "The Differential Diagnosis of Malarial Fevers," *MR* 25

(January 5, 1884): 1–4. On the problem of diagnosis in this period, see John Duffy, "The Impact of Malaria on the South," in Savitt and Young, eds., *Disease and Distinctiveness in the American South,* 33.

18. Simon Baruch, "A Plea against Prophylactic Injections after Normal Labor," *NYMJ* 39 (January 5, 1884): 12–15. For the wider context of the debate over this innovation see Leavitt, *Brought to Bed,* 142–70, esp. 158.

19. Baruch, "Plea against Prophylactic Injections," 13.

20. "The Prevention and Treatment of Puerperal Fever," editorial, *MR* 25 (January 5, 1884): 14–16. Baruch apparently wrote this editorial himself: on January 26, 1884, Fordyce Barker wrote him: "When I read the Editorial in the Record of January 5th I said to myself, 'Who the devil can have written this!' I am sure that I shall always hereafter recognize your mortal type in anything of yours that I read, even if your name does not appear."

21. Barker to Baruch, January 26, 1884, Simon Baruch papers.

22. *DAMB,* 765, 886–87; William B. Atkinson, ed., *A Biographical Dictionary of Contemporary American Physicians and Surgeons,* 2d ed. rev. (Philadelphia: Brinton, 1880), 260. Baruch summarized the controversy in "Some American Contributions to the History of Modern Therapy," *TG* 3d ser., 19 (February 15, 1903): 89–90. On the importance of elite medical societies to the physician's career, see Rothstein, *American Physicians in the 19th Century,* 201–7.

23. Simon Baruch, "Objectionable Features of Certain Methods of Prophylaxis against Puerperal Fever," *MR* 25 (February 16, 1884): 178–81; Barker to Baruch, February 11, 1884, Simon Baruch papers.

24. Simon Baruch, "The Prevention of Puerperal Infection: A Study of Antiseptic Practice in the Maternity Hospitals of Paris, Prague, Berlin, Parma, Glasgow, Copenhagen, and New York," *NYMJ* 39 (March 22, 1884): 322–27.

25. Baruch quotes from the letter in "The Routine Use of the Vaginal Douche after Normal Childbirth," *GMJ* 40 (July 1885): 27–30.

26. Records of Montefiore Hospital (in the director's office in 1958); minutes of the Executive Committee (bound from 1884 to 1898) and of the Board of Directors (1884–89). See also Dorothy Levenson, *Montefiore: The Hospital as Social Instrument, 1884–1984* (New York: Farrar, Straus & Giroux, 1984), 7, 27.

27. Simon Baruch, "Tracheotomy in Croup and Diphtheria," *MR* 26 (November 15, 1884): 534–36.

28. Simon Baruch, "The Management of the Third Stage of Labor," *American Journal of Obstetrics* 18 (April 1885): 359–75 and 18 (May 1885): 502–18; Simon Baruch, "The Therapeutic Significance of the Cervical Follicles," *NYMJ* 41 (June 1885): 715–20 and 42 (July 4, 1885): 11–15.

29. Membership records at the New York Academy of Medicine.

30. Simon Baruch, "The Relation of Rest to the Success of Antiseptic Surgery, with Remarks on 'Listerism,'" *MR* 29 (January 30, 1886): 124–26.

31. Simon Baruch, "Do Antipyretics as at Present Employed Modify the Duration or Mortality of Typhoid Fever?" *MR* 31 (January 8, 1887): 33–35.

32. Simon Baruch and Edward S. Peck, "An Interesting Case of Hysterical Amblyopia in the Male," *MR* 32 (November 19, 1887): 649–51; Atkinson, ed., *Biographical Dictionary of American Physicians and Surgeons,* 14–15 of addi-

tions; Ernest Jones, *The Life and Work of Sigmund Freud*, Vol. 1, *1856–1900: The Formative Years and the Great Discoveries* (New York: Basic Books, 1953), 238. In later life Baruch was sometimes considered an alienist because of his success in treating mental ills by hydrotherapy, a form of treatment already widespread in Europe when Baruch and Peck wrote this article.

33. Baruch and Peck, "Interesting Case of Hysterical Amblyopia." For Baruch's belief that physicians should seek every possible source of physical disturbance leading to nervous conditions *before* attacking the eyes and nose, urethra, "or worst of all, the uterus and ovaries," see Baruch, "Relation of Peripheral Irritation to Disease," 263–75.

34. Simon Baruch, "Therapeutic Memoranda on Diphtheria with Special Reference to the Value of Large Doses of Oil of Turpentine," *MR* 32 (December 24, 1887): 784–90. This article elicited an objection from S. B. H. Nichols, *MR* 33 (February 11, 1888): 169–70. Baruch's reply appeared in *MR* 33 (February 25, 1888): 231.

35. Henry Burton Sands, "An Account of a Case in Which Recovery Took Place after Laparotomy Had Been Performed for Septic Peritonitis Due to a Perforation of the Vermiform Appendix," *NYMJ* 47 (February 25, 1888): 197–205, reproduces notes of the case which Baruch made on the first day. Fitz presented his paper ("Perforating Inflammation of the Vermiform Appendix") at the Association of American Physicians in 1886; it appeared in the first volume of the association's transactions in that year.

36. Baruch gave accounts of the case in "Pathognomonic Signs of Perforating Appendicitis," *MR* 41 (April 30, 1892): 489; and "The General Practitioner in the Development of Appendicitis Management," *MR* 48 (March 30, 1912): 601–4. See also his discussion of John A. Wyeth, "Appendicitis Strictly a Surgical Lesion," *Trans. NYAM* 2d ser., 2 (1895): 254–66.

37. *DAMB*, 1075–76.

38. *DAMB*, 169–70. On the relationship between Sands and Bull and for a comprehensive account of the development of medical thinking about this condition, see Dale C. Smith, "A Historical Overview of the Recognition of Appendicitis," *New York State Journal of Medicine* 86 (1986): 571–83, 639–47.

39. Sands, "Account of a Case," 198, 204; Baruch, "Pathognomonic Signs" and "The General Practitioner." According to Smith, "Historical Overview," 642, this case "provided Sands with the success he had been seeking and, more importantly, with a solid clinical foundation from which to dispute [Reginald Heber] Fitz [who favored medical management and drainage if an abscess formed]."

40. John A. Wyeth, "The Present Status of the Surgery of the Vermiform Appendix," *International Journal of Surgery* (July 1892): 170–71.

41. *New York Sun*, February 22, 1888.

42. Of Josef's American debut at the Metropolitan Opera House on November 29, 1887, the *New York Times* critic, W. J. Henderson, reported: "Men shouted 'Bravo!' and women waved their handkerchiefs. Pianists of repute were moved almost to tears. Some wiped moisture from their eyes. The child had astonished the assembly. He was a marvel." Quoted in the Introduction to Josef Hofmann, *Piano Playing with Piano Questions Answered* (1920; rpt. New York: Dover, 1976), v–vi; *New York World*, February 24, 1888.

43. *DAMB*, 1079–80, 517–19, 649–52; *DAB*, 2:199.

44. *New York Times,* February 3, 1888.
45. Ibid., February 21, 1888.
46. Simon Baruch, letter to *MR* on its two thousandth weekly publication 75 (March 27, 1909): 529.
47. *DAMB,* 418; *DAB,* 3:472–73. According to Richard W. Schwarz, *John Harvey Kellogg, M.D.* (Nashville: Southern Publishing Association, 1970), 31, it was Flint who introduced Kellogg to some of the earlier writings on the medical uses of water.
48. *New York Herald,* February 21, 1888; *New York Times, Sun,* and *Herald,* all of February 22. The *Morning Journal,* February 22, printed the story accurately.
49. *New York Times* and *Herald,* both of February 23, 1888.
50. *New York Star,* February 24, 1888.
51. *New York World,* February 21, 1888. According to Gregor Benko in the Introduction to Hofmann, *Piano Playing,* vi, "Throughout his life, Hofmann denied that the strenuous schedule had fatigued him at all."
52. Undated clipping in Simon Baruch papers.
53. Allan McLane Hamilton, *Recollections of an Alienist: Personal and Professional* (New York: George H. Doran, 1916), 136.
54. Baruch's Physician's casebook, 54–58. Mention of this symptom appeared in the press only once, in the *Herald,* February 21, 1888.
55. "The Overworked Boy Pianist," editorial, *MR* 33 (February 25, 1888): 221.
56. Simon Baruch, letter to *MR* 75 (March 27, 1909): 529.
57. Interview with Dr. Baruch in *New York Sun,* January 21, 1912, including a picture of him with Josef, taken February 26, 1888.

13. The Apostle of Cleanliness

1. Works Progress Administration, Federal Writers' Project, *Entertaining a Nation: The Career of Long Branch* (Long Branch, N.J.: Houghton Mifflin, 1940), 1–4, 45. The Baruchs apparently first summered in Long Branch around 1885; in "A Clinical Study of the Etiology and Treatment of Summer Diarrhoea of Infants," *Medical News* (Philadelphia) 53 (July 1888): 9, Baruch refers to his practice for three summers past at "one of the most popular summer resorts."
2. Works Progress Administration, Federal Writers' Project, *Entertaining a Nation,* 37, 38, 45, 100.
3. Letter from Bernard Baruch to *Asbury Park Sunday Press,* February 9, 1958; Works Progress Administration, Federal Writers' Project, *Entertaining a Nation,* 73, 104.
4. Simon Baruch, "The General Practitioner in the Development of Appendicitis Management," *MR* 81 (March 30, 1912): 602–4; Simon Baruch, "Pathognomonic Signs of Perforating Appendicitis," *MR* 41 (April 30, 1892): 489.
5. Works Progress Administration, Federal Writers' Project, *Entertaining a Nation,* 2, 25, 56–57, 86. Susan E. Cayleff, *Wash and Be Healed: The Water-Cure Movement and Women's Health* (Philadelphia: Temple University Press, 1987), 162–63, attributes the decline of American water-cure establishments partly to the growing popularity of such seaside resorts as Long Branch after the Civil War. For a different explanation, see Harvey Green, *Fit for America:*

Health, Fitness, and Sport in American Society (Baltimore: Johns Hopkins University Press, 1986), 54–67.

6. Simon Baruch, "Conditions Indicating Change of Air and Baths in the Summer Diarrhoea of Children," *Medical News* (Philadelphia) 60 (June 18, 1892): 681–82.

7. Mary E. Herrick, "The Tenement-House: Its Influence upon the Child," *Journal of Social Science* 24 (August 1892): 25–33; Bertha H. Smith, "The Public Baths," *Outlook* 75 (March 4, 1905): 567–77; Lucy Cleveland, "The Public Baths of New York City," *Modern Sanitation* 4 (March 1908): 1–14; David Glassberg, "The Design of Reform: The Public Bath Movement in America," *American Studies* 20 (Fall 1979): 5–21. Marilyn Thornton Williams, *Washing "The Great Unwashed": Public Baths in Urban America, 1840–1920* (Columbus: Ohio State University Press, 1991), 30, has noted that many urban slum dwellers were not in the habit of bathing regularly and that the few tubs that did exist in tenements were likely to be used as storage areas or coal bins. See also Richard L. Bushman and Claudia L. Bushman, "The Early History of Cleanliness in America," *Journal of American History* 74 (March 1988): 1213–38.

8. Riis, *Battle with the Slum*, 281; Riis, *How the Other Half Lives* (New York: C. Scribner's Sons, 1890), Appendix, 299–301, 304; Riis, *The Children of the Poor* (New York: C. Scribner's Sons, 1892), 94 n. Wilson G. Smillie, "The Period of Great Epidemics in the United States, 1800–1875," in Top, ed., *History of American Epidemiology*, 58, 69, 71; Robert H. Bremner, "The Big Flat: History of a New York Tenement House," *American Historical Review* 64 (October 1958): 61; Herrick, "Tenement-House," 29–33. According to Williams, *Washing "The Great Unwashed,"* 66, when owners of low-rent urban housing did finally add bathing facilities after 1900, they did so mainly to compete with new tenements that were built to include baths.

9. Simon Baruch, "A Plea for Public Baths, Together with an Inexpensive Method for Their Hygienic Utilization," *DG* 7 (May 1891): 98; Riis, *Battle with the Slum*, 282; G. W. W. Hanger, "Public Baths in the United States," *Bulletin of the Bureau of Labor* 9 (1904): 1256, 1262, 1328. On the problem of sewage in the waters where New York's floating baths were anchored, see John Duffy, *A History of Public Health in New York City, 1866–1966* (New York: Russell Sage Foundation, 1974), 517–19.

10. This paragraph and the next are based on Simon Baruch, "Public Baths," editorial, *Times and Register* (Philadelphia), (August 24, 1889): 397–98. See also *New York World*, August 30, 1889. Baruch's early courtship of the press was important; according to Williams, *Washing "The Great Unwashed,"* the press actively supported baths in all five of the cities she studied (Boston, Philadelphia, New York, Baltimore, and Chicago).

11. John Brisben Walker to Baruch, June 13, 1890.

12. Simon Baruch, "The Status of Water in Modern Medicine—An Address Delivered Before the Social Science Association at Saratoga Springs, N.Y.," *D&HG* 8 (June 1892): 99–101 and (July 1892): 119–22, quote from 121.

13. Ibid., 121. For the constitution of the Social Science Association, see L. L. Bernard and Jessie Bernard, *Origins of American Sociology: The Social Science Movement in the United States* (New York: Russell & Russell, 1943), 543.

14. Harvey E. Fisk, "The Introduction of Public Rain Baths in America: A

Historical Sketch," *Sanitarian* 36 (June 1896): 481–501, p. 20 of reprint in Baruch's papers.

15. Baruch, "Plea for Public Baths," 94–96; Bernard Baruch, *My Own Story,* 3. That promoters of public baths in Baruch's day insisted not only on separate areas for men and women but on separate entrances may owe something to notorious sexual practices related to mixed bathing in late Roman antiquity and the High Middle Ages, uses reflected in the colloquial persistence of the Italian *bagnio* (bath) for brothel. On the continuing connection between bathing and sexual license in late nineteenth-century Chicago, see Lloyd Wendt and Herman Kogan, *Lords of the Levee: The Story of Bathhouse John and Hinky Dink* (Indianapolis: Bobbs-Merrill, 1943), 15–19. I wish to thank James C. Fisher, Jr., for calling my attention to this work. Contrary to the supposition of Glassberg, "Design of Reform," 12, Bathhouse John Coughlin took his name as a proprietor and promoter of private, not public, baths.

16. There is a copy of the report among Baruch's papers. Williams, *Washing "The Great Unwashed,"* chap. 2 and 131–34, sees as a classic progressive urban reform solution the idea that the city government should take responsibility for the people's health (which marked the movement in all five cities she studied). It also seems highly probable, as she notes, that Baruch, freshly returned from Europe, was influenced by the idea derived from Virchow and then prevailing in Germany that governments are responsible for the health of the people.

17. Baruch's report as chair of the Committee on Hygiene of the Medical Society of New York County.

18. This comment was written in by Baruch as a later footnote to the committee report. Williams, *Washing "The Great Unwashed,"* 53, notes that, whereas the leadership of the bath movement in Boston, Philadelphia, Baltimore, and Chicago was united and cohesive and hence effective, the movement's leaders in New York City "were not unified and never organized as a group." She attributes delays in erecting baths in New York partly to this disorganization.

19. Cyrus Edson to Baruch, October 24, November 15, 1890.

20. Fisk, "Introduction of Public Rain Baths," reprint, 5–6; F. S. Longworth, General Agent of the New York AICP, to Baruch, November 28, 29, 1890; William G. Hamilton, Chairman of the AICP Committee on Baths, to Baruch, December 23, 1890.

21. *New York Sun,* December 3, 1890; *New York World,* December 4, 1890.

22. This paragraph and the next are based on Baruch, "Plea for Public Baths," 92–95. For the generally backward and unpleasant status of the bathroom at that time, see Lawrence Wright, *Clean and Decent: The Fascinating History of the Bathroom and the Water Closet and of Sundry Habits, Fashions and Accessories of the Toilet Principally in Great Britain, France, and America* (London: Routledge & Paul, 1960), 199–216.

23. Wright, *Clean and Decent,* 151.

24. Hanger, "Public Baths," 1363–65.

25. Clipping in Simon Baruch's papers, "Free Public Baths," *MR* (December 6, 1890): n.p.

26. Cyrus Edson to Baruch, November 15, 1890; *New York Sun,* December 3, 1890; William G. Hamilton to Baruch, December 23, 1890, January 5, 1891;

Baruch to E. M. Carpenter, Superintendent of the New York Juvenile Asylum, March 17, 1891; Carpenter to Baruch, March 18, 1891.

27. There is an undated clipping of this article among Dr. Baruch's papers, as well as a letter dated April 13, 1891, from William Paul Gerhard, a civil engineer, referring to "yesterday's Herald." On Gerhard, who specialized in the planning and installation of public bath equipment, see Williams, *Washing "The Great Unwashed,"* 128–29.

28. Frederick Peterson to Baruch, April 17, 1891; Baruch, "Plea for Public Baths," 89; Baruch to Hamilton, April 4, 1891, printed in the AICP booklet among Baruch's papers; Hamilton to Baruch, April 6, 1891. On the AICP's exclusion of Baruch and the general disunity of bath advocates in New York, see Williams, *Washing "The Great Unwashed,"* 53.

29. De F. Folsom to Baruch, March 18, 1891.

30. Hamilton wrote to Baruch on April 15 protesting this "wrong"; Baruch wrote in the margin of the letter, "Personal Interests?"

31. Wm. M. Speer, secretary to Mayor Grant, to Baruch, April 15, 1891; Fisk, "Introduction of Public Rain Baths," 12. See Williams, *Washing "The Great Unwashed,"* 52, on the Grant administration's lack of responsiveness.

32. *New York Evening Post,* April 21, 1891.

33. Flegenheimer to Baruch, May 1, 9, 12, 1891.

34. Flegenheimer to Baruch, May 19, 1891. The "friends of the free bath movement" were probably members of the AICP.

35. Flegenheimer to Baruch, May 20, 1891.

36. Baruch, "Plea for Public Baths," 97–99; *Medical News* (Philadelphia) (June 27, 1891): 723–24, carried favorable comment on this article. Baruch always pressed for inexpensive, modest baths, readily accessible to slum dwellers; ironically, according to Williams, *Washing "The Great Unwashed,"* 59–61, 134, 136, New York, in contrast to Boston, Philadelphia, and Chicago, built large, elaborate baths.

37. Flegenheimer to Baruch, June 5, 1891.

38. Simon Baruch, "A Plea for Baths," *MR* 39 (May 30, 1891): 628; *New York Herald,* June 1, 1891; clipping from *New York Sun,* dated only June 1891. According to Williams, *Washing "The Great Unwashed,"* businessmen were generally well represented among bath advocates in the five cities she studied. On the development of soap manufacture as a response, not a stimulus, to demand, see Bushman and Bushman, "Early History of Cleanliness," 1233–36.

39. "Public Baths," editorial, *GMJ* 52 (June 1891): 603.

40. Day to Baruch, June 17, 1891; Lassar to Baruch, July 4, 1891; Sulzberger to Baruch, August 26, 1891; Douglas to Baruch, September 17, 1891; Fenner to Baruch, September 30, 1891.

41. Baruch kept the invitation in a scrapbook. The *New York Recorder,* August 18, noted his response.

42. "The People's Bath," editorial, *Medical News* (Philadelphia) 59 (September 19, 1891): 334; Gould also praised Baruch in lectures, as he wrote to Baruch, February 14, 1892.

43. Bell to Baruch, September 19 and 30, 1891; Fisk, "Introduction of Public Rain Baths," 11; clipping of letter from Baruch to Bell, editor of the *Sanitarian,* June 1895. Williams, *Washing "The Great Unwashed,"* 44, notes the impor-

tance of Baruch's influence in the AICP's decision to build the People's Baths on the Lower East Side in 1891.

44. Flegenheimer to Baruch, October 20, 22, 1891.
45. Clipping from unnamed New York paper, July 1895; Fisk, "Introduction of Public Rain Baths," reprint, 7. Williams, *Washing "The Great Unwashed,"* 64–66, 94–95, 136–37, emphasizes underusage as one factor in the eventual decline of public baths but notes their educational value. According to Judith Walzer Leavitt, *The Healthiest City: Milwaukee and the Politics of Health Reform* (Princeton: Princeton University Press, 1982), 198, the Abraham Lincoln Settlement bath was "probably the most popular of the efforts to maintain health in the city environment."
46. Fisk, "Introduction of Public Rain Baths," 11; Bell to Baruch, November 16, 1891.
47. Smith, "Public Baths," 571. According to Williams, *Washing "The Great Un-washed,"* 44–45, Tammany forces did not perceive great popular demand for baths.
48. Riis, *Battle with the Slum,* 63.
49. Interview with Brown in the *Albany Evening Journal,* April 27, 1895; Brown to Baruch, July 17, 1895. On Brown, whom Williams considers (together with Baruch) New York's leading bath proponent, see Williams, *Washing "The Great Unwashed,"* 43; see also her Appendix I, 139, for the text of the 1892 bath law.
50. Charles E. Rosenberg, *The Cholera Years: The United States in 1832, 1849 and 1866* (Chicago: University of Chicago Press, 1962); Edmund Charles Wendt, ed., *A Treatise on Asiatic Cholera* (New York: W. Wood, 1885), 147–50, 208–15; Hesketh Pearson, *Oscar Wilde: His Life and Wit* (New York: Harper and Brothers, 1946), 5.
51. Frank Luther Mott, *A History of American Magazines, 1885–1905* (Cambridge, Mass.: Harvard University Press, 1957), 311, discusses signs of cholera panic in the lay press in 1892; "The Approach of Cholera," editorial, *D&HG* 8 (September 1892): 170–71.
52. "Some Points on the Cholera Scare," editorial, *D&HG* 8 (October 1892): 189–90.
53. De F Folsom to Baruch, November 1, 1892; the editorial appeared on October 21. Max Lerner, *America as a Civilization* (New York: Simon & Schuster, 1957), 250, suggests that Americans' preoccupation with bodily cleanliness may represent an effort to shut out the sights and smells of industrialism or to separate themselves from the marks of manual labor.
54. Otto Kempner to Baruch, November 8, 1892.
55. "Success of the People's Bath," editorial, *D&HG* 8 (November 1892): 210–11.
56. David Leventritt to Baruch, November 22, 1892. There is no evidence that Baruch again began trying to form a committee at this time.
57. Kempner to Baruch, December 8, 1892; copy of bill in Baruch's papers.
58. Bryant to Baruch, February 23, 1893; Baruch had asked Bryant's opinion of the bill; Kempner to Baruch, February 27, 1893.
59. In his letter to the editor, *Sanitarian* (June 1895), Baruch said Commissioner Bryant had "aided and encouraged" him and was instrumental in securing the cooperation of the president of the New York Board of Health. Along with Baruch, Bryant was one of those whose endorsements were published

in the AICP bath booklet of spring or summer 1891. Bryant to Baruch, March 7, 1893.

60. "A Bureau of Public Baths," editorial, *MR* 43 (March 11, 1893): 306.
61. This paragraph and the next two are based on Simon Baruch, "The Bureau of Public Baths," letter to the editor, *MR* 43 (March 25, 1893): 381–82.
62. Smith, "Public Baths," 573.
63. Gilroy to Baruch, November 28, 1890; Baruch in *Chicago Record-Herald,* April 22, 1910.
64. "Public Baths in New York City," editorial, *GMJ* 56 (March 1893): 314-16. See Williams, *Washing "The Great Unwashed,"* 66, on the disappointing patronage of New York's baths (7,500,056 in 1920) compared to the actual capacity of over 20 million baths yearly.
65. "Public Baths," editorial, *JB* 7 (March 1893): 77–78.
66. Fisk, "Introduction of Public Rain Baths," 14.

14. "Ikey, Ikey, save the soap"

1. Louis Wagner, President of Board of Directors of City Trusts, Philadelphia, to Baruch, August 18, November 18, 1893; Louis Otto Heiland to Baruch, May 1, 1915. See Williams, *Washing "The Great Unwashed,"* 96–98, on the belated beginning of the movement in Philadelphia.
2. Clippings from the *Daily Inter Ocean,* February 24, 1893, January 14, 1894; *Chicago Sunday Herald,* April 30, 1893; *Chicago Evening Journal,* February 24, 1893. There is a picture of Dr. Wellington among Dr. Baruch's papers. On the baths at Hull-House, located in the basement of the gymnasium and operated as the chief activity of the well-baby clinic under the supervision of Dr. Alice Hamilton, see Barbara Sicherman, *Alice Hamilton: A Life in Letters* (Cambridge, Mass.: Harvard University Press, 1984), 115, 119. Hamilton found that she could "overcome the mothers' resistance to bathing by anointing the babies with olive oil." On the success of Chicago's public bath advocates (uniquely women, both lay and medical) in the face of unreformed city governments, see Williams, *Washing "The Great Unwashed,"* 82–95.
3. Clippings from *New York Sun,* February 3, 1895; *New York World,* August 7, 1894; *Brooklyn Eagle,* January 29, 1895; *American Medico-Surgical Bulletin* (May 15, 1895): 578–80; *GMJ* (May 1895): 415–16; *Mail and Express,* September 14, 1895; *New York Times,* May 7, 1899; undated report of the Riverside Association among Baruch's papers; Fisk, "Introduction of Public Rain Baths," p. 17 of reprint in Baruch's papers.
4. Clippings from *Chicago Inter-Ocean,* January 14, 1894; *Chicago Evening Journal,* January 18, 1894; undated note from H. E. Crampton to Baruch containing figures on baths through July 1894.
5. R. W. Gilder to Baruch, August 30, September 28, 1894; subpoena dated November 19; Cyrus Edson, New York City Commissioner of Health, to Baruch, November 22, 1894.
6. None of this correspondence appears in Baruch's papers, perhaps because he gave it to his son Herman, who used it to write "The History of the Public Rain Bath in America," *Sanitarian* (October 1896): 209–302; the story appears on p. 3 of a reprint of that article in Baruch's papers. On Baruch's failure to join the subcommittee of the Committee of Seventy, see Williams, *Washing*

"*The Great Unwashed,*" 47, 53. Williams suggests that the subcommittee rejected Baruch's membership "probably because of his identification with the regular Democratic party." But, as she herself notes (46), anti-Tammany forces encompassed a wide spectrum of political, civic, and religious affiliations. It seems more likely that it was William Gaston Hamilton, chair of the subcommittee, who vetoed Baruch's membership, recalling their many clashes within the AICP.

7. Arnold W. Brunner to Baruch, January 7, 1895; William Paul Gerhard to Baruch, January 11, 14, 1895; George H. Rohe, Superintendent of Maryland Hospital for the Insane (now Spring Grove), to Baruch, January 12, 1895; Goodwin Brown to Baruch, January 19, 23, 1895. On the invisibility of Baruch's part in securing passage of this, the only mandatory public bath law in the United States, see Williams, *Washing "The Great Unwashed,"* 43, 53; she notes that despite Baruch's work, Brown "later claimed sole credit for its passage."

8. Clippings from the *Sun* and the *Brooklyn Eagle,* dated by Baruch.

9. Brown to Baruch, January 23, February 5, 26, July 17, 1895, March 16, 1896; there are copies of the bill among Baruch's papers, in the *Albany Evening Journal,* April 27, 1895, and in Williams, *Washing "The Great Unwashed,"* Appendix II, 140.

10. Brown to Baruch, March 14, April 19, 1895. In view of this correspondence, it is difficult to understand Brown's later insistence on sole credit for passage of the 1895 law: see Williams, *Washing "The Great Unwashed,"* 43, 53.

11. Clippings dated by Baruch; Francis B. Lee, member of New Jersey Commission on Penal Laws, to Baruch, December 28, 1895. Williams, *Washing "The Great Unwashed,"* 42–43, considers Brown, along with Baruch, one of the founders of the movement for municipal baths.

12. Cyrus Edson to Baruch, April 24, 26, 1895. Baruch was invited to the meeting twice: Edson to Baruch, May 1, 1895, and secretary of the Health Department to Baruch, April 30, 1895.

13. Clippings from unnamed newspapers; *New York Evening Telegram,* May 2, 1895.

14. Arnold W. Brunner to Baruch, May 6, 18, 21, 25, 1895; William G. Hamilton to Baruch, April 6, 1891; William Paul Gerhard to Baruch, April 13, 1891. In a typescript entitled "Faulty Bathing" among Baruch's papers, he says, p. 12, that the AICP installed ring-shaped overhead showers which he considered inferior to the forty-five-degree angle head designed by Oscar Lassar and used in Germany.

15. Brunner to Baruch, May 31, 1895; Charles G. Wilson, President of the New York City Board of Health, to Baruch, June 6, 1895; "A Landmark in Public Hygiene," editorial, *Medical Record* 47 (June 22, 1895): 788–89; Cyrus Edson to Baruch, July 6, 1895; Wilson to Baruch, September 5, 1895; George B. Fowler, Commissioner of Health Department, to Baruch, September 30, 1895.

16. Pamphlet issued by Executive Committee of Fifty, dated October 25, 1895, in Baruch's papers.

17. Ibid.

18. Ibid.; Brunner to Baruch, November 9, 1895.

19. Francis B. Lee to Baruch about baths in Trenton, December 13, 28, 1895; Dr.

Pearce Bailey to Baruch about baths in Boston, December 29, 1895; Theodore Diller to Baruch about baths in Pittsburgh, March 14, 1896; clipping from *Trenton Daily State Gazette,* January 8, 1896. The clipping from the *Citizen,* in Baruch's papers, came with a letter from Sarah Lowrie, secretary of the Public Baths Association of Philadelphia, February 28, 1896.

20. Secretary of New York Health Department to Baruch, April 7, 1896; William G. Hamilton to Baruch, June 12, 1896. The Hull-House baths made it easy for mothers to bathe their children.
21. Francis B. Lee to Baruch, June 17, 1896.
22. The date of this letter is unclear.
23. Fisk, "Introduction of Public Rain Baths," 1–21 in reprint.
24. Moreau Morris, M.D., "More about the Public Rain Bath in America," *Sanitarian* (July 1896), quoted in Herman Baruch, "The History of the Public Rain Bath," 1–4 of reprint. Morris, who had been New York's health commissioner and superintendent of the Health Department in the 1860s and 1870s, had also served on the Tenement House Committee of 1884.
25. Ibid., 2–4.
26. Wellington to Baruch, November 18, 1896.
27. Clippings from *Chicago Tribune,* February 21, 1897.
28. The report does not appear among Baruch's papers; he refers to it in "The Present Status of the Bath Question," editorial, *Medical Record* 51 (May 8, 1897): 659–60. In a note among his papers, scribbled in his own hand on the back of a typewritten extract from the minutes of the New York Academy of Medicine meetings of May 20 and June 3, 1897, he claimed authorship of this editorial. In this same note Baruch absolved Mayor Strong from blame for his bath committee's errors and delays.
29. Baruch, "Present Status of the Bath Question." The following four paragraphs are from this source.
30. Clipping from *New York Herald,* May 10, 1897. Compare Baruch's reaction with Williams, *Washing "The Great Unwashed,"* 50, characterizing the 1897 mayor's committee report as an "important document" and the "first major work on the subject to appear in this country."
31. George B. Fowler to Baruch, May 19, 1897; Baruch's note at the bottom of Fowler's letter is dated May 20, 1897.
32. Typed extract from academy minutes, May 20, June 3, 1897, in Baruch's papers.
33. Baruch's note to himself, see note 28 above. Williams, *Washing "The Great Unwashed,"* 51, recounts the meeting between the academy committee and Mayor Strong but notes that the Rivington site was followed by several located in parks.
34. Clipping from *New York World,* June 4, 1897. Though Baruch absolved Strong, he must have enjoyed the cartoon, for he had many copies made of it. Williams, *Washing "The Great Unwashed,"* 53, says that Strong firmly supported public baths but failed for lack of leadership and political experience and out of confusion caused by the 1896 law and uncertainty over the impending consolidation of Greater New York.
35. Clipping of Baruch's letter to editor of *New York Times,* written June 5, no publication date but presumably published on June 5, along with the *Times* editorial to which Baruch's letter responded.

36. Collis to Baruch, June 6, 1897. It is uncertain whether Baruch and the academy committee were the decisive factors in this dilemma; see Williams, *Washing "The Great Unwashed,"* 51.
37. Strong to Academy Committee, June 17, 1897; clipping from *New York Evening Journal,* June 22, 1897; Deputy Commissioner of Public Works to Baruch, October 15, 1897; Maurice F. Holahan, President of Board of Public Improvements, to Baruch, January 14, 1898; Henry S. Kearney, Commissioner of Public Buildings, Lighting and Supplies, to Baruch, January 17, 24, 1898; Lincoln Steffens, *The Shame of the Cities* (1904; rpt. New York: P. Smith, 1948), 297.
38. Kearney to Baruch, October 18, 1898.
39. Clipping from the *Philadelphia Evening Telegraph,* December 1, 1898.
40. Anne Beadenkopf, "The Baltimore Public Baths and Their Founder, the Rev. Thomas M. Beadenkopf," *Maryland Historical Magazine* 45 (September 1950): 206. The New York expenditure was for the floating baths. Williams, *Washing "The Great Unwashed,"* analyzes the differential rates of the movement's success in the five cities she studied; see chap. 7, esp. 132, for the explanation that, as in Baltimore, reform administrations were not necessarily helpful, whereas in Chicago the exclusively female leadership had great success despite machine administrations.
41. Henry S. Kearney, Commissioner of Public Buildings, Lighting and Supplies, to Baruch, March 10, 1899; Mayor's secretary to Baruch, March 8, 1899. Baruch, letter to the editor written May 10, 1899, in an undated clipping from *New York Tribune.*
42. Baruch, letter to the editor written May 10, 1899.
43. O'Connor, *Hell's Kitchen,* 145.
44. Clippings from the *Buffalo Commercial* and *Buffalo Evening News,* April 19, 1900. See Williams, *Washing "The Great Unwashed,"* 28, on the importance of urban rivalry in the spread of the public bath idea.
45. Wellington to Baruch, May 26, 1900. Williams, *Washing "The Great Unwashed,"* 53, blames disunity among bath proponents as a major factor in the movement's slow progress in New York City.
46. Unpaged clipping. Williams, *Washing "The Great Unwashed,"* 43, credits Brown with introducing showers into state institutions for the insane. She describes him as "a leading force in insuring the passage" of the New York bath legislation of 1892 and 1895.
47. A. N. Bell, "About the Introduction of Public Bath," *Sanitarian* (July 1900), unpaged clipping. Perhaps because she relied on lay rather than medical publications, Williams, *Washing "The Great Unwashed,"* 43, is apparently unaware that Baruch disputed Brown's claim.
48. The award was sent not to Baruch but to "The Administration of the Public Baths of the City of New York" (George Livingston, Commissioner of Public Works, to Baruch, June 12, 1903). Benjamin D. Woodward, executive assistant commissioner general, U.S. Commission to the Paris Exposition of 1900, wrote Baruch that he had traced the award to the Bureau of Public Buildings and Offices, where the staff who received it had spent $3 to frame it; though willing to deliver it to its rightful owner, they would not do so without reimbursement.
49. Undated clippings from unnamed newspaper.
50. Riis, *Battle with the Slum,* 281. According to Williams, *Washing "The Great*

Unwashed," 66–67, New York's public baths were underused, as was true elsewhere also (135). She attributes the eventual decline of baths partly to this fact. For a literary reflection of the relief the baths offered in summer heat, see *Call It Sleep,* Henry Roth's classic novel of Jewish life in New York at the turn of the century (1934; rpt. New York: Avon Books, 1964), 262–63.

51. Riis, *Battle with the Slum,* 283; Smith, "Public Baths," 577; Cleveland, "Public Baths of New York City," 9, 11, 13, 14. According to Duffy, *Public Health in New York City,* 517–19, New York City had twelve municipal bathhouses by 1912, with funds appropriated for a thirteenth; for a table showing their opening year, construction cost, and land cost, see Williams, *Washing "The Great Unwashed,"* 57.

52. Clippings in Baruch papers from *Chicago Record-Herald* and *Chicago Daily Tribune,* April 22, 1910. Across the page on which these clippings are mounted, Baruch wrote "Fulfillment." This building, at 1911 West Twentieth Street (now Cullerton Street), still stands in the Pilsen area of Chicago in the 1990s. The words "Chicago Public Bath" remain visible over the door of the building, which is now used for some other purpose. Chicago's Municipal Order League had recommended naming that city's first municipal bath for Baruch in 1894, but after Mayor Carter Harrison's assassination, the bath was named to honor his memory instead.

53. Baruch quoted in Williams, *Washing "The Great Unwashed,"* 43.

54. In Baltimore in late 1959, four years after bath facilities were required in each dwelling unit, the city ordered the public baths closed (*Baltimore Sun,* October 23, 1959); ironically, in October 1960 the *New York Times* reported that *Tribunu Ludu,* the Communist party organ of Poland, had published and supported an appeal for the construction of public baths throughout Baruch's native land. According to Williams, *Washing "The Great Unwashed,"* 67, most of New York City's baths were renovated by the Works Progress Administration in the 1930s and continued to operate after World War II. Manhattan's last bath was closed in 1971 as an economy measure. In 1959 the city of Chicago turned over fourteen public bath sites to the Chicago Park District; these baths have gradually ceased operation as the surrounding homes have been equipped with plumbing. As late as January 1990, however, the Park District continued to operate showers in Pulaski Park, and the people continued to make use of them (Robert Willoughby of the Chicago Park District Administration to author, January 10, 1990).

15. The Gospel of Hydrotherapy

1. For a full explication of the physician's dilemma in this period, see Warner, *Therapeutic Perspective.*

2. *R&LMJ* (May 1866): 488.

3. Simon Baruch, "The Management of Chronic Diseases," *D&HG* 8 (January 1892): 1–2; Simon Baruch, "The Modern Management of Pneumonia," *ODJM&S* 13 (July–December 1911): 17–18.

4. Baruch, "Modern Management of Pneumonia."

5. Simon Baruch, "Do Antipyretics as at Present Employed Modify the Duration or Mortality of Typhoid Fever?" *MR* 31 (January 8, 1887): 33–35.

6. William H. Welch, "The Cartwright Lectures on the General Pathology of

Fever," *MR* 33 (April 28, 1888): 457–64; Baruch quoted from this paper in "The Treatment of Typhoid Fever," *MR* 35 (February 16, 1889): 175–78.

7. Baruch, "Treatment of Typhoid Fever," 175. On the overreaction to clinical thermometry (and the widespread idea that physicians could treat disease merely by lowering temperature) that followed the publication of Carl Wunderlich's work in 1866, see Walter Sneader, *Drug Discovery: The Evolution of Modern Medicines* (Chichester, England: Wiley, 1985), 81; Sneader notes that "traditional" methods of reducing fever were reintroduced at that time, including cold water and drugs such as quinine. For an exploration of this interval, see Jan R. McTavish, "Antipyretic Treatment and Typhoid Fever: 1860–1900," *Journal of the History of Medicine and Allied Sciences* 42 (October 1987): 486–506. Because McTavish deliberately excludes "various theories of pathology and their relationship to antipyretic practice," he generally disregards the fact that antipyresis alone was not the goal of Brand or of Baruch. Several decades elapsed before researchers amassed data to support Brand's (and Baruch's) empirical observations that cold baths strengthen powers of resistance in typhoid patients (or, as McTavish mentions in note 29, exert tonic effects).

8. Baruch, "Treatment of Typhoid Fever," 177.

9. Simon Baruch, "The Value of Water in Modern Therapeutics; A Clinical Study of Methods of Application in Various Diseases and Their Results," *DG* 4 (April 1889): 37. McTavish, "Antipyretic Treatment," 501, n. 62, cites Horatio C. Wood's 1890 text on therapeutics on the overwhelming statistical evidence that the Brand bath reduced mortality from typhoid. Nonetheless, McTavish, 505, suggests that sanitary reforms and other factors were responsible for lowered typhoid mortality. Brand's data, however, were based on cases treated, not on overall decline in typhoid deaths in the general population.

10. Simon Baruch, "Instruction in Hydrotherapy," *MR* 73 (January 18, 1908): 93.

11. Baruch translated Brand's letter and included it in "The Cold-Water Treatment of Typhoid Fever," *MR* 35 (April 20, 1889): 435.

12. Simon Baruch, "A Plea for the Practical Utilization of Hydrotherapy," *GMJ* 50 (January 1890): 53. For a description of the difficulty of typhoid diagnosis and the Brand method of treatment, see Thomas Mann, *Buddenbrooks* (1901; rpt. New York: Pocket Books, Cardinal Edition, 1957), 638–39.

13. Baruch, "Plea for the Practical Utilization of Hydrotherapy," 29–30.

14. Thomas Carlyle, *The Correspondence of Thomas Carlyle and Ralph Waldo Emerson, 1834–1872* (Boston: Houghton Mifflin, [1884?]), 235–36; Charles Robert Darwin, *Autobiography. With Original Omissions Restored; Edited and with an Appendix and Notes by his Grand-daughter, Nora Barlow* (London: Collins, 1958), 117–22. On the popularity of American hydropathic establishments during the nineteenth century, see Harry B. Weiss and Howard R. Kemble, *The Great American Water-Cure Craze: A History of Hydropathy in the United States* (Trenton, N.J.: Past Times Press, 1967); and Cayleff, *Wash and Be Healed*.

15. Baruch, "Plea for the Practical Utilization of Hydrotherapy," 24.

16. Ibid., 25–26.

17. Ibid., 31–39. Writing in 1941, when the physiological effects of hydrotherapy still lacked full scientific explanation, Henry E. Sigerist, "American Spas in

Historical Perspective," in Felix Marti-Ibañez, ed., *Henry E. Sigerist on the History of Medicine* (New York: MD Publications, 1960), 73, observed that "experience has preceded science in medicine more than once."

18. Baruch, "Plea for the Practical Utilization of Hydrotherapy," 40. On the tendency to equate therapies based on the healing power of nature with endorsement of sectarianism see Warner, *Therapeutic Perspective,* 20–21.

19. Baruch, "Plea for the Practical Utilization of Hydrotherapy," 40.

20. Ibid., 41.

21. William Bierman, *Physical Medicine in General Practice,* 2d ed. (New York: P. B. Hoeber, 1947), 513. Baruch, "Plea for the Practical Utilization of Hydrotherapy," 44–45. For a description of similar work by the dynamic Battle Creek surgeon and nutritionist John Harvey Kellogg, see Schwarz, *John Harvey Kellogg,* 48–51. Baruch read Kellogg's work and referred to it in his own publications.

22. Baruch, "Plea for the Practical Utilization of Hydrotherapy," 42. Marcel Proust, *Jean Santeuil,* trans. Gerard Hopkins (New York: Simon & Schuster, 1956), 25, narrates an example of the "warm water" versus "cold water" debate in which Jean [Proust?] was the "nervous" subject. On the development and role of the designation "neurasthenia," see Sicherman, "Uses of a Diagnosis," 25–38.

23. Baruch, "Plea for the Practical Utilization of Hydrotherapy," 45–52. Baruch, who frequently chided others for failing to give directions as specific in hydrotherapy as in drug therapy, may have been precluded by space limitations from doing so here. As it stands, this article ran a full thirty pages (24–54) in *Gaillard's Medical Journal.*

24. Ibid., 53. Compare McTavish, "Antipyretic Treatment," 505.

25. This case must have occurred during the summer of 1887, after Baruch had begun to use cold baths for typhoid (but not the very cold Brand bath) and before the Welch lecture on fever in the spring of 1888; Baruch's most complete account of this shattering failure appears in "May the Mortality from Typhoid Fever Be Diminished?" *GMJ* 52 (January 1891): 3–4.

26. Garrison, *Introduction,* 1st ed., 242.

27. Discussion following Baruch, "The Treatment of Typhoid Fever: A Review of Recent Discussions," *MR* 37 (March 22, 1890): 335.

28. This paragraph and the next eight are taken from Simon Baruch, "Hydrotherapy in Europe," correspondence, *MR* 38 (October 11, 1890): 422–24.

29. Garrison, *Introduction,* 1st ed., 585.

30. R. Fortescue Fox, *The Principles and Practice of Medical Hydrology Being the Science of Treatment by Water and Baths* (London: University of London Press, 1913), 27. Concerning Winternitz's similar influence on Kellogg, see Schwarz, *John Harvey Kellogg,* 34.

31. Garrison, *Introduction,* 1st ed., 658.

32. Sebastian Kneipp, *The Only Authorized and Complete English Edition: My Water-Cure; Tested for More Than Thirty-Five Years and Published for the Cure of Diseases and the Preservation of Health,* translated from his 36th ed. (Kempten, Bavaria, 1894); this edition ("by Sebastian Kneipp, Secret Chamberlain of the Pope") contains the prefaces and information about previous editions used above, as well as those up to the fiftieth edition of the German version, which also appeared in 1894.

33. Baruch later noted this fact (but not its significance for the patient) in "Kneipp's Water Cure in the Light of Medical History," *NYMJ* 62 (October 26, 1895): 522–25. See also "The Pope Tries Hydrotherapy," editorial, *MR* 45 (April 14, 1894): 467.

34. Rene Dubos and Jean Dubos, *The White Plague: Tuberculosis, Man and Society* (Boston: Little, Brown, 1952), 104–5, 186, 262, n. 1.

35. Baruch, "A Survey of the Koch Experimental Field" and "The War on Tuberculosis," *DG* 7 (January 1891): 1, 12; clippings from *New York Herald*, December 1890.

36. Clippings from the *New York Herald*, December 1890.

37. Simon Baruch, Report as Chairman of the Attending Staff of Montefiore, October 30, 1885; Simon Baruch, "The Cure of Pulmonary Tuberculosis Upon the Principle of Nutrition," *DG* 7 (November 1891): 230–31. On the treatment of tuberculosis at Montefiore, see Levenson, *Montefiore*, 29–31, 51–56.

38. Quoted in Baruch, "Survey of the Koch Experimental Field," 5. John Harvey Kellogg was conducting similar research with hydrotherapy in tuberculosis at Battle Creek, Michigan.

39. "Salutatory," Baruch's first editorial in *DG* 7 (January 1891): 11.

40. This paragraph and the next are taken from Baruch, "Survey of the Koch Experimental Field," 1–5.

41. "The War on Tuberculosis," *DG* 7 (January 1891): 11–12.

42. Simon Baruch, "The 'Lymph,'" *DG* 7 (February 1891): 34.

43. Simon Baruch, "Simplified Therapeusis of Phthisis," *DG* 7 (February 1891): 31–33; Simon Baruch, "Koch's Lymph," *DG* 7 (May 1891): 7.

44. This paragraph and the next are drawn from *New York Herald*, June 16, 1891.

45. Dubos and Dubos, *White Plague*, 105–9.

46. Some of these cases are described in Simon Baruch, "The Successful Treatment of Chronic Diseases: A Plea for Their More Methodical Management," *D&HG* 8 (March 1892): 40–42.

47. Simon Baruch, "The Management of Chronic Diseases," *D&HG* 8 (January 1892): 1–3; this is the first of five sections which constitute this article. The following four sections appeared under the modified title given in note 46.

48. *D&HG* 8 (January 1892): 1–3; (February 1892): 20–23; (March 1892): 39–43; (April 1892): 59–64; (May 1892): 84–86. Much of Baruch's clinical evidence for this paper came from his patients at Montefiore.

49. *D&HG* 8 (May 1892): 84–85.

50. *Trans. AMA* 19 (1868): table, 164.

51. Quoted in *R&LMJ* 8 (August 1869): 153.

52. Jones, *Life and Work of Sigmund Freud*, 235.

53. *New York Tribune*, March 29, 1903.

54. Quoted in Thomas Neville Bonner, *Medicine in Chicago, 1850–1950: A Chapter in the Social and Scientific Development of a City* (Madison: American History Research Center, 1957), 205.

55. He was defended against one such charge in "The People's Baths," editorial, *GMJ* 53 (October 1891): 398–99. Simon Baruch, *The Uses of Water in Modern Medicine*, 2 vols. (Detroit: G. S. Davis, 1892), 1:xi–xiii; published in the Physician's Leisure Library, series 6, this work was translated into German by Dr. Friedrich Grosse and published as *Das Wasser in der Ärztlichen Praxis* (Stuttgart: Christliches Verlagshaus, 1895).

56. Letter to *NYMJ* 56 (December 24, 1892): 719.
57. Simon Baruch, "Practical Data on the Application of Water in Some Intractable Diseases," *JB* 7 (February 1893): 46–49. Baruch edited this journal, the first one he refers to in the quote above, from December 1891 to December 1893. On September 10, 1891, Charles E. de M. Sajous of Philadelphia, editor in chief of the *Annual of the Universal Medical Sciences,* asked Baruch to edit a section on climatology, balneology, and hydrotherapy. It appears that Baruch succeeded in getting a department for hydrotherapy alone (Sajous to Baruch, September 28, 1891, and subsequent correspondence).
58. The paper was published in several journals: Simon Baruch, "Therapeutic Reflections," *MR* 44 (November 4, 1893): 577–81; and "Therapeutic Reflections: A Plea for Physiological Remedies," *JB* 7 (December 1893): 416–26, with the discussion that followed given on 426–29. This paragraph and the next are based on the longer version.
59. In his last book, *An Epitome of Hydrotherapy for Physicians, Architects and Nurses* (Philadelphia: W. B. Saunders, 1920), 172–73, Baruch referred to experiments of his own at Montefiore and at the Riverside Hydriatric Institute after 1895, confirming that cold baths increase the number of circulating leucocytes. He also quoted Chicago pathologist Ludwig Hektoen on the importance of leucocytes in the body's defense against the pneumococcus.
60. Discussion, *JB* 7 (December 1893): 426–29.
61. Gustavus Eliot, "The Treatment of Enteric Fever," *MR* 44 (November 18, 1893): 640–44; Baruch, "Logic vs Sentiment in Therapeutics," correspondence, *MR* 44 (December 23, 1893): 829–31; Adolph Rupp, "Tubbing in Typhoid," correspondence, *MR* 45 (January 6, 1894): 29; Dr. A. B. Ball to Baruch, January 6, 1894.
62. Charles E. Page, "Hygienic versus Drug Therapy for Typhoid Fever," *MR* 45 (April 28, 1894): 518–20; Page to Baruch, May 12, 1894. John Harvey Kellogg of Battle Creek, Michigan, was another respected regular physician who was influenced by European work with scientific hydrotherapy and who tried to secure its acceptance in America; see Schwarz, *John Harvey Kellogg,* 34, 48–49, 90.
63. Simon Baruch, "Kneipp's Water Cure in the Light of Medical History," *NYMJ* 62 (October 26, 1895): 522–25. The information about the Riverside Association clinic is taken from Simon Baruch, "Physiological Basis and Clinical Effects of Hydrotherapy in Chronic Disease," *Maryland Medical Journal* 48 (October 1905): 410.
64. Baruch's publisher in New York was William Wood and Co.; in London, Bailliére, Tindall and Cox. The French edition, translated by G. Collet, was called *Le pratique de l'hydrothérapie* (Paris: J. B. Bailliére et fils, 1910). On this book's priority, see Weiss and Kemble, *Great American Water-Cure Craze,* 65. In 1901 John Harvey Kellogg's *Rational Hydrotherapy* appeared, incorporating twenty-seven years of experimentation with the physiological effects of water. According to Schwarz, *John Harvey Kellogg,* 90, it sold fifteen thousand copies within three years and was long recognized by physicians as "the most important single treatise on hydrotherapy." Kellogg, who admired Baruch, wrote a tribute to him in 1914, under the title "A Remarkably Useful Life"; typescript copy in Baruch's papers.
65. Baruch, "Lessons of Half a Century of Medicine," *ODJM&S* 11 (July 1910):

2; Baruch, "Physiological Basis and Clinical Effects," 410; Baruch, *The Principles and Practice of Hydrotherapy,* 3d ed. (1908), 530–31.

66. Baruch, editorial, "Financial Prospects of the Physician," *D&HG* 8 (January 1892): 12–14. Baruch frequently wrote on this subject.

67. He was editor of the *Dietetic Gazette* (the *Dietetic and Hygienic Gazette* after January 1892) from January 1891 to May 1893; coeditor of *Gaillard's Medical Journal* from January 1891 to February 1899; editor of the *Journal of Balneology* from December 1891 to December 1893; editor of the section on hydrotherapy of the *Annual of the Universal Medical Sciences* for an uncertain time after September 1891; New York editor of the *Medical Times and Register* of Philadelphia in August 1889, for how long I do not know. On October 31, 1891, he wrote to H. A. Hare, editor of the *Therapeutic Gazette,* offering to edit a hydrotherapy department.

68. Lea Bros. and Co., Publishers, to Baruch, December 8, 1891; Baruch to Lea Bros., December 10, 1891; Lea Bros. to Baruch, December 11, 1891.

69. Gabriel Baum, the lawyer, to author; Baum recalled that many of the debtors in this instance were racing touts who traveled with the horses and had no property holdings.

70. Bernard Baruch, *My Own Story,* 177–79; Coit, *Mr. Baruch,* 110–11. Before any other dispensation, Dr. Baruch's will (according to a copy among his papers) provided for the payment of $20,000 to his son Bernard, "in accord with a verbal agreement made many years ago."

71. Simon Baruch, "Observations on German Therapeutics," *MR* 62 (December 20, 1902): 972–75. In "The Claims of Water as a Therapeutic Agent," *MR* 75 (February 27, 1909): 341, Baruch explained that the "water cure system" of the *Naturärzte* had made such inroads on the regulars' practices that they appointed a commission headed by Adolf Kussmaul to investigate the need for revising the medical curriculum. Baruch credited the subsequent inclusion of hydrotherapy to the commission's report, which found "faith in prescriptions" among the educated waning in favor of confidence in diet and water.

72. Among many writings in which Baruch recommended the teaching of hydrotherapy are "The First Hydriatric Clinic," editorial, *JB* 7 (January 1893): 6; "Faulty Hydrotherapy," *JAMA* (May 15, 1897): 938–40; "Hydrotherapy in Chronic Diseases," *NYMJ* 69 (April 1, 1899): 450; and "Observations on German Therapeutics," *MR* 62 (December 20, 1902): 975. Baruch resigned as professor of hydrotherapeutics in the New York Post-Graduate Medical School in the spring of 1906 (George N. Miller, secretary, to Baruch, May 9, 1906). He described his hope for disciples in an address before the Interurban Club, published as "Instruction in Hydrotherapy," *MR* 73 (January 18, 1908): 92–95.

73. Permission to quote correspondence pertaining to Baruch's Columbia appointment was granted by Mr. Herpers, secretary of the university, in 1958. Baruch's salary was decoded at the secretary's office. Baruch, "Instruction in Hydrotherapy," 92–95. For a description of Columbia's medical school during Baruch's tenure, see Walsh, *History of Medicine in New York,* 2:443–49.

74. The lecture was published in *MR* 75 (February 27, 1909): 337–41.

75. The ice baths Baruch condemned later became accepted procedure in heat-stroke, in the belief that temperature must be reduced as rapidly as possible

to prevent brain damage. Baruch's low mortality figure with less dramatic treatment may have been the result of his care in stimulating the peripheral circulation while the patient was in the bath. William Osler, between the sixth edition (1906) and the seventh (1909) of his *Principles and Practice of Medicine,* steeply upgraded his section on hydrotherapy in typhoid fever, noting its beneficial effects on the nervous system, on fever, on the heart rate and blood pressure, on the lungs, on the incidence of bedsores, and on the mortality rate. In the 1908 edition of *Principles and Practice of Hydrotherapy,* 527, Baruch cited Osler's enthusiasm for the Brand bath as early as 1895: "Were the Brand method more heroic still he would use it, because it saves life."

76. Simon Baruch, "The Management of Sunstroke—a Lesson in Hydrotherapy," *International Clinics* 22d ser., 2 (1912): 1–13. The only other published lecture I have located, among the many Baruch gave at Columbia, is "The Treatment of Pulmonary Tuberculosis by Hydrotherapy," *International Clinics* 23d ser., 3 (1913): 116–26.

77. Frances A. Hellebrandt, *Simon Baruch: Introduction to the Man and His Work,* Special Bulletin of the Baruch Center of Physical Medicine and Rehabilitation of the Medical College of Virginia, Richmond (July 29, 1950), 5.

78. Letters from members of the class of 1913 to the author, February and March 1958. Of forty-eight members living in 1958, twenty replied to an inquiry about Dr. Baruch. My description of him as a lecturer is a composite of their replies.

79. Baruch to Lambert, April 20, 1913.

80. Baruch to Lambert, April 28, 1913; Emil Roy Posner, "A Physiotherapist Looks at Physiotherapy," *American Mercury* 71 (July 1950): 48. In a letter to Frances A. Hellebrandt, July 24, 1950, Posner said that the incident was "personally" related to him by two of Baruch's assistants, "whose names I have and can furnish." Eight years later, Posner's widow was unable to supply the names (letter to author, December 2, 1958).

81. Walsh, *History of Medicine in New York,* 2:443.

82. Simon Baruch, "Hydrotherapy in Acute Diseases," *Illinois Medical Journal* 18 (August 1910): 217.

83. Simon Baruch, "A Substitute for Fresh Air," letter to editor, *MR* 82 (November 16, 1912): 904–5.

84. Baruch, "Lessons of Half a Century in Medicine," 15. Some of Baruch's colleagues were terrified at the thought of incurring his disapproval; Dr. Hobart A. Hare, professor at Jefferson Medical College and author of a textbook on therapeutics then in its tenth edition, wrote Baruch on March 2, 1909, asking assurance that his was not the unnamed text Baruch had recently criticized.

85. Baruch, "Treatment of Pulmonary Tuberculosis," 116.

86. Butler to Baruch, May 6, 1913; Baruch to Butler, September 23, 1913. It is possible that Baruch's faculty appointment was a casualty of Columbia's transition to clinical full-time, which began in 1911–12; see Walsh, *History of Medicine in New York,* 2:448.

87. A McGehee Harvey and Victor A. McKusick, eds., *Osler's Textbook Revisited* (New York: Appleton-Century-Crofts, 1967), 69.

16. The Wizard of Spas

1. "The Hot Springs Reservation," editorial, *New York Sun,* March 26, 1912; *Saratoga Sun,* June 18, 1913. According to the *New York Sun,* August 15, 1915, Governor Hughes's interest in reviving Saratoga as a spa resulted in state ownership and the creation of the Saratoga Reservation Commission; see Chapter 569 of the Laws of 1909.

2. Hermann Oelrichs of San Francisco to Baruch, March 13, 26, 1906; minutes of meeting of San Francisco County Medical Society in *MR* 69 (April 14, 1906); card dated February 10, 1906, granting Baruch privileges in the Bohemian Club for two weeks.

3. The *San Francisco Call* and *San Francisco Chronicle,* February 14, 1906, and the *San Louis Obispo* [?], February 15, 1906; an editorial in the *San Francisco Call* of February 25 said Baruch was "employed" by the Southern Pacific. His denial appeared in the *Independent* of Santa Barbara, February 26, 1906. The Southern Pacific did not give Baruch ideas he did not have earlier; in "Practical Data on European Health Resorts and Sanitaria," *Medical News* (Philadelphia) 17 (July 10, 1897): 33–42, he had praised American resources and urged their development to stop the annual exodus to European spas.

4. L. H. Nutting to T. J. Anderson, January 8, 1906. On the importance of health-related activities to the development of southern California and on the role of physicians as advertising agents, see John E. Baur, *The Health Seekers of Southern California, 1870–1900* (San Marino, Calif.: Huntington Library, 1959); I am indebted to Ronald L. Numbers for this reference. Baruch considered his California efforts completely successful; in the 1908 edition of *The Principles and Practice of Hydrotherapy,* 530, he listed the Hotel El Paso de Robles alongside four other "good hotels" in various parts of the United States as having hydrotherapeutic installations superior to those he had seen in Germany or France.

5. Hugh Bradley, *Such Was Saratoga* (New York: Doubleday, Doran, 1940), 72–73; David M. Ellis, James A. Frost, Harold C. Syrett, and Harry J. Carman, *A Short History of New York State* (Ithaca: Cornell University Press, 1957), 617.

6. Bradley, *Such Was Saratoga,* 152, 196–99. Writing in 1941, Henry E. Sigerist, "American Spas in Historical Perspective," 71, noted with nostalgia that "the glories of the old days when Southern landlords, New York millionaires, adventurers and expensive prostitutes mixed in glamorous intercourse are revived from time to time in novels such as Edna Ferber's *Saratoga Trunk."*

7. Baruch's Saratoga letters and clippings are filled with references to the depletion and adulteration that occurred at the turn of the century. On the history of this episode, see Henry E. Sigerist, "Towards a Renaissance of the American Spa," in Milton I. Roemer, ed., *Henry E. Sigerist on the Sociology of Medicine* (New York: MD Publications, 1960), 249.

8. Chapter 17 deals with Baruch's medical editorship of the *Sun;* Peabody to Baruch, August 29, 1912.

9. *Saratoga Sun,* June 18, 1913, September 16, 1914; Bradley, *Such Was Saratoga,* 241–75.

10. Dates of the congress appear on Baruch's tickets; R. Fortescue Fox, Secretary of the Section on Therapeutics, to Baruch, July 8, 1913; cable from Brunton in Baruch's papers.

11. Undated clipping from *London Express,* with picture of Baruch; Baruch, letter to editor, *MR* 84 (November 1, 1913): 809; Baruch, "The Need of Instruction in the Remedial Uses of Water," Address before Therapeutic Section of International Medical Congress in London, *TG* 3d ser., 29 (November 15, 1913): 762–63.

12. Irving G. Rouillard, Commission Secretary, to Baruch, August 12, 1913, gives the contents of the cable and says it was sent in response to a cable from Baruch. Baruch to Peabody, December 18, 1913, says he was asked to make the tour; this is the impression he usually gave. Other evidence indicates that he offered to do so; see, for example, the *Saratogian,* December 23, 1913, and Albert J. Wittson's letter to the editor, ibid., July 19, 1919.

13. Peabody to Baruch, August 16, 1913.

14. *New York Times,* September 20, 1913; typed itinerary in Baruch's Saratoga correspondence. Wittson was a brother of Gerard Wittkowsky, the patient in the successful appendicitis surgery of 1887.

15. Peabody to Baruch, September 18, 1913; J. F. Humphrey of Saratoga to Baruch, April 13, 1914, discusses Ferris's legislative experience as lunacy commissioner; *New York Sun,* August 15, 1915, mentions his work at Watkins Glen.

16. Full-page feature about Saratoga, with interviews and picture of Ferris, *New York Sun,* August 15, 1915.

17. There is no draft or copy of a reply from Baruch to Ferris's note of September [18–21?] and no further letter from Ferris until November 19. Ferris had a residence at the Wolcott in New York City in September, and it is possible that they spoke by telephone. A telegram from Peabody, September 21, informed Baruch of Ferris's authority to arrange for Haertl's expenses.

18. *DAB,* s.v. "George Foster Peabody." Eleven years after Spencer Trask's death, Peabody married his widow, Katrina, a playwright, patron of the arts, and friend of Dr. Baruch. After her death two years later, Peabody converted the Trask estate called Yaddo into an artists' retreat of the same name, a use it still serves today; see Bradford Smith, "Parnassus, U.S.A.," *Saturday Review,* August 2, 1958, p. 40.

19. Peabody to Baruch, October 5, 1913. Although Baruch refused payment for his services, the state reimbursed him $1,458.00 for his expenses and Dr. Wittson's.

20. Among many letters concerning Haertl's value to the commission are Rouillard to Baruch, November 17, 1913, and Ferris to Baruch, November 19, 1913. "Saratoga as a Health and Recreation Resort," *Medical Times* 41 (October 1913): 291–93, is probably the article to which Baruch referred when he wrote Peabody on November 12, 1913, that he was enclosing some "publicity work" he had done to help the cause.

21. Baruch to Peabody, January 26, 1914. A four-column article in the *Saratogian,* November 10, 1914, was enough to undo all of the counterpropaganda; it described a meeting, concerned with getting state funds, attended by physicians, businessmen, and officials of the Delaware and Hudson Railroad and the Hudson Valley Railroad.

22. Baruch's letter to the *Albany Argus* was reprinted in the *Saratoga Sun* on March 31, 1914, and is discussed in J. F. Humphrey to Baruch, April 3, and Baruch to Humphrey, April 6, 1914. Rouillard to Baruch, April 8, 15, 1914.

23. In writing on June 14 that he would do the work but reject the honorarium,

Baruch emphasized his willingness to serve the commission without pay. Ferris was on salary. On April 1, 1915, shortly before Ferris left the commission, Baruch wrote the commission engineer, Charles G. Anthony, that he would have done more for Saratoga but "had not the frank and actual support of the Medical Expert."

24. Baruch to Peabody, June 26, 1914; Peabody to Baruch, July 3, evidently refers to another letter from Baruch of which there is no copy in Baruch's correspondence.

25. Peabody to Baruch, July 3, 1914.

26. Baruch to Ferris, July 4, 1914.

27. Ferris to Baruch, October 22, 1914; Baruch to Ferris, August 21, 1914; Ferris to Baruch, August 22, 1914.

28. Baruch wrote Ferris, May 22, 1914, "It was my intention as you know to give the Saratoga colleagues a course in Hydrotherapy but this has been side-tracked."

29. Peabody's letter is not in Baruch's correspondence; Baruch's reply is dated September 16, 1914; draft of letter to Reick, returned by Peabody, September 13, 1914.

30. "Saratoga Springs and the Medical Profession," editorial, *New York Sun,* September 14, 1914.

31. Peabody to Baruch, September 18, 1914.

32. Peabody to Baruch, October 9, 1914; Baruch to Ferris, October 22, 1914.

33. Anthony, the commission engineer, wrote Baruch on April 23, 1915, that Ferris's appointment had been renewed for two more months.

34. "Some of Our Health Resorts," editorial, *New York Sun,* March 16, 1915, reprinted in the *Saratogian,* undated clipping.

35. *New York Sun,* May 21, 1915; *Saratogian,* May 24, 1915; Simon Baruch, "The Giving of Nauheim Baths in This Country," *MR* 87 (June 12, 1915): 972–75.

36. Correspondence between Baruch and Herbert Ant, commission chemist, from December 6, 1915, to March 27, 1916. Simon Baruch, "Carbon Dioxide Baths. Observations on Their Action," *NYMJ* 103 (May 13, 1916): 913–17; *Saratogian,* May 19, 1916, February 23, 1917. Two articles in Sidney Licht, ed., *Medical Hydrology* (New Haven: Elizabeth Licht, 1963), reflect more recent research supporting Baruch's argument for adding salines to natural carbon dioxide waters: Walter S. McClellan, "Carbon Dioxide Baths," 311, states that the release of carbon dioxide is related to mineral content (the greater the salinity, the slower the escape of the gas and the greater the therapeutic efficacy); Victor R. Ott, "Spa Therapy in Cardiovascular Disorders," 362, explains that "the highest possible carbon dioxide content in the bathtub is optimal, for the higher the gradient between carbon dioxide tension in the water and the carbon dioxide partial pressure in the human tissues, the stronger will be the percutaneous diffusion and action on the nervous and circulatory systems."

37. Peabody wrote Baruch, August 22, 1913, that Pratt had purchased lands the state desired for the development of Saratoga so as to resell them to the state at what Peabody considered exorbitant prices; carbon of Baruch's letter to Saratoga physicians, May 22, 1916.

38. Moriarta to Baruch, May 24, 1916; Bradley, *Such Was Saratoga,* 227; May to Baruch and Baright to Baruch, both dated June 10, 1916.

39. Dr. John M. Swan of Rochester to Pratt, carbon to Baruch, June 13, 1916;

Baright to Baruch, June 10, 1916. That the name "Nauheim bath" has persisted as Baruch used it, to indicate any therapeutic bath containing carbon dioxide, is clear from McClellan, "Carbon Dioxide Baths," 311.

40. Baruch to Swan, June 18, 1916.
41. Baruch's revelation of this warning is discussed in Jones to Baruch, March 1, 1918.
42. *Saratogian,* May 18, 1916.
43. Baruch to Swan, June 18, 1916.
44. "Nauheim Treatment in Saratoga," editorial, *MR* 89 (June 3, 1916): 1002–3.
45. Simon Baruch, "The Therapeutic Resources of the Saratoga Springs," *NYMJ* 103 (June 10, 1916): 1105–9.
46. Simon Baruch, "The Therapeutic Resources of Our Spas," *NYMJ* 103 (June 10, 1916): 1135; Simon Baruch, "Nauheim Baths at Saratoga," letter to editor, *MR* 89 (June 10, 1916): 1054.
47. Simon Baruch, "The Nauheim Method," *MR* 89 (June 17, 1916): 1074–81. A more recent rationale of carbon dioxide baths, little different from Baruch's, appeared in Bierman, *Physical Medicine in General Practice,* 35–38. For even later explanations of the physiological effects of CO_2 baths, see McClellan, "Carbon Dioxide Baths," 316–19, and Ott, "Spa Therapy in Cardiovascular Disorders," 350–55. Both McClellan and Ott confirm Baruch's clinical observations (carbon dioxide baths slow the heart; diminish the blood pressure—especially abnormally high systolic rates; and increase respiration of carbon dioxide). Ott, 351–52, offers a "working hypothesis" based on indirect biochemical effects, including chemical substances (especially acetycholine) set free in the epidermis that produce vasodilation and autonomic stimulation. This proposed mode of action is contrary to Baruch's thesis that the baths caused constriction of the peripheral circulation and consequently strengthened the action of the heart.
48. Referred to and quoted in Albert J. Wittson, "Saratoga Springs for Cardiovascular Diseases," letter to the editor, *MR* 90 (July 29, 1916): 204, clipping in Baruch's papers.
49. Ibid. On America's continuing failure to keep pace with Europe in the study of mineral springs, see Baur, *Health Seekers of Southern California,* 101–2.
50. Louis W. Noland to Baruch, August 29, 1916; Baruch to Superintendent Jones, October [?], 1916.
51. Baruch to Downs, November 21, 1916; Baruch to Jones, November 23, 1916; Baruch to Pratt, December 4, 1917 [should read 1916].
52. Baruch to Downs, February 7, 1917. There are many such sketches in Baruch's papers.
53. Superintendent Jones to Baruch, March 1, 1918; Baruch to Osler, carbon, December 20, 1918; copy of Osler's letter to Baruch, January 7, 1919.
54. Baruch to Sherry, carbon, January 31, 1919.
55. Peabody to Baruch, February 4, 1919.
56. Peabody to Baruch, August 22, 1919, enclosing copies of letters from Peabody to Hon. George R. Van Namee, Secretary to Governor Smith, August 22, 1919, and to Charles R. Miller, editor of the *New York Times,* August 22, 1919.
57. Sigerist, "American Spas in Historical Perspective," 74–76, describes the study of Saratoga's mineral springs, which began eight years after Dr. Baruch's death under a commission headed by his son Bernard. An advocate of

medical education and research in balneology, Sigerist, who called Simon Baruch "a physician of vision," said that the foundation of the Simon Baruch Research Institute in the 1930s had "marked a date in the history of American medicine" that signified that America was beginning to catch up with Europe. Noting that Saratoga "gave 23,245 charity treatments in 1939 to 1940," Sigerist (whose *Socialized Medicine in the Soviet Union* [New York: Norton, 1937], 181, had called the opening of health resorts to workers "one of Soviet medicine's most brilliant achievements") added that inasmuch as a "cure" required about eighteen treatments, the number of medical indigents Saratoga accommodated was very small out of a national population of 130 million. In "Living under the Shadow," in Max Pinner and Benjamin F. Miller, eds., *When Doctors Are Patients* (New York: Norton, 1952), 11, Sigerist attributed his survival during World War II, despite high blood pressure and severe work overloads, to his annual stays of several weeks at Saratoga.

17. Dr. Baruch of the *Sun*

1. In a letter to Baruch, April 9, 1903, Wyeth claims authorship of an editorial published on April 7. Baruch's son Herman gave the dates of Baruch's editorship in *Centennial of the Medical College of Virginia, 1838–1938* (New York: New York Alumni Association, Medical College of Virginia, 1937). According to Frank M. O'Brien, *The Story of the Sun, New York, 1833–1928* (New York: D. Appleton, 1928), 236, the *Sun* announced authorship of only two articles: Francis P. Church's "Is There a Santa Claus?" and Harold Mac-Donald Anderson's "Lindbergh Flies Alone." Baruch's work is mentioned in "The Newspaper and the Physician," editorial, *Medical Times* 40 (November 1912): 333. On Shrady's editorship at the *Herald*, see Walsh, *History of Medicine in New York*, 2:350. There are discussions of medical journalism in Garrison, *Introduction*, 663; Frank Luther Mott, *American Journalism: A History of Newspapers in the United States through 250 Years, 1690 to 1940* (New York: Macmillan, 1950), 519–615; Martin Gardner, *Fads and Fallacies in the Name of Science* (New York: Dover, 1957), 4–5; and James H. Cassedy, "Muckraking and Medicine: Samuel Hopkins Adams," *American Quarterly* 16 (1964): 85–99. See also John C. Burnham, *How Superstition Won and Science Lost: Popularizing Science and Health in the United States* (New Brunswick: Rutgers University Press, 1987).
2. "Medical Editors a Real Necessity," reprint from the *Medical Times* 40 (November 1912): 318–20. Under this arrangement Baruch must have approved the lengthy interview published in the *Sun* of November 21, 1915, in which he expressed agreement with the Chicago physician who declined to perform major abdominal surgery to sustain life in a baby born with monstrous deformities. Baruch said he would have acted exactly as Dr. Harry J. Haiselden had done, given the same circumstances. My thanks to Martin S. Pernick for a copy of this two-page interview. On the value that Frank Munsey, who bought the *Sun* in 1916, placed on news stories and editorial articles on scientific subjects, see O'Brien, *Story of the Sun*, 209–10.
3. Baruch spoke of his editorial duties in an address before the International Medical Congress, London, August 1913, published as "The Need of Instruction in the Remedial Uses of Water," *TG* 3d ser., 29 (November 1913): 768.

4. February 20, December 9, 1912. All dates standing alone in the following notes in this chapter identify *Sun* editorials attributed to Baruch.
5. January 17, 21, March 8, 1912, October 22, 1913, September 6, 1914, February 9, 1916.
6. June 15, November 18, 1912, June 23, August 11, 1913, January 6 (cartoon, January 9), April 15, September 1, November 1, 1914, April 5, June 20, December 6, 1916, January 7, 1917.
7. March 21, 1912, December 27, 1914, January 22, February 27, 1915, May 5, 1916, March 27, 1917.
8. April 12, 1912, July 12, 1913, October 12, 1914, February 9, 1915.
9. March 9, 12, June 13, July 6, August 13, October 11, 1912, May 22, June 22, 1913, February 11, May 15, November 8, 1914, February 22, March 31, 1915.
10. December 22, 1912, September 15, December 17, 1913, January 19, August 6, 1914, March 28, 1915.
11. May 2, August 22, October 4, 1912, January 6, 1913.
12. February 26, April 29, October 13, November 22, December 12, 29, 1912, February 16, July 17, November 24, December 21, 1913, July 27, August 9, 1914.
13. July 19, December 9, 1912, July 3, 6, 11, 13, 16, 24, 28, 30, August 3, 11, 17, 18, 24, 30, September 2, 12, 21, 22, 28, October 17, November 23, 1916. For a detailed description of this epidemic, see Guenter B. Risse, "Epidemics and History: Ecological Perspectives and Social Responses," in Elizabeth Fee and Daniel M. Fox, eds., *AIDS: The Burdens of History* (Berkeley: University of California Press, 1988), 48–56.
14. March 4, September 15, October 24, 1912, January 13, 1913, January 26, 1914.
15. September 28, November 9, 1914.
16. January 18, March 16, March 31, 1912, June 22, 1914, April 23, May 2, 1916.
17. June 29, October 26, 1913, February 2, March 19, May 17, 1914.
18. January 26, May 28, 1913.
19. Baruch, "Medical Editors a Real Necessity."
20. Editorial, *JAMA* 69 (November 10, 1917): 1641.
21. *New York Sun,* January 12, 1912.
22. January 14, 1912.
23. Arthur Farlow to the *Sun,* January 25, 1912; Baruch to Stimson and Farlow in the *Sun,* February 1, 1912; August Stetson to Baruch, February 1, 1912; Frederick Peabody to Baruch, February 10, 1912; Edward S. van Zile to the *Sun,* February 24, 1912. The dispute among Christian Scientists delighted Peabody, a Boston lawyer, who wrote Baruch: "In a quiet way I have from time to time endeavored to facilitate hostilities."
24. September 22, 1912. The *Sun* of the next day reported the reaction of numerous New York physicians.
25. October 2, 1912. For a more balanced view of Roosevelt's activities in this connection, see James Harvey Young, *Pure Food: Securing the Federal Food and Drug Act of 1906* (Princeton: Princeton University Press, 1989), 190–93, 254.
26. Undated clipping in Baruch's papers; I did not find this editorial in going through the *Sun;* it was probably written in November. The other material about Works is contained in a clipping from *Good Health* dated September 1912.
27. The *Sun* of December 10, 1912, published a reply from the alert Christian Science Committee on Publication but permitted itself an editorial note

longer than the letter of protest. "The Evolution of Mental Healing," January 12, 1914, pretends to view the popular mental cults with tolerance, as vestiges of primitive beliefs in amulets, talismans, and the like.

28. A letter to *MR* 81 (January 27, 1912): 176–77 questions whether Christian Scientists can distinguish smallpox from acne and asks why they must be paid when Jesus Christ worked for nothing.

29. March 7, 1912, January 23, February 7, 24, April 8, 14, 1913, April 9, 1914.

30. August 10, 1916, March 28, 1914.

31. July 28, September 8, November 4, 1912, April 12, May 11, October 13, 1913, February 22, October 4, December 31, 1914, March 21, 1915.

32. August 25, September 21, 1912, February 2, November 3, 1913, December 31, 1914, November 20, 1915; Simon Baruch to Bernard Baruch (carbon), June 23, 1918. For a comprehensive history of patent medicines, see James Harvey Young, *The Toadstool Millionaires: A Social History of Patent Medicines in America before Federal Regulation* (Princeton: Princeton University Press, 1961).

33. April 26, 1912, January 31, February 1, July 6, November 23, 1913, November 11, 1914.

34. March 2, 1912, July 6, 1913.

35. January 28, 1912, January 20, March 9, June 27, August 10, 1913. The *Sun* of March 4, 1913, reported an official investigation of the financial resources of people using the city dispensaries.

36. February 12, October 28, 1912, March 3, May 2, 1913, June 15, 1914, August 15, 1916. From 1903 to 1906 Baruch debated with Tiberius von Györy, *Universitätsdocent* in Budapest, over priority in the recognition of puerperal fever's contagiousness; Baruch championed Oliver Wendell Holmes, Györy favored Ignaz P. Semmelweis. Frank P. Murphy discusses Baruch's scholarship in "Bibliography of Ignaz P. Semmelweis, 1818–1865," *Bulletin of the History of Medicine* 20 (1946): 653–707; see also Genevieve Miller, "In Praise of Amateurs: Medical History in America before Garrison," *Bulletin of the History of Medicine* 47 (November–December 1973): 614.

37. February 20, April 7, December 9, 1912, December 29, 1913, January 21, 1917. Chauncey D. Leake, "Medical Caricature in the United States," *Bulletin of the Society of Medical History of Chicago* 4 (April 1928): 14–15.

38. February 5, 23, December 6, 1912, February 14, 1915, January 14, 1917; Torney's secretary to Baruch, February 19, 1912; Stokes to Baruch, February 23, March 15, 1912.

39. September 7, November 10, 1912, May 21, 1914. According to Hume, *Victories of Army Medicine,* 102–3, the U.S. Army was the first to practice compulsory typhoid vaccination, starting in 1909. Widespread vaccination did not come until later; in the meantime, typhoid prevention was a sanitary problem.

40. May 24, 28, October 11, November 13, 1912, January 20, March 30, April 20, 1914, February 24, March 19, May 21, 1916. See also Duffy, *History of Public Health in New York City,* 519–21, on the severity of the city's water pollution problem in this period.

41. Simon Baruch, "Important Investigations in Sterilized Milk," *JB* 7 (November 1893): 395; Baruch, "Lessons of Half a Century in Medicine," 16; *New York Sun,* May 15, 1916. On the complex questions underlying support for

certification as opposed to pasteurization, see Manfred J. Waserman, "Henry L. Coit and the Certified Milk Movement in the Development of Modern Pediatrics," *Bulletin of the History of Medicine* 46 (1972): 359–90.

42. *New York Globe and Commercial,* March 13, 1907; *New York Evening Journal,* March 14, 1907; and other clippings from unidentified newspapers.

43. Rhoda Truax, *The Doctors Jacobi* (Boston: Little, Brown, 1952), 249–50. Baruch paid tribute to Straus in *Sun* editorials on April 20 and November 22, 1913, and September 12, 1917.

44. April 4, September 1, 14, November 5, 1912, September 28, 1913.

45. June 22, July 22, 1912, June 8, September 28, 1913, February 23, May 1, June 19, July 8, August 13, 17, October 6, 16, 18, 1916, February 18, 1917.

46. January 23, February 2, 1912; Ellis, Frost, Syrett, and Carman, *Short History of New York State,* 368–69. See also Waserman, "Quest for a National Health Department," 353–80.

47. January 18, 24, February 10, 1913. Baruch also favored the transfer of the Baltimore station; see *Baltimore Star,* May 19, 1913.

48. March 2, 1915; *MR* (May 22, 1915): 864; Baruch to Blue (carbon), May 15, 1915.

49. February 4, 1914, March 27, 1915, March 7, April 22, 1916. The transfer finally took place on March 1, 1921, just three months before Baruch died.

50. March 24, September 4, 1912.

51. April 19, December 14, 1912, March 10, July 27, November 28, 1913, March 14, April 17, 1914.

52. April 30, 1914.

53. December 24, 1912, February 25, March 2, 31, 1913, July 31, 1914.

54. March 27, November 27, 1912, November 14, 1914, January 17, 27, July 9, September 28, 1916. The dates of Baruch's polio editorials are given in note 13 above.

55. November 17, 1912, January 17, April 4, 1913, November 16, 20, December 5, 1914.

56. February 8, 1912. By 1913, Baruch had decided it might be better to keep health matters in the Public Health Service; see "The Owen Health Bill," editorial, *New York Sun,* February 24, 1913.

57. January 31, February 20, April 16, 21, 1913.

58. September 29, October 3, 1912, July 1, 2, 30, November 7, 1914, February 26, March 30, 1915, February 19, November 22, December 21, 1916, March 27, April 1, 1917; "Effect of the War on the Consumption of Narcotic Drugs" (unsigned article on the *Sun* editorial page, rather than an editorial), December 23, 1917. From 1915 to 1917 Baruch served as chairman of a committee on drug addiction set up by the National Committee on Prisons and Prison Labor. He also testified before a joint legislative committee on January 11, 1918, urging that addicts be treated in hospitals under government supervision (*New York American* and *New York City Herald,* both of January 12, 1918). For a comprehensive history of efforts to regulate narcotics in the United States, see David F. Musto, *The American Disease: Origins of Narcotic Control* (New Haven: Yale University Press, 1973).

59. August 9, October 17, 1912, February 21, 1913, November 7, 1914; Mitchell to Baruch, October 19, 1912; undated draft of Belle's speech.

60. April 29, July 18, November 14, 1912, February 14, 17, July 20, 1913, March

19, 1915; "A Symposium on Prohibition," Viereck's *American Monthly,* June 5, 1918.

61. September 30, 1913, April 12, 1914.
62. March 16, 1916, January 29, March 4, 17, April 16, 1917. Simon Baruch, "Alcohol in Peace and War," *MR* 91 (June 9, 1917): 981–85, and "The Nutritive Value of Yeast," *MR* 91 (June 16, 1917): 1053. In response to a summary of these two articles in the *New York Times,* June 19, 1917, Graham Lusk wrote a letter published on June 27. Baruch saved a copy of the letter he sent to Senate members, together with the more than thirty replies he received.
63. November 25, December 3, 1914.
64. June 21, 1913, January 14, 1916, October 31, 1917.
65. May 18, November 7, 16, December 23, 1912, April 20, 1913, February 4, 1914, March 27, 1915, March 7, April 22, 1916.
66. The *Sun* of September 1, 1912, carried Baruch's views on euthanasia; other physicians interviewed who favored legalizing euthanasia were not willing to give their names, as Baruch did.
67. March 25, 1914. For the context of Baruch's eugenics writings, see Daniel J. Kevles, *In the Name of Eugenics: Genetics and the Uses of Human Heredity* (New York: Knopf, 1985).
68. November 11, 1912, June 27, 1913, July 13, 1913.
69. Even so outspoken an evolutionist as Clarence Darrow viewed sterilization as a denial of Darwinism; see Darrow, "The Eugenics Cult," *American Mercury* 8 (June 1926): 129–37.
70. April 21, 1912, November 20, 1913.
71. Quoted in Garrison, *Introduction* (1917), 710–11. For the context of the sterilization movement, see Philip R. Reilly, *The Surgical Solution: A History of Involuntary Sterilization in the United States* (Baltimore: Johns Hopkins University Press, 1991).
72. Garrison, *Introduction* (1913), 663.
73. According to Leake, "Medical Caricature," 14–16, *Life* began a systematic campaign against the medical profession in 1908. See also Mott, *History of American Magazines, 1885–1905,* 556–68, esp. 562, on the editor's "favorite crusade" against vivisection. Despite *Life*'s "barbed paragraphs" and "pictures that were sometimes really distressing," thousands of doctors, Mott notes, "kept the attractive little periodical in their waiting rooms, thus dispensing a wit often more therapeutic than medicine."

18. "Before I go hence"

1. Dr. Baruch's niece Martha Machol to author, May 1958, recalls his custom of working late in the night during a visit at her Berlin home, probably in 1913. On the strikingly similar hard-driving work habits of Baruch's contemporary and fellow advocate of scientific hydrotherapy, see Schwarz, *John Harvey Kellogg,* 128–36.
2. Baruch to "Annie," Bernard Baruch's wife; although the carbon of this letter is dated "N. Y. May 12, 1916," it was probably written a few days later; it was on May 12 that the news of his attack appeared in the *Baltimore Sun.*
3. H. A. Hare to Baruch, November 25, 1890; clippings from *Medical Week*

(undated) and *MR* (December 16, 1893); J. H. Kellogg, *Rational Hydrotherapy,* 3d ed. rev. (Philadelphia: F. A. Davis, 1906), 1160–62; Harry P. Loomis to Baruch, November 19, [?]; Simon Baruch, address to Interurban Club, published as "Instruction in Hydrotherapy," *MR* 73 (January 18, 1908): 92–95; Joseph H. Pratt to Baruch, February 8, 1909.

4. Deneen to Baruch, January 21, 1907. Charles S. Deneen was Republican governor of Illinois from 1905 to 1913.
5. According to the *New York American,* November 28, 1917, Hartwig then had two daughters; Bernard, one son and two daughters; Herman, two sons; and Sailing, three sons. Simon saved a group of poems he wrote about family get-togethers.
6. Baruch dated the *Times* clipping August 7, 1911; Alden March, Sunday editor of the *Times,* to Baruch, November 28, 1911, forwarded a check in payment for the poem, which he said had appeared on August 20.
7. The *New York Times,* November 28, 1917, gave full coverage to the party; accounts also appeared in the *New York American* and the *Sun* of the same date.
8. Baruch to Albert D. Ferris, Saratoga Springs Medical Supervisor, April 23, 1915; McCombs to Baruch, telegram, November 21, 1912; McAdoo to Baruch, February 16, 1915; Blue to Baruch, August 10, 1916.
9. *NYMJ* 104 (August 26, 1916): 430. The *Sun* editorials on polio are listed in Chapter 17.
10. Atherton Seidell, "Vitamines and Nutritional Diseases: A Stable Form of Vitamine, Efficient in the Prevention and Cure of Certain Nutritional Deficiency Diseases," Reprint 325 from *Public Health Reports* (February 18, 1916), 364–70; Baruch saved two of these reprints. Meltzer to Baruch, July 29, 1916.
11. Top, ed., *History of American Epidemiology,* 87; Mendel to Baruch, telegram and letter, July 29, 1916; carbon to Baruch's form letter, September 16, 1916. I have attempted to reconstruct Baruch's method of preparation from Atherton Seidell to Baruch, July 29, 1916, and Baruch to Mr. Prince and Mr. Mulhauser (brewers), August 12, 1916.
12. On Ehrlich see Patricia Spain Ward, "The American Reception of Salvarsan," *Journal of the History of Medicine and Allied Sciences* 36 (January 1981): 46.
13. *MR* 89 (June 17, 1916): 1074; letters to author from Louis Shalet, M.D., of Long Island, October 26, 1959, and Irving J. Sands, M.D., of Brooklyn, March 3, 1958; Dr. Shalet recalls meeting Baruch on the Staten Island ferry in 1914. Baruch's Sea View correspondence extends from February 1 to April 19, 1918.
14. Clipping from the *Baltimore American,* dated only May 1913; the *Baltimore Star,* May 19, 1913. See Williams, *Washing "The Great Unwashed,"* chap. 6, esp. 125–30, on the association's history and the yearly memorial services it held for Baruch for five years after his death. It ceased activities, including publication of the *Journal,* in the early 1930s.
15. *Sun* editorials on this subject appeared on April 28, July 23, 1913, April 15, 1914, August 10, 26, September 5, 6, 8, December 2, 1915, March 27, April 4, May 29, June 27, August 12, October 5, 7, 19, December 11, 1916, and February 4, 14, March 30, July 23, 1917.
16. Baruch to Daniels, carbon, November 17, December 9, 1914; Daniels to Baruch, November 15, 1916; Martin to Baruch, March 31, 1917.

17. *New York Times,* December 29, 1914; invitation to German Medical Society.
18. Drafts of Baruch's statement in his papers; he tried in vain to locate his naturalization papers in 1912 and again after the loyalty question arose. His certificate of naturalization, now at the South Caroliniana Library in Columbia, is dated January 19, 1871.
19. Baruch to Franklin Martin, September 3, 1917; Major Edgar King, Surgeon-General's Office, to Baruch, September 10, 1917; Lt. Col. C. C. McCulloch to Baruch, September 10, 1917; telegram from Major Pearce Bailey to Baruch, October 22, 1917; telegram from Surgeon-General William C. Gorgas to Baruch, October 24, 1917; telegram from Baruch to Gorgas, October 25, 1917; *New York Evening Post,* October 29, 1917.
20. Baruch to Martin, January 22, 1918; Simon Baruch, "Devices for Sanitation of Trenches," *JAMA* 69 (November 17, 1917): 1694–95; Simon Baruch, "Disposal of Excreta in the Trenches," *Military Surgeon* 42 (January 1918): 75–84; Simon Baruch, "Substitute Metallic Containers for Latrine Purposes," *Military Surgeon* 43 (July 1918): 121–25.
21. C. Burns Craig, Medical Reserve Corps, to Baruch, January 30, 1918; Baruch to Surgeon-General, February 19, 1918; Dr. Samuel Newman to author, October 29, 1959; Franklin Martin to Baruch, April 12, 1916. Baruch's editorials on the needs of the medical corps appeared on September 10, 1912, November 23, 1914, May 7, July 2, 1916, March 25, 26, June 24, July 26, 1917. He also wrote a signed article on the editorial page of the *Sun,* August 9, 1917; "Preparedness in the Medical Corps," *NYMJ* 104 (August 12, 1916): 334–35; and "Doctors in the Army," letter to the *New York Times,* March 23, 1918.
22. *New York Times,* July 12, 1914.
23. Simon Baruch to oldest son, Hartwig, carbon, July 24, 1914.
24. Of the nine memos Baruch saved, those bearing dates range from January 30, 1912, to April 2, 1914. The late Gabriel Baum of Camden told the author that his father and uncle, Herman and Mannes Baum, never expected repayment of the money they had spent on Dr. Baruch's medical education.
25. Memo dated November 23, 1912.
26. Letter in Bernard Baruch's office in 1956, dated only 1919.
27. Coit, *Mr. Baruch,* 61; Dr. Baruch to Hartwig, July 24, 1914. In a will dated July 25, 1919, Baruch credited three of his sons with contributing to his "maintenance and comfort and that of my wife during the past seventeen years." He also wrote Hartwig that he personally spent around $800 a year, "most of which I still earn, while she has not enough with $6000.00 a year."
28. "Is Obesity Increasing?" December 22, 1912. Other *Sun* editorials about modern woman appeared on March 7, 14, April 12, July 24, August 14, September 21, 1912, January 2, March 15, 1913.
29. I know of no result of this study other than the various interviews, letters, and speeches cited below. Baruch was apparently unacquainted with H. J. Mozans, *Woman in Science, with an Introductory Chapter on Woman's Long Struggle for Things of the Mind* (New York: D. Appleton, 1913), a pioneering work of women's history written under a pseudonym by John A. Zahm, a C.S.C. (reprinted by MIT Press in 1974 and the University of Notre Dame Press in 1991). For more recent overviews, see Margaret Alic, *Hypatia's Heritage: A History of Women in Science from Antiquity to the Late Nineteenth Century* (London: Women's Press, 1986); and Londa Schiebinger, *The Mind*

Has No Sex? Women in the Origins of Modern Medicine (Cambridge, Mass.: Harvard University Press, 1989).

30. Undated proof from the *New York Times* of a letter Baruch wrote August 12, 1915. Although the elderly Baruch insisted on "woman's place," as a young man he had championed equal rights. When the first woman applied for membership in the Hebrew Benevolent Association of Camden, he argued that the association constitution (which he had helped to write) provided "that *all* Israelites are entitled to membership. There can be no distinction of sex." See minutes of Hebrew Benevolent Association, April 21, 1878.

31. Belle to the *New York Times,* February 14, 1915. On the slowness of many southern women to support the vote for women, see Anne Firor Scott, *The Southern Lady: From Pedestal to Politics, 1830–1930* (Chicago: University of Chicago Press, 1970), 169–72.

32. *New York Times,* February 7, 1914; in a letter to the *New York Times,* February 14, 1914, Belle stated that her report was "well received" even though only a small minority of antisuffragists belonged to the Federation of Women's Clubs. The *New York American,* February 7, 1914, ran a large headline: "2000 Suffrage Women at Astor Hiss Mrs. Baruch: Spirited Defense of Anti-Suffrage by Doctor's Wife Excites a Meeting." Baruch to *New York Times,* February 10, 1914.

33. Dr. Baruch to Hartwig, carbon, July 24, 1914.

34. "Feminism Is a Bar to Social Betterment: And the Affiliation of Suffrage and Feminism," undated reprint, apparently from the *Century Magazine;* speech by Baruch quoted in the *Pittsburgh Leader* and the *Pittsburgh Dispatch,* January 24, 1915. The history of women artists was largely unknown at that time: one of the first full historical surveys of women artists was a 1977 exhibit entitled "Women Artists: 1550–1950"; see Robert Hughes, "Rediscovered—Women Painters," *Time,* January 10, 1977, pp. 60–63. See also Karen Petersen and J. J. Wilson, *Women Artists: Recognition and Reappraisal from the Early Middle Ages to the Twentieth Century* (New York: New York University Press, 1976).

35. This paragraph and the next are based on letters to the *New York Times* from Baruch and Beard, July 4, 11, 18, August 1, 12, 1915, and undated proof of letter written by Baruch on July 7, 1915. There is now a vast literature documenting efforts, on biological grounds, to delimit women's activities; see, for example, Ruth Hubbard, Mary Sue Henefin, and Barbara Fried, eds., *Women Look at Biology Looking at Women: A Collection of Feminist Critiques* (Cambridge, Mass.: Schenkman, 1979). In 1946, Macmillan published Mary R. Beard's *Woman as Force in History: A Study in Traditions and Realities;* see Nancy F Cott, "Mary Ritter Beard," in Barbara Sicherman and Carol Hurd Green, eds., *Notable American Women: The Modern Period* (Cambridge, Mass.: Belknap Press of Harvard University Press, 1980), 71–73.

36. When Baruch made this statement in 1915, Marie Curie had already become the first person in history to win two Nobel prizes: in physics in 1903 for the discovery of radioactivity (with Henri Becquerel and her husband, Pierre); and in chemistry in 1911 for the discovery of radium and the study of its properties. Pierre was killed in a traffic accident in Paris in 1906, long before Marie won her second Nobel award. It seems likely that Baruch's adamant refusal to recognize creativity even in the gifted Madame Curie resulted from associating women scientists with the feminism he detested. For the context

of this association, see Margaret W. Rossiter, *Women Scientists in America: Struggles and Strategies to 1940* (Baltimore: Johns Hopkins University Press, 1982), 100–128.

37. On the difficulties women physicians faced in finding internships and hospital staff positions, see Mary Roth Walsh, *"Doctors Wanted: No Women Need Apply": Sexual Barriers in the Medical Profession, 1835–1975* (New Haven: Yale University Press, 1977), 219–24; and Regina Markell Morantz-Sanchez, *Sympathy and Science: Women Physicians in America* (New York: Oxford University Press, 1985), 159–60, 233, 317.

38. H. M. Dermitt, secretary of the Civic Club of Allegheny County, Pennsylvania, to Baruch, December 9, 1916; Baruch's reply, carbon, December 12, confirms news of Belle's conversion to suffrage.

39. *New York Times,* January 5, 1913.

40. Baruch to Williams, carbon, August 11, 1917.

41. *New York Times,* December 8, 1912; souvenirs of the encampment among Baruch's papers; *Confederate Veteran* 22 (December 1914): 545–48, and (August 1915): 343; L. H. Hill to Baruch, one letter dated only 1915, the other August 18, 1915; Daniel Parker to Baruch, August 13, 1915. According to Coit, *Mr. Baruch,* 43, Simon also "let loose the bloodcurdling rebel yell" one night at the Metropolitan Opera House when the orchestra played "Dixie."

42. "Reminiscences of a Confederate Surgeon," reprint from the *Long Branch Record,* September 24, 1915.

43. "Robert Edward Lee—the Man and the Soldier," no place or date of publication, 6, 9, 11–12. On February 21, 1917, Baruch wrote similar thoughts to Yates Snowden, professor of history at the University of South Carolina, together with the observation that his opinions "may not yet find an echo in the entire South"; Yates Snowden Papers, South Caroliniana Library, University of South Carolina, Columbia.

44. Undated clipping, probably 1918, from *New York Herald.*

45. *New York Sun,* December 2, 1913, noted the opening of the hospital.

46. Baruch to Marks, carbon, November 1, 1917. According to the *New York Evening Post,* October 29, 1917, Marks was responsible for having the bath named in Baruch's honor.

47. Wyeth's tributes to Baruch are to be found in Wyeth, "The Present Status of the Surgery of the Vermiform Appendix," *International Journal of Surgery* 5 (July 1892): 170, and in the discussion following Wyeth, "Appendicitis Strictly a Surgical Lesion," *Trans. NYAM* 2d ser., 2 (1894): 266; in "Surgery in Bright's Disease," editorial [by Wyeth], *New York Sun,* April 7, 1903, and in Wyeth, "The Technic of Appendectomy," read in the Section on Surgery and Anatomy of the American Medical Association at the Fifty-Eighth Annual Session, held at Atlantic City, June 1907, reprint from an unidentified journal in Baruch's papers.

48. Baruch to Wyeth, carbon, April 12, 1903.

49. Albert J. Wittson to Baruch, February 8, 1907, in Baruch's papers; Baruch to Wittson, February 10, 1907, Simon Baruch Papers, South Caroliniana Library, University of South Carolina, Columbia.

50. Howard A. Kelly to Baruch, May 27, 1912, concerning what Baruch considered an injustice to him in the historical portion of Howard A. Kelly and Elizabeth Hurdon, *The Vermiform Appendix and Its Diseases* (Philadelphia:

W. B. Saunders, 1905); Baruch to Fielding H. Garrison, carbon, December 1, 1914, concerning a similar neglect of Baruch's priority in the first edition of Garrison's *Introduction* (1913); Garrison to Baruch, December 2, 1914.

51. *New York Times,* March 26, 1919; Alfred W. Crosby, *America's Forgotten Pandemic: The Influenza of 1918* (New York: Cambridge University Press, 1989); first published as *Epidemic and Peace, 1918* (Westport, Conn.: Greenwood Press, 1976). Simon Baruch, "Influenza—a Comparison," *MR* 95 (January 11, 1919): 52–55; Simon Baruch, "Influenza—a Therapeutic Lesson," *Therapeutic Gazette* 3d ser., 35 (June 15, 1919): 393–95; Simon Baruch, *An Epitome of Hydrotherapy for Physicians, Architects and Nurses* (Philadelphia: W. B. Saunders, 1920, reprinted in 1950 by the Doctor Simon Baruch Foundation and distributed by the Baruch Committee on Physical Medicine and Rehabilitation), 165–75 on pneumonia, quote on 171. For data describing reduced mortality rates under osteopathic treatment, similarly localized and based on similar rationale, see Norman Gevitz, *The D.O.'s: Osteopathic Medicine in America* (Baltimore: Johns Hopkins University Press, 1982), 71–72. On the successful use of hydrotherapy by naval surgeons among influenza victims aboard the USS *Solace* in 1919, see Baruch *Epitome,* 61–64.

52. Morris Fishbein, "The End of Eclecticism," *American Mercury* 8 (June 1926): 328; Fishbein was the editor of the *JAMA* from 1924 to 1950. Baruch dedicated the *Epitome* to Bernard, "in appreciation of his filial devotion and unstinting support of the author's life work." The Simon Baruch Foundation, which Bernard established, reprinted the *Epitome* in a limited edition in 1950.

53. Baruch to Albert Warren Ferris, medical adviser to the Saratoga Reservation Commission, July 4, 1914.

54. In "'Physiological Remedies' at the Pan-American Medical Congress," editorial, *Journal of Balneology* 7 (September 1893): 303, Baruch defined his "mission." The same idea pervades all of his writings on hydrotherapy, including hundreds of editorials in the *Dietetic and Hygienic Gazette, Gaillard's Medical Journal,* and the *Journal of Balneology.*

55. *New York Times,* April 12, 1959. The "Aquapeutic," which sold for $69.95, worked on the principle of the whirlpool bath described in Baruch's *Epitome,* 133–39.

56. Undated handwritten draft in Baruch's papers.

57. Samuel Newman to author, October 29, 1959.

58. Draft of letter from Baruch to Le Brun, May 6, 1920, on the reverse of Le Brun's letter to Baruch, May 3.

59. Undated clipping from the *Public Ledger* in Baruch's papers.

60. *New York Times,* May 8, 1921.

61. Baruch to "My dear Son," carbon, May 16, 1921; according to his own numbering, one page of this letter is missing from his papers.

62. Arthur M. Crane to the Speakman Company of Wilmington, Delaware, May 16, 1921, carbon in Baruch's papers.

63. *New York Times,* June 3, 1921.

64. Bernard Baruch, *My Own Story,* 50–51, says that Dr. Baruch had a stroke and lost the power of speech shortly before his death but retained his other faculties almost to the end. Rabbi Bernard J. Bamberger of Congregation Shaaray Tefila (formerly the West End Synagogue) wrote the author (No-

vember 22, 1960) that "judging from what I have heard from Mr. B. M. Baruch and others, Dr. Baruch, though a member of the Congregation, was never particularly interested in its activities; Mrs. Baruch, however, was more devout and observant."

65. *New York Times,* June 6, 1921. "F. de S. M." wrote the article about Simon Baruch in *The Jewish Encyclopedia* (New York: Funk and Wagnalls, 1943), 2:561–62. Baruch's will was published in the *Times,* June 29, 1921.

66. Quoted in Laurence Farmer, ed., *Doctors' Legacy: A Selection of Physicians' Letters, 1721–1954* (New York: Harper, 1955), 196–97.

Notes on Sources

Manuscripts

After Simon Baruch's death in 1921, his papers passed into the hands of his third son, Herman Baruch, a physician and ambassador to the Netherlands in the Truman administration. They remained in Herman's family until 1956, when Simon's second son, Bernard, arranged for them to be temporarily deposited at The Johns Hopkins University Institute of the History of Medicine for my use in this study. All letters, clippings, and memorabilia mentioned in the text or notes and not otherwise identified were located in this collection while I used it in Baltimore between 1956 and 1961.

The present location of this collection is a mystery. I returned it to Bernard Baruch in 1961, after finishing this manuscript in its original form. In 1978, when I next attempted to locate it, Harold Epstein, formerly Bernard Baruch's personal secretary, recalled that he had placed it at Princeton, along with Bernard's papers, after Bernard's death in 1965. Princeton, however, holds only a few Simon Baruch letters, all personal, all written to Bernard. I have been unable to relocate the papers I used, either in such likely repositories as the Waring Historical Library of the Medical University of South Carolina, Charleston; the South Caroliniana Library, University of South Carolina, Columbia; or the Tompkins-McCaw Library of the Medical College of Virginia, Richmond. Nor is this collection listed in published directories of manuscript collections in the United States.

[While gathering illustrations as this manuscript is about to go to the printer, I have discovered through a serendipitous telephone call with Jodi Koste, archivist at the Tompkins-McCaw Library of the Medical College of Virginia, that, contrary to information given me in 1978, the Simon Baruch papers I used are indeed located there. They are part of what is called the Simon Baruch Collection, but they are no longer in the topical/chronological order I gave them as a condition of my use during the 1950s. In the intervening years someone has taped each letter to a sheet of paper and arranged them all chronologically, presenting an insur-

361

mountable obstacle to archival processing. Thus these papers have never been listed in national directories of manuscript collections. They are, however, available for unrestricted scholarly use. As the Simon Baruch Collection has no inventory, I do not know whether it contains all of the materials Bernard Baruch provided for my use in writing this book. I have therefore retained endnote references to "Simon Baruch papers," to indicate materials I used which may—or may not—be found in the Simon Baruch Collection in Richmond.]

For the years between 1881 and 1921, which Dr. Baruch spent in New York City, his papers provided a full record of his professional interests and activities. He saved much of his large incoming correspondence, drafts or carbon copies of many outgoing letters, physician's registers, casebooks, newspaper and journal clippings, blueprints of hydrotherapeutic apparatus and public baths, bills, canceled checks for several of his last years, typescripts and proofs of his books, cards of referring physicians, invitations to and programs of social and professional events, drafts of lecture notes and speeches, pamphlets, and reprints.

Baruch had a highly developed autobiographical instinct. He filled numerous scrapbooks, often gluing letters on top of one another. He sometimes altered materials before having them photocopied, wrote over statements in newspaper clippings and reprints, or added marginal comments. Although the resulting self-consciousness of the collection sometimes made the biographer's task more difficult, it often provided welcome clues to his attitude about himself and others. The papers temporarily deposited in Baltimore included few materials of a purely personal nature, but they provided a full record of Simon Baruch's professional life after 1881.

For the years between 1840 and 1881, the only manuscripts in Dr. Baruch's papers were a love letter to Belle Wolfe, his future wife, written in 1867; a letter appointing him to the Executive Committee of the State Board of Health; and a number of entries in his physician's register and casebooks. His notes on Eli Geddings's lectures at the Medical College of South Carolina are now in Special Collections, Robert W. Woodruff Library, Emory University, Atlanta. I used items from the Hentz Family Papers, Manigault Family Papers, and Battle Family Papers in the Southern Historical Collection at the University of North Carolina Library, to round out a picture of the southern medical student's life just before the Civil War.

In the South Caroliniana Library at the University of South Carolina, the Mary Amarinthia Snowden Papers contain two letters Baruch wrote to her during the Civil War; Baruch's 1917 letter to Yates Snowden is in the Yates Snowden Papers. The Manning Family Papers at the South Caroliniana Library contain the draft of an agreement, dated 1878, between Baruch and Marie Barbot for running a farm. In the Simon Baruch Papers in the same library are a letter Dr. Baruch wrote to Dr. Albert S. Wittson in 1907 and eight letters Dr. Baruch wrote to Dr. Alexander Salley of Orangeburg between 1865 and 1870. The long, thoughtful letters to Salley provide many descriptions of medical practice in Reconstruction South Carolina, along with Baruch's political opinions, impressions of colleagues, and occasional references to personal affairs.

I also made use of a letter from Andrew Dickson White in the Daniel Coit Gilman Papers at the Johns Hopkins University and of one from Belle Baruch to Bernard Baruch in Bernard's New York City office.

Archival Sources

Dr. Baruch's naturalization papers, dated January 19, 1871, are in the Simon Baruch Papers at the South Caroliniana Library in Columbia. In the Library of the Medical University of South Carolina in Charleston, and in the Tompkins-McCaw Library and Dean's Office of the Medical College of Virginia in Richmond, are various materials bearing on Dr. Baruch's medical education. The most useful are the faculty circulars, comparable to the college catalogs of today, registers of matriculants and graduates, and lists of winning students' essays.

In the War Department Collection of Confederate Records in the National Archives, some Baruch items are located in records of the Adjutant and Inspector General's Office and Office of the Secretary of War; others are collected in the dust jacket bearing Dr. Baruch's name.

His marriage license is in the Bureau of Records and Statistics of the Department of Health of the City of New York, Borough of Manhattan. I found minutes of the Hebrew Benevolent Association of Camden in the possession of the association secretary in March 1958. Baruch's land purchases in South Carolina are on record in the office of the Clerk of Court of Kershaw County, Camden, South Carolina.

In the office of the director of the Montefiore Hospital for Chronic Diseases (now Montefiore Hospital and Medical Center) in New York City I found minutes of meetings of the Executive Committee and Board of Directors as well as Baruch's annual reports as chief of staff. Fellowship records of the New York Academy of Medicine are located in the Academy Library.

Baruch's real estate transactions in Long Branch, New Jersey, are recorded in the office of the Clerk of Monmouth County, Freehold. The *Transactions of the South Carolina Medical Association* and the *Annual Reports of the State Board of Health of South Carolina* are available at the National Library of Medicine in Bethesda, Md. The Medical College of Virginia in Richmond has a file of the *Proceedings and Journal of the American Association for Promoting Hygiene and Public Baths*.

I found records and correspondence concerning Baruch's tenure at Columbia College of Physicians and Surgeons in the Office of the Secretary of the University.

Interviews and Correspondence

Because Simon Baruch was eighty years old at his death in 1921, few people who knew him were still alive at the time of this writing in the 1950s. Notable and helpful exceptions were his son Bernard; his niece Martha Machol of London; and Gabriel Baum of Camden, son of Simon's benefactor, Mannes. All three gave generously of their time in writing or conversing about their recollections.

From a list of forty-eight survivors of the Class of 1913 at Columbia College of Physicians and Surgeons secured for me by Patti Levington Atwater, twenty-two responded to my request for impressions of Dr. Baruch during his tenure on the Columbia faculty. Valuable reminiscences came from Dr. Charles I. Allen of Wadesboro, North Carolina; Dr. James W. Babcock of New York City; Dr. John H. Carlisle of Passaic, New Jersey; Dr. Z. Lawrence Griesemer of Elizabeth, New Jersey; Dr. William B. Hetzel of Pittsburgh; Dr. Maurice Lenz of New York

City; Dr. Norman B. McWilliams of Williamstown, Massachusetts; Dr. Irving J. Sands of Brooklyn; and Dr. Everett W. Shank of Dayton, Ohio.

Author's queries in the *New York Times* and the *Carolina Israelite* brought helpful replies from Henry Savage, Jr., and Dr. and Mrs. W. Robin Zemp of Camden; Lynch Horry Deas Boykin, Jr., of Charlotte, North Carolina; Dr. Gatewood Workman of Davidson, North Carolina; Dr. Samuel Newman of Danville, Virginia; Eppa Huntington IV of Richmond; William T. Sanger, Chancellor Emeritus of the Medical College of Virginia; and Dr. Louis Shalet of Jamaica, Long Island.

In May 1960, the Joseph Valentino family of Elberon, New Jersey, permitted me to look through the Anchorage, formerly Dr. Baruch's summer house in Long Branch; Frank R. Valentino was most helpful in locating information about the Anchorage as it looked in Dr. Baruch's day.

Dr. Baruch's major bibliographer, Dr. Frances A. Hellebrandt, showed unparalleled generosity in sharing the results of biographical research which she carried out over a period of six years at the Baruch Center of Physical Medicine and Rehabilitation at the Medical College of Virginia. In addition to answering my questions, she kindly relinquished many of the materials she had gathered, including photographs, typed copies of newspaper materials, and correspondence.

Others who generously shared the results of pertinent research were Dr. Joseph I. Waring, historian of South Carolina medicine; Margaret L. Coit, biographer of Bernard Baruch; and Jacob Rader Marcus, director of the American Jewish Archives.

Simon Baruch's Published Works

In the course of his long, active career, Dr. Baruch wrote three books and more than 130 articles, in addition to hundreds of editorials in the various medical journals he edited. There are several published bibliographies. The earliest was compiled during World War II by Annabell W. Furman, librarian of the Medical College of the State of South Carolina. Prefaced by a biographical sketch by Hillyer Rudisill, Jr., and organized by topic ("General Medicine," "Surgery," "Spa Therapy," and so on), this bibliography was published in September 1944 as a Special Issue (the "Baruch Number") of the *Library Bulletin of the Medical College of the State of South Carolina*.

Dr. Frances A. Hellebrandt published a more complete listing, arranged chronologically, in *Simon Baruch: Introduction to the Man and his Work* (Special Bulletin of the Baruch Center of Physical Medicine and Rehabilitation of the Medical College of Virginia, Richmond, July 29, 1950). In its forty-four pages, Dr. Hellebrandt's bibliography lists not only articles, books, and editorials in journals Baruch edited but also many of the letters he wrote to the editors of newspapers and medical periodicals. Her work constitutes an accurate and nearly comprehensive compilation of Dr. Baruch's published works, with the exception of his medical editorials in the *New York Sun*.

There is no mention of Baruch in particular or medical editorship in general either in Frank M. O'Brien, *The Story of the Sun, New York, 1833–1918* (New York: George H. Doran, 1918), or in Edward P. Mitchell, *Memoirs of an Editor: Fifty Years of American Journalism* (New York: Charles Scribner's Sons, 1924). Nor are there official records of Baruch's position with the *Sun* (Lee B. Wood, executive editor, *New York World-Telegram and the Sun,* to author, May 21, 1957, and Thomas W. Dewart, president of the *New York Sun, Inc.,* to author, October 11, 1957). Nonetheless, the fact of Baruch's editorship is well established. Baruch himself often referred to it in published medical articles, and his papers contain many clippings of his editorials, letters in reference to them, memoranda listing titles of editorials and dates of publication, and scattered records of payments received from the *Sun.* According to Dr. Baruch's son Herman, in *Centennial of The Medical College of Virginia, 1838–1938* (privately published by the New York Alumni Association, Medical College of Virginia, New York City, June 1, 1937), Dr. Baruch's *Sun* editorship extended from 1912 to 1918. I gathered the editorials discussed in Chapter 17 of this study by reading the *Sun's* editorial pages during these six years. Most of the more than six hundred health-related editorials published in this period are so characteristic of Baruch in style and content that there is no question of his authorship.

Newspapers and Periodicals

For the period of Dr. Baruch's residence in South Carolina, the most useful newspapers were the *Camden Weekly Journal,* the *Camden Journal,* and the *Fairfield Herald* of Winnsboro. Files of all three are located at the South Caroliniana Library in Columbia. Among the most helpful medical journals for this period were the *Transactions of the South Carolina Medical Association* and the *Richmond Medical Journal* (later the *Richmond and Louisville Medical Journal* and, finally, when located in New York City, *Gaillard's Medical Journal*). The *Freedmen's Record* yielded useful comments by northern teachers on the contemporary social and economic scene.

Among Dr. Baruch's papers, his extensive collection of newspaper clippings provided a rich source of such material for the period from 1881 to his death in 1921. Indispensable medical journals were the *Medical Record,* the *New York Medical Journal, Transactions of the American Medical Association,* and *Transactions of the New York Academy of Medicine.* Among the most useful lay periodicals for this period were the *American Mercury,* the *Outlook,* and the *Journal of Social Science.*

Published Contemporary Sources

Atlas to Accompany Official Records of the War of the Rebellion. Washington, D.C.: U.S. Government Printing Office, 1881.

Barnes, Joseph K., et al., eds. *The Medical and Surgical History of the War of the Rebellion.* 6 vols. Washington, D.C.: U.S. Government Printing Office, 1870–88.

Bartholow, Roberts. *A Practical Treatise on Materia Medica and Therapeutics.* New and enlarged ed. New York: D. Appleton, 1878.

Baruch, Herman. "The History of the Public Rain Bath in America." *Sanitarian* 36 (October 1896): 299–302.

Billings, John Shaw. "The National Board of Health and National Quarantine." *Transactions of the American Medical Association* 31 (1880): 435–64.

Carlyle, Thomas. *The Correspondence of Thomas Carlyle and Ralph Waldo Emerson, 1834–1872.* Boston: Houghton Mifflin, [1884?].

Childs, Arney Robinson, ed. *The Private Journal of Henry William Ravenel, 1859–1887.* Columbia: University of South Carolina Press, 1947.

Clarke, Edward H., et al. *A Century of American Medicine, 1776–1876.* Philadelphia: H. C. Lea, 1876.

Cleveland, Lucy. "The Public Baths of New York City." *Modern Sanitation* 4 (March 1908): 1–14.

Committee on the Abuse of Medical Charities. "The Abuses of Medical Charity." *Transactions of the American Medical Association* 31 (1880): 987–1000.

Darrow, Clarence. "The Eugenics Cult." *American Mercury* 8 (June 1926): 129–37.

Darwin, Charles Robert. *Autobiography. With Original Omissions Restored; Edited and with an Appendix and Notes by his Grand-daughter, Nora Barlow.* London: Collins, 1958.

Davis, Michael M., Jr. *Immigrant Health and the Community.* New York: Harper & Brothers, 1921.

Dorland, W. A. Newman. *The American Illustrated Medical Dictionary.* 22d ed. Philadelphia: W. B. Saunders, 1951.

Dunglison, Robley. *Medical Lexicon: A Dictionary of Medical Science.* 1st ed. 1833; rev. eds. Philadelphia: Blanchard and Lea, 1857, and Philadelphia: H. C. Lea, 1874.

Farmer, Laurence, ed. *Doctors' Legacy: A Selection of Physicians' Letters, 1721–1954.* New York: Harper, 1955.

Fisk, Harvey E. "The Introduction of Public Rain Baths in America: A Historical Sketch." *Sanitarian* 36 (1896): 481–501.

Flint, Austin, ed. *Sanitary Memoirs of the War of the Rebellion Collected and Published by the United States Sanitary Commission: Contributions Relating to the Causation and Prevention of Disease, and to Camp Diseases Together with a Report of the Diseases, etc., among the Prisoners at Andersonville, Georgia.* New York: United States Sanitary Commission, 1867.

Fox, R. Fortescue. *The Principles and Practice of Medical Hydrology Being the Science of Treatment by Water and Baths.* London: University of London Press, 1913.

Garrison, Fielding H. *An Introduction to the History of Medicine.* 1st and 2d eds. Philadelphia: W. B. Saunders, 1913 and 1917.

Geddings, Eli. "Report of the Committee on Medical Education." *Transactions of the American Medical Association* 22 (1871): 113–51.

Grant, U. S. "The Vicksburg Campaign." In Robert Underwood Johnson and Clarence Clough Buel, eds., *Battles and Leaders of the Civil War.* 4 vols. New York: Century, 1887–88.

Hamilton, Allan McLane. *Recollections of an Alienist: Personal and Professional.* New York: George H. Doran, 1916.

Hanger, G. W. W. "Public Baths in the United States." *Bulletin of the Bureau of Labor* 9 (1904), *The Exhibit of the United States Bureau of Labor at the Louisiana Purchase Exposition,* 1245–1367.

Harwell, Richard Barksdale, ed. *The Confederate Reader.* New York: Longmans, 1957.

Herrick, Mary E. "The Tenement-House: Its Influence upon the Child." *Journal of Social Science* 24 (August 1892): 25–33.

Hofmann, Josef. *Piano Playing with Piano Questions Answered.* 1920. Reprint. New York: Dover, 1976.

Holmes, O. W. *Currents and Counter-currents in Medical Science.* Boston: Ticknor and Fields, 1861.

Jacquette, Henrietta Stratton, ed. *The South after Gettysburg: Letters of Cornelia Hancock, 1863–1868.* New York: T. Y. Crowell, 1956.

Kellogg, J. H. *Rational Hydrotherapy.* 3d ed., rev. Philadelphia: F. A. Davis, 1906.

Kelly, Howard A., and Elizabeth Hurdon. *The Vermiform Appendix and Its Diseases.* Philadelphia: W. B. Saunders, 1905.

Longstreet, James. *Manassas to Appomattox.* Philadelphia: J. B. Lippincott, 1896.

Marcus, Jacob Rader, ed. *Memoirs of American Jews, 1775–1865.* 3 vols. Philadelphia: Jewish Publication Society of America, 1955–56.

Martin, Isabella D., and Myrta Lockett Avary, eds. *A Diary from Dixie, as Written by Mary Boykin Chesnut, Wife of James Chesnut, Jr., United States Senator from South Carolina, 1859–1861, and Afterward Aide to Jefferson Davis and a Brigadier General in the Confederate Army.* New York: D. Appleton, 1905.

Mazyck, Arthur, comp. *Guide to Charleston Illustrated: Being A Sketch of the History of Charleston, S.C., with Some Account of Its Present Condition, with Numerous Engravings.* Charleston: Walker, Evans and Cogswell, 1875.

Mitchell, Edward P. *Memoirs of an Editor: Fifty Years of American Journalism.* New York: Charles Scribner's Sons, 1924.

Page, Charles E. "Hygienic versus Drug Therapy for Typhoid Fever." *Medical Record* 45 (April 28, 1894): 518–20.

Paine, Robert T. *Pauperism in Great Cities: Its Four Chief Causes.* N.p.: N.p., 1893?

Pike, James S. *The Prostrate State: South Carolina under Negro Government.* New York: D. Appleton, 1874.

Porcher, F. P. *Resources of the Southern Fields and Forests, Medical, Economical and Agricultural. Being Also a Medical Botany of the Confederate States; With Practical Information on the Useful Properties of the Trees, Plants and Shrubs.* Charleston: Steampower Press of Evans & Cogswell, 1863.

Reynolds, M. "The Progress of Medical Science, An Address before the Medical Association of Sumter County, South Carolina." *Charleston Medical Journal and Review* n.s., 2 (October 1874): 199–212.

Riis, Jacob. *The Battle with the Slum.* New York: Macmillan, 1902.

——. *The Children of the Poor.* New York: C. Scribner's Sons, 1892.

——. *Children of the Tenements.* New York: Macmillan, 1903.

——. *How the Other Half Lives.* New York: C. Scribner's Sons, 1890.

Sands, Henry Burton. "An Account of a Case in Which Recovery Took Place after Laparotomy Had Been Performed for Septic Peritonitis Due to a Perforation of the Vermiform Appendix." *New York Medical Journal* 47 (February 25, 1888): 197–205.

Sangston, Lawrence. *The Battle of the North by a Member of the Maryland Legislature.* Baltimore: Ball, Kelly, Hedian and Pier, 1863.

Seidell, Atherton, "Vitamines and Nutritional Diseases: A Stable Form of Vitamine, Efficient in the Prevention and Cure of Certain Nutritional Deficiency Disease." Reprint 325 from *Public Health Reports* (February 18, 1916).

Simons, Manning. "Report on the Climatology and Epidemics of South Carolina." *Transactions of the American Medical Association* 23 (1872): 272–331.

——. "Report of the Committee on State Medicine and Public Hygiene." *Transactions of the American Medical Association* (1878): 81–89.

Slocum, H. W. "Final Operations of Sherman's Army." In Robert Underwood

Johnson and Clarence Clough Buel, eds., *Battles and Leaders of the Civil War,* 4 vols. New York: Century, 1887–88.

―――. "Sherman's March from Savannah to Bentonville." In Robert Underwood Johnson and Clarence Clough Buel, eds., *Battles and Leaders of the Civil War.* 4 vols. New York: Century, 1887–88.

Smith, Bertha H. "The Public Baths." *Outlook* 75 (March 4, 1905): 567–77.

South Carolina Women in the Confederacy: Records Collected by Mrs. A. T. Smythe, Miss M. B. Poppenheim, and Mrs. Thomas Taylor. Columbia, S.C.: State Co., 1903.

Steffens, Lincoln. *The Shame of the Cities.* 1904. Reprint. New York: P. Smith, 1948.

Stillé, Charles J. *History of the U.S. Sanitary Commission: Being the General Report of Its Work during the War of the Rebellion.* Philadelphia: J. B. Lippincott, 1866.

Taylor, J. J. *The Physician as a Business Man; Or, How to Obtain the Best Financial Results in the Practice of Medicine.* Philadelphia: Medical World, 1891.

Thorpe, Francis N., comp. and ed. *The Federal and State Constitutions, Colonial Charters, and Other Organic Laws of the States, Territories, and Colonies Now or Heretofore Forming the United States of America, Compiled and Edited under the Act of Congress of June 30, 1906.* 7 vols. Washington, D.C.: U.S. Government Printing Office, 1909.

Toner, J. M. "Obituary of Eli Geddings." *Transactions of the American Medical Association* 30 (1879): 819–23.

Watson, Irving A. *Physicians and Surgeons of America.* Concord, N.H.: Republican Press Association, 1896.

Welch, William H. "The Cartwright Lectures on the General Pathology of Fever." *Medical Record* 33 (April 28, 1888): 457–64.

Wendt, Edmund Charles, ed. *A Treatise on Asiatic Cholera.* New York: W. Wood, 1885.

Wood, Horatio C., Jr., and Arthur Osol. *The Dispensatory of the United States of America.* 23d ed. Philadelphia: J. B. Lippincott, 1943.

Wyeth, John A. "Appendicitis Strictly a Surgical Lesion." *Transactions of the New York Academy of Medicine* 2d ser., 2 (1895): 254–66.

―――. "The Present Status of the Surgery of the Vermiform Appendix." *International Journal of Surgery* 5 (July 1892): 170–71.

―――. *With Sabre and Scalpel: The Autobiography of a Soldier and Surgeon.* New York: Harper & Brothers, 1914.

Secondary Works

Adams, George Worthington. "Confederate Medicine." *Journal of Southern History* 6 (May 1940): 151–66.

―――. *Doctors in Blue: The Medical History of the Union Army in the Civil War.* New York: Schuman, 1952.

Arrowsmith, Lewis G. "The Young Doctor in New York." *American Mercury* 22 (January 1931): 1–10.

Atkinson, William B., ed. *A Biographical Dictionary of Contemporary American Physicians and Surgeons.* 2d ed. rev. Philadelphia: D. G. Brinton, 1880.

―――. *The Physicians and Surgeons of the United States.* Philadelphia: Charles Robson, 1878.

Atwater, Edward C. "Internal Medicine." In Ronald L. Numbers, ed., *The Edu-*

cation of American Physicians: Historical Essays, 143–74. Berkeley: University of California Press, 1980.

Ball, William Watts. *The State That Forgot: South Carolina's Surrender to Democracy.* Indianapolis: Bobbs-Merrill, 1932.

Baruch, Bernard M. *Baruch: My Own Story.* New York: Henry Holt, 1957.

Baur, John E. *The Health Seekers of Southern California, 1870–1900.* San Marino, Calif.: Huntington Library, 1959.

Beadenkopf, Anne. "The Baltimore Public Baths and Their Founder, the Rev. Thomas M. Beadenkopf." *Maryland Historical Magazine* 45 (September 1950): 201–14.

Berman, Alex. "The Heroic Approach in 19th Century Therapeutics." In Judith Walzer Leavitt and Ronald L. Numbers, eds., *Sickness and Health in America: Readings in the History of Medicine and Public Health,* 77–86. Madison: University of Wisconsin Press, 1978.

Bernard, L. L., and Jessie Bernard. *Origins of American Sociology: The Social Science Movement in the United States.* New York: Russell & Russell, 1943.

Berthoff, Rowland T. "Southern Attitudes toward Immigration, 1865–1914." *Journal of Southern History* 17 (August 1951): 328–60.

Bierman, William. *Physical Medicine in General Practice.* 2d ed. New York: P. B. Hoeber, 1947.

Blake, John B. "Anatomy." In Ronald L. Numbers, ed., *The Education of American Physicians: Historical Essays,* 29–47. Berkeley: University of California Press, 1980.

Blake, Nelson M. *Water for the Cities.* Syracuse: Syracuse University Press, 1956.

Blanton, Wyndham B. "The Egyptian Building and Its Place in Medicine." *Bulletin of the Medical College of Virginia* 37 (February 1940): 8–9.

———. *Medicine in Virginia in the Nineteenth Century.* Richmond: Richard, Garrett and Massie, 1933.

Bluestein, Bonnie Ellen. *A New York Medical Man: William Alexander Hammond, M.D. (1828–1900), Neurologist.* Ann Arbor, Mich.: University Microfilms, 1979.

Bonner, Thomas Neville. *Medicine in Chicago, 1850–1950: A Chapter in the Social and Scientific Development of a City.* Madison: American History Research Center, 1957.

Bradley, Hugh. *Such Was Saratoga.* New York: Doubleday, Doran, 1940.

Breeden, James O. "Disease and Southern Distinctiveness." In Todd L. Savitt and James Harvey Young, eds., *Disease and Distinctiveness in the American South,* 1–28. Knoxville: University of Tennessee Press, 1988.

———. *Joseph Jones, M.D.: Scientist of the Old South.* Lexington: University Press of Kentucky, 1975.

Bremner, Robert H. "The Big Flat: History of a New York Tenement House." *American Historical Review* 64 (October 1958): 54–62.

Brewster, Lawrence F. "Planters from the Low-Country and Their Summer Travels." *Proceedings of the South Carolina Historical Association,* 1943.

Brieger, Gert H. "Surgery." In Ronald L. Numbers, ed., *The Education of American Physicians: Historical Essays,* 175–204. Berkeley: University of California Press, 1980.

———. "Therapeutic Conflicts and the American Medical Profession in the 1860's." *Bulletin of the History of Medicine* 41 (May–June 1967): 215–22.

Brogan, D. W. *The American Character.* New York: Knopf, 1944.

Bryan, Thomas Conn. *Confederate Georgia*. Athens: University of Georgia Press, 1953.

Burnham, John C. *How Superstition Won and Science Lost: Popularizing Science and Health in the United States*. New Brunswick: Rutgers University Press, 1987.

Bushman, Richard L., and Claudia L. Bushman. "The Early History of Cleanliness in America." *Journal of American History* 74 (March 1988): 1213–38.

Carrigan, Jo Ann. "Yellow Fever: Scourge of the South." In Todd L. Savitt and James Harvey Young, eds., *Disease and Distinctiveness in the American South*, 55–78. Knoxville: University of Tennessee Press, 1988.

Cash, W. J. *The Mind of the South*. 1941. Reprint. Garden City, N.Y.: Doubleday Anchor Books, 1954.

Cassedy, James H. *American Medicine and Statistical Thinking, 1800–1860*. Cambridge, Mass.: Harvard University Press, 1984.

———. "The Flamboyant Colonel Waring: An Anti-Contagionist Holds the American Stage in the Age of Pasteur and Koch." *Bulletin of the History of Medicine* 36 (March–April 1962): 163–76.

———. *Medicine and American Growth, 1800–1860*. Madison: University of Wisconsin Press, 1986.

———. "Muckraking and Medicine: Samuel Hopkins Adams." *American Quarterly* 16 (1964): 85–99.

———. "The Registration Area and American Vital Statistics: Development of a Health Research Resource, 1885–1915." *Bulletin of the History of Medicine* 39 (1965): 221–31.

Cayleff, Susan E. *Wash and Be Healed: The Water-Cure Movement and Women's Health*. Philadelphia: Temple University Press, 1987.

Centennial Memorial of the Medical College of the State of South Carolina, 1824–1924. Charleston, 1924.

Cobb, William Montague. *The First Negro Medical Society: A History of the Medico-Chirurgical Society of the District of Columbia, 1884–1939*. Washington, D.C.: Associated Publishers, 1939.

Coit, Margaret L. *Mr. Baruch*. Boston: Houghton Mifflin, 1957.

Conkin, Paul K. *Gone with the Ivy: A Biography of Vanderbilt University*. Knoxville: University of Tennessee Press, 1985.

Cott, Nancy F. "Mary Ritter Beard." In Barbara Sicherman and Carol Hurd Green, eds., *Notable American Women: The Modern Period, A Biographical Dictionary*, 71–73. Cambridge, Mass.: Belknap Press of Harvard University Press, 1980.

Coulter, E. Merton. *The Confederate States of America, 1861–1865*. Baton Rouge: Louisiana State University Press, 1950.

Coulter, John S. *Physical Therapy*. Vol. 8 in E. B. Krumbhar, ed., *Clio Medica: A Series of Primers on the History of Medicine*. New York: Paul B. Hoeber, 1932.

Cowen, David L. "Materia Medica and Pharmacology." In Ronald L. Numbers, ed., *The Education of American Physicians: Historical Essays*, 95–121. Berkeley: University of California Press, 1980.

Crosby, Alfred W. *America's Forgotten Pandemic: The Influenza of 1918*. New York: Cambridge University Press, 1989. First published as *Epidemic and Peace, 1918*. Westport, Conn.: Greenwood Press, 1976.

Cunningham, H. H. "Confederate General Hospitals: Establishment and Organization." *Journal of Southern History* 20 (August 1954): 376–95.

————. "The Confederate Medical Officer in the Field." *U.S. Armed Forces Medical Journal* 9 (November 1958): 1580–1605.

————. *Doctors in Gray: The Confederate Medical Service.* Baton Rouge: Louisiana State University Press, 1958.

DeCasseres, Benjamin. "Ben Butler." *American Mercury* 20 (July 1930): 353–61.

Donald, David. *Lincoln Reconsidered: Essays on the Civil War Era.* New York: Knopf, 1956.

Dowdey, Clifford. *Death of a Nation: The Story of Lee and His Men at Gettysburg.* New York: Knopf, 1958.

Dubos, Rene, and Jean Dubos. *The White Plague: Tuberculosis, Man and Society.* Boston: Little, Brown, 1952.

Duffy, John. *A History of Public Health in New York City, 1866–1966.* New York: Russell Sage Foundation, 1974.

————. "The Impact of Malaria on the South." In Todd L. Savitt and James Harvey Young, eds., *Disease and Distinctiveness in the American South,* 29–54. Knoxville: University of Tennessee Press, 1988.

————. "Medical Practice in the Ante Bellum South." *Journal of Southern History* 25 (February 1959): 53–72.

————. "One Hundred Years of the *New Orleans Medical and Surgical Journal.*" Reprinted from the *Louisiana Historical Quarterly* 40 (January 1957).

————. *Sword of Pestilence: The New Orleans Yellow Fever Epidemic of 1853.* Baton Rouge: Louisiana State University Press, 1966.

————. "Yellow Fever in the Continental United States during the Nineteenth Century." *Bulletin of the New York Academy of Medicine* 44 (June 1968): 687–701.

Durden, Robert Franklin. *James Shepherd Pike: Republicanism and the American Negro, 1850–1882.* Durham: Duke University Press, 1957.

Ellis, David M., James A. Frost, Harold C. Syrett, and Harry J. Carman. *A Short History of New York State.* Ithaca: Cornell University Press, 1957.

Ellis, John H. "The New Orleans Yellow Fever Epidemic in 1878: A Note on the Affective History of Societies and Communities." *Clio Medica* 12 (June–September 1977): 189–216.

Fishbein, Morris. "The End of Eclecticism." *American Mercury* 8 (July 1926): 327–33.

————. *A History of the A.M.A., 1847 to 1947.* Philadelphia: W. B. Saunders, 1947.

Fleming, Walter Lynwood. *Documentary History of Reconstruction: Political, Military, Social, Religious, Education and Industrial: 1865 to Present Time.* 2 vols. Cleveland: A. H. Clarke, 1907.

————. *The Sequel of Appomattox: A Chronicle of the Reunion of the States.* New Haven: Yale University Press, 1919.

Franke, Norman H. *Pharmaceutical Conditions and Drug Supply in the Confederacy.* Madison: American Institute of the History of Pharmacy, 1955.

Freeman, Douglas Southall. *Lee's Lieutenants: A Study in Command.* 3 vols. New York: C. Scribner's Sons, 1942–44.

Furman, Annabel W., comp. Baruch Number. Special Issue, *Library Bulletin of the Medical College of the State of South Carolina* (September 1944): 1–20.

Fye, Bruce. "Active Euthanasia: An Historical Survey of Its Conceptual Origins and Introduction to Medical Thought." *Bulletin of the History of Medicine* 52 (Winter 1978): 492–502.

Gardner, Martin. *Fads and Fallacies in the Name of Science.* New York: Dover, 1957.

Garrison, Fielding H., and Leslie T. Morton, comps. *Medical Bibliography: An Annotated Check-List of Texts Illustrating the History of Medicine.* 2d ed. London: Grafton, 1954.

Geer, William M. "Francis Lieber at the South Carolina College." *Proceedings of the South Carolina Historical Association* (1943): 3–22.

Gevitz, Norman. *The D.O.'s: Osteopathic Medicine in America.* Baltimore: Johns Hopkins University Press, 1982.

———, ed. *Other Healers: Unorthodox Medicine in America.* Baltimore: Johns Hopkins University Press, 1988.

Gifford, G. Edmund, Jr. "The Charleston Physician-Naturalists." *Bulletin of the History of Medicine* 49 (1975): 556–74.

Gildersleeve, Basil. *The Creed of the Old South, 1865–1915.* Baltimore: Johns Hopkins Press, 1915.

Glasgow, Ellen. *Barren Ground.* New York: Doubleday, Page, 1925.

Glassberg, David. "The Design of Reform: The Public Bath Movement in America." *American Studies* 20 (Fall 1979): 5–21.

Glazer, Nathan. *American Judaism.* Chicago: University of Chicago Press, 1957.

Green, Harvey. *Fit for America: Health, Fitness, and Sport in American Society.* Baltimore: Johns Hopkins University Press, 1986.

Greenwood, Major. "Miasma and Contagion." In E. Ashworth Underwood, ed., *Science, Medicine and History: Essays on the Evolution of Scientific Thought and Medical Practice Written in Honor of Charles Singer,* 2:501–7. 2 vols. London: Oxford University Press, 1953.

Gregory, Frederick. "The Impact of Darwinian Evolution on Protestant Theology in the Nineteenth Century." In David C. Lindberg and Ronald L. Numbers, eds., *God and Nature: Historical Essays on the Encounter between Christianity and Science,* 369–90. Berkeley: University of California Press, 1986.

Gritzer, Glenn, and Arnold Arluke. *The Making of Rehabilitation: A Political Economy of Medical Specialization, 1890–1980.* Berkeley: University of California Press, 1985.

Guttmacher, Alan F. *Bootlegging Bodies: A History of Bodysnatching.* Fort Wayne, Ind.: Public Library of Fort Wayne and Allen County, 1955.

Harrow, Benjamin. "Simon Baruch." *Dictionary of American Biography.* 2: 29–30. New York: Charles Scribner's Sons, 1929.

Hartshorn, W. Morgan, comp. and ed. *History of the New York Polyclinic Medical School and Hospital.* New York and Camden, N.J.: Haddon Craftsmen, 1942.

Harvey, A. McGehee, and Victor A. McKusick, eds. *Osler's Textbook Revisited.* New York: Appleton-Century-Crofts, 1967.

Haygood, Tamara Miner. *Henry William Ravenel, 1814–1887: South Carolina Scientist in the Civil War Era.* Tuscaloosa: University of Alabama Press, 1987.

Hellebrandt, Frances A. *Simon Baruch: Introduction to the Man and His Work.* Special Bulletin of the Baruch Center of Physical Medicine and Rehabilitation of the Medical College of Virginia, July 29, 1950, pp. 1–44.

Hoffmann, P. *Geschichte der Stadt Schwersenz und ihrer Schützengilde.* Posen, 1912.

Hoke, Thelma Vaine, comp. and ed. "The First 125 Years, 1838–1963." *Bulletin of the Medical College of Virginia* 61 (Fall 1963): 1–96.

Holifield, E. Brooks. "Science and Theology in the Old South." In Ronald L. Numbers and Todd L. Savitt, eds., *Science and Medicine in the Old South*, 127–43. Baton Rouge: Louisiana State University Press, 1989.

———. "The Wealth of Nineteenth-Century American Physicians." *Bulletin of the History of Medicine* 64 (Spring 1990): 79–85.

Hubbard, Ruth, Mary Sue Henefin, and Barbara Fried, eds. *Women Look at Biology Looking at Women: A Collection of Feminist Critiques*. Cambridge, Mass.: Schenkman, 1979.

Hufford, David J. *American Healing Systems: An Introduction and Exploration*. Conference booklet. Philadelphia: University of Pennsylvania, 1984.

Hume, E. E. *Victories of Army Medicine*. Philadelphia: J. B. Lippincott, 1943.

Hunter, Thomas Marshall. "Medical Service for the Yankee Soldier." Ph.D dissertation, University of Maryland, 1952.

Jones, Bill M. *Health-Seekers in the Southwest, 1817–1900*. Norman: University of Oklahoma Press, 1967.

Jones, Ernest. *The Life and Work of Sigmund Freud*. Vol 1, *1856–1900: The Formative Years and the Great Discoveries*. New York: Basic Books, 1953.

Kaufman, Martin. *American Medical Education: The Formative Years, 1765–1910*. Westport, Conn.: Greenwood Press, 1976.

———. *Homeopathy in America: The Rise and Fall of a Medical Heresy*. Baltimore: Johns Hopkins University Press, 1971.

Kaufman, Martin, Stuart Galishoff, and Todd L. Savitt, eds. *Dictionary of American Medical Biography*. 3 vols. Westport, Conn.: Greenwood Press, 1984.

Kelly, Howard A., and Walter L. Burrage, eds. *American Medical Biographies*. Baltimore: Norman Remington, 1920.

———. *Dictionary of American Medical Biography*. New York: D. Appleton, 1928.

Kevles, Daniel J. *In the Name of Eugenics: Genetics and the Uses of Human Heredity*. New York: Knopf, 1985.

Keys, Thomas E., and Frank H. Krusen. "Dr. Simon Baruch and His Fight for Free Public Baths." *Archives of Physical Medicine* 26 (September 1945): 549–57.

Kirkland, Thomas J., and Robert M. Kennedy. *Historic Camden*. 2 vols. Columbia, S.C.: State Co., 1905–26.

Konopka, Stanislas. *Les relations culturelles entre la France et la Pologne dans le domaine de la médecine*. Warsaw: Société Polonaise d'Histoire de la Médecine, 1958.

Korn, Bertram W. *American Jewry and the Civil War*. 1951. Reprint. Cleveland: World, Meridian Paperback, 1961.

Leake, Chauncey D. "Medical Caricature in the United States." *Bulletin of the Society of Medical History of Chicago* 4 (April 1928): 1–29.

Leavitt, Judith Walzer. *Brought to Bed: Child-Bearing in America, 1750–1950*. New York: Oxford University Press, 1986.

———. *The Healthiest City: Milwaukee and the Politics of Health Reform*. Princeton: Princeton University Press, 1982.

Lerner, Max. *America as a Civilization*. New York: Simon & Schuster, 1957.

Levenson, Dorothy. *Montefiore: The Hospital as Social Instrument, 1884–1984*. New York: Farrar, Straus & Giroux, 1984.

Liebenau, Jonathan. *Medical Science and Medical Industry: The Formation of the American Pharmaceutical Industry*. Baltimore: Johns Hopkins University Press, 1987.

Livingstone, David N. *Darwin's Forgotten Defenders: The Encounter between Evangelical Theology and Evolutionary Thought.* Grand Rapids, Mich.: William B. Eerdmans, 1987.

Longo, Lawrence D. "Obstetrics and Gynecology." In Ronald L. Numbers, ed., *The Education of American Physicians: Historical Essays,* 205–55. Berkeley: University of California Press, 1980.

Lubell, Samuel. *Revolt of the Moderates.* New York: Harper, 1956.

Marcus, Jacob Rader. *The Rise and Destiny of the German Jew.* Cincinnati: Jewish Publication Society of America, 1934.

Maulitz, Russell C. "Pathology." In Ronald L. Numbers, ed., *The Education of American Physicians: Historical Essays,* 122–42. Berkeley: University of California Press, 1980.

Maxwell, William Quentin. *Lincoln's Fifth Wheel: The Political History of the U.S. Sanitary Commission.* New York: Longmans, Green, 1956.

May, J. Thomas. "A 19th-Century Medical Care Program for Blacks: The Case of the Freedmen's Bureau." *Anthropological Quarterly* 46 (July 1973): 160–71.

McClellan, Walter S. "Carbon Dioxide Baths." In Sidney Licht, ed., *Medical Hydrology,* 311–20. New Haven: Elizabeth Licht, 1963.

McPherson, James M. *Battle Cry of Freedom: The Civil War Era.* New York: Oxford University Press, 1988.

McTavish, Jan R. "Antipyretic Treatment and Typhoid Fever: 1860–1900." *Journal of the History of Medicine and Allied Sciences* 42 (October 1987): 486–506.

Mencken, H. L. *Prejudices: Sixth Series.* New York: Knopf, 1927.

Miers, Earl Schenk. *The Great Rebellion: The Emergence of the American Conscience.* Cleveland: World, 1958.

Miller, Francis Trevelyan, ed. *The Photographic History of the Civil War in Ten Volumes.* New York: Review of Reviews, 1911.

Miller, Genevieve. "In Praise of Amateurs: Medical History in America before Garrison." *Bulletin of the History of Medicine* 47 (November–December 1973): 586–615.

Mohr, James C. *Abortion in America: The Origins and Evolution of National Policy.* New York: Oxford University Press, 1978.

Moore, James R. *The Post-Darwinian Controversies: A Study of the Protestant Struggle to Come to Terms with Darwin in Great Britain and America, 1870–1900.* Cambridge: Cambridge University Press, 1979.

Morantz-Sanchez, Regina Markell. *Sympathy and Science: Women Physicians in America.* New York: Oxford University Press, 1985.

Mott, Frank Luther. *American Journalism: A History of Newspapers in the United States through 250 Years, 1690 to 1940.* New York: Macmillan, 1941.

———. *A History of American Magazines.* 5 vols. Cambridge, Mass.: Harvard University Press, 1930–68.

Mozans, H. J. *Woman in Science, with an Introductory Chapter on Woman's Long Struggle for Things of the Mind.* 1913. Reprint. Cambridge, Mass.: MIT Press, 1974.

Murphy, Frank P. "Bibliography of Ignaz P. Semmelweis, 1818–1865." *Bulletin of the History of Medicine* 20 (1946): 653–707.

Musto, David F. *The American Disease: Origins of Narcotic Control.* New Haven: Yale University Press, 1973.

Newman, Charles. *The Evolution of Medical Education in the Nineteenth Century.* London: Oxford University Press, 1957.

Norwood, William F. *Medical Education in the United States before the Civil War.* Philadelphia: University of Pennsylvania Press, 1944.

Numbers, Ronald L. *Creation by Natural Law: Laplace's Nebular Hypothesis in American Thought.* Seattle: University of Washington Press, 1977.

———. "Do-It-Yourself the Sectarian Way." In Judith Walzer Leavitt and Ronald L. Numbers, eds., *Sickness and Health in America: Readings in the History of Medicine and Public Health,* 87–96. Madison: University of Wisconsin Press, 1978.

———. *Prophetess of Health: A Study of Ellen G. White.* New York: Harper & Row, 1976.

———, ed. *The Education of American Physicians: Historical Essays.* Berkeley: University of California Press, 1980.

Numbers, Ronald L., and Janet S. Numbers. "Science in the Old South: A Reappraisal." *Journal of Southern History* 48 (May 1982): 163–84.

Numbers, Ronald L., and Todd L. Savitt, eds. *Science and Medicine in the Old South.* Baton Rouge: Louisiana State University Press, 1989.

O'Brien, Frank M. *The Story of the Sun, New York, 1833–1928.* New ed. New York: D. Appleton, 1928.

O'Brien, Michael, and David Moltke-Hansen, eds. *Intellectual Life in Antebellum Charleston.* Knoxville: University of Tennessee Press, 1986.

O'Connor, Richard. *Hell's Kitchen: The Roaring Days of New York's Wild West Side.* Philadelphia: Lippincott, 1958.

O'Donovan, Michael (pseud.). *The Stories of Frank O'Connor.* New York: Knopf, 1952.

Olesko, Kathryn M. "Physics Instruction in Prussian Secondary Schools before 1859." *Osiris* 2d ser., 5 (1989): 94–120.

Packard, Francis R. *History of Medicine in the United States.* 2 vols. New York: Paul B. Hoeber, 1931.

Patton, James W. "Facets of the South." *Journal of Southern History* 23 (February 1957): 3–24.

Pearson, Hesketh. *Oscar Wilde: His Life and Wit.* New York: Harper and Brothers, 1946.

Petersen, Karen, and J. J. Wilson. *Women Artists: Recognition and Reappraisal from the Early Middle Ages to the Twentieth Century.* New York: New York University Press, 1976.

Pinner, Max, and Benjamin F. Miller, eds. *When Doctors Are Patients.* New York: Norton, 1952.

Posner, Emil Roy. "A Physiotherapist Looks at Physiotherapy." *American Mercury* 71 (July 1950): 46–58.

Proust, Marcel. *Jean Santeuil.* Translated by Gerard Hopkins. New York: Simon & Schuster, 1956.

Reilly, Philip R. *The Surgical Solution: A History of Involuntary Sterilization in the United States.* Baltimore: Johns Hopkins University Press, 1991.

Remington's Pharmaceutical Sciences. 15th ed. Easton, Pa.: Mack, 1975.

Richmond, Phyllis Allen. "American Attitudes toward the Germ Theory of Disease (1860–1880)." In Gert H. Brieger, ed., *Theory and Practice in American Medicine: Historical Studies from the Journal of the History of Medicine and Allied Sciences,* 58–84. New York: Science History Publications, 1976.

Risse, Guenter B. "Epidemics and History: Ecological Perspectives and Social

Responses." In Elizabeth Fee and Daniel M. Fox, eds., *AIDS: The Burden of History,* 33–66. Berkeley: University of California Press, 1988.

Risse, Guenter B., Ronald L. Numbers, and Judith Walzer Leavitt, eds. *Medicine without Doctors: Home Health Care in American History.* New York: Science History Publications/USA, 1977.

Roberts, Jon H. *Darwinism and the Divine in America: Protestant Intellectuals and Organic Evolution, 1859–1900.* Madison: University of Wisconsin Press, 1988.

Rose, Willie Lee. *Rehearsal for Reconstruction: The Port Royal Experiment.* Indianapolis: Bobbs-Merrill, 1964.

Rosen, George. *Fees and Fee Bills: Some Economic Aspects of Medical Practice in Nineteenth Century America.* Supp. 6 to the *Bulletin of the History of Medicine.* Baltimore: Johns Hopkins Press, 1946.

———. *The Structure of American Medical Practice, 1875–1941.* Edited by Charles E. Rosenberg. Philadelphia: University of Pennsylvania Press, 1983.

Rosenberg, Charles E. *The Cholera Years: The United States in 1832, 1849 and 1866.* Chicago: University of Chicago Press, 1966.

———. "The Practice of Medicine in New York a Century Ago." In Judith Walzer Leavitt and Ronald L. Numbers, eds., *Sickness and Health in America: Readings in the History of Medicine and Public Health,* 55–74. Madison: University of Wisconsin Press, 1978.

———. "Social Class and Medical Care in 19th-Century America: The Rise and Fall of the Dispensary." In Judith Walzer Leavitt and Ronald L. Numbers, eds., *Sickness and Health in America: Readings in the History of Medicine and Public Health,* 157–72. Madison: University of Wisconsin Press, 1978.

———. "The Therapeutic Revolution: Medicine, Meaning, and Social Change in Nineteenth-Century America." In Morris J. Vogel and Charles E. Rosenberg, eds., *The Therapeutic Revolution: Essays in the Social History of American Medicine,* 3–26. Philadelphia: University of Pennsylvania Press, 1979.

Rossiter, Margaret W. *Women Scientists in America: Struggles and Strategies to 1940.* Baltimore: Johns Hopkins University Press, 1982.

Rothstein, William G. *American Physicians in the 19th Century: From Sects to Science.* Baltimore: Johns Hopkins University Press, 1972.

Salley, Alexander S., Jr. *The History of Orangeburg County, South Carolina, from Its First Settlement to the Close of the Revolutionary War.* Orangeburg, S.C.: R. L. Berry, Printer, 1898.

Savitt, Todd L. *Medicine and Slavery: The Diseases and Health Care of Blacks in Antebellum Virginia.* Urbana: University of Illinois Press, 1978.

Savitt, Todd L., and James Harvey Young, eds. *Disease and Distinctiveness in the American South.* Knoxville: University of Tennessee Press, 1988.

Schiebinger, Londa. *The Mind Has No Sex? Women in the Origins of Modern Science.* Cambridge, Mass.: Harvard University Press, 1989.

Schullian, Dorothy M. "Unfolded Out of the Folds." *Bulletin of the Medical Library Association* 40 (April 1952): 135–43.

Schwarz, Richard W. *John Harvey Kellogg, M.D.* Nashville: Southern Publishing Association, 1970.

Scott, Anne Firor. *The Southern Lady: From Pedestal to Politics, 1830–1930.* Chicago: University of Chicago Press, 1970.

Sears, Paul B. *Charles Darwin: The Naturalist as a Cultural Force.* New York: Scribner, 1950.

Shafer, Henry Burnell. *The American Medical Profession, 1783–1850.* New York: Columbia University Press, 1936.

Sharpe, William D. "Confederate Medical Services during the War between the States." *Academy of Medicine of New Jersey Bulletin* 11 (March 1965): 28–40.

Sheehy, Gail. "The Man Who Changed the World." *Vanity Fair* 53 (February 1990): 108–25, 180–89.

Shryock, Richard H. *The Development of Modern Medicine: An Interpretation of the Social and Scientific Factors Involved.* New York: Knopf, 1947.

Simkins, Francis B., and Robert H. Woody. *South Carolina during Reconstruction.* Chapel Hill: University of North Carolina Press, 1932.

Sicherman, Barbara. *Alice Hamilton: A Life in Letters.* Cambridge, Mass.: Harvard University Press, 1984.

———. "The Uses of a Diagnosis: Doctors, Patients, and Neurasthenia." In Judith Walzer Leavitt and Ronald L. Numbers, eds., *Sickness and Health in America: Readings in the History of Medicine and Public Health,* 25–38. Madison: University of Wisconsin Press, 1978.

Sicherman, Barbara, and Carol Hurd Green, eds. *Notable American Women: The Modern Period.* Cambridge, Mass.: Belknap Press of Harvard University Press, 1980.

Sigerist, Henry E. "American Spas in Historical Perspective." In Felix Marti-Ibañez, ed., *Henry E. Sigerist on the History of Medicine,* 66–79. New York: MD Publications, 1960.

———. "Living under the Shadow." In Max Pinner and Benjamin F. Miller, eds., *When Doctors Are Patients,* 3–17. New York: Norton, 1952.

———. *Socialized Medicine in the Soviet Union.* New York: Norton, 1937.

———. "Towards a Renaissance of the American Spa." In Milton I. Roemer, ed., *Henry E. Sigerist on the Sociology of Medicine,* 248–55. New York: MD Publications, 1960.

Smillie, Wilson G. "The Period of Great Epidemics in the United States, 1800–1875." In Franklin H. Top, ed., *The History of American Epidemiology,* 58–71. St. Louis: Mosby, 1952.

Smith, Bradford. "Parnassus, U.S.A." *Saturday Review,* August 2, 1958, p. 40.

Smith, Dale C. "A Historical Overview of the Recognition of Appendicitis." *New York State Journal of Medicine* 86 (1986): 571–83, 639–47.

Sneader, Walter. *Drug Discovery: The Evolution of Modern Medicines.* Chichester, England: Wiley, 1985.

South Carolina Medical Association. *A Brief History of the South Carolina Medical Association to Which Are Added Short Historical Sketches of Various Medical Institutions and Societies of South Carolina.* Charleston: South Carolina Medical Association, 1948.

Stampp, Kenneth M., and Leon F. Litwack. *Reconstruction: An Anthology of Revisionist Writings.* Baton Rouge: Louisiana State University Press, 1969.

Starke, Hermann. *Zur Geschichte des Königlichen Friedrich-Wilhelms-Gymnasiums zu Posen.* Posen: Herzbach, 1884.

Stephens, Lester D. *Ancient Animals and Other Wondrous Things: The Story of Francis Simmons Holmes, Paleontologist and Curator of the Charleston Museum.* Charleston: Charleston Museum, 1988.

———. *Joseph LeConte: Gentle Prophet of Evolution.* Baton Rouge: Louisiana State University Press, 1982.

Stern, B. J. *Should We Be Vaccinated? A Study of the Controversy in Its Historical and Scientific Aspects.* New York: Harper & Brothers, 1927.

Stevenson, Isobel. "Medical Literature of the Civil War Era." *Ciba Symposia* 3 (April 1941): 908–18.

Temkin, Owsei. "On the History of 'Morality and Syphilis.'" In Owsei Temkin, *The Double Face of Janus and Other Essays in the History of Medicine,* 472–84. Baltimore: Johns Hopkins University Press, 1977.

Thomas, Benjamin P. *Abraham Lincoln.* New York: Knopf, 1952.

Top, Franklin H., ed. *The History of American Epidemiology.* St. Louis: Mosby, 1952.

Townsend, Jonathan M. "Francis Peyre Porcher, M.D." *Annals of Medical History,* 3d ser., 1 (1939): 177–88.

Truax, Rhoda. *The Doctors Jacobi.* Boston: Little, Brown, 1952.

Turner, Ernest Sackville. *Taking the Cure.* London: Joseph, 1967.

Underwood, E. Ashworth, ed. *Science, Medicine and History: Essays on the Evolution of Scientific Thought and Medical Practice Written in Honor of Charles Singer.* 2 vols. London: Oxford University Press, 1953.

Van Ingen, Philip. *The New York Academy of Medicine: Its First Hundred Years.* New York: Columbia University Press, 1949.

Vogel, Morris J., and Charles E. Rosenberg, eds. *The Therapeutic Revolution: Essays in the Social History of American Medicine.* Philadelphia: University of Pennsylvania Press, 1979.

Walsh, James J. *History of Medicine in New York: Three Centuries of Medical Progress.* 5 vols. New York: National Americana Society, 1919.

Walsh, Mary Roth. *"Doctors Wanted: No Women Need Apply": Sexual Barriers in the Medical Profession, 1835–1975.* New Haven: Yale University Press, 1977.

Ward, Patricia Spain. "The American Reception of Salvarsan." *Journal of the History of Medicine and Allied Sciences* 36 (January 1981): 44–62.

Waring, Joseph Ioor. *A History of Medicine in South Carolina, 1825–1900.* Columbia: South Carolina Medical Association, 1967.

———. *A History of Medicine in South Carolina, 1900–1970.* Columbia: South Carolina Medical Association, 1971.

Warner, John Harley. "The Idea of Southern Medical Distinctiveness: Medical Knowledge and Practice in the Old South." In Ronald L. Numbers and Todd L. Savitt, eds., *Science and Medicine in the Old South,* 179–205. Baton Rouge: Louisiana State University Press, 1989.

———. "The Nature-Trusting Heresy: American Physicians and the Concept of Healing Power of Nature in the 1850s and 1860s." *Perspectives in American History* 11 (1978): 291–324.

———. *The Therapeutic Perspective: Medical Practice, Knowledge, and Identity in America, 1820–1885.* Cambridge, Mass.: Harvard University Press, 1986.

Warner, Margaret. "Local Control versus National Interest: The Debate over Southern Public Health, 1878–1884. *Journal of Southern History* 50 (August 1984): 407–28.

Warschauer, Adolf. "Die Entstehung einer judischen Gemeinde." In Ludwig Geiger, ed., *Zeitschrift für die Geschichte der Juden in Deutschland,* 3:170–81. Braunschweig, 1890.

Waserman, Manfred J. "Henry L. Coit and the Certified Milk Movement in the Development of Modern Pediatrics." *Bulletin of the History of Medicine* 46 (July–August 1972): 359–90.

————. "The Quest for a National Health Department in the Progressive Era." *Bulletin of the History of Medicine* 49 (Fall 1975): 353–80.

Weaver, George H. "Surgeons as Prisoners of War: Agreement Providing for Their Unconditional Release during the Civil War." *Bulletin of the Society of the Medical History of Chicago* 4 (January 1933): 249–55.

Weiss, Harry B., and Howard R. Kemble. *The Great American Water-Cure Craze: A History of Hydropathy in the United States.* Trenton, N.J.: Past Times Press, 1967.

Wendt, Lloyd, and Herman Kogan. *Lords of the Levee: The Story of Bathhouse John and Hinky Dink.* Indianapolis: Bobbs-Merrill, 1943.

Wescoe, W. Clarke. "Preceptors as General Educators in Medicine." *Journal of Medical Education* 31 (September 1956): 598–603.

Whorton, James. "Chemistry." In Ronald L. Numbers, ed., *The Education of American Physicians: Historical Essays,* 72–94. Berkeley: University of California Press, 1980.

Williams, Marilyn Thornton. *Washing "The Great Unwashed": Public Baths in Urban America, 1840–1920.* Columbus: Ohio State University Press, 1991.

Williams, Ralph Chester. *The United States Public Health Service, 1798–1950.* Washington, D.C.: Commissioned Officers Association of the U.S. Public Health Service, 1951.

Williamson, Joel. *After Slavery: The Negro in South Carolina during Reconstruction, 1861–1877.* Chapel Hill: University of North Carolina Press, 1965.

Wilson, Robert. "Some Historical Aspects of the Medical College of the State of S.C." In *A Brief History of the South Carolina Medical Association,* 142–46. Charleston: South Carolina Medical Association, 1948.

Wittke, Carl. *The German Language Press in America.* Lexington: University of Kentucky Press, 1957.

Woodward, C. Vann. *Origins of the New South, 1877–1913.* Baton Rouge: Louisiana State University Press, 1951.

————. "The Political Legacy of Reconstruction." In Kenneth M. Stampp and Leon F. Litwack, eds., *Reconstruction: An Anthology of Revisionist Writings,* 516–31. Baton Rouge: Louisiana State University Press, 1969.

————. *Reunion and Reaction: The Compromise of 1877 and the End of Reconstruction.* Boston: Little, Brown, 1951.

————, ed. *Mary Chesnut's Civil War.* New Haven: Yale University Press, 1981.

Woodward, C. Vann, and Elisabeth Muhlenfeld. *The Private Mary Chesnut: The Unpublished Civil War Diaries.* New York: Oxford University Press, 1984.

Works Progress Administration, Federal Writers' Project. *Entertaining a Nation: The Career of Long Branch.* Long Branch, N.J.: Houghton Mifflin, 1940.

Wright, Lawrence. *Clean and Decent: The Fascinating History of the Bathroom and the Water Closet and of Sundry Habits, Fashions and Accessories of the Toilet Principally in Great Britain, France, and America.* London: Routledge & Paul, 1960.

Young, James Harvey. *Pure Food: Securing the Federal Food and Drug Act of 1906.* Princeton: Princeton University Press, 1989.

————. *The Toadstool Millionaires: A Social History of Patent Medicines in America before Federal Regulation.* Princeton: Princeton University Press, 1961.

Index

Abbey, Henry (manager of Josef Hofmann's American concert tour, 1887–88), 156–57, 158, 159, 160, 162

"An Account of a Case in Which Recovery Took Place After Laparotomy Had Been Performed for Septic Peritonitis Due to a Perforation of the Vermiform Appendix" (Henry Burton Sands, on case SB brought to him in 1887), 329n35

Ackerknecht, Erwin H., on biography, xiii

Addams, Jane (Hull-House founder and leader of public bath movement in Chicago), 184–85, 186 [caption]

Agassiz, Louis, 8–9, 12

Albany Argus, on Saratoga Springs reclamation, 237

Albany Evening Journal, on Goodwin Brown, Albany resident, as founder of public bath movement, 188

Alcohol, 32, 48, 60, 66, 109, 291. *See also* Liquors; Whiskey; SB and Alcohol: SB on Beer; SB on Prohibition; SB on Wine

American Gynecological Society, 150

American hellebore (indigenous plant source of veratrum viride), 88

American Journal of Obstetrics, 152

American Medical Association, 9, 23, 72, 87, 88, 90, 95, 106, 141, 219, 240, 252, 259, 290

American Public Health Association, 175, 176

Ammonia, in typhoid fever, 60

Amputation, 23, 34, 37–38

Anatomy, 9, 10–11, 23–24, 299n19

Anderson, R. H., 40

Anderson County, South Carolina, physicians: request of, for legislation making their services liens on patients' crops and property (1873), 101–2

Anesthetics, 23, 31, 36–37, 116, 225, 260, 305n29, 319n23. *See also* SB on Chloroform

Anodynes, 29, 32, 53

Antietam (Sharpsburg, Maryland), 37 [illustration and caption], 66

Antimony, 65

Antiphlogistics (anti-inflammatory substances), 28, 94

Anti-Semitism, 243; in South during Civil War, 40

Antisepsis, 116; puerperal, 149–51, 153; in appendicitis surgery, 156; after amputation in Civil War, 37–38

Antispasmodics. *See* SB and Chloral hydrate; SB and Potassium bromide

Appendicitis, surgical treatment of. *See* under SB

Appomattox, 138, 140

Apprenticeship, medical; advantages and weaknesses, 7, 298n8; customary fees, 297n3. *See also* under SB

Army Argus, and anti-Semitism, 40

Army of Northern Virginia, 31, 41, 44, 52, 53, 57

Aromatics (substances with spicy fragrance and stimulant properties), 29

Astringents (substances that cause contraction and arrest discharges), 29, 99

Atomizer, 79

Auscultation (act of listening for sounds within the body), 31, 53, 301n35, 310n31. *See also* Physical diagnosis

Auxiliary relief associations in Civil War, 40

Bacteriology, 108, 229

Bailey (SB's friend and fellow surgeon-captive), 38

Balneology, 221; Henry Sigerist urges education and research in, 349–50n57

Baltimore, Maryland, 38, 39, 49, 200 [caption], 274. *See also* SB and Fort McHenry

About the Author

Patricia Spain Ward received her bachelor's degree from the University of Colorado, her master's from The Johns Hopkins University, and her doctorate from the University of Wisconsin-Madison, where she was a Maurice L. Richardson Fellow in the History of Medicine. Her publications include medical biographies in *Notable American Women, 1607–1950,* the *Dictionary of American Biography,* the *Biographical Dictionary of Social Welfare in America,* and *American National Biography;* studies of the American reception of Salvarsan for the treatment of syphilis, of the role of penicillin production in Soviet-American relations at the close of World War II, of the physician-brothers, Richard Clarke Cabot and Hugh Cabot, and of Andrew Ivy and Krebiozen at the University of Illinois; monograph-length histories of women in pharmacy and of the impact on Illinois medicine of Abraham Flexner's survey of American medical schools; and a study of the first antitrust case against organized medicine (1938–1943). Formerly Campus Historian of the University of Illinois at Chicago, she is Adjunct Assistant Professor of Medical Humanities at the University of Illinois College of Medicine at Chicago. She has held research grants from the National Institute of Mental Health and the National Library of Medicine and is currently writing a biography of Hugh Cabot under a grant from the National Endowment for the Humanities.